INHERENTLY-SUSTAINABLE
TECHNOLOGY DEVELOPMENT

INHERENTLY-SUSTAINABLE TECHNOLOGY DEVELOPMENT

ARJUN B. CHHETRI AND M. RAFIQUL ISLAM

Civil And Resources Engineering
Dalhousie University, Halifax, Nova Scotia Canada

Nova Science Publishers, Inc.
New York

For permission to use material from this book please contact us:
Telephone 631-231-7269; Fax 631-231-8175
Web Site: http://www.novapublishers.com

NOTICE TO THE READER

LIBRARY OF CONGRESS CATALOGING-IN-PUBLICATION DATA

Available Upon Request

ISBN 978-1-60456-180-7

Published by Nova Science Publishers, Inc. ✦ New York

Dedication

I would like to dedicate this book to my late father Bed Bahadur Chhetri and my mother Hari Maya Chhetri. My father was truly an inspiration to me to achieve my educational goal. Even though he had no formal education, he had the mission of providing education to everyone in the Lamjung district of Nepal, struggled a lot and was able to establish several schools in the area. However, at his later life, he was worried on that the so called modern education left several unintended footprints in the society. Educating a person to him was more of an imparting the knowledge to transform the society in a positive way, keeping the indigenous knowledge intact and serving the society without any vested interests. He was also a role model for revolutionizing agriculture system in the whole district. Similarly, my mother, a true believer in the spirit of 'giving' to others, works so hard even at the age of late sixties and always inspires and guides me for my future endeavors. I am fortunate to be blessed with such wonderful parents. Without their vision and inspiration, this book would not have been possible.

Arjun B. Chhetri

In keeping with the first author, I would like to dedicate this work to my parents, Alhaj M. Sulaiman, a life-long educator and Hamida Banu, a lifelong homemaker. Ironically, if this book that proposes a recipe for developing inherently sustainable technologies were written and implemented 60 years ago, my parents didn't have to suffer from debilitating diseases, such as asthma and Alzheimer's.

M. Rafiqul Islam

CONTENTS

PREFACE

In his 'prophetic' (as quoted by a critique) book, Al Gore quoted a highly successful maverick geologist remarking that "in order to find oil, you've got to be honest" (Gore, 1992). For Gore himself, a journalist turned politician, this statement was remarkable. After losing the 2000 presidential election to the Republican candidate George W. Bush, he would convert this career-ending last act of a professional politician into the first act of life after politics. What catches the eye is the pathway and his method. Emerging in his new avatar as the 'honest' lay spokesperson on matters of science, technology and the environment, the former vice-president and Senator would proceed to distance himself from the political intentions informing his entire previous incarnation, including a lengthy public track record of statements and actions, as an elected official.

Pause for a moment to take the full measure of this achievement. In the information age, notably in the fields of both journalism and politics, honesty and transparency seem to have been widely abandoned and even repudiated. At the very highest levels of the current administration in Washington, officials speaking on the record to The New York Times — but not for attribution — bluntly dismiss any inherent value in truthful observation and reporting of actual phenomena. One of them said that "the reality-based community" — referring to practically everyone outside the administration, still "believe that solutions emerge from your judicious study of discernible reality." However, he and other officials now saw themselves wielding sufficient authority to "create our own reality", as he explained to one journalist. "And while you're studying that reality -- judiciously, as you will -- we'll act again," he added, "creating other new realities, which you can study too, and that's how things will sort out. We're history's actors ... and you, all of you, will be left to just study what we do (Suskind, 2004)". Even George Orwell's mantra, "Who controls the past controls the future: who controls the present controls the past." seems profound in the context of today's politics and journalism.

For Al Gore — vice-president of the preceding administration — honesty is... a buzzword, but his invocation of the concept amid such an environment lends a crusading quality to his lecturing and writing. For science and knowledge, on the other hand, honesty is not just a buzzword. It is the starting point. The authors proceeded to undertake the investigation that gave rise to this book because they could find no contemporary work clarifying how the lack of honesty could launch research in the direction of ignorance. It is with considerable eloquence and infallible logic, then, that this book makes the connection between technology development and honesty. From there it proceeds to discuss how, given such a starting point, it is necessary to emulate nature in order to develop sustainable technologies for many applications, ranging from energy to pharmacy and health care.

Although Al Gore is identified as its most prominent popularizer, a very different viewpoint currently prevails concerning sustainability and its basis. The prevailing wisdom is that

1. carbon dioxide (and even carbon the element), as an essential component of life itself, is the culprit; and that
2. it must be annihilated in order to save the planet that suffers from the threat of extinction due to global warming.

How honest is this doctrine? If all energy sources were shifted out of carbon and into nuclear materials, would we have a perfect earth, healthy and ready to sustain life for eternity? This is not the form in which the proponents of this false sustainability thesis deliver their argument. Instead, nuclear energy is proposed as a replacement for gas turbines, much as electric cars are proposed to replace gasoline-driven ones, and the fluorescent light to replace incandescent light. (To see where this ends, it is sufficient only to recall that incandescent light itself was originally proposed as a supplement of and-or substitute for natural sunlight...). The list can be lengthened, to include plastic insulators replacing natural ones, etc. — but the general idea, which is the important thing, is that of improving human welfare on the basis of replacing what is natural with what is artificial.

According to the current trendy doctrine of sustainability, which seems to be based on a doctrine of 'better living through better chemistry', it is this transition from natural to artificial that is supposed to overcome the asserted evils of carbon and excessive reliance on other natural energy sources like the sun. Where is this argument headed? It seems to make our European ancestors, who wasted centuries disputing how, when and whether we would fall off the Earth's edge, look very logical and profoundly wise. Instead of following others down that garden path, the authors examine the root of the problem, one that has continued to dog the modern age since the Renaissance. They see a disturbing pattern of abuse of logic during the modern era, an era rife with Eurocentric prejudices about the inherent superiority of European civilization and science over anything else on the face of the earth, and argue that science that was true to itself would not allow the development in the first place of technologies that all turned out to be unsustainable as time progressed. The task the authors set themselves on this score is not easy. Every theory of consequence from the last 350 years had to be scrutinized and deconstructed. The authors sought to uncover some link in the application of any of these theories to a sustainable technology — but they report finding, in the end, not a one.

As others have argued elsewhere, human beings cannot create enough carbon dioxide to trigger a global shift in the functioning of the heating-cooling engine that regulates the geology as well as the atmosphere of this planet[2]. Human societies nevertheless do possess the ability to create products that never existed in nature that would cause unpredictable and catastrophic consequences: nuclear energy is certainly yet another such product. The authors point out that during the production of such artificial energy (e.g., enriching of uranium through numerous stages of centrifuges), one would end up generating more carbon dioxide – something that everyone wants to get rid of. In their view this is further evidence that, in the

Information Age, we are riding the same disastrous roller-coaster initiated since the European Renaissance as "New Science".

That was a scientific revolution — revolutionary precisely to the extent that it demystified tangible causes and tangible effects of natural physical processes and phenomena. However, the authors argue that its philosophical underpinnings contaminated and compromised that remarkable achievement with a toxic prejudice. Decking itself out as Christian, and advertising itself down the centuries as "European", this outlook nurtured an irrational prejudice against any of the thought-material or scientific effort achieved outside Christian societies of Europe and North America. This outlook also wrote off as hocus-pocus the entire body of scientific achievement registered in the ancient pre-Graeco-Roman civilizations of the Eastern world, along with the achievements of other non-Christian societies of Africa and the Americas (before European "discovery").

The authors demonstrate how all the solutions that are being offered to the current environmental mess will make existing methods and processes of harnessing energy sources even more unsustainable. Along this line, they assemble much information normally excluded from the strictly scientific discourse but that nevertheless weighs significantly when it comes time to apply discoveries in the form of technologies. The authors document a possible explanation for the repeated downward spiral attending the principal "breakthrough" innovations in technology. This is a pathway they and their research group have described as the HSSA Syndrome, "HSSA" standing for "Honey → Sugar → Saccharin™ → Aspartame™ (Zatzman, 2007).

Undertaking to investigate how was it possible to package so many technological disasters as efficient alternatives, the authors show how the conventional definition of efficiency itself makes it impossible to see how these technologies made every one of the larger processes into which they were introduced less efficient. Introducing the concept of global efficiency, the authors show that efficiency declines as we move away from nature. For example, the global efficiency of nuclear energy can be an order of magnitude less than what one would calculate in terms of conventional efficiency.

Can it be that no one up to now had unraveled the science of our current technological disaster? Arguing that the role of intention, i.e., of the direction in which the scientific research effort itself was undertaken in the first place, has not been sufficiently recognized, the authors propose explicitly to include the role of intention in the line of technology development they advocate. No amount of disinformation, they point out, can render a technology sustainable that was not well-intended, that was not directed at improving overall human welfare or at what many today call "humanizing the environment". This is not only a matter of claiming to be honest — not least in the matter of finding oil. Rather, it is a matter of recognizing the role of intention and being honest as the starting point of a technology's development.

What impact would this have on the current mode of technology development? Would DDT have been inflicted? Would Freon have been released to eat its hole in the ozone layer? Would the world be awash in artificial plastic (hard or soft) with its near unmanageable waste burdens? Would synthesized pharmaceutical "medicines" be ravaging human health? Would the mishandling of antibiotics unleashed so many tragedies? Imagine: no non-stick Teflon on cookware, no tactical nuclear weapons, no Vioxx, no Prozac... The authors contend that, if the mode of technology development proposed by the authors were used, we would not have to wait for 50-plus years to discover how this toxic shock has falsified every promise. They buttress this claim with an impressive list of many prominent breakthroughs of the modern age, all of which ended up breaking the promise that they originally made. What the authors mean about the role of intention in defrauding future generations thus becomes clear.

What has inspired the authors to seek development of inherently sustainable technologies? For some, to look anywhere other than Europe (and North America) — and the dominant Eurocentric outlook and discourse — is unthinkable. One recent work seriously suggests that all essential components of true sustainability were prefigured in the works of Victorian thinkers in 19-th century Britain (Lumley and Armstrong, 2004). The authors of the present work summon an impressive body of evidence in support of their indictment of Eurocentric prejudices and unanticipated consequences flowing from them. Generally speaking, there has been a strong bias throughout the current industrial and financial system of dominant Western economies against the more qualitative and less quantitative approaches to science and engineering. There have also been many cases where — on the grounds of "lack of hard numbers" and the difficulty of quantifying much of what actually happens with natural materials that are not directly interfered with by means of some "shock-and-awe" type of engineering process — natural sources of materials and their pathways have been dismissed as innovative technological alternatives to artificial (usually chemically-engineered) solutions. Has this bias operated to distort thinking, to lead to an unjustified dismissal of nature-based solutions as something that would do little or nothing to extend the lifetime of the current industrial and financial system of dominant Western economies at the cost of the environment? The question of whether these prejudices have so seriously strengthened the hand of the global North at the expense of the global South is clearly a life-and-death question for the entire planet. The authors make a strong case for the thesis that no serious investigation of sustainable technology development, much less inherently sustainable, i.e., nature-based, technological development, can be permitted routinely to pigeon-hole such concerns as "political" and therefore of no significance for the actual work of scientists and engineers.

Looking at cultures that actually used to produce truly sustainable technologies, the authors show how they met the fundamental requirement of sustainable technology development: that is, their intention was good. With good intention, Rudolf Diesel would have been allowed to conduct his research with vegetable oil, Indian researchers would have been allowed to follow up their research on *neem* and herbal medicine, the Arabs would be allowed to rekindle their knowledge torch that was extinguished at the dawn of the European renaissance... It is after, and on the basis of, resolving this problem intention/direction that the authors propose to emulate nature. For them, nature is the only role model for sustainable technology development. The results here are eye-opening: by demonstrating what was wrong with the previous technology development mode, they set up a paradigm shift. For these technologies, one need not worry about long-term consequences: they will be as sustainable as nature itself. This seemingly novel idea was already well understood by... the Mughal emperor who built the Taj Mahal centuries ago, before anyone ever dreamed of the strictly scientific controls of, say, ISO 900x.

The authors answer practically all the questions that continue to dog the current mode of technology development. Employing the human-scaled logic of good intentions that prevailed in the thought material of cultures from the beginnings of the ancient world up to the end of the European Middle Ages, and informed by the authors' own review of the scientific content of some of this thought-material, it is shown that sustainable technology development is possible, and a good thing. The Eurocentric culture in which modern technology development emerged, however, has had a spotty record when it comes to establishing the truth. People may have forgotten, or deem it irrelevant, that Christmas (December 25) — the most important date in the Christian calendar — is rooted in a timelessly ancient pre-Christian practice having nothing whatever to do with the nativity of Jesus Christ. A true knowledge-seeker, on the other hand, cannot be oblivious to facts of this kind. Before Al Gore discovered and mentioned it, were the peoples of India, China, the Mayan civilization or the Inca unaware of the role of honesty in science and technology? Some thousand years before Europeans would stop bickering over the flatness of the Earth and/or its central position in the Universe, were the Arabs not already aware of the circumference of the Earth and even its actual, i.e., non-spherical, shape? To ask these questions is to begin to answer them, and the authors' reading of, and reflection on, these matters provides the basis underpinning the dexterity they bring to mastering all consequentially dynamic aspects of technology development.

The authors have correctly identified both the source and the pathway of the truth. The individual's actual journey settles the question of whether the end-result will be positive or negative in its impact. Mustering and balancing its societal and technical arguments in this manner, linking the normally highly technical issues of technologies and their sustainability with the very necessity and nobility of the human project, the authors and this book have produced a remarkable as well as unique contribution to the discussion and the literature.

G.V. Chilingarian
University of Southern California

REFERENCES

Gore, A., 1992, *Earth in the Balance: Ecology and the Human Spirit*, Houghton Mifflin Company, Boston, New York, London, 407 pp.

Lumley, S. and Armstrong, P., 2004, "Some of the Nineteenth Century Origins of the Sustainability Concept", Env. Devlopment and Sustainability, vol 6, no, 3, Sept, 367-378.

Sorokhtin, O.S., Chilingar, G.V. and Khilyuk, L.F., 2007. *Global Warming and Global Cooling, Evolution of Climate on Earth* . Developments in Earth & Environmental Sciences. Elsevier, pp 313.

Suskind, R. 2004. "Without a doubt", [Sunday] New York Times Magazine (17 October).

Zatzman, G., 2007. "The Honey → Sugar → Saccharin™ → Aspartame™ Syndrome: A Note", *Journal of Nature Science and Sustainable Technology* {ISSN 1933-0324}, vol. 1, no. 3, 397-401.

ACKNOWLEDGEMENTS

We, the authors, are grateful to many colleagues, friends and all members of our research group that have, in many ways, contributed to this book. In particular, we would like recognize the contribution of Dr. Chefi Ketata, Dr. Martin Tango, Dr. Henrietta Mann, Dr. Govind Raj Pokharel, Bishnu Hari Adhikari, and M. Parvez Islam for their valuable advice and support during the writing of this book. Gary Zatzman, CEO of EEC Research Organisation played a pivotal role in both defining and solving the problem of sustainability. David Prior, CEO of Veridity Environmental Technology, provided us with many useful and inspirational suggestions.

We are most deeply thankful to members of our families, for their support, and encouragement and most importantly their patience, perseverance and tolerance during the writing of this book.

Chapter 1

INTRODUCTION

This book deals with analyzing the historical outlook of technology development illustrating the in-depth study of the driving forces behind technology development before renaissance hit the modern age. It is shown that previous civilizations did have a long-term outlook, which was drastically altered in the post-renaissance culture. The assessment of delinearized history of technology development showed that modern technology development mode is inherently unsustainable. The role of intension in technology development has been investigated. It is shown that aphenomenal intention would lead to reversal of 'intended' outcome of a technology. Conventional engineered processes are driven by an economic model that is wasteful and profit driven, along with the built-in inability to consider the long-term for humanity. In contrary, Nature operates at zero-waste, hence all waste-based technologies are anti-nature. Existing development mode has taken such a short-term approach that every mechanism has been created to make the world environment continuously worse. The absence of good intention can only bring long-term disaster.

Current model of technology development focuses only to the tangible benefit which falls into unsustainable technology in long-term. This means, it can foresee only the tangible benefits as well as impacts, however, the intangible benefits and impacts are solely overlooks. Today's global environmental problems such as global warming and climate change are the impacts of caused by unsustainable technology development. The engineering approach we have taken has several assumptions such as linear, static, steady state, periodic never exists in nature. During pre-renaissance period, natural phenomenon and processes were the models for development which is not the case in pre-renaissance period. As a consequence, instead of being addressed keeping sustainability in mind, the limitations of the older technology's speed and scale of productivity were leap-frogged by diverging onto the anti-nature path. In longer term, those technologies such as mechanical power from water wheel had no negative impacts to the environment as each and every part could be replaced, recycled and renewed. Modern engineering based development completely missed this principle leading it to unsustainable in long-term. Hence, none of the technologies could benefit society that is developed without good intensions.

Modern technological developments are based on synthetic chemicals that are highly toxic to human and the environment. They are extremely energy dependent and require highly skilled work force for their design, manufacturing, operation and maintenance. These technologies are highly capital intensive and beyond the reach of common people. Consumption of fossil fuels in an unsustainable rate and use of highly toxic chemicals and catalysts in fossil fuel refining make the situation worse. Modern technologies are fully based on refined fossil fuel resources, which are inherently toxic to the natural environment. The other petroleum products such as plastics, a symbol of modern civilization, is the most devastating item made from petroleum by-products. A series of modern technologies developed such as microwave, antioxidants, coke, use of glycol, simulated wood or plastic glass, pesticides, use of cell phone are few examples of synthetic based modern technologies, even though they were promised to ease the life of human being, are becoming life threatening technologies.

The developing countries, which are not affected by the impacts of these technologies are now engaged in taking pride in introducing these technologies, often paid with borrowed (at very high interest rate) money, much of which is spent for hiring consultants and buying the technologies from 'donor'countries. Yet, the 'technology transfer' to the developing countries becomes the major slogan of NGOs, multinational companies and big corporations to 'enhance' their livelihood. Neither those development models nor these transferred technologies became successful in developing countries simply because they are not appropriate for particular purpose and the environment. However, it is generally misunderstood that a technology that suits in one place is universally good for other areas too. It could be true if and only if the technology is based on the universal principle of science of nature. To-date, such technology has been illusive in the modern Age.

Inherently sustainable technologies are those which are simple and benign, yet can effectively achieve the particular purpose. The technology should be suitable to the environment, socio-economy and culture in which it is intended to be used. Inherently sustainable technologies are to be developed based on the social priorities, local financial feasibility, demographic characteristics, technical considerations and gender perspectives that meet the needs of local people. Making better use of locally available material, human resources and indigenous knowledge, independent of energy requirement of today's technology of the 'rich', are the keys to the development of inherently sustainable technology development.

This book is truly a treasure of knowledge and of the latest research findings. Unlike majority of books on sustainable technology development, this book does not stop at questioning fundamental issues of current technological development *modus operandi,* instead, it offers simple and practical solutions identifying the roots of problems currently being faced by the society. Various types of sustainable energy technologies suitable for cooking, heating, lighting, transportation and industrial usage are presented. Pathways of conventional fossil fuel based technologies including their impacts to human and the environment is illustrated. A detailed analysis of problems of synthetic fuels and benefits of using nature based resources are also catalogued. For the first time, it has been included the newly established revolutionary concept of the direct use of crude oil in a jet engine. This will not only save trillions of dollars spent on fossil fuel refining but also help protect the degrading natural environment. The role of current technology development in global environmental perspectives are clearly spelt out. Several environment friendly energy technologies are discussed for industrial and transportation end uses. Conventional water and waste water management models are analyzed and a knowledge based model along with the involvement of community is presented. Use of hydraulic power, steam power and modern forms of energy for agro-processing appropriate to the particular use are detailed.

Current practices of food freezing and refrigeration, chemical preservation, pasteurization and their impacts to natural enzymes are scientifically illustrated and several alternatives are offered. Modern agriculture production involves the use of synthetic fertilizers, toxic pesticides, chemical preservatives and plastic materials for its packaging, all of which are extremely harmful. Pathways of pesticides, fertilizers and plastics and their impacts are presented. Impacts of other additives used during food processing and preservation and packaging have also been included. Natural and non toxic-alternatives based on the latest research results are presented as alternatives. Pathways and impacts of different drinking fluids available in the market for the adults as well as for children such as Coke, Pepsi, bottled water, sports drinks etc. are scientifically analyzed and appropriate suggestion for their improvement are included.

Various personal care and health products currently in use are toxic and harmful to human and the environment. A series of natural health and personal care products such as soaps, cosmetics, paints, polish and, natural pesticides and natural coloring agents are presented. Replacement to the synthetic chemicals from natural products is also included. It was recently revealed that technologies which were overlooked for their ill effects for several years such as laser printers, photocopiers and similar other products. Natural substitutes of some office gadgets such as ink, toners and papers are also presented. Inherently sustainable bio-based technology alternatives to the synthetic plastic based technologies including insulators are discussed. Because synthetic chemicals, which are inherent to the current technology development mode, are primarily responsible for global environmental and health problems, there is no hope for rescuing the world without a paradigm shift in current technology development mode. Finally, this book concludes that the new technology development mode must foster the development of natural products, which are inherently beneficial to human and the environment. This book offers an excellent theoretical as well as applied scientific base for students, environmentalists, entrepreneurs, research organizations, policy makers and industries.

1.1. TOWARDS DEVELOPING INHERENTLY SUSTAINABLE TECHNOLOGIES

True sustainability is linked to long-term, hence, the consideration of intangibles (Khan and Islam, 2007a). Even though for millennia the notion of intangibles was in the core of various civilizations, such as Indian, Chinese, Egyptian, Babylonian, and others, this notion has been largely neglected in the post-renaissance era (Zatzman and Islam, 2007a). It can be argued that the lack of consideration of intangibles in the modern age is deliberate, due to focus on short-term. In the words of John Maynard Lord Keynes, who believed that historical time had nothing to do with establishing the truth or falsehood of economic doctrine, "In the long run, we are all dead" (cited by Zatzman and Islam, 2007b).

Because economics is the driver of modern engineering, short-term is the guiding principle behind all engineering calculations. This focuses on short-term poses a serious problem in terms of scientific investigation. The science of tangibles says: there's no need, or room, for intangibles unless one can verify their presence and role with some experimental program - experimental meaning controlled conditions, probably in a laboratory, with experiments that are designed through the same science that one is set out to 'prove'. In contrast, Khan and Islam (2007a; 2007b) argued that the science of tangibles so far has not been able to account for disastrous outcomes of numerous modern technologies. The same way, scientists cannot determine the cause of global warming with the science that assumes all molecules are identical, thereby, making it impossible to distinguish between organic CO_2 and industrial CO_2, scientists cannot determine the cause of diabetes unless there is a paradigm shift that distinguishes between sucrose in honey and sucrose in Aspartame (Chhetri and Islam, 2007a).

There is a widespread notion that, with Science, many practical problems of daily existence can be solved that could not be solved otherwise. This notion is especially popular among engineers. However, it must be admitted that this idea is also very much part of contemporary culture. Certainly in the countries of what is broadly known as the Triad — the Anglo-American bloc (*i.e.*, the United States, Canada, Britain and Australia), the other countries of Europe & Russia, plus Japan — it is one of the hallmarks of what is generally accepted as a modern outlook.

Elsewhere (Islam, 2003), this point has been identified and associated with what is called "the roller-coaster ride of the Information Age". For example: no sooner is a "daily life problem" like insomnia identified than the pharmaceutical industry produces a pill to help one fall asleep. Then, however, the problem of meeting the demands of daily life to wake up on time to get to work, etc., emerges, and another pill — this one to help one "wake up" to full consciousness — is developed and marketed. Similarly, sugar is identified as a latent dietary time-bomb and in almost no time flat, a "solution" is proffered consisting of a choice among "sugar-free" substitutes. It hardly ends there, as the sugar-free substitutionalists then end up in deadly warfare, *e.g.*, the Aspartamers *versus* the Saccharinisers, over whose substitute causes more lab rats to die more horrible deaths from dosages that, when scaled to anything in the range of adult human body-mass indices, bear no relation to any known pattern of human consumption of sugar even over an entire lifetime.

The serious point masked throughout this dreadful comedy is precisely the temporal criterion that each of these "solutions" was addressing in the first place. In every case, the litmus-test applied to the proposed intervening substance is: its performance over the period of time t = "right now". Everything else — including consequences for the human body or even initial acceptability to a functioning living organism — is deemed to fall in the category of "side effects" before being rudely sloughed off as "someone else's problem". The assumption underlying this practice is that the Science that addresses problems at the point where $t + \Delta t \to t$ is the only useful or profitable "science". It follows that any science that takes of care of anything other than the short term is "blue sky" or otherwise "doesn't count", *i.e.*, isn't going to make anyone a billionaire.

The first part of this chapter deals with analyzing the historical outlook of technology development. This chapter presents an in-depth study of the driving forces behind technology development before renaissance hit the modern age. It is shown that previous civilizations did have a long-term outlook, which was drastically altered in the post-renaissance culture. This part also identifies 'intention' as the most important player in determining sustainability of a process.

The second part of this chapter investigates the role of intention on technology development. It is shown that aphenomenal intention would lead to reversal of 'intended' outcome of a technology. If we follow the path of human intentions as a social form, how humans as individuals and collectives arrange their lives, we find that Intention is not a wish or an aspiration. Rather, it is a plan, a way to create a pathway. This section posits that the overwhelmingly intention governing contemporary economic and social existence is the Establishment plan to control, contain, and sell off the whole world, again and again, and attempting to obliterate the natural world by transforming everything in it to products. In this, the technology development has merely been a tool for sustaining status quo, which is aphenomenal in the context of nature, where everything is dynamic (Zatzman et al., 2007a; Zatzman et al., 2007b). This chapter follows some of the dangerous pathways of contemporary attempts to control nature, and the community at large and suggests another path for the world community.

1.2. DELINEARIZED HISTORY OF TECHNOLOGY DEVELOPMENT

The approach to knowledge in this chapter has challenged many previous assumptions, not only in their contents but especially their "linearity" and implicit assumption of a more or less smooth continuous path of knowledge from the past into the present and the future. That is what this chapter has set out to "de-linearize". This section is based on three papers recently written by Zatzman et al (2007a; 2007b;2007c).

1.2.1. Introduction

It is becoming increasingly clear that the current mode of technology development is not sustainable (Mittelstaedt, 2007). Most agree with Nobel Chemistry laureate Dr Robert Curl that the current technological marvels are 'technological disasters'. Few, however, understand the root cause of this failure. This failure now endangers the future of entire species, including our own. Many theories put forward— including those branded as 'conspiracy theories', 'pseudoscience', 'creationism', etc. —but none provide answers to the questions that face the current perilous state of the world.

This lack of sound, fundamentally correct theories is felt in every sector. The outcome is seen in the prevailing popular mood throughout Western countries that "*there is no alternative*". This so-called TINA syndrome was recently identified once again by Zatzman and Islam (2007b), who credited former British Prime Minister (now Baroness) Margaret Thatcher with its enunciation during the 1980s as the secular equivalent of Holy Write among Anglo-American policymakers. The essence of this approach upholds and promotes the status-quo as the only way to move forward.

The situation has meanwhile become so desperate that some Nobel laureates (e.g., Robert Curl) or environmental activists (e.g., David Suzuki) openly despair Humanity's acquisition of technology in the first place as a form of societal 'Original Sin'. Others have pinpointed the severe pollution burdens mounting especially in the energy resource exploitation sector to single out petroleum operations and the petroleum industry for special blame. In the context of increasing oil prices, the petroleum sector has become an almost trivially easy target, and this situation has been compounded by more recent pronouncements from current US President George W. Bush about "oil addiction". Even his most ardent detractors have welcomed this particular comment as a signal insight (Khan and Islam, 2007a). Numerous alternate fuel projects have been launched — but they propose the same inefficient and contaminated processes that got us into trouble with fossil fuel.

Albert Einstein famously stated, "The thinking that got you into the problem, is not going to get you out." Today, there is no evidence that modern Eurocentric civilization is ready to propose a way out of this technological conundrum. The symptoms are ubiquitous, from toxic addiction (Mittelstaedt, 2006a) to global warming (Chhetri and Zatzman, 2008). How is the crying need to treat these symptoms being addressed, however? Soon after it was revealed that the farmers of India have been committing suicide in record numbers, and that the much-vaunted 'green revolution' was actually a fraud keeping humanity in a chokehold (Saunders, 2007), the Congressional Medal of Honour was bestowed on Dr Norman Borlaug. This is the individual who orchestrated the key experimental research undertaken with Mexican maize in the 1940s that underpinned the eventual introduction of costly chemical pesticides, herbicides and other 'aids' for enhancing the productivity of individual tillers throughout the Third World, in one crop after another (Editorial, 2007).

In the chemical sector (food, drug, and lifestyle), similar absurdities continue to abound. Recently, chemical companies 'celebrated' 100 years of PVC, as though PVC has done Humanity good. Yet, China is being accused of using PVC and other toxic chemicals in children's toys, leading to the recall (only in USA and Europe) of millions of toys (CBC, 2007). Weeks before, the head of China's Food and Drug Administration was executed for allowing unwanted chemicals in drugs. That followed weeks of other major scandals (or accusations) regarding Chinese chemical treatment of food and health products (*e.g.*, toothpaste) earmarked for export to United States. In this same year, debates have been raging around the possible connections to chemical fertilizer, chemical pesticides, genetically modified crops, and you-name-it to honey bee Colony Collapse Disorder (CCD) among European honey bees (Zatzman et al., 2007a).

At one level, the official discourse is rigidly maintained that hormones are no more just hormones and stem cell research is absolutely necessary because there is no substitute to real (natural) cells. Yet, even Prince Charles "gets it". Recently, he joined the choir of pro-nature scientists by asking the Sheikhs of Abu Dhabi (site of the second-highest rate of child diabetes in the world), "Have you considered banning McDonald's?" The Prince might not be willing to admit the connection of British-invented sugar culture to diabetes, but he is delighted to report he owns an organic farm.

Somehow, when it comes to scientists, trained with the science of tangibles, this organic product is 'not necessarily' better than other products, such as chemically-grown using toxic pesticide. One food scientist wrote to one of the authors that "I have yet to be convinced that the history of a molecule affects its function and that natural is necessarily better." Apart from the all-pervasive culture of fear that prevents one's taking a stand in case a lawsuit looms on the horizon (in geology, the identical syndrome hides behind the frequently-encountered claim that 'the possibility of finding oil cannot be ruled out entirely'), this comment from a food scientist contains a wry reminder of what has corrupted modern science in the most insidious manner. This has been the dilemma of modern age. Scientists today do not, or find that they cannot, simply uphold the truth. Those that speak, when they speak, uphold self-interest and the status quo. If natural is not necessarily better than artificial, and if chemicals are just chemicals, why should we have a different branch called food science? For that matter, why differentiate chemical engineering, nuclear engineering, pharmacy, military science, or anything else any longer? With such an attitude, why not declare defeat and place them all hereafter under a single umbrella: the Science of Disinformation. Only recently, by the way, comparing opinion polling methodologies in general with the results of actually surveying in detail a defined population from and in a developing country, Shapiro *et al.* (2007) were able to elaborate in some detail the *modus operandi* of this science of disinformation. Has the overall state of the scientific world become so grim that the general public has to resort to trusting social-political activists — *e.g.*, Al Gore's *An Inconvenient Truth*, Michael Moore's *Sicko!* and even a relative novice like Morgan Spurlock and his documentary, *Supersize Me!* — ahead of professionally knowledgeable scientists? This chapter attempts to find the cause of such helplessness in a science whose modernity seems to consist entirely of promoting only the culture of tangibles under the slogan "More is better — because there is more of it."

1.2.2. About Linking "History", "Time" and Delinearization: Some Introductory Remarks

Why should we study history, particularly in the context of technology development? Is history useful for increasing our knowledge? The issue here is *not* whether new knowledge accumulates on the basis of using earlier established findings, with the entire body of knowledge then being passed on to later generations. The real issue is: *on what basis does an individual investigator cognize the existing state of knowledge*? If the individual investigator cognizes the existing state of knowledge on the basis of his/her own re-investigation of the bigger picture surrounding his/her field of interest, that is a conscious approach, one which shows that the investigator operating according to conscience.

If, on the other hand one accepts as given the so-called conclusions reached up to now by others, such a consideration could introduce a problem: what were the *pathways* by which those earlier conclusions were reached? An investigator who declines to investigate those pathways is negating conscience.

Such negating of conscience is not a good thing for anyone to undertake. However, the fact is there were for a long time external or surrounding conditions asserting an undue or improper influence on this front. What if, for example, there exists an authority (like the Church of Rome, during the European Middle Ages) that steps into the picture as my-way-or-the-highway (actually: rack-and-thumbscrews) Knowledge Central, certifying certain conclusions while at the same time banishing all thinking or writing that leads to any other conclusions? Then the individual's scientific investigation itself and reporting will be colored and influenced by the looming threat of censorship and-or the actual exercise of that censorship. (The latter could occur at the cost of one's career and 'pato' [="personal access to oxygen"].)

Against this, mere interest on the part of the investigator to find something out, mere curiosity, won't be enough. The investigator him/herself has to be driven by some particular consciousness of the importance for humanity of his/her own investigative effort. Of course, the Church agrees — but insists only that one have to have the Church's conscience ("everything we have certified is the Truth; anything that contradicts, or conflicts with, the conclusions we certified is Error; those who defend Error are agents of Satan who must be destroyed").

This would account for Galileo's resorting to defensive maneuvers (claiming he was not out to disprove Scripture) — a tactic of conceding a small Lie in order to be able to continue nailing down a larger more important Truth. Why mix such hypocrisy into such matters? Because *it had worked for other investigators in the past*. What was new in Galileo's case was the decision of the Church of that time not to permit him that private space in which to maneuver, in order to make of him an example with which to threaten less-talented researchers coming after him. The worst we can say against Galileo after that point is that, once an investigator (in order to get along in life) goes along with this, s/he destroys some part of her/his usefulness as an investigator. This destruction is even more meaningful because it is likely to change the direction of the conscience pathway of the investigator, for example, leading him/her to pursue money instead of the truth.

The historical movement in this material illustrates the importance of retaining the earliest and most ancient knowledge. However, it leaves open the question of what was actually authoritative about earlier knowledge for later generations. The unstated but key point is that the authority was vested in the unchanging character of the key conclusions. That is to say: this authority was never vested in the integrity and depth of probing by earlier investigators and investigations into all the various pathways and possibilities.

In medieval Europe, the resort to experimental methods does not arise on the basis of rejecting or breaking with Church authority. Rather it is justified instead by a Christian-theological argument, along the following lines:

a) knowledge of God is what makes humans right-thinking and good and capable of having their souls saved in Eternity;
b) this knowledge should be accessible wherever humans live and work; and
c) the means should be at hand for any right-thinking individual to verify the Truth or eliminate the Error in their knowledge.

These "means" are then formulated as the starting point of what becomes "scientific method".

So, as a result (combining here the matter of the absence of any sovereign authority for the scientific investigator's conscience, and the Christian-theological justification for certain methods of investigation that might not appear to have been provided by any previously-existing authority), even with scientific methods such as experiments, the conscience of an investigator who separated his/her responsibility for the Truth from the claims of Church authority — but without opposing or rebelling against that authority — could not ensure that his/her investigation could or would increase knowledge of the truth.

There is another feature that is crucial regarding the consequences of vesting authority in a Central Knowledge-Certifier. For thousands of years, Indian mathematics were excelling in increasing knowledge yet nobody knew about its findings for millennia outside of the villages or small surrounding territories — because there did not exist any notion of *publication of results and findings* for others. Contrast this with the enormous propaganda ascribing so many of the further advancements in the New Science of tangibles to the system that emerged of scholarly publication and dissemination of fellow researchers' findings and results. This development is largely ascribed to "learning the lessons" of the burning of the libraries of Constantinople in 1453 which deprived Western civilization of so much ancient learning.

The issue is publication, and yet at the same time, the issue is *not just* publication. Rather, it is: on what basis does publication of new findings and research take place? Our point here is that publication will serve to advance knowledge in rapid and great strides *if and only if* authority is vested in the integrity and depth of probing by earlier investigators and investigations into all the various pathways and possibilities. Otherwise, this societal necessity and usefulness for publication becomes readily and easily subverted by... the Culture of Patents, the exclusivity of "intellectual property" or what might be described today as "Monopoly Right".

If & only if we put first the matter of the *actual conduct* of scientific investigations and the 'politics' attaching to that conduct (meaning: the *ways and means* by which new results are enabled to build humanity's store of knowledge) — *then & only then* can we hope to reconstruct the actual line of development. With the actual knowledge of this line of development, for any given case, we can then proceed to critique, isolate and eliminate the thinking and underlying ideological outlook that keep scientific work and its contents travelling down the wrong path on some given problem or question. The issue is not just to oppose the Establishment in theory, in words. The issue is rather to oppose the Establishment in practice, beginning with vesting authority regarding matters of science and present state of knowledge in the integrity and depth of probing by earlier investigators and investigations to date into all the various pathways and possibilities of a given subject-matter.

1.2.3. Delinearized History of Time and Knowledge — The Starting Point

All starting-points are arbitrary. However, according to a well-worn notion, "if you don't know where you're going, any path can take you there." (This idea has been recorded among peoples of many very different times and places — in the U.S., by the U.S. baseball celebrity Yogi Berra of the late 20th century to the Arabian desert, attributed to Prophet Muhammad, the founding messenger of Islamic religion in the 7th century CE in a famous *hadith*.) This paper sets out to investigate the notions of delinearized historical rendering of scientific and technological development. That process has become firmly established in the world's thinking as entirely western, if not indeed today overwhelming based in or dependent upon the United States. Our starting-point? The synthesis, over the five centuries that followed the life of the Prophet Muhammad, of ancient learning by the Arab scholars inspired by Islam.

The Summary

At the PDO Planetarium of Oman, Dr. Marwan Shwaiki recounted for us an arrestingly delinearized history of the Arab contribution to world scientific and technical culture. What follows is our distillation of some of the main outlines:

Human civilization is synonymous with working with nature. For thousands of years of known history, we know that man marveled in using mathematics to design technologies that created the basis of sustaining life on this planet. In this design, the natural system had been used as a model. For thousands of years, the sun was recognized as the source of energy that is needed to sustain life. For thousands of years, improvements were made over natural systems without violating natural principles of sustainability. The length of a shadow was used by ancient civilizations in the Middle East to regulate the flow of water for irrigation – a process still in presence in some parts, known as the *fallaj* system. At nights, stars and other celestial bodies were used to ascertain water flow. This is old, but by no means obsolete, technology. In fact, this technology is far superior to the irrigation implanted in the modern age that relies on deep- water exploitation.

For thousands of years of known history, stars were used to navigate. It was no illusion, even for those who believed in myths and legends: stars and celestial bodies are dynamic. This dynamic nature nourished poetry and other imaginings about these natural illuminated bodies for thousands of years. The Babylonians started these stories, as far as one can find out from known history. Babylonian civilization is credited with dividing the heavenly bodies in 12 groups, known as the Zodiac. The Babylonians are also credited with the sexagesimal principle of dividing the circle into 360 degrees and each degree into 60 minutes. They are not, however, the responsible for created confusion between the unit of time (second and minute) and space (Zatzman, 2007). Their vision was more set on the time domain. The Babylonians had noticed that the sun returned to its original location among the stars once every 365 days. They named this length of time a "year". They also noticed that the moon made almost 12 revolutions during that period. Therefore, they divided the year into 12 parts and each of them was named a "month". Hence, the Babylonians were the first to conceive of the divisions of the astronomical clock.

Along came Egyptian civilization, which followed the path opened by the Babylonians. They understood even in those days, the sun is not just a star, and the earth is not just a planet. In a continuous advancement of knowledge, they added more constellations to those already identified by the Babylonians. They divided the sky into 36 groups starting with the brightest star, Sirius. They believed (on the basis of their own calculations) that the sun took 10 days to cross over each of the 36 constellations. That was what they were proposing *thousands of years before the Gregorian calendar fixed the number of days to some 365*. Remarkably, this latter fixation would actually violate natural laws; in any event, it was something of which the Egyptians had no part. The Gregorian "solution" was larded with a Eurocentric bias, one that solved the problem of the days that failed to add up by simply wiping out 12 days (Unix users can see this for themselves if they issue the command "cal 1752" in a terminal session).

It was the Greeks — some of whom, *e.g.*, Ptolemy, travelled to Egypt to gather knowledge — who brought the total number of constellations to 48. This was a remarkable achievement. Even after thousands more years of civilization and the discovery of constellations in the southern sky, — something previously inaccessible to the peoples to whose history we have access — the total number of constellations was declared to be 88 in 1930. Of course, the Greek version of the same knowledge contained many myths and legends, but it always portrayed the eternal conflict between good and evil, between ugly and beautiful, and between right and wrong.

The emergence of Islam in the Arabian Peninsula catapulted Arabs to gather knowledge on a scale and at a pace unprecedented in its time. Even before this, they were less concerned with constellations as groups of stars, and far more focused on individual stars and using them effectively to navigate. (Not by accident, star constellations' names are of Greek origin, while the names of individual stars are mostly of Arabic in origin.) In the modern astronomical atlas, some 200 of the 400 brightest stars are given names of Arabic origin. Arabs, just like ancient Indians, also gave particular importance to the moon. Based on the movement of the moon among the stars, the Arabs divided the sky and its stars into 28 sections naming them *manazil*, meaning the mansions of the moon. The moon is "hosted" in each mansion for a day and a night. Thus, the pre-Islamic Arabs based their calendar on the moon, although they noted the accumulating differences between the solar and lunar calendars. They also had many myths surrounding the sun, moon, and the stars. While Greek myths focused on kings and gods, however, Arab myths were more focused on individuals and families.

Prehistoric Indians and Chinese assumed that the Earth had the shape of a shell borne by four huge elephants standing on a gigantic turtle. Similarly, some of the inhabitants of Asia Minor envisaged that the Earth was in the form of a huge disk carried by three gigantic whales floating on the water. The ancient inhabitants of Africa believed that the sun sets into a "lower world" every evening and that huge elephants pushed it back all night in order to rise the next morning. Even the ancient Egyptians imagined the sky in the shape of a huge woman surrounding the Earth and decorated from the inside with the stars. This was in sharp contrast to the ancient Greek belief that the stars were part of a huge sphere. Ptolemy refined the ancient Greek knowledge of astronomy by imagining a large sphere with the stars located on the outer surface. He thought that all the planets known at the time - Mercury, Venus, Mars, Jupiter and Saturn - were revolving within this huge sphere, together with the sun and the moon.

The ancient Greeks, including Aristotle, assumed that the orbits of these celestial bodies were perfectly circular and that the bodies would keep revolving forever. For Aristotle, such perfection manifested symmetric arrangements. His followers continue to use this model. Scientifically speaking the spherical model is nothing different from the huge elephant on a gigantic turtle model and so on. What precipitated over the centuries following Ptolemy is an Eurocentric bias that any models that the Greek proposed is inherently superior than the models proposed by Ancient Indians, Africans, or Chinese. In the bigger picture, however, we know now that the pathways of celestial bodies are non-symmetric and dynamic. Only with this non-symmetric model can one explain retrograde motion of the planets – a phenomenon that most ancient civilizations even noticed. Eurocentric views, however, would continue to promote a single theory that saw the Earth as the centre of the Universe. In Ptolemy's word: "During its rotation round the Earth, a planet also rotates in a small circle. On return to its orbit, it appears to us as if it is going back to the west." Of course, this assertion, albeit false, explained the observation of retrograde motion. Because it explains a phenomenon, it becomes true – the essence of pragmatic approach led to the belief that the Earth is indeed the centre of the Universe – a belief that would dominate the Eurocentric world for over thousand years.

The knowledge gathered about astronomy by the ancient Chinese and Indians was both extensive and profound. The Chinese were particularly proficient in recording astronomical incidents. The Indians excelled in calculations and had established important astronomical observatories. It was the Arabs of the post-Islamic renaissance that would lead the world for many centuries, setting an example of how to benefit from knowledge of the previous civilizations. Underlying this synthesizing capacity was a strong motive to seek the truth about everything.

Among other reasons for this, a most important reason one was that every practicing Muslim is required to offer formal prayer five times a day, all relating to the position of the sun in the horizon. They are also required to fast one month of the year and offer pilgrimage to Mecca once in a lifetime, no matter how far they resided (as long as they can afford the trip).

Most importantly, they were motivated by the *hadith* of The Prophet that clearly outlined, "It is obligatory for every Muslim man and woman to seek Knowledge through science (as in process)". This was a significant point of departure diverging extremely sharply away from the Hellenized conception that would form the basis of what later became "Western civilization" at the end of the European Middle Ages. Greek thought from its earliest forms associated the passage of time not with the unfolding of new further knowledge about a phenomenon, but rather with decay and the onset of increasing disorder. Its conceptions of the Ideal, of the Forms etc. are all entire and complete unto themselves, and — most significantly— they standing *outside* Time, truth being identified with a point in which everything stands still. (Even today, conventional models based on the "New Science" of tangibles unfolded since the 17th century discloses its debt to these Greek models by virtue of its obsession with the steady state as what is considered the "reference-point" from which to discuss many physical phenomena, as though there was such a state anywhere in nature…) Implicitly, on the basis of such a standpoint, consciousness and knowledge exist in the here-and-now — after the Past and before the Future unfurls. (Again, today, conventional scientific models treat time as the independent variable, in which one may go forward or backward, whereas time in nature cannot be made to go backward — even if a process is reversible.) All this has a significant, but rarely articulated, consequence for how Nature and its truths would be cognized. According to this arrangement, the individual's knowledge of the truth at any given moment, frozen outside of Time, is *co-extensive* with whatever is being observed, noted, studied, etc.

The Islamic view diverged sharply by distinguishing belief, knowledge (*i.e.*, some conscious awareness of the truth), and truth (or actuality). In this arrangement, the individual's knowledge of the truth or of nature is always fragmentary and also time-dependent. Furthermore, how, whether or even where knowledge is gathered cannot be subordinated to the individual's present state of belief(s), desires or prejudices. In the Islamic view, a person seeking knowledge of the truth cannot be biased against the source of knowledge, be it in the form of geographical location or tangible status of a people. Muslims felt compelled to become what we term as 'scientist' or independent thinker, each person deriving their inspiration from the *Qu'ran* and the *hadith* of Prophet Muhammad. Hence, they had no difficulty gaining knowledge from the experience of their predecessors in different fields of science and mathematics. They were solely responsible for bringing back the writings of Greek Aristotle and Ptolemy and the Indian Brahmagupta in the same breath. Neither were their role models: they were simply their ancestors whose knowledge Muslims didn't want to squander. They started the greatest translation campaign in the history of mankind, to convert the written works of previous civilizations into Arabic. In due course, they had gained all prior knowledge of astronomy, and that enabled them to become the world leaders in that field of science for five successive centuries. Even their political leaders were fond of science and knowledge. One remarkable pioneer of knowledge was Caliph Al-Mamoon, one of the Abbasite rulers. Some one thousand years before Europeans were debating how flat the Earth is, Al-Mamoon and his scholars already knew the earth is spherical (although — significantly — *not* in the European perfect-sphere sense), but he wanted them to find out the circumference of the Earth. Al-Mamoon sent out two highly competent scientific expeditions. Working independently, they were to measure the circumference of the Earth. The first expedition went to Sinjar, a very flat desert in Iraq. At a certain point, on latitude 35 degrees north, they fixed a post into the ground and tied a rope to it. Then they started to walk carefully northwards, in order to make the North pole appear one degree higher in the sky. Each time the end of the rope was reached, the expedition fixed another post and stretched another rope from it until their destination was reached: latitude 36 degrees north. They recorded the total length of the ropes and returned to the original starting point at 35 degrees north. From there, they repeated the experiment heading south this time. They continued walking and stretching ropes between posts until the North pole dropped in the sky by one degree, when they reached the latitude of 34 degrees.

The second of Almamon's expeditions did the same thing but in the Kufa desert. When they had finished the task, both expeditions returned to Al-Mamoon and told him the total length of the rope used for measuring the length of one degree of the Earth's circumference. Taking the average of all expeditions, the length of one degree amounted to 56.6 Arabic miles. The Arabic mile is equal to 1973 metres. Therefore, according to the measurements made by the two expeditions, the Earth's circumference is equal to 40,252 kilometres. Nowadays, the figure is held to be 40,075 kilometres. So, how does it compare with the circumference of the earth as we know today? Today, It is known to be 40,075 km if measured through the equator, a difference of less than 200 km. Contrast that with the debate that was taking place in Europe over the earth being flat many centuries later. Another important aspect, this was the first time in known history, a state sponsored fundamental research. The motive of Caliph Mamoon was not to capture more land and history shows that these rulers were not the recipient of any tax. In fact, all rulers paid zakat, the obligatory charity, for the wealth they possessed, the entire amount going to the poor. Also, the judicial system was separate from the administration. Judicial system being always in the hands of the 'most righteous', rather than most 'powerful'. In fact, during the entire Ottoman period, even the state language was not Arabic. For administration, it was Turkish for communication with the headquarters and local languages for the local communication.

Some eight centuries later, we come to the heart of Eurocentric attitude to science and knowledge. In 16th century, Copernicus identified, "The Earth is not located in the center of the universe but the sun is. The earth and the planets rotate around the Sun." This simple observation of the truth could not be tolerated by the Catholic Church. For the Catholic Church, the Earth was the centre of the universe, with possibly the Vatican at its epicenter! They would not realize there is no room for blind faith and prejudice in seeking knowledge or the truth. Galeleo, yet another Church member offered another blow to the Eurocentric dogma. Galileo saw the earth moving. In his words, "O people! Beware that your Earth, which you think stationary, is in fact rotating. We are living on a great pendulum." Galileo wasn't just a 'terrorist' interested in blasphemy. He discovered the four great moons of Jupiter. He was the inventor of the clock pendulum and the "Laws of Motion". The Church could not bear Galileo's boldness. He was put on trial. Confronted with such tyranny, Galileo, who was by then old and weak, yielded and temporarily changed his mind. But while he was going out of the court, he stamped his feet in anger saying: "But you are still rotating Earth!" This was the beginning of New Science that would dominate the world until today.

Until the works of the Spanish Muslims, all translations were limited to science without particular attention to what would be considered philosophical. Averröes was the first one to venture into even purely philosophical work, particularly that of Aristotle. It is well acknowledged that without this translation, Aristotle's work would disappear from public access. This is indeed a bifurcation point in time. Muslims used older knowledge to increase their knowledge, Eurocentrics took that knowledge to increase their ignorance. As a consequence, one can easily see how all atrocities ranging from the mediaeval Crusades (at the Mediterranean edge of western Asia) to modern-day Crusades (in the Gulf region of western Asia) has only focused on promoting the aphenomenal model and how prior knowledge was destroyed or distorted in order to achieve 'quick victories'.

A Discussion

What we see here is a difference in attitude between standpoints maintained pre- and post Thomas Aquinas, the father of Eurocentric philosophy. Before his time, truth was bound up with knowledge, and could be augmented by subsequent inquiry. After that point, on the other hand, the correctness or quality of knowledge has rendered as a function of its conformity with the experience or theories of the elite (called 'laws'). Before, personal experience was just 'personal'. After, the experience of the elite has become a commodity that can be purchased as a source of knowledge. Before, the source of knowledge was individual endeavor, research, and critical thinking. After, it became dogma, blind faith, and the power of external (aphenomenal) forces. After Thomas Aquinas, few Europeans have engaged in *increasing* knowledge *per se*. If they did, they were severely persecuted. Copernicus (1473-1543) is just one example. What was his offence? The Earth moves around a stationary sun. It was not complete knowledge (it is important to note that 'complete' knowledge is anti-knowledge), but it was knowledge in the right direction. His theory contradicted that of Ptolemy and in general the Catholic church. Yet, Wikepedia wrote this about him: "While the heliocentric theory had been formulated by Greek, Indian and Muslim savants centuries before Copernicus, his reiteration that the sun — rather than the Earth — is at the center of the solar system is considered among the most important landmarks in the history of modern science." While there is some recognition that Copernicus's knowledge was not *new* knowledge, it did not prevent European scientists from making statements that would sanctify Copernicus. Goethe, for instance, wrote:

> "Of all discoveries and opinions, none may have exerted a greater effect on the human spirit than the doctrine of Copernicus. The world had scarcely become known as round and complete in itself when it was asked to waive the tremendous privilege of being the center of the universe. Never, perhaps, was a greater demand made on mankind — for by this admission so many things vanished in mist and smoke! What became of our Eden, our world of innocence, piety and poetry; the testimony of the senses; the conviction of a poetic — religious faith? No wonder his contemporaries did not wish to let all this go and offered every possible resistance to a doctrine which in its converts authorized and demanded a freedom of view and greatness of thought so far unknown, indeed not even dreamed of."

In the above statement, there are three items to note: 1) there is no reference to Copernicus's knowledge being prior knowledge; 2) there is no comment on what the problem was with Copernicus's theory; 3) there is no explanation to why religious fanatics continued to stifle knowledge and how to handle them in the future.

What would be the knowledge-based approach here? To begin with, to ask whether the theory contradicts the truth. European scholars did not ask this question. They compared with words in the *Holy Bible* — a standard whose authenticity, impossible to establish unambiguously, was itself subject to interpretation. When we ask the question "Is such-and-such true?", we cannot simply define the truth as we wish. We have to state clearly the standard measure of this truth. For Muslim scientists prior ot the European Renaissance, the *Qu'ran* formed the standard. Here is the relevant passage Chapter 36 (36-40) from the *Qu'ran* addressing the matters of whether the sun is 'stationary', the earth stands at the centre of the solar system, or the moon is a planet:

لَا ٱلشَّمْسُ (كَٱلْعُرْجُونِ ٱلْقَدِيمِ ٣٩) وَٱلْقَمَرَ قَدَّرْنَـٰهُ مَنَازِلَ حَتَّىٰ عَادَ (ٱلْعَزِيزِ ٱلْعَلِيمِ ٣٨) وَٱلشَّمْسُ تَجْرِى لِمُسْتَقَرٍّ لَّهَا ذَٰلِكَ تَقْدِيرُ
(٤٠) ٱلْقَمَرَ وَلَا ٱلَّيْلُ سَابِقُ ٱلنَّهَارِ وَكُلٌّ فِى فَلَكٍ يَسْبَحُونَ يَنبَغِى لَهَا أَن تُدْرِكَ

One possible translation: "And the sun runs on its fixed course for a term (appointed). That is the Decree (the word comes from 'qadr' as in 'proportioned' or 'balanced') of the All-Mighty (Al-Aziz) and the All-Knowing (Al-Aleem, the root word being *ilm* or science). And the moon, We have measured (or proportioned, again coming from the root word, 'qadr') for it locations (literally meaning 'mansion') till it returns like the old dried curved date stalk. It is not for the sun to overtake the moon, nor does the night outstrip the day. They all float, each in an orbit."

When did you find out that sun is not stationary? What is the speed and how does the solar orbit look like? See the following table (Zatzman et al., 2007c).

Bibliographic Entry	Result (w/surrounding text)	Standardized Result
Chaisson, Eric, & McMillan, Steve. *Astronomy Today*.New Jersey: Prentice-Hall, 1993: 533.	"Measurements of gas velocities in the solar neighborhood show that the sun, and everything in its vicinity, orbits the galactic center at a speed of about 220 km/s …."	220 km/s
"Milky Way Galaxy " *The New Encyclopedia Britannica*.15th ed. Chicago: Encyclopaedia Britannica, 1998: 131.	"The Sun, which is located relatively far from the nucleus, moves at an estimated speed of about 225 km per second (140 miles per second) in a nearly circular orbit."	225 km/s
Goldsmith, Donald. *The Astronomers*.New York: St. Martin's Press, 1991: 39.	"If the solar system … were not moving in orbit around the center, we would fall straight in toward it, arriving a hundred million years from now. But because we do move (at about 150 miles per second) along a nearly circular path …."	240 km/s
Norton, Arthur P. *Norton's Star Atlas*.New York: Longman Scientific & Technical, 1978: 92.	"… the sun's neighborhood, including the Sun itself, are moving around the centre of our Galaxy in approximately circular orbits with velocities of the order of 250 km/s."	250 km/s
Recer, Paul (Associated Press). Radio Astronomers Measure Sun's Orbit Around Milky Way. *Houston Chronicle.* 1 June 1990.	"Using a radio telescope system that measures celestial distances 500 times more accurately than the Hubble Space Telescope, astronomers plotted the motion of the Milky Way and found that the sun and its family of planets were orbiting the galaxy at about 135 miles per second." "The sun circles the Milky Way at a speed of about 486,000 miles per hour."	217 km/s

With 20/20 hindsight, many write these days that the speed of the sun could be predicted using Newton's law. What is missing in this assertion is that Newton's law is absolute and all hypotheses behind Newton's gravitational law are absolutely true. In addition, it also assumes that we know exactly how the gravitational attractions are imparted from various celestial bodies — a proposition that stands (not to put too fine a point on it) "over the moon"!

Along came Galileo (1564-1642). Today, he is considered to be the "father of modern astronomy," as the "father of modern physics", and as the "father of science". As usual, the Church found reasons to ask Galileo to stop promoting his ideas. However, Galileo really was not a 'rebel'. He remained submissive to the Church and never challenged the original dogma of the Church that promotes the aphenomenal model. Consider the following quote from Wikipedia:

Psalm 93:1, Psalm 96:10, and Chronicles 16:30 state that "the world is firmly established, it cannot be moved." Psalm 104:5 says, "[the LORD] set the earth on its foundations; it can never be moved." Ecclesiastes 1:5 states that "the sun rises and the sun sets, and hurries back to where it rises."

Table 1.1. Science and the Scientists

Scientist	Period	Specialization	Remarks
Isaac Newton	1643-1717	Physics: Laws of motion, conservation of momentum, laws of gravitation, properties of matter Light and Sound: Visible spectrum of light, law of cooling, speed of sound, theory of color, diffraction Heat: law of cooling Mathematics: generalized binomial theorem, power series, Newton's method	God governs all, knows all that is or can be done; wrote more on religion than he did on natural science; much left unpublished at his death
J.C. Maxwell	1831-1879	Physics: Maxwell's equation: electricity, magnetism and inductance, first true color photograph Mathematics:Maxwell's distribution, dimentional analysis, Optics: optics and color vision	Scots Presbyterian (a Protestant sect outside the "established " Church of England)
A.M. Ampère	1775-1836	Physics: relation between electricity and magnetism, Ampere's circuital law,	
M. Faraday	1979-1867	Physics: electromagnetism, Faraday's law of induction Chemistry: electrochemistry, Benzene, bunsen burner, oxidation numbers, anode, cathode, electrode, ion.	He kept religion and science strictly apart because they are different from the direct communications between God and the soul
J.C.F. Gauss	1777-1855	Number theory, differential geometry, geodesy, electrostatics, astronomy, optics, magnetism, Gauss-Seidel, Gauss-Newton method,	Gauss was deeply religious and conservative

Table 1.1. Science and the Scientists (Continued)

Scientist	Period	Specialization	Remarks
D. Bernoulli	1700-1782	Bernoulli's equation/Theorem, An ideal fluid flow, conservation of energy	Calvinist faith
H.P.G.Darcy	1803-1858	Darcy's Law on fluid flow, permeability constant, Darcy-Weisbach equation	
P.S. Laplace	1749-1827	Laplace differential equation, capillary action, double refraction, the velocity of sound, the theory of heat, elastic fluids, Laplace transformation, nebular hypothesis, origin of solar system, existence of black hole, mathematical astronomy, celestial and classical mechanics, Young-Laplace equation in surface tension	Replying to someone asking if he believed in the existence of God, Laplace said: "Je n'en ai besoin de cette hypothèse [*I have no need of that hypothesis at all*]."
Albert Einstein	1879-1955	theory of relativity, statistical mechanics, quantum theory, Theory of Brownian Movement, The Evolution of Physics	Jewish; conventional separation of scientific from personal views, but dismissed quantum theory with the remark that "God does not play dice with the world"
Robert Boyle	1627-1691	kinetic theory, Boyle's law,	
J.A.C.Charles	1746-1823	Charle's Law (Ideal gas law), La Charliere's principle	
C. Darwin	1809-1882	The origin of species, natural selection, evolution theory	
A.L. Lavoisier	1743-1794	Theory of combustion, laws of conservation of mass,	
Gregor Mendel	1822-1884	Genetics, hybrid	Catholic religious orders
A. G. Bell	1847-1922	Inventor of the telephone	Scots Presbyterian
John Dalton	1766-1844	Dalton's law of partial pressures	
O.&W. Wright	1871-1948; 1867-1912	Air place	
James Watt	1736-1819	Steam engine	

Galileo defended heliocentrism, and claimed it was not contrary to those Scripture passages. He took Augustine's position on Scripture: not to take every passage literally, particularly when the scripture in question is a book of poetry and songs, not a book of instructions or history. The writers of the Scripture wrote from the perspective of the terrestrial world, and from that vantage point the sun does rise and set. In fact, it is the earth's rotation which gives the impression of the sun in motion across the sky.

Galileo's trouble did not come from the Establishment because he contradicted Aristotle's principle. For instance, Galileo contradicted Aristotle's notion that the moon is a perfect sphere or the heavy object would fall faster than lighter objects directly proportional to weight, etc. Amazingly both the Establishment and Galileo continued to be enamoured with Aristotle while bickerly fighting with each other. Could the original premise that Aristotle worked on be the same as that of the Church as well as Galileo's? Why didn't he rebel against this first premise?

Galileo's contributions to technology, as the inventor of geometric and military compass suitable by gunners and surveyors, are notable. There, even Aristotle would agree, this was indeed τεχνε (*techne*) or "useful knowledge" — useful to the Establishment, of course.

What happens if we embark from another starting-point, employing a different mode of discourse apparently more familiar in its uses of conventional mathematical conceptions?

Table 1.1 shows the affiliations of various European scientists. Scientists are usually nervous about the talk on religion/science mix-up. The enlightened ones know that the conventional discourses from either the conventional-religious or tangibles-science starting-points end up going off the rails. However, they don't see *the reason* they go off the rails. It's not because they are mutually antagonistic. It's because they each support maintaining people in a state of ignorance and powerlessness, only from opposite directions that meet on the plane of utter and complete aphenomenality. The conventional religious guys substitute, to greater or lesser degrees, the "mind" of the God of conventional religion for the human brain of the individual scientific investigator. So this means not only human reason but human conscience is severely circumscribed in, or even kept altogether out of, scientific theory and practice. The conventional science-of-tangibles guys, on the other hand, declare or assume quite arbitrarily that the so-called "laws" they are discovering or using in the form of governing equations etc exist outside the characteristic time of any natural process. So singular phenomena are either marginalised or over-emphasised as exceptions to law. EITHER WAY (religious or tangibles route), nothing can be verified and asserted with conviction because neither the origin, pathway nor intention/aim of anything can be demonstrated on its own terms. Scientists who have good experimental technique are always a good thing, but today will such a conventionally-skilled scientific worker no matter how high the quality of that skill, address and solve the problems that cry out for solution? We need scientists with convictions, who can and do work with the courage of their conviction both in identifying the real problem, its cutting edge and its solution-path. In this table, the position/disposition of Laplace & Einstein are interesting. The Scots Presbyterians [Maxwell, Faraday] are interesting because they had no social standing in England (only in Scotland were the Presbyterians powerful, although not an "established" church), so they had to fight to defend their standing among the scientists of their time. Alexander Graham Bell came to America and escaped all that nonsense.

1.2.4. A Reflection on the Purposes of Science

There is a widespread notion that, *with Science, many practical problems of daily existence can be solved that could not be solved otherwise.* This notion is especially popular among engineers. However, it must be admitted that this idea is also very much part of contemporary culture. Certainly in the countries of what is broadly known as the Triad — the Anglo-American bloc (*i.e.*, the United States, Canada, Britain and Australia), the other countries of Europe & Russia, plus Japan — it is one of the hallmarks of what is generally accepted as a modern outlook.

Here we have rendered the proposition in its most innocent-sounding form. If we zero in on the essence of this proposition, however, we stumble across something potentially far more contentious. People are inured to associating *"many practical problems of daily existence"* quite unconsciously with the immediate, the short term, that period in which time *t* stands at "right now". In order to define that period objectively, it must first be appreciated that, the moment a particular point in time has been identified, actual time has already moved on. So, in reality, time *t* is always and everywhere actually "*t* + Δ*t*". Hence, it follows that "right now" may be understood, and even "experienced", as the point at which *t* + Δ*t* → *t*, because at this point, in effect, Δ*t* → 0.

Here, however, we have to ask: is Science actually undertaken to address and deal with this rather singular point at which *t* + Δ*t* → *t*? Are the highest and best purposes of Science, or is indeed any other socially positive purpose, particularly well-served by addressing and dealing only or mainly or primarily with an immediate reality conditioned by the "Δ*t* → 0" criterion?

Elsewhere (Islam, 2003), this point has been identified and associated with what is called "the roller-coaster ride of the Information Age". For example: no sooner is a "daily life problem" like insomnia identified than the pharmaceutical industry produces a pill to help one fall asleep. Then, however, the problem of meeting the demands of daily life to wake up on time to get to work, etc., emerges, and another pill — this one to help one "wake up" to full consciousness — is developed and marketed. Similarly, sugar is identified as a latent dietary time-bomb and in almost no time flat, a "solution" is proffered consisting of a choice among "sugar-free" substitutes. It hardly ends there, as the sugar-free substitutionalists then end up in deadly warfare, *e.g.*, the Aspartamers *versus* the Saccharinisers, over whose substitute causes more lab rats to die more horrible deaths from dosages that, when scaled to anything in the range of adult human body-mass indices, bear no relation to any known pattern of human consumption of sugar even over an entire lifetime.

The serious point masked throughout this dreadful comedy is precisely the temporal criterion that each of these "solutions" was addressing in the first place. In every case, the litmus-test applied to the proposed intervening substance is: its performance over the period of time *t* = "right now". Everything else — including consequences for the human body or even initial acceptability to a functioning living organism — is deemed to fall in the category of "side effects" before being rudely sloughed off as "someone else's problem". The assumption underlying this practice is that the Science that addresses problems at the point where *t* + Δ*t* → *t* is the only useful or profitable "science". It follows that any science that takes of care of anything other than the short term is "blue sky" or otherwise "doesn't count", *i.e.*, isn't going to make anyone a billionaire.

Does there exist anything, anywhere in nature or society, that be taken care of mainly, only or primarily in the short term? Is such a notion consistent or inconsistent with what makes us human? Even positing this question stirs waters that run very, very deep. For example, the theoretical physicist Stephen Hawking created a huge best-seller in recent years with his reflection on this problem, arrestingly entitled "A Brief History of Time". This paper repositions and discusses the problem of Time, short-term and long-term, by setting out what can best be described as its "de-linearized" history.

1.2.5. Time-conceptions, the Tangible-intangible Nexus, and the Social Role of Knowledge

As already mentioned above: the very moment a particular point in time has been identified, actual time has already moved on. Therefore, in reality, time t is always and everywhere actually "$t + \Delta t$". There is a subtlety introduced here: the observer cannot be detached from the process or phenomenon being observed. This is indeed an important truth that cognitive psychology, with reference to the human personality in general, explored in some depth during the 20th century. However, its application to the actual practice of scientific investigation has yet to be elaborated. Quite to the contrary: since Newton, one of the bedrock premises of the so-called "hard sciences" (physics, chemistry, biology, geology and all the engineering disciplines associated with these bodies of scientific knowledge) has been that the observer observes and speaks from *outside* the reference-frame of the phenomenon or process being studied.

Of course, the immediate consciousness of the scientific investigator as a human observer, at time t = "right now", is precisely that s/he is indeed independent of the phenomenon or process being studied. Far from being a merely static contradiction, however, this indicates that, as an inevitable byproduct of uncritically accepting that immediate consciousness as the definitive reality, an actual loss of information has already taken place: information about the relationship between the observer and the phenomenon or process being studied. In this relationship, the "I" of the individual has become the "relate", meaning: the element that connects the observer as part of the reference frame to everything else in the reference frame.

What about this information loss? It should alert us to the risk we start to run if we conflate knowledge of the truth entirely and exclusively with what has been observed and recorded from within the moment in which $t + \Delta t \rightarrow t$. The chief error and limitation in the doctrine known to philosophy as empiricism — which says the only reliable knowledge is inductive and is generated by experiment, experience, and-or the human sensorium (sight, hearing, taste, touch or smell) — resides in its failure to grasp this objective fact of the continuance of time, independently of anyone. This state of affairs is rife with profound implications for assessing what constitutes reliable knowledge of the truth and distinguishing it from a catalogue of perceptions larded with pattern-matchings of varying degrees of elegance.

What is needed is to advance the analysis further from this point. The difficulties involved are palpable. First, it becomes necessary to propose a new level of generality. This would be a level of generality of consideration in which the evident contributions to our knowledge of the truth deriving from moment-to-moment observations based on the human sensorium and various data-collection methods and measuring systems on the one hand, and on the other hand the positioning of where these phenomena fit into a bigger picture with time considered over the long term, can both be accommodated. For this task, the existing methods of what has been called, since the 17th century, "New Science" — *viz.*, to effect a "division of labour" between, on the one hand, the collection and cataloguing of observations of a process or phenomenon and, on the other hand, the generalizing of larger meanings and patterns from the riot of data collected and catalogued — seem ever clumsier and more inadequate. In today's Information Age, we stand literally awash in collections of data about anything and everything on scales heretofore unimagined (Zatzman and Ialam, 2007a).

	Physically incommensurable	Quantifiable
TANGIBLE?	TO SOME DEGREE: NO	TO LARGE DEGREE: YES
INTANGIBLE?	TO LARGE DEGREE: YES	TO SOME DEGREE: NO

Figure 1. Tangibility/Measurability matrix (Zatzman & Islam, 2007a).

Here a very old idea can be summoned into service with a highly modern twist. The old idea is to distinguish what is tangible from what is intangible. The modern twist is to classify as "intangible" all those features that exist within a process or phenomenon but have not yet acquired or developed a tangible expression. Then, the differences between the physical commensurability and measurability of tangible and intangible elements have to be arranged systematically. The following matrix is suggestive:

This matrix and its spectra suggest *pairing* tangible with intangible components, according to some relate that combines their relative commensurability and quantifiability, and to consider phenomena or processes as a *nexus* of tangible and intangible components. Note that this position stands 180 degrees opposite the general dispositions of conventional "New Science". According to the conventional standpoint, in the name of ensuring that the truth of the tangible doesn't get mixed up with superstition, religion, gobbledy-gook, or subjective biases, all notions of the intangible are to be banished to the margins.

It is the progress of (actual) *time* which provides the implicit connection between greater or lesser tangibility/intangibility. That "actual time" is what has been discussed extensively elsewhere (Zatzman & Islam, 2007a) as "characteristic time" in the case of natural processes, designated symbolically as $t_{NATURAL}$, or as "historical time" in the case of social processes, designated symbolically as $t_{HISTORICAL}$. Either of these is consistent with the idea of *time as a fourth dimension*. This stands in stark contrast, however, to the conventional notion of *time as the independent variable* developed throughout New Science since Newton — what is best characterised as t_{LINEAR} (Zatzman & Islam, 2007a)

A more explicit index of this tangible-intangible nexus, also related to the passage of actual time, is the state of our *information, i.e.,* our previous or existing relevant knowledge. This is less like data and more like understanding, taking "understanding" to refer to the fruit of conscious participation of individuals in definite acts of 'finding out' (Zatzman & Islam, 2007a)

Time and information here have their tangible expressions, *e.g.,* as "duration", or as "data". However, it is their intangible role that is decisive in mediating our ability as humans to make use of knowledge of the truth for socially positive ends and humanize the environment, natural or social. These are the activities that secure humanity's long term. No human social problem is without some human social solution. Whoever would increase knowledge is bound to disturb the *status quo*, but even so, a person must increase his/her knowledge of the truth. The essence of human social agency lies on the path of pursuing knowledge.

1.2.6. Delinearized History of Time, Science, and Truth

Thousands of years ago, Indian philosophers commented about the role of time, as a space (or dimension), in unraveling the truth, the essential component of knowledge (Zatzman and Islam, 2007b). The phrase used by Ancient Indian philosophers was that *the world reveals itself*. Scientifically, it would mean that time is the dimension in which all the other dimensions completely unfold, so that truth becomes continuously known to humans, who use science (as in critical thinking). Another very well-known principle from Ancient India is the connection among *Chetna* (inspiration), *dharma* (inherent property), *karma* (deeds arising from *Chetna*), and *chakra* (wheel, symbolizing closed loop of a sustainable life style). Each of these concepts scientifically bears the intangible meanings, which cannot be expressed with conventional European mathematical approach (Joseph, 2000). Only recently, Ketata et al. (2006a; 2006b; 2006c; 2006d) recognized this fact and introduced a series of mathematical tools that can utilize the concept of meaningful zero and infinity in computational methods.

These ancient principles contain some of the most useful hints, extending far back into the oldest known human civilizations, of true sustainability as a state of affairs requiring the involvement of infinite time as a condition of maintaining a correct analysis as well as ensuring positive pro-social conclusions (Khan and Islam, 2007b). Moving from Ancient India to Ancient China, the Chinese philosophers provide one with some very useful insight into very similar principles of sustainability and knowledge. The well-known statement, although rarely connected to science, of Confucius (551-479 B.C.) relates unraveling of the truth to creating *balance* (the statement is: *Strive for balance that remains quiet within*). For Confucius, balance had the essential condition of 'quiet within'. This idea is of the essence of intangibles in the "knowledge" sense (Zatzman and Islam, 2007b).

In The *Qu'ran* (first and only version compiled in mid-7th century), humans' time on earth and time in nature are all part of one vast expanse of time. This position is entirely consistent with the notion that the world reveals itself. In terms of the role of intention, the most famous saying of The Prophet — the very first cited in the Bukhari's collection of the *hadiths* — is that any deed is based on the intention (Hadiths of The Prophet, 2007). A review of human history reveals that what is commonly cast or understood as "the perpetual conflict between Good and Evil" has always been in fact about opposing intentions. The Good has always been characterized by an intention to serve a larger community, while Evil has been characterized as the intention to serve a self-interest. What was known in Ancient India as the purpose of life (serving humanity) is promoted in the Qur'an as serving self interest in the long-term (as in infinity, see discussion later). Because nature itself is such that any act of serving others leads to serving the self in the long term, it is conceivable that all acts of serving others in fact amount to self-interest in the long-term (Islam, 2005b). In terms of *balance*, The *Qu'ran* promoted the notion of *qadar* (as in *Faqaddarahu*, فَقَدَّرَهُ, meaning 'thereby proportioned him', 80:19, The Qur'an), meaning proportionate or balanced in space as well as time. The *Qu'ran* is also specific about the beginning and end of human life. Personal communication with a PhD from MIT (as reported in Abou-Kassem et al., 2007) resulted in the following discussion. The word 'aakherat'(اخِرَة) is repeatedly used in The *Qu'ran* whenever the need for taking a long-term approach is highlighted. The word "*aakherat*" (as in *Al-aakherat*[1], الْآخِرَة , 2:4 The Qur'an) is the feminine form of the adjective "*aakher*" (أخِر), meaning "last", as in last one to arrive, or generally last one to take place. This is the simple or immediate meaning. A wider connotation: the word *aakher*, meaning the last when it describes a period of time, also connotes the infinite in that period. Thus, *Aakherat* referring to the life after, means it is an infinite life. This calls for the notion that while man is considered mortal, in fact man is eternal. Man's body is mortal but his *self* is eternal. This is the only kind of creation with this quality, being eternal. Hence, man approaches divine nature with the attribute of being eternal, that is the existence in $+\infty$ of time while differs with the attribute of having a beginning, meaning man lacks the existence in time $= 0$. The same after-life is sometimes referred to as *ukhraa* (أخرى), the feminine form of *aakhar*. Note the slight difference from the previous *aakher*, meaning last. The word *aakhar* means 'second', but used only when there is no 'third' (Arabic and Sanskrit distinguish grammatically between one, two and more than two, unlike European languages that distinguish between one and more-than-one, as reported by Islam and Zatzman (2006). This *ukhraa* is not used in The *Qu'ran*. In contrast to *aakherat*, two words are used in The *Qu'ran*. One is *ulaa* (as in Al-Ulaa, الْأُولَى, meaning The First, 92:13, The Qur'an). So, the life in this world is the 'first life' in contrast to the life after. The other word is *dunya* (as in Al-Dunya,الدُّنْيَا, 79:38, The Qur'an), which means the 'nearer' or 'lower'. So this life is nearer to us time-wise and also of lower quality. This Qur'anic description of human life, his role in this world and his eternal life is quite consistent with other oriental philosophies that considerably predate the period in which The *Qur'an* was first compiled in its tangible form.

There is a notion widespread in the Western world that the monotheistic premises of each of the three Abrahamic religions — Judaism, Christianity and Islam — point to broad but unstated other cultural common ground. The historical record suggests such has not been the case, however, when it comes to certain fundamental premises of the outlook on and approaches taken to science and scientific method.

The position of mainstream Greek, *i.e.*, Eurocentric, philosophy on the key question of the nature of the existence of the world external to any human observer is: *everything is either A or not-A*. That is Aristotle's law of the excluded middle which assumes time $t = $ "right now" (Zatzman and Islam, 2007b). Scientifically, this assumption is the beginning of what would be termed as steady-state models, for which Δt approaches 0. This model is devoid of the time component, a spurious state even if a time-dependent term is added in order to render the model 'dynamic' (Abou-Kassem et al., 2007). Aristotle's model finds its own root in Ancient Greek philosophy (or mythology) that assumes that 'time begins when Chaos of the Void ended' (Islam, 2005b). Quite similar to what Aristotle's law of excluded middle, the original philosophy also disconnected both time function and human intention by invoking the assumption, "the gods can interrupt human intention at any time or place". This assertion essentially eliminates any relationship between individual human acts with a sense responsibility. This particular aspect was discussed in details by Zatzman and Islam (2007b)

---

[1] "Al" stands for "The".

who identified the time function and the intention as the most important factors in conducting scientific research. Their argument will be presented later in this section.

The minority position of Greek philosophy, put forward by Heraclitus, was that matter is essentially atomic and that, at such a level, everything is in endless flux. Mainstream Greek philosophy of Heraclitus' own time buried his views because of their subversive implication that nature is essentially chaotic. Such an inference threatened the Greek mainstream view that Chaos was the Void that had preceded the coming into existence of the world, and that a natural order came into existence putting an end to chaos.

What Heraclitus had produced was in fact a most precise description of what the human observer actually perceives of the world. However, he did not account for time at all, so changes in nature at this atomic level incorporated no particular direction or intention. In the last half of the 18th century, John Dalton reasserted the atomic view of matter, albeit now stripped of Heraclitus' metaphysical discussion and explanations. Newton's laws of motion dominated the scientific discourse of his day, so Dalton rationalized this modernized atomic view with Newton's object masses and, and we end up with matter composed of atoms rendered as spherical balls in three-dimensional space, continuously in motion throughout three-dimensional space ... within time considered as an independent variable. This line of research seals any hope for incorporating time as a continuous function, which would effectively make the process infinite-dimensional.

Zatzman and Islam (2007b) have offered extensive review of Aristotle's philosophy and provided one with scientific explanation of why that philosophy is equivalent to launching the science of tangibles. In economic life, tangible goods and services and their circulation provide the vehicles whereby intentions become, and define, actions. Locked inside those tangible goods and services, inaccessible to direct observation or measurement, are intangible relations – among the producers of the goods and services and between the producer and Nature – whose extent, cooperativeness, antagonism and other characteristic features are also framed and bounded by intentions at another level, in which the differing interests of producers and their employers are mutually engaged. In economic terms, Zatzman and Islam (2007b) identified two sources of distortion in this process. They are: 1) linearization of complex societal non-linear dependencies (functions and relationships) through the introduction of the theories of marginal utility (MU); and 2) lines in the plane intersect as long as they are not parallel, *i.e.*, as long as the equation-relationships they are supposed to represent are not redundant. The first source removes very important information pertaining to social interactions and the second source enables the use of the "=" sign, where everything to its left is equated to everything to its right. Equated quantities cannot only be manipulated, but – especially – interchanged, according to the impeccable logic, as sound as Aristotle (who first propounded it), which says: two quantities each equal to a third quantity must themselves be equal to one another or, symbolically, that 'A = C' and 'B = C' implies that 'A = B'. Scientific implications of this logic will be discussed in the latter part of this section. Here, in philosophical sense, the introduction of this logic led to the development of a 'solution'. As further arguments will be built on this 'a solution', soon this 'a solution' will become 'the solution' as all relevant information are removed during the introduction of the aphenomenal process. This would lead to the emergence of 'equilibrium', 'steady state', and various other phenomena in all branches of New Science. It won't be noticeable to common people that these are not natural systems. If anyone questions the non-existence of such a process, s/he will be marginalized as 'conspiracy theorists', 'pseudo-scientists', and numerous other derogatory designations. This line of thinking would explain why practically all scientists up until Newton had tremendous difficulty with the Establishment in Europe. In the post-Renaissance world, the collision between scientists and the Establishment was erased — *not* because the Establishment became pro-science, but more likely because the New Scientists became equally obsessed with tangibles, devoid of time function as well as intention (Zatzman and Islam, 2007a). Theoretically, both of these groups subscribed to the same set of misconceptions or aphenomenal bases that launched the technology development in the post-renaissance era. Khan and Islam (2007a) identified these misconceptions as:

1) Chemicals are chemicals or energy is energy (meaning they are not function of the pathway and are measured as a function of a single dimension); 2) If you cannot see, it doesn't exist (only tangible expressions, as 'measurable by certain standard' are counted); 3) Simulation equals emulation (if there is agreement between reality and prediction at a given point in time, the entire process is being emulated). Zatzman and Islam (2007a) and Khan and Islam (2007a) attributed these misconceptions to the pragmatic approach (whatever works must be true), which can be traced back original Greek philosophy.

The immediate consequence of the science of tangibles is that every decision that emerges is scientifically false. The removal of a dimension and ignoring the consequences is inherent to this consequence (Mustafiz, 2006). Because time is the most important dimension, the omission of this dimension has the severest consequences. Time also forms the pathway of the science of intangibles. Intention, on the other hand, forms the root or foundation of the science of intangibles. Ignoring any of these would render the process aphenomenal. Zatzman and Islam (2007b) cited a number of examples to establish this assertion. One of them is as follows:

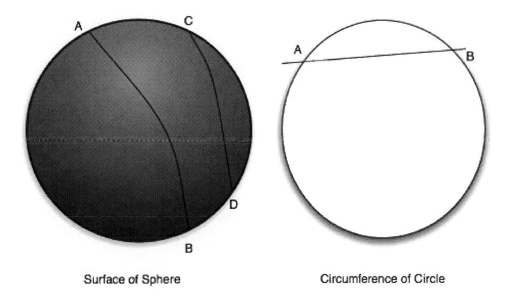

Surface of Sphere   Circumference of Circle

Figure 1.1. Sphere and Circle Compared (redrawn from Zatzman and Islam, 2007b).

Compare the circle to the sphere, in Figure 1.1 above. The shortest distance between two points A and B on the circle's circumference is a straight (secant) line joining them, whereas the curved arc of the circumference between the two points A and B is always longer than the secant. The shortest distance between two points on the surface of a sphere, on the other hand, is always a curve and can never be a straight line. Furthermore, between two points A and B lying on any great-circle of the sphere (*i.e.*, lying along any of an infinite number of circles that may be drawn around the surface of the sphere whose diameter is identical to that of the sphere itself) and between any other two points, say C and D, a curved line of the same length joining each pair of points will subtend a different amount of arc. For the points not on the great-circle, the same length-distance will subtend a greater arc than for points on a great-circle; curvature *k* in each case is uniform but different. On the other hand, what makes a circle circular rather than, say, elliptical, is precisely the condition whereby equal distances along its circumference subtend equal arcs, because curvature *k* anywhere along the circumference of a circle is the same.

Is anyone whose comprehension remains confined to cases of the circle in flat planar space likely to infer or extrapolate from such knowledge whatever they would need in order to grasp and use such differences found on the curved surface of the sphere? Of course not: indeed, any solution or solutions obtained for a problem formulated in two-dimensional space can often appear utterly aphenomenal when transferred or translated to three-dimensional space. In terms of the originating example of the fundamental metrics of the two kinds of surfaces: to those working in the environment of spherical surface-space, it becomes quickly obvious the shortest distance between two points that stand really close to one another on the surface of a sphere will approximate a straight line. In fact, of course, it is actually a curve and the idea that "the shortest distance between two points is a straight line" remains something that only approximates the situation in an extremely restricted subspace on the surface of a sphere. In a pragmatic sense, it is quite acceptable to propose that the shortest distance between two points is a straight line. However, in a real world which is anything but linear, this statement cannot form the basis for subsequent logical development as it would falsify all subsequent logical trains. Zatzman and Islam (2007b) called this attempt to simplify a model used to account for complex phenomena by chopping dimensions away at the outset (with the idea of adding them back in at the end) was "about as practicable as trying to make water run uphill."

The above point is further expounded by giving a simple, yet thought-provoking example (Zatzman and Islam, 2007a). This example involves an experiment carried out without the knowledge of the findings of Galileo and Newton. Someone could observe and write up everything about an experiment involving dropping a weighty lead ball from the top of the Tower of Pisa. On another occasion the same could be done for an experiment entailing dropping a feather from the top of the Tower. Comparing the two, the key observation might well be that the lead ball fell to the ground faster and, from that fact, it might even be speculated that the difference in the time taken to reach the ground was a function of the difference in the weight of the feather and the lead ball. They argued that no matter how much more precise the measuring of the two experiments became, in the absence of any other knowledge or discovery it would be difficult to overthrow or reject this line of reasoning. Now, let's say the measuring devices available for subsequent repetition of this pair of experiments over the next 10, 20 or 30 years develop digital readouts, to three or four decimal places of accuracy. Quite apart from what engineering marvels these 'precision clocks' have led to, the fact would remain that this advancement in engineering does not help correcting the conclusion. In fact, the engineering advancement without regard to the basis of fundamental science would actually increase confidence toward the wrong conclusion. This is the situation for which engineering (making of precision clocks) only serves to strengthen the prejudice of the science of tangibles.

Another example was cited by Abou-Kassem et al. (2007). This one involves the discussion of the speed of light. It is 'well recognized' in the New Science world that the speed of light is the maximum achievable speed. The argument is based on the famous Einstein's equation of $E=mc^2$. However, scientific scrutiny of this 'well recognized' statement in Physics shows that this statement is aphenomenal. When it is stated what is the speed of light, it is asserted that this is the speed of light (or radiation) within a vacuum. Then, when one asks what is a vacuum, it emerges that the vacuum in true sense[2] does not exist and one must resort to a definition, rather than a phenomenal state.

Historically, there were always a debate about the limit of speed of light, but only in the post-renaissance culture that speed of light became a 'constant'. For example note the following quote from Wikipedia (Website 1):

"Many early Muslim philosophers initially agreed with Aristotle's view that light has an infinite speed. In the 1000s, however, the Iraqi Muslim scientist, Ibn al-Haytham (Alhacen), the "father of optics", using an early experimental scientific method in his Book of Optics, discovered that light has a finite speed. Some of his contemporaries, notably the Persian Muslim philosopher and physicist Avicenna, also agreed with Alhacen that light has a finite speed. Avicenna "observed that if the perception of light is due to the emission of some sort of particles by a luminous source, the speed of light must be finite."

The 14th century scholar Sayana wrote in a comment on verse Rigveda 1.50.4 (1700–1100 BCE—the early Vedic period): "Thus it is remembered: [O Sun] you who traverse 2202 yojanas [ca. 14,000 to 30,000 km] in half a nimesa [ca. 0.1 to 0.2 s]", corresponding to between 65,000 and 300,000 km/s, for high values of yojana and low values of nimesa consistent with the actual speed of light."

In modern science, the justification of a constant c is given through yet another definition – that of vacuum itself. The official NIST site (on Fundamental Physics constant) lists this constant as having a value of 299 792 458 m/s, with a standard uncertainty of zero (stated as 'exact'). Now, all of a sudden, a definition, rather than a phenomenon (measurable quantity) becomes the basis for future measurements. It is so because the fundamental SI unit of length, the meter, has been defined since October 21, 1983[3], one meter being the distance light travels in a vacuum in 1/299,792,458 of a second. This implies that any further increase in the precision of the measurement of the speed of light will actually change the length of the meter, the speed of light being maintained at 299,792,458 m/s. This is equivalent to changing the base of a logical train from reality to aphenomenality and effectively creating a process

---

[2] Merriam-Webster online dictionary lists the four meanings of vacuum, none phenomenal:

1: emptiness of space

2a: a space absolutely devoid of matter *b:* a space partially exhausted (as to the highest degree possible) by artificial means (as an air pump) *c:* a degree of rarefaction below atmospheric pressure

3 a : a state or condition resembling a vacuum : VOID <the power *vacuum* in Indochina after the departure of the French -- Norman Cousins> b: a state of isolation from outside influences <people who live in a *vacuum*...so that the world outside them is of no moment -- W. S. Maugham>*4:* a device creating or utilizing a partial vacuum.

[3] Decided at the Seventh Conférence générale des poids et mesures (CGPM; the same acronym is used in English, standing for "General Conference on Weights and Measures". It is one of the three organizations established to maintain the International System of Units (SI) under the terms of the Convention du Mètre (Metre Convention) of 1875. It meets in Paris every four to six years.

that penalizes any improvement in discovering the truth (the true speed of light in this case). Abou-Kassem et al. (2007) argued that this definition of meter is not scientifically any more precise than the original definition that was instituted by the French in 1770's in the following form: one meter is defined as 1/10,000,000 the distance from the North Pole to the Equator (going through Paris). They also discussed the spurious arrangement of introducing the unit of time as a second. It wasn't until 1832 that the concept of second was attached to the SI arrangement. The original definition was 1 second = 1 mean solar day/864,000. As late as 1960 the ephemeris second, defined as a fraction of the tropical year, officially became part of the new SI system. It was soon recognized that both mean solar day and mean tropical year both vary, albeit slightly, more 'precise' (apparent assertion being more precise means closer to the truth) unit was introduced in 1967. It was defined as 9,192,631,770 cycles of the vibration of the cesium 133 atom. The assumption here is that vibration of cesium 133 atom is exact, this assumption being the basis of Atomic clock. Only recently, it has been revealed that this assumption is not correct, creating an added source of error in the entire evaluation of the speed of light. On the other hand, if purely scientific approach is taken, one would realize that the true speed of light is neither constant nor the highest achievable speed. Clayton and Moffat (1999) discussed the phenomenon of variable light speed. Also, Schewe and Stein (1999) discussed the possibility of very low speed of light. In 1998, the research group of Lene Hau showed that the speed of light can be brought down to as low as 61 km/hour (17 m/s) by manipulating the energy level of the medium (Hau et al., 1999). Two years later, the same research group reported near halting of light (Liu et al., 2001). The work of Bajcsy et al. (2003) falls under the same category except that they identified the tiny mirror-like behavior of the media, rather than simply low energy level. More recent work on the subject deals with controlling light rather than observing its natural behavior (Ginsberg et al., 2007). Abou-Kassem et al. (2007) used the arguments provided by previous physicists and constructed the following graph. It is clear from the graph (Figure 1.2) that the assumption that 'speed of light', 'vacuum', and 'unit of time', 'unit of distance' are some arbitrarily set constants do not change the true nature of nature, which remains continuously dynamic. Note that media density can be converted into media energy, only if continuous transition between energy and mass is considered. Such transition, as will be clearer in the following section, is rarely talked about in the context of engineering (Khan et al., 2007a). This graph also reveals that that once definitions and assertions have been accepted in face values and are not subject to further scrutiny, the possibility of increasing knowledge (as in being closer to discover the truth about nature) is diminished.

Recently, a chemical engineer argued that the above graph is only a trivial manifestation of what Bose-Einstein theory would have predicted some 100 years ago. According to him, Bose-Einstein theory predicts the speed of light within an infinitely dense medium must be zero. Similar to the attitude expressed by the food scientist (in the Introduction of the present chapter), this line of thinking unfortunately characterizes modern-day education in which scientists become so focused on obvious tangible expressions that they are incapable to thinking beyond the most tangible aspect of the research. Recently (2001), Eric Cornell, Wolfgang Ketterle, and Carl Wieman were awarded Nobel Prize for "for the achievement of Bose-Einstein condensation in dilute gases of alkali atoms, and for early fundamental studies of the properties of the condensates". Their work, however, far from vindicating science of tangibles, has in fact made it more necessary to take an alternate approach. Eric Cornell's most popular invited lecture is titled: Stone Cold Science: Things Get Weird Around

Absolute Zero. This 'weird'-ness cannot be predicted with the science of tangibles. One further citation of Eric Cornell is: "What was God thinking? Science can't tell" (Cornell, 2005). Far from being content that all discoveries have been made and, therefore, there is nothing more to discover, a true researcher in pursuit of knowledge readily picks up on these shortcomings of conventional thinking, and as history frequently shows, it is within the inquisitive mind that answers reside. Ironically, this would also mean, discoveries are made because one is not afraid to make mistakes and, more importantly, theorize without fear of the Establishment. Satyendranath Bose, who did not have a PhD, himself did his part of the mistake. In fact, as the following quote from Wikipedia shows (Website 2), his findings were initially discarded by mainstream journals and he had to resort to sending Einstein his original work. It was only then that Einstein introduced the idea from light to mass (photon to atom) and the paper was finally published. If Bose did not have the tenacity and if Einstein did not have the decency to consider thinking "outside the box", one could not begin to think what would be the state of laser and all the gadgets that we take for granted today.

"Physics journals refused to publish Bose's paper. It was their contention that he had presented to them a simple mistake, and Bose's findings were ignored. Discouraged, he wrote to Albert Einstein, who immediately agreed with him. His theory finally achieved respect when Einstein sent his own paper in support of Bose's to Zeitschrift für Physik, asking that they be published together. This was done in 1924." (from Website 2, 2007)

In the core of any scientific research, the attitude must be such that there is no blind faith or automatic acceptance of an existing principle. In this particular case of Nobel Prize winning work of Eric Cornell, he would not be able to observe anomalies if he took Bose-Einstein theory as absolute true (Tung *et al.*, 2006). In fact, all experimental observations indicate, there has to be major adjustments, if not re-formulation, made to the Bose-Einstein theory, as evidenced by follow up research that won Nobel Prize in 2005 (discussion below).

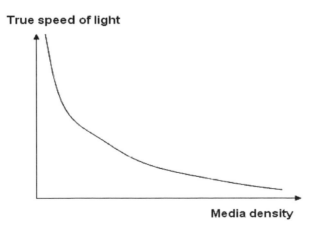

Figure 1.2. Speed of light as a function of media density (redrawn from Abou-Kassem et al., 2007).

As recently as 2005, Nobel Prize in Physics was awarded jointly to Roy Glauber 'for his contribution to the quantum theory of optical coherence' and to John Hall and Theodor Hänsch 'for their contributions to the development of laser-based precision spectroscopy, including the optical frequency comb technique'. Indeed these discoveries have something to

or did not include general or widespread publication. Thus, there could well have been almost as much total reliable knowledge 1400 years ago as today, but creative people's access and availability to that mass of reliable knowledge would have been far narrower. Only recently it is discovered that Islamic scholars were doing mathematics some 1000 years ago of the same order that are thought to be discovered in the 1970s (Lu and Steinhardt, 2007) – with the difference being that our mathematics can only track symmetry, something that does not exist in nature (Zatzman and Islam, 2007a). The picture below is an example of fractal mathematical design which is symmetric, however, different from the ancient architectural designs.

Photographs below show that in Islamic medieval period, fractal mathematics wasn't the one that dictated architectural designs.

(above two photographs taken from Turkish Airline travel magazine, Skylife, August, 2007)

Knowledge definitely is not within the modern age. Recently, a three-dimensional PET-scan of a relic known as the 'Antikythera Mechanism' has demonstrated that it was actually a universal navigational computing device – with the difference being that our current-day versions rely on GPS, tracked and maintained by satellite (Freeth et al., 2006). Only recently, Ketata et al. (2007a) recognized that computational techniques that are based on ancient, but nonlinear counting techniques, such as Abacus, are far more superior to the linear computing. Even in the field of medicine, one would be shocked to find out what Ibn Sina ('Avicenna') said regarding nature being the source of all cure still holds true (Crugg and Newman, 2001) – with the proviso that not a single quality given by nature in the originating source material of, for example, some of the most advanced pharmaceuticals used to "treat" cancer remains intact after being subject to mass production and accordingly stripped of its powers actually to cure and not merely "treat", i.e., delay, the onset or progress of symptoms. Therefore, there are examples from the history that show that knowledge is directly linked with intangibles and in fact, only when intangibles are included that science leads to knowledge (Vaziri et al., 2007).

Thomas Aquinas (1225-1274 AD) took the logic of Averröes and introduced it to Europe with a simple yet highly consequential modification: he would color the (only) creator as God and define the collection of Catholic church documentation on what eventuated in the neighborhood of Jerusalem some millennium ago as the only communication of God to mankind (hence the title, *bible* – the (only) Book). If Aristotle was the one who introduced the notion of removing intention and time function from all philosophical discourse, Thomas Aquinas is the one who legitimized the concept and introduced this as the only Science (as in process to gaining knowledge). Even though, Thomas Aquinas is known to have adapted the logic of Averröes, his pathway as well as prescribed origin of acquiring knowledge was diametrically opposite to the science introduced by Averröes. This is because the intrinsic features of both God and *bible* were dissimilar to the (only) creator and *Qu'ran*, respectively (Armstrong, 1994). For old Europe and the rest of the world that it would eventually dominate, this act of Thomas Aquinas indeed became the bifurcation point between two pathways, with origin, consequent logic, and the end being starkly opposite. With Aristotle's logic, something either is or is not: if one is 'true', the other must be false. Because, Averröes' 'the creator' and Thomas Aquinas's 'God' both are used to denominate monotheist faith, the concept of science and religion became a matter of conflicting paradox (Pickover, 2004). Averröes called the (only) creator as 'The Truth' (In Qu'ranic Arabic, the word 'the Truth' and 'the Creator' refer to the same entity). His first premise pertained to the book (*Qu'ran*) that said, "Verily unto Us is the first and the last (of everything)"(89.13). Contrast this to a "modern" view of a creator. In Carl Sagan's words (Hawking, 1988), "This is also a book about God...or perhaps about the absence of God. The word God fills these pages. Hawking embarks on a quest to answer Einstein's famous question about whether God had any choice in creating the universe. Hawking is attempting, as he explicitly states, to understand the mind of God. And this makes all the more unexpected the conclusion of the effort, at least so far: a universe with no edge in space, no beginning or end in time, and nothing for a Creator to do."

In recent days, there has been a superflux of Creationists who brought back the original Eurocentric logic and 'prove' the existence of God, falsehood of Darwin's theory of natural selection, and others. They used impoverished form of the deductive logic to achieve these objectives. Logic is only a form. The form cannot be higher than the content addressed by the form. If the content consists of defective or erroneous observations of natural phenomena, no clever logical maneuvers will save one's argument. The problem is not reducible to the logical truth of one's premises or assumptions. The problem is if actual facts of nature violate or disprove the assumptions being used. Then one is in serious trouble.

These Creationists also discuss limitations in deductive logic. The implication is that other kinds of logic might be just fine, the main alternative being inductive logic. The problem with this logic emerges when the observations of actual phenomena that form its content turn out to be insufficient or not necessary. Inductive logic is fine if and only if its propositions are based on, or express, necessary and-or sufficient conditions.

In Europe, Mediaeval philosophy from about 800 through about 1350 CE thought that Reason, in the sense of human reasoning power, was a gift from God, and was the same for everybody. Differences were ascribed to degree of one's faith in God — actually in Jesus Christ as one's personal savior— or lack thereof. Philosophers not belonging to the Church elites the late 1600s onward began to notice the cases where this was false or did not lead to socially positive conclusions — for example, Church persecution of scientific researchers. These philosophers developed the notion of right reason. This contains within it a not-very-well-worked-out, but nevertheless rough idea, of intention. This then itself also divided into two. Those who believed the world outside me was my idea, that its material existence independent of the will or existence of any particular observer was questionable and impossible to affirm, looked at this intention only from the ethical-moral standpoint. On the other hand, those who have no problem with affirming the existence of the natural world, with humans in it, had no problem seeing intention as direction. The ethical-moral part is then recast as conscience, and the material basis of conscience is consciousness.

The focus on tangibles started in Europe with the dominance of Church and European Christian faith. This later translated into New Science that promoted the Science of Tangibles with doctrinal ferver (Church near the Kremlin, above; and gold-covered *bible* below).

The content of this consciousness and its social character has not remained static. It has undergone evolutionary transformations. Humans are both self-aware and also aware of others beyond immediate kin. They are social in an extended way that has not been found in any other species on this earth. This kind of socialization has become as necessary to individuals' adult existence as kinship relations are before one leaves the family surrounding in which they were initially brought into the world.

The process of this social development of humans' lives has given rise to elaborate systems of handling symbols and other abstract representations of immediate reality or ideas. In the process of communicating of others the results of our reasoning process, meanwhile, all manner of shortcuts were developed. From the usefulness of such shortcuts for purposes of communicating the results of a reasoning process, however, it does not follow at all that the reasoning process can be improved by means of shortcuts. There is no shorcut that can be substituted for the starting point of any reasoning process. This is always and everywhere the same: data of actual phenomena honestly/conscientiously observed, acquired and recorded.

Answers to questions about the existence of God [or the existence of anything, for that matter] cannot be positioned within any of these processes just described. They are matters of a belief that has formed into a conviction. There is no process of "proof" for any affirmation — either to oneself or to others — that anyone or anything in particular exists. There is no logic or other device that, by itself, can guarantee or provide such "proof". Even when it comes to scientific thinking, "science" that is developed with what is called "complete objectivity", i.e., without pro-social, human convictions, will always end up being used to enhance someone's short term at the expense of a lot of other people's long term.

In the Qur'an, the first premise is clearly outlined in the principle of shahada. As outlined earlier in the context of Averröes's work, the Quran repeatedly outlines the first premise and asserts the path of knowledge as the one that is based on this premise. Take for instance, the second chapter (second only to the first introductory chapter). It states:

الٓـمٓ (١) ذَٰلِكَ ٱلْكِتَٰبُ لَا رَيْبَ فِيهِ هُدًى لِّلْمُتَّقِينَ (٢) ٱلَّذِينَ يُؤْمِنُونَ بِٱلْغَيْبِ وَيُقِيمُونَ ٱلصَّلَوٰةَ وَمِمَّا رَزَقْنَٰهُمْ يُنفِقُونَ (٣) وَٱلَّذِينَ يُؤْمِنُونَ بِمَآ أُنزِلَ إِلَيْكَ وَمَآ أُنزِلَ مِن قَبْلِكَ وَبِٱلْءَاخِرَةِ هُمْ يُوقِنُونَ (٤) أُو۟لَٰٓئِكَ عَلَىٰ هُدًى مِّن رَّبِّهِمْ وَأُو۟لَٰٓئِكَ هُمُ ٱلْمُفْلِحُونَ (٥)

Approximate meaning being:

> (1) Alif. Lam. Mim. [note: no one knows the meaning of this – not even prophet Muhammad]
> (2) This is the Scripture whereof there is no doubt, a guidance unto those who are on the right path. (3) Who believe in the in intangibles, and establish communication (between God and oneself), and spend (in charity) of that We have bestowed upon them; (4) And who believe in that which is revealed unto thee (Muhammad) and that which was revealed before thee, and are certain of the Hereafter (long-term). (4) These depend on guidance from their Lord. These are the successful. (5) As for the Disbelievers, Whether thou warn them or thou warn them not it is all one for them; they believe not. [Chapter 2: Sura Bakara, The Qur'an]

This divergence in pathways was noted by Zatzman and Islam (2007a). Historically, challenging the first premise, where the divergence is set, has become such a taboo that there is no documented case of anyone challenging it and surviving the wrath of the Establishment (Church alone in the past, Church and Imperialism after the Renaissance). Even challenging some of the cursory premises have been hazardous, as demonstrated by Galileo. Today, we continue to avoid challenging the first premise and even in the information age it continues to be hazardous, if not fatal, to challenge the first premise or secondary premises. It has been possible to keep this modus operandi because new "laws" have been passed to protect 'freedom of religion' and, of late, 'freedom of speech'. For special-interest groups, this opens a Pandora's box for creating 'us *vs* them', 'clash of civilizations' and every aphenomenal model now in evidence (Zatzman and Islam, 2007b).

Avoiding discussion of any theological nature, Zatzman and Islam (2007a) nevertheless managed to challenge the first premise. Rather than basing the first premise on the Truth *à la* Averröes, they mentioned the importance of individual acts. Each action would have three components: 1) origin (intention); 2) pathway; 3) consequence (end). Averröes talked about origin being the truth; they talked about intention that is real. How can an intention be real or false? They equate real with natural. Their work outlines fundamental features of nature and shows there can be only two options: natural (true) or artificial (false). The paper shows Aristotle's logic of anything being 'either A or not-A' is useful only to discern between true (real) and false (artificial). In order to ensure the end being real, the paper introduces the recently developed criterion of Khan (2006) and Khan and Islam (2007b). If something is convergent when time is extended to infinity, the end is assured to be real. In fact, if this criterion is used, one can be spared of questioning the 'intention' of an action. If any doubt, one should simply investigate where the activity will end up if time, t goes to infinity.

This absence of discussion of whatever happened to the tangible-intangible nexus involved at each stage of any of these developments is no merely accidental or random fact in the world. It flows directly from a Eurocentric bias that pervades, well beyond Europe and North America, the gathering and summation of scientific knowledge everywhere. Certainly, it is by no means a property inherent - either in technology as such, or in the norms and demands of the scientific method *per se*, or even within historical development - that time is considered so intangible as to merit being either ignored as a fourth dimension, or conflated with tangible space as something varying independently of any process underway within any or all dimensions of three-dimensional space. Recently, Mustafiz et al. (2007) identified the need of including a continuous time function as starting point of acquiring knowledge. According to them, the knowledge dimension does not get launched unless time as a continuous function is introduced. They further show that the knowledge dimension is not only possible, it is necessary. The knowledge is conditioned not only by the quantity of information gathered in the process of conducting research, but also by the depth of that research, *i.e.*, the intensity of one's participation in finding things out. In and of themselves, the facts of nature's existence and of our existence within it neither guarantee nor demonstrate our consciousness of either, or the extent of that consciousness. Our perceptual apparatus enables us to record a large number of discrete items of data about the surrounding environment. Much of this information we organize naturally and indeed unconsciously. The rest we organize according to the level to which we have trained, and-or come to use, our own brains. Hence, neither can it be affirmed that we arrive at knowledge directly or merely through perception, nor can we affirm being in possession at any point in time of a reliable proof or guarantee that our knowledge of anything in nature is complete.

Historically, what Thomas Aquinas model did to European philosophy is the same as what Newton's model did to the New Science. The next section examines Newton's models. Here it would suffice to say that Newton's approach was not any different from the approach of Thomas Aquinas or even Aristotle. One exception among scientists in Europe was Albert Einstein, who introduced the notion of time as the fourth dimension. However, no one followed up on this aspect of Einstein's work and it was considered that the addition of a time term in the Newton's so-called steady state models will suffice. Mustafiz (2006) recognized the need of including the time dimension as a continuous function and set the stage for modeling science of intangibles (Abou-Kassem et al., 2007).

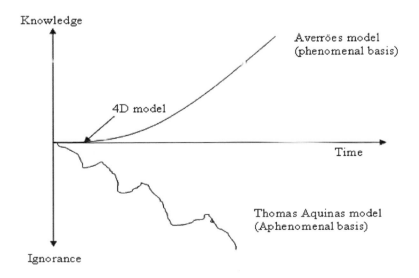

Figure 1.3. Logically, a phenomenal basis is required as the first condition to sustainable technology development. This foundation can be the Truth as the original of any inspiration or it can be 'true intention', which is the essence of intangibles (modified from Zatzman and Islam, 2007b and Mustafiz et al., 2007).

Table 1.2. Criterion, origin, pathway and end of scientific methods in some of the leading civilizations of world history

People	Criterion	Origin	Pathway	End
Zatzman and Islam (2007b)	$\Delta t \to \infty$	Intention	$f(t)$	Consequences
Khan (2006)	$\Delta t \to \infty$	Intention	Natural	Sustainability
(Zatzman and Islam, 2007b)	$\Delta t \to \infty$	Intention	Natural	Natural (used $\Delta t \to \infty$ to validate intention)
Einstein	t as 4th-D	"God does not play dice…"	Natural	N/A
Newton	$\Delta t \to 0$	"external force" (1st Law)	No difference between natural & artificial	Universe will run down like a clock
Aquinas	Bible	Acceptance of Divine Order	All *knowledge* & *truth* reside in God; *choice* resides with Man	Heaven and Hell
Averröes	Al- Furqan الفرقان (meaning The Criterion, title of Chapter 25 of *The Qur'an*) stands for *Qur'an*	Intention (first *hadith*)	*Amal saliha* (good deed, de-pending on good intention)	Accomplished (as in *Muflehoon*, ٱلْمُفْلِحُونَ , 2:5), Good ($+\infty$) Losers (as in *Khasheroon*, ٱلْخَـٰسِرُونَ, 58:19), Evil ($-\infty$)
Aristotle	*A* or *not-A* ($\Delta t=0$)	Natural law	Natural or arti-ficial agency	*Ευδαιμονια* (*Eudaimonia*, tr. "happiness", actually more like "Man in harmony with universe")
Ancient India	Serving others; "world reveals itself"	Inspiration (*Chetna*)	*Karma* (deed with inspiration, *chetna*)	Karma, salvation through merger with Creator
Ancient Greek (pre-Socratics)	t begins when Chaos of the void ended	the Gods can interrupt human intention at any time or place	N/A	N/A
Ancient China (Confucius)	N/A	Kindness	Quiet (intangible?)	Balance

Table 1.2 summarizes the historical development in terms of scientific criterion, origin, pathway and consequences of the principal cultural approaches to reckoning, and reconciling, the tangible-intangible nexus.

With this above table, we present a table (Table 1.3) that shows the characteristic features of Nature. These are true features and are not based on perception. They are true because there are no example of their opposites.

Table 1.3. Typical features of natural processes as compared to the claims of artificial processes (Adapted from Khan and Islam, 2007a)

Features of Nature and natural materials	
Feature no.	Feature
1	Complex
2	Chaotic
3	Unpredictable
4	Unique (every component is different), *i.e.*, forms may appear similar or even "self-similar", but their contents alter with passage of time
5	Productive
6	Non-symmetric, *i.e.*, forms may appear similar or even "self-similar", but their contents alter with passage of time
7	Non-uniform, *i.e.*, forms may appear similar or even "self-similar", but their contents alter with passage of time
8	Heterogeneous, diverse, *i.e.*, forms may appear similar or even "self-similar", but their contents alter with passage of time
9	Internal
10	Anisotropic
11	Bottom-up
12	Multifunctional
13	Dynamic
14	Irreversible
15	Open system
16	True
17	Self healing
18	Nonlinear
19	Multi-dimensional
20	Infinite degree of freedom
21	Non-trainable
22	Infinite
23	Intangible
24	Open
25	Flexible

Table 1.4. How the Natural features are violated in the first premise of various 'laws' and theories of the science of tangibles (Zatzman et al., 2007c)

Law or theory	First premise	Features violated (see Table 1.3)
Conservation of mass	Nothing can be created or destroyed	None
Lavoisier's deduction	Perfect seal	15
Phlogiston theory	Phlogiston exists	16
Theory of relativity	Everything (including time) is a function of time	None
$E = m c^2$	Mass of an object is constant	13
	Speed of light is constant	13
	Nothing else contributes to E	14, 19, 20, 24
Planck's theory	Nature continuously degrading to heat dead	5, 17, 22
Charles	Fixed mass (closed system), ideal gas, Constant pressure,	24, 3, 7
Boyles	A fixed mass (closed system) of ideal gas at fixed temperature	24, 3, 7
Kelvin's	Kelvin temperature scale is derived from Carnot cycle and based on the properties of ideal gas	3, 8, 14, 15
Thermodynamics 1st law	Energy conservation (The first law of the thermodynamics is no more valid when a relationship of mass and energy exists)	None
Thermodynamics 2nd law	Based on Carnot cycle which is operable under the assumptions of ideal gas (imaginary volume), reversible process, adiabatic process (closed system)	3, 8, 14, 15
Thermodynamics 0th law	Thermal equilibrium	10, 15
Poiseuille	Incompressible uniform viscous liquid (Newtonian fluid) in a rigid, non-capillary, straight pipe	25, 7
Bernouilli	No energy loss to the sounding, no transition between mass and energy	15
Newton's 1st law	A body can be at rest and can have a constant velocity	Non-steady state, 13
Newton's 2nd law	Mass of an object is constant Force is proportional to acceleration External force exists	13 18
Newton's 3rd law	The action and reaction are equal	3
Newton's viscosity law	Uniform flow, constant viscosity	7, 13
Newton's calculus	Limit $\Delta t \rightarrow 0$	22

Table 1.5. Analysis of "breakthrough" technologies

Product	Promise (knowledge at t= 'right now'	Current knowledge (closer to reality)
Microwave oven	Instant cooking (bursting with nutrition)	97% of the nutrients destroyed; produces dioxin from baby bottles
Fluorescent light (white light)	Simulates the sunlight and can eliminate 'cabin fever'	Used for torturing people, causes severe depression
Prozac (the wonder drug)	80% effective in reducing depression	Increases suicidal behavior
Anti-oxidants	Reduces aging symptoms	Gives lung cancer
Vioxx	Best drug for arthritis pain, no side effect	Increases the chance of heart attack
Coke	Refreshing, revitalizing	Dehydrates; used as a pesticide in India
Transfat	Should replace saturated fats, incl. high-fiber diets	Primary source of obesity and asthma
Simulated wood, plastic gloss	Improve the appearance of wood	Contains formaldehyde that causes Alzheimer
Cell phone	Empowers, keep connected	Gives brain cancer, decreases sperm count among men.
Chemical hair colors	Keeps young, gives appeal	Gives skin cancer
Chemical fertilizer	Increases crop yield, makes soil fertile	Harmful crop; soil damaged
Chocolate and 'refined' sweets	Increases human body volume, increasing appeal	Increases obesity epidemic and related diseases
Pesticides, MTBE	Improves performance	Damages the ecosystem
Desalination	Purifies water	Necessary minerals removed
Wood paint/varnish	Improves durability	Numerous toxic chemicals released
Leather technology	Won't wrinkle, more durable	Toxic chemicals
Freon, aerosol, etc.	Replaced ammonia that was 'corrosive'	Global harms immeasurable and should be discarded

Source: Zatzman and Islam, 2007b.

Now, in Table 1.4, we summarize many currently used 'laws' and theories, all of which emerged from the New Science after renaissance. Note how the first premises of practically all of these theories violate fundamental features of Nature. Only conservation of mass that in fact has root in ancient times and theory of relativity do not have an aphenomenal first premise. It is important to note that only recently Kvitco (2007) discredited Einstein's relativity altogether. However, he did not elaborate on the first premise of the theory. Our contention is, Einstein's relativity theory appears to be spurious if processed through the science of tangibles. So far, there is no evidence that the first premise of the theory of relativity, as Einstein envisioned, is aphenomenal. Now, if New Science has given us only theories and 'laws' that have spurious first premise, Averröes criterion would make New Science aphenomenal. This is indeed found in modern technologies that have resulted in 'technological disasters', reversing originally declared 'intention' for every technology. This is shown in Table 1.4.

1.2.7. Other Considerations in Mathematics and Science

In both Sanskrit and Arabic, grammatical 'number' is: singular, two-fold, or 'plural' (meaning: more than two). This is important because adjectives and verbs have to agree with the number of the noun serving as the subject of the sentence. In *all* European languages, there is simply: singular, meaning one only or fraction-of-one, and plural, meaning more-than-one.

In the tribal languages that we know about or that still exist and that go back to the period from 40 000 to 12 000 years ago (before last Ice Age), there is no way to enumerate quantities past about 20 or 30. This might have something to do with how many lived together or in close contact in communities BEFORE versus AFTER the emergence of settled locales based on agriculture and animal husbandry.

The ancient Greeks have only very general ideas of large numbers, thus there is the myriad, meaning 10,000 --- but it is for counting much larger numbers in "units" of 10, 000.

Ancient India houses several mathematical traditions that tackle very large numbers, most interestingly the Jaina mathematicians. It seems instead of fractions/rational numbers, the Jaina mathematicians redefine a whole so it has a very very large number of "units" which exist in nature in some meaningful form. So for example the circuit of the sum around the earth can be measured in minutes of arc; that becomes the unit. Then the sun's circuit during the year is defined by the hundreds of millions of minutes in the total arc. The next threshold number is the number of such years that "the world" has existed according to the Jain priests' calculations, which is then crores of lakhs of minutes-of-arc.

Although schemas of this kind neatly skirt the apparent contradictions of fractions (what logic does a fraction have within a system that enumerates units by a decimal positioning system?), decimal representation was entirely normal in Indian maths of the late classical period, because this was or could be made consistent with the positioning system of representing number-values. However, these were numbers that existed as the result of subdividing by 10s, 100s, 1000s etc.

What the Indian mathematicians did not come up with was anything that would "reduce" 25 over 100, which could be represented as "0.25", to "1/4". And going the other way, Egyptian and Babylonian mathematics had fractions, but not positional representation of numerical value --- so they too could not make the link.

Well into the 19th century, a value such as "66-2/3" was meaningful mainly only as the aliquot third part of 200. As "66.666..." on a number line, just ahead of 66.5 and just less than 66.75, it would have been meaningful mainly to people like the research mathematician Riemann, trying in the 1860s to define the real line as an infinitely divisible and ultimately non-denumerable continuum of numbers. There was really little if any notion of physically measuring such a quantity from any natural phenomenon.

Numbers in the Qur'an

As mentioned earlier, the Qu'ran is the only document that has survived in its original form for over 1400 years. This is also the only document that has used the word *ilm* (Science, as in the process) a great many times. With this science, great strides were made for many centuries toward increasing knowledge and making tangible progress in human society. However, focus on tangible was not the reason for this tangible progress. It was instead focus on intangibles. Just after the introductory chapter, Chapter 2 (verses 3-4) outlines the conditions for true guidance. The first condition is set out to be 'believing in the intangibles' (the Arabic word being, "Al-Ghaib", الغيب).

الَّذِينَ يُؤْمِنُونَ بِالْغَيْبِ وَيُقِيمُونَ الصَّلَوٰةَ وَمِمَّا رَزَقْنَٰهُمْ يُنفِقُونَ (٣)

(approximate translation of the meaning: those who believe in the intangible, establishes communication, and spends in charity from their lawful belongings)

It is no surprise that this document has the mention of very few numbers, all of which, nevertheless have very significant meaning that is the subject to future research. In this chapter, we will simply state the numbers that appear in the Qur'an. To begin with there is no word in Arabic that would bear similar meaning as in European mathematics. The word most commonly used as an equivalent to number is, 'rukm', رقم, as in Chapter 83, verse 9, كِتَٰبٌ مَّرْقُومٌ, *kitabum markum*, which means 'written record'. The word rukm has a number of other meanings, such as ornament, engrave, mark or sign, all indicating for 'something to be known'. It seems, this word in Arabic stands for tangible expressions of an intangible and not something that is an image or aphenomenal, valid only for a time, t= 'right now'. Note that there is no mention of zero in the Qur'an, even though the Arabic equivalent word, *cipher*, existed even before the Qur'an came into tangible existence. There are *hadiths* of the prophet mentioning the word, *cipher*, which stood for 'nothing' or 'empty'. This word, in fact, has been adapted into the English language (as used in 'decipher'), once again standing for 'meaningless' or empty zeros. (At the same time, it is a place-holder: it can serve a function during computation without itself being a number. This raises an interesting point. According to the science of tangibles, in the matter of chemical reactions that can only take place in the presence of certain catalysts, it is repeated everywhere with almost the force of religious fervour: a catalyst does not take part in the reaction! Why don't the proponents of this "logic" not insist just as fervently that 0 as a placeholder takes no part in the computation?) The introduction of 0 in computation was introduced by the Arab who adapted the concept and the symbol from Ancient India. The influence of India in post-prophet Muhammad Arab mathematics is so dominant that even the Indian numerals replaced original Arab numerals (now adopted in European mathematics) that were actually more scientific than than the Indian counterpart (e.g. every numeral represents the numeric value by the number of angle that it forms).

The Quran did not use any numeral, but used the following numbers in various concepts (some examples are given).

Number One (in the context of 'there is only one *ilah*[4]'):
(قل إنما هو اله *واحد* وإنني بريء مما تشركون)
(سورة الأنعام, الآية 19) Chapter 6, verse 19
Number Two (in the context of 'do not choose two *ilah*'s)
(قال تعالى:(وقال الله لا تتخذوا إلهين *اثنين* إنما هو إله واحد
(سورة النحل, الآية 51) Chapter 17, verse 51

---

[4] The word, *ilah*, is erroneously translated as 'god', the actual meaning is closer to shelter-giver, as in husbandry. *Al-Ilah* stands for 'the only shelter giver', which might explain why it is commonly translated as the 'God'.

Number Three (in the context of 'not uttering Three (Trinity), stop because Allah is the only One *ilah*)

(ولا تقولوا **ثلاثة** انتهوا خيرا لكم)

(سورة النساء, الآية 171) Chapter 4, verse 171

Number Four (in the context of allowing aphenomenal model worshippers for months for free movement)

(فسيحوا فالأرض **أربعة** أشهر)Chapter 9, verse 2

(سورة التوبة, الآية 2)

Number Five (in the context of the actual number of men in the story of the people of the Cave)

(ويقولون **خمسة** سادسهم كلبهم رجما بالغيب)

(سورة الكهف، الآية22) Chapter 18, verse 22

Number Six (in the context of creating the Universe in six *yaum*'s[5])

(إن ربكم الله الذي خلق السماوات و الأرض في **ستة** أيام)

(سورة الأعراف,الآية 54) Chapter 7, verse 54

Number Seven (in the context of seven gates in hell)

Chapter (ها **سبعة** أبواب لكل باب منهم جزء مقسوم)

(سورة الحجر, الآية 44) Chapter 15, verse 44

Number Eight (in the context of eight angels upholding the Throne on the day of judgment, when there would be no secret)

(ويحمل عرش ربك فوقهم يومئذ **ثمانية**)

(سورة الحاقة, الآية 17) Chapter 69, verse 17

Number Nine (in the context of nine persons making mischief and not reforming, during the period of *Thamud*, the ones who built the crystal valley in Jordan)

(وكان في المدينة **تسعة** رهط يفسدون في الأرض)

(سورة النمل, الآية48) Chapter 27, verse 48

Number 10 (in the context of fasting for 10 days if a pilgrim cannot afford to sacrifice an animal)

(تلك **عشرة** كامل)

(سورة البقرة, لآية196) Chapter 2, verse 196

Number 11(in the context of Prophet Joseph's description of his dream of 11 planets[6], the sun, and the moon prostrating toward him):

أحد عشر كوكبا والشمس و القمر رأيتهم لي ساجدين

(سورة يوسف, لآية 4)Chapter 12, verse 4

Number 12 (in the context of the number of months in a year as per Divine order)

(إن عدة الشهور عند الله **اثنا عشر** شهرا في كتاب الله

(سورة التوبة, الآية 36)Chapter 9, verse 36

Number 19 (in the context of

(عليها **تسعة عشر**)

(سورة المدثر, الآية 30) Chapter 74, verse 30

---

[5] The word, *yaum* is errorneously translated as 'day'. It is closer to phase. This is supported by other statements that are indicative of phase and not 'day', for instance, 'the day of judgment' is called '*yaum addin*'. For 'day', as in daylight, there is a different word, *nahar* in Arabic. Also, in Arabic, Earth day begins when the sun sets.

[6] The Arabic word is: كوكبًا, *kawakeb*. There are other words in Arabic to describe planets as well. The distinction of these terminologies is beyond the scope of this paper.

Number 20 (in the context of 20 steadfast righteous people overcoming attack from 200 unrighteous ones)

(إن يكن منكم **عشرون** صابرون يغلبوا مائتين)

(سورة الأنفال,الآية 65) Chaper 8, verse 65

Number 30 (in the context of ordained bearing and weaning of a child for 30 months and maturity for man by 40 years)

(وحمله وفصاله **ثلاثون** شهرا)

(سورة الأحقاف, الآية 15) Chapter 46, verse 15

Number 40 (in the context of assigning 40 nights of solitude)

(وإذ واعدنا موسى **أربعين** ليلة ثم اتخذتم العجل من بعده وأنتم ظالمون)

(سورة البقرة, الآية 15) Chapter 2, verse 15

Number 50 (in the context of Noah spending 950 (1000 minus 50) years before the flood struck)

(ولقد أرسلنا نوحا إلى قومه فلبث فيهم ألف سنة إلا **خمسين** عاما)

(سورة العنكبوت, الآية 14) Chapter 29, verse 14

Number 60 (in the context of feeding 60 needy people in case someone is unable to fast two consecutive months as penalty to violating family code of conduct)

(فمن لم يستطع فإطعام **ستين** مسكينا)

(سورة المجادلة, الآية 4) Chapter 58, verse 4

Number 70 (in the context of the length of the chain holding captives in hell)

(ثم في سلسة ذرعها **سبعون** ذراعا فسلكوه)

(سورة الحاقة, الآية 32) Chapter 69, verse 32

Number 80 (in the context of punishment in the form of number of lashes for unfounded allegation against a chaste woman)

فاجلدوهم **ثمانون** جلدة ولا تقبلوا منهم شهادة أبدا

(سورة النور, الآية 4) Chapter 24, verse 4

Number 90 (in the context of two disputants (brothers) coming to David and asking to settle the dispute, one of them having nine and 90 ewes still wanted the other one's only one)

وهذا أخي له تسع **وتسعون** نعجة ولي نعجة واحدة

(سورة ص, الآية 22) Chapter 38, verse 22

Number 100 (in the context of someone being dead for 100 years yet answering "a day or part of a day" when asked "How long did you tarry (thus)?"

قل بل لبثت **مائة** عام

(سورة البقرة, الآية 259) Chapter 2, verse 259

Number 200 (In the context of 20 righteous with steadfastness vanquishing 200 of the attackers)

إن يكن منكم عشرون صابرون يغلبوا **مائتين**

(سورة الأنفال,الآية 65) Chapter 8, verse 65

Number 300 (In the context of habitants of the cave sleeping for 300 years and nine days)

ولبثوا في كهفهم **ثلاث مائة** سنين و ازدادوا تسعا

(سورة الكهف, الآية 25) Chapter 18, verse 25

Number 1000 and 2000 (in the context of 1000 righteous people that are steadfast vanquishing 2000 attackers)[7]

وإن يكن منكم *ألف* يغلبوا *الفين* بإذن الله

(سورة الأنفال, الآية 66) Chapter 8, verse 66

Number 3000 (in the context of 3000 angels sent down to help the righteous who were under attack by wrongdoers)

إذ تقول للمؤمنين ألن يكفيكم أن يمدكم ربكم *بثلاثة آلاف* من الملائكة منزلين

(سورة آل عمران, الآية 124) Chapter 3, verse 124

Number 5000 (in the context of increasing the number of angels from 3000 to 5000 in order to help the righteous (see above))

هذا يمددكم ربكم *بخمسة آلاف* من الملائكة مسومين

(سورة آل عمران, 125) Chapter 3, verse 125

Number 100,000 (in the context of Jonah being dispatched to a locality of 100,000 or more who were initially misguided)

وأرسلناه إلى *مائة ألف* أو يزيدون

(سورة الصافات, الآية 147), Chapter 37, verse 147

Fractions

Fractions in the Qur'an are principally used to denote natural division, as applied in sharing or just division of properties. Consequently, most divisions deal with family heritage laws. Following are some examples.

Number One Over Two (in the context of family heritage law)

ولكم *نصف* ما ترك أزواجكم إن لم يكن لهن ولد

(سورة النساء, الآية 12) Chapter 4, verse 12

Number One over Three (in the context of family heritage law)

إن لم يكن له ولد وورثه أبواه فلأمه *الثلث*

(سورة النساء, الآية 11) Chapter 4, verse 11

Number One over Four (in the context of family heritage law)

(قال تعالى:(فإن كان لهن ولد فلكم *الربع* مما تركن

(سورة النساء, الآية 12) Chapter 4, verse 12

Number One over Five (in the context of distribution of war booty[8])

واعلموا إنما غنمتم من شيء فإن لله *خمسه*

(سورة الأنفال, الآية 41) Chapter 8, verse 41

Number One over Six (in the context of family heritage law)

فإن كان له إخوة فلأمه *السدس*

(سورة النساء,الآية 11) Chapter 4, verse 11

Number One over Eight (in the context of family heritage law)

(قال تعالى:(فإن كان لكم ولد فلهن *الثمن* مما تركتم

(سورة النساء, الآية 12) Chapter 4, verse 12

---

[7] Note how the same verse stated earlier 20 righteous people vanquishing 200 attackers, as compared to 1000 righteous vanquishing 2000 attackers – the relationship is definitely not linear.

[8] It is important to note the war booty in Quranic context applies strictly to defensive war. There was only one offensive war during the entire period of the revelation of the Qur'an. This war (the last one) had no casualty, generated no war booty, and was followed by general amnesty for the very people who attacked the Prophet's group in the form of four wars in less than 10 years.

Natural Ranking

Various numeral rankings are used in the Qur'an. Following are some of the examples:

First (in the context of first one to be obedient to Allah)

قول إني أمرت أن أكون *أول* من أسلم

(سورة الأنعام, الآية 14) Chapter 6, verse 14

Second (in the context of the second one as a companion of the prophet when he was migrating from Mecca to Medina, being driven out by Arab pagans)[9]

إلا تنصروه فقد نصره الله إذ أخرجه الذين كفروا *ثاني اثنين*

(سورة التوبة, الآية 40) Chapter 9, verse 40

Third (in the context of adding a third messenger because first two were not heeded)

إذ أرسلنا إليهم اثنين فكذبوهما فعززنا *بثالث* فقالوا إنا إليكم مرسلون

(سورة يس, الآية14) Chapter 36, verse 14

Fourth (in the context of no secret can be kept from Allah as he makes the fourth when three human beings consult in secret)

ما يكون من نجوى ثلاثة إلا هو *رابعهم*

(سورة المجادلة, الآية 7) Chapter 58, verse 7

Fifth (in the context of taking a fifth oath invoking one's innocence in absence of material witness)

والخامسة أن لعنة الله عليه إن كان من الكاذبين

(سورة النور, الآية 7) Chapter 24, verse 7

Sixth (in the context of the sixth companion (a dog) of the inhabitants of the cave)

ويقولون خمسة *سادسهم* كلبهم رجما بالغيب

(سورة الكهف, الآية22) Chapter 18, verse 22

Eighth (in the context of the eighth companion (a dog) of the inhabitants of the cave, as hearsay)

ويقولون سبعة *وثامنهم* كلبهم

(سورة الكهف, الآية 22) Chapter 18, verse 22

Mathematical Operations

Mathematical operations in the Qur'an are all natural, i.e., addition to increase, subtract to decrease, multiply to strike or counter, and divide to breakdown in among natural recipients or compartments. No operation that is spurious would yield any result. These operations were mainly used by 7th century onward Muslims to calculate compulsory charity as well as just share of heritage properties. Examples are given below:

Addition (in the context of 300 and 9 years spent by the inhabitants of the cave)

(قال تعالى:(ولبثوا في كهفهم *ثلاث مائة سنين* و *ازدادوا تسعا*

(سورة الكهف, الآية 25) Chapter 8, verse 25

The operation is: 300 + 9

---

[9] Note that second, ثانيَ (*thani*), in Arabic only applies to ranking. The unit of time, 'second' is incorrectly translated in Arabic as *thani*. Such artificial time unit does not exist in Quranic Arabic (Zatzman, 2007).

Subtraction (in the context of Noah spending 1000 minus 50 years with his tribe)

ولقد أرسلنا نوحا إلى قومه فلبث فيهم *ألف سنة إلا خمسين عاما*

(سورة العنكبوت, الآية 14) Chapter 29, verse 14

The operation: 1000 – 50

Multiplication (in the context of righteous people fighting attackers and vanquishing them even when outnumbered)[10]

إن يكن منكم *عشرون* صابرون يغلبوا *مائتين*

وإن يكن منكم *ألف* يغلبوا *ألفين* بإذن الله

(سورة الأنفال, الآية 65, 66) Chapter 8, verses 65, 66

The operation: 20 striking against 200; 1000 striking against 2000

Division (in the context of fractions allocated to various recipients of a heritage)

إن لم يكن له ولد وورثه أبواه فلأمه *الثلث* فإن كان له إخوة فلأمه *السدس*

(سورة النساء, الآية 11) Chapter 4, verse 11

The Number Seven and its Multiple in the Qur'an

In the last year, a book called (إشراقات الرقم سبعة في القران الكريم), which won The Dubai International Holy Quran Award, talked about the number seven in the Qur'an. The book mentioned many things about number seven and its multiple and here a few examples:

1. The fact that there are seven heavens[11] were said seven times in the Quran:

    (سورة البقرة, الآية 29) Chapter 2, verse 29

    (سورة الإسراء, الآية 44)Chapter 17, verse 44

    (سورة المؤمنون, الآية 86)Chapter 23, verse 86

    (سورة فصلت, الآية 12) Chapter 41, verse 12

    (سورة الطلاق, الآية 12) Chapter 65, verse 12

    (سورة الملك, الآية 3) Chapter 67, verse 3

    (سورة نوح, الآية 15) Chapter 71, verse 15

2. The fact of creation the earth and heavens in six *yaums* also mention seven times:

    (سورة الأعراف, الآية 54) Chapter 7, verse 54

    (سورة يونس, الآية 3) Chapter 10, verse 3

    (سورة هود,الآية 7)Chapter 11, verse 7

    (سورة الفرقان, الآية 59) Chapter 25, verse 59

    (سورة السجدة,الآية 32) Chapter 32, verse 32

---

[10] The root word used for 'multiplication' in Arabic is ضرب, which stands for numerous meanings. For example (Chapter and verse numbers from the Quran are indicated):

  To travel, to get out: 3:156; 4:101; 38:44; 73:20; 2:273.

  To strike: 2:60,73; 7:160; 8:12; 20:77; 24:31; 26:63; 37:93; 47:4.

  To beat: 8:50; 47:27.

  To set up: 43:58; 57:13.

  To give (examples): 14:24,45; 16:75,76,112; 18:32,45; 24:35; 30:28,58; 36:78; 39:27,29; 43:17; 59:21; 66:10,11.

  To take away, to ignore: 43:5.

  To condemn: 2:61.

  To seal, to draw over: 18:11.

  To cover: 24:31.

  To explain: 13:17.

[11] In Qur'an, paradise (سَمَوَأتٍ: The word used is .(celestial)is different from heaven (jannah or garden which also stands for sky or a layer of stars.

(سورة ق, الآية 38) Chapter 50, verse 38

(سورة الحديد, الآية 4) Chapter 57, verse 4

3. The number of السور and the number of الآيات between the first time number seven was mention and the last time are a multiple of number seven:

    First time (سورة البقرة (2), الآية 29) Chapter 2, verse 29

    Last time (سورة النبأ (78), الآية 12)Chapter 78, verse 12

    So, that:

    78 – 2 = 77 = 7 * 11

    The numbers of الآيات between them are 5649 = 7 * 807

4. The number of السور (Chapters) that begin with the praise of Allah are seven :

    (سورة الإسراء, الآية 1)Chapter 17, verse 1

    (سورة الحديد, الآية1) Chapter 57, verse 1

    (سورة الحشر, الآية1) Chapter 59, verse 1

    (سورة الصف, الآية 1) Chapter 61, verse 1

    (سورة الجمعة, الآية 1) Chapter 62, verse 1

    (سورة التغابن, الآية 1) Chapter 64, verse 1

    (سورة الأعلى, الآية 1) Chapter 87, verse 1

1.2.8. Modeling Natural Phenomena in Multiple Dimensions

In relatively recent history, Einstein was the first scientist to recognize time as the fourth dimension. This recognition explained the transition from mass to energy and made it possible for scientists to consider combining mass- and energy-balance equations. The first use of the fourth dimension, however, was not by a physicist. Hermann Minkowski (1864-1909), a mathematician, used the fourth dimension to 'solve' the space-time continuum. In 1914, Gunnar Nordström (1881-1923), a theoretical physicist, included four dimensions in his gravitational theory, a theory that can be called the first general theory of relativity (Ravndal, 2003). His work on splitting of five-dimensional space into Einstein's and Maxwell's equations in four dimension was the first recognition of more than 4 dimensions in modeling reality. Years later (1921), Kaluza (1885-1954) combined Maxwell's theory of electromagnetism and Einstein's theory of general relativity to develop a unified theory (Kaku and O'Keefe, 1994). This theory was useful for modeling galaxies, solar systems, and spacecraft for outer space travel. In 1926, Oskar Klein (1894-1977) hypothesized that the fourth spatial dimension is curled up in a circle of very small radius, so that a particle moving a short distance along that axis would return to where it began. This is perhaps the first non-linear, albeit circular, approximation of infinitely small distance in multi-dimensional analysis (as opposed to Newton's Δx approaching linearity). The distance a particle can travel before reaching its initial position is said to be the size of the dimension. This extra dimension is a compact set, and the phenomenon of having a space-time with compact dimensions is referred to as compactification. Following this initial development, many researchers worked on the development string theory and its variations (e.g. superstring theory), a detailed description of which is available in a recent textbook (Becker et al., 2007). It is generally recognized that the string theory or its variations do not explain physical phenomena. However, only Abou-Kassem et al. (2007) attributed this short-coming to spurious assumptions of various models and presented them in line with aphenomenal models that are incorrectly promoted as the correct models. One of these assumptions involves the cylindrical shape assumption. The research group of Wessen (e.g. Wessen et al., 2000) eliminated this assumption and was 'successful' in solving space-time-continuum problems (Wessen, 2002). With time, many more dimensions have been recognized (as many as 11, as discussed by Caroll, 2004), but few have ventured into the possibility of modeling infinite dimension. Yet, this is precisely what is needed in solving natural phenomena (Mustafiz et al., 2007).

In groundwater and hydrology applications, Bear (1972) is credited to highlighting the need for including greater dimensions in order for a natural value to be representative. He introduced the concept of Representative Elemental Volume (REV) that would essentially mean that unless a certain dimension is used, the value can fluctuate to such an extent that it is not meaningful. Islam (2002) used the same concept to introduce through numerical modeling that the volume of the sample is of extreme importance, both in physical and numerical modeling. Figure 1.4 shows his finding.

In the previous section, the shortest distance between two points has been discussed in the context of dimensionality. Such discussion is also of importance in determining the relationship between truth and dimensionality. Decades ago, in a discussion on fractals, a professor asked the allegorical question: How long is the Mississippi River? (Prof. M.R. Islam, personal communication). It was in line with the ground breaking work of Mandelbrot (1967) who would later be known as the father of fractals. The intention behind this question was to demonstrate that the distance between two points depends on the scale used. It is easily understood by discussing the distance measured by an airplane, by a surveyor that uses a scale of 10s of meters, a surveyor that uses scale of 1 meter, a surveyor that uses his feet, then all the way down to an ant that measure its feet to even measure distances over pebbles. Figure 1.5 shows the effect of distance reported between two points for various dimensions used. To-date, 12 dimensions have been identified. It is conceivable that this trend will continue and in the future many more dimensions will be revealed. The question one should ask is what is the true distance between the two points are being monitored in the following figure? As the dimension is increased, the distance is increased. Is there a limit to this trend? This was not the question that was answered by Benoît Mandelbrot. Instead, he introduced the concept of self-similarity and revolutionized 20th century mathematics. However, a close scrutiny of nature would reveal such self similarity is non-existent, making the fractal mathematics aphenomenal.

Mustafiz et al. (2007) discussed the effect of linearization (which means the dimensions are reduced to 1) on the predicted value. This work has been further extended to multiphase flow, for which more dimensions (philosophically) are added (Islam et al., 2007). As expected, the effect of linearization of a higher order phenomenon gives even greater discrepancy between 1D and 3D results, quite similar to what was observed by Islam and Chilingar (1995) over a decade ago. The important point to be made in this graph is that the inclusion of time as a continuous function, there is no need to include a finite number of dimensions, as has been the practice thus far in Physics and Cosmology. The use of time as a continuous function introduces infinite dimension. This dimension was characterized as 'Knowledge dimension' by Mustafiz (2006).

In engineering applications, the need for modeling with multiple dimensional approach comes from practical need of explaining the existence of chaotic behavior (Ketata et al., 2007b; 2007c). Even though it has been long been recognized that nature is chaotic, very little modeling work has been extended in order to simulate chaos deterministically (Ketata et al.,

2006c; 2006d). In the past, Islam and Nandakumar (1986) attempted to model multiple solutions as well as the bifurcation point for porous media problems with mixed convection. This work was later expanded by Islam and Nandakumar (1990) and others. More recently, similar attempt has been made in other disciplines (e.g. Coriell et al., 1998).

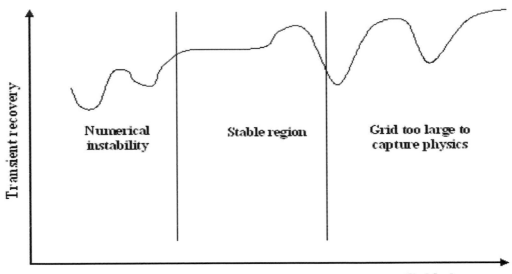

Figure 1.4. The effect of numerical grid sizes on the prediction of fluid flow behavior (From Islam, 2002).

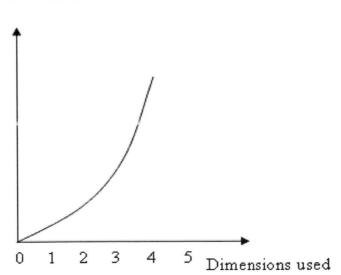

Figure 1.5. Relationship between dimensions used and measured distance (modified from Abou-Kassem et al., 2007).

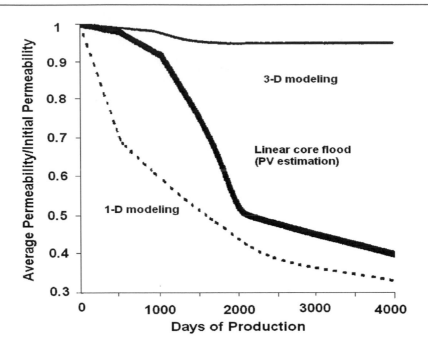

Figure 1.6. The effect of dimensionality on outcome (from Islam and Chilingar, 1995).

One of the first attempts to relate multiple solutions to dimensional analysis was reported by Islam and Chilingar (1995). In the context of microbial movement within a porous medium, a prime candidate for nonlinear dynamics, they showed that by simply changing the dimension of the model, the outcome will change drastically (Figure 1.6) Such recognition was found to be useful in other analyses involving porous media characterization, which is prone to multiple solutions (Katz et al., 1995).

Transition from Mathematics of Tangibles to Mathematics of Intangibles

The publication of the book, *Principia Mathematica* by Sir Isaac Newton at the end of 17th century has been the most significant development in European-centered civilization. It is also evident that some of the most important assumptions of Newton were just as aphenomenal as the assertion of Thomas Aquinas, except Newton did not talk about Theology (Zatzman and Islam, 2007a). By examining the first assumptions involved, Zatzman and Islam (2007b) were able to characterize Newton's laws as aphenomenal, for three reasons that they 1) remove time-consciousness (nature is truly dynamic); 2) recognize the role of 'external force' (equivalent to 'gods playing with human intention in pre-Aristotle Greek philosophy); and 3) do not include the role of intention. In brief, Newton's law ignore, albeit implicitly, all intangibles from nature science.

Zatzman and Islam (2007b) identified the most significant contribution of Newton in mathematics as the famous definition of the derivative as the limit of a difference quotient involving changes in space or in time as small as anyone might like, but not zero, *viz.*

$$\frac{d}{dt}f(t) = \lim_{\Delta t \to 0} \frac{f(t + \Delta t) - f(t)}{\Delta t}$$

[1]

Economic Index

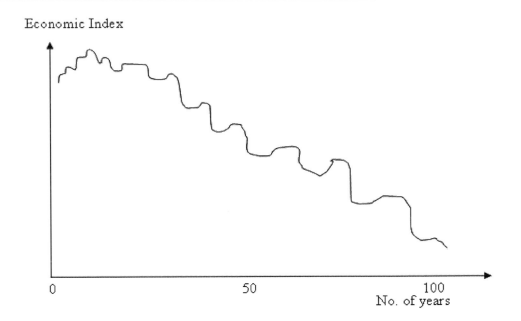

0   50   100
                     No. of years

Figure 1.7. Economic wellbeing is known to fluctuate with time (adapted from Abou-Kassem et al., 2007).

Without regards to further conditions being defined as to when and where differentiation would produce a meaningful result, it was entirely possible to arrive at "derivatives" that would generate values in the range of a function at points of the domain where the function was not defined or did not exist. Indeed: it took another century following Newton's death before mathematicians would work out the conditions – especially the requirements for continuity of the function to be differentiated within the domain of values – in which its derivative (the name given to the ratio-quotient generated by the limit formula) could be applied and yield reliable results. Kline (1972) detailed the problems involving this breakthrough formulation of Newton. However, no one in the past did propose an alternative to this differential formulation, at least not explicitly. The following figure (Figure 1.7) illustrates this difficulty.

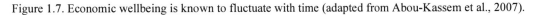

In this figure, economic index (it may be one of many indicators) is plotted as a function of time. In nature, all functions are very similar. They do have local trends as well as global trend (in time). One can imagine how the slope of this graph on a very small time frame would quite arbitrary and how devastating it would be to take that slope to a long-term. One can easily show the trend, emerging from Newton's differential quotient would be diametrically opposite to the real trend. In order to offer a substitute taking derivative at an infinitely small space, Zatzman and Islam (2007b) provided the following procedure. They took a simplified example to the implication of Newton's formula (Figure 8).

It is assumed that the sine function illustrated above represents some physical phenomenon. Using Newton's difference-quotient formula (see Eq. 1), the instantaneous rate of change anywhere along the graph-line of this function, which will be continuous anywhere within the interval $(-\infty, +\infty)$, $i.e.$, $-\infty \leq t \leq +\infty$, can be computed stepwise as follows (Figure 9):

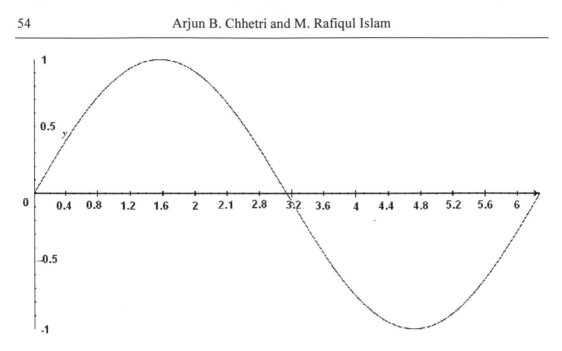

Figure 1.8. Graphic representation, in Cartesian coordinates, of the classic simple function $f(t)=\sin t$.

$$\frac{d}{dt}f(t) = \lim_{\Delta t \to 0}\frac{\sin(t+\Delta t)-\sin t}{\Delta t} = \lim_{\Delta t \to 0}\frac{\sin t \cos \Delta t + \sin \Delta t \cos t - \sin t}{\Delta t}$$

As Δt approaches 0, cos Δt approaches cos 0, which is 1. Meanwhile, because sin x approaches x for decreasingly small values of x, the term $\dfrac{\sin \Delta t}{\Delta t}$, also becomes unity. So:

$$\frac{d}{dt}f(t) = \lim_{\Delta t \to 0}\frac{\sin(t+\Delta t)-\sin t}{\Delta t} = \lim_{\Delta t \to 0}\frac{\sin t \cos \Delta t + \sin \Delta t \cos t - \sin t}{\Delta t} =$$

$$\lim_{\Delta t \to 0}\frac{\sin t + \sin \Delta t \cos t - \sin t}{\Delta t} =$$

$$\lim_{\Delta t \to 0}\frac{\sin \Delta t \cos t}{\Delta t} = \lim_{\Delta t \to 0}\frac{\sin \Delta t}{\Delta t}\cos t = \lim_{\Delta t \to 0}\cos t = \cos t$$

$$\lim_{\Delta t \to 0}\frac{\sin \Delta t \cos t}{\Delta t} = \lim_{\Delta t \to 0}\frac{\sin \Delta t}{\Delta t}\cos t = \lim_{\Delta t \to 0}\cos t = \cos t$$

Figure 1.9. Generating the first derivative $f'(t)$ for the function $f(t) = \sin t$ using Newton's difference-quotient formula (Zatzman et al., 2007b)

This means that, as one moves continuously along the domain t, the *instantaneous rate of change* along the curve represented by the graph for $f(t)$ can be computed by evaluating the cosine of t at that value on the horizontal axis. What is being described is change *within* the function; *the function itself, of course, has not changed.* As this particular function happens to be periodic, it will cycle through the same values as the operational output described by this graph proceeds through subsequent cycles. This makes it quite easy to see that the function itself describes a steady-state condition, which may not be phenomenal, but by taking the derivative one is not imposing any additional feature to the function. In fact, however, even if the function were some polynomial, anything lying on the path of its graph (for instance,

Figure 1.7) would represent the steady-state operation of that function: steadiness of state is not reducible to some trait peculiar to periodic functions. Contrast this to Newton's method, which implicitly invokes the notion of approximating instantaneous moments of curvature, or infinitely small segments, by means of straight lines. This linearization is done at an infinitely small scale, so that common observers cannot argue about the validity of the linearization. However, when the same function is integrated, people are surprised that the original function is not recovered except of special cases (see further development below). Zatzman and Islam (2007b) argued that this linearization within a bold and utterly unprecedented Newton's approach, contains a trap for the unwary: going backward or forward in space or in time is a matter of indifference. This 'time travel' has the potential of invoking aphenomenal state (contrary to natural or phenomenal state), later to legitimize it as the 'only solution', falsifying the entire scientific process. If natural reality is to be modeled as it actually unfolds, however, the requisite mathematics has to close the door on, and not permit the possibility of, treating time as reversible. In lieu of invoking linear slope, they suggested the construction of a difference quotient based on evaluating the limit at some arbitrary common value like 0, a finite constant real value c were used instead. A new derivative may be defined as shown in Figure 1.10.

Two immediate notes must accompany this development. First, even though c is stated to be a positive number greater than zero, it is not arbitrary. The actual value of c should be at least greater than characteristic value of the process. The notion of Representative Elemental Volume (REV), as first promoted by Bear (1972) is useful in determining a reasonable value for c. The other note is, using c that approaches 0 (Newton's approximation) cannot be introduced, even when the characteristic value is very small (e.g. phenomena at nano scale). This is because, zero in European mathematics refers to 'nothing' or 'void', which is aphenomenal (Ketata et al., 2006b). On the other hand, when it comes to 'meaningful' (Ketata et al., 2006b; 2006c) the value of c can not only approach zero or even infinity, it can actually be set to those values. Scientifically, 'meaningful' zero and infinity are both intangibles and do qualify to be used in the science of intangibles.

From Figure 1.10, it becomes clear that we are dealing with multiple, in fact: infinite, solutions. Mustafiz et al. (2007) argued that such should be the case when one is modeling Nature or intangibles. Abou-Kassem et al. (2007) argue that Newton's derivative is also prone to infinite solutions, with the exception that this possibility is not apparent and is not discussed by even the most prolific researchers. This argument is discussed later in this section.

In a different discourse, Abou-Kassem et al. (2006) introduced the so-called Engineering approach in order to solve reservoir engineering problems. Abou-Kassem et al. (2006) pointed out that there is no need to go through this process of expressing in differential equation form (avoiding Newton's ratio-quotient), followed by discretization. In fact, by setting up the algebraic equations directly, one can make the process simple and yet maintain accuracy (Mustafiz et al., 2007).

Figure 1.11 shows how formulation with the engineering approach ends up with the same linear algebraic equations if the inside steps are avoided. Even though the engineering approach was known for decades (known as the control volume approach), no one identified in the past the advantage of removing in-between steps.

$$f'(t) = \frac{d_c}{dt} f(t) = \lim_{\Delta t \to c} \frac{\sin(t + \Delta t) - \sin t}{\Delta t} = \lim_{\Delta t \to c} \frac{\sin t \cos \Delta t + \sin \Delta t \cos t - \sin t}{\Delta t}$$

Now, as Δt approaches c, cos Δt approaches cos c, which is anywhere in the interval [-1,+1]. Meanwhile, the term $\dfrac{\sin \Delta t}{\Delta t}$ may fall anywhere in the interval $[-\dfrac{\sqrt{3}}{2}, +\dfrac{1}{c}]$. Applying these maxima and minima generates the open interval $-(2 \sin t + \dfrac{1}{c} \cos t) \leq \dfrac{d_c}{dt} f(t) \leq \dfrac{1}{c} \cos t$, in which:

- at $t = 0$ (+2$k\pi$), $\dfrac{d_c}{dt} f(t)$ converges to a single value, viz., $\dfrac{1}{c}$, which is positive (> 0);

- at $t = \dfrac{\pi}{6}$: $-(2 + \dfrac{\sqrt{3}}{2c}) \leq \dfrac{d_c}{dt} f(t) \leq \dfrac{\sqrt{3}}{2c}$, which straddles 0;

- at $t = \dfrac{\pi}{4}$: $-\sqrt{2}(1 + \dfrac{1}{2c}) \leq \dfrac{d_c}{dt} f(t) \leq \dfrac{\sqrt{2}}{2c}$, which straddles 0;

- at $t = \dfrac{\pi}{3}$: $-(\sqrt{3} + \dfrac{1}{2c}) \leq \dfrac{d_c}{dt} f(t) \leq \dfrac{1}{2c}$, which straddles 0;

- at $t = \dfrac{\pi}{2}$: $-2) \leq \dfrac{d_c}{dt} f(t) \leq 0$, which is mainly negative (≤ 0);

- at $t = \dfrac{2\pi}{3}$: $-(\sqrt{3} - \dfrac{1}{c}/) \leq \dfrac{d_c}{dt} f(t) \leq -\dfrac{1}{2c}$, which is entirely negative (<0);

- at $t = \dfrac{3\pi}{4}$: $-\sqrt{2}(1 - \dfrac{1}{2c}) \leq \dfrac{d_c}{dt} f(t) \leq -\dfrac{\sqrt{2}}{2c}$, which is entirely negative (<0) and reduces,

- at $c = 1$, to $-\dfrac{\sqrt{2}}{2}$.

From here, heading towards $t = \pi$, other features emerge:

- At $t = \dfrac{5\pi}{6}$, $\dfrac{d_c}{dt} f(t)$ lies somewhere between $-(1 - \dfrac{\sqrt{3}}{2c})$ and $-\dfrac{\sqrt{3}}{2c}$, in which:

- for $c = \dfrac{\sqrt{3}}{2}$, $-1 \leq f'(t) \leq 0$;
  $\scriptstyle \Delta t \to c$

- for $\dfrac{\sqrt{3}}{2} < c < \sqrt{3}$, while for $c > \sqrt{3}$, $f'(t) < 0$; and
  $\scriptstyle \Delta t \to c$

- for $c = \sqrt{3}$, $f'(t) = -0.5$;
  $\scriptstyle \Delta t \to c$

- At $t = \pi$: $-\dfrac{1}{c} \leq \dfrac{d_c}{dt} f(t) \leq \dfrac{1}{c}$

Figure 1.10. Generating family of first derivatives, $\{ f'(t) = \dfrac{d_c}{dt} f(t) \}$, for $f(t) = \sin t$ using modified $\scriptstyle \Delta t \to c$ difference-quotient.

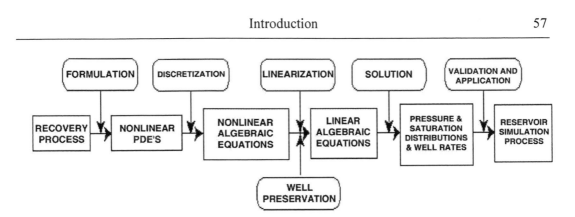

Figure 1.11. Major steps used to develop reservoir simulators (redrawn from Abou-Kassem et al., 2006).

In analyzing further the role of mathematical manipulation in solving a natural problem, Abou-Kassem et al. (2007) cited the example of the manipulation of the simple function, y =5. Following steps show how this function simple function can take route of knowledge or ignorance, based on the information that is exposed or hidden, respectively.

Step 1: $y = 5$. This is an algebraic equation that means, y is a constant with a value of 5. This statement is an expression of tangibles, which becomes clear if the assumptions are pointed out. The assumptions are (Islam and Zatzman, 2007a): a) y has the same dimension as 5 (meaning dimensionless); b) nothing else matters (this one actually is a clarification of the condition a). Therefore, the above function implies that y cannot be a function of anything (including space and time). The mere fact that there is nothing in nature that is constant makes the function aphenomenal. However, subsequent manipulations (as in Step 2) make the process even more convoluted.

Step 2: $dy/dx = 0$. This simple derivation is legitimate in calculus that originates from Newton's ratio of quotient theory. In this, even partial derivative would be allowed with equal legitimacy as nothing states in conventional calculus that such operation is illegitimate. By adding this derivative in x (as in x direction in Cartesian coordinate), a spurious operation is performed. In fact, if Step 1 is true, one can add any dimension to this the differential would still be 0 – statement that is 'technically' true but hides background information that becomes evident in Step 3.

Step 3: If one integrates dy/dx, one obtains, y = C, where C is a constant that can have infinite number of values, depending on which special case it is being solved for. All of a sudden, it is clear that the original function. All of a sudden, it is clear that the original function (y=5) has disappeared.

Step 4: One special case of $y=C$ is, y=5. To get back the original and unique function (as in Step 1), one now is required to have boundary conditions that are no longer attached to the mathematical formulation. If a special case of C=5 is created, similarly one can have $y=1$, 2, 3, 4, 5, 6,... How does one know which solution will give the 'true' solution. Based on pragmatism (whatever works is true, see Zatzman and Islam (2007b) for further details), one resorts to eliminating solutions that do not meet the immediate need. In this particular case, all but one solution are called 'spurious' solutions, because they failed to match the solution of interest, i.e., y=5.

This simple example shows how imposing Newton's differential and integrating procedure convolutes the entire process, while losing information that would allow anyone to trace back the original algebraic function. On the other hand, if one is looking at an actual phenomenon, then $dy/dx = 0$ could mean that we are at the very start of something, or at the very end of something. However, we actually don't know, because, in physical nature, spatial transformations that do not incorporate a time element are like the two-dimensional person who could be sleeping or dancing. If we look at $\partial y/\partial x$, on the other hand, then we have to look also at $\Delta y/\Delta t$, and then we also have to consider the situation where $\Delta y/\Delta x=0$ but $\Delta y/\Delta t$ is non-0. This might very well be a branch-point, a point of bifurcation or, generally speaking, something marking a change from an old state to a new state. Branch-points in physical natural reality clearly imply infinite solutions, since the process could go, literally, anywhere from that branch-point. This approach of locating bifurcation phenomena has eluded previous researchers engaged in modeling chaos (Gleick, 1987).

The engineering implication of the Newtonian approach was highlighted recently by Abou-Kassem et al. (2007). The following steps were highlighted. Note the similarity of these steps with the one shown above regarding a simpler function.

Step 1)   Mass balance + Darcy's law → It is an algebraic equation.
Step 2a)   Time variable is added to it through Newton's differential quotient → time increment is allowed to approach to 0.
Step 2b)   Space variable is added through Newton's differential quotient → space increment is allowed to approach 0.
Step 2c)   differential equations emerge, burying assumptions added in 2a and 2b.
Step 3)   Differential equation integrated analytically, original solutions will not be recovered. The integrated values will have the possibility of having infinite solutions, depending on the boundary conditions, initial conditions, etc.
Step 4)   Three special cases (out of infinite number of solutions possible) are identified as part of the integrated solution of the Differential equation in Step 3. They are:
Step 4a)   Steady state, compressible. This is Mass balance and Darcy's law as in Step 1.
Step 4b)   Unsteady state, slightly compressible fluid. This is the typical equation that gives rise to the Diffusivity equation. This one would have liquid density as the only equation of state (density as a function of pressure).
Step 4c)   Unsteady state, compressible fluid case. This is the typical gas flow equation. This would have gas compressibility (z factor that is a function of pressure and temperature). Here the term 'unsteady' means there is a time derivative. As time extends to infinity, this term drops off, making the model steady state. This alone shows that these 'unsteady state' models are not dynamic models and do not emulate nature that is dynamic at all time.

This development is seen as a great accomplishment of modern mathematics. We started off with one equation, but ended up with three equations that describe other fluids. The pragmatic approach says, if the results are okay, the process must be okay.

Step 5) Because analytical methods are very limited in solving a PDE and require their additional assumptions regarding boundary conditions, numerical techniques were introduced. This one essentially involves discretization through Taylor series approximation and subsequent elimination of higher order terms, arguing that at higher order they are too small (e.g. if Δx is less than 1, Δx^2 is $\ll 1$; $\Delta x^3 \lll 1$).

Step 6) The removal of higher order terms, as in Step 5, is equivalent to eliminating the additions of space and time variables as in Steps 2a and 2b. We, therefore, recover original mass balance and Darcy's law (Momentum balance equation) as in Step 1. The Engineering approach works with these algebraic equations (Step 1) rather than working with PDE and subsequent discretized forms. This explains why Engineering approach coefficients are the same as the 'mathematical approach' coefficients.

When we go from y=5 to dy/dx = 0, we add the possibility of adding an infinite series. When we then go from dy/dx to y = constant, we are left with infinite solutions, all because of the previous addition. On the other hand, if we do this integration numerically (by invoking Taylor series approximation), we end up having the original solution only if we ignore the left over terms of the infinite series that may or may not be convergent. It is important to see the actual derivation of Taylor series expansion. This really *is* magical --- as in *aphenomenal*!

1.3. THE ROLE OF INTENTION IN TECHNOLOGY DEVELOPMENT

All human actions have 'intention' as the root. Even though, 'intention' had been an integral part of oriental culture in all aspects of life, including technology development, it has been stripped off from technology development in the post-renaissance world. The previous section outlines the reason behind this dissociation of intention from the pathway of an action. Mass production and non-benevolent marketing schemes are not compatible of consciousness of intention. This section presents the role of intention in determining the fate of a technology.

Recently, Chhetri (2007) has established that by taking long-term (intangible) approach the outcome is reversed from the one that emerges from short-term (tangible) approach. He made this observation in relation to energy efficiency of various energy sources. By focusing on just heating value, one comes up with a ranking that diverges into what is observed as the global warming phenomenon. On the other hand, if long-term approach was taken, none of the previously perpetrated technologies would be considered 'efficient' and would long been replaced with truly efficient (global efficiency-wise) technologies, avoiding the currently faced energy crisis. Zatzman and Islam (2007a) equated real with natural and further argued that sustainability of an action is similar to sustainability of a process. An action to be sustainable (or real), it must have its origin real to begin with. If the origin of any action is the intention, they argued, intention must play a role in defining success of an action, and subsequently, the process that is developed by these actions.

It has long been accepted that Nature is self-sufficient and complete, rendering it as the true teacher of how to develop sustainable technologies. From the standpoint of human intention, this self-sufficiency and completeness is actually a standard for declaring Nature perfect. "Perfect" here, however, does not mean that Nature is in one fixed unchanging state. On the contrary, it is the capacity of Nature to evolve and sustain that makes it such an excellent teacher. This perfection makes it possible and necessary for Humanity to learn from Nature not to fix Nature but to improve its own condition and prospects within Nature, in all periods and for any timescale. The significance of such emulating of Nature is subtle but crucial: it is that technological or other development undertaken within the natural environment only for some limited short term must necessarily, sooner or later, end up violating something fundamental or characteristic within Nature. Understanding the effect of intangibles and the relations of intangible to tangible is important for reaching appropriate decisions affecting the welfare of the society and the nature as well. A number of aspects of natural phenomena have been discussed here to find out the relationship between intangible and tangible. The target of this study is to provide strong basis to the sustainability model. The mass and energy balance equation has provided and explained to support the influence of intangibles and the role of intention.

1.3.1. Origin of Intention

For the last 200 years the role of intention in all social endeavors has been either ignored or carefully put aside. This includes practically all scientific analyses, and coincides with the commercialization of practically everything in our lives, including education (Islam, 2003). The moment any action is judged against a commercial value, it is assumed that the intention of the action does not have any bearing on the action. This detachment from intention, which is actually the driver of all actions, is so embedded in all analyses that our research found no model that considers this factor in any model of the modern age.

Every action is preceded by intention. Every civilization, ranging from ancient Indian to European culture has recognized the role of intention. For instance, the relationship between 'Chetna' (inspiration) and 'Karma' (deed) was outlined in Mahabharat and in the scripts of Buddha. In Europe, the ancient criminal justice system was based on 'guilty mind' (*mens rea*). The most famous saying of the Prophet and the first one cited in the collection of Bukhari [Hadith of Bukari 1944] is that any deed is based on the intention. A review of human history reveals that the perpetual conflict between good and evil has always been about opposing intentions. The good has always been characterized by the intention to serve a larger community while evil has been characterized as the intention to serve a self interest. Because nature itself is such that any act of serving others leads to serving the self in the long term, it is conceivable that all acts of serving others in fact amount to self interest in the long-term (Islam, 2005). Some see this as the approach of obliquity. History also tells us that ruling entities have always covered up their intentions. From ancient Pharaohs to contemporary ruling elites, rulers have invariably maintained the façade of their good intentions. Whenever this covering up became exposed, the principle of "the King has been ill-advised" has been invoked. While the onset of the information age has begun to make it difficult to cover up intentions, recent events in this new millennium show clearly that covering up intentions is bound to be very costly and will have short-term consequences. The US invasion and occupation of Iraq for trumped-up reasons is the most recent example, with tragic ramifications for humankind (Keenan, 2005; Singh 2005).

Few would dispute seeking peace is the loftiest goal of humans in society, yet human history is marred by war (Kohn, 2000). Since the beginning of the 20th century wars have given impetus to economic and technological breakthroughs as research and the development of better weapons of destruction, and their production create jobs and potential new products to be sold in the civilian economy. In the United States a war president is almost certain to be re-elected, and talking war is considered to be presidential. Ronald Reagan, the Star Wars president, was considered the most popular president ever, although the war (named for a popular science fiction television program) was to be about developing weapons systems to control outer space by the US against its perceived enemies. This scheme required such an enormous outlay of the collective wealth of the US that it was deemed, after long debate, unworkable. However, it has become a vastly successful commercial enterprise. Star Wars toys, stories, and movies are one of the most popular forms of entertainment even for adults. In the prevailing US culture, dominance is synonymous with weapons of mass destruction, which can be simultaneously morphed into consumer products engineered to becoming part of the human cultural space (Carey, 1995).

1.3.2. Nature for Sale

Energy

The sun shines 1.3 kW of energy per square meter on us, yet we burn some 50 million barrels of crude oil daily to have energy for our daily needs (International Energy Annual 2003). This crude oil is refined with numerous toxic additives that are particularly harmful when burned in all combustion engines. Natural gas is another form of energy on which we have become dependent. This gas is processed (to remove water, carbon dioxide, etc.) with toxic chemicals, such as, glycol, Diethylamine (DEA), and others. Even very small parts of these toxic chemicals are dangerous to humans, particularly when they too are burned, in every turbine and other type engines, and the gas stoves in our kitchens. Natural gas is also used to make fertilizers that can only be compared with drugs – the more taken the more needed. The ensuing dependency severely compromises inherent metabolic systems, and in the case of fertilizers, depleting the soil of its inherent nutrients. The cycle of poisoning does not stop here. Plastics are made from the toxic waste left after refining oil, 2.5 million tons of it every day. They are laid out on everything, from baby bottles (that emit dioxin when microwaved) and children's toys to carpets, wall paints, and pillow fillings. To make them user-friendly, more toxins are added. Meanwhile governmental agencies bombard the public is with slogans recommending, "Reduce, Reuse, and Recycle", knowing fully well that every cycle of re-use makes these plastics more toxic and oxidized, using very important oxygen molecules to produce even more harmful chemicals. This plastic is particularly poisonous when heated, yet they are marketed on non-stick™ cookware and recommend incineration as the ultimate fate of these plastics (Justo & Veeraragavan 2002).

No Air

Cigarettes (nicotine added tobacco) were introduced into the personal and public space less than 100 years ago, advertised as glamorous for women and masculine for men, who inhale toxic smoke directly into the lungs. Thus far, the only attempt to stop this human destruction, after years of research and law suits by the public, has been to put warnings on cigarette packs, and increase the price by value added taxes in the US and Canada. In the vast majority of developing countries, people who cannot afford food enough to sustain themselves, smoke billions of dollars of cigarettes daily, profiting only the entities that produce and sell these weapons of mass destruction. In addition many of these same countries are tobacco producers, whose economies to date are dependent on this crop and although countries in Latin America and Africa have taken measures to prevent youthful smoking, Big Tobacco is leading an offensive against such measures in these areas of the world (Cevallos, 2006).

Water

Nature offers free water through rainfall that, after passing through soil, becomes potable by picking up essential minerals. Every nation has access to this water, which is best consumed without any additive. Yet throughout the western world people have little option to drink this fresh water since the water supply system is infused with chlorine, possibly the most potent poison readily soluble in water. Chlorination of water was first introduced in England in 1908 and the US and Canada soon followed suit (Christman, 1998). "Products and services that result in 45% of the U.S. gross domestic product are rooted in chlorine chemistry. In addition to water disinfectants and pharmaceuticals, chlorine is critical to 25% of all medical plastics, 70% of all disposable medical applications, and 95% of crop protection chemicals; it also plays a significant role in the production of soaps and detergents, aluminum, and pulp and paper. The chlor-alkali sector is a solid job producer in the U.S., with a payroll of more than $360 million and more than 37,000jobs" (Bernstein, 2004).

In addition, many cities in the US and Canada have added fluoride to the water, as was recommended by the US Dental Association, the same Dental Association that once promoted the addition of fluoride in toothpaste, followed by the 'invention' of fluoride-free toothpaste. This form of corporate control is so intense, that there are now discussions about the efficacy of adding Aspirin™ and even Lipitor™ to drinking water (Chemical and Engineering News Editorial, 2006). Chlorinated water has become synonymous with some government/corporate definitions of health. Even the World Health Organization of the UN deems chlorinated water the only potable water. Human civilization has survived and indeed thrived for thousands of years, yet we are forced to believe today's civilization cannot survive without the addition of a toxic chlorine tablet. Countries that once had the most access to drinking water have become the most behind in accessing 'potable' water.

Food

Nature offers us free food in the form of plants and animals that feed on these plants. As infants, the best food is mother's milk, which is also free. However, every aspect of the food chain has been engineered, making each 'process' inherently toxic, so that now mother's milk contains traces of all the toxins the mother has ingested and the presence of plastic in umbilical cords (Hooper et al. 2000; Darnerud et al. 2001). The food we eat has a very high price tag because it has become a matter of public policy to throw away excess food to avoid 'price shock' (Hanson, 1993; Richardson, 1998).

Few doubt that processed and 'engineered' food is the cause of obesity (the second biggest killer in North America), yet the developed countries continue to flood Asia and Africa with processed food product technology. In the modern age, there is not a single famine that could not be averted by the West, yet it remains the imposed savior of the world, particularly the developing world. The developed countries have made a contribution to civilization in the form of the plastic bottle to carry water, yet people in Somalia have carried their water in clay containers since they learned to make pottery. Which water is less contaminated? Anyone capable of browsing the website would know the dangers of plastic bottles and with any knowledge of science would understand that leaching doesn't stop just because we cannot measure the amount leached with available technology (Islam, 2005).

1.3.3. The Science of Inefficiency

Historically, human efficiency has been synonymous with doing more with less – the essence of waste minimization. In the Western capitalist world, wasting is built in to the system. Canada, the only country that topped the UN-designated best place to live five years in a row is also the country that has the most energy consumption per capita (Islam, 2003). If cold climate is an indicator of energy needs, Canada's per capita energy consumption is much higher than colder parts of the world, such as Alaska, Norway, Siberia, and others (National Energy Pricing Review, 1996). In the developing world, Kuwait spends 40% of its energy needs in burning fossil fuel so this tiny country can be cooled with air conditioning (Islam ,2004).

In contemporary Western society, there is an all- pervasive perception that intentions don't count. Nobel Laureate Linus Pauling – prizewinner both for Chemistry and for peace, transmuted his work into the notion that humanity could live better with itself and with nature through the widest possible use and/or ingestion of chemicals, that chemicals are chemicals, i.e that knowledge of chemical structure discloses everything we need to know about physical matter- that all chemicals of the same structure are identical regardless of how differently they may actually have been generated or existed in their current form (Pauling, 1954). Paralleling this idea, the Nobel Laureate in Economics, Joseph Stiglitz, has redefined the entire field and science of economics along the line of the notion that information is destiny. Such dogmas have proven especially harmful for health and quality of life in the developed world and for basic economic welfare in the developing countries of Africa, Asia and Latin America. (Godoy et al., 2000) Scientists need to be asking if the catchphrase 'chemicals are chemicals' is true, every nation that fell or was pushed into the trap of chemical fertilizer use by agribusiness, is now searching for ways to escape its myriad problems. If money, or investment, is "destiny" why do we see repeated economic collapse in developing countries proportional to the money invested from developed donor countries? Figure 1.12 illustrates this point. Following a term of service as the head of the World Bank, it was Prof. Stiglitz, in an August 2003 speech in Bangladesh, stated that "the World Bank and IMF only serve the interest of developed countries". From the time institutions in these countries overhauled their basic posture during the Kennedy Administration, guided by the theories of "economic takeoff" (Rostow, 1960), and reoriented and realigned their policies in the closest possible collaboration with the United States' Agency for International Development (AID) programs, such an outcome could never have been in doubt.

According to the U.S. motivational guru Brian Tracy, "today the greatest single source of wealth is between your ears". Human beings, by their labour, are the source of all wealth, yet modern civilization equates wealth with reducing the human population. With the exceptions of the U.S. and Canada, where population increases are now attributable entirely to immigration while the effective birth rate is zero and the natural rate of increase is below zero, population decline is the actual trend throughout the "developed" parts of the world. Yet, assistance from western industrial countries to countries of the developing world, whence the majority of immigrants originates, has been growing specifically in the form of aid to promote zero population growth – a hobby horse of George W Bush's grandfather Prescott Bush and of his father George H.W. Bush (Tarpley & Chaitkin, 1992) – as a solution to their underdevelopment. In these countries, an entire two generations of governments have routinely emulated the West, coming to consider population as their greatest impediment to prosperity. Countries rich with the resources of human population are considered to be the poorest (UNICEF, 2001).

The 'chemicals are chemicals' mantra can make stone (picture above) ground flour the same as the steel-ground one; organic fertilizer the same as the synthetic one; the sunlight the same as the fluorescent light, and eventually Lenin the same as the Tsar who was overthrown by him (picture below). This is the essence of the aphenomenal model.

1.3.4. The Myth of Emulating Nature –The Aphenomenal Model

Few humans dispute that man is the most intelligent creation on this planet. No one disputes that nature is perfect (especially in the sense of complete). In fact, nature is so fully-formed and comprehensive that emulating nature has formed the basis for virtually all branches of knowledge, ranging from natural justice and dialectics of the social system to technology development. Unfortunately, however, no modern technology truly as yet emulates the *science* of nature. It has been quite the opposite: observations of nature have rarely been translated into pro-nature process development. Rather, it is the aphenomenal model (Khan et al. 2005) that which asserts relations between phenomena that do not exist, based on obscuring anything that contradicts a pre-determined outcome, followed by its justification through disinformation, that has taken the lead in all aspects of social life (Zatzman et al. 2007a).

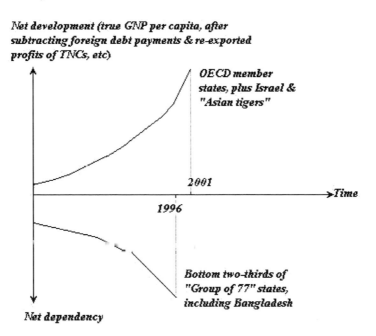

Figure 1.12. As a result of the overextension of credit and subsequent manipulation (by the creditors: Paris Club etc) of the increasingly desperate condition of those placed in their debt, nostrums about "development" remain a chimera and cruel illusion in the lives of literally billions of people in many parts of Africa, Asia and Latin America. (Here the curves are developed from the year 1960.)

Figure 1.13. This picture from Guatemala shows large barren lands that once were filled with trees. These trees were uprooted to make way for the chemical fertilizer driven agriculture. Since chemical fertilizers have been discredited and the need for more fertilizers has skyrocketed, farmers have to abandon the vast land and look for making money from selling the trees! *(Photo courtesy of David Prior)*

Even though it is widely accepted in the social framework that pro-nature arrangements such as would ensure natural justice and social equity, are absent – and not by accident but by design, few paid attention to the problem in so-called natural science. Today, some of the most important technological breakthroughs have been mere manifestations of the *linearization* of nature science: nature linearized by focusing only on its external features. Linearization forms the basis for the first line of disinformation involved (Shapiro et al. 2007).

Nature is non-linear and the claim of emulating nature with linear formulae is inherently untrue. Today, computers process information exactly opposite to how the human brain does. Turbines produce electrical energy while polluting the environment beyond repair even as electric eels produce much higher-intensity electricity while cleaning the environment (Shapiro et al. 2007). Batteries store very little electricity while producing very toxic spent materials. Synthetic plastic materials look like natural plastic, yet their syntheses follow an exactly opposite path. Furthermore, synthetic plastics do not have a single positive impact on the environment, whereas natural plastic materials do not have a single negative impact. In medical science, every promise made at the onset of commercialization proven to be opposite what actually happened: witness Prozac™, Vioxx™, Viagra™, etc.

Nature did not allow a single product to impact the long-term negatively. Even the deadliest venom (e.g., cobra, poisoned arrow, tree frog) have numerous beneficial effects in the long-term. This catalogue carries on in all directions: microwave cooking, fluorescent lighting, nuclear energy, cellular phones, refrigeration cycles to combustion cycles. In essence, nature continues to improve matters in its quality, as modern technologies continue to degrade the same into baser qualities.

Nature thrives on diversity and flexibility, gaining strength from heterogeneity, whereas the quest for homogeneity seems to motivate much of modern engineering. In its non-linearity, Nature inherently promotes multiplicity of solutions. Modern applied science, however, continues to define problems as linearly as possible, promoting "single"-ness of solution, while particularly avoiding non-linear problems. Nature is inherently sustainable and promotes zero-waste, both in mass and energy. Engineering solutions today start with a "safety factor" while promoting an obsession with excess (hence, waste). Nature is truly transient, never showing any exact repeatability or steady state. Engineering today is obsessed with standards and replicability, always seeking "steady-state" solutions. Similar observation can be made for socio-economical development.

How could this happen? Our research shows that none of these technologies emerged from any good intention. 'Good', here, implies long-term good, or good for the general public. The promoters of these products are not incapable of developing 'good' products, they are rather incapable of seeing that 'doing good is good business'. In business development, self-interest in the short-term reigns supreme and promoters of these models are so focused in their short-term gains beyond the quarterly profit. They are quite aware that their motive of amassing profit at the expense of natural justice would offend any consumer, so they resort to hiding their motives right from the beginning. This kind of mendacity results, for example, leads to the corruption of scientific research. Recently two medical researchers, one in Norway and one in South Korea have admitted to faking their research data [Associated Press 2006]. Research has become a race to patent potential money-making developments and Nobel prizes that lead to more money, in the name of assisting humanity. The offending research institutions attempt to single out individual researchers to blame, the one rotten apple, to obscure their own culpability and the future of funding of their projects. Researchers and scientists work in a pressure cooker culture of getting there first.

In this, the fault of the consumer lies with the lack of research. In fact, consumers have been so captivated by the short-term and external gains themselves, that they cannot read between the lines that the overwhelming corporate message is "Shut up and buy!". Often, they forget the reason behind buying a product other than the fact that it was on sale, or was seen on TV, or the neighbor has one (Bernays, 1923).

False Promises

1) In 1960, when birth control pills were first introduced, each pill contained 10 times more male hormone than necessary to abort the egg. The promise behind this was the Liberation of women. Soon after, the anti-nausea drug thalidomide was introduced for pregnant women. The promise here was that women could have easy pregnancies by removing nausea. In reality, 20% of babies who mothers were on the drug became severely deformed. This drug was banned in 1962 but now it is making a comeback. Today, even a 12 year old can get prescribed for birth control pills (at least in Canada) and the same industry is busy producing 'correction pills' that would 'eliminate' the inherent injustice of woman's biology by stopping menstruation altogether (McLeans, Dec. 2005).

2) In 1940's, baby disposable diapers were introduced. The inventor, Marion Donovan noticed that her babies would 'nearly instantaneously' wet their cloth diapers as soon as they were changed. In 1946, she introduced the 'breakthrough' technology of disposable waterproof diaper. Did the habit of 'nearly instantaneously' wetting the diaper go away? Of course not. In fact, the first name of these diapers was 'the boat', indicating it was meant to keep babies afloat on their own urine! However we are convinced that disposable diapers are synonymous with keeping the babies dry and civilized. Cotton nappies are expensive, and even considered germ carriers now (Islam, 2003).

Overall, modern development and social progress can be characterized by its driver, greed. Nature, on the other hand, operates on the basis of need and therefore there is no need to make false promises or to institute opacity if one wishes to introduce pro-nature development. The result of the greed-driven social development has led to the current 'technological disaster' (as stated by Robert Curl, a Nobel Laureate in Chemistry). This process has led to a sharp decline in a population that cares for nature, while the number of people focused on self interest and short-term gains has skyrocketed. During this time, the quality of human health has suffered tremendously. For instance, in last 50 years, there has been an increase of 50 times per capita in the use of sugar ('refined', externally processed, carbohydrate) plastic ('wrinkle free' leather or fabric, 'durable' wood, cheap water container), fertilizer ('refined' biomass), spirit ('refined' alcohol), cigarettes ('refined' tobacco), chemicals ('preservatives', Pasteurization, antibiotics), and 'remediative' surgery, while the 'life' expectancy has increased somewhat In the words of Albert Einstein, this 'life' isn't worth living. Unfortunately, this 'life' is being promoted as the only life human beings should live for. Figure 1.12 illustrates this point.

1.3.5. WHY IS THE CURRENT DEVELOPMENT MODE ANTI-NATURE?

As discussed earlier in this article, the current process is driven by an economic model that is wasteful and profit driven, along with the built-in inability to consider the long-term. Nature is infinite and operates at zero-waste, hence waste-based technology is anti-nature. By taking the short-term approach, mechanisms have been created that make the world environment continuously worse. (Figure 1.14 elaborates this aspect for technology development. However, it may be readily extrapolated to other aspects of social development, including politics and education. The absence of good intention can only bring long-term disaster.

Early civilizations considered themselves the guardians and caretakers of all living things on the lands they inhabited, and held themselves responsible for future generations. Indigenous American Nations considered themselves one with all around them. There was no special word for Nature, no separation: plants, animals, and humans were considered interdependent. In this world it was the coming of the European invader, funded by their own rulers at home, that led to the eventual corporatizing of the earth which all living things share in common, into a commodity to be broken up at will, through wars and land appropriation. The advent of property laws made "legal" after the fact, what had actually been acts of misappropriation. In nineteenth-century America, following the Civil War, specifically in order to to protect and encourage corporate property, this "right" to retain control or ownership of *any* form of property – especially property already accounted as a business asset (whether it originated as a natural resource or as a claim on someone else's labour) but acquired without "colour of right" (*i.e.*, before there existed any law specifically defining or dealing with its legal existence as property (Latta, 1961)– was consciously elaborated as an exception to the Rule of Law. As the result of wars and other struggles waged to protect this corporatized form of property and the technological development that stemming from it – including associated long-term toxic effects – the world now finds itself in an environmental crisis (Rich, 1994).

The deepening of this crisis is marked by a simultaneous extension of corporate abuse of Humanity's rights of access to fresh air, clean water and other absolute necessities, alongside a growing rebellion by the human productive forces sustaining these corporations as their market, against government accommodation of the abusers and their abuses. Today, water and air have become commodities. Governments and corporations now own access to water. Overuse by industry and agriculture have made it into a scarce commodity over which future wars will be waged (Barlow & Clarke 2002; Holden & Thubani 1996). Contaminated by industrial and agricultural runoff, the sale of bottled water, or home filters to the public who can afford it, is promoted as 'uncontaminated'. Pollution itself, created by chemical poisons released into the air by industry, agriculture, and the automobile, has become a money-making commodity – with the sale of pollution 'credits' from one polluter to another. Home filters to 'clean' the air in homes and public buildings, promote clean air, again for those who can afford it, autos in many places are required to have catalytic converters to filter out poisons emitted from the burning of fuel, to keep down air pollution. At the same time corporate activity, with its virtual immunity from prosecution, legal sanctions or legal responsibility in its home bases and main markets, is purchased and maintained by trying to dump unwanted wastes in various parts of Africa and Asia. This is arousing more and more people in the rest of the world against corporate fiat and dictate, energizing in its wake a rapidly widening discussion of alternative arrangements for Humanity's continued existence on this planet. Accordingly, the intention to control nature has become the last remaining pathway by which corporations hope to ensure a constant, never-ending stream of profit – and a battleground on which the fate of Humanity for generations to come may be decided.

The most efficacious route by which humans can begin to restore the earth to some kind of balance is through education. By "education" is meant the ability to look at the world unencumbered by preconceived notions. Thus, it is neither job skills training, nor the ability to earn more money, nor what takes place in institutions calling themselves universities by operating in a bubble, separated from real life around them, as the captives of corporate intentions. Education as it has been up to now – the instrument by which modern society prepares the next generation of workers according to the needs of capital in the short term – is utterly inadequate for the demands of the Information Age.

Transition to Tangible

Throughout the 20th century and to date, the intention of all business models (the amalgamation of entities that come together by law for the purposes of doing business) has been to try to sell everything on this planet: not only manufactured products and the food we must buy to eat, but also the very bodies of humans through our labor, our body parts as consumer items (breast modification for women, penile implants for men, internal organs as replacement parts, etc.), animals as pets, health, transportation, education, culture, war, and even the very air we breathe and the water we drink, all natural resources – all *for a price*, all for sale only. Nothing is sold that does not profit the seller all the way down the extraction and production chain.

The drive to corporatization started in Britain in the 16th century. Systematically, most of the world's land was converted into 'property' 'owned' by individuals, and later by corporate entities (which enjoy the rights and personality of individuals under the law). The first act of the Bolshevik Revolution of 1917 was to eliminate such private property in land. The entire social system elaborated from and on the basis of that act, on one-sixth of the earth's surface, threw into a chronic crisis the economy in the rest of the world. In the United States and Europe in particular the regime of private property – not only in land, but in means of production in general, including factories, distribution networks, etc. – still held sway. However, increasingly in these countries, the State was interposed

1. as guarantor of all parts of socially necessary services that were of minimal profit to private capital;
2. as guarantor of all high-risk energy development projects; and
3. as financier of parasitic spending on, and the endless and guaranteed market for, weapons systems of every description. In these and other ways, the self-interest of private property and its unquenchable appetite for gain could still carry on – only disguised as government-approved and, therefore, somehow pro-social.

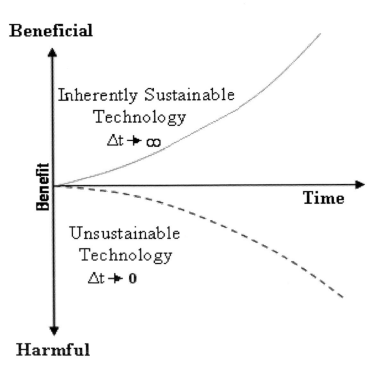

Figure 1.14. Direction of sustainability (Redrawn from Khan and Islam, 2007a).

With the disappearance after 1989-1991 of the regime of socialist social property in the

Soviet Union and eastern Europe, the chronic crisis of the established capitalist world order did not come to an end. On the contrary, the crisis itself has deepened by becoming more chronic, with serious decay in social indices from alcoholism to infant mortality and premature death throughout the former socialist countries as well as a change in some of the forms of this crisis. In addition to certain individual countries such as the Republic of Cuba and the Democratic People's Republic of Korea which still maintain a socialist system as a barrier against the revival of private property in general, there are today a number of economic blocs that have formed – most dramatically and recently ASEAN in China and southeast Asia, and the ALBA project led by Cuba and Venezuela in Latin America and envisioned eventually to incorporate Argentina, Brazil, Chile, Ecuador and Bolivia as well – on the basis of reining in previously absolute freedom for private property, especially in the form of foreign credits or foreign direct investment from U.S. or European sources, to overrule the needs of individual member-states.

1.3.6. Development of a Sustainable Model

The sustainability model developed by Khan and Islam (2007a) provides the basis of the direction of the sustainable technology. According to this model, a process is sustainable if and only if it travels a path that is beneficial for an infinite span of time. Otherwise the process must diverge in a direction that is not beneficial in the long run. Pro-nature technology is the long-term solution; anti-nature solutions are all that will come from schemas that comprehend, or analyze, or plan to handle change on the basis of any approach in which time-changes, or Δt, are examined only as they approach 0 (zero) that have been designed or selected as being good for time $t =$ 'right now' (equivalent to the idea of $\Delta t \rightarrow 0$). Of course, in nature, time "stops" nowhere, there is no such thing as steady state, and hence, regardless of the self-evident tangibility of the technologies themselves, the "reality" in which they are supposed to function usefully is itself non-existent – what can be described as "aphenomenal" – and cannot be placed on the graph (Figure 1.15). "Good" technology can be developed – if and only if it travels a path that is beneficial for an infinite span of time. In Figure 1.15, this concept is incorporated in the notion of '*time tending to Infinity*', which (among other things) implies also that time-changes instead of approaching 0 (zero) could instead approach Infinity, *i.e.*, $\Delta t \rightarrow \infty$. In this study, it has been introduced the term 'perception' which was found important at the beginning of any process. Perception varies person to person. It is very subjective and there is no way to prove if a perception is true or wrong; its effect is immediate. Perception is completely one's personal opinion developed from one's experience without appropriate knowledge. That is why perception can not be used as the base of the model. However, if perception is used in the model, the model would look like as follows (Figure 1.15).

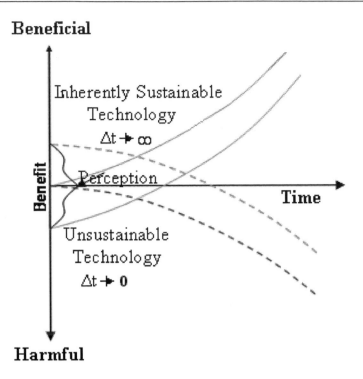

Figure 1.15. Direction of sustainability (Modified from Khan and Islam, 2007a).

Problem with the Current Model

Any current model of technology development focuses only to transient tangible benefit which falls into unsustainable technology at the end. For example, conventional engineering analysis today, in which electrical power generation is routine, common and widespread, would condemn as unsustainable the technology that converts the rotary motion of a wheel fixed in position over a flowing water course (river or stream) into useful work in the form of mechanical energy available immediately within a workplace constructed around the installation of this water wheel. However, every component of this arrangement can be renewed, replaced or maintained entirely from naturally available materials (wood for the wheel, keeping the water flow source undimmed or otherwise unobstructed), whereas vast tracts of nature have to be destroyed one way or another to sustain electrical power generation. Instead of being addressed keeping sustainability in mind, the limitations of the older technology's speed and scale of productivity were leap-frogged by diverging onto the anti-nature path. A century later the headlines would read: "Does Power Corrupt?" in an attempt to signal the devastating side effect of electrical energy (Mittelstaedt, 2007). The very fact that alternate current does not exist in nature should have alerted scientists that electrical energy is not sustainable. Instead, electrical energy has been made into norm and today's civilization is measured by how many buildings are light during the night (Figure 1.16). In this, even steam energy is marginalized unless turbines are run with nuclear energy.

A single analysis would have indicated decades ago that electrical heat or electrical light cannot be beneficial for the human being. However, this analysis would require researching beyond the immediate tangible and in the modern age there seems to be giant step backward toward tangibles. Energy technologies that survived the commercialization test ended up making things more focused on tangible (Khan and Islam, 2007b).

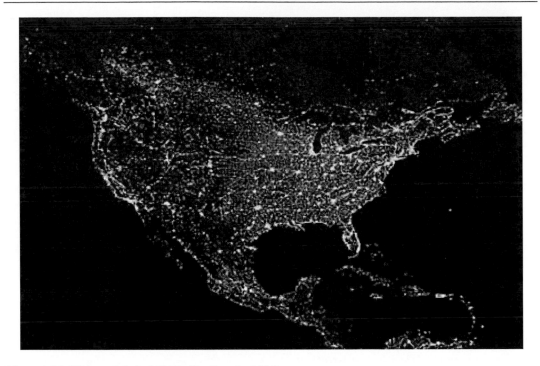

Figure 1.16. USA at night by NASA (Soulincode, 2006).

If the products are analyzed with the implementation years and the time required to be exhausted, it is found that no non-natural products are sustainable (Figure 1.17). The effect of some products continues even after extinction of those products. For example, chemical such as DDT is still found in bird dropping (Guano) though DDT is no more practiced. These droppings stimulate the growth of mosses and plankton in the ponds, which feed various insects, which in turn support small birds, called snow buntings (Schmid, 2005). Therefore, it is found that some pollutants never end due to their biological connections. Microoven, simulated wood, non-stick cooking jar, Freon, DDT, PVC etc were flourished during last several decades with lots of promises, however, those promises became falsehood with progressing time. For instance, Freon changed its facade after 57 years, DDT after 30 years, PVC after 30 years; non-stick Teflon after 50 years; Enron after 15 years and VIOXX after 3 years; everything that is untrue will change its front after a finite time (DDT, 2006; PVC, 2006; Teflon, 2006; Enron, 2006; VIOXX 2006). Truth will not. In that sense, truth is the only steady state. However, none of the current technology with transient tangible model is steady and therefore, based on false promises (Zatzman and Islam, 2007b).

In this decade, Australia and some other countries have banned the use of incandescent light bulb which produces artificial light (Maclaren, 2007). Teflon is considered to be used as a non toxic, low frictional surface. However, its constituents are cancer causing. Teflon degrades at high temperature and that is why its uses in cookeries are alarming in the future. Even with the technological improvement, at least 70 percent of all new drugs introduced in the United States in the past 25 years come from nature despite the use of sophisticated techniques to design products in the laboratory (Steenhuysen, 2007). Their study indicates that a back-to-nature approach might yield better possibilities for companies looking for the next blockbuster drug.

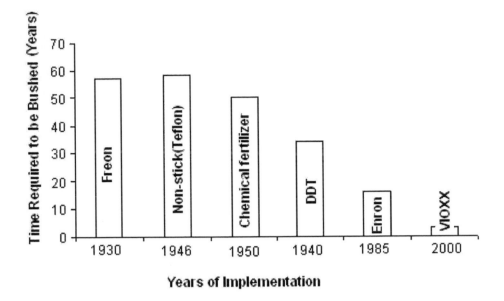

Figure 1.17. Bushed out time of false promised products

The Importance of Truth as a Criterion

In technology development, it is important to take a holistic approach. The only single criterion that one can use is the reality criterion. A reality is something that doesn't change with time going to infinity. This is the criterion, Khan (2006) used to define sustainability. If the ranking of a number of options is performed based on this criterion that would equivalent to the real (phenomenal) ranking. This ranking is absolute and must be the basis for comparison of various options. This ranking is given in the left most column of Table 1.7. In technology development, this natural (real) ranking is practically never used. Based on other ranking criteria, most of the ranking is reversed, meaning the natural order is turned up side down. However, there are some criteria that would give the same ranking as the natural one, but that does not mean that the criterion is legitimate. For instance, the heating value for honey is the highest. However, this does not mean the process is correct, or — putting it in terms of the syllogism that launched Section 2 — it reaffirms that "all Americans do not speak French", *i.e.*, something we already knew all along. This table is discussed in Section 8 *infra* as a starting-point for establishing a "reality index" that would allow a ranking according to how close the product is to being natural.

In engineering calculations, the most commonly used criterion is the efficiency, which deals with output over input. Ironically, an infinite efficiency would mean someone has produced something out of nothing – an absurd concept as an engineering creation. However, if nature does that, it operates on 100% efficiency. For instance, every photon coming out of the sun gets used. So, for a plant the efficiency is limited (less than 100%) because it is incapable of absorbing every photon it is coming in contact with, but it will become 100% if every photon is accounted for. This is why maximizing efficiency as a man-made engineering practice is not a legitimate objective. However, if the concept of efficiency is used in terms of overall performance, the definition of efficiency has to be changed. With this new definition (called 'global efficiency' by Khan et al., 2007b and Chhetri, 2007), the efficiency calculations will be significantly different from conventional efficiency that only considers a small object of practical interest. As an example, consider an air conditioner running outdoor. The air in front of the air conditioner is indeed chilled, while air behind the device will be heated. For instance, if cooling efficiency calculations are performed on an air conditioner running outdoor, the conventional calculations would show finite efficiency, albeit not 100%, as determined by measuring temperature in front of the air conditioner and dividing the work by the work done to operate the air conditioner. Contrast this to the same efficiency calculation if temperature all around are considered. The process will be proven to be utterly inefficient and will become obvious the operation is not a cooling process at all. Clearly, cooling efficiency of the process that is actually heating is absurd. Consider now, with an air conditioner running with direct solar heating. An absorption cooling system means there is no moving part and the solar heat is being converted into cool air. The solar heat is not the result of an engineered process. What would, then, be the efficiency of this system and how would this cooling efficiency compare with the previous one? Three aspects emerge from this discussion. First, global efficiency is the only one that can measure true merit of a process. Secondly, the only efficiency that one can use to compare various technological options is the global efficiency. Thirdly, if one process involves natural options, it cannot be compared with a process that is totally 'engineered'. For instance, efficiency in the latter example (as output/input) is infinity considering no engineered energy has been imparted on the air conditioner.

Table 1.7. Synthesised and natural pathways of organic compounds as energy sources, ranked and compared according to selected criteria (from Zatzman et al. 2007b)

Natural (real) ranking ("top" rank means most acceptable)	Aphenomenal ranking by the following criteria			
	Bio-degradability	Efficiency[1,] e.g., $\eta = \dfrac{Outp - Inp}{Inp} \times 100$	Profit margin	Heating value (cal/g)
1. Honey 2. Sugar 3. Sacchharine 4. Aspartame	2 3 4 1	4 "sweetness /g" 3 2 1	4 3 2 1	1 2 3 4
1. Organic wood 2. Chemically-treated wood 3. Chemically grown, Chemically treated wood 4. Genetically-altered wood	1 REVERSES 2 depending on 3 applic'n, 4 e.g., durability	4 REVERSES if 3 toxicity is 2 considered 1	4 REVERSES if 3 organic wood 2 treated with 1 organic chemicals	4 3 2 1

Table 1.7. (Continued)

Natural (real) ranking ("top" rank means most acceptable)	Aphenomenal ranking by the following criteria			
	Bio-degradability	Efficiency[1], e.g., $\eta = \dfrac{Outp - Inp}{Inp} \times 100$	Profit margin	Heating value (cal/g)
1. Solar 2. Gas 3. Electrical 4. Electromagnetic 5. Nuclear	Not applicable	*5* # Efficiency *4* can-not be *3* calculated for *2* direct solar *#*	*5* *4* *3* *2* *1*	*5* # - Heating *4* value cannot *3* be *2* calculated for *#* direct solar
1. Clay or wood ash 2. Olive oil + wood ash 3. Veg oil+NaOH 4. Mineral oil + NaOH 5. Synthetic oil + NaOH 6. 100% synthet ic (soap-free soap)	*1* Anti- *3* bacterial soap *4* won't use *5* olive oil; *6* volume needed *2* for cleaning unit area	*6* REVERSES if *5* global is *4* considered *3* *2* *1*	*6* *5* *4* *3* *2* *1*	*4* # 1 cannot be *6* ranked *5* *3* *2* *#*
1. Ammonia 2. Freon 3. Non-Freon synthetic	*1* *2* *3*	Unknown	*3* *2* *1*	Not applicable
1. Methanol 2. Glycol 3. Synthetic polymers (low dose)	*1* *2* *3*	*1* For hydrate *2* control *3*	*3* *2* *1*	Not applicable
1. Sunlight 2. Vegetable oil light 3. Candle light 4. Gas light 5. Incandescent light 6. Fluorescent light	Not applicable	*6* *5* *4* *3* *2* *1*	*6* *5* *4* *3* *2* *1*	Not applicable

[1] This efficiency is local efficiency that deals with arbitrarily set size of sample.

* calorie/gm is a negative indicator 'weight watchers' (that are interested in minimizing calorie) and is a positive indicator for energy drink makers (that are interested in maximizing calorie).

No engineering design is complete until economic calculations are performed. There lies the need for maximizing profit margin. Indeed, the profit margin is the single-most criterion used for developing a technology ever since renaissance that saw the emergence of short-term approach in an unparalleled pace. As Table 1.6 indicates, natural rankings generally are reversed if the criterion of profit maximization is used. This affirms once again how modern economics has turned pro-nature techniques upside down (Zatzman and Islam, 2007a).

Violation of Characteristic Time

Another problem of the current technology is that it violates the natural characteristic time. The characteristics time is similar to natural life cycle to any living being. However, characteristics time does not include any modification of life cycle time due to non-natural human intervention. For instance, the life span of an unconfined natural chicken can be up to 10 years, yet table fowls or broilers reach adult size and are slaughtered at six weeks of age (PAD, 2006). The characteristics time for broiler chicken has been violated due to human intervention. This study has emphasized on characteristic time because of its pro-nature definition. Anything found in the nature grown and obtained naturally is reached to its contents both in tangibles and intangibles. However, anything produced either by internal genetically intervention or external chemical fertilizer along with pesticide utilization can not be good for human consumption for both long term and short term benefit. The notion of this violation is only to produce more to obtain short-term tangible benefits trading off with other intangible benefits which are more important.

1.3.7. Observation of Nature: Importance of Intangibles

Nature is directly observed and recorded only in tangible aspects detectable with current technologies. Accordingly, much of what could only be taking place as a result of intangible but very active orderliness within nature is promoted – according to this exclusively and narrowly tangible standard – as being "disorder". The greatest confusion is created when this misapprehension is then labeled "chaotic," and its energy balance on this basis portrayed as headed towards "heat death", or "entropy", or the complete dissipation of any further possibility of extracting "useful work".

Reality is quite different. In nature, there is not a single entity that is linear, symmetric or homogeneous. In Globe, there isn't a single process that is steady or even periodic. Natural processes are chaotic, but not in the sense of being either arbitrary or inherently tending towards entropy. Rather, they are chaotic in the sense that what is essentially orderly and characteristic only unfolds with the passage of time within the cycle or frequency that is characteristic of the given process at some particular point. What the process looks like at that point is neither precisely predictable previous to that point nor precisely reconstructible or reproducible after that point: the path of such a process is defined as chaotic on the basis of its being a periodic, non-linear and non-arbitrary.

Nature is chaotic. However, the laws of motion developed by Newton can not explain the chaotic motion of Nature due to its assumptions which contradicts with the reality of Nature. The experimental validity of Newton's laws of motion is only limited to describe instantaneous macroscopic and tangible phenomena, however, microscopic and intangible phenomena are ignored. The classical dynamics, as represented by Newton's laws of motion, emphasizes fixed and unique initial conditions, stability, and equilibrium of a body in motion (Ketata et al., 2007a). However, the fundamental assumption of constant mass alone is adequate to conflict Newton's laws of motion. Ketata et al. (2007a) formulated the following relation to describe the body in continuous motion in one space:

$$m = \frac{F}{\left((6t + 2) + \left(3t^2 + 2t + 1\right)^2\right)ce^u}$$ [1]

where

F is the force on the body;

$u = t^3 + t^2 + t + 1$;

and c is a constant.

The above relation demonstrates that the mass of a body in motion depends on time whether F varies over time or not. This is absolutely the contradiction of first law of motion. Similarly, the acceleration of a body in motion is not proportional to the force acting on the body because mass is not constant. Again, this is a contradiction of second law of motion.

Here it is found that time is the biggest issue which, in fact, dictates the correctness of Newton's laws of motion. Considering only instantaneous time ($\Delta t \rightarrow 0$), Newton's laws of motion will be experimentally valid with some error, however, considering the infinite time span ($\Delta t \rightarrow \infty$), the laws can not be applicable. That is why sustainable technologies which include short term to long term benefit can not be explained by Newton's laws. To overcome this difficulty, it is necessary to break out of '$\Delta t \rightarrow 0$', in order to include intangibles, which is the essence of pro-nature technology development.

In terms of the well-known laws of conservation of mass (m), energy (E) and momentum (p), the overall balance, B, within Nature may be defined as some function of all of them:

$$B = f(m, E, p)$$ [2]

The perfection without stasis that is Nature means that everything that remains in balance within it is constantly improving with time. That is:

$$\frac{dB}{dt} > 0.$$ [3]

If the proposed process has all concerned elements such that each element is following this pathway, none of the remaining elements of the mass balance discussed later will present any difficulty. Because the final product is being considered as time extends to infinity, the positive ("> 0") direction is assured.

Pro-nature technology, which is non-linear, increases its orderliness on a path that converges at infinity after providing maximum benefits over the intervening time. This is achievable only to the extent that such technologics employ processes as they operate within nature, or use materials whose internal chemistry has been refined entirely within the natural environment and whose subsequent processing has added nothing else from nature in any manner other than its characteristic form. Any and every other technology is anti-nature. The worst among them are self-consciously linear, "increasing" order artificially by means of successive superpositions that supposedly take side-effects and negative consequences into account as they are detected. This enables the delivery of maximum power, or efficiency, etc. for some extremely short term, without regard to coherence or overall sustainability and at the cost of manifold detrimental consequences carrying on long after the "great advances" of the original anti-nature technology have dissipated. Further disinformation lies with declaring the resulting product 'affordable', 'inexpensive', 'necessary' and other self serving and utterly false attributes while increasing only very short terms costs. Any product that is anti-nature would turn out to be prohibitively costly if long-term costs are included. The case in point is the tobacco technology. In Nova Scotia alone, 1300 patients die each year of cancer emerging directly from smoking (Islam, 2003). These deaths cost us 60 billion dollars in body part alone. How expensive cigarette should be? The fact is, if intangibles are included in any economic analysis, a picture very different from what is conventionally portrayed will emerge (Zatzman and Islam, 2007b).

Any linearized model can be limited or unlimited, depending on the characteristics of the process (Figure 1.18). The "limited linearized model" has two important characteristics: more tangible features than intangible, and a finite, limited amount of disorder or imbalance. Because only linearized models are man-made, nature has time to react to the disorder created by this limited model, and it may, therefore, be surmised that such models are unlikely to cause damage that is irreparable.

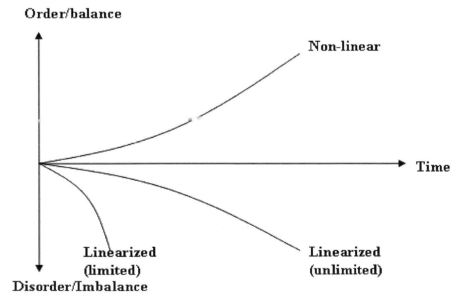

Figure 1.18. Pathway of nature and anti-nature (Modified from Khan and Islam, 2007a).

The unlimited linearized model is characterized by long-term effects little understood but far more damaging, with more intangible features than tangible and an unlimited degree of disorder, or imbalance. Contemporary policy-making processes help conceal a great deal of actual or potential imbalance from immediate view or detection – a classic problem with introducing new pharmaceuticals, for example. Since a drug has to pass the test of not showing allergic reactions, many such drugs make it into the market after being "tweaked" to delay the onset of what are euphemistically called "contra-indications." An elaborate and tremendously expensive process of clinical trials is unfolded to mask such "tweaking", mobilizing the most heavily invested shareholders of these giant companies to resist anything that would delay the opportunity to recoup their investment in the marketplace. The growing incidence of suicide among consumers of Prozac® and other SSRI-type anti-depressant drugs, and of heart-disease "complications" among consumers of "Cox-2" type drugs for relief from chronic pain, are evidence of the consequences of the unlimited linearized model and of how much more difficult any prevention of such consequences is (Miralai, 2006). In forms of concentrations, unlimited pertains to intangible.

Here is another "homier" example of how the unlimited linearized model delays the appearance of symptoms: if food is left outside, in 2-3 days, it will cause food poisoning provoking diarrhea. However, if the food is placed in artificial refrigeration, the food will retain some appearance of 'freshness' even after several weeks – although its quality will be much worse than the 'rotten' food that was left outside. Another more exotic but non-industrial example can be seen in the reaction to snake venom. The initial reaction is immediate. If the victim survives, there is no long-term negative consequence. Used as a natural source or input to a naturally-based process, snake venom itself possesses numerous long-term benefits and is known for its anti-depressed nature.

Repositioning cost-benefit analysis away from such short-term considerations as the cheapness of synthesized substitutes, etc to the more fundamental tangible/intangible criterion of long-term costs and benefits, the following summary emerges: tangible losses are very limited, but intangible losses are not.

1.3.8. Intangible Cause to Tangible Consequence

Short-term intangible effects are difficult to understand, but consideration of the treatment procedures employed by homeopaths may serve to illustrate. The most characteristic principle of homeopathy is that the potency of a remedy can be enhanced by dilution, an inconsistency with the known laws of chemistry (Homeopathy, 2006). In some case, the dilution is so high that it is extremely unlikely that one molecule of the original solution would be present in that dilution. As there is no detectable mechanism to this, the effect of the molecule cannot always be understood and that is why the homeopathy still remains controversial to the modern science of tangible. However, the trace ingredient of dilution is not always ignorable. Recently, Rey (2003) studied the thermoluminescence of ultra-high dilution of lithium chloride and sodium chloride and found the emitted light specific of the original salts dissolved initially. The dilution was beyond Avogadro's number ($\sim 6.0 \times 10^{23}$ atoms per mole) – but its effect was visible. In other words: when concentration of a substance descends to below detection level, it cannot be ignored, as its effects remain present. This is where greater care needs to be taken in addressing the harmful potential of chemicals in low concentrations. Lowering the concentration cannot escape the difficulty – a significant consideration when it comes to managing toxicity. Relying on low concentration as any guarantee of safety defeats the purpose when the detection threshold used to regulate as to what is "safe" is itself higher than the lowest concentrations at which these toxins may be occurring or accumulating in the environment. Although the science that will identify the accumulation of effects from toxic concentrations before they reach the threshold of regulatory detection remains to be established, the point is already clear: tangible effects may proceed from causes that can remain intangible for some unknown period of time.

Mobile phones are considered to be one of the biggest inventions of modern life for communication. So far, the alert of using mobile phone was limited only to the human brain damage for non-natural electro magnetic frequency. An official Finnish study found that people who used the phones for more than 10 years were 40 per cent more likely to get a brain tumor on the same side as they held the handset (Lean and Shawcross, 2007). However, recently it has been observed that mobile frequency also cause serious problem to the other living being of nature, which are very important for use to balance the ecological system. Recently, an abrupt disappearance of the bees that pollinate crops has been noticed especially in USA as well as some other countries of Europe (Lean and Shawcross, 2007). The plausible explanation of this disappearance is that radiation from mobile phones interferes with bees' navigation systems, preventing the famously home loving species from finding their way back to their hives. Most of the world's crops depend on pollination by bees. That is why a massive food shortage has been anticipated due to the extinction of these bees due to radiation given off by the mobile phones. Albert Einstein once said that if the bees disappeared, "man would have only four years of life left" (Lean and Shawcross, 2007). This is how a non-natural hi-tech instrument poses tangible effect in the long run due to its intangible causes.

1.3.9. The Science of Intention

Consider the transition highlighted in Table 1.7. Society started off with natural use products. Any alteration in these natural products ended up making these products toxic in the long term. The question becomes, why did we allow this transition? For the perpetrators, it is clearly greed. For the victims (consumers), it is ignorance. In a way, both of them suffer from the same focus on tangibles. None of these products would have a chance, if people were consciously making decisions before any of their actions (Manders, 1978). This consciousness can come only with the awareness of intentions. In the past, this important intangible has been ignored.

Intention should essentially mean good intention and has to be guided by the conscience, which is unique to human beings and is the core of what sets humans apart from other animals. Other animals, fortunately, act uniquely on instinct and hence do not risk violating their natural traits. This is also true of every other entity, including, one could argue, the inanimate objects. Only human beings have the ability to intervene in order to alter the natural course of nature. If this intervention is motivated by greed or self interest in the short-term, this intervention will invariably lead to disasters.

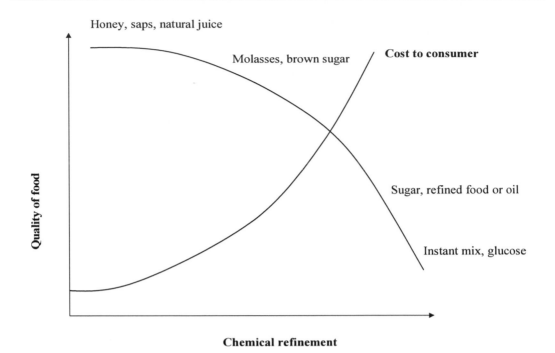

Figure 1.18. The outcome of greed-driven technology. The same applies to quality of human beings that have been 'refined' with the greed-driven education system or to the quality of human health of people who adopted this anti-Nature culture.

If human beings do not succeed in reversing this pattern, nature will make adjustments in order to alleviate the long-term harm of greed-driven initiatives. Here, we include effects that result from man-made activities. For instance, the use of 'refined' oil in combustion engines has led to global warming that destabilized the entire climate system. The reaction of nature is not the 'wrath of God', it is rather the ongoing effort to revert the current trend. The emergence of numerous diseases among humans is not 'God's revenge', it is the reaction of human bodies (a very natural system) trying to resist the ill effect of viruses. Note that viruses do not have natural microstructures or forms, they are rather the product of anti-nature processes (Gelderblom, 2006). Similar statement can be made for all chemicals that have been introduced since the industrial revolution, ranging from DDT to Freon.

1.3.10. How does One Revert?

It would be easy to say we can solve all our human and environmental problems by resorting to some atavistic memory of living in some imagined past. Fortunately, all tangible features of nature are dynamic and unidimensional and there is no way we can revert to a former physical existence. Any claims that this is possible, surely falls into the category of the perpetrators of the aphenomenal model. Take for instance, the following transition:

Sugar cane sap → molasses → sugar → saccharine → Asparteme

Table 1.7. Various transitions as a product of the greed-based development

```
Wood → plastic;
Glass → PVC, fiberglass;
Cotton → polyester;
Natural fiber → synthetic fiber;
Clay and limestone→ cement;
Molasses → Sugar → NutraSweet;
Fermented flower extract →perfume;
Water filter (Hubble bubble) → cigarette filter;
Graphite, clay → chalk → marker;
Vegetable paint → plastic paint;
Natural marble → artificial marble;
Clay tile → ceramic tile → vinyl and plastic;
Wool → polyester;
Silk → synthetic;
Bone → hard plastic;
Vegetable glue → plastic glue;
Organic fertilizer → chemical fertilizer;
Adaptation → bioengineering
```

Modern science tells us this transition has been devastating. So, *where* do we revert? Some suggest going back to molasses or brown sugar. But current methods of producing molasses are unacceptable. Today, developing countries engaged in these processes embrace toxic chemistry such as arsenic use to bleach molasses, while wealthy countries wouldn't hesitate to collect toxic residues from sugar factories to sell as molasses or brown sugars (some would even paint it brown (add "food coloring" to increase profitability). Others propose, 'Organic' sugar, at an extra cost. And although organic sugar means the sugar cane was not tainted with toxic pesticides or the use of chemical fertilizers, it doesn't guarantee that the 'refining' process itself was free from toxic chemicals (in fact, no sugar mill uses organic bleach). Similar statements can be made for other exotic varieties of sugar products that are currently flooding the market (including 'fair trade', kosher, etc.) None of these 'alternatives' can be considered good because, all of them have the same intention behind their marketing, which is to increase the profitability of the product, using the cheapest available means.

A late 20th century view of the world has emerged in Western nations, led by the US, which posits the world, including nature, as a market. Here everything is for sale, includin how people think and feel. As theories of the world, market based approaches need not only to be evaluated in terms of their success or failure, but also in terms of the symbolic and cultural effects they make possible by placing a cash value on people's needs.

Unless intention is changed, the pathway that we have traveled cannot be changed. Intentions can only change with knowledge. Knowledge can only come with long-term vision, which is the essence of education that is not equated with training or learning of skills.

It helps us to see how focusing on the short-term has made it possible that whatever we long for eludes us. It is the kind of knowledge that allows us to see and plan for the long-term, mindful of where the path of our actions can take us. With this kind of knowledge, even in the short-term, doing good can be good business.

2. ENERGY TECHNOLOGIES

2.1. COOKING

Introduction

To meet the energy demand of increased population, the use of fossil fuel has significantly increased in the recent years. Fossil fuels are used mainly to meet the demand for transportation (land, air and water), industries and domestic uses. Cooking is one of the major activities in our daily life. Conventionally, various fuels such as natural gas, coal, kerosene, fuelwood, charcoal, rice husk, dung and pellets are employed for cooking purposes. There are some newer technologies such as biogas, solar, electrical and microwave technologies that are also increasingly becoming popular. However, their health, economic impacts and efficiency depends on what type of cooking technology is used. Various types of cooking technologies, their impacts and benefits have been discussed below.

2.1.1. Fossil Fuel

Coal, natural gas and kerosene are the major cooking fuels used. Coal and natural gas are burned directly for cooking in the stoves or are converted into electricity and then cooked in electric ovens.

Cooking with Kerosene

Kerosene is one of the major components of the refinery that is being used as fuels for aviation, domestic cooking, heating and lighting. In developing countries, kerosene is mainly used for cooking in metal stoves and lighting in rural areas, where it is used to fuel space heaters in urban areas. Burning kerosene as a fuel causes several toxic gas and particulate emission, creating health problems to the users. This is also one of the contributors to greenhouse gas emission.

Table 2.1.1. Kerosene fraction from a typical crude analysis*

Particulars	Total original crude oil	Distillate kerosene
Boiling point range ^{0}C	-	149-232
Yield on crude %wt	100	12.25-13.55
Specific gravity @15.5^{0}C	0.869	0.785
Total sulfur %wt	2.5	0.15
Mercaptan sulfur %wt	-	0.006
Paraffins, % wt	-	62
Naphthenes, %wt	-	20
Aromatics %wt	-	18
Smoke point mm	-	28
Freezing point ^{0}C	-	-54.5
Aniline point ^{0}C	-	15
Wax content, %wt	5.5	trace
Kinematics viscosity @38^{0}C mm^2/s	9.6	1.15
Acidity, mgKOH/g	0.15	0.02
Total nitrogen, ppm	1200	-
Total ash, % wt	0.006	-
Vandium, ppm	27	-
Nickel, ppm	7	-
Carbon residue, %wt	5.2	-
Asphatlenes, % wt	1.4	-
Molecular wt (average)	-	150

* based on Kuwait export crude in Nepal (Singh and Mahato, 2003).

Kerosene is a hydrocarbon fraction obtained by fractional distillation of crude oil. The major component of the kerosene oil is paraffin type oil followed by naphthenes and aromatic hydrocarbons with varying carbon of $C_{10}H_{14}$ to $C_{10}H_{16}$. The characteristics of kerosene oil may vary depending upon the sources of crude oil, but Table 2.1.1 is a typical analytical characteristic of kerosene oil based on Kuwait export crude oil in Nepal (Singh and Mahato, 2003).

The use of kerosene has several environmental and health problems. Burning of kerosene produces large amounts of carbon products such as solid carbon, particulate matters, carbon dioxide, and sulfur dioxide. It also produces polycyclic aromatic hydrocarbons which are considered to be human carcinogen. The environmental problem created by kerosene burning is also linked with soil, water and other ecological parameters. Burning kerosene in inefficient stoves and poorly ventilated areas pose serious health threat of the inhabitants. Several eye and respiratory diseases are seen while burning kerosene in millions of households in the world. Indoor air quality is a genuine concern for much of the population engaged in agriculture and industries affecting the local air quality.

Burning of kerosene for different purposes has several health impacts. An excess of lung cancer was seen in a large cohort of Japanese workers exposed to kerosene and other fossil fuels (IARC,1989). A Japanese study showed that an excess of stomach cancer was observed amongst workers possibly exposed to kerosene and machine oils. Some case-control studies found an association between lung cancer and the use of kerosene stoves for cooking amongst women in Hong Kong. Long-term exposures to "low" concentrations of kerosene have been reported to produce non-specific CNS effects such as nervousness, loss of appetite and nausea (Ritchie et al., 2001). Kim Oanh et al. (2002) reported that the kerosene stove had the highest emission of 11 polycyclic aromatic hydrocarbons (PAHs) 28 mg/ kg compared to sawdust and wood fueled stove. Chronic exposure of kerosene causes dermatitis. Lung effects have also been reported for long-term exposure. Hence replacement of kerosene is necessary with natural fuels available such as plant hydrocarbons or even of fossil fuel origin but not processed through anti-nature means. Pathway of kerosene is presented in Figure 2.1.1.

Hence the use of kerosene is not only creating environmental problems but also social problems in the societies. Kerosene and other oil import dependency are very high in developing countries resulting in draining valuable hard currency.

Cooking with Natural Gas

Natural gas is one of the major cooking fuels in the developed and emerging developed countries. Natural gas is considered to be clean cooking options. However, cooking with natural gas has several health and environmental problems. The New York Time (2006) reported that significantly higher frequency of cough and phlegm was found among those in homes cooking with gas. The report showed that 10.2 percent children of those using gas, were reported both chronic cough and phlegm compared with 7.6 percent whose kitchens had electric ranges. Breathing efficiency of the residents using gas stoves were found lower compared to the electric stoves. Nitrogen dioxide has been considered a prime suspect as the cause of difficulties arising from stove emissions, in part because of studies with rats. Besides nitrogen dioxide, gas burning produces a variety of other substances including carbon monoxide, sulfur dioxide, formaldehyde and hydrogen cyanide all of which are highly toxic gases. The situation becomes worse when these fuels are contaminated with the catalysts and other synthetic additives (Islam and Zatzman, 2007a).

A recent study showed that the fumes given off by gas cooking may have harmful effects on human lung cells (BBC, 2001). There are tiny particles of pollution produced when gas is burnt that has inflammatory effect when passed through the lungs. This is one of the causes of the breathing problems and various respiratory diseases. It was reported that the use of gas for cooking is associated with an increased risk of respiratory symptoms and impaired lung functions in women (Jarvis et al., 1996). It was further reported that Gas cooking was associated with an increased risk of awakening with shortness of breath and asthma among women.

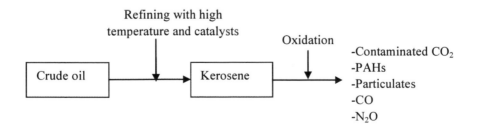

Figure 2.1.1. Pathway of kerosene burning (Chhetri and Islam, 2008).

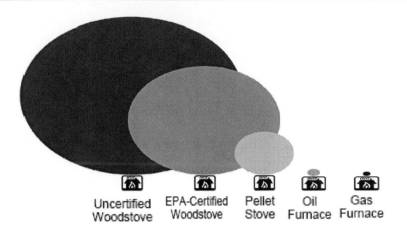

Figure 2.1.2. Particulate emission from different stoves (source: EPA, 2003).

Natural gas processing involves the use of glycols for water dehydration and methanolamines (MEA), diethanolamine (DEA) and triethanolamine (TEA) for carbon dioxide and hydrogen sulfide removal. These chemicals cannot be completely recycled and the natural gas contains some of these chemicals in it. The pathways analysis of the natural gas burning shows that glycols and amines produce carbon monoxide and other toxic gases (Matsuoka et al., 2005). This carbon monoxide is poisonous for humans and plants and remains persistent in the atmosphere affecting public health and the environment.

EPA (2003) developed a model for particulate emission from wood and fossil fuels stoves (Figure 2.1.2). This analysis shows that gas stove has lowest emission and woodstove has the highest emission. Cooking on stoves or furnaces in which oil or kerosene is burnt, the total life cycle emission needs to be considered. During crude oil refining, huge amounts of energy and various toxic catalysts and chemicals, such as hydrofluoric acid, sulfuric acid, platinum, and nickel are used. Such processes increase the possibility of generating heavier CO_2 not favored by plants for the photosynthesis process. Also the refining processes are costly and they pose many other environmental problems from processing to end use such as oil spills and leaking, which may greatly affect the biodiversity.

Chhetri et al. (2007a) argued that the emission from woodstoves which is an organic source and emission from refined fossil fuels which is contaminated with toxic catalysts and chemicals are not the same and have different impacts in human health and environment. CO_2 released from wood stoves is newer and better quality than CO_2 produced from fossil fuel burnings. The reason is that in the photosynthesis reactions plants often show preferences for one carbon isotope over another. The process discriminates against the heavy ^{13}C isotope (Bice, 2001, NOAA, 2005). Service (1998) reported that natural gas contains two carbon isotopes ^{13}C and [12]C. Thermogenic process of natural gas formation often produces heavier and more ^{13}C isotope (Zou et al., 2006). On the other hand, the CO_2 from the wood stoves is lighter and fresher. Therefore, the CO_2 release from fossil fuel burnings contains heavier ^{13}C isotope and less preferred by the plants. Based on this assumption, the emission of CO_2, particulates and their impacts is presented in Figure 2.1.3. Similar findings are also reported by Kjallstrand and Olsson (2004). According to them, the installation of a pellet burner and a change to wood pellets as fuel normally decreases the emissions remarkably.

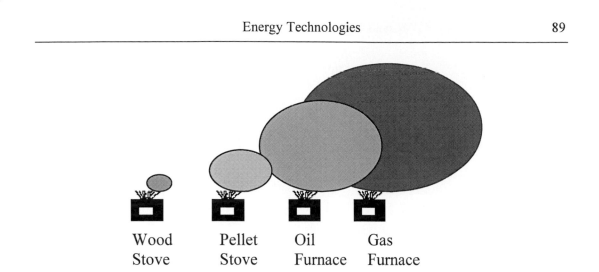

Figure 2.1.3. Life cycle emission of CO_2 for different fuel stoves (Chhetri et al., 2007a).

Moreover, cooking is greatly influenced by the fuel used for heating. If cooking is done through combustion, the CO_2 produced has a different quality based on the age of the fuel burned. The younger the fuel burnt, the better CO_2 is produced. For example, the CO_2 produced by wood burning is best among the CO_2 produced by burning wood, coal, charcoal, pellets, kerosene, oil and gas (Figure 2.1.3). In addition to CO_2, there are other products emitted from burning fuels, such as volatile organic compounds and aromatic hydrocarbons. These products are less harmful in case of wood burning than coal, oil, and gas. Because, these fossil fuels are older than wood, as well as many toxic chemicals and catalysts are used in during their processing or refining (Khan and Islam, 2007b). For example, glycol, methylethylamine, diethylamines and triethylamines are often used during gas processing (Lakkhal et al., 2005). Different electrical and combustion sources for cooking are shown in Figure 2.1.4 In the Figure the longer box size represents the more negative impacts on health and environment.

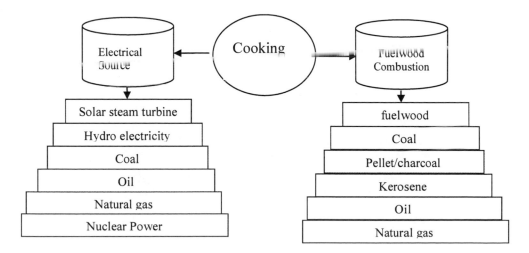

Figure 2.1.4. Pictorial views of electrical and combustion source for cooking, the size corresponds to the impacts (i.e, emissions and life cycle analysis) (Chhetri et al., 2007a).

A new concept on effects of fuel types on food quality have been established (Chhetri at al., 2007a). Different types of fuels have different levels of impacts on food quality. If cooking is done using electricity, the fuel source by which electricity is produced needs to be considered. For example, cooking by electricity produced through hydro source and solar heated steam turbines are better compared to the electricity produced through the gas turbine, oil or nuclear sources. Considered are their emission and impacts in various stages of life cycle.

In Figure 2.1.5, the relation between the fuel sources and quality of food is pictorially shown. Bigger oval shapes represent the better food quality. Among six different fuels wood stoves got the biggest and microwave got the smallest oval shape. In the other word, burning wood for cooking is the best option compared to other fossil fuel burning and electrical and electromagnetic heating. It is considered that the heating source has a great impact on the food quality. Cooking food by fuelwood combustion will produce the best food quality compared to other sources. Heating the food electrically (electrical heater) or electromagnetically (microwave), the reaction occurs at the molecular level that may alter the food structure. Therefore, in terms of food quality, electrical heating or microwave heating could have adverse impact on the food quality (Chhetri et al., 2006b).

2.1.2. Cooking Stoves (Wood, Charcoal, Rice Husk, Dung, Straw, Pellets)

Various types of cookstoves from three stone stove to computerized stoves are in operation in the world. The use of stove depends on the type of fuel being used, the living standard of the people and the purpose for which the stove is used. More than 3 billion people use fuel wood in traditional or improved stoves to cook worldwide (GTZ, 1997). In the context of world's energy supply, fuel wood is far more important than nuclear energy as the former is serving more people than the later (European Committee for Solar Cooking Research, 1995). In addition to the fuelwood stoves, there are charcoal stoves, rice husk stoves, dung, straw and pellet stoves depending on the availability of biomass in particular location.

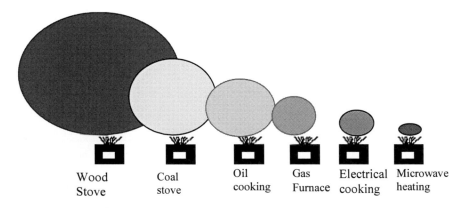

Figure 2.1.5. Food quality based on the fuel source used (Chhetri et al., 2007a).

Conventional woodstoves are generally inefficient stoves and emits particulate matter from wood combustion. However, the CO_2 emitted from woodstoves are natural and non toxic. Pathway of wood stoves is shown in Figure 2.1.6 (left). Just designing an oil-water trap to capture the particulate matters from wood burning will make the wood burning inherently safe. Similar would be the case when charcoal, rice husk, dung, straw are burnt in cookstoves. Biomass burning in cooking stoves does not have any environmental or health impacts. However, the efficiency of the stoves could determine the economy of the stoves and amount of energy consumption is directly related to the economy of the system. As the global efficiency of biomass stoves is significantly higher, economy and efficiency of biomass stove should not be an issue (Chhetri, 2007).

Pellet Stoves

Pellet stoves are very sophisticated and expensive stoves (Figure 2.1.6). The pellets are generally made from biomass sources such as sawdust or bamboo with or without binders. Binders generally used are limestone, dolomite, bentonite, hydrated lime and carbonic additives such as coal and coke breeze. High pressure, high heat and conveyor belts are used to manufacture the high energy intensive making the fuel expensive.

Pellet stoves utilize electronically controlled combustion, blowers, and heat exchangers for heating. Pellet-burning appliances rely on sophisticated computers and circuit boards. These stoves are extremely expensive and are beyond the reach of most people. Prices of the Pellet stoves range from about US$1700 to US$3000 or more for the stove, and from US$150 to US$400 for installation (CHI Associates, 1998). These are high energy intensive stoves as they use electricity in addition to the pellet as fuel. High heat or other forms of energy is also used during pellet making for crushing, grinding, transportation through conveyor belts. Moreover, the use of carbonic additives may result in various toxic emissions from these stoves and plants are likely to reject this contaminated CO_2. Pellet stoves release the carcinogenic benzene as the predominant aromatic compound (Olsson and Kjallstrand, 2004). The pellet burner emits benzene as the major aromatic compound, whereas the stove and boiler emit phenolic antioxidants together with benzene. Pellet stoves are one of the EPA certified stoves.

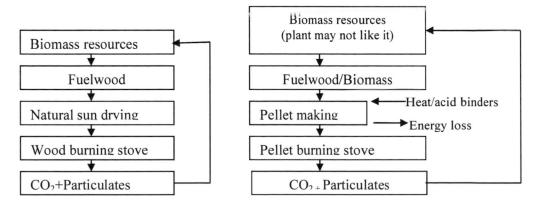

Figure 2.1.6. Pathways of wood stoves (left) and pellet stoves (right)(Chhetri et al., 2007a).

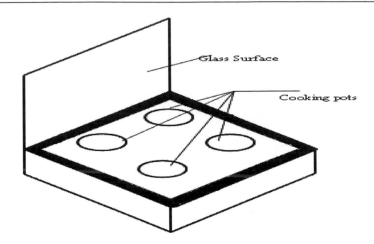

Figure 2.1.7. Box type solar cooker (Khan et al., 2007a).

2.1.3. Solar Cooking

Solar energy is the most ubiquitous energy source on earth. Other form of energy such as biomass, wind, ocean thermal, geothermal and others are the secondary form of solar energy. Solar energy has application in many areas including direct heat utilization and electricity generation through solar thermal technology as well as photovoltaic conversion. However, utilization of direct solar energy for cooking is most economical and beneficial from health point of view. Cooking through solar energy has been very popular these days and the technology is widespread. This is popular especially in the rural and semi urban areas where electricity cost is high and getting biomass resources is difficult. There is a huge potential for this technology in the tropical and subtropical countries where there are over 300 sunny days in a year. This type of solar radiation is possible in Asian and pacific reason including other parts of the world. The use of solar cookers in several places in the world including South Africa in appreciable fuel and time savings as well as increased energy security for households using commercial fuels (Wentzel and Pouris, 2007). Solar energy is a free source and utilization of heat energy directly without any conversion does not pose any threat to the natural environment.

There are various types of solar cookers in use for domestic of institutional purposes. A solar box cooker with pots is shown in the Figure 2.1.7. A shallow glass covered chamber, coated black inside and insulated all around, is exposed to the sun until the temperature inside exceeds 100^{0}C which is sufficient to cook food. Some more heat input can be achieved by having an exterior reflector at four corners. Box type solar cookers are popular, as they are simple to make. Four pots can be placed on the stove at once. Instead of a box type cooker, another option is a panel cooker. This cooker concentrates the sun's rays onto a pot placed inside a plastic bag or under a glass bowl. In parabolic and panel cookers, heat is concentrated in the pot. Thus, it is comparatively faster to use than a box cooker. Solar cookers can be built on the wall of a house (Arab, 2005).

Concentrating cookers can be built for institutional purposes such as schools, army camps, hostels and other institutional purposes. Indian army has built a solar cooker in Ladakh the elevation of which is 4000 meters from sea level using parabolic reflectors for steam production which is used for cooking (Refocus, 2005). These types of cookers are also suitable for residential schools, school hostels and other institutions. Due to no negative environmental and health impacts and long life with no moving parts, solar cooking systems are found economically viable options.

There are still several social issues connected to solar cooking technology developed today. Solar cookers have not become the total solution for cooking problems rather they are add-on cooking device with specific potential benefits and offering more choice and flexibility to consumers. Hence, solar cooking is considered an opportunity for added benefit in particular location of situations.

2.1.4. Biogas Cooking

Almost half of the world's population residing in the developing countries use fuelwood, kerosene and agricultural residues as energy sources for cooking and space heating. As providing electricity to this population is far beyond imagination at least for several years to come, there should be other alternative energy options for this population. Consumption of forest firewood would put high pressure in biomass resources until biomass is used in a sustainable manner.

Biogas is produced from household wastes, such as kitchen waste, sewage sludge and cattle dung. A simple dome type digester is constructed and these waste materials are digested at temperature ranging from 15-45^{0}C. In this process, methane gas is produced by anaerobic digestion of these organic materials. As the sewage sludge is also used as an input to the biogas digesters, this would help reduce the cost of sewage sludge treatment and the slurry produced from the digestor can be used as fertilizer to grow the crops. This biogas can be used for cooking, heating and transportation. Figure 2.1.8 shows a biogas digester inlet where organic materials are fed into the digester. In addition to these waste materials, biogas can be produced from water hyacinth, tree leaves and any other decomposable carbonaceous materials. Biogas stoves are simple technologies and could be easily manufactured in any place where biogas is feasible.

Figure 2.1.8. Biogas digester inlet (Courtesy: CHOICE humanitarian Nepal).

Cooking from biogas is a clean and environmentally friendly option. The CO_2 it produces after burning is readily recyclable by plants as it is from the organic materials. It is sometimes accounted that CO_2 emission from the biogas plants by leaking is a greenhouse gas. This is not true. This CO_2 is directly used for photosynthetic by plants. However, if the waste from municipal waste contains pesticides and heavy metal contamination, it is likely that the CO_2 produced will be contaminated by these synthetic chemicals may not be recycled by plants (Chhetri et al., 2007a).

The other advantage of using biogas is that the slurry can be used for agricultural production. Biogas digester systems produce high value energy from the waste biomass and this is a truly zero waste system. Even the hot gases can be used to heat water to use for household purposes such as space heating and bathing. The extra biogas if any can be used to run engine to produce electricity or can be used in vehicles for transportation. Biogas can be produced even from human excreta resulting in improved sanitation. Hence biogas technology is the most efficient and beneficial technology. This is one of the most suitable and inherently sustainable technologies.

2.1.5. Microwave and Electric Cooking

Microwave Cooking

In conventional heating of food items, energy transfer takes place by conduction and/or convection due to thermal gradient whereas in microwave heating, the heat is produced within the food molecules due to high rotation at applied frequency (~2.45GHz) of polar water molecules. Food processing has important impact on various constituents of food such as phenolic compounds, flavonoids and others components. Flavonoids as natural antioxidants have demonstrated a wide range of biochemical and pharmacological effects, including a reduced risk of coronary heart disease, stroke and lung cancer. Vallejo et al. (2003) showed that 55% loss of chlorogenic acid occurred in potato, 65% quercetin content loss was found in tomato and 97% of the flavonoids were lost when fresh broccoli was microwaved.

Lopez et al.(2004) evaluated the changes on fresh avogado purees after microwave treatment. The study reported that 19 compounds were extracted from avogado and four new compounds were found in avogado leaves. The main compounds found after the microwave processing of avogado were aldehydes, ketones, alcohols and maillard. The chromatographic analysis of various compounds from avogado leaves reported to be increased were furfural acid, tarpenoids, estragole, and 2-hexenal [E] after the microwave application. The level of terpenoids and estragole showed an increment when microwave exposure time was increased. The microwave time and pH value played a major role in extracting these volatiles. The more the exposure time, the higher were the concentration of volatile compounds. These volatiles have severe health impacts. Aldehydes are primarily mucous membrane irritants. They cause eye, nose, and throat irritation. Some aldehydes such as formaldehyde are carcinogenic and in combination with other irritants may lead to an increase in the carcinogenicity of other compounds, such as polycyclic aromatic hydrocarbons (PAHs). The maillard is also reported to be carcinogen and maillard molecules are antinutritional. Maillard molecules pose toxic effects such as risks to the vascular system and kidney in diabetics.

Table 2.1.1. Comparison of fresh and processed cumin seeds after conventional and microwave heating by GC analysis for hydrocarbon and aldehyde presence (Behera et al., 2004)

Compounds	Fresh sample %	Conventional roasting (125°C, 10 min) %	Microwave heating (730W, 10 min) %
Monoterpenes	56.4	58.1	45.0
Sesquiterpenes	0.108	-	0.085
Aldehydes	43.2	41.0	50.0
Alcohols	0.3	0.73	7.68
Ratio of Aldehyde/ hydrocarbons	0765	0.705	1.11

Behera et al. (2004) reported that the volatile oils such as aldehyde level increased and changes were observed in the optical rotation values of the cumin seeds after the microwave processing. They also compared the changes in aldehyde level, monoterpenes, alcohols and other hydrocarbons with conventional heating and microwave heating (Table 2.1.1). The difference in optical rotation could be one of the indicators of structural change occurred in the volatiles. The experimental results and the GC analysis confirmed the presence of major constituents; terpene hydrocarbons (a-pinene, b-pinene, sabinene, p-cymene, terpinene), aldehydes (cuminaldehyde, p-mentha-1,3-dien-7-al, p-mentha-1,4-dien-7-al) and alcohols (cumin alcohol, perilla alcohol, trans-verbenol, fenchol).

The characteristic flavor of cumin seeds is basically contributed by aldehydes. The higher ratio of aldehydes to hydrocarbons indicates that there is more retention of the flavour in microwave heating than conventional roasting. Moreover, the retained aldehydes and hydrocarbons which may undergo structural changes after the microwave heating are likely to behave differently.

Khraisheh et al (2004) evaluated the quality and structural changes in terms of shrinkage behavior in potato during microwave and convective drying. The main attribute considered was the ascorbic acid (vitamin C) retention and rehydratibility of the potato samples as it is one of the major indicator of quality. The report showed that the ascorbic acid retention was dependent on air temperature, moisture content and microwave power. The destruction of vitamin C was reported in the microwave-dried sample followed by higher loss of moisture. Microwave heating causes insufficient moisture content in food. A similar study reported that about 70% of the Vitamin C is destroyed during microwave cooking of the potato dish and loss of the same further increased due to reduced moisture and longer cooking time (Burg and Fraile, 1995). The loss of vitamin C occurs due to both enzymatic and thermal degradation. By comparing with regular heating, one can easily determine the degradation particular to microwave.

More than 80 volatile compounds were detected after baking of eight cultivars of potato in a microwave oven (Oruna-Concha, 2002). It was reported that the lipid degradation and maillard reaction of sugar degradation were the main sources of more than 80 flavour volatile components identified. Some of the volatile compounds identified after the microwave baking were Hexane, Ethylbenzene, Dimethylbenzenes, Propylbenzene, Benzaldehydes and several others. The sources of these volatiles were the lipids in the potato flesh. The other volatiles found after the maillard reaction or sugar degradation were furfural, phenylacetaldehyde, methylbutanal and several others. Sulfur compounds identified after microwave baking of potato were dimethyl sulfide, disulfide, trisulfide and tetrasulfide along with several other compounds from methoxypyrazines. However, the study does not differentiate the volatiles before and after the microwave baking of different cultivars of potato flesh. Due to the microwave irradiation, these volatiles may not be compatible with the body of living beings due to radiation effects. A detailed study is necessary to investigate the health impacts of these volatiles and the potential emission of volatiles to the atmosphere during and after baking.

Canumir et al. (2002) studied the exposure of *Escherichia coli* to microwave treatments of apple juice. The study reported that there was a significant reduction in microbial population in apple juice. Apple juice pasteurisation at 720–900 W for 60–90 s resulted in a 2–4 logs microbial population reduction. The observations from the experiment indicates that inactivation of *E. coli* is due to heat as they can resist only certain level of exposure to heat. The total impact in the apple juice is a function of time, temperature and concentration of dry solid matters present in the fluid. However, the pasturaization cannot kill all the microbes. Thus, it is important to know whether reducing certain level of bacterial for particular application exacerbates such treatment or not. Moreover, the pasteurization destroys the nutrients and useful microbes when exposed to high temperature for longer duration. In this process, it is important to note that the products that emerge after destruction of bacteria with microwave are not the same as those emerging from naturally heated bacteria. It is likely that microwave will create toxins after destroying organic molecules.

Microwaves are promoted for its uniform heating quality. However, various studies reported that heating of containerized liquids with microwaves may cause flow and thermal stratification inside the container. Due to variations in product characteristics (such as viscosity) and in equipment factors, the patterns of temperature distribution in heated liquids (static or flowing) can be quite complex (Tajchakavit, and Ramaswamy, 1995). Moreover, the power level and frequency of the microwave input are critical process factors in microwave heating. Also, power output by the magnetron changes as it heats up over time. The lower frequency microwave (915MHz) has higher depth of penetration than the higher frequency (2450 MHz) microwaves. Due to microwave heating, there is a number of spatially heterogeneous heating effects that may cause hot or cold spots that compromise the quality and safety of the food products (Nott and Hall, 1999). The complex heating patterns in microwave are the functions of material variations (sample-shape and -size as well as the water-, salt-, and sugar-contents, etc.) and processing variations (heating time, power delivery, etc.).

It is reported that the non-uniform heating by microwaves may lead to survival of foodborne pathogens, including *Salmonella* and *L. monocytogenes*, in certain locations of foods heated at selected internal locations to endpoint temperatures that would normally be lethal. Studies demonstrated that the measured internal temperature of poultry does not indicate the extent of inactivation of surface-inoculated *Salmonella* on poultry due to lower temperatures at the product surface (Schnepf, and Barbeau, 1989). Alvarez et al (1999) studied the effect of microwave heating to pasteurize milk products and did not recommend because it is difficult to achieve the uniform distribution of heat that ensures all of the milk to heat up to required pasteurization temperature for specified time. Required pasteurization can be availed through longer exposure. However, extended microwave heating condition adversely affects the flavor and other properties of milk including vitamins.

Sierra (2000) carried out a study on the effects of continuous-flow microwave heating of milk on the stability of vitamins B1 and B2. The analysis carried out by ion-pair reverse-phase high-performance liquid chromatography at 90 °C holding time was raised to 30 s or 60 s, the content of vitamin B1 was lowered (3% and 5%, respectively). Microwave application for heating milk and milk products caused formation of significant amount of Cholesterol Oxidation Products (COPs) which are very harmful for the human health (Herzallah, 2005). This also makes to think of the other similar food products which may produce similar harmful products due to microwave treatment.

The effect of drying time of the macaroni beads due to microwave heating in the fluidized bed drying time was studied Goksu et al (2005). The drying time in the fluidized bed was reduced by 50% when heating with microwave compared to conventional fluidized bed drying. However, this study did not study the composition, quality, volatile compounds formed during microwave heating. These quantities are important for the food quality. Merely focusing on drying time as the single most important factor is patently aphenomenal and, therefore, unsustainable (Khan, 2006).

The time-temperature profiles of selected starch-water systems subjected to microwave processing were established and the effect of microwave radiation on the physico-chemical properties and structure of potato and tapioca starches was studied by Lewandowicz et al (Lewandowicz, 1997). Microwave radiation affected the temperature and moisture contents with strong correlation between moisture content and rate of temperature rise. The major changes observed in potato starch was the change in its crystal structure from type B to type A. The tapioca starch under went similar changes. This observation clearly shows that there are structural changes due to microwave irradiation in food particles. Kratchanova et al (2004) obsersed destruction of the parenchymal cells of orange peel and also found that the specific surface and the water absorption capacity of the orange tissue, and the endogenous enzymes of the peels were inactivated due to microwave heating. Anytime an organic material is subject to structure change invoked by unnatural phenomena, the outcome is severely damaging (Islam, 2005).

Electromagnetic irradiation from microwave oven harms food, and converts substances cooked in it to dangerous toxic and carcinogenic products. Even extremely short exposure to raw, cooked or frozen vegetables convert their plant alkaloids into carcinogens. Russian researchers also reported a marked acceleration of structural degradation leading to a decreased food value (Mercola, 2005). Among the changes observed were – deceased bio-availability of vitamin B complex, vitamin C, vitamin E, essential minerals and lipotropics factors in all food tested. Various kinds of damage to many plant substances, such as alkaloids, glucosides, galactosides and nitrilosides were reported. Milk and cereal grains heated by microwave convert some amino acids into carcinogens.

There are several effects observed due to the consumption of microwave heated food. Microwave irradiation creates non-thermal, irreversible byproducts (Porcelli et al, 1997) that may be unknown, hence, unprocessable by our body and, in turn, likely to be accumulated as a waste. Hormone production affected and/or altered by continually eating microwaved foods leading to the secretion of hormones that could attack to any 'foreign' compounds opposite to digestion. Micronutrients, essential for approximately 65% of all known enzymes, have been considerably reduced in modern diets, due to food refinement, canning, refrigeration and additives resulting in drops in metabolic activities. This symptom is reported to be accelerated due to microwave heating. De Villiers (1994) identified the reduction as the cause of phenomenal increase of Western and industrial diseases, many of them with genetic associations. Consumption of microwaved food causes loss of memory, concentration, emotional instability, and irritability. This will depend on what type of special hormone will be secreted in order to cope with microwaved products.

Cooking in Electric Ovens

Coking in electrically heated ovens, electric rings and grills have been very popular in the urban homes and fast food restaurants. It is generally understood that electrical heating has no emission in the kitchen and is a clean cooking option. However, several studies show that there are large amount of particulate emissions from electric ovens. Dennekamp et al. (2001) measured experimentally that bacon fried on gas or electric rings emitted particles of diameters in the size range of 50-100 nm. It was further observed that substantial concentrations of NO_X were generated during cooking on gas and four rings for 15 minutes produced 5 minute peaks of about 1000 ppb nitrogen dioxide and about 2000 ppb nitric oxide.

It has been reported that exposure to electromagnetic field to the children has been associated with child leukemia. Enviroharvest Inc (2006) reported that children under the age of 14, who live near the power lines and if exposed to magnetic fields have a greater risk of dying from leukemia. Electromagnetic fields are ubiquitous in urban areas and people are exposed in one or the other ways. People could be exposed from the public power lines, electrical and electronics appliance in homes such as oven, furnace, dryers, stoves etc. Because several epidemiological studies on humans have indicated a link between electromagnetic frequencies (EMFs) and serious health problems, US EPA 1990 recommended that EMFs be classified as a Class B carcinogen which is a probable human carcinogen and joined the ranks of formaldehyde, DDT, dioxins and PCBs (Van Venden, 2006).

Electric power lines coming to home, substations close by, transformers home wiring, computers, electric blankets and water beds, electric clocks, fluorescent light bulbs, electric oven, microwave oven and radars are the technologies from which people are exposed to electromagnetic field at residence. As people have to stay close to the electric oven during cooking, the exposure could be in the longer duration possibly affecting the health of inhabitants. Hence cooking through any form of electricity is anti-natural and is inherently unsustainable process. If we consider the global efficiency of the fossil fuels which are burned to produce electricity for cooking, this will not be justifiable due to its life cycles environmental impacts (Chhetri, 2007). Examples of electromagnetic radiation sickness have been reported to be sleep disturbances, dizziness, heart palpitations, headache, blurry sight, swelling, nausea, a burning skin, vibrations, electrical currents in the body, pressure on the breast, cramps, high blood pressure and general unwell-being (Van Venden, 2006). Hence from health and environmental perspectives, cooking in electrical appliances is to be avoided as much as possible.

2.1.6. Cooking from Wind and Nuclear Electricity

Wind energy is considered an environmentally friendly energy source. Yet, there are several environmental issues related to wind energy. Wind energy is generally used to produce electricity and generate motive power for pumping and milling. Generation of electricity from wind does not produce CO_2 emission except for the parts manufacturing. The use of wind energy in milling grains makes the farm products ready for cooking. Wind power can also be utilized for ground water pumping which is essential ingredient of cooking. Hence wind energy indirectly can play a greater role in cooking. However, converting wind to electricity is not a good to better option, meaning it is not a pro-nature process and hence not sustainable.

None of the studies shows any differences in cooking by electricity from different sources. Modern engineering is based on the linearization and "chemicals are chemicals" or "energy is energy" mode (Khan and Islam, 2007a). As all chemicals are not same (C_2H_5OH from refinery and from grains are different), the electricity from hydropower and electricity from nuclear should be different. The only problem is our current level of knowledge cannot distinguish the difference from two sources. Chhetri (2007) characterized the energy source in terms of their value and argued that electricity from two sources could be different. They argued that at least if we considered the global efficiency of hydropower and nuclear energy, the overall impact on the health and environment from nuclear energy (from exploration to electricity production) would be far higher than hydropower.

Cooking in electricity is not only the use of heat of conduction but also radiation and electromagnetic energy that can play great role in cooking. The interaction of food molecule and electromagnetic heat and radiation would of course have some impacts on the food quality. It can be felt that anything cooked using kerosene can be distinguished from the taste of the food in whatever controlled vessel is used for cooking. This means cooking would interfere with the food molecules and the intrinsic quality of food could be altered. This would not be the case while cooking from coal or wood burning. Thus, cooking in electricity is not a natural process and cooking from nuclear electricity could be the worst possible damage in the food locally and environment globally. This is not detected mainly because the tool is absent but does not mean that it does not exist (Zatzman and Islam, 2007a).

2.2. HEATING

2.2.1. Fossil Fuel

Fossil fuels are the major fuels used for space heating, and supplying industrial process heating. There are several ways fossil fuels are being used for heating. Table 2.2.1 shows various types of fossil and wood fuels with their respective heating values. This indicates the maximum amount of hear released during combustion. However, all heat cannot be utilized as some of it is lost from equipment and material absorption. Hence, it is impossible that heat conversion efficiency of any fuel is 100%. The global efficiency of any fuel from exploration of fossil fuels to the combustion at the end use devices is to be considered to calculate the global efficiency. Moreover, their impacts to the natural environment and human health as well as the values of such energy which the society looks at them are other main factors that need to be considered during global efficiency calculation. Depending upon the location and living standards, different fuels are used for home and industrial heating space.

Table 2.2.1. Average heat content of various fuels (Wilson and Morril, 1997)

Fuel Type	BTU/Unit	Kilocalories/Unit
Kerosene (No.1 Fuel Oil)	134,000/gallon	8912/litres
Burner fuel oil (No.2 Oil)	140,000/gallon	9320/litres
Electricity	3413/kW	860/kWh
Natural gas	1,000,000 thousand cu.ft.	7139/cubic meter
Propane	91,600/gallon	6098/litre
Anthracite coal	27,800,000/ton	6354,286/cubic meter
Hardwood (20% moisture)	24,000,000/cord	1,687,500/cubic meter
Pine (20% moisture)	18,000,000/cord	1,265,625/cubic meter
Wood pellets (pellet stoves)	36,000,000	8228572/tonne

Kerosene Heating

Kerosene is one of the major fuel components used for space heating in urban and suburban areas of developing and developed countries. Different types of kerosene heaters are available in the market, in which kerosene is directly burned to generate heat. These are portable heaters and can be used to heat desired places by moving closer to where heat is needed. Despite having good heating values, burning kerosene is not a desired heating option. This produces large amounts of particulates, aromatic hydrocarbons and irritating smell. Orme and Leksmono (2002) reported that unvented kerosene heater releases 600 mg/h of volatiles organic compounds. The particulates may cause respiratory problems of the inhabitants (Triche et al., 2005). In most of the countries, kerosene is imported from abroad spending hard currencies and at the same time the use creates health and environmental impacts. Hence, kerosene heating is not a sustainable option from both environmental and economic point of view.

Burner Fuel Oil Heating

Similar with the kerosene, this is also oil used to fire the burners of various types of engines. This fuel oil is used to produce process heat for industrial operations. The fuel is burned in relatively high temperatures. The high temperature oxidation products from the fuel oils will produce toxic carbon dioxide, carbon monoxide, NOx and other particulates. Various volatile organic compounds (VOCs) such as benzene, toluene, ethyl benzene, xylenes are released during industrial operations due to the use of refined burner oil which is already contains heavy metals and chemicals used as catalysts used during refining fossil fuels (Orme and Leksmono (2002). The combustion process also releases CO_2, CO, NOx, NO and other toxic gases which cause several health problems including respiratory and cardiovascular illnesses (COMEAP, 2004).

It is reported that heating oil burners emit particulate matter (PM), oxides of nitrogen (NOx), sulfur dioxide (SO_2), mercury (Hg), carbon dioxide (CO_2) and other pollutants during burning (NESCAUM, 2005). These pollutants have direct health impacts, contribute to the formation of ozone and fine particulate matter, cause regional haze, contribute to acid deposition and nitrification of water bodies, add to the global mercury pool and contribute to the build-up of greenhouse gasses in the atmosphere. The combustion of heating oil is a significant source of SO_2 emissions (Table 2.2.2). The burning of heating oil also significantly contributes to total CO_2 emissions. Emission of solid particles and condensable liquid droplets are generated from most combustion sources including heating oil burners which have health and environmental impacts.

Burning of heating oils produces nitrogen dioxide (NO_2) and the secondary oxidants that are formed in the atmosphere contribute to numerous adverse health outcomes. NO_2 causes respiratory distress, respiratory infection, and irreversible lung damage (NESCAUM, 2005). These are exacerbated by the secondary oxidants that are produced including ozone and fine particulate matter contributing to the formation of acid rain. SO_2 is one of the most important sources of emission from home heating oil. Increased level of SO_2 in the atmosphere can cause wheezing, breathing difficulty, and shortness of breath. SO_2 also contributes to cardiovascular disease, respiratory illness, and impaired lung function especially in individuals with pulmonary diseases including asthma. Sulfur dioxide also contributes to acid rain and related crop and vegetation damage (NESCAUM, 2005). Due to the profound health and environmental issues, burning of heating oil for heating purposes whether it is for home or industrial heating is not sustainable for the long-term.

Natural Gas Heating

Natural gas is a mixture containing mainly methane and other trace impurities. Burning natural gas for both domestic and industrial electricity is very common these days especially in developed countries. It is generally understood that natural gas burning is a clean option. However, natural gas burning for space heating and producing industrial process heat has several health and environmental problems. AEHA (1998) blamed natural gas as the most important source of indoor air pollution responsible for generating illness that even surpasses even pesticides and passive tobacco smoke. This may be the worst form of fuel for chemically susceptible individual.

Natural gas contains chemical pollutant that can worsen both the classical allergy and chemicals sensitivity not because of its inherent quality but due to MEA, DEA, TEA and others (Chhetri and Islam, 2006a). The combustion gases, unburned fuel and chemical additives can be major sources of indoor air pollution (AEHA, 1998). There are several other studies that show that there is a link between natural gas heating emission and asthma. Research indicates that even everyday natural gas exposure increases asthma attacks, causing waking with shortness of breath, reduced lung function, and increased airway obstruction (The Lancet, 1996). It is an often ignored threat as effects can be asymptomatic, with causes easily misdiagnosed. Hence, despite much touted cleaner fuel, with current refining techniques, it turns out that natural gas burning for energy production in any purposes has health and environmental impacts and can never be considered as a sustainable energy solution (Chhetri and Islam, 2006a).

Coal Heating

The main indoor pollutants from coal combustion are carbon monoxide, nitrogen oxides, sulfurous oxides, particles, and volatile organic compounds. Some recent studies examining coal home heating have found increased occurrence of respiratory symptoms such as phlegm and cough in adults (Pope and Xu, 1993) and school children (Jedrychowski et al., 1998; Qian et al., 2004). Children living in homes where coal was used as the primary heating fuel experienced 45% greater lower respiratory illness (primarily acute bronchitis) (Baker et al., 2006).

Table 2.2.2. Air emission rates for home oil burners (USEPA, 1998)

Pollutant	Emission Rate in lbs/MMBTU
PM total	0.012
PM condensable	0.0094
PM filterable	0.0030
CO	0.036
TOC/VOC (non methane)	0.0051
NOx	0.13
SOx 0.05%	0.05
Sox 0.25%	0.26

Coal burning produced lots of sulfur emission, which not only affects the public health but also is a precursor for acid rain deposition which is one of the century's major environmental problems. Coal cleaning process involves the addition of several synthetic chemicals for its cleaning before its processing. The catalysts used in coal refining are also one of the reasons for creating environmental problems. Heating from the coal in home and industries is carried in two ways. First, coal can be burned in the heaters or stoves directly and the heat can be used for space heating and industrial processes. The other method is coal is heated to produce steam from water and the steam is used to run the turbines to produce electricity and the electricity can be used for heating purposes. Direct burning of coal has less environmental impacts, higher efficiencies. But the electricity production mode creates more environmental problems and has lower global efficiencies. Compare to the other sources heat production, coal should be less harmful than oil heating or natural gas burning to produce heat.

2.2.2. Solar Heating (Passive Heating and Cooling, Direct Heating)

Solar energy is an important, clean, free and abundantly available energy resource. The heat and light radiated by sun has a major role in balancing the temperature of the earth, produces oxygen and organic chemicals through photosynthesis, maintaining carbon and water cycle on earth. The sun produces enormous amount of energy through sustained nuclear fission reaction. The solar energy received on earth in the form of radiation is used for heating water, space and industrial processes. Solar energy received on ground level is affected by atmospheric clarity and latitude. Solar energy has spectrums from infra-red to ultraviolet frequencies (Rao and Parulekhar, 1999).

Passive Heating

The use of solar energy for heating is not a new concept and has been used since the pre-historic time. Solar heating is used either in active form or passive form. In passive solar heating, there are no special devices for energy conversion. Solar energy can also be used for passive cooling in addition to heating. In this passive heating, all solar gains are brought in through windows and minimum use is made of pumps or fans to distribute heating or cooling effect. Passive heating techniques use building elements such as walls, windows, floors and roofs, in addition to exterior building elements and landscaping, to control heat generated by solar radiation. Solar heating designs collect and store thermal energy from direct sunlight. Passive cooling minimizes the effects of solar radiation through shading or generating air flows with convection through ventilation.

Management of day lighting is the utilization of natural daylight that greatly contributes to efficient heating. The benefits of using passive solar techniques include simplicity and economically viable options. Once the sunlight is in from the windows, a well insulated and air-tight building envelope helps prevent heat loss and allows the solar heat to provide more of the heating needed in desired place. The window system is a crucial component of the energy-efficient building envelope (Figure 2.2.1). Where as common double-glazed windows let heat escape, high performance windows, with insulated frames, multiple glazing, and insulating glass spacers can reduce heat loss by more than half. Orientation of the space to be heated and materials characteristics in which passive heating is applied play very important role in passive heating. Management of daylight is also an important aspect of passive heating.

Passive Cooling

Expensive air conditioning in homes using costly and environmentally damaging refined fossil fuels can be greatly reduced or sometimes completely eliminated by using passive solar cooling technique. Heat from solar radiation and heated air is kept away from reaching the building during passive solar cooling designing. Internal heat gains by materials and occupants are exhausted through natural ventilation. In order to keeps the solar radiation out, fixed or adjustable shading devices or using special glazing windows. It has been reported that over 90% solar gains can be reduced by using shading devices keeping the desired amount of light admitting inside (Duncan and Swartman, 1995). Good insulation, reducing window size and using reflective materials in walls and roofs of building could help to control the external heat gain. Provision of cross ventilation keeping in view the direction of prevailing winds also plays an important role in passive solar cooling in buildings.

Direct Solar Heating

Direct use of solar energy is carried out by using some conversion or concentration devices in order to collect the diffuse radiant energy from sun. There are various types of devices in use for this purpose. A parabolic trough concentrates light on a line where as a parabolic dish concentrates light on a point. Parabolic dish that can concentrate energy at one point can be used for cooking purposes. There are several types of flat plate solar collectors being used for direct water and air heating system.

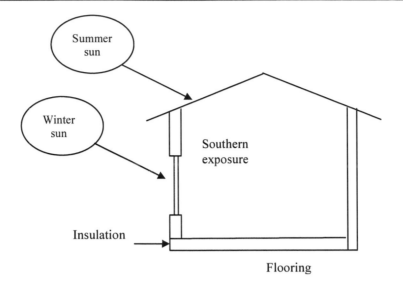

Figure 2.2.1. Schematic for passive solar heating.

Solar Air Heating

Solar heating is carried out simply by using the greenhouse principle. The high intensity and shorter wave length sunlight enters the glass surface but heat is absorbed by the cold air inside leaving the low intensity and longer wave length sun light. The longer wave length sunlight does not reflect back to outside and continue to heat the surface inside. The hot air inside can be circulated in the desired places through the pipes and duct system (Figure 2.2.2). This is one of the most economical and environmental friendly systems as there are no emission in this process.

Solar Hot Water System

One of the important applications of direct solar energy is water heating in domestic hot water systems. Domestic hot water heating load is approximately 20% of the total household energy consumption. By using direct solar energy to heat water will reduce large amount of domestic fossil fuel consumption. A solar water system typically uses glazed collectors mounted on a roof and connected to a storage tank. Fluid is pumped to the collectors where it is warmed by the sun, then returned to a heat exchanger where it heats the water in a storage tank. Modern solar water heaters are relatively easy to maintain and can pay for themselves with energy savings over their lifetime. Moreover, large and commercial systems can dramatically cut heating costs, making them ideal for businesses, such as restaurants, car washes, laundry facilities and fitness centres. A typical solar hot water system is shown in Figure 2.2.3.

Oil Heating System

Water heating system has certain limitations. Water can be heated up to 100^0C maximum. However, if the heating fluid is vegetable oil or waste cooking oil, it can be heated over 300^0C. The heat from the oil can be transferred through certain heat exchangers in order to suit the desired purposes. Hence heating the oil can significantly increase the efficiency. Khan et al. (2005b;2007d) developed an oil heating system in which a parabolic concentrator was used to concentrate the solar energy. Hence by changing the one-time fluid as a heating medium can have several advantages. Vegetable oil is a one-time use fluid and there is no environmental impacts using such natural oils.

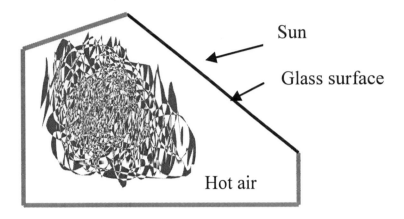

Figure 2.2.2. Solar hot air system.

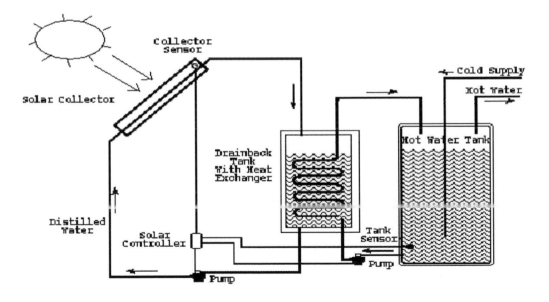

Figure 2.2.3. Solar hot water system (After Sustainable Building Sourcebook, 2006).

Similar technique can be utilized for space heating from direct solar energy. Solar energy can be used through the heliostats to concentrate solar power into high temperature power house, where superheated steam can be produced and turbines can be run through the superheated steams to produce electricity. The use of direct solar energy offers higher efficiency and at the same time there are no environmental impacts. Thus using direct solar energy in domestic and industrial application is an inherently sustainable option even though electricity is not good for energy quality.

2.2.3. Geothermal

Geothermal heating is one of the most efficient ways to heat a building. Geothermal heating is much more efficient than air heat pumps and other supplemental electric heat used in warmer climates. The thermal energy from geothermal sources can be obtained in the forms of hot water, steam, geothermal brine and mixture of these fluids. These fluids can be extracted by driving deep production well in the geothermal fields at a depth from 300-3000 metres (Rao and Parulekhar, 1999). These fluids can be obtained either by pumping or natural pressure. Geothermal energy can be used for baths and therapy, district heating and space heating, hot water irrigation in cold countries, air conditioning, greenhouse heating, process heat, electrical power generation and mineral extraction from the geothermal fluids. As this is naturally occuring heat on the earth's crust, utilizing this heat through the transfer of heat will not have any negative impact to health and the environment. However, the salty brine should be managed carefully so as not to increase the salinity of the agriculture fields on the farming areas. The conversion of geothermal energy into electricity from binary cycles or flash systems is not a natural phenomenon, and hence can not be sustainable. However, the use of geothermal energy as direct heat source is inherently sustainable technology and is technically feasible and economically viable in most of the cases.

2.2.4. Hydropower

The only way to space and water heating through hydropower involves the use of electricity generated from hydropower. As hydro power is a clean energy source, it is considered least hazardous solution to produce electricity. Hydro electricity can be used for water or air heating and can be circulated in the desired areas for space heating. The heated water can be used for bathing, cooking of cleaning clothes and utensils. Conversion of hydro electricity into heat reduces the global efficiency significantly. However, using this high quality energy for space and water heating is not economically feasible and cannot be socially justifiable. This has also the possibility of creating health problems due to the electric and electromagnetic fields created in transmission lines or conversion gadgets. Heating from electricity from hydropower is likely to be better in many respects as compared to the heat generated by gas, oil or nuclear power. In any circumstances, using hydro electricity for heating is not a sustainable choice from energy consumption perspectives. This is due to the anti-natural feature of AC or DC current.

2.2.5. Direct Heating Engines

Heat engines are the engines that produce heat and electricity utilizing the temperature difference between the two points at different temperatures. For example, in a burning cooking stoves, the temperature is very high. The temperature in the nearby atmosphere is significantly lower as compared to cooking fire temperature. Using this difference in temperature at very short distance, a very high quality heat or electricity can be generated and be used either for direct heating of electrical heating. This is not a new technology but has been in use since the invention of sterling engines. Moreover, the ocean thermal energy also uses the similar principle of temperature difference between the top layer of water and some hundred meters down the ocean. There are some new simplified heat engines to produce heat or electricity recently discussed by Khan et al. (2007d).

This technology can be applied in places where enormous amount of heat is wasted in industrial and household applications. There is no by-product of this process and there is no environmental impact as such. Stirling engines will convert any temperature difference directly into movement or motive power. Earlier, there were acoustic heat engines with no moving parts that used to convert heat into intense acountic power and could be directly used in acoustic refrigerators to provide heat driven refrigeration. Electricity could also be generated via a linear alternator or other electroacoustic power transducer (Website 3).

2.2.6. Biomass Heating (Wood, Biogas, Charcoal, Rice Husk, Dung, Straw)

Home and industrial heating by burning wood is the oldest method of heating. Figure 2.2.4 shows the share of biomass including wood combustion in home and industrial burners. Wood biomass includes wood chips from forestry operations, residues from lumber, pulp/paper, and furniture mills, and fuel wood for space heating. It has been reported that the largest single source of wood energy is black liquor a residue of pulp, paper, and paperboard production. Black liquor supplies over 50% of these industries' energy requirements (EIA, 2004a). Lumber mills and furniture manufacturers use chips, sawdust and bark for nearly 60% of their energy requirements. A small but growing amount of wood is co-fired with coal in utility power plants. Cordwood, wood chips, and pellets made from sawdust are used for space and water heating in buildings, including in over two million households as primary or supplemental heating fuels.

Wood is the freshest fuel amongst the biomass fuels including fossil fuels which also originated from biomass. Burning wood is not an inherently "dirty process" that causes serious air pollution. However, it is likely that if wood is burned in a inefficient stove, it may produce particulates of incomplete combustion (PICs). With improved technologies wood heating offers several benefits. In home heating, the particulate matters are the major problems which can be trapped by oil water mixture at the exhaust (Khan et al., 2007a). In industrial burners, due to the high heating temperature and area, there are less particulates of incomplete combustion. A typical industrial biomass burning system is shown in Figure 2.2.5 that has high conversion efficiency and fewer pollutants.

The other important benefit of wood burning is that it has negligible amounts of sulfur, a major precursor to acid rain. Burning wood creates enough awareness as the point emission are obvious and people can take precautions. However, in case of fossil fuels, the environmental impacts occurs in long term and cannot be corrected once they are released into the atmosphere as they are not generally seen at the source. For instance, the catalysts and chemicals such as lead, mercury, and chromium are released in large amount burning fossil fuel burning but nothing is visible. They are later on found contaminating water source and air and it is impossible to treat them.

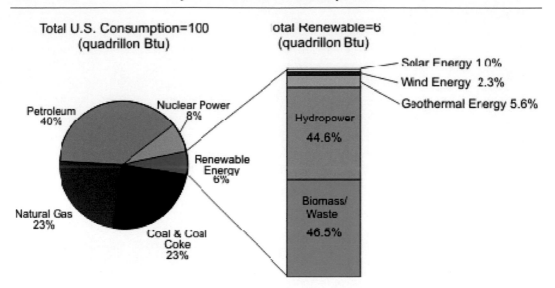

Figure 2.2.4. Contribution of Renewable Energy to U.S. Energy Consumption, 2004 (EIA, 2004a).

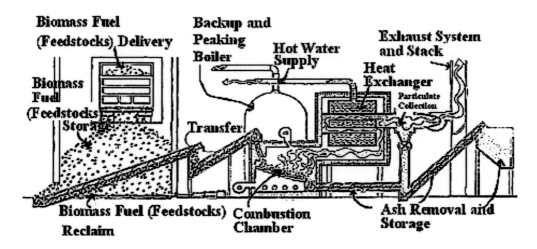

Figure 2.2.5. Industrial Biomass Heating System Description (Natural Resource Canada, 2004).

Biomass heating does not contribute to global warming. The CO_2 produced from the wood burning is readily used by plants during photosynthesis. The CO_2 is fresh CO_2 as it comes from the wood fuel of age less than 100 years, unlike in case of fossil fuels that is old fuel and was buried millions of years under high pressure and temperature. Hence, using wood for heating or cooking does not add CO_2 into the atmosphere and hence a clean burning fuel.

Burning biomass is not only beneficial from the environmental point of view but also from economical point of view. Tables 2.2.3 and 2.2.4 show the cost comparison of the different fuels for life cycle. The data show the power of 150 KW systems necessary to heat 800 m^2 area. It is seen that despite biomass system has higher initial costs, it has lowest fuel cost annually. The waste biomass utilization revealed the cheapest among the other fuels. This shows that biomass is not only clean energy from but also economical in the long-term.

Table 2.2.3. Biomass heating for 800 m² area and 150 kW (Natural Resource Canada, 2004)

Fuel	Oil	Wood chips
Initial cost	$ 21000	$ 80,000
Annual O and M cost	$ 1000	$ 8,000
Annual fuel cost	$ 18,000	$ 1,700

Table 2.2.4. Unit cost for heating 800 m² and 150 kW (Natural Resource Canada, 2004)

Fuel	Price	Cost of heat ($/GJ)
Electricity	$ 0.08/kWh	22.5
Propane	$ 0.40/L	15.60
Fuel Oil	$ 0.30/L	8.50
Gas	$ 0.20/m³	5.80
Mill residues	$ 10/tonne	1.70
Tree chips	$ 40/tonne	6.70

It is generally stated that using wood as a fuel is the major cause of deforestation and this will provide less plants to absorb carbon dioxide which accelerates the global warming. However, there is a natural cycles of growth, maturity, decay and re- growth of trees and forests. A healthy forest is a living community of plants and animals. When trees are used for energy, a part of the forests carbon bank is diverted from the natural decay and natural forest fire cycle into our homes to heat.

Harvesting biomass has become an important issue for a long time and sustainability of forest is usually questioned while talking about wood energy. However, the key to ecologically sound and sustainable wood energy use is to ensure that the forest remains healthy, maintains a stable level of variously aged trees and provides a good habitat for a diversity of other species, both plants and animals.

Similar to heat generated with wood burning, heating through biogas is another sustainable alternative. Biogas is usually produced from the waste biomass which it not wasted. Producing biogas is a value addition to the waste and at the same time is a reduction of the waste treatment load. The emission from biogas is of completely organic origin and there are no negative environmental impacts due to the use of biogas for heating or any other purposes. Charcoal is a naturally processed wood to increase the fuel density and burning charcoal not a bad option. Rice husk can be effectively burned in stoves as a biomass source. Animal dung and straw can either be directly used for heating by burning or can be converted to biogas that can heat the required area. Hence, burning biomass is an environmentally clean and sustainable energy options, unlike fossil fuels which causes several environmental and health impacts.

2.3. LIGHTING

Lighting is one of the major uses of electricity in the world. Worldwide, grid-based electric lighting consumes 19% of total global electricity production, slightly more electricity than used by the nations of OECD Europe for all purposes (EIA, 2006a). It is further reported that lighting requires as much electricity as is produced by all gas-fired generation and 15% more than produced by either hydro or nuclear power. The annual cost of this service including energy, lighting equipment and labor is USD 360 billion, which is roughly 1% of global GDP. Electricity used by lighting is also a major source of CO_2 emissions, equivalent to 70% of those from the world's cars.

Lighting is one of the very important human needs to perform various types of operation. Light can be derived in two ways: natural and artificial. Natural light is the light received from the sun in the day time and from the moon in the night time. Creating light by burning plant and vegetable oils is also considered a natural way of producing light. Artificial light can be created by converting solar energy into electricity, burning fossil fuels directly such as kerosene, generating electricity by burning fossil fuels, electricity from hydropower, from energy stored in batteries, generating gas by wood gasification among others. Human eyes have certain capacity to see the things in different spectrum of light. Artificial light has entirely different spectrum than natural light. Hence source from which light is received makes a big difference in the vision as well as in human health.

It is generally understood that the eye is the only organ for vision. Most recent research revealed the connection of eye nerves to brain, it is reported that light also mediates and controls a large number of biological processes in the human body (Van Bommel, 2006). Light has also important functions that control biological clocks and some of the hormones in the human body system. Light has been in use to treat people with depressions and sleep disorders (SLTBR, 2005). The troublesome irregular sleep-wake pattern of Alzheimer patients can often be healed with bright morning light (Van Someren, 2000). Natural light in the morning synchronizes the individual body clock to the earth's 24-h light dark rotational cycle. It has also been reported that humans got most of the information from the light through the retina.

2.3.1. Fossil Fuel Based Lighting

Kerosene Oil and its Use

As the fossil fuel is considered the major drivers for economic development, it is also a major source for artificial lighting. Kerosene is one of the major components of the refinery that is being used as fuels for lighting but is also used for aviation fuel, domestic cooking, heating and lighting. In developing countries, kerosene is mainly used for lighting in rural and suburban areas. Globally, one in three people got lighting from kerosene and other fuels, this is equivalent to the 20% of global lighting cost (Mills, 2002). It was further reported that household fuel-based lighting is responsible for annual energy consumption of 96 billion litres of kerosene (or 3603 petajoules, PJ), this also equates to 1.7 million barrels of oil annually. Fuel-based lighting results in 244 million metric tonnes of carbon dioxide emissions to the atmosphere each year. Ordinary wick-based kerosene lamps are the most common type of fuel-based lighting in developing countries. One estimate puts the estimate for India at over 100 million wick-based kerosene lamps (Louineau et al 1994). Because the kerosene is considered to be used by lower income group people, it is generally subsidized in developing countries, kerosene pricing and subsidies are often the source of political and social unrest, hoarding, and scarcity (Business Week Online, 2000; NepalNews.com, 2000). Hence, the use of kerosene is not only creating environmental problems but also social ones. Kerosene and other oil import dependency are very high in developing countries resulting in draining valuable hard currency. The kerosene-based lighting is inefficient, does not fully serve the purpose for reading and working at night, impose high cost on poor people and poses serious health threat. Despite spending of huge sum of money for lighting, people receive low level of service.

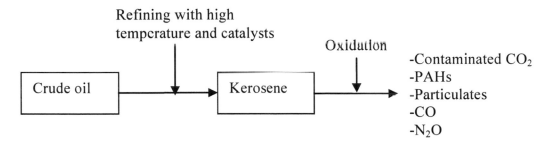

Figure 2.3.1. Pathway of kerosene burning (Chhetri and Islam, 2008).

Burning of kerosene for different purposes has several health impacts. An excess of lung cancer was seen in a large cohort of Japanese workers exposed to kerosene and other fossil fuels (IARC, 1989). Similar Japanese study showed that an excess of stomach cancer was observed amongst workers possibly exposed to kerosene and machine oils. Some case-control studies found an association between lung cancer and the use of kerosene stoves for cooking amongst women in Hong Kong. Long-term exposures to "low" concentrations of kerosene have been reported to produce non-specific CNS effects such as nervousness, loss of appetite and nausea (Ritchie et al., 2001). Kim Oanh et al. (2002) reported that the kerosene stove had the highest emission of 11 polycyclic aromatic hydrocarbons (PAHs) 28 mg/ kg compared to sawdust and wood fueled stove. Chronic exposure of kerosene causes dermatitis. Lung effects have also been reported for long-term exposure. Hence replacement of kerosene is necessary with natural fuels available such as plant hydrocarbons. Pathway of kerosene is presented in Figure 2.3.1.

Kerosene is a hydrocarbon fraction obtained by fractional distillation of crude oil. The major component of the kerosene oil is paraffin type oil followed by naphthenes and aromatic hydrocarbons with varying carbon of $C_{10}H_{14}$ to $C_{10}H_{16}$. The characteristics of kerosene oil may vary depending upon the sources of crude oil, but Table 2.3.1 is a typical analytical characteristic of kerosene oil based on Kuwait export crude oil in Nepal (Singh and Mahato, 2003).

Kerosene oil is extensively used for heating and lighting in developing countries. It is sometimes used as fuel for tractors and light vehicles. It is also used as thinners in paint and varnishes. Kerosene is also used by some metal cutting industries as a cheap fuel. This has applications in some small scale boilers in industries. In Nepal and India, kerosene is mainly used for cooking in household and providing lighting in rural areas where there is no electricity (Chhetri and Islam, 2008).

In India, at least 70–80 million rural households still depend on kerosene lamps for meeting a basic need such as lighting (MNES, 2001). Kerosene-based lighting devices used widely in rural areas include kerosene wick lamps, hurricane lanterns, kerosene petromax, and non-pressure mantle lamps. In rural India, kerosene lighting is practiced even in the electrified households as kerosene becomes cheaper than electricity and electricity is simply not reliable. It was reported that the total kerosene consumption in India during 2000/01 was approximately 11.5MT out of which about 60% was used in rural areas (MoPNG, 2000). Kerosene is a subsidized commodity in India, Nepal and some other developing countries. However, kerosene is also available in free market at higher price. It is thus obvious that there is still a large kerosene market in developing countries such as India and Nepal. Similar is the case in other developing countries.

Table 2.3.1. Kerosene fraction from a typical crude analysis*

Particulars	Total original crude oil	Distillate kerosene
Boiling point range ^{0}C	-	149-232
Yield on crude %wt	100	12.25-13.55
Specific gravity @15.5^{0}C	0.869	0.785
Total sulfur %wt	2.5	0.15
Mercaptan sulfur %wt	-	0.006
Paraffins, % wt	-	62
Naphthenes, %wt	-	20
Aromatics %wt	-	18
Smoke point mm	-	28
Freezing point ^{0}C	-	-54.5
Aniline point ^{0}C	-	15
Wax content, %wt	5.5	trace
Kinematics viscosity @38^{0}C mm^2/s	9.6	1.15
Acidity, mgKOH/g	0.15	0.02
Total nitrogen, ppm	1200	-
Total ash, % wt	0.006	-
Vandium, ppm	27	-
Nickel, ppm	7	-
Carbon residue, %wt	5.2	-
Asphaltenes, % wt	1.4	-
Molecular wt (average)	-	150

* based on Kuwait export crude in Nepal (Singh and Mahato, 2003).

The use of kerosene has several environmental and health problems. Burning of kerosene produces considerable carbon products, such as solid carbon, particulate matters, carbon dioxide, and sulfur dioxide. It also produces polycyclic aromatic hydrocarbons which are considered to be human carcinogen. The environmental problem created by kerosene burning is also linked with soil, water and other ecological parameters. In most of the developing countries, kerosene is imported from other countries and is heavily subsidized for rural people. Burning kerosene in "inefficient stoves" and poorly ventilated areas pose serious health threat of the inhabitants. Several eye and respiratory diseases is seen while burning kerosene in millions of households in the world. Indoor air quality is a genuine concern for much of the population engaged in agriculture and industries affecting the local air quality. Global air quality has been worsened in the last decades due to the use of synthetic chemicals in industries. The use of plastic has done irreversible damage to the air quality and we are practically breathing in air which is severely contaminated with plastic emission.

2.3.2. Electric Lighting

Electricity need for global lighting use is distributed approximately 28% to the residential sector, 48% to the service sector, 16% to the industrial sector, and 8% to street and other lighting (Mills, 2002; Mills, 2005). The corresponding carbon dioxide emissions are 1.775 billion metric tonnes per year during that period. Lighting electricity demand in the 23 International Energy Agency (IEA) countries represents approximately half of the world's total lighting use that represents an amount of primary energy of 3600 PJ ($48 billion), equal to 115% of that used to provide household electric lighting in all IEA countries, and 244 MT carbon dioxide emissions. The demand of lighting energy is increasing rapidly in the world. According to IEA (2006b), the demand of lighting energy will increase 80% higher as that of today if without rapid action for alternatives. Most of this lighting comes from electricity produced either from hydro or nuclear electricity generation or from electricity generated from fossil fuels. Electricity used by lighting is also a major source of CO_2 emissions, equivalent to 70% of the global emission released from the world's cars (IEA, 2006b). It is also reported that 19% of the global electricity generation is taken for lighting alone and the global CO_2 emission is three times than CO_2 emission from aviation (Black, 2006). The total CO_2 emission from lighting is about 900 million tonnes per year (IEA, 2004a). This amount is derived for electricity generation and fuel based lighting. Lighting alone takes up 3% of global oil supply. It is estimated that global demand for artificial light will be 80% higher by 2030 with current economic and energy efficiency trends. According to (IEA, 2004a), if all the end users install only efficient lamps, ballasts and controls (which is impossible) over the life cycle of the lighting service, global lighting electricity demand in 2030 would be just 2,618 TWh. This is almost unchanged from 2005 and would actually be lower between 2010 and 2030 (see the LLCC from 2008 scenario in Figure 2.3.2). The biggest consumer of electricity is the fluorescent tube being used for lighting in commercial and public sector buildings that account for 43% of the electricity used for lighting. The local efficiency of these tubes varies between 15% - 60%.

Modern lighting generated from electricity has several environmental problems. Light is converted from electricity produced by hydro or nuclear power and electricity from fossil fuel burning. Lighting is one of the major sources of greenhouse gas emissions, especially CO_2 emission. In case of hydro electricity, CO_2 emission occurs due to the use of fossil fuels during manufacturing of turbines, generators, penstock pipes, transmission line and other equipment and end use appliances. In case of electricity produced from nuclear power, CO_2 emission occurs during its project life cycle beginning uranium from exploration, mining, leaching, fuel procession, enrichment cycles and other processes as fossil fuels are used for various operations. Even though it has been claimed that nuclear power generation is CO_2 free, considering the life cycle CO_2 emission of the nuclear power system, it appears that nuclear power plants emit significant amount of CO_2. Mortimer (1989) reported that nuclear power releases 4-5 times more CO_2 than equivalent power production from other renewable energy systems. During electricity production from nuclear systems, in addition to the nuclear radiations, various wastes such as gloves, clothing, tools, equipment and others which are contaminated with radioactivity and disposal of such waste is debatable.

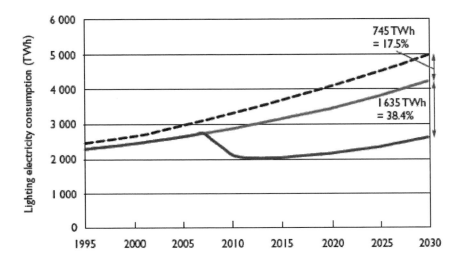

Figure 2.3.2. Global Lighting Electricity Consumption in 1995–2030 Under the No Policies, Current Policies and LLCC (least life cycle cost) from 2008 Scenarios (IEA, 2004).

Similar impacts into the human health and environment occur in the process of burning fossil fuels to produce lighting. Burning diesel for electricity generation emit large amount of heavy metals, toxic gases and particulates. According to EPA (2002), emission from mobile diesel sources such as trucks produces, acetaldehyde, acrolein, benzene, 1,3-butadiene, ethylbenzene, formaldehyde, n-hexane, naphthalene, styrene, toluene, xylene among others. These are highly toxic and carcinogenic compounds affecting human health and the environment. Similar emission is expected from stationery sources by diesel burning. Burning natural gas to produce electricity has also several environmental problems. As glycols and amines are used during gas processing, even traces of glycol in the gas streams produce carbon monoxide which is a poisonous gas (Matsuoka et al., 2005). During a study of carcinogenetic and toxicity of propylene glycol on animals, the skin tumor incidence was observed (CERHR, 2003). Glycol may form toxic alcohol inside human body if ingested as fermentation may take place. Production of light converting the solar energy through photovoltaic conversion has been very popular in rural and isolated areas. Despite the fact that solar is freely available in nature, the light produced from solar is the most valuable among all sources. Moreover, solar lighting is generated in the day time and stored to use power in the night time that necessitates the use of batteries which are very toxic products consisting of heavy metals and toxic acids such as sulfuric acid. Solar cells itself consist of several heavy metals and the safe disposal of cells as well as batteries is a great problems these days. Thus, it appears that production of lighting from electricity has several health and environment impacts.

Lighting the streets in the night time involves huge loss of light energy creating very high light pollution. Baskill (2006) mentioned that lighting the whole streets all night creates light pollution which is not only the waste of money but also affects human health and environment. The orange smog of night-time light pollution denies millions of people the right to enjoy the beauty of the night sky. A large part of light is wastes from most light fittings. It is reported that more than 300 megawatts worth of light is wasted towards sky from UK streetlights alone which is equivalent to a worth of about $190m Baskill (2006). It was further mentioned that intrusive nuisance lighting can cause stress, leading to deterioration in health, heart attacks, and even thoughts of suicide. It is reported that exposure to light at night time may also increase the risk of cancer because a kind of hormone which is produced in absence of light in human body is not produced due to the presence of night time light.

Prescott (2006) argues that global energy demand can be lowered by installing efficient compact fluorescent light bulbs. The argument is compact fluorescent light bulbs emit 70% less carbon dioxide. However, fluorescent light bulbs (including compact fluorescent light bulbs) and high intensity discharge laps are the two most common type of mercury containing lamps. High intensity discharge lamps include mercury vapor lamps, metal halide and high-pressure sodium lamps. The vapor lamps lights are filled with inert gases that continuously radiate very toxic light. Oxidation of mercury is high temperature bulbs creates several by products and toxicity and disposal of these light bulbs are the major causes for the lake and river pollution (Islam et al., 2006). This mercury is accumulates in fish which is consumed by public. Hence, changing from incandescent light bulb to compact fluorescent light bulbs in not an accomplishment, instead it is bad to worse model.

Lighting from electricity has several other problems in health. Reuters (2004) reported that exposure to the night light has incidences of increase of cancers especially in the children due to childhood leukemia. It was mentioned that exposure to much more light at night that disrupts the body's circadian rhythms, or internal clock, and suppresses the normal nocturnal production of the hormone melatonin that is linked to an increased risk of certain cancers. Pauley (2004) reported the link of light at night has a indirect link to generate cancer in human. It was further reported that about 40,000 women die each year from breast cancer, and the cause of 50% of the breast cancers in the US is unknown. The electric light is the hallmark of modern life in the industrialized world and could possibly be linked to the higher rates of breast cancer. According to Quinn et al. (1999), young children who sleep with light on have substantially higher risk of developing nearsightedness as they get older. The study showed that 34% of the children who slept with a night-light before age 2 tested, 34 percent were found myopic. During sleep time, even low level of light can penetrate the eyelids and make the eye work while they should be at rest. This finding is in line with the notion that the greater ambient night time light levels associated with industrialization may be a factor in the high incidence of myopia in developed nations (Quinn et al., 1999). Hence, all kinds of light from electricity generation have one or the other health and environmental impact in short term as well as long term and are not sustainable.

2.3.2. Natural Lighting

Sunlight in the day time and moon light in the night time are the truly natural lights. Sunlight is not only crucial for vision but without which life does not sustain. Photosynthesis wouldn't occur without sunlight, vitamin D wouldn't form, human life-protecting skin pigments wouldn't exist. Natural sunlight is very important for our brain to operate as some 70% of all our sensors are located on the retina (Islam et al., 2006). The light we use to see also is the light that illuminates our brain. The artificial light does exactly opposite. Photosynthesis can not occur with artificial light. It is so toxic that a person can feel delusion in no time if persistently exposed to the artificial light.

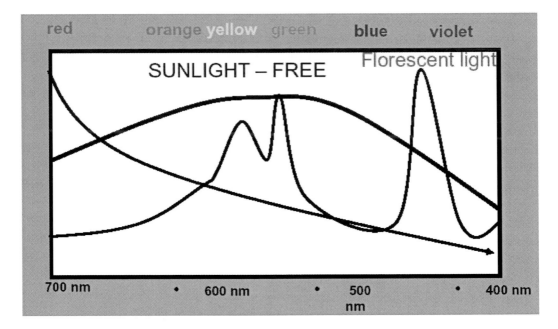

Figure 2.3.3. Spectrum of natural sunlight, electric bulb and compact florescent light (after Islam, 2003).

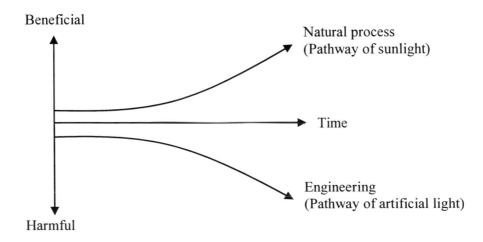

Figure 2.3.4. Pathway of natural sunlight and artificial electric light (redrawn from Islam et al., 2006).

Management of daylighting can save large amount of lighting loads globally. Bodart and De Derde (2002) reported that proper management of daylighting can reduce artificial lighting consumption from 50 to 80%. The global primary energy saving coming not only from the reduction of the lighting consumption but also from the reduction of lighting internal loads could reach 40%, for a type of glazing usually used in office buildings.

Figure 2.3.3 shows the spectrum of sunlight, electric bulb and florescent bulb. The sunlight which is free in nature and the most abundant energy source has vision range in all of its spectrums. However, this is not seen in other two bulbs. The florescent bulb is seen worst among others as it has little visible range. There is a transition between natural and artificial lights which is plus-infinity to minus-infinity. This transition is depicted in the following Figure 2.3.4. The transition further depicts that 100% free sunlight which is very good for human health has been made extremely toxic and costly during the transformation from free sunlight to incandescent bulb and florescent bulb. However, natural lighting is the perfect kind of lighting for human eyes. On the contrary, light from electricity or fossil fuels is artificial light, which has no health benefits.

2.3.3. Plant and Vegetable Oil Based Lighting

Lighting from Bio-hydrocarbons

Due to the problems associated with electric and fuel based lighting, alternatives, such as, plant and vegetable-based oils could be serious considered as potential sources of light. There are more than 350 oil-bearing crops identified globally which are considered as potential alternative fuels for diesel engines (Pryor et al., 1982). These oils can be directly burned in the lamps, stoves and other devices for heating, lighting and cooking. Chhetri and Islam (2008) discussed about the various types of bio-hydrocarbons available in Nepal as the potential alternatives for replacing kerosene burning and electricity lighting. These bio-hydrocarbons are the volatile oils obtained from certain plants caraway or dill, pine trees and citrus fruits contain number of large hydrocarbons known as terpenes with molecular formula $C_{10}H_{16}$. These hydrocarbons exists both as aliphatic compounds such as alkatriene or more as allicyclic compounds such as limonene, 1-methyl-4-isopropenyl cyclohexane, alpha pinene or 2,6,6-trimethyl-bi-cyclo (3.1.3)-2-heptene, beta pinene, delta-3-carene etc (Singh and Mahato, 2003). Other plant based bio-hydrocarbons include sesquiterpenes $C_{15}H_{24}$, diterpenes $C_{20}H_{32}$, triterpenes $C_{30}H_{48}$, and polyterpenes $(C_{10}H_{16})_n$. Rubber is also a plant based hydrocarbon which has polymer or isoprene C_5H8 hydrocarbon group which is an open chain polyterpene. Besides these, a number of species from Euphorbia and Ficus also yield plant hydrocarbons that can be used kerosene substitution (Chhetri and Islam, 2008). However, in the context of Nepal, Pine oil, Jatropha oil and Sea buckthorn oil which are found economically and technically feasible are the major bio-hydrocarbons that can replace kerosene, and diesel fuels. These three sources are described in more detail.

Pine Oils

It is reported that mid-hill areas of Nepal has 11 million plant species of *pinus roxburghii and higher altitude hills are occupied by Pinus wallichiana*. Both these trees oozes out copious resinous materials during summer called oleoresin. Distillation of this liquid yields about 16-20% w/w of transparent oil called turpentine oil and about 76-80 % solid resin (Singh and Mahato, 2003). Pine oil is being produced in substantial quantities in Nepal by some public and private industries. A major part of this is used for medicinal purposes and varnish products. However, every year thousands of litres are wasted due to various reasons. The price of turpentine is similar to that of kerosene. The price of turpentine can further be reduced by producing them locally in rural areas. This will not only produce bio-hydrocarbon for kerosene replacement but also saves cutting down the pine trees keeping the environment safe (Chhetri and Islam, 2008). Constituents of the oil terpentine extracted from gun oleoresin of Pinus roxburghii Sargent of the mid hills of Nepal contains the following hydrocarbons verified by gas liquid chromatography analysis (Table 2.3.2).

Table 2.3.2. GLC analysis of terpentine oil from Pinus roxburghii of Nepal (Singh and Mahato, 2003)

Hydrocarbons	Molecular formula	% Constituents
Delta 3 Carene	$C_{10}H_{16}$	49.10
Alpha Pinene	$C_{10}H_{16}$	27.97
Beta pinene	$C_{10}H_{16}$	16.07
Para Cymene	$C_{10}H_{14}$	6.83
Gama Terpinene	$C_{10}H_{16}$	0.23
Limonene	$C_{10}H_{16}$	Trace
Total		100

Table 2.3.3. Solvent property of terpentine and paraffinic hydrocarbon (Singh and Mahato, 2003)

Hydrocarbons	Boiling point (^{0}C)	Solubility parameter	Viscosity @20^{0}C	Flash point (^{0}C)
Paraffinic	81	8.2	0.89	3
Turpentine	150-170	8.1	1.26	33

Table 2.3.4. Comparison of fuel characteristics of kerosene and bio-hydrocarbons (Singh and Mahato, 2003)

Characteristics	Kerosene	Bio-hydrocarbons from pine
Flash point ^{0}C	Min 35	33
Distillation		
% recovered below 200^{0}C	Min 20	98
FBP ^{0}C	Max 300	170
Specific gravity	0.785	0.856
Calorific value (cal/g)	10045	9560

The solvent properties of Terpentine and Paraffinic hydrocarbons as given in Table 2.3.3 (Singh and Mahato, 2003). The boiling point of paraffinic hydrocarbon is 81^{0}C and Terpentine hydrocarbon is 150-170^{0}C. Terpentine hydrocarbon has higher viscosity and higher flash point compared to paraffinic hydrocarbon. Both have similar solubility characteristics.

Figure 4 summarizes the fuel comparison between kerosene and bio-hydrocarbons. Bio-hydrocarbons have similar flash point as that of kerosene. The bio-hydrocarbons can be extracted at lower distillation temperature than kerosene. Kerosene has slightly higher calorific value.

Jatropha Oil

Jatropha carcus is a tropical plant grown successfully in arid and semi arid climates. This plant can be grown in tropical America, tropical and subtropical areas of Africa, Asia and Europe. This can be grown in sodic, saline, degraded and eroded soil. This plant can be termed as multipurpose plant as it has many attributes and considerable potential for diverse use. This plant can be grown in diverse areas, ranging from extremely low to high rainfall areas. The plant sheds its leaves to counter extreme drought in low rainfall and prolonged rainless periods (Openshaw, 2000). It can be used to reclaim land as hedge or a live fence to contain farm animals into cultivated lands. It can also be used for erosion control. The plant produces many useful products especially the seed that produces oil is of most importance. Moreover, the seed cakes, the stem, the stem juice are also useful.

Jatropha is a versatile plant which can be used for numerous purposes. Every part of the plant, from the leaf to the root is very useful. The major use of Jatropha is the seed oil which can be directly blended in the diesel engines or can be converted into biodiesel by a process called transesterification. Gubitz et al (1999) reported the fatty acid content of Jatropha oil (Table 5).

The comprehensive uses of Jatropha are illustrated in Figure 6 (Chhetri et al., 2007b). The oil from Jatropha can be used for various purposes such as a base for paint and varnishes, lubricant, heating oil, feedstock to make biodiesel, as a fuel oil for cooking. It can also be used in cosmetics and medicines, natural soap making and use as drying oil. The oil contains a high percentage of monounsaturated oleic and polyunsaturated linoleic acid indicating it has a semi-drying property. This oil has been used as natural pesticides such as to control malaria. Henning (1997) reported that Jatropha was used to treat malaria in Mali. The extracts from leaves, bark and seeds were used as purgative. The leaf can be used to treat external Inflammation. The root extracts are reported to be used as treatment for Pneumonia and Syphilis (Henning, 1997). The seeds or fruits were used as contraceptives as well as abortifacient. There are reports that diseases such as paralysis, gout and skin diseases can be treated as well. The latex from the stems has also been used to promote healing of wounds, refractory ulcers, septic gums and as a styptic in cuts and bruises. Hence Jatropha has multiple uses and is truly a zero waste system.

Table 2.3.5. Fatty acid composition of Jatropha oil (Gubitz et al, 1999)

Fatty acid, %		
Myristic acid	14:0	0-0.1
Palmitic acid	16:0	14.1-15.3
Stearic acid	18:0	3.7-9.8

Table 2.3.5 – Continued

Fatty acid, %		
Arachidic acid	20:0	0-0.3
Behenic acid	22:0	0-1.2
Palmitoleic acid	16:1	0-1.3
Oleic acid	18:1	34.3-45.8
Linoleic acid	18:2	29.0-44.2
Linoleic acid	18:3	0-0.3

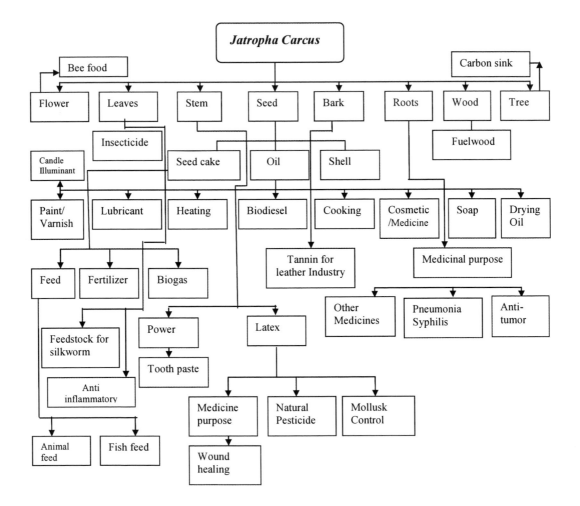

Figure 2.3.5. Multiple and zero waste use of Jatropha (Chhetri et al, 2007b).

Chemical, physical and fuel parameter of *Jatropha carcus* oil is presented in Table 2.3.6 The characteristics shows that Jatropha oil can either be used directly as fuel for burning in lamps or can be converted to biodiesel to replace the use of petrodiesel.

Table 2.3.6. Comparison of properties of diesel, Jatropha oil and biodiesel (Reddy and Ramesh, 2005)

Properties	Diesel	Jatropha oil	Biodiesel
Density (kg/m^3)	840	918	880
Viscosity (cSt)	4.59	49.9	5.65
Calorific value (kJ/kg)	42390	39774	38450
Flash point (^{0}C)	75	240	170
Cetane number	45-55	45	50
Carbon residue	0.1	0.44	Not available

Figure 2.3.6. Jatropha oil burning (Chhetri et al., 2007b)

Figure 2.3.6 is the Jatropha oil burning in a small traditional lamp. There are various designs of lamps available to burn kerosene, most of which can be replaced with Jatropha oil without any modification.

Kerosene is utilized commonly in pressure stoves for cooking in countless households and commercial enterprises of developing countries. In many countries, kerosene is heavily subsidized by the government and is always a burden to the national economy of many countries. Boswell (2003) designed an experimental institutional stove to burn Jatropha oil directly for cooking. This is also a pressurized stove. The oil consumption rate for this particular stove was 0.7 litres of Jatropha oil per hour giving a stable flame and low level of smoke and particulate matters. Thermal cracking of oil at elevated temperatures results un the formation of solid and partially combusted products that are prone to be deposited on inner tube surface. The stove designed took this into account and made a provision to clean mechanically through some orifices build into it. This stove was built based on the parts available in the Nepalese and Indian market and petroleum fuel can also be burned without any modification (Boswell, 2000). The geometry of the stove allows adequate air for combustion and promotes secondary combustion of the fuel in the upper area as well. After pressurization of fuel, it passes through the pipe and admitted to a vaporizer prior to combustion. Vaporization is promoted by preheating the fuel before it goes to the nozzle. The vaporizer is housed in a flame stabilizer that enhances temperature around vaporizer and assists for fuel vaporization. The fuel burning starts after the vaporized oil is fired with flame stabilizer.

Seabuckthorn Oil

Seabuckthorn is a diversified group of plant species distributed naturally in Asia and Europe. The importance of Seabuckthorn in soil conservation and in off farm income generating activities in Hindu Kush Himalaya (HKH) region is adequately addressed by Lu (1992). Throughout in the HKH region, people have been using it for centuries, in various ways. Wider distribution and adaptation, extensive and well-developed root system, rapid regeneration, compact canopy and coverage are important attributes with which it protects soil from wind and water erosion (Chhetri and Islam, 2008).

Although several species and sub-species are introduced, two species of Seabuckthorn are found in different geographical regions of the world including Northern Himalayan districts of Nepal; namely *Hippophae salicifolia* D.Don and *Hippophae tibetana* Schlecht. It is a multipurpose and economically important plant with lesser degree of acknowledgement in Nepal to date. Fruit of the plant is used since a long time as *Chuk* (traditional vinegar), processed locally from the extracted juice. Due to the introduction of new technologies, the fruit extract is used for production of jam, juice and jelly. Juice is manufactured for commercial purpose in some areas. In terms of other application, it has been estimated that there is enough vitamin C in the berries of the Sea Buckthorn plants of the world to meet the dietary requirements of the entire human population. Branches and trunks in some areas are also used as fuel wood. Seabuckthorn fixes atmospheric nitrogen into nutrient so that it helps to reclaim the lost soil fertility. Seabuckthorn is one of the precious gifts by the nature to the high mountain communities. The Eurasian recognized Seabuckthorn long ago that had multidimensional traditional use in the local community. During last decades, people have further developed better understanding about this plant. The former USSR, China and Mongolia are pioneer countries who started its extensive cultivation some 50 years ago (Schroeder and Yao, 1995). It is also found in Europe Western Canada and several other countries.

Nepal, a Himalayan country offers the distribution of Seabuckthorn throughout the country in the high mountains. Herbarium records for Nepal indicate availability of Seabuckthorn in some districts, while the potential vegetation map indicated iso-potential sites for Seabuckthorn forests for more than 21 districts of northern Nepal. The growing conditions, yet known, are believed to be suitable for this plant primarily in the North-West Nepal. National Herbarium and plant Laboratory, Plant Research Division, Nepal at Godavari has specimens of three species of *Hippophae*, namely, *H. salicifolia*, D. Don, *H. tibetana* Schlecht and *Hippophae rhamnoides* L. However, only former two species are identified in the high mountain areas of Nepal.

The morphological structure of Seabuckthorn shows much variation. It includes small shrubs of 20 to 70 cm average heights to medium sized trees up to height of 1 to 5 m (Lu, 1992). According to Lu (1998), though it is a hydrophyte, yet it has developed some xerophytic features. In China some exceptional trees of 16 meters high with trunk girth 5.3 m, and crown diameter of 16.1 meter were observed (Lu, 1992). Other studies show that Seabuckthorn is extremely variable in height from small bush less than 50 cm to a tree more than 20 m high. In Nepal where only 2 species are found so far, they range from 20 cm high shrubs of *H. tibetana* to 8 to 10 meter high with trunk diameter 50 to 70 cm medium sized trees of *H. salicifolia* (Lu, 1992). It is a dioecious plant species. The leaves are small, 3 to 8 cm long and 0.4 to 1cm wide, linear, lanceolate and covered with silvery stellate scale on the backside to reflect sunshine and to reduce moisture loss.

Table 2.3.7. Fatty Acid composition of Sea Buckthorn oil *(Lu, 1992)*

Ingredient	Seed Oil	Pulp Oil	Fruit Residue Oil
Unsaturated fatty acids	87%	67%	70%
Saturated fatty acids	13%	33%	30%

The seed contains 10 to 12 % of oil depending upon the species of the plant. However, the seed collected from Dolpa contains 7.6 % oil, 17.56 % protein and 4 percent tannin (Lu, 1992). *H. tibetana* contains 19.51 % oil which is the highest among all the species of *Hippophae* (Lu, 1992). The seed oil contains 12 to 20% saturated fatty acids and 88.3 to 89.1% unsaturated fatty acids (Schroeder and Yao, 1995), as shown in Table 2.3.7. Because of low oil content, solvent extraction process is used. However, current use of petroleum ethers and others products for solvent extraction should be replaced by grain alcohols for the sustainability in the long-term. Sea buckthorn oil contains vitamins A, E and K and which are used in various fields of food, drug and cosmetics (Lu, 1992). The chemical composition of two species of Seabuckthorn seed is given below. As other oils, the oil contained in sea buckthorn can be burned to for lighting.

Algal Oil

Thousands of species of algae and micro-algae are available in different parts of the world. Some species of algae are so rich in oil that it accounts for over 50% of their mass (Danielo, 2005). National Renewable Energy Laboratory of USA has identified over 300 species of algae as varied as diatoms and green algae in salt water and fresh water which are rich in oil. Algae are available in ponds and lakes in significant quantity. Being similar in properties with other vegetable oils, this oil can also be burned for lighting, heating and cooking to replace kerosene in developing countries. In fact these algae can be promoted in waste lands to yield valuable oils. There exists approximately 100,000 known species of unicellular microscopic algae, called diatoms (Danielo, 2005). Among them, certain species are particularly rich in oil content. They carry photosynthesis as big plants and are the large sink for CO_2. Utilizing the algae oil not only helps to develop green fuels but also fix CO_2 in the environment. Hence, algal oil produced from the waste land could be a good source for bio-hydrocarbons that easily replace kerosene for cooking, heating and lighting. The oil can also be converted to biodiesel to replace petrodiesel.

These are non edible oils that have been discussed for lighting. There are thousands of other plant hydrocarbons that can be extracted to generate light. Depending on the location where production of edible oils such as olive oil, mustard oil, soybean oil, sunflower and other edible oils are in excess, these oils can be burned to generate light. If synthetic fertilizers and pesticides are not used during production, they remain truly organic and completely biodegradable. These organic sources generate natural light spectrum and are useful for eyes, health and environment. The plant bio-hydrocarbons and oils are renewable sources and sustainable for the long-term fulfilling the sustainability criteria developed by Khan et al. (2005a).

Environmental Benefits of Bio-hydrocarbons

The promotion of bio-hydrocarbons that can be exploited from the indigenous plant resources that can replace the use of imported kerosene. Plant oils are clean burning fuels that show no problems of respiratory and eye diseases. Since the kerosene burning emits sulfur compounds, shifting from kerosene to bio-hydrocarbons can reduce sulfur emission, thereby, help to reduce acid rain deposition. Plants that yield bio-hydrocarbons are the large sink for carbon dioxide. However, it should be noted that the CO_2 which is contaminated with heavy metals and toxic chemicals are not acceptable to plants (Chhetri et al., 2007a). Hence the only way to curb global warming is to stop producing industrial CO_2. Only the natural CO_2 which is not contaminated with synthetic chemicals will be recycled by plants (Chhetri and Islam, 2007b).

There is a prevalent misconception that biofuels are expensive compared to commercial fuels. This occurs due to the calculation of the local efficiency for particular fuel system. However, if global efficiency is considered, the economics of biofuels is justifiable proving it economical in the long-term. Biofuels production such as Jatropha oil has several by-products. Each of these by-products can be utilized and revenue can be generated. For example, Jatropha oil, every part of the plant is extremely valuable from food to medicine (Figure 2.3.2). Similar benefits can be obtained from the by-products of pine oil production. The remaining part from the turpentine can be used for medicinal purpose and varnish production. In case of Seabuckthorn, residues after expelling oil can also be used for medicinal purpose. All of these plant species yielding bio-hydrocarbons are the zero-waste plants and have multiple uses leaving no environmental impacts. There are hundreds of plants that can yield bio-hydrocarbons, most of them can be used as fuels in various forms.

Economic Development

Development and management of the plants species for extracting oils have a positive impact on the environment, saving huge environmental costs. The cultivation of plants has several positive impacts on soil and ecosystem such as root systems enhance soil stability against heavy rain or dry season. Clean fuels make positive impacts on health, which will have positive impacts on the economy. Cultivation of the plants for oils also has direct employment benefits. Goldemberg (2003) reported various jobs created by different renewable energy technologies (Table 9). The jobs created for ethanol are one of the highest. As suggested by Wood (2005), Jatropha offers five times more employment than crops to produce ethanol. Jatropha will stand for highest employment possibility among all the renewable energy sources. Similar contribution could be seen if analyzed for pine oil, Seabuckthorn and algae oil production.

Table 2.3.8. Jobs in Energy Production (Goldemberg, 2003)

Sector	Jobs (person-years), TWh
Petroleum	260
Offshore oil	265
Natural gas	250
Coal	370
Nuclear	75
Wood energy	1000
Hydro	250
Minihydro	120
Wind	918
Photovoltaics	7600
Ethanol (from sugarcane)	4000

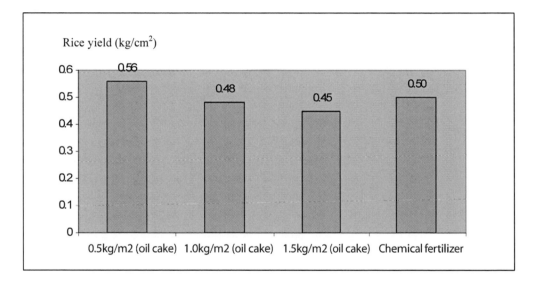

Figure 2.3.7. Effect of Jatropha oil cake on de-hulled rice yield (Boswell et al., 2000).

Mitigation of industrial carbon dioxide emission has positive environmental and economical impacts in local, regional and global scale. Rural enterprises based on oil plant oil seed resources may promote social stability and cohesion in the community. Indigenous plant oil resources can contribute to national energy security by supplementing imported fossil fuels. It was reported that *Jatropha carcus* oil cakes have been utilized directly as an organic fertilizer to grow paddy and vegetables. Figure 2.3.7 shows the impact of oil cake in rice production compared to chemicals fertilizer. It is observed that oil cake yields higher production than chemical fertilizers. The use of soil cake works as soil conditioners keeping the soil quality suitable for next crop. Similar economy can be observed in case of pine and Seabuckthorn resources. The development of community based enterprises would help significantly to enhance the economy of the areas where these plants are feasible (Khan et al., 2007a). The cultivation of plants that yield bio-hydrocarbons has no environmental impacts.

Production of bio-hydrocarbons for clean energy options is technically feasible, environmentally appealing, socially responsible and economically attractive in the long term (Islam, 2004; Khan and Islam, 2007a).

2.3.5. Biogas Lighting

Biogas as a Fuel for Lighting

Biogas is considered one of the most important fuels for lighting in the areas where there is no electricity (Chhetri and Islam, 2008). Burning kerosene is the most conventional alternative in such areas. As discussed earlier, fuel based lighting and lighting generated by electricity have several health and environmental problems. They also significantly contribute greenhouse gas emission. Biogas lighting is promoted in many parts of the world such as India and Nepal to replace kerosene lighting. A study carried out BSP (2002) reported that after the introduction of biogas plants the consumption of kerosene has been reduced significantly for cooking and lighting in rural areas of Nepal. The Ujeli lamps are most popular lamp in Nepal to burn biogas for lighting (Chhetri and Islam, 2008). The gas consumption of these lamps is between 150 and 200 liters per hour. The light produced by biogas fed Ujeli lamps are comparable with that of a 60-watt light bulb. Figure 2.3.8 shows a typical lamp in which biogas is filled to produce light. Depending on design of lamps, the gas consumption varies.

There are more than 2.5 million small and large biogas plants installed in India which are mainly used for cooking (Jash and Basu, 1999). The conventional biogas digester does not always produce enough biogas for lighting and cooking. It was reported that small digesters that consume about 12 kg of dung per day were designed to generate biogas solely for lighting purpose (Figure 2.3.9). From the size of this digester, 0.45 to 0.5 m^3/day of biogas production was recorded which is sufficient to light a small house for 4 hours daily.

Benefits of Biogas Lighting

Biogas is a clean gas produced by the decomposition organic matters by microbes. There are no additional chemicals or catalysts necessary for the biogas production. Biogas lighting has the following advantages.

Positive Impact on Health, Sanitation and Safety

In order to enhance the biogas production, most of the household build and connect the toilets to the biogas digesters. This gives opportunity for better management of human faeces and prevents water and food products contaminating. The water contamination otherwise could cause dysentery and tapeworm infestation (BSP, 2002). It was reported that the incidence of these problems were higher in non-biogas household than the households having biogas digesters. The danger of fire hazards due to kerosene burning lamps accidents was also considerably lowered after the introduction of biogas lighting in several incidences. Hence biogas systems have also positive impact on increased household safety.

Figure 2.3.8. Biogas Lamp (Bunny and Besselink, 2005).

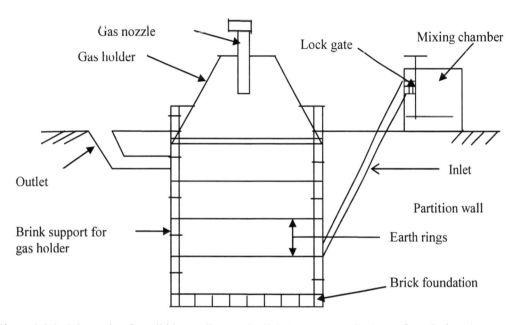

Figure 2.3.9. Schematic of small biogas digester for lighting purpose (Redrawn from Jash and Basu, 1999).

Benefit on Agriculture and Sustainable Land Use

The biogas slurry is an important source of nutrients for agriculture. In the areas where biogas plants were installed, the use of liquid and composted biogas slurry increased considerably. Due to the bio-slurry use as fertilizer, the use of chemical fertilizer was found reduced by about 9 percent (BSP, 2002). About 10 percent increase in maize yield and 18 percent increase in cabbage yield were reported with the application of digested slurry.

Environmental Benefits

Introduction of biogas digesters help to reduce the import of kerosene from abroad. There is a large amount of CO_2 avoidance due to the transition from kerosene to biogas lighting. Biogas is an organic product and the CO_2 produced by biogas burning is a natural CO_2 and does not contribute to global warming as it is readily recycled by plants. Even the methane leaked during production and burning is converted to CO_2 and is a part of global carbon cycle.

Socio-economic Benefits

Biogas can be produced in any small scale in the household to big scale in the landfills and municipal waste treatment systems. Making biogas digesters doe not need highly skilled work force. Hence local people in the communities can themselves be the resource persons for biogas digesters construction and make their living working in the communities. The other advantage is that once the people's health is not affected, people can be socially motivated for their own and community works. Because of the production of good fertilizer, more people have practiced farming enhancing their economy. Since their energy is produced from the waste, they can utilize their money for other enterprises. Conventionally, women are considered responsible for collecting firewood for their cooking in developing countries. Lighting from biogas would also reduce the environmental and health cost significantly. Hence biogas is an inherently sustainable technology as it has no negative environmental impact and has significant positive social and economic impact to the society.

2.4. FOSSIL FUEL REFINING AND PROCESSING

Introduction

The history of development of oil and gas is compared with that of modern civilization. Oil and gas are considered the backbone of the modern economic systems. Modern transportation systems from car to aircrafts are designed based on the oil, gas and other fossil fuel use. Since the use of fossil fuels creates several environmental and health problems, the increasing dependence on fossil fuels is making the situation worse. The total energy consumption in 2004 was equivalent to approximately 200 million barrels of oil per day which is about 14.5 terawatts, over 85% of which comes from fossil fuels (Service, 2005). Globally, about 30 billion tons of CO_2 is produced annually from fossil fuels, which includes oil, coal and natural gas (EIA, 2004b). The industrial CO_2 is solely responsible for the current global warming and climate change problems the world is facing today (Chhetri and Islam, 2007a).

Refining crude oil and processing natural gas use large amount of toxic chemicals and catalysts including heavy metals. These heavy metals contaminate the end products and are burnt along with the fuels producing various toxic by-products. The pathways of these toxic chemicals and catalysts show that they largely affect the environment and public health. The use of toxic catalysts is creates many environmental effects that are make irreversible damage to the global ecosystem. The synthetic based technology development is anti-natural and there is no hope to reverse the global environmental problems to reverse until and unless the current engineering practices follow the natural path which is inherently sustainable. The use of natural catalysts and chemicals should be considered as the backbone for the future development. The crude oil is a truly non-toxic natural and biodegradable product but the way we refine it is responsible for all the problems created by refined oil on earth. The refined oil is hard to biodegrade and toxic to all living things. Hence, either we need to use natural catalysts and chemicals which do not render refined oil and gas a toxic product or we need to design a vehicle that directly runs on crude oil based on its natural properties.

2.4.1. Pathways of Oil Refining

Fossil fuels derived from the petroleum reservoirs is refined in order to suit the various application purposes from car fuels to aeroplane and space fuels. It is a complex mixture of hydrocarbons varying in composition depending on its source. Depending on the number of carbon atoms the molecules contain and their arrangement, the hydrocarbons in the crude oil have different boiling points. In order to take the advantage of the difference in boiling point of different components in the mixture, fractional distillation is used to separate the hydrocarbons from the crude oil. Figure 2.4.1 is the fractional distillating column in which the temperature is lower at the top and increased as it goes down of the column.

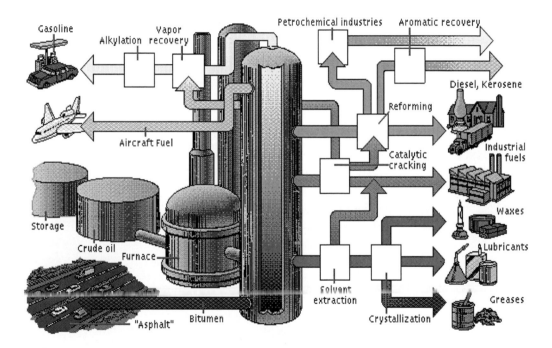

Figure 2.4.1. Fractional distillation unit for hydrocarbon refining (Website 4).

Through fractional distillation, crude oil is refined into various products such as such as gasoline, diesel, aircraft fuel, kerosene, asphalt, waxes and others. In this process, the fractions of crude oil are divided out successively by their increasing molecular weight and boiling temperature. Gasoline has a low molecular weight and vaporizes at a fairly low temperature and it will be separated out before any other component. The leftover oil goes through the similar process at higher temperature in which jet fuel is separated out. The distillation process continues until all the fractions are separated.

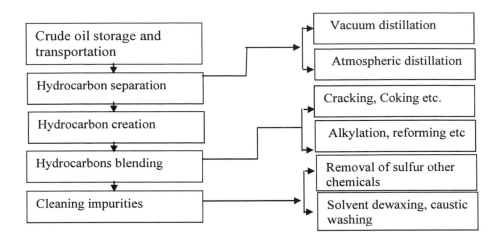

Figure 2.4.2. General activities in oil refining (Chhetri et al., 2007a).

Figure 2.4.2 gives a general schematic of the activities from storage of crude oil to the complete refining process. The stored crude oil is transported to separation unit where either vacuum distillation or atmospheric distillation is used for hydrocarbon separation. Various grades of hydrocarbons are created after distillation. These are again used for the production of different types of hydrocarbon compounds. Chemical impurities of crude oil such as sulfur or wax are separated.

Petroleum refining begins with the distillation, or fractionation, of crude oils into separate hydrocarbon groups. The resultant products of petroleum are directly related to the properties of the crude processed. Most of the distillation products are further processed into more conventionally usable products changing the size and structure of the carbon chain through several processes by cracking, reforming and other conversion processes. Table 2.4.1 summarizes various processes involved in the oil refining, purpose of particular process, the feedstock input in the refining unit and products of distillation. In order to remove the impurities in the products and improve the quality, extraction, hydrotreating and sweetening are applied. Hence, an integrated refinery consists of fractionation, conversion, treatment and blending including petrochemicals processing units.

Fractional distillation is the process of separation of crude oil in atmospheric and vacuum distillation towers into groups of hydrocarbon compounds of different boiling points. The hydrocarbon conversion process, in which the size and structure of hydrocarbon molecules consist of thermal and catalytic cracking for the decomposition, alkylation and polymerization for combining the hydrocarbon molecules and rearranging with catalytic reforming. To remove or separate the naphthenes, aromatics and other undesirable compounds, various treatment processes such as dissolving adsorption and precipitation are carried out. In addition to this, desalting, drying, hydrodesulfurizing, solvent refining, sweetening, solvent extraction, and solvent dewaxing are also done to remove impurities from the fractions. Other activities such as formulating and blending are carried out to produce finish products with desired properties. Refining operations also include the treatment of waste waters contaminated due to the petroleum operations, solid waste management, process water treatment and cooling and sulfur recovery. Other auxiliary operations include power generation and management for process operations, flare system, supply of air, nitrogen, steam and other necessary system inputs along with the administrative management of the whole refining systems keeping into consideration the environmental factors around the operational unit.

Table 2.4.1. Various processes and products in oil refining process (OSHA, 1999)

Process name	Action	Method	Purpose	Feedstock(s)	Product(s)
FRACTIONATION PROCESSES					
atmospheric distillation	separation	thermal	separate fractions	desalted crude oil	gas, gas oil, distillate, residual
vacuum distillation	separation	thermal	Separate w/o cracking	Atmospheric tower residual	gas, gas oil, lube, residual
CONVERSION PROCESSED - DECOMPOSITION					
catalytic cracking	alteration	catalytic	upgrade gasoline	Gas oil coke, distillate	Gasoline/petrochemical feedstock
coking	polymerize	thermal	convert vacuum residuals	Gas oil coke, distillate	gasoline, petrochemical feedstock
hydrocracking	hydrogenate	catalytic	convert to lighter HCs	Gas oil, cracked oil residual,	lighter higher quality products
hydrogen steam reforming	decompose	catalytic/thermal	produce hydrogen	Desulfurized gas, O2, steam	hydrogen, CO, CO_2
steam cracking	decompose	thermal	crack large molecules	Atm tower, heavy fuel/ distillate	Cracked naphtha, coke, residual
visbreaking	decompose	thermal	reduce viscosity	Atm tower residual	Distillate tar
CONVERSION PROCEESES-UNIFICATION					
alkylation	combining	catalytic	Unit olefins and isoparaffins	Tower isobutane/ cracker olefin	Iso-octane (alkylate)
grease compounding	combining	thermal	Combine soap and oils	Lube oil, fatty acid, alky metal	Lubricating grease
polymerizing	polymerize	catalytic	Unite 2 or more olefins	Cracker olefins	High-octane naphtha, petrochemical stocks
CONVERSION PROCESSES - ALTERATION OR REARRANGEMENT					
Catalytic reforming	Alteration/ dehydration	catalytic	Upgrade low octane naphtha	Coker/ hydro-cracker naphtha	High oct. Reformate/ aromatic
isomerization	rearrange	catalytic	straight chain to branch	Butane, pentane, hexane	Isobutane/ pentane/ hexane
TREATMENT PROCESSES					
amine treating	Treatment	Absorption	Remove acidic contaminants	Sour gas, HCs w/CO_2 & H_2S	Acid free gases & liquid HCs
desalting	Dehydration	Absorption	Remove contaminants	Crude oil	Desalted crude oil
drying	Treatment	Abspt/ therm	Remove H_2O & sulfur cmpds	Liq HCs, LPG, alky feedstk	Sweet & dry hydrocarbons
furfural extraction	Solvent extr.	Absorption	Upgrade mid distillate & lubes	Cycle oils & lube feed-stocks	High quality diesel & lube oil

Table 2.4.1. Continued.

Process name	Action	Method	Purpose	Feedstock(s)	Product(s)
hyfrodesulfarization	Treatment	Catalytic	Remove sulfur, contaminants	High-sulfur residual/ gas oil	Desulfurized olefins
hydrotreating	Hydrogenation	Catalytic	saturate HC's	Residuals, cracked HC's	Cracker feed, distillate, lube
phenol extraction	Solvent extr.	Abspt/ therm	Improve visc. index, color	Lube oil base stocks	High quality lube oils
solvent deasphalting	Treatment	Absorption	Remove asphalt	Vac. tower residual, propane	Heavy lube oil, asphalt
solvent dewaxing	Treatment	Cool/ filter	Remove wax from lube stocks	Vac. tower lube oils	Dewaxed lube basestock
solvent extraction	Solvent extr.	Abspt/ precip.	Separate unsat. oils	Gas oil, reformate, distillate	High-octane gasoline

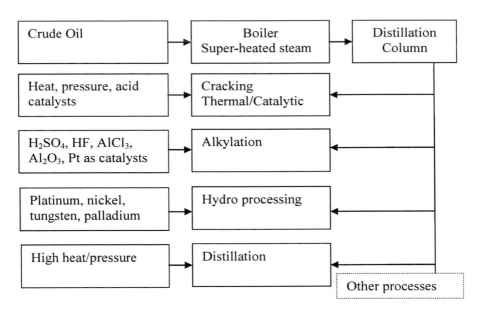

Figure 2.4.3. Pathway of oil refining process (Chhetri et al., 2007a).

The pathways of oil refining illustrate that the oil refining process utilizes highly toxic catalysts and chemicals, and the emission from oil burning also becomes extremely toxic (Chhetri and Islam, 2007b). Figure 6 shows the pathway of oil refining. During cracking of the hydrocarbon molecules, different types of acid catalysts are used along with high heat and pressure. The process of employing the breaking of hydrocarbon molecules is the thermal cracking. During alkylation, sulfuric acids, hydrogen fluorides, aluminum chlorides and platinum are used as catalysts. Platinum, nickel, tungsten, palladium and other catalysts are used during hydro processing. In distillation, high heat and pressure are used as catalysts. The use of highly toxic chemicals and catalysts creates several environmental problems as these are highly toxic chemicals and catalysts. Their use will contaminate the air, water and land in different aspect. Use of such chemicals is not a sustainable option. The pathway analysis shows that current oil refining process is inherently unsustainable.

2.4.2. Pathways of Natural Gas Processing

Natural gas is a mixture of methane, ethane, propane, butane and other hydrocarbons, water vapor, oil and condensates, hydrogen sulfides, carbon dioxide, nitrogen, some other gases and solid particles. The free water and water vapors are corrosive to the transportation equipment. Hydrates can plug the gas accessories creating several flow problems. Other gas mixtures such as hydrogen sulfide and carbon dioxide are known to lower the heating value of natural gas by reducing its overall fuel efficiency. There are certain restrictions imposed on major transportation pipelines on the make-up of the natural gas that is allowed into the pipeline called pipe 'line quality' gas. This makes mandatory that natural gas is purified before it is sent to transportation pipelines. The gas processing is aimed at preventing corrosion, environmental and safety hazards associated with transport of natural gas.

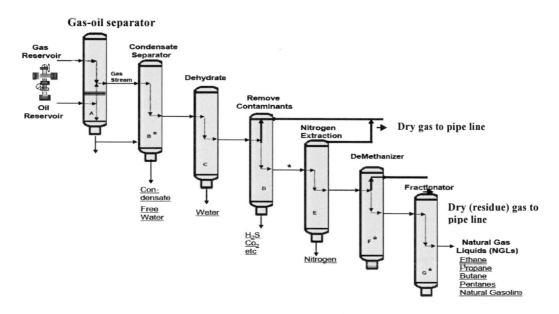

Figure2.4.4. Generalized natural gas processing schematic (Modified from EIA, 2006).

The presence of water in natural gas creates several problems. Liquid water and natural gas can form solid ice-like hydrates that can plug valves and fittings in the pipeline (Nallinson, 2004). Natural gas containing liquid water is corrosive, especially if it contains carbon dioxide and hydrogen sulfide. Water vapor in natural gas transport systems may condense causing a sluggish flow. Hence, the removal of free water, water vapors, and condensates is a very important step during gas processing. Other impurities of natural gas, such as, carbon dioxide and hydrogen sulfide generally called as acid gases must be removed from the natural gas prior to its transportation (Chakma, 1999). Hydrogen sulfide is a toxic and corrosive gas which is rapidly oxidized to form sulfur dioxide in the atmosphere (Basu et al., 2004). Oxides of nitrogen found in traces in the natural gas may cause ozone layer depletion and global warming. Figure 2.4.4 is the schematic of general gas processing system.

Figure 2.4.5 illustrates the pathway of natural gas processing from reserves to end uses. This figure also shows various emissions from natural gas processing from different steps. After the exploration and production, natural gas stream is sent through the processing systems. Glycol dehydration is used for water removal from the natural gas stream. Similarly, methanolamines (MEA) and Diethanolamine (DEA) are used for removing H_2S and CO_2 from the gas streams. Since these chemicals are used for gas processing, it is impossible to completely free the gas from these chemicals. Glycols and amines are very toxic chemicals. Burning of glycols produces carbon monoxide and when the natural gas is burned in the stoves, it is possible that the emission produces carbon monoxide. Carbon monoxide is a poisonous gas and very harmful for the health and environment. Similarly, amines are also toxic chemicals and burning the gas contaminated by amines produces toxic emissions. Despite the prevalent notion that natural gas burning is clean, the emission is not free from environmental problems. It is reported that one of the highly toxic compounds released in natural gas stoves burning (LPG in stoves) is isobutane which causes hypoxia in the human body (Sugie et al, 2004).

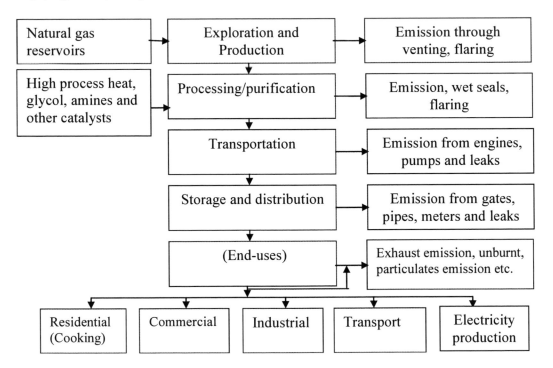

Figure 2.4.5. Pathway of natural gas (Chhetri et al., 2007a).

Pathway of Glycol

Matsuoka et al (2005) reported a study on electro oxidation of methanol and glycol and found that electro-oxidation of ethylene glycol at 400mV form glycolate, oxalate and formate (Figure 2.4.6). The glycolate was obtained by three-electron oxidation of ethylene glycol, and was an electrochemically active product even at 400mV, which led to the further oxidation of glycolate. Oxalate was found stable, no further oxidation was seen and was termed as "non-poisoning path" The other product of glycol oxidation is called formate which is termed as poisoning path or "CO poisoning path". The glycolate formation decreased from 40-18 % and formate increased from 15-20% between 400 and 500mV. Thus, ethylene glycol oxidation produced CO instead of CO_2 and follows the poisoning path over 500 mV. The glycol oxidation produces glycol aldehyde as intermediate products.

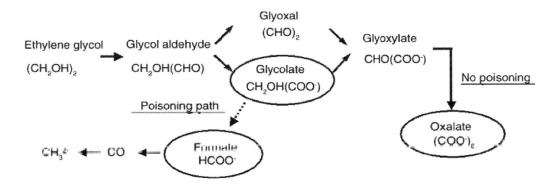

Figure 2.4.6. Ethylene Glycol Oxidation Pathway in Alkaline Solution (After Matsuoka et al., 2005).

Glycol ethers are known to produce toxic metabolites such as the teratogenic methoxyacetic acid during biodegradation, the biological treatment of glycol ethers can be hazardous (Fischer and Hahn, 2005). Abiotic degradation experiments with ethylene glycol showed that the by-products are monoethylether (EGME) and toxic aldehydes, e.g. methoxy acetaldehyde (MALD). Glycol passes into body through inhalation, ingestion or skin. Toxicity of ethylene glycol causes depression and kidney damage (MSDS, 2005). High concentration levels can interfere with the ability of the blood to carry oxygen causing headache and a blue color to the skin and lips (*methemoglobinemia*), collapse and even death. High exposure may affect the nervous system and may damage the red blood cells leading to anemia (low blood count). During a study of carcinogenetic and toxicity of propylene glycol on animals, the skin tumor incidence was observed (CERHR, 2003). Glycol may form toxic alcohol inside human body if ingested as fermentation may take place. Samuel and Steinman (1995) reported that laboratory report on animals have proved DEA to be a carcinogen with major impact in kidney, liver and brain. Nitrosamine, a byproduct of DEA, is also considered a probable carcinogen. Thus DEA, TEA and MEA used in natural gas processing will have significant impact on the human health as well as in the environment. Hence the use of glycols in gas processing is not a sustainable option.

Pathways of Amines and their Toxicity

Amines are considered to be toxic chemicals. It was reported that occupational asthma was found in a patient handling of a cutting fluid containing diethanolamine (Piipari *et al.*, 1998). Toninello (2006) reported that the oxidation products of some biogenic amines appear to be also carcinogenic. DEA also reversibly inhibits phosphatidylcholine synthesis by blocking chorine uptake (Lehman-McKeeman and Gamsky, 1999). Systemic toxicity occurs in many tissue types, including the nervous system, liver, kidney, and blood system that may cause increased blood pressure, diuresis, salivation, and pupillary dilation. Diethanolamine causes mild skin irritation to the rabbit at concentrations above 5%, and severe ocular irritation at concentrations above 50% (Beyer *et al.,* 1983). Ingestion of diethylamine causes severe gastrointestinal pain, vomiting, and diarrhea, and may result in perforation of the stomach possibly due to the oxidation products and fermentation products. Due to these reasons, the use of amines gas processing is not an environmentally friendly option.

2.4.3. Additives in Oil Refining and Gas Processing and their Functions

Oil refining and natural gas processing is a very expensive process in terms of operation and management. These operations involve the use of several chemicals and catalysts which are very expensive. Moreover, these catalysts and chemicals pose a great threat to the natural environment including air and water pollution. Air and water pollution will finally have impacts on the health of human, animals and plants. For instance, the use of catalysts such as lead during crude oil refining to produce gasoline has been a serious environmental problems. Burning gasoline emits toxic gases including lead particle and oxidation of lead in the air forms lead oxide, which is a poisonous compound affecting lives of every living things. The major cause of water pollution due to heavy metals such as mercury and chromium is also caused by the use of these metals in oil refining. Table 2.4.2 shows the details of oil refining process and catalysts used in the operations.

Table 2.4.2. Details of oil refining process and various types of catalyst used

Process	Description	Catalyst/Heat/ pressure used
Distillation Processes	It basically relies on the difference of boiling point of various fluids. Density has also important role to pay in distillation. The lightest hydrocarbon at the top and heaviest residue at the bottom is separated.	Heat
Coking and Thermal process	Coking unit converts heavy feedstocks into solid coke and lower boiling hydrocarbons products which are suitable to offer refinery units to convert to higher value transportation fuel. This is a severe thermal cracking process to form coke. Coke contains high boiling point hydrocarbon and some volatiles which are removed my calcining at temperature 1095-1260 ^{0}C. Coke is allowed sufficient time to remain in high temperature heaters hence called delayed cooking.	Heat
Thermal Cracking	The crude oil is subjected to both pressure and large molecules are broken into small ones to produce additional gasoline. The naphtha fraction is useful for making many petrochemicals. Heating naphtha in the absence of air makes the molecules split into shorter ones.	Excessive Heat and pressure

Process	Description	Catalyst/Heat/ pressure used
Catalytic Cracking	Converts heavy oils into high gasoline, less heavy oils and lighter gases. Paraffin's are converted to C3 and C4 hydrocarbons. Benzene ring of aromatic hydrocarbons are broken. Crude oil is cracked with longer hydrocarbons. Larger hydrocarbons split into shorter ones at low temperatures if a catalyst is used. This process is called catalytic cracking. The products include useful short chain hydrocarbons.	Nickels, Zeolites, Acid treated natural alumina silicates, amorphous and crystalline synthetic silica alumina catalyst
Hydro-processing	Hydroprocessing (325 0C and 50 atm) includes both hydro cracking (350 0C and 200 atm) and hydrotreating. Hydrotreating involves the addition of hydrogen atoms to molecules without actually breaking the molecule into smaller pieces and improves the quality of various products (e.g., by removing sulfur, nitrogen, oxygen, metals, and waxes and by converting olefins to saturated compounds). Hydrocracking breaks longer molecules into smaller ones. This is a more severe operation using higher heat and longer contact time. Hydrocracking reactors contain fixed, multiple catalyst beds.	Platinum, Tungsten, palladium, nickel, crystalline mixture of silica alumina. Cobalt and Molybdenum oxide on alumina nickel oxide, nickel thiomolybdate tungsten and nickel sulfide and vanadium oxides, nickel thiomolybdate (sulfur removal) and nickel molybdenum (for nitrogen removal)
Alkylation	Alkylation or "polymerization" - forming longer molecules from smaller ones. Another process is isomerization where straight chain molecules are made into higher octane branched molecules. The reaction requires an acid catalyst at low temperatures and low pressures. The acid composition is usually kept at about 50% making the mixture very corrosive.	Sulfuric acid, or hydrofluoric acid, HF (1-40 degrees Celsius, 1-10 atm). Platinum on $AlCl_3/Al_2O_3$ catalyst uses as new alkylation catalyst
Catalytic Reforming	This uses heat, moderate pressure and fixed bed catalysts to turn naphtha, short carbon chain molecule fraction, into high-octane gasoline components - mainly aromatics.	Catalyst used is a platinum (Pt) metal on an alumina (Al_2O_3) base.
Treating Non hydrocarbons	Treating can involve chemical reaction and/or physical separation. Typical examples of treating are chemical sweetening, acid treating, caustic washing, hydrotreating, drying, solvent extraction, and solvent dewaxing.	

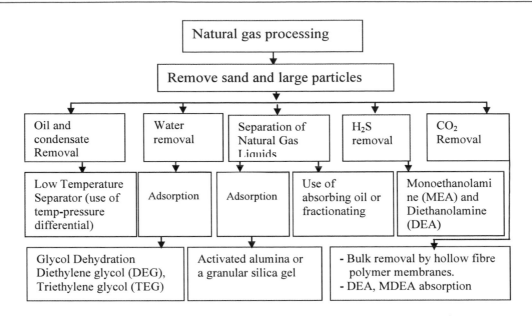

Figure 2.4.7. Natural gas processing methods (Chhetri and Islam, 2006a).

Additives Used in Gas Processing

Figure 2.4.7 illustrates the details of removing contaminants and chemicals as well as catalysts used during natural gas processing. This generalized scheme includes all necessary steps depending on the types of ingredients available in a particular gas. Removing water, carbon dioxide, hydrogen sulfide, nitrogen, helium, natural gas liquids and water vapors are to be removed from the natural gas streams. Water removal from natural gas stream is carried out using adsorption from glycol dehydration. The natural gas liquids such as ethane, propane, butane, pentane and gasoline are separated from methane using cryogenic and absorption methods. Currently, hydrogen sulfide and carbon dioxides are removed by using Monoethanolamine (MEA) and Diethanolamine (DEA) absorption or using polymeric membranes.

2.4.4. Natural Alternative Catalysts for Oil Refining and Gas Processing

The catalysts and chemicals used in oil refining and gas processing develop the major pathways for creating several environmental problems including global warming and climate change. This problem can be overcome by two ways. First, this problem can be avoided using natural catalysts and chemicals in oil refining and gas processing instead of toxic heavy metals such as lead, chromium, mercury etc. Secondly, the design of engines that can be run directly with the crude oil. The use of natural catalysts such as zeolites, natural alumina silicates, amorphous and crystalline silica alumina catalyst, clay and others would prevent oil refining process from contributing environmental pollution. Similarly, the use of clay absorption instead of glycol dehydration, use of natural amines extracted from hemp seeds instead of synthetic amines for carbon dioxide removal and vegetable oils for hydrogen sulfide removal are truly environmentally friendly options for natural gas processing (Chhetri and Islam, 2006a). The use of direct crude oil is discussed in the subsequent chapter.

2.4.5. Direct Use of Crude Oil in a Jet Engine

Conventional engines are not suitable for running on crude oil and gas without refining. The use of crude oil and natural gas directly without refining requires designing of new engine based on the properties of the crude. A jet engine has been designed recently in order to convert saw dust waste to electricity (Chhetri and Islam, 2007c). This is one of the most efficient technologies since it can use a variety of fuels for combustion. This jet engine is designed in such a way that saw dust is sprayed from the top where the air blower works to produce a jet. Some startup fuel such as organic alcohol is used to start up the engine. Once the engine is started, the saw dust and blower will be enough to create power for the engine to run. The main advantage of this jet engine is that it can use a variety of fuels such as waste vegetable oil and tree leaves. It is reported that this engine has a possibility to use crude oil directly. The possibility of directly using of crude oil can eliminate the various toxic and expensive refining processes which alone reduce large amounts of greenhouse gas emission into the atmosphere. Hence, this technology is envisaged as one of the most sustainable technologies among the others currently available.

2.4.6. CO_2 Emission, Natural and Industrial CO_2 and Global Warming

Carbon dioxide has been considered as the major cause for the global warming. However, there is no scientific evidence that all carbon dioxides are responsible for global warming. Carbon dioxide is the most essential compound for the biodiversity to be maintained on earth. Without carbon dioxide, no photosynthesis occurs and without photosynthesis, there will be no global food cycle continues. Yet, carbon dioxide as such is touted as a major precursor for global warming.

Chhetri and Islam (2007a) classified CO_2 as natural and industrial CO_2. They showed that the CO_2 which is obtained by burning any biomass fuels including crude oil without adding any synthetic additives is a natural CO_2. Natural CO_2 is recycled by plants for photosynthesis to produce food for consumers. Plants have inherent mechanism to discriminate the natural and industrial CO_2 and take only natural CO_2 as an input for photosynthesis. Farquhar et al.(1989) reported that plants favor a lighter form of carbon dioxide for photosynthesis and discriminate against heavier isotopes of carbon. The CO_2 produced by burning refined fossil fuels which involves the use of various toxic additives is contaminated by these chemicals and this CO_2 is not acceptable to plants. This is because the pathway the fuel travels from refinery to combustion devices makes the refined product inherently toxic (Chhetri et al., 2007a). However, if the CO_2 comes from wood burning, which has no chemical additives, this CO_2 will be most favored by plants (Chhetri et al., 2007a). Moreover, if the CO_2 comes from biomass pellets which involve the use of acidic additives, it will not be accepted by plants as it is contaminated CO_2. As the CO_2 contaminated by toxic chemicals is not accepted by plants, this CO_2 accumulates in the atmosphere and works as the heat trap in the atmospheric layer resulting in global warming. This analysis provides the distinction between the natural and industrial CO_2 and their impact in the global warming and climate change.

2.5. GLOBAL ENERGY SCENARIO

2.5.1. Global Energy Problems

Energy is the single most important factor that affects the prosperity of any society. Richard Smalley, a Nobel laureate in chemistry in his paper on "Future Global Energy Prosperity: The Terawatt Challenge" ranked 'energy' at the top of the 10 global problems that includes energy, water, food, environment, poverty, terrorism and war, diseases, education, democracy and population. Energy problem has been considered serious as it is believed that the main energy carrier, the global fossil fuel production has already reached to its maximum capacity (Smalley, 2005). The issue of energy has also been pressing due to their negative impacts to the global environment. In the other way, the energy problem is global not due to the depletion of fossil fuels but due to their serious impacts on ecosystem which is detrimental to the existence of humankind on earth. The global energy problem is a complex problem that no nation or block of nations acting alone can solve it. This is a problem that confronts humanity collectively. The search for solutions to the current energy problem should recognize the value of equitable sharing of burdens and rewards on a global scale. However, this has not been the case to date.

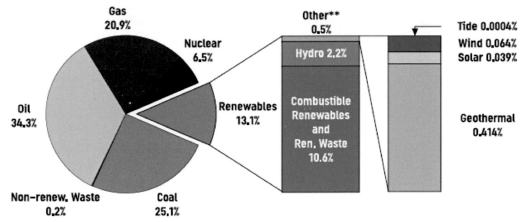

Figure 2.5.1. Fuel shares of world total primary energy supply for 2004 (IEA, 2007).

Fossil fuels have become the major driving factors of modern economic development (Figure 2.5.1). Over 80% of energy is supplied through fossil fuels (IEA, 2007). However, recent hikes in petroleum prices have shown severe impacts on the global economic scenario. The global energy scenario is tainted by the widening gap between the discovery of the petroleum reserves and the rate of production. Environmentally, fossil fuel burning is the major cause of producing greenhouse gases, which are major precursors for the current global warming problem. The alternatives sought to date are also based on the petroleum resources as primary energy input. There is not a single energy source which can be considered the solution for all energy problems. An integrated use of energy resources such as solar, hydro, biomass, wind, geothermal and hydrogen could open up opportunities for the sustainable energy in the future. One can gain very significantly on global efficiency by using various energy sources directly. Current science is highly influenced by the distinction of renewable and non-renewable energy sources. Proper science indicates that the distinction between renewable and non-renewable is superficial, devoid of a any scientific basis. By removing this distinction and applying knowledge-based processing and refining schemes, one can shift the current energy consumption base from 'non-renewable' to readily renewable one.

The modern economic development is largely dependent on the consumption of large amount of fossil fuels. Due to this reason, fossil fuel resources are considered sharply depleting. With the current consumption rate, the oil use will reach to its highest level within this decade. For example, humans today collectively consume the equivalent of a steady 14.5 trilling watts of power and 80% of that comes from fossil fuel (Smalley, 2005). Moreover, oil prices have skyrocketed and have shown severe impacts on all economic sectors. Yet, oil is expected to remain the dominant energy resource in decades to come with its total share of world energy consumption (Figure 2.5.2). This analysis indicates that except hydropower resources, the consumption of other resources will still continue to rise.

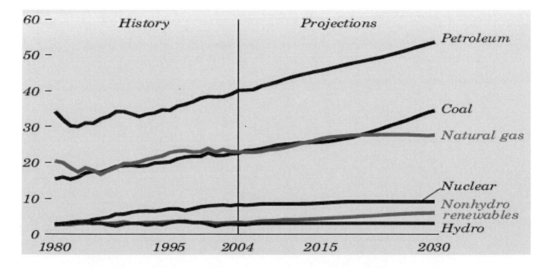

Figure 2.5.2. Global Energy Consumption by Fuel Type (Quadrillion Btu) (EIA, 2006a).

Worldwide oil consumption is expected to rise from 80 million barrels per day in 2003 to 98 million barrels per day in 2015 and then to 118 million barrels per day in 2030 (EIA, 2006a). Transportation and industries are the major sectors for oil demand in the future (Figure 2.5.3). The transportation sector accounts for about 60% of the total projected increase in oil demand in the next two decades followed by the industrial sector. Similarly, natural gas demand is expected to rise by an average of 2.4 % per year over the 2003-2030 period and coal use by an average of 2.5% per year. Total world natural gas consumption is projected to rise from 95 trillion cubic feet in 2003 to 134 trillion cubic feet in 2015 and 182 trillion cubic feet in 2030 (EIA, 2006a). The oil demand in residential and commercial sector will also increase constantly. The residential oil consumption demand increases much lower than other sectoral oil demand, which means almost half of the world's population with access to modern form of energy, will continue to depend on the traditional fuel resources.

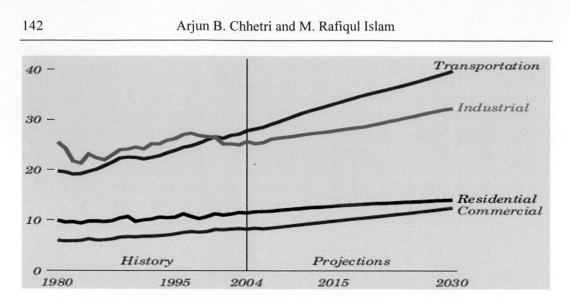

Figure 2.5.3. Delivered Energy Consumption by Sector (quadrillion Btu) (EIA, 2006a).

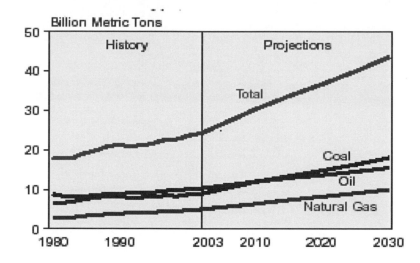

Figure 2.5.4. World CO_2 Emissions by oil, coal and natural gas, 1970-2025 (adopted from EIA, 2005).

Burning of fossil fuel has several environmental problems. Due to the increased use of fossil fuels, the world carbon dioxide emission is increasing severely and is expected to grow continuously in the future. Currently, the total CO_2 emission from all fossil fuel sources is about 30 billion tons per year (Figure 2.5.4). The total CO_2 emission from all fossil fuels is projected to be almost 44 billion tons by 2030 which exceeds 1990 levels by more than double (EIA, 2006b). At present, the CO_2 emission is at the highest level in 125,000 years (Service, 2005).

The current technology development mode is completely unsustainable (Khan and Islam, 2007a). Due to the use of unsustainable technologies, the energy production and consumption usually have an environmental downside, which may in turn threaten human health and quality of life. Impacts on atmospheric composition, deforestation leading to soil erosion and siltation of water bodies, the disposal of nuclear fuel waste, and occasional catastrophic accidents such as Chernobyl and Bhopal are some of the widely recognized problems.

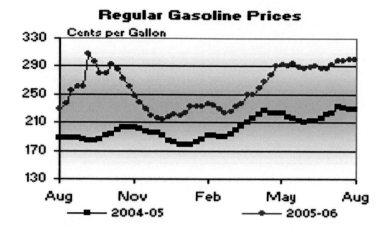

Figure 2.5.5. Regular gasoline price (EIA, 2006c).

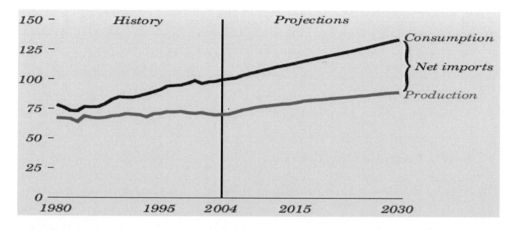

Figure 2.5.6. Total energy production, consumption and imports for US from 1980-2030 (quadrillion Btu) (EIA, 2006a).

The price of petroleum products is constantly increasing due to two reasons. First, the global oil consumption is increasing due to the increased industrial demand, higher number of vehicles, increase in urbanization and higher population. The industrial and transportation sector demand is rapidly increasing and is expected to increase in the future. The current oil consumption rate is much higher than the discovery of new oil reserves. Secondly, the fossil fuel use is subjected to meet the strict environmental regulations such as low sulfur fuel, unleaded gasoline, etc. This increases the price of the fuel. Figure 4 shows the rising trend of regular gasoline prices in USA from early 2006 to date. The US energy demand is significantly increasing. To meet the increasing demand, the US imports will also increase. Figure 5 indicates the net import of energy on a Btu basis projected to meet a growing share of total U.S. energy demand (EIA, 2006a). It is projected that the net imports are expected to constitute 32 percent and 33 percent of total U.S. energy consumption in 2025 and 2030, respectively, which is up from 29 percent in 2004.

The modern economic development is highly dependent on the energy resources and their effective utilization. There is a great disparity between the rate at which the fossil fuel is being used up and the rate at which the new reserves are found. Moreover, the new and renewable energy resources are not being developed at the pace to replace the fossil fuel. Most of the energy resources, which are claimed to replace the fossil fuel is again based on the fossil fuel for their primary energy resources. The alternatives being developed are based on chemical technologies which are hazardous to the environment. The technology development follows the degradation of chemical technologies as honey---> sugar--->saccharine--->aspartame syndrome (Islam et al, 2006). The artificial light which is alternative to the natural light has several impacts to the human health. Schernhammer (2006) reported a modestly elevated risk of breast cancer after longer period of rotating night work. Melatonin-depleted blood from premenopausal women exposed to light at night stimulates growth of human breast cancer xenografts in nude rats (Blask, et al., 2005). The gasoline engine which replaced steam engine became worse than its earlier counterpart. Modern gasoline and diesel engine use the fuel which is refined by using highly toxic chemicals and catalysts. The biodiesel which is touted to replace the petroleum diesel uses similar toxic chemicals and catalysts, such as, methanol and sodium hydroxide, producing similar exhausts gas as that of petroleum diesel. This principle applies in every technological development. The major problem facing the energy development is that the conventional policies are meant to maintain the status quo and all the technological development taking place are anti-nature. Hence a comprehensive policy that includes analysis of global energy problems and possible solutions based on natural principle and natural products is necessary to meet the global energy challenges in sustainable way.

2.5.2. Global Energy Status: Model for Prospective Solution

The global energy consumption share from different sources is shown in Table 2.5.1. The analysis carried out by EIA (2006a) showed that oil remains the dominant energy source followed by coal and natural gas. It is projected that the nuclear energy production will also increase by more than two times by the year 2030. Energy sources such as biomass, solar, and hydro will not be increased significantly compared to the total energy consumption. Renewable energy sources supply 17% of the world's primary energy. They include traditional biomass, large and small hydropower, wind, solar geothermal, and biofuels (Martinot, 2005).

The total global energy consumption today is approximately 14.5 terawatts, equivalent to 220 million barrels of oil per day (Smalley, 2005). The global population rise will to settle somewhere in 10 billion by 2050 based on the current average population increase (WEC, 2005). The per capita energy consumption is still rising in the developing countries as well as in developed countries. However, almost half of the world's population in the developing countries still relies on traditional biomass sources to meet their energy needs. Smalley (2005) argued that to meet the energy requirements for almost 10 billion people on the Earth by 2050, approximately 60 terawatts of energy is required, which is equivalent to some 900 million barrels of oil per day. According to him, major reservoirs of the oil will have been used up by that time. Thus, there should be some alternatives to fulfill such huge energy requirement to maintain the growing economic development.

Table 2.5.1. World Total Energy Consumption by Source from 1990-2030 (Quadrillion Btu) (EIA, 2006b)

Source	History				Projections				Ave. Annual
	1990	2002	2003	2010	2015	2020	2025	2030	% Change
Oil	136.1	158.7	162.1	191.0	210.5	229.8	254.9	277.5	2.0
Natural Gas	75.20	95.90	99.10	126.6	149.1	170.1	189.8	218.5	3.0
Coal	89.40	96.80	100.4	132.2	152.9	176.5	202.8	231.5	3.1
Nuclear	20.40	26.70	26.50	28.90	31.10	32.90	34.00	34.70	1.0
Others	28.30	32.20	32.70	45.80	50.60	58.80	64.10	73.20	3.0
Total	47.30	410.3	420.7	524.2	594.2	666.0	745.6	835.4	2.6

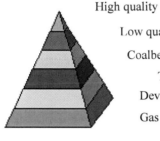

High quality
Low quality
Coalbed gas
Tight gas
Devonion shale gas
Gas hydrates

Light Oil $>20^0$API

Heavy Oil (10-20^{0}API)

Bitumen <10^{0}API

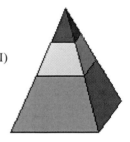

Figure 2.5.7. Worldwide Oil and Natural Gas Resource Base (after Stosur, 2000).

The point that Smalley does not make is that the need for an alternate source does not arise from the apparent depletion of petroleum basins. In fact, some 60% of a petroleum reservoir is left unrecovered even when a reservoir is called 'depleted' (Stosur, 2000). It is expected that with more appropriate technologies, the current recoverable reserves will double. It is well known that the world has more heavy oil and tar sands than the 'recoverable' light oil (Figure 2.5.7). It is expected that technologies will emerge so that heavy oil, tar sands, and even coal are extracted and processed economically without compromising the environment. This will need drastic change in practically all aspects of oil and gas operations (Khan and Islam, 2007b). However, the immediate outcome would be that all negative impacts of petroleum operations and usage will be eradicated, erasing the boundary between renewable and non-renewable energy sources.

Figure 2.5.7 indicates the similar trend for natural gas reserves. The conventional technology is able to recover lighter gases, which are relatively at lower depths. Recently, more focus is being placed to develop technologies in order to recover the coalbed methane. There are still large reserves of tight gas, devonian shale gas and gas hydrates. It is expected that new technologies will emerge to economically recover the deeper gas and hydrates so that natural gas can contribute significantly to the global fuel scenario. The problem with natural gas industry currently is that it uses highly toxic glycol for dehydration and amines for the removal of carbon dioxide and hydrogen sulfide (Chhetri and Islam, 2006a). Oxidation of glycol produces carbon monoxide which is highly poisonous gas and amines form carcinogens with other oxidation products. Hence, the use of processed natural gas is hazardous to human health and the environment. Chhetri and Islam (2006a) proposed the use of natural clay material for the dehydration of natural gas and use of natural oil to remove the carbon dioxide and hydrogen sulfides from the natural gas streams. This offers truly natural alternative for the gas processing which has no environmental impacts and at the same time reduces the gas processing cost significantly.

Smalley (2005) also missed the most important reason why the correctly used *modus operandi* in energy management is unsustainable. With current practices, thousands of toxic chemicals are produced at every stage of the operation. Many of these toxic products are manufactured deliberately in name of value addition (The Globe and Mail, 2006). These products would have no room to be circulated in a civic society if it was not for the lack of long-term economic considerations (Zatzman and Islam, 2007a). These products are routinely touted as cheap alternatives to natural products. This has two immediate problems associated to it. First, natural products used to be the most abundant and, hence, the cheapest. The fact that they became more expensive and often rare has nothing to do with free market economy and natural justice. In fact, this is the testimony of the type of manipulation and market distortion that have become synonymous with Enron, World dot com and others, which failed due to corrupt management policies. The second problem with touting toxic materials as cheap (hence, affordable) is that the long term costs are hidden. If long term costs and liabilities were incorporated, none of the products would remotely emerge as cheap.

It has been considered that most of the economic hydropower sources have been already exploited. However, hydropower is a continuous source and still there exists huge untapped hydropower resources. Moreover, there is a huge potential to generate power from ocean thermal and tidal energy sources. These resources have great promise but yet to be commercialized. These sources are more feasible in isolated islands as power transportation in such islands is difficult. Tidal energy has also a great potential but depends on the sea tides, which are intermittent. Biomass is a truly renewable source of energy, however, sustainable harvesting and replenishment is a major challenge in utilizing this resource. This is the major energy source for almost half of the world's population residing in the developing countries. It is also argued that increasing the use of biomass energy would limit the arable land to grow food for increased population. Global share of biomass energy is less than 1% (Martinot, 2005). Even though it is location specific, wind energy is a clean energy source and its development is increasing rapidly. This will be an effective supplement for other renewable energy resource to meet the global energy requirement for the long term.

Nuclear energy has been the most debated source of energy. It has been argued that the development of nuclear energy reduces the greenhouse gas emission. The detailed analysis showed that the nuclear energy creates unrecoverable environmental impacts because of the nuclear radiations and particle emission, which have very long half life. The nuclear disasters which the world has already witnessed are not affordable. The safe disposal of nuclear waste has yet to be worked out and is proving to be an absurd concept. Bradley (2006) reported that the disposal of spent fuel has been in debate for a long time and has not yet been solved.

Hydrogen energy is considered as the major energy carrier for the 21st century but the current mode of hydrogen production is not sustainable. Use of electricity to electrolyze to produce electricity becomes a vicious cycle which has very little or no benefit. The search of hydrogen production from biological method is an innovative idea which is yet to be established commercially. The most debated problem in hydrogen energy is the storage and transportation of energy. However, hydrogen production using the solar heating has a good promise. Geothermal energy involves high drilling costs reducing its economic feasibility.

The geothermal electricity generation is characterized by low efficiency. However, the application of direct heat for industrial processes or other uses would contribute significantly. The problems and prospect of each of the energy sources are discussed below.

Solar Energy

Solar is the most important source of energy in terms of life survival as well as in terms of energy source. Service (2005) reported that the earth receives 170,000 terawatts of energy every moment everyday. This means that every hour, earth's surface receives more energy from the sun than what humans consume in an entire year. The only challenge is how to use this huge energy source in a sustainable way for the benefit of mankind. The conventional way of utilizing solar electric energy is extremely inefficient. For example, solar electric conversion has efficiency of approximately 15%. This is further reduced if global efficiency is considered (Khan et al., 2007d). Despite the availability of such huge source of energy, the current technological development is unable to exploit this resource to fulfill the global energy requirements due to lack of appropriate technology.

As argued by Service (2005), solar energy is one of the most expensive renewable energy technologies on the current market and far more expensive than the competition (Table 2.5.2). Solar energy is mostly used for water heating and lighting. For water heating, the direct solar energy is utilized. Even though the initial investment cost of the direct water heating system is comparatively high, it is a one-time investment that lasts for 20-30 years, it becomes economical in the long term. The efficiency of the conventional heating system can be significantly increased by using waste vegetable oil as heating fluid instead of directly heating water (Khan et al., 2007d). The maximum theoretical temperature for water heating is 100^0C whereas heating the vegetable oil using solar concentrators can increase the temperature some three folds higher than that of conventional water heating. The energy of heated oil can then be transferred through suitable heat exchangers for various processes including industrial and household processes. Hence, direct application of solar energy has very high efficiency with no negative environmental impacts.

Khan et al.(2007d) developed a thermally driven refrigeration system that runs on single pressure cycle. This refrigerator runs on single pressure refrigeration cycle which is a thermally driven cycle using three fluids. Thermal driving force is derived from direct use of solar energy. This is very efficient system which has no moving parts and have extremely high efficiency. Similarly, Khan et al. (2007d) developed a direct solar heating system that utilizes the waste vegetable oil as thermal fluid. With parabolic solar collector, the temperature of the fluid can reach more than 300^0 Celsius with efficiency more than 70%. Direct use of solar energy for heating or generating solar electricity can significantly contribute to the global energy problem. Recently it has been reported that heat engines can be used in order to capitalize from heat differences at any place. Such heat engines can even run in a low-temperature difference (Website 4). It is envisaged that the temperature difference of a wood fired stove and outside temperature can be effectively used to run such heat engines. Such a principle is utilized in the ocean thermal technology, where temperature difference between the two anticlines of the sea could potentially generate a heat difference of 10^0-20^0 Celsius.

Lighting is one of the most widespread uses of solar energy. The current technological development has gone in such a direction that creates artificial crisis for energy. We first shade the sunlight by erecting some structures and create artificial light using fossil fuels to light billions of homes, offices and industries. If we can properly utilizing day light at least during the day, it would save huge money, health and environment.

Table 2.5.2. Unit Cost of Various Energy Technologies

Energy Technology	Cost per kW ($)	Reference
Solar	0.25-0.50	Service (2005)
Wind	0.05-0.07	Service (2005)
Natural gas	0.025-0.05	Service (2005)
Coal	0.01-0.04	Service (2005)
Nuclear	0.037	Uranium Information Center, 2006

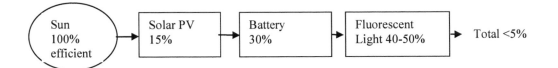

Figure 2.5.8. Pathway of generating artificial light from natural sun light (Chhetri, 2007).

A large amount of fossil fuels are being burnt just to create artificial lighting which produces severe environmental problems and impact on living beings. Developing technologies to create healthy light for the night time with renewable sources such as light from biogas from wastes would provide an environmental friendly and zero waste solution. Figure 2.5.8 shows the pathway of producing light from solar energy. The efficiency of such solar panel is around 15%. The solar panels are made of silicon cells, which are very inefficient in hot climate areas and are inherently toxic as they consist of heavy metals, such as, silicon, chromium, lead and others. The energy is stored in batteries for night time operations. These batteries are exhaustible and have short life even if they are rechargeable. The batteries have maximum efficiency of some 30 % (Fraas et al., 1986). Conversion from batteries into fluorescent light has efficiency of about 40-50%. Thus considering local efficiency of all the components in the system in Figure 6, the global efficiency of the system is less than 5%. Sunlight which is perfectly natural and 100% efficient, is converted to less than 5% efficient artificial light, which is toxic and harmful to human health. Solar panels are widely used for lighting in isolated areas where other sources of energy are not available. Moreover, the embodied energy of the solar cells is very high and emits huge amount of CO_2 due to the fossil fuel use during manufacturing of the solar cells. The most modern batteries are more toxic than earlier types, filled with mostly heavy metals. The batteries are covered with plastic and toxic inside are one of the most environmental polluting components (Islam et al., 2006). The severity is particularly intense when they are allowed to oxidize. Note that oxidation takes place at any temperature. The final converter into artificial light is the 'inert' gas filled tubes continue to radiate very toxic light. Thus the value of light from sunlight to artificial toxic light has decreased as the steps of processing increased. It is obvious that the more technology is processed, the more harmful it becomes and has the less value in terms of environmental impact and global efficiency (Figure 2.5.9). This illustration is equally valid for each and every technology developed after the industrial revolution (Zatzman and Islam, 2007a; Khan and Islam, 2007a).

Despite sun being the largest energy source, the solar electricity with current technology cannot be the solution for the global energy problem. Use of electricity for various end uses is also debatable. For example, using electricity for cooking is not a natural phenomenon. Microwave cooking is most fashionable way of cooking in modern society. It has been reported that microwave cooking destroyed more than 97% flavonoids in broccoli, 55% chlorogenic acid loss occurred in potato and 65% quercetin content loss was reported in Tomato (Vallejo et al., 2003). There are several other unnatural compounds formed during electric and electromagnetic cooking which are considered to be carcinogenic based on their pathway analysis. Hence, electricity is not considered good for cooking healthy food.

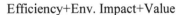

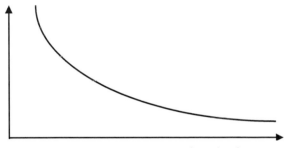

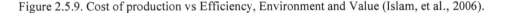

Cost of production

Figure 2.5.9. Cost of production vs Efficiency, Environment and Value (Islam, et al., 2006).

Hydropower

Hydropower today provides approximately 19% of the world's electricity consumption (WEC, 2001). Growing evidence of global environmental problems is due to the use of fossil fuels to meet industrial, commercial and domestic requirements. In order to achieve solutions to the environmental problems that the world is facing today requires long term potential actions for sustainable energy development and resource management. Hydropower is one of such renewable energy sources that provide clean energy options for economic development. However, large hydropower development has several environmental and socio-economical consequences. Submergence of upstream land due to large dams creates social as well as environmental problems. The change in the concentration of minerals due to the large volume of water would change the soil microorganism interaction affecting the biodiversity in the area. Submergence of land area results in the displacement of inhabitants in the project areas, changing the land use pattern which would significantly affect the social features, albeit being site specific.

Pokharel et al.(2007) reported that only small, mini and micro-hydro systems, which do not have negative impacts to the environment are sustainable and manageable by the local community. The world hydropower potential is approximately 2360 GW of which approximately 700 GW has already been exploited WEC (2001). The development of half of the total hydro potential could lead to the reduction of approximately 13% greenhouse gas emission due to avoidance to the use of fossil fuel (WEC, 2001). A careful planning and development of hydropower projects to have the minimum social and environmental impact in the project areas is crucial. Hydropower, especially the small, mini and micro-hydro power development is a key to addressing the global environmental problems caused due to the energy generation.

Ocean Thermal, Wave and Tidal Energy

Ocean Thermal Energy Conversion (OTEC) utilizes the useful energy due to the temperature difference of surface water and water at a depth of approximately 1000 meters which would provide a temperature difference of approximately 20^0C. OTEC is very useful energy source in the islands as it is difficult to supply energy from inlands due to the transportation problems. Even though this is a clean source of energy, governments and developers are reluctant to invest in this technology because it is yet to be tested. OTEC is in the early stages of development and pilot studies. The capital cost for OTEC is very high because of heat exchangers, long pipes and large turbines (Tanner, 1995). The global efficiency OTEC becomes lower due to the involvement of series of units such as pumps, evaporator, condenser, separator, turbines and generators. However, this is a clean source of energy and could contribute significantly in the islands and coastal areas and has great potential to avoid emission of greenhouse gases.

Thorpe (1998) reported that wave energy alone can contribute approximately 10% of the current level of world electricity supply. Currently, tidal and wave energy represent a largely ignored renewable energy resources. The worldwide potential of wave power is in the order of 1-10 TW (Voss, 1979). Even though wave energy is in the early stages of development, it holds a good promise and is an effective alternative of the greenhouse gas emission due to the use of fossil fuels. Similarly, the global potential of tidal energy is approximately 3 TW but only in certain locations of the world exists natural conditions for technical and economic viability (Voss, 1979). However, more research and technological development towards utilizing these clean resources would have great impact in the future energy scenario. Finally, the potential of this tidal energy directly, rather than generating electricity, must be studied.

Wind Energy

The world market for wind energy technologies has grown dramatically in recent years. Before 2000, a small number of European companies dominated the production of wind turbines but the situation substantially changed when wind power development in US, China, and India substantially increased. Global wind power generating capacity has reached to 59,322 megawatts (MW) as of 2005 (GWEC, 2006). This is 25% growth over one year period. Wind is the world's fastest-growing energy source on a percentage basis. The wind turbines installed in the year 2005 alone was 11,769 MW (GWEC, 2006). Figure 2.5.10 shows the wind power capacity of world's top ten wind producing countries. It has further been reported that by 2010, wind energy alone will save enough greenhouse gas emissions to meet one third of the European Union's Kyoto obligation (GWEC, 2006). North America has the highest capacity installed in 2005, 37% higher than the previous year. Similarly the growth of wind energy capacity in Canada was 53% in 2005 (GWEC, 2006). Asian countries especially India and China have experienced strong growth of over 46% of installed capacity, bringing in total capacity to 7135 MW. In 2005 alone, the Asian continent accounted for 19% of new installations.

Despite wind energy is a clean and natural source of energy, it generally cannot compete with fossil fuel resources if environmental impact of fossil fuels is not considered. It is considered feasible only in the places where there is no fossil fuel and needs the quick installation. There are various policies in place to support wind power development globally. The Clean Development Mechanism (CDM) of Kyoto Protocol supports fund for wind energy development. However, due to the significant bureaucratic formalities, the approval of the projects is very slow and tedious. The baselining, additionality and certified emission reduction have to be fulfilled as prerequisite for CDM funding. Besides this, investors should demonstrate that emission reductions are "additional" to any that would occur in the absence of the certified project activities. The past experience showed that by 2003, only 49 projects out of 1030 submitted were approved (Pershing and Cedric, 2002). Thus, the CDM model cannot help fulfill the Kyoto emission reduction requirements practically. Since wind energy is highly location specific, local community organization, co-operatives, local and provincial government should be the part of the wind power development in order to achieve the true sustainability in its development (Chhetri et al., 2006a).

Even though wind energy is considered a clean energy source, there are several adverse environmental impacts associated with it. It creates noise in the areas where large wind farms have been installed. The wind turbines can scatter electromagnetic communication signals and create problems for flying creatures such as airplane threatening the security of several lives. Moreover, converting wind to electricity is not good to better option, meaning it is not a pro-nature process and hence not sustainable. It is widely considered that wind energy can contribute significantly for the reduction of greenhouse gas emission. However, decreasing greenhouse gas emission is not an accomplishment. In fact, the technology development should be in such a way that none of the technologies are allowed to emit greenhouse gases.

Bioenergy

Biomass remained the most important source of energy from the beginning of civilization. Biomass includes wood fuels, agro-fuels and waste or byproducts (Figure 2.5.11). Almost half of the world's population, especially people in the developing countries, is heavily dependent on this source. This will remain an important source of energy for humanity as this is a readily renewable source. Replenishment of biomass in sustainable way is essential to maintaining the largest carbon sink in the planet. IEA (2004) reported that the use of biomass in developing countries will increase from 886 mtoe in 1997 to 1103 mtoe in 2020 at annual growth rate of 1%. Biomass resources are potentially the world's largest and most sustainable energy source - a renewable resource comprising 220 billion oven-dry tonnes (about 4500 EJ) of annual primary production (Hall & Rao, 1999). The annual bio-energy potential is about 2900 EJ, though only 270 EJ could be considered available on a sustainable basis and at competitive prices. The key issue is not the availability of biomass but sustainable management and delivery of energy to those who are in real need.

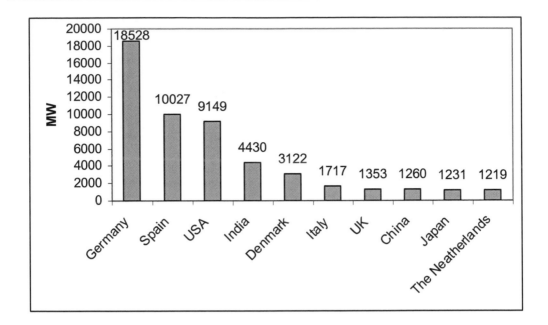

Figure 2.5.10. Top ten wind producing (source: GWEC, 2006).

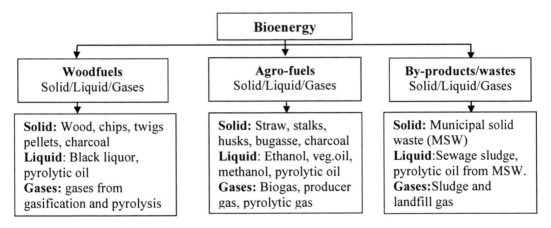

Figure 2.5.11. Bioenergy classification based on source.

Fuelwood

Wood is the most abundantly available and widely used resources especially in developing countries. It is a most conventional and major form of biomass used for cooking, heating and converting into other forms of energy such as liquid or gas. Wood is either directly harvested for cooking and space heating or can be from waste streams from various industries. Combustion of wood in traditional stoves has relatively low efficiency in the ranges of 10-14 % (Shastri et al., 2002). Chhetri (1997) reported from the experimental investigation that some of the stoves designed precisely reached the efficiency of up to 20 %. Some improved cookstoves have efficiency up to 25% (Kaoma and Kasali, 1994). However, the conventional efficiency calculation is based on calculating the local efficiency considering only the energy input and heat output in the system itself. This method does not consider the utilization of byproducts, the fresh CO_2 released after wood burning which is essential for the plant photosynthesis, use of exhaust heat for household water heating, use of ash as surfactant or as fertilizer and good sources of natural minerals such silica, potassium, sodium, calcium and others.

Wood ash is very rich source of silica which is an important source for industrial applications. The ash also contains various minerals such as potassium, sodium, magnesium, calcium and others. Conventionally, ash has been in use as a source of fertilizer because of its high mineral content. It is also a truly natural detergent. Sodium or potassium can also be extracted from wood ash to use as saponification agent for soap making from vegetable oils and animal or fish fats. A fine wood ash is a very good raw material for making non toxic tooth paste. Chhetri and Islam (2006b) reported that wood ash can be extracted to use as natural catalyst for the transesterification of vegetable oil to produce biodiesel for diesel substitute. Rahman et al. (2004) reported that Maple wood ash has the potential to adsorb both Arsenic (III) and Arsenic (V) from contaminated aqueous streams at low concentration levels without any chemical treatment. Static tests showed up to 80% arsenic removal and in various dynamic column tests the arsenic concentration was reduced from 500 ppb to lower than 5ppb. Moreover, in eastern culture, ash is used traditionally as a water disinfecting agent possibly because of some mineral content in it. However, detailed scientific research on this topic is only beginning to surface (Rahman et al., 2006). Hence, by-products of wood burning have several beneficial applications keeping the environment clean and safe provided wood is harvested and replenished in a sustainable way.

Khan et al., (2007a) developed an energy efficient stove fuelled by compacted saw dust that utilizes exhaust heat coming from flue gas for household water heating. A simple heat exchanger was used to transfer heat from flue gas to cold water. They also designed an oil-water trap to trap all particulate matters emitted from wood combustion. The particulates or the carbon soot collected from oil-water mixture is a very good nano-material which has very high industrial demand. The soot can be used as a non toxic paint also. When the particulates are trapped into oil-water trap and the heat is extracted for water heating, the CO_2 emitted is a 'fresh' or 'new' CO_2 which is most favored by plants during photosynthesis (Chhetri et al, 2007a). Combustion of woodfuel thus does not contribute to the greenhouse effect. Other products of combustion such as NOx and formaldehyde are also not harmful compared to the similar products from fossil fuel burning. The heat loss in the heater itself will contribute small amount of heat loss that lowers the local efficiency somewhat. Assuming the 5-10% radiation and conduction loss, the global efficiency of wood combustion in the stove is considered to be more than 90%. Thus, wood combustion in effectively designed stoves has one of the highest efficiency among the combustion technologies.

Energy from waste is the second-largest source of biomass energy. The main contributors of this source are municipal solid waste (MSW), manufacturing waste, and landfill gases. These wastes can be converted to energy by anaerobic digestion to produce biogas which can be used for cooking, fuel for transportation and lighting. Ethanol from corn or sugar cane and biodiesel from waste vegetable oils and animal fats are major sources. Charcoal and pellets are made from firewood. Agro-fuel is another important source of energy which is grown naturally, planted for food production purposes or planted as energy crops. Ethanol, biogas and pyrolytic gases are produced from agro-fuels and used for transportation and stationery engines. By-products of biomass or wastes generated from domestic and public activities generate large amount of organic waste which are important sources of energy. Utilizing waste as energy source not only helps to solve the energy problem but also support clean the environment leading to zero-waste living. There are several technologies to convert biomass into electricity such as gasification and conventional steam cycles through the pyrolytic gases. However, large amount of energy is involved during such processes and the efficiency is significantly reduced and thus is not technically attractive. Moreover, biomass to electricity conversion utilizes various catalysts which make the system costly.

Liquid Biofuels

Bioethanol

Biofuels have been drawing considerable attention recently due to the disadvantages of fossil fuels (emission of green house gases, unsustainable supply) that produce large amount of CO_2 during a combustion process. Among the liquid biofuels, ethanol has the major contribution in the transportation sector. Lignocellulosic biomass contains 40-60% of cellulose and 20-40% of hemi cellulose two third of which are polysaccharides that can be hydrolyzed to sugars and then fermented to ethanol. Ethanol can be easily burned in today's internal combustion engines to substitute gasoline.

The worldwide gasoline use in transportation industry is about 1200 billion liters/year (Martinot, 2005). The total ethanol production as of 2004 is approximately 32 billion litres/year. Brazil is the leading country to use ethanol as transportation fuel. Globally, there is a huge gap between the gasoline use and supply of ethanol to substitute the gasoline in the current market. Ethanol is being produced from various biomass sources such as corn, sugarcane, sweet sorghum, switch grass and other food grains. During the pretreatment, the biomass is sized, cleaned and pretreated with low concentration acid to hydrolyze the hemicellulose and expose for hydrolysis. Different kinds of acids, bases, high temperature steam and carbon dioxides are used for pretreatment. In acid hydrolysis, dilute sulfuric acid, hydrochloric acid or nitric acids are used. In alkaline treatment, sodium hydroxide and calcium hydroxide are most common. One of the major objectives of the pretreatments is to remove the lignin part, which cannot be fermented and convert the hemicellulose into fermentable sugars. Pretreatments are generally done by physical methods includes high steam pressure explosion process, CO_2 explosion, nitrogen explosion and hot water treatment. Biological pretreatment includes treatment of biomass by fungus. After the pretreatment, the cellulose is hydrolyzed into glucose sugar with concentrated hydrochloric or sulfuric acids or enzymes as catalysts.

The ethanol production process is highly toxic as the process utilizes various toxic chemicals in series of processes. Hydrochloric and sulfuric acids, synthetic sodium hydroxide and calcium hydroxide are highly toxic and corrosive chemicals. The enzyme hydrolysis method uses various synthetic surfactants to accelerate the reaction. The products of burning such contaminated fuel would emit toxic pollutants and pose severe environmental and health problems. These toxic chemicals contribute to water pollution that makes water treatment process unsafe and expensive. The pretreatment, hydrolysis and other processes used high heat and pressure, which themselves require fossil fuel combustion. Thus the conventional method of using the fossil fuel as primary energy input to methanol production makes the whole process unsustainable. Enzymatic hydrolysis is technically feasible and environmentally sound, acid hydrolysis is available more commercially.

Biodiesel

Due to the several environmental impacts caused by burning petrodiesel, considerable efforts have been made to develop biodiesel to replace petrodiesel. Biodiesel is produced from the transesterification of vegetable oils using alcohols such as methanol or ethanol as medium and hydroxides of potassium and sodium as catalysts. Despite the fact that biodiesel is produced from the renewable resources such as vegetable oil, the pathway of conventional biodiesel is similar to that of petrodiesel. A recent EPA (2002) report indicated that even though biodiesel has less toxic pollution compared to petroleum diesel, combustion of biodiesel still produces all types of toxic emission as that of petrodiesel such as benzene, acetaldehyde, toluene, formaldehyde, acrolein, PAHs, xylene (Table 2.5.4). The use of excessive heat, chemicals, and catalysts adds toxicity in the resulting biodiesel and makes the process expensive, highly unsustainable and create similar impacts on the environment. Various additives used for biodiesel production lead to the formation of sediments and other insoluble residues making the biodiesel even worse. Formation of sediment or gum can result in operational problems with plugging and fouling at the end-use equipment. Moreover, since current biodiesel production is dependent on the methanol from oil refineries, there is no future of developing biodiesel if fossil fuels are considered depleting. If the methanol can be made from organic waste, then this methanol could not only help to utilize waste to produce valuable production, but also would be a non toxic product unlike refinery methanol. Refinery methanol is considered one of the major contributors that contribute weathering of the rubber parts in the engine due to use of biodiesel.

Table 2.5.4. Difference in average toxic effects at two biodiesel blend levels (EPA, 2002)

Toxins	Average % change compared to base fuel	
	20% biodiesel	100% biodiesel
Acetaldehyde	-7.10	-14.40
Acrolein	-1.50	-8.50
Benzene	16.50	-0.80
1,3-butadiene	39.00	-12.30
Ethylbenzene	-44.90	-61.00
Formaldehyde	-7.80	-15.10
n-hexane	-48.70	-12.10
Naphthalene	-13.80	-26.70
Styrene	-3.70	39.30
Toluene	19.90	13.30
Xylene	-12.30	-39.50

Several studies have been done to make the biodiesel fuel competitive to the petrodiesel. Feedstock and processing are the major activities which make the biodiesel fuel more expensive. Hence, development of least cost process and cheap feedstock are of prime concern today. Boocock et al. (1996) developed a method for biodiesel production at room temperature without any additional heat. This process uses methanol as alcoholysis medium, tetrahydrofuran (THF) from biological origin to create oil dominant one phase system in which methanolysis speeds up dramatically faster. The separation of THF is also not difficult as its boiling point is similar to that of methanol. Mahajan et al. (2006) reported that using

THF as a co-solvent, the mass transfer problems from during the transesterification reaction for developing methanol oil system as oil dominated one phase system. The main objective of mixing THF is to convert low acid number vegetable oils into standard biodiesel in a single chemical reaction using certain catalysts. Mixing THF reduces the mechanical mixing that is conventional done during transesterification reaction.

It was recently reported that excellent results were obtained for biodiesel making from an alkaline transesterification reaction of soybean oil using ultrasonic mixing (Colucci et al., 2005). Ultrasonic agitation offers complete mixing at lower temperature (25-60^0C) and increases the reaction rate for to five times higher than those reported for mechanical agitation. The possible reasons for this was considered due to the increase in interfacial area and activity of microscopic and macroscopic bubbles formed when ultrasonic waves of 20 kHz were applied in two phase reaction system. Similar study reported that by using ultrasounds (28-40 kHz) for mixing, catalysts requirements were reduced 2-3 times lower than conventional method and reaction took place in much shorter (10-40 minutes) time (Stavarache et al., 2006). Biodiesel yields obtained when 28 kHz frequency was 98-99%. Zhu and Tsuchiya (2005) reported that using ultrasound for biodiesel production does not need external heating and stirring apparatus leading to a compact design for producing biodiesel fuels. Even though ultrasound could play big role in processing and economics of biodiesel, the catalysts and fossil methanol being used for the reaction still remains problematic due to their toxicity. Generating ultrasound energy using fossil fuels could eventually lead to the environmental problems. Hence some natural source for creating ultrasound energy using solar energy could be a better option for its long term sustainability.

Chhetri and Islam (2006b) developed a process that uses truly natural catalysts and non toxic chemicals to use in the biodiesel as catalysts and the alcoholysis medium. Natural catalysts such as hydroxides from wood ash and methanol from renewable green source can make the biodiesel process truly green. Recently it has been reported sugar, which is a non-toxic and inexpensive, can be used as catalysts for biodiesel production (Toda et al., 2005). However, they used sulfuric acid for the sulphonation to form the aromatic rings to use as catalysts. Biodiesel could be contaminated by the sulfuric acid creating similar problems as that of conventional biodiesel. If sugar can be used from natural origin which has no synthetic chemicals in it and without sulphonation, this could become a good non-toxic catalyst. It has also been reported that charred sugar as solid catalysts could be reused for several time. Using natural sugar as natural catalysts could help in reducing the toxicity in the waste stream. The feedstock for biodiesel has a great role to play in order to reduce the higher cost of biodiesel. Non edible oils such as Jatropha, pongamia and others can revolutionize the biodiesel industry as this will not have competition with the food for humans.

Liquid biofuels are considered major transportation fuels for future. Producing liquid biofuels such as ethanol and biodiesel with natural methods without using toxic catalysts and chemicals will significantly contribute for keeping the environment safe. Since these fuels are produced from various biomass feedstocks, this can make countries independent from importing fossil fuels from abroad. Development of these biofuels would offer opportunity for energy securities as these are renewable fuels sustainable for longer term. Despite these biofuels are considered slightly costlier than fossil fuels, these fuels are cheaper if one considers the environmental benefits compared to their counterparts. Fossil fuels are highly operated by few corporations and none of the public or communities have any inputs for their development making rest of the world vulnerable in terms of economics. Development of biofuels on the other hand can be easily produced by communities or even individuals that will eventually lead to economically attractive and sustainable in the long term.

Nuclear Energy

Nuclear energy comes from uranium, a metal mined from the natural ores. Nuclear energy is produced from the fission process where splitting of the nuclei takes place to produce heat. In the nuclear reactor, the energy produced is used to heat the water to make the steam and the steam turbine run the generator to produce electricity. Naturally occurring uranium consists of approximately 99.28 percent ^{238}U and 0.71 percent ^{235}U. Uranium-235, uranium-238, Plutonium 239 are the fissile materials which produces fission reaction in today's nuclear power plant, however, ^{235}U is the main fissile material used for energy production (Letcher and Williamson, 2004). However, the concentration of natural uranium is not feasible for current conversion technology and needs substantial enrichment. EIA (2005) reported that most of the ores in the United States contains 0.05-0.3% uranium oxide (U_3O_8) ^{235}U is enriched from a concentration of 0.7 % to approximately 2-5 %. Enrichment of uranium consists of various processes such as gaseous-diffusion and centrifugal isotope separation. Because the uranium separation achieved per diffusion is extremely low, the gas must pass through some 1400 stages to obtain a product with a concentration of 3-4% (Uranium Enrichment, 2006). EIA (2006b) reported that the total world nuclear energy consumption was 2.523 trillion kWh. Based on the current trend, the total nuclear power development projected for 2030 is 3.239 trillion kWh. It seems that the nuclear energy will not take the major share of energy supply even by 2030.

Nuclear energy has severe environmental concerns (Chhetri, 2007). One of the major concerns of the nuclear fuel is the safe disposal of spent fuel either from the spent fuel of the reactors or waste from reprocessing plants. The gaseous diffusion process has a possibility of UF6 release from the 'enriched' uranium. This process emits highly radioactive radiation, gases and rays such as α and β particles. Wise Uranium Project (2005) reported that the half lives of natural uranium isotopes U-234 is 244,500 years, U-235 is 7.03 x 10^8 years and that of U-238 are 4.468 x 10^9 years. These are the half lives for natural uranium. But when the uranium is 'enriched', these might have longer half lives than natural uranium and nature does not recognize such 'enriched' uranium and hence does not biodegrade. The α radiation from uranium processing has high possibility of causing cancer to the living body, the danger being higher with enriched uranium. The combustion products of depleted uranium such as uranium trioxide (UO_3) and others do not behave as that of natural uranium and has several health hazards (Salbu et al., 2005).

Nuclear power plants pose environmental threats in many ways. First, the nuclear reactors release radioactive waste which is extremely harmful to the human and environment. The extraction of uranium, mining, milling, conversion to Uranium hexafluoride also produces radioactive waste. Moreover, various uranium processing steps such as extraction, mining, milling, conversion and enrichment process uses huge amount of fossil fuel producing lots of carbon dioxide and other air emissions. Thus, nuclear power plant are not reducing global CO_2 emission but adding hazardous pollution into the environment. The sequestration of spent uranium inside the geological traps will pose long term effects to the biodiversity and global environment. Moreover, the cooling systems require huge amount of water which is much higher than used by any other fossil fuel plants. The impact of hot water discharged on large water bodies and aquatic systems are more significant than any other fuel processing technologies. Most importantly, the possible failure of the nuclear power plants could create big catastrophic accidents with severe consequences for living beings.

It is claimed that nuclear power plants are one of the most efficient technologies. The local efficiency of nuclear energy conversion has been reported to reach up to 50% (Ion, 1997). Uranium extraction consists of expensive leaching process during mining as well as hundreds of stages of gas diffusion or centrifugation required for the uranium enrichment. A conventional mining has efficiency of about 80% efficiency (Website 5). In a milling process, which is a chemical plant and usually uses sulfuric acid for leaching, about 90 % of the uranium is extracted (Website 5). There is also a significant conversion loss in the conversion of uranium to UF6, the efficiency of which is usually considered less than 70%, and enrichment efficiency is less than 20%. Considering the 50% thermal to net electric conversion and 90% efficiency in transmission and distribution, the global efficiency of the nuclear processing technology is considered to be lower than 5%. If we consider the environmental impact caused by radioactive hazards and the cost of the overall system including disposal of uranium spent fuel, the global efficiency would be further lowered. As nuclear technology uses large amount of fossil fuel for its processing, the life of nuclear technology will last until the fossil fuel remain in use. Moreover, the total uranium available in the world is considered exhaustible. However, as a natural process, formation of uranium should continue for ever as every process on earth is reversible.

Service (2005) reported that despite number of discussions in political arena, there is not a single nuclear power plant built in USA after 1973. He further argued that even if we want to supply $1/3^{rd}$ of the energy demand which is approximately 10 Terrawatt (TW) by 2050, that means 10,000 nuclear power plants each producing a gigawatt of power are needed. This is equivalent to opening one reactor every other day for next 50 years, which is beyond imagination. High upfront capital costs, waste disposal, corporate liability and nuclear proliferation are the major concerns while developing nuclear energy. Thus nuclear energy is not going to be the panacea for the global energy supply as many argue today.

The extreme hot summer in Europe is restricting nuclear energy generation and showing up the limits of nuclear power Godoy (2006). The heat waves have led authorities in France, Germany, Spain and elsewhere in Europe to override their own environmental norms on the maximum temperature of water drained from the plants' cooling systems. The justification offered to support this issue was to guarantee the provision of electricity for the country. Of the 58 nuclear power plants, 37 are situated at the bank of the rivers and use them as outlet for water from their cooling system. The environmental rules limit the maximum temperature for waste water in order to protect river flora and fauna. Hot water temperature likely leads to high concentrations of ammociac which is potentially toxic to river fauna. It was recently reported that one of eight Spanish nuclear reactors was shut down due to the high temperatures recorded in the river Ebro, into which the reactor drains the water used in its cooling system. It indicates that nuclear energy has several limitations for its use. Generating electricity at the cost of environment is based on extremely short-term approach and is truly anti-natural. This is one of the several misinformation yet given to the public from the scientific community who touted nuclear energy as cleaner fuel.

Despite huge sum of money has been spent in favor of nuclear energy in order to advocate nuclear energy is clean and does not contribute global warming, this perpetration is no longer valid. The nuclear industry still lacks to find the answers of several environmental and public safety concerns. All part of nuclear fuel cycle from uranium mining, milling, enrichment and processing emit hazardous radiation. Nuclear accidents, leaks and releases of radiation are common phenomena in the nuclear industry. There is no safe level of nuclear radiation in any form of the operation of nuclear activities. There is not a single place on the earth where the waste of the enriched uranium can be safely disposed. Despite industries' repetitively assurance for safe disposal of waste, the problem remains unsolved and never be solved. Moreover, hot summers due to global warming are hitting to the water resources such as rivers, an essential component of cooling system in the nuclear plants. This is no more explanation needed to tell that global warming is showing the limits of nuclear power plants and nuclear power plants are destroying the natural environment irreversibly.

Nuclear power is promoted as a solution to the global warming based on the consideration that CO_2 is not emitted from the power plant. However, considerable fossil fuels are used during mining, milling, fuel enrichment, manufacturing and plant and equipment construction. Considering the life cycle CO_2 emission of the nuclear power system, it appears that nuclear power plants emit significant amount of CO_2 from mining to production. Mortimer (1989) reported that nuclear power releases 4-5 times more CO_2 than equivalent power production from other renewable energy systems. Besides this, nuclear industry generates various wastes such as gloves, clothing, tools, equipment and others which are contaminated with radioactivity and disposal of such waste is debatable. Hence, ignoring the history of nuclear issues and fundamental realities of the nuclear fuel cycle, the power generation from nuclear plants is absurd model. The nuclear energy neither solves the global energy problem nor helps in reversing global warming.

Geothermal Energy

Geothermal energy is the naturally available energy stored as heat in the earth's interior part. This energy source, as natural steam, hot brine and hot water, has been exploited for decades to generate electricity as well as both in space heating and industrial processes. The heat is transferred from depth to sub-surface regions initially by conduction and then by convection, with geothermal fluids acting as the heat carrier. These geothermal fluids are primarily rainwater penetrated into the Earth's crust from the recharge which is then heated in contact with the hot rocks, accumulated in aquifers at high pressures and temperatures more than $300^{\circ}C$. The temperature in the core of the earth is in the order of $4000^{\circ}C$, while active volcanoes erupt lava at about $1200^{\circ}C$ and thermal springs can reach up to $350^{\circ}C$ (WEC,2001). Average geothermal gradient inside the Earth is $30^{0}C$ for each 1000m depth (Rao and Parulekar, 1999). The hydro geothermal energy sources are available in the form of hot water, hot brine and steam at depth less than 3000 m. Petro-geothermal energy resources consists of hot dry rocks at depth below 2000m. The temperature available in the form of mixture of hot water and steam is up to $200^{0}C$.

The efficiency of electricity production from the geothermal source is in the range of 10–17% (Barbier, 2002). The geothermal fluid consists of different types of particulate matters and molten impurities which needs a centrifugation to protect the turbine from weathering. It is clear that conversion of geothermal energy to electricity is not attractive option. However, the direct use of heat for space heating and various industrial processes would significantly increase the thermal efficiency of system. The CO_2 reduction due to the use of geothermal energy would be an added advantage. Geothermal energy is a free source and is an environmental-friendly energy source. The efficiency of geothermal energy can be significantly increased by using thermal fluids such as vegetable oil which can be heated up to 400^0C (Khan et al., 2006a; Khan et al., 2007d). Considering the thermal application without electricity production, the global efficiency of the geothermal energy could be over than 60%. However, geothermal energy involves high drilling costs, which also depend on the type of geology, salinity of fluid, and the constituent particulates in the fluid. WEC (2001) report showed that the total worldwide use of geothermal power offers a contribution both to energy saving (around 26 million tons of oil per year) and to CO_2 emission reduction (80 million tons/year if compared with equivalent oil-fuelled production).

Hydrogen Energy

Hydrogen is a clean fuel and an energy carrier which can be used for broad range of application from transportation to electricity production. Hydrogen has a high energy value and produces no pollution after combustion. Hydrogen is found in many organic compounds such as gasoline, natural gas, methanol, propane and biomass. Hydrogen is produced by electrolysis of water or by applying heat to hydrocarbons which is called hydrogen reforming. Currently, most hydrogen is produced by reforming from the natural gas. Hydrogen is used to produce electricity using fuel cells. The conventional way of producing electricity from hydrogen is that electricity is used to electrolyze water to separate hydrogen and the hydrogen produced is to produce electricity. Electricity production by using electricity for electrolysis becomes a vicious cycle is not an attractive option. Mills et al. (2005) reported that very high temperature reactors with direct solar heating for hydrogen production are attractive options. In the Sulfur–Iodine process, there are virtually no by-products and harmful emissions (Figure 2.5.12). The reaction products such as sulfuric acid can be decomposed at 850^0C and hydrogen formed during the reaction can be decomposed at 400^0C. The systems efficiency can be further enhanced if the waste heat generated during the reaction can be utilized for other purposes such as for desalination process. It was reported that the very high temperature reactors could achieve efficiency of up to 70% (Mills et al., 2005).

International Energy Agency (IEA, 2004) projected that if current policies were not changed, the world's energy demand in 2030 would be 60% higher than in 2003 and the CO_2 emissions would increase by even more than 60%. Due to this reason, non-carbon based energy are being more emphasized. As the energy combustion is responsible for producing various greenhouse gases including CO_2, the non-carbon energy source such as hydrogen that do not produce CO_2 holds good promise. Hydrogen can be used for both mobile and stationary applications. Hydrogen is the stored fuel for fuel cells for the transportation vehicles with water as emission products. Despite being attractive from the environmental point of view, the current cost of hydrogen is very high for the production, storage, transportation and distribution. Since hydrogen is a secondary source of energy, the primary energy source and the primary energy input are very important two factors that determine the economy and feasibility. Reforming natural gas uses very high heat and catalysts making the process problematic to the environment due to toxic effects of catalysts (Khan and Islam, 2007b). The catalysts used in the natural gas processing such as glycol produces carbon monoxide during combustion and oxidation products of amines are carcinogenic (Chhetri and Islam, 2006a). As natural gas has direct application as fuel, reforming the natural gas to produce hydrogen is not a feasible solution. Gasification of biomass has also been envisaged as one of the major future source of hydrogen production. However, biomass gasification and then breakdown of gas into hydrogen will significantly reduce the efficiency of the systems.

The only feasible option would be to use the waste biomass for this purpose. Hydrogen production from some bacteria or algae through photosynthesis could be a prospective option for its long-term sustainability. This process may become economical in the long term as it does not need high energy for the process and the global efficiency could go significantly high.

Ramesohl and Merten (2006) argued that there is a fear of restrictions to an enhanced growth of hydrogen production from renewable energy sources. This is absolutely wrong assumption. Renewable energy sources such as solar can be a good option to split the water into hydrogen and oxygen so that hydrogen can be used for desired application. In addition to the environmental and energy issue, safety concerns for the production, storage, transportation and use should be taken into consideration so as to provide enough security of the system. Hydrogen will play a major role in energy scenario in the years to come. The energy policy should be formulated in such a way that the total energy consumption and greenhouse gas emission should be in complete balance.

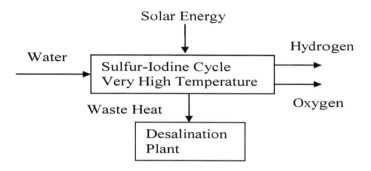

Figure 2.5.12. Very high temperature reactor with desalination plant (After Mills et al., 2005).

Impact of Energy Technology and Policy on Global Energy Scenario

Currently, fossil fuels provide over 80 % of the world's energy demand. EIA (2006d) estimated that the world's total energy consumption will rise by 59% between 1999 and 2020. The same report predicts a 20-year increase of carbon dioxide emissions by 60%. It is clear that the fossil fuel will still remain the mainstream of the global energy demand and supply scenario. Supplying this huge quantity of energy demand is a big challenge. Due to the environmental problems caused by the use of fossil fuels, series of environmental problems including global warming is inevitable (Chhetri and Islam, 2007a). However, recent studies indicate that toxicity and other negative effects are the results of all environmental problems emerged from oil refining and natural gas processing (Khan and Islam, 2007b; Chhetri and Islam, 2007b). This global energy demand must be met in a sustainable way with least or no impacts on the natural environment. However, the current development trend does not seem to move in that direction. A paradigm shift in the conventional energy conversion technologies and policy is necessary in order to achieve the true sustainability in technology development and environmental management (Khan and Islam, 2007a).

The US policy for the development of hydrogen fuel cells operated cars focused on cutting down the oil import from foreign countries, to get out of 'oil addiction'. President George Bush in his speech mentioned that running vehicles on hydrogen fuel cells would help reduce oil consumption, as the technology does not require gasoline, and lower pollution, as water is the only emission (Loven, 2006). Of course, hydrogen is a great fuel, however as mentioned earlier, most of the energy coming from splitting water through electrolysis will be spent to electrolyze itself and forms the vicious cycle of electricity generation using electricity. Moreover, the fuel cells are extremely expensive and toxic for now and the hydrogen transportation requires a news distribution system to replace today's natural gas distributing stations. A recent study shows that most expensive components of fuel cell are the high-purity catalysts, pure hydrogen and synthetic membranes (Mills et al., 2005). These three elements are unnatural elements and should be replaced with natural catalysts and bio membranes. If hydrogen is produced using direct solar energy which is the most abundant and free energy source on the earth, it will be a feasible option. Production of hydrogen from biological sources using bacteria is another option which may be sustainable in the long term. However, these technologies, despite having good prospect for the future, have received little attention from the scientific community or the general public.

Ethanol is another strong alternative as touted by George Bush as an antidote to the 'oil addiction' for United States (Fialka and Ball, 2006). Ethanol is produced from the biomass sources such as corn, sugarcane, switchgrass and other cellulose sources. Currently, it does not appear likely that ethanol can compete with gasoline. However, the ethanol conversion technologies are also not truly sustainable. These technologies are usually based on the use of toxic chemical additives that makes the whole process unsustainable. For example, ethanol production process from switchgrass involves acid hydrolysis as major production process. Bakker et al., (2004) reported that the concentrated sulfuric acid at 1:1-4:1 (acid: biomass ratio) is generally used for breaking down the biomass before it is sent to fermentation. Because of the use of highly toxic acids, the fermentation inhibitors such as 5-hydroxymethylfurfural (5-HMF) and furfural acid are produced. They reduce the conversion efficiency significantly. The use of toxic acids for the ethanol production creates several environmental problems. Moreover, there are other shortcomings the ethanol industry is considered to be facing today such as inadequate infrastructures, higher fuel cost and conversion system performance. Only biological methods of fermentation may stand as sustainable ethanol production technology in the future.

A strong policy intervention guided by science and good intension is necessary to develop the ethanol base industry. The US policy to replace more than 75% of oil imports from the Middle East by 2025 will never be realized with the status quo on the technological development. The projection of Energy Information Administration indicates that US will import more than 70 % in 2025 compared to 62% oil import in 2005. Corn or sugarcane based ethanol industry is also blamed to have competition with the food industry. However, the waste cellulose materials could be considered as feedstock to avoid such competition. Brazil is one of the best examples where ethanol and other biofuels made the country independent of the foreign oil import.

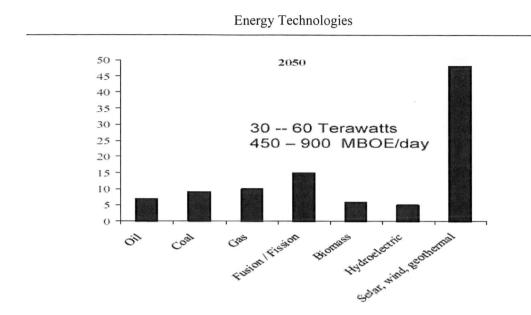

Figure 2.5.13. Energy mix projected for 2050 (After Smalley, 2003).

Energy Demand in Emerging Economies

Recently, Asia has emerged as prospective biggest consumer of the energy in the world. India and China, characterized by the largest population and higher economic growth rate, the demand of energy is dramatically increasing. According to Kuroda (2006), over the last 10 years, China grew at an average annual rate of 9.1% and India at a rate of 6.3%. The most forecasters see continued rapid growth in these countries in the years ahead - likely 8% to 9% in China and 7% to 8% for India. The projection of the Asian Development Bank showed an estimated average GDP growth of 6.6% across the developing economies of Asia and the Pacific to be continued in the coming years. In order to maintain this economic growth, the developing countries need large amount of energy for its industrial operation. Butler (2005) presented that the Chinese economy grew by 49% between 1999 and 2004. China increased its oil import in 2004 by 990,000 barrels a day of additional amount than it had on 2003. Similar consumption pattern could be seen in India in the years to come. The energy demand is significantly increasing in the East Asian countries such as Taiwan, Korea, Thailand, Indonesia, Malaysia and other countries as well. The increasing global energy demand would put great pressure in fossil fuel resources resulting in the worse environmental consequences ahead.

Conventional Global Energy Model

Richard E. Smalley, a Nobel Laureate in chemistry in 1996, forecasted that based on the current population growth and increase in energy demand, the global energy demand in 2050 for about 10 billion population, would be approximately 60 Terrawatts which is 900 million barrels of oil per day. The projection in Figure 16 indicated that fuel sources such as solar, wind and geothermal would play singificant role in the global energy supply (Smalley, 2003). The second significant energy source suggested is nuclear energy. As discussed earlier, the nuclear power can never be the solution to the global energy problem, rather it deteriorates the global environment with impacts in order of magnitude higher than the current level. The energy sources such as wind, solar and geothermal need to be utilized as they are freely available in nature. However, Service (2005) argued that putting 10% efficient solar panels to harvest 20 TW of energy requires 0.16% of earth's land. Moreover, the current photovoltaic technology has long term environmental impacts. Various heavy metals such as lead, chromium along with silicon are used to make solar panels. The storage batteries also have several toxic chemicals. With increasing awareness of environmental impact, there can not be a safe place to dispose these anti-natural chemicals. None of the process reactions is reversible and there is practically no hope to rehabilitate these chemicals back to nature. Thus, photovoltaics neither solve energy problem nor are friendly to the environment. Geothermal energy has vast potential but electricity production from this energy source loses significant efficiency.

Renewable vs Non-Renewable: No Boundary as Such

Figure 2.5.14 shows that as the natural processing time increases, the energy content of the natural fuels increases from wood to natural gas. The average energy value of wood is 18 MJ/kg (Hall, and Overend, 1987) and energy content of coal, oil and natural gas are 39.3MJ/kg, 53.6MJ/kg and 51.6MJ.kg, respectively (Website 6). Moreover, this shows that the renewable and non-renewable energy sources have no boundary. It is true that solar, geothermal, hydro and wind sources are being renewed at every second based on the global natural cycle. The fossil fuel soures are solar energy stored by the trees in the form of carbon and due to the temperature and pressure, they emerge as coal, oil or natural gas after millions of years. Biomass is renewed from a few days to a few hundreds years (as a tree can live up top several hundred years). These processes continue for ever. There is not a single point where fossil fuel has started or stopped its formation. So, why these fuels are called non-renewable? The current technology development mode is based on extremely short term approach as our solution of the problems start with the basic assumption of 'Δt tends to 0'. Only technologies that fulfill the criteria of time approaching infinity are sustainable (Khan and Islam, 2007a). The only problem with fossil fuel technology is that they are made more toxic after they are refined using high heat, toxic chemicals and catalysts.

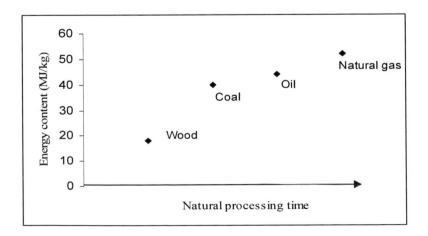

Figure 2.5.14. Energy content of different fuels (MJ/kg) (Chhetri, 2007)

It is clear that fossil fuel would contribute significant amount of energy even by 2050. It is widely considered that fossil fuels will be used up soon. However, there are still huge reserves of fossil fuel. The current estimation on the total reserves is based on the exploration to-date. As the number of drillings or exploration activities increases, more recoverable reserves can be found (Figure 2.5.15c). In fact, Figure 2.5.15 is equally valid if the abscissa is replaced by 'time' and ordinate is replaced by 'exploratory drillings' (Figure 2.5.15b). For every energy source, more exploration will lead to larger fuel reserve. This relationship makes the reserve of any fuel type truly infinity. This relationship alone can be used as a basis for developing technologies that exploit local energy sources.

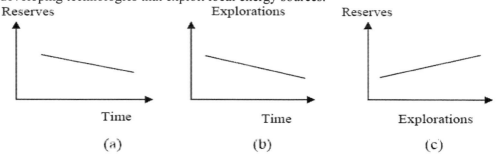

(a)   (b)   (c)

Figure 2.5.15. Fossil fuel reserves and exploration activities (Chhetri, 2007).

Table 2.5.5. US crude oil and natural gas reserve (Million barrels)

	Year	Reserve	% Increment
Crude Oil Reserve	1998	21,034	
	1999	217,65	3.5%
	2000	22,045	1.3%
	2001	22,446	1.8%
Natural Gas	1998	164,041	
	1999	167,406	2.1%
	2000	177,427	6.0%
	2001	183,460	3.4%

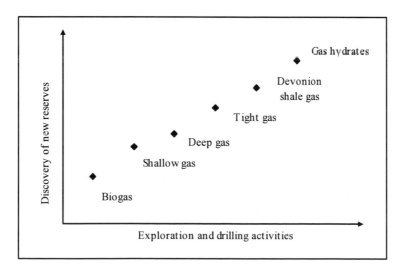

Figure 2.5.16. Discovery of natural gas reserves with exploration activities (Chhetri, 2007).

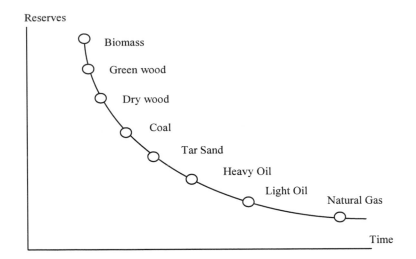

Figure 2.5.17. Continuity of resource base (Chhetri, 2007).

The US oil and natural gas reserves reported by EIA (2000;2002) showed that the reserves over the years have increased (Table 2.5.5). This additional reserves were estimated after the analysis of geological and engineering data. Hence, as the number of exploration increases, the reserves will also increase.

The discovery trend of natural gas reserves increases as exploration activities or drillings is increased (Figure 2.5.16). Biogas in naturally formed in swamps, paddy fields and other places due to the natural degradation of other organic materials. As illustrated in Figure 2.5.7, there are huge gas reservoirs including deep gas, tight gas, Devonian shale gas and gas hydrates, which are not yet exploited. The current exploration level is limited to shallow gas, which is a small fraction of the total natural gas reserve. Hence, by increasing the number of exploration activities, more and more reserves can be found which indicates the availability of unlimited amount of fossil fuels. As the natural processes continue, formation of natural gas also continues for ever. This is applicable to other fossil fuel resources such as coal, light and heavy oil, bitumen and tar sands.

Figure 2.5.17 shows the variation of resource base with time starting from biomass to natural gas. Due to natural activities, the biomass which is available in huge quantities on earth, undergoes various changes. With heat and pressure on the interior of the earth, formation of fossil fuel starts due to the degradation of organic matters from the microbial activities. The slope of the graph indicates that the volume of reserve decreases as it is further processed. Hence, there is more coal than oil and more oil than natural gas, meaning unlimited resources. Moreover, the energy content per unit mass of the fuel increases as the natural processing time increases (Figure 2.5.14). The biomass resource is renewable and the biological activities continue on the earth, the process of formation of fossil fuel also continues for ever. Hence the conventional boundary of renewable and non-renewable is dismantled and concluded that there is no boundary between the renewable and non-renewable as all natural processes are renewable (Chhetri, 2007). The only problem with fossil fuel arises from the use of toxic chemicals and catalysts during oil refining and gas processing. Provided the fossil fuels are processed using the natural and non-toxic catalysts and chemicals, or make use of crude oil or gas directly, fossil fuel will still remain as a good supplement in the global energy scenario in the days to come.

Sustainable Energy Model

Smalley (2005) argued that the potential of biomass is limited by the need to use arable land to grow food. However, biomass is regenerable and utilizing only the waste biomass could contribute significantly without competing with food sources. As half of the world's population now is surviving on biomass as mainstream fuel, a small intervention in the traditional technology could have significant impact on the economy and environment. Khan et al. (2007a) developed a high efficiency zero-waste cookstove with particulate trap mechanism from the exhaust and showed that the stove is almost 90% efficient considering its multiple uses. The stove is completely safe from the health point of view because the particulates which are considered to cause health hazard are trapped in an oil-water trap, leaving the clean gas essential for plants for photosynthesis. The soot collected in the oil water trap could be the excellent nano-materials for the future industries. Moreover, this can be used as non-toxic paints. Use of such stoves could siginifcantly increase the energy sustainability in the future. Thus, biomass could still remain the mainstream fuel for billions of people in the world in the several years to come.

Chhetri et al (2007) showed the pathways of oil refining. His findings revealed that the environmental problems are created when the refining process uses highly toxic chemicals and catalysts. The problem is caused due to the synthetic chemical based technologies making the earth full of synthetic chemcials. According to the pathway analysis carried out Islam (2004) there is nothing harmful in the crude oil. Chhetri and Islam (2007c) discussed about a jet engine that can run in any kind of solid (saw dust) or liquid including crude oil to produce electricity. This gives an idea that majority of environmental problems can be avoided simply using crude oil directly. This will not only save larger amount of money spent on expensive refineries for their refining but also have no negative impact on the environment at all. As the crude oil is completely biodegradable, the CO_2 produced by burning crude oil could be easily recycled by the plants (AlDarbi et al., 2005; Chhetri and Islam, 2007a). This necessitates the reinventing the wheel-desiging new vehicles that can run in crude oil.

Based on the utilization of sustainable energy resources, energy projections for next 50 years are shown in Figure 2.5.18 (Chhetri, 2007). Fossil fuel use is envisaged to use directly as crude oil without refining. Fossil fuels are to be considered as the alternative sources rather than mainstream fuels. The reason behind this is that they are slow forming renewable energy sources. The use of biomass in a sustainable manner will remain pre-dominant for majority of people especially in the developing countries even in the future. Hydropower, especially the vast ocean thermal and wave energy resources, could be exploited as this is a free energy source. Wind energy and geothermal sources would also contribute significantly. Since the most abundant energy source available on the earth is solar energy, the direct application of energy is the only solution of the global energy problem. It is considered that solar energy could be the significant contributor to solving the energy problems universally. It is just a matter of how the world can exploit this vast resource (170,000 TW) which could be the only panacea of the global energy problem. Solar hydrogen and direct solar energy should remain the dominating energy source for their environmental benefits and sustainability. Hence, technology development based on the principle of nature is the only solution to the current problem. Only the current technology development mode needs to be reversed to pro-nature technology development. The conventional engineering technologies violate characteristics time of nature in almost all aspects and are anti-natural. Only knowledge based technology development and management which follows the principle of nature would be instrumental in solving the global energy problem. Khan and Islam (2007a) showed that only the technologies which are environmentally appealing, economically attractive and socially responsible are sustainable in the long-term.

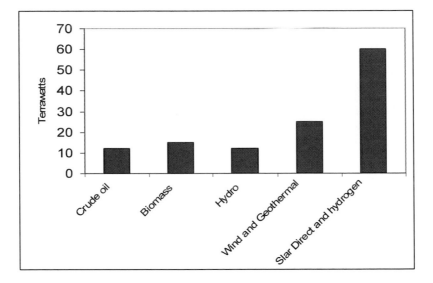

Figure 2.5.18. Energy projection for next 50 years (Chhetri 2007)

2.5.3. Reversing Global Warming

Global warming has been a subject of discussion from late seventies. It is perpetrated that the building up of carbon dioxide in the atmosphere results in irreversible climate change. Even though carbon dioxide has been blamed as the sole cause for the global warming, there is no scientific basis that all carbon dioxides are responsible for global warming. Chhetri and Islam (2007a) developed a new concept that describes that all carbon dioxides do not contribute to global warming. Based on this concept, carbon dioxide is characterized as 'natural' and 'industrial' carbon dioxide based on various the origins it comes from and the pathway it travels. In the process of civilization, all kinds of activities can increase CO_2 output into the atmosphere, but precisely which activities can be held responsible for consequent global warming? Both the activity and its CO_2 output are necessary, but neither by itself is sufficient, for establishing what the impact may be and whether it is deleterious. The world economy entered the Age of Petroleum mostly since the rise of industrial-financial monopoly in one sector of production after another in Europe and America, before and following the First World War. Corresponding to this has been the widest possible extension of chemical engineering – especially the chemistry of hydrocarbon combination, hydrocarbon catalysis, hydrocarbon manipulation and rebonding – on which the refining and processing of crude oil into fuel and myriad byproducts such as plastics and other synthetic materials crucially depend. As a result, there is today no activity, be it production or consumption, in any society that is tied to the production and distribution of such output in which adding to the CO_2 burden in the atmosphere can be avoided or significantly mitigated. In these developments, carbon and CO_2 are in fact vectors carrying many other actually toxic compounds and byproducts of these chemically-engineered processes.

Atmospheric absorption of carbon and CO_2 from human activities or other natural non-industrial activities would normally be continuous. However, what occurs with hydrocarbon complexes combined with inorganic and other substances that occur nowhere in nature is much less predictable, and – on the available evidence – not benign, either. From a certain standpoint, there is logic in attempting to estimate the effects of these other phenomena by taking carbon and CO_2 levels as vectors. However, there has never been any justification to assume the CO_2 level itself is the malign element. Whether the consideration is refining for automobile fuels, processing synthetic plastics, or concocting synthetic crude, behind a great deal of the propaganda about "global warming" stands a huge battle among oligopolies, cartels and monopolies over market share. The science of "global warming" is precisely the only route on which to separate the key question of what is necessary to produce goods and services that are Nature-friendly from the toxification of the environment as byproducts of the anti-Nature bias of chemical engineering in the clutches of the oil barons.

Current Status of Greenhouse Gas Emission

Industrial activities, especially related to the burning of fossil fuels, are major contributors of global greenhouse gas emissions. Climate change due to anthropogenic greenhouse gas (GHG) emissions is a growing concern for global society. In the third assessment report, the Intergovernmental Panel on Climate Change (IPCC) provides the strongest evidence so far that the global warming of the last 50 years is due largely to human activity and the CO_2 emissions that arise when burning fossil fuel (Farahani et al., 2004). Service (2005) reported that the CO_2 level now is at the highest point in 125,000 years Approximately 30 billion tons of CO_2 is released from fossil fuel burning each year. The CO_2 concentration level in the atmosphere traced back in 1750 was reported to be 280 ± 10ppm (IPCC, 2001). It has risen continuously since then and the CO_2 level reported in 1999 was 367 ppm. The present atmospheric CO_2 concentration level has not been exceeded during the past 420,000 years (IPCC, 2001; Houghton et al., 2001; Houghton, 2004).

The latest 150 years were a period of global warming (Figure 2.5.19). Global mean surface temperatures have increased 0.5-1.0°F since the late 19th century. The 20th century's 10 warmest years all occurred in the last 15 years of the century. Of these, 1998 was the warmest year on record. Sea level has risen 4-8 inches globally over the past century. Worldwide precipitation over land has increased by about one percent.

The industrial emission of CO_2 consists of process emission and production emission. Coal mining, oil refining, gas processing, petroleum fuel combustion, pulp and paper industry, ammonia, petroleum refining, iron and steel, aluminum, electricity generation and cement production are the major industries responsible for producing various types of greenhouse gases. In addition to this, transportation sector has also large share of greenhouse gas emission. Greenhouse gas emission from bioresources is also significant. However, National Energy Board of Canada does not consider CO_2 from biomass as contribution to greenhouse problems (Hughes and Scott, 1997). The justification emerges from the fact that greenhouse gas emission from bioresources such as fuelwood, agricultural waste, charcoal is carbon neutral as the plants recycle this CO_2. However, if various additives are added during the production of fuel such as pellet making and charcoal production, the CO_2 produced is no longer carbon neutral. For instance, pellet making involves the addition of binders such as carbonic additives, coal and coke breeze which emit carcinogenic benzene as a major aromatic compound (Chhetri at al., 2007a). The CO_2 contaminated with synthetic chemical additives is not favored by plants for photosynthesis and as a result, CO_2 accumulates in the atmosphere. Moreover, deforestation, especially the unsustainable harvesting of biomass due to urbanization and to fulfill the industrial biomass requirement also results in net CO_2 emission from bioresources.

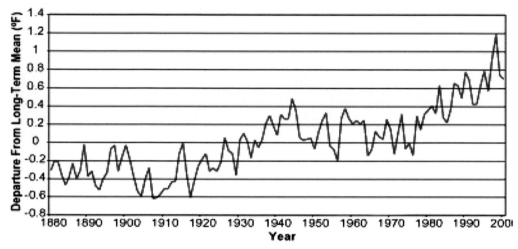

Figure 2.5.19. Global Temperature Changes from1880 to 2000 (Modified after EPA Global Warming Site: US National Climate Data Center 2001).

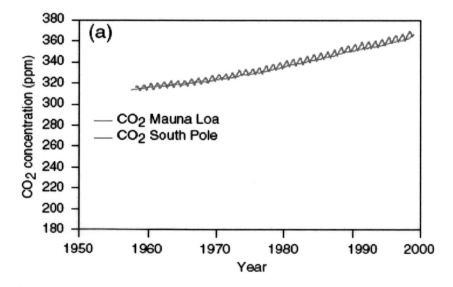

Figure 2.5.20. Variation in atmospheric CO_2 concentration (IPCC, 2001).

IEO (2005) estimated that worldwide CO_2 emission from the consumption of fossil fuels was 24,409 million metric tons in 2002 and it is projected to reach to 33284 million metric tons in 2015 and 38,790 million tons in 2025. Similarly worldwide CO_2 production from consumption and flaring of fossil fuel in 2003 was 25,162.07 million metric tones. The USA alone had a share of 5802.08 million tones of CO_2 emission in 2003 (IEA, 2005). Current CO_2 emission levels are expected to continue increasing in the future as fossil fuel consumption is sharply increasing (WEC, 2006). The projection showed that emission from all sources are emitted to grow by 36% in 2010 (to 18.24 Gt/y) and by 76% in 2020 to 23.31 Gt/y (compared to the 2000 base level). Variation of CO_2 concentration at different time scales is presented in Figure 2.5.20. This figure shows the increase in CO_2 emission exponentially after 1950. However, present methodology does not classify CO_2 based on its source. Industrial activities during this period also went up exponentially. Because of this industrial growth and extensive use of fossil fuels, the level of 'industrial' CO_2 emission increased sharply. The worldwide oil supply in 1970 was approximately 49 million barrels per day but the supply increased to approximately 84 million barrels per day (EIA, 2006). NOAA (2005) defined annual mean growth rate of CO_2 as the sum of all CO_2 added to, and removed from, the atmosphere during the year by human activities and by natural processes.

Some recent studies by Khilyuk and Chilingar (2004) reported that the human contribution to global warming is negligible. The global forces of nature such as solar radiation, outgassing from the Ocean and the atmosphere and microbial functions are driving the Earth's climate (Khilyuk and Chilingar, 2006). These studies showed that the CO_2 emissions from human induced activities is far less in quantity than the natural CO_2 emission from Ocean and volcanic eruptions. This line of argument is used by others to demonstrate that the cause of global warming is at least a contentious issue (Goldschmidt, 2005). These studies fail to explain the differences between the natural and human induced CO_2 and their possible impacts on global warming. Moreover, the CO_2 from ocean and natural forest fires were a part of the natural climatic cycle even when no global warming was noticed. All the global forces mentioned by Khilyuk and Chilingar (2006) are also affected by human interventions. For example, more than 85,000 chemicals being used worldwide for various industrial and agricultural activities are exposed in one or the other way to the atmosphere or ocean water bodies that contaminate the CO_2 (Global Pesticide Campaigner, 2004). The CO_2 produced from fossil fuel burning is not acceptable to the plants for their photosynthesis and for this reason, most organic plant matters are depleted in carbon ratio $\delta^{13}C$ (Farquhar et al., 1989; NOAA, 2005a). Finally the notion of 'insignificant' has been used in the past to allow unsustainable practices, such as pollution of harbors, commercial fishing and massive production of toxic chemicals that were deemed to be "Magic Solutions" (Khan and Islam, 2007a). Today, banning of chemicals and pharmaceutical products has become almost a daily affair (The Globe and Mail, 2006; The New York Times, 2006a). None of these products was deemed 'significant' or harmful when they were introduced. Khan and Islam (2007a) have recently catalogued an array of such ill-fated products that were made available to 'solve' a critical solution (Environment Canada, 2006). In all these engineering observations, a general misconception is perpetrated, that is: if the harmful effect of a product can be tolerated in the short-term, the negative impact of the product is 'insignificant'. A recent study by Miralai (2006) showed that the impact of any synthetic chemical increases in the lower concentration unlike in organic or natural chemicals of which the benefit increases for the lower concentration.

Crude oil →Gasolene+Solid residue+diesel+kerosene+volatile HC+ numerous petroleum products
Solid residue +hydrogen+metal (and others) →plastic
Plastic+Oxygen →4000 toxic chemicals (including 80 known carcinogens)

Figure 2.5.21. The crude oil pathway (Islam, 2004).

Khilyuk and Chilingar (2006) explained an adiabatic model developed by Khilyuk et al. (1994) for the atmosphere together with a sensitivity analysis to evaluate the effects of human induced CO_2 emissions on the global temperature. The model showed that due to the human induced CO_2, the global temperature rise is negligible. However, considering that the adiabatic condition in the atmosphere is one of the most linear thoughts and the basic assumption of this model is incorrect (Khan et al., 2007a). For an adiabatic condition, the following three assumptions are made: perfect vacuum between system and surrounding area, perfect reflector around the system like the thermo flux mechanism to resist radiation and zero heat diffusivity material that isolates the system. None of these conditions can be fulfilled in the atmosphere. Moreover, the study reported that increased emissions of carbon dioxide and water vapor are important for agriculture and biological protection and the CO_2 from fossil fuel combustion is non toxic. However, their finding is in contradiction to the fact that plants discriminate against heavier CO_2 and favor CO_2 with lighter carbon isotope ratios. As all chemicals are not the same, all CO_2 is not the same. The CO_2 from power plants is highly toxic as various toxic chemicals are added during the refining and processing of fossil fuels (Chhetri et al., 2007a; Chhetri and Islam, 2007c; Khan and Islam, 2007a). Since the CO_2 from fossil fuel burning is contaminated with various toxic chemicals, plants do not readily synthesize it. Note that practically all catalysts used are either chemically synthesized or are denatured by concentrating them to a more beneficial state (Khan and Islam, 2007a). The CO_2 rejected from plants accumulates in the atmosphere and is fully responsible for global warming. According to Thomas and Nowak (2006), human activities have already demonstrably changed global climate, and further, much greater changes are expected throughout this century. The emissions of CO_2 and other greenhouse gases will further accelerate global warming. Some future climatic consequences of human induced CO_2 emissions, for example some warming and sea-level rise, cannot be prevented, and human societies will have to adapt to these changes. Other consequences can perhaps be prevented by reducing CO_2 emissions.

Figure 2.5.21 is the crude oil pathway. The crude oil is refined to convert into various products including plastics. More than four million tons of plastics are produced from 84 million barrels of oil per day. It has been further reported that plastic burning produces more than 4000 toxic chemicals 80 of which are known carcinogens (Islam, 2004).

Various other greenhouse gases, in addition to CO_2, have contributed to global warming. The concentration of other greenhouse gases increased significantly in the period 1750-2001. Several classes of halogenated compounds such as chlorine, bromine, fluorine are also greenhouse gases and are the direct result of industrial activities. None of these compounds was in existence before 1750 but are found in significant concentration in the atmosphere after that period (Table 2.5.6). Chlorofluorocarbons (CFCs), hydrohloroflorocarbons (HCFCs) which contains chlorine and halocarbons such as bromoflorocarbons which contain bromine are considered potent greenhouse gases. The sulfur hexafluoride (SF_6) which is emitted from various industrial activities such as aluminum industry, semi-conductor manufacturing, electric power transmission and distribution, magnesium casting and from nuclear power generating plants also considered a potent greenhouse gas. Table 2.5.6 shows that the concentration of these chemicals has significantly increased in the atmosphere after 1750. For example, the CFC-11 was not present in the atmosphere before 1750. However, the concentration after 1750 reached to 256 ppt after 1750. It is important to note here that these chemicals are totally synthetic in nature cannot be manufactured under natural conditions. This would explain why the future pathway of these chemicals is so rarely reported.

The transportation sector consumes a quarter of the world's energy, and accounts for some 25% of total CO_2 emissions, 80% of which is attributed to road transport (EIA, 2006b). Projections for Annex I countries indicate that, without new CO_2 mitigation measures, road transport CO_2 emissions might grow from 2500 million tones in 1990 to 3500 to 5100 million tones in 2020. The fossil fuel consumption by the transportation sector is also sharply increasing in the Non Annex I countries as well. Thus the total greenhouse gas emission from transportation will rise in the future. It is reported that as much as 90% of global biomass burning is human-initiated and that such burning is increasing with time (NASA, 1999). Forest products are the major source of biomass along with agricultural as well as household wastes. The CO_2 from biomass has long been considered to be the source of feedstock during photosynthesis by plants. Therefore the increase in CO_2 from biomass burning can not be considered to be unsustainable, as long as the biomass is not contaminated through 'processing' before burning. CO_2 from unaltered biomass is distinguished from CO_2 emitted from processed fuels. To date, any processing involves the addition of toxic chemicals. Even if the produced gases do not show detectable concentration of toxic products, it is conceivable that the associated CO_2 will be different from CO_2 of organic origin. The CO_2 emission from biomass which is contaminated with various chemical additives during processing has been calculated and deducted from the CO_2 which is good for the photosynthesis that does not contribute to global warming.

Classification of Carbon Dioxide

Carbon dioxide is classified in to two types. Previous theories were based on the "Chemicals are Chemicals" approach of the two time Nobel Laureate Linus Pauling's vitamin C and antioxidant experiments. This approach advanced the principle that whether it is from natural or synthetic sources and irrespective of the pathways it travels, vitamin C is same. It essentially disconnects a chemical product from its historical pathway. Even though, the role of pathways has been understood by many civilizations for centuries, systematic studies questioning their principle is a very recent phenomenon. For instance, only recently Gale et al. (1995) reported that vitamin C did not lower death rates among elderly people, and may actually have increased the risks of dying. Moreover, ß carotene supplementation may do more harm than good in patients with long cancer (Josefson, 2003). Obviously such a conclusion can not be made if subjects were taking vitamin C from natural sources. In fact, the practices of people who live the longest lives indicate clearly that natural products do not have any negative impact on human health. More recently it is reported that antioxidant supplement including vitamin C should be avoided by patients being treated as the cancer cells gobbles up vitamin C faster than normal cells which might give greater protection for tumors rather than normal cells (Agus et al.,1999).

Table 2.5.6. Concentrations, global warming Potentials (GWPs), and atmospheric lifetimes of GHGs (IPCC, 2001)

Gas	Pre-1750 concen-tration	Current topospheric concentration	GWP (100-yr time horizon)	Life time (years)
carbon dioxide (CO_2)	280 ppm	374.9	1	varies
methane (CH_4)	730ppb	1852ppb	23	12
nitrous oxide (N_2O)	270	319ppb	296	114
CFC-11 (trichlorofluoromethane) (CCl_3F)	0	256 ppt	4600	45
CFC-12 (dichlorodifluoromethane) (CCl_2F_2)	0	546 ppt	10600	100
CFC-113 (trichlorotrifluoroethane) ($C_2Cl_3F_3$)	0	80 ppt	6000	85
carbon tetrachloride (CCl_4)	0	94 ppt	1800	35
methyl chloroform (CH_3CCl_3)	0	28 ppt	140	4.8
HCFC-22 (chlorodifluoromethane) ($CHClF_2$)	0	158 ppt	1700	11.9
HFC-23 (fluoroform) (CHF_3)	0	14 ppt	12000	260
perfluoroethane (C_2F_6)	0	3 ppt	11900	10000
sulfur hexafluoride (SF_6)	0	5.21 ppt	22200	3200
trifluoromethyl sulfur pentafluoride (SF_5CF_3)	0	0.12 ppt	18000	3200

Antioxidants that are presently in nature are known to act as anti-aging agents that are different from those which are synthetically manufactured. The previously used hypothesis that "Chemicals are Chemicals" fails to distinguish between the characteristics of synthetic and natural vitamins and antioxidants. The impact of synthetic antioxidants and vitamin C in body metabolism would be different than that of natural sources. Numerous other cases can be cited demonstrating that the pathway involved in producing the final product is of utmost importance. Some examples have recently been investigated by Islam and co-workers (Islam, 2004; Khan and Islam, 2007a; Zatzman and Islam, 2007a). If the pathway is considered, it becomes clear that organic produce is not the same as non organic produce, natural products are not the same as bioengineered products, natural pesticides are not the same as chemical pesticides, natural leather is not same as synthetic plastic, natural fibers are not the same as synthetic fibers, natural wood is not same as fiber- reinforced plastic etc. (Islam, 2006a). In addition to being the only ones that are good for the long-term, natural products are also extremely efficient and economically attractive. Numerous examples are given in Khan and Islam (2007a). Unlike synthetic hydrocarbons, natural vegetable oils are reported to be easily degraded by bacteria (AlDarbi et al., 2005). Application of wood ash to remove arsenic from aqueous streams is more effective than removing by any synthetic chemicals (Rahman, et al., 2004; Wassiuddin et al., 2002). Using the same analogy, carbon dioxide has also been classified based on the source from where it is emitted, the pathway it traveled and age of the source from which it came from (Khan and Islam, 2007a).

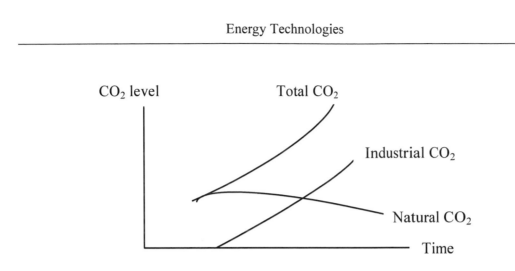

Figure 2.5.22. Total, industrial and natural CO_2 trend (Chhetri and Islam, 2007a).

Similarly, present methodology does not classify CO_2 based on its source. Because of the industrial growth and extensive use of fossil fuels, the level of 'industrial' CO_2 emission increased sharply (Figure 2.5.22). At the same time, the level of 'natural' CO_2 which comes by burning biomass went down due to deforestation. However, researchers, industry and government are focused on the total CO_2, which is not correct in terms of its impacts on global warming. NOAA (2005) defined annual mean growth rate of CO_2 as the sum of all CO_2 added to, and removed from the atmosphere during the year by human activities and by natural processes. 'Natural' CO_2 cannot be same as that of 'industrial' CO_2 and should be examined separately.

Plants favor a lighter form of carbon dioxide for photosynthesis and discriminate against heavier isotopes of carbon (Farquhar et al., 1989). Since the fossil fuel refining involves the use of various toxic additives, the carbon dioxide emitted from these fuels is contaminated and is not favored by plants. If CO_2 comes from wood burning, which has no chemical additives, this CO_2 will be most favored by plants. This is because the pathway the fuel travels from refinery to combustion devices makes the refined product inherently toxic (Chhetri et al., 2007a). The 'industrial' CO_2 which the plants do not synthesize accumulates in the atmosphere. The accumulation of this rejected CO_2 must be accounted in order to assess the impact of human activities on global warming. This analysis provided a basis for discerning 'natural' CO_2 from "man-made or industrial CO_2", which could be correlated with global warming.

Water and its Role in Global Warming

Water is one of the components of natural transport phenomenon. Natural transport phenomenon is a flow of complex physical processes. The flow process consists of production, storage and transport of fluids, electricity, heat and momentum (Figure 2.5.23). The most essential material components of these processes are water and air which are also the indicators of natural climate. Oceans, rivers and lakes form both the source and sink of major water transport systems. Because water is the most abundant matter on earth, any impact on the overall mass balance of water is certain to impact the global climate. The interaction between water and air in order to sustain life on this planet is a testimony to the harmony of nature. Water is the most potent solvent and also has very high heat storage capacity. Any movement of water through the surface and the Earth's crust can act as a vehicle for energy distribution. However, the only source of energy is the sun and sunlight is the most essential ingredient for sustaining life on earth. The overall process in nature is inherently sustainable, yet truly dynamic. There isn't one phenomenon that can be characterized as cyclic. Only recently, scientists have discovered that water has memory. Each phenomenon in nature occurs due to some driving force such as pressure for fluid flow, electrical potential for the flow of electricity, thermal gradient for heat, and chemical potential for a chemical reaction to take place. Natural transport phenomena cannot be explained by simple mechanistic views of physical processes by a function of one variable. Even though Einstein pointed out the possibility of the existence of a fourth dimension a century ago, the notion of extending this dimensionality to infinite numbers of variables is only now coming to light (Islam, 2006a). A simple flow model of natural transport phenomenon is presented in Figure 2.5.23. This model shows that nature has numerous interconnected processes such as production of heat, vapor, electricity and light, storage of heat and fluid and flow of heat as well as fluids. All these processes continue for infinite time and are inherently sustainable. Any technologies that are based on natural principles are sustainable (Khan and Islam, 2007a).

Water plays a crucial role in the natural climatic system and hence in global warming. Water is the most essential as well as the most abundant ingredient of life. Just as 70% of the earth's surface is covered with water, 70% of the human body is constituted of water. Even though the value and sanctity of water has been well known for thousands of years in eastern cultures, scientists in the west are only now beginning to break out of the "Chemicals are Chemicals" mode and examine the concept that water has memory, and that numerous intangibles (most notably the pathway and intention behind human intervention) are important factors in defining the value of water (Islam, 2006b).

At the industrial/commercial level however, preposterous treatment practices such as the addition of chlorine to 'purify'; the use toxic chemicals (soap) to get rid of dirt (the most potent natural cleaning agent (Islam, 2006b); the use of glycol (very toxic) for freezing or drying (getting rid of water) a product; use of chemical CO_2 to render water into a dehydrating agent (opposite to what is promoted as 'refreshing'), then again demineralization followed by the addition of extra oxygen and ozone to 'vitalize'; the list seems to continue forever. Chlorine treatment of water is common in the west and is synonymous with civilization. Similarly, transportation in copper pipe and distribution through stainless steel (enforced with heavy metal), storage in synthetic plastic containers and metal tanks, and mixing of ground water with surface water (itself collected from 'purified' sewage water) are common practices in 'developed' countries. More recent 'innovations' such as Ozone, UV and even H_2O_2 are proving to be worse than any other technology. Overall, water remains the most abundant resource, yet 'water war' is considered to be the most certain destiny of the 21st century. What Robert Curl (a Novel Laureate in Chemistry) termed as a 'technological disaster', modern technology development schemes seem to have targeted the most abundant resource (Islam, 2006b).

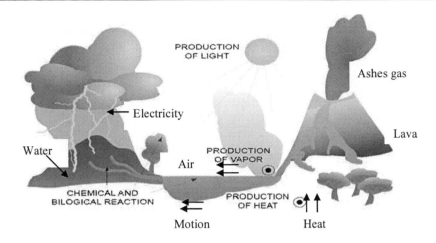

Figure 2.5.23. Natural transport phenomenon (after Fuchs, 1999).

The greenhouse gas effect is thought to be one of the major mechanisms by which the radiative factors of the atmosphere influence the global climate. Moreover, the radiative regime of the radiative characteristics of the atmosphere is largely determined by some optically active component such as CO_2 and other gases, water vapor and aerosols (Kondratyev and Cracknell, 1998). As most of the incoming solar radiation passes through atmosphere and is absorbed by the Earth's surface, the direct heating of the surface water and evaporation of moisture results in heat transfer from the Earth's surface to the atmosphere. The transport of heat by the atmosphere leads to the transient weather system. The latent heat released due to the condensation of water vapors and the clouds play an important role in reflecting incoming short-wave solar radiation and absorbing and emitting long wave radiation. Aerosols such as volcanic dust and the particulates of fossil fuel combustion are important factors in determining the behavior of the climate system. Kondratyev and Cracknell (1998) reported that the conventional theory of calculating global warming potential only account for CO_2 ignoring the contribution of water vapor and other gases in global warming. Their calculation scheme took into account the other components affecting the absorption of radiation including CO_2, water vapor, N_2, O_2, CH_4, NOx, CO, SO_2, nitric acid, ethylene, acetylene, ethane, formaldehyde, chlorofluorocarbons, ammonia and aerosol formation of different chemical composition and various sizes. However, this theory fails to explain the effect of pure water vapor and the water vapor that is contaminated with chemical contaminants.

The impact of water vapor on climate change depends on the quality of water evaporated, its interaction with the atmospheric particulates of different chemical composition and size of the aerosols. The majority of chemicals that reach to water body are very toxic and radioactive, the particulates being continuously released into the atmosphere. The chemicals also reach to water bodies by leakage, transportation loss and as by-products of pesticides, herbicide and water disinfectants. The industrial wastes, which are contaminated with these chemicals finally reach to the water body and contaminate the entire water system. The particulates of these chemicals and aerosols when mixed with water vapor may increase the absorption characteristics in the atmosphere thereby increasing the possibility of trapping more heat. However, pure water vapor is one of the most essential components of the natural climate system and will have no impacts in global warming. Moreover, most of the water vapors will end up transforming into rain near the Earth's surface and will have no effect on the absorption and reflection. The water vapor in the warmer part of the earth could rise to higher altitudes as they are more buoyant. As the temperature decreases in the higher altitude, the water vapor gets colder, and it will hold less water vapor, reducing the possibility of increasing global warming.

It has been recently reported that water has memory (Tschulakow et al., 2005). Because of this property, the assumption of the impact of water vapor to global warming cannot be explained without the knowledge of memory. The impact will depend on the pathway it traveled before and after the formation of vapor from water. Gilbert and Zhang (2003) reported that the nanoparticles change the crystal structure when they are wet. The change of structure taking place in the nanoparticles in the water vapor and aerosols in the atmosphere have profound impact in the climate change. This relation has been explained based on the memory characteristics of water and its pathway analysis. It is reported that water crystals are entirely sensitive to the external environment and take different shape based on the input (Emoto, 2004). Moreover, the history of water memory can be traced by its pathway analysis. The memory of water might have a significant role to play in the technological development (Hossain and Islam, 2006). Recent attempts have been directed towards understanding the role of history on the fundamental properties of water. These models take into account the intangible properties of water. This line of investigation can address the global warming phenomenon. The memory of water not only has impacts on energy and ecosystems but also has a key role to play in the global climate scenario.

Characterization of Energy Sources

Energy is conventionally classified, valued or measured based on the absolute output from a system. The absolute value represents the steady state of energy source. However, modern science recognizes that such a state does not exist and every form of energy is at a state of flux. Each form of energy has a set of characteristics features. Anytime these features are violated through human intervention, the quality of the energy form declines. This analysis enables one to assign greater quality index to a form of energy that is closest to its natural state. Consequently, the heat coming from wood burning and the heat coming from electrical power will have different impacts on the quality, the only thing that comes in contact. Just as all chemicals are not the same, different forms of heat coming from different energy sources are not the same. The energy sources are characterized based on the global efficiency of each technology considering the environmental impact of the technology and overall value of energy systems (Chhetri, 2007).

Various energy sources are also classified according to their global efficiency. Conventionally, energy efficiency is defined for a component or service as the amount of energy required in the production of that component or service; for example, the amount of cement that can be produced with one billion Btu of energy. Energy efficiency is improved when a given level of service is provided with reduced amounts of energy inputs, or services or products are increased for a given amount of energy input. However, the global efficiency of a system is defined as the efficiency calculated based on the energy input at various stages of system operation, products output, the possibility of multiple use of energy in the system, the use of the system by products and its impacts to the environment. The global efficiency calculation considers the source of the fuel, the pathways the energy system travels, conversion systems and impacts to the human health and environment and intermediate as well as by products of the energy system. Chhetri (2007) calculated the global efficiency of various energy systems. For example, the global efficiency of coal burning to produce electricity is calculated considering the efficiency of the entire operations from coal mining to electricity transmission (Figure 2.5.24). The coal to electricity production without considering the environmental impacts has a global efficiency of 12.40% (Chhetri, 2007). The efficiency can be improved by using the fly ash for other purposes such as making cement, if toxic catalysts are not used during coal conversion or cracking. Some chemicals such as of Fe-Mn oxides or some acidic compounds are added during coal cleaning and refining before they are burned (Guo et al., 2004). These additives contaminate the CO_2 making it toxic. A large amount of sulfur and arsenic are also released during coal burning. The global efficiency of the whole system is thus reduced even if we consider the environmental impacts of coal burning.

The global efficiency of wood combustion has been calculated to be more than 90% (Chhetri et al., 2007a). Similarly, the global efficiency of nuclear power generation was lower than 5%. Nuclear waste storage has been the subject of discussion for a long time and no feasible methods have been successfully worked out yet. Development of nuclear power generation also utilizes fossil fuel during various process operations contributing to the emission of CO_2. The major problem of nuclear power generation is the generation of toxic nuclear waste. Nuclear waste is a big problem which cannot be utilized and is almost impossible to store safely.

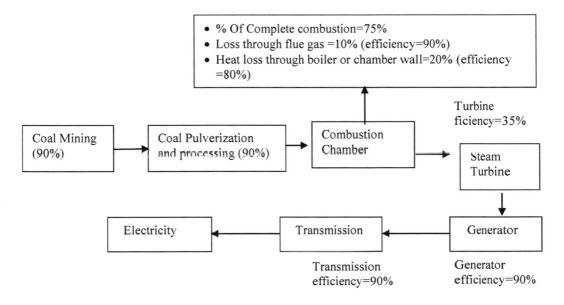

Figure 2.5.24. Global efficiency of coal to electricity system calculated based on Chhetri (2007).

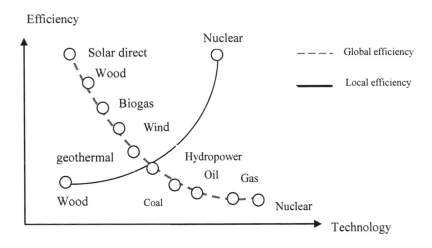

Figure 2.4.25. Global and local efficiency of different energy sources (Chhetri, 2007)

Figure 2.5.25 shows the global and local efficiency of various energy technologies calculated by Chhetri (2007). They showed that global efficiencies of higher quality energy sources are higher than those of lower quality energy sources. With their ranking, solar energy source (when applied directly) is the most efficient, while nuclear energy is least efficient among many forms of energy studied. Chhetri (2007) demonstrated that previous finding fail to discover this logical ranking because the focus had been on local efficiency. For instance, nuclear energy is generally considered to be highly efficient which is a true observation if one's analysis is limited to one component of the overall process. If global efficiency is considered, of course the fuel enrichment alone involves numerous centrifugation stages. This enrichment alone will render the global efficiency very low.

The Kyoto Protocol and Global Warming

Based on the conclusion that current global warming and climate change is due to the emission of greenhouse gases by industrial activities, the Kyoto Protocol was negotiated by more than 160 nations in 1997, aiming to reduce greenhouse gases primarily CO_2 (EIA, 2005). In this Protocol, the industrial nations (Annex-I countries) have committed to making substantial reductions in their emission of greenhouse gases by 2012. For the first time, the Kyoto Protocol includes an international agreement for the reduction of emission of greenhouse gases. Global warming is a major environmental concern. It is especially the case in many developed countries, where the greenhouse gas emissions responsible for this change are concentrated. As a result, uncertainties and fears about possible consequences for the development of manufacturing activities in the future. According to the Third Assessment Report of the Intergovernmental Panel on Climate Change (IPPC) which brings together the world's leading experts in this field, globally averaged surface temperature is projected to increase by between minimum of 1.4^0C and maximum of 5.8°C from 1990 to 2100 under a business-as-usual projection. This temperature rise corresponds to a sea level rise of 9 cm to a maximum of 88 cm. More recently, chief scientific advisor to UK government estimated an increase of 3^0C in the coming decade. Despite desserting views and skepticism (Lindzen, 2002; Lindzen, 2006;Carter, 2006) it is being increasingly clear that global warming is not a natural phenomenon and emerges from industrial practices that are not sustainable (Khan, 2006).

The Kyoto Protocol has set special targets in order to reduce greenhouse gas emission from Annex-I countries as outlined by Article 2 of the Protocol. Various measures suggested reducing the greenhouse gas emissions are promotion of sustainable development, enhancement of energy efficiency, protection and enhancement of sinks and reservoirs of greenhouse, promotion of sustainable forms of agriculture in light of climate change considerations, methane reduction through waste management and promotion of increased use of new and renewable forms of energy. Article 3 as major provision of the Kyoto Protocol reflects agreement that all parties must reduce their greenhouse gas emission level 5% below their 1990 levels during the 'commitment period' between 2008 and 2012. Some countries, including the US, Canada, European Union countries and Japan, will have to reduce emissions up to 8 percent below 1990 level. Some on this list including Australia and Iceland will be allowed to increase emissions by varying amounts up to 10%. The other features of the Protocol is that the parties included in Annex B may participate in emissions trading for the purposes of fulfilling their commitments. Clean Development Mechanism (CDM) is defined under article 12 to assist sustainable development for developing countries. Annex I countries could count reductions in greenhouse gases achieved in this way against their own targets.

Despite a series of targets for emission reduction, the Kyoto Protocol has many flaws. The standards for emission reduction are not based on scientific facts. The time scale proposed for reducing emission levels also had no justification. The standards emission level taken as of 1990 had also no basis. Developing countries such as China and India as newly emerging economies were excluded from meeting the targets. Emission trading has become 'license to pollute' for industrialized countries and big corporations. This situation has become worse due to the introduction of emission trading. The CDM instituted to assist developing countries is not functional. Moreover, there are significant bureaucratic formalities that slow down the project approval for CDM granting to develop clean energy technologies. The main difficulties in making the CDM work arise from the dual issues of 'additionality' and 'baselining'. To obtain a 'certified emission reduction', that is, new emission rights, from investments in developing countries, investors must demonstrate that emission reductions are 'additional' to any that would occur in the absence of the certified project activities. The monitoring and administration of such emission certification would be a cost burden for relatively small companies. As a result, only the big companies which can administer and monitor the certification would get the benefits. The present targets of greenhouse gas emission in industrialized countries are not tough enough for 2008-2012. Such provisions are affected by many factors and would likely become a license to pollute that will enable global emission to further increase. The Kyoto Protocol doesn't even set a long-term goal for atmospheric concentrations of CO_2, so the Kyoto protocol does not hold good promise to achieve its set targets. Possibly the most important shortcoming of the Kyoto protocol is in its failure to recommend any change in the current process of energy production and utilization. Any change in the current practice can alter the global warming scenario drastically. For instance, if toxic chemicals were not used in crude oil refining, allowable CO_2 emission would increase very significantly. Such analysis is absent in most of the previous work (Khan, 2006; Khan and Islam, 2007b).

The intergovernmental Panel on Climate Change stated that there was a "discernible" human influence on climate; and that the observed warming trend is "unlikely to be entirely natural in origin" (IPCC, 2001). The Third Assessment Report of IPCC stated "There is new and stronger evidence that most of the warming observed over the last 50 years is attributable to human activities." Khilyuk and Chilingar (2004) reported that the CO_2 concentration in the atmosphere between 1958 to 1978 was proportional to the CO_2 emission due to the burning of fossil fuel. In 1978, CO_2 emissions into the atmosphere due to fossil fuel burning stopped rising and were stable for nine years. They concluded that if fossil fuels burning were the main cause, the atmospheric concentration should stop rising and thus, fossil fuel burning is not the cause of the greenhouse effect. However, this assumption is extremely short sighted and global climate certainly does not work linearly, as envisioned by Khilyuk and Chilingar (2004). Moreover, the 'Greenhouse Effect One-Layer Model' proposed by Khilyuk and Chilingar (2003; 2004) assumes adiabatic conditions in the atmosphere that do not practically exist. The authors have concluded that the human-induced emission of carbon dioxide and other greenhouse gases have a very small effect on global warming. This is due to the limitation of the current linear computer models which cannot predict temperature effects on the atmosphere other than the low level. Similar arguments were made while promoting dichlorodifluoromethane (CFC-12) to environmental problems incurred by ammonia and other refrigerants after decades of use, CFC-12 was banned in USA in 1996 for its impacts on stratospheric ozone layer depletion and global warming. Khan and Islam (2007a) presented detailed list of technologies that were based on spurious promises. Zatzman and Islam (2007a) complemented this list by providing a detailed list of economic models that are also counter productive. The potential impact of microbial activities on the mass and content of gaseous mixtures in Earth's atmosphere on a global scale was explained (Khilyuk and Chilingar, 2004). However, this study does not distinguish between biological sources of greenhouse gas emission such as from microbial activities, and industrial sources such as fossil fuel burning. They inhibit different characteristics as they derive from diverse origins and travel different paths which obviously, have significant impact on atmospheric processes.

Current climate models have several problems. Scientists have agreed on the likely rise in the global temperature over the next century. However, the current global climatic models can predict only global average temperatures. Projection of climate change in a particular region is considered to be beyond current human ability. Atmospheric Ocean General Circulation Models (AOGCM) are used by IPCC to model climatic feactures, however, these models are not accurate enough to provide reliable forecast on how climate may change. They are linear models and cannot forecast complex climatic features. Some climate models are based on CO_2 doubling and transient scenarios. However, the effect of climate while doubling the concentration of CO_2 in the atmosphere cannot predict the climate in other scenarios. These models are insensitive to the difference between natural and industrial greenhouse gases. There are some simple models in use which use fewer dimensions than complex models and do not predict complex systems. The Earth System Models of Intermediate Complexity (EMIC) are used to bridge the gap between the complex and simple models, however, these models are not suitable to assess the regional aspect of climate change (IPCC, 2001).

Unsustainable technologies are the major cause of global climate change. Sustainable technologies can be developed following the principles of nature. In nature, all functions are inherently sustainable, efficient and functional for an unlimited time period. In other words, as far as natural processes are concerned, 'time tends to Infinity'. This can be expressed as t

or, for that matter, $\Delta t \to \infty$. By following the same path as the functions inherent in nature, an inherently sustainable technology can be developed (Khan and Islam, 2005a). The 'time criterion' is a defining factor in the sustainability and virtually infinite durability of natural functions. Figure 2.5.26 shows the direction of nature-based, inherently sustainable technology, as contrasted with an unsustainable technology. The path of sustainable technology is its long-term durability and environmentally wholesome impact, while unsustainable technology is marked by Δt approaching 0. Presently, the most commonly used theme in technology development is to select technologies that are good for t='right now', or $\Delta t=0$. In reality, such models are devoid of any real basis (termed "aphenomenal" by Khan et al., (2005a) and should not be applied in technology development if we seek sustainability for economic, social and environmental purposes. While developing the technology for any particular climatic model, this sustainability criterion is truly instrumental. The great flaw of conventional climate models is that they are focused on the extremely short term, t='right now', or $\Delta t=0$. Hence, the Kyoto protocol without development of technologies that are inherently sustainable is not beneficial to solve the global warming problems.

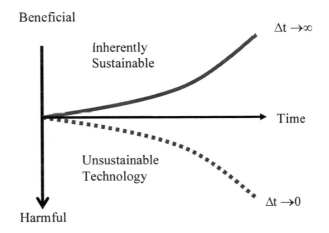

Figure 2.5.26. Direction of sustainable/green technology (redrawn from Islam, 2005).

Sustainable Energy Development

Technology has a vital role to play in modern society. One of the major causes of present day environmental problems is the use of unsustainable technologies that are inherently unsustainable. The use of thousands of toxic chemicals in fossil fuel refining, industrial processes to the products of personal care such as body lotion, cosmetics, soaps and others has polluted much of the world in which we live (The Globe and Mail 2006; Chhetri et al., 2007c). Present day technologies arc based on the use of fossil fuel in the form of primary energy supply, production or processing, and the feedstock for products, such as plastic. Every stage of this development involves the generation of toxic waste, rendering product harmful to the environment. According to the criterion presented by Khan and Islam (2005a; 2005 b), toxicity of products mainly comes from the addition of chemical compounds that are toxic. This leads to continuously degrading quality of the feedstock. Today, it is becoming increasingly clear that the "chemical addition" that once was synonymous with modern civilization is the principal cause of numerous health problems including cancer and diabetes. A detailed list of these chemicals has been presented by Khan and Islam (2006 b).

Proposing wrong solution for various problems has made the situation progressively worse. For instance, USA is the biggest consumer of milk, most of which is 'fortified' with calcium. Yet, USA ranks at the top of the list of osteoporosis patients per capita in the world. Similar standards are made about the use of vitamins, antioxidants, sugarfree diet etc. Potato farms on Prince Edward Island in eastern Canada are considered a hot bed for cancer (The Epoch Times, 2006). Chlorothalonil, a fungicide, which is widely used in the potato fields, is considered a carcinogen. US EPA has classified chlorothalonil as a known carcinogen that can cause a variety of ill effects including skin and eye irritation, reproductive disorders kidney damage and cancer. Environment Canada (2006) published lists of chemicals which were banned at different times. This indicates that all the toxic chemicals used today are not beneficial and will be banned from use some day. This trend continues for each and every technological development. However, few studies have integrated these findings to develop a comprehensive cause and effect model. This comprehensive scientific model developed by Khan and Islam (2007a) is applied for screening unsustainable and harmful technologies right at the onset. Some recently developed technologies that are sustainable for the long term are presented.

One of the sustainable technologies presented here is the true green biodiesel model (Chhetri and Islam, 2006b). As an alternative to petrodiesel, biodiesel is a renewable fuel that is derived from vegetable oils and animal fats. However, the existing biodiesel production process is neither completely 'green' nor renewable because it utilizes fossil fuels, mainly natural gas, as an input for methanol production. Conventional biodiesel production process entails the use of fossil fuels such as methane as an input to methanol. It has been reported that up to 35% of the total primary energy requirement for biodiesel production comes from fossil fuel (Carraretto et al., 2004). Methanol makes up about 10% of the feed stock input and since most methanols are currently produced from natural gas, biodiesel is not completely renewable (Gerpen et al., 2004). The catalysts and chemicals currently in use for biodiesel production are highly caustic and toxic. The synthetic catalysts used for the transesterification process are sulfuric acid; sodium hydroxide and potassium hydroxide, which are highly toxic and corrosive chemicals. The pathway for conventional biodiesel production and petrodiesel production follows a similar path (Figure 2.5.27). Both the fuels have similar emission of pollutants such as benzene, acetaldehyde, toluene, formaldehyde, acrolein, PAHs, xylene (EPA, 2002). However, the biodiesel has fewer pollutants in quantity than petrodiesel.

Chhetri and Islam (2006b) developed a process that rendered the biodiesel production process truly green. This process used waste vegetable oil as biodiesel feedstock. The catalysts and chemicals used in the process were non-toxic, inexpensive and natural catalysts. The catalysts used were sodium hydroxide obtained from the electrolysis of natural sea salt and potassium hydroxide from wood ash. The new process substituted the fossil fuel based methanol with ethanol produced by grain based renewable products. Use of natural catalysts and non toxic chemicals overcame the limitation of the existing process. Fossil fuel was replaced by direct solar energy for heating, making the biodiesel production process independent of fossil fuel consumption.

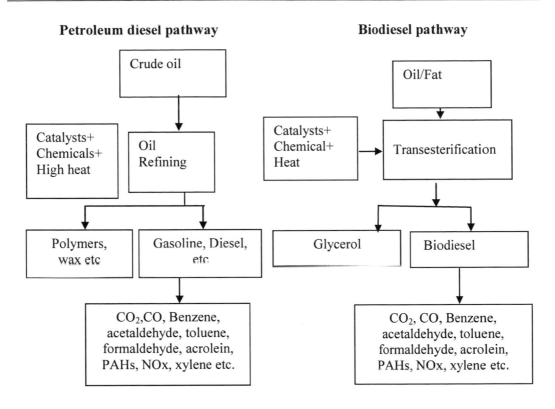

Figure 2.5.27. Pathway of mineral diesel and conventional biodiesel (Chhetri and Islam, 2006b).

Khan et al. (2007b) developed a criterion to test the sustainability of the green biodiesel. According to this criterion, any technology to be sustainable in the long term, it should be environmentally appealing, economically attractive and socially responsible. The technology should continue for infinite time maintaining the indicators functional for all time horizons. For a green biodiesel, the total environmental benefits, social benefits and economics benefits are higher than the input for all time horizons. For example, in case of environmental benefits, green biodiesel burning produces 'natural' CO_2 which can be readily synthesized by plants. The formaldehyde produced during biodiesel burning is also not harmful as there are no toxic additives involved in the biodiesel production process. The plants and vegetable for biodiesel feedstock production also have positive environmental impacts. Thus switching from petrodiesel to biodiesel fulfils the condition $\dfrac{dCn_t}{dt} \geq 0$ where Cn is the total environmental capital of life cycle process of biodiesel production. Similarly, the total social benefit (Cs) $\dfrac{dCs_t}{dt} \geq 0$ and economic benefit (Ce) $\dfrac{dCe_t}{dt} \geq 0$ by switching from mineral diesel to biodiesel (Khan et al., 2007b). Figure 2.5.28 gives a sustainable regime for an energy system for infinite time and fulfills the environmental, social and economic indicators. Biodiesel can be used in practically all areas where petrodiesel is being used. This substitution will help to significantly reduce the CO_2 responsible for current global warming problem.

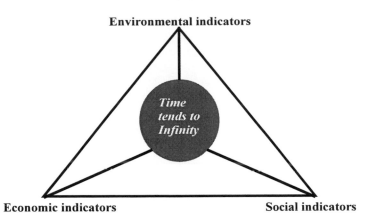

Environmental indicators

Time tends to Infinity

Economic indicators   **Social indicators**

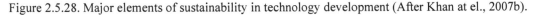

Figure 2.5.28. Major elements of sustainability in technology development (After Khan at el., 2007b).

Development of bioethanol in natural way is another sustainable technology that offers replacement for gasoline engines. The conventional bioethanol production from various feedstocks such as switchgrass and other biomass involves use of chemicals for its breakdown in various stages. For example, the ethanol production process from switchgrass involves acid hydrolysis as a major production process. It is reported that the conversion of switchgrass into bioethanol use concentrated sulfuric acid at 4:1 (acid biomass ratio) which makes the process unsustaniable; produced fuel is a highly toxic fuel and produces formentation inhibitors such as 5-hydroxymethylfurfural (5-HMF) and furfural acid during the hydrolysis process which reduces the efficiency (Bakker et al, 2004). Moreover, the conventional bioethanol production also consumes huge fossil fuel as primary energy input making the ethanol production dependent on fossil fuels.

Development of bioenergy on a large scale requires the deployment of environmentally acceptable, low cost energy crops as well as sustainable technologies to harness them with the least environmental impact. Sugarcane, corn, switchgrass and other ligocellulogic biomass are the major feed stocks for ethanol production. The model developed by Chhetri and Islam (2006b) for green biodiesel can also be applied to make the bioethanol production process truly green. They proposed the use of non toxic chemicals and natural catalysts to make the bioethanol process truly environmental friendly. The technology has been tested for long term sustainability using a set of sustainability criteria. The ethanol produced using the natural and non toxic catalysts will produce natural CO_2 after combustion and has no impacts on global warming.

Recently, the direct use of crude oil is of great interest. Crude oil itself is comparatively cleaner than distillates as it contains less sulfur and toxic metals. The use of crude oil for various applications is to be promoted. This will not only help to maintain the environment because of its less toxic nature but also be less costly as it avoids expensive catalytic refining processes. Several studies have been conducted to investigate the electricity generation from saw dust (Sweis, 2004; Venkataraman et al., 2004; Calle et al., 2005). Figure 2.5.29 shows the schematic of a scaled model developed by Prof. Islam in collaboration with Veridity Environmental Technologies (Halifax, Nova Scotia, Canada). A raw sawdust silo is equipped with a powered auger sawdust feeder. The saw dust is inserted inside another feeding chamber that is equipped with a powered grinder that pulverizes sawdust into wood flour. The chamber is attached to a heat exchanger that dries the saw dust before it enters into the grinder. The wood flour is fed into the combustion chamber with a powered auger wood flour feeder. The pulverization of sawdust increases the surface area of the particles very significantly. The additional energy required to run the feeder and the grinder is provided by the electricity generated by the generator itself, requiring no additional energy investment. In addition the pulverization chamber is also used to dry the saw dust. The removal of moisture increases flammability of the feedstock. The combustion chamber itself is equipped with a start-up fuel injector that uses biofuel. Note that initial temperature required to startup the combustion chamber is quite high and cannot be achieved without a liquid fuel. The exhaust of the combustion chamber is circulated through a heat exchanger in order to dry sawdust prior to pulverization. As the combustion fluids escape the combustion chamber, they turn the drive shaft blades rotate to turn the drive shaft, which in turn, turns the compressor turbine blades. The power generator is placed directly under the main drive shaft.

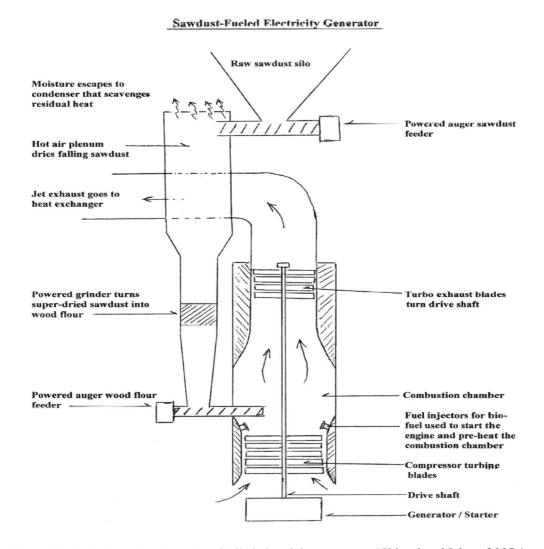

Figure 2.5.29. Schematic of sawdust fuelled electricity generator (Chhetri and Islam, 2007c)

Fernandes and Brooks (2003) compared black carbon (BC) derived from various sources. One interesting feature of this study was that they studied the impact of different sources on the composition, extractability and bioavailability of resulting BC. By using molecular fingerprints, the concluded that fossil BC may be more refractory than plant derived BC. This is an important finding as only recently there has been some advocacy that BC from fossil fuel may have cooling effect, nullifying the contention that fossil fuel burning is the biggest contributor to global warming. It is possible that BC from fossil fuel has higher refractory ability, however, there is no study available to date to quantify the cooling effect and to determine the overall effect of BC from fossil fuel. As for the other effects, BC from fossil appear to be on the harmful side as compared to BC from organic matters. For instance, vegetarian fire residues, straw ash and wood charcoals had only residual concentrations of n-alkanes (<9 µg/g) and polyclyclic aromatic (PAHs) of less than 0.2 µg/g. These concentrations compared with Diesel soot, urban dust and chimney soot PAH concentrations of greater than 8 µg/g and n-alkanes greater than 20 µg/g (Fernandes and Brooks, 2003).

This design shows that even the solid fuels can be used to produce electricity at high efficiencies. Burning of saw dust produces fresh carbon dioxide compared burning of fossil fuels which produces older carbon dioxide (Chhetri et al., 2007a). The use of crude oil (which is liquid) in such a systems will be even more efficient than solid fuel. If the crude oil is used directly similar to saw dust electricity generator, the environmental problems associated with fossil fuel use and refining can be minimized increasing the economical efficiency of the fossil fuel use.

Development of Zero Waste Energy Systems

Waste generation has become synonymous with Modern civilization (Islam, 2004; Khan and Islam, 2005b). This trend has the most profound impact on energy and mass utilization. Conventional energy systems are most inefficient technologies (Chhetri, 2007). The more is wastes, the more inefficient the system is. Almost all industrial and chemical processes produce wastes and most of them are toxic. The wastes not only reduce the efficiency of a system but also pose severe impacts on health and environment leading to further degradation of global efficiency. The treatment of this toxic waste is also highly expensive. Plastics derivatives from refined oil are more toxic than original feedstocks; the oxidation of a plastic tire at high temperature produces toxics such as dioxin. The more refined the products are, the more wastes are generated. Zero waste technologies here are analogous to the 'five zeros' of Olympic logo which are zero emissions, zero resource waste, zero waste in activities, zero use of toxics and zero waste in the product life cycle. This model, originally developed by Lakhal and H'Midi (2003) was called the Olympic Green Chain model. This model was used by Khan (2006) for proposing an array of zero waste technologies.

Zero waste technologies help to eliminate the production of industrial CO_2. The utilization of waste as an energy source offers multiple solutions for energy as well as mitigation of environmental problems. Production of energy from waste reduces the cost of waste treatment and at the same time gives added value to the waste products. This enhances the global efficiency of the system. Local efficiency does not consider the exploration and processing, total transmission and distribution losses, the environmental and social cost associated with the system and the possible uses of by-products. Solar energy is free energy, extremely efficient. Direct solar energy is a benign technology. Khan et al. (2007d) developed a direct solar heating unit to heat the waste vegetable oil as heat transfer medium (Figure 2.5.30). The solar concentrator can heat the oil to more than 300^0C which is maximum of 100^0C in case of water. The heat can be transferred through heat exchanger for space heating, water heating or any other purposes. In the case of direct oil heating, the global efficiency of the system is more than 80%. No waste is generated in the system.

Khan et al.(2007d) developed a heating/cooling and refrigeration system that uses direct solar heat without converting into electricity (Figure 2.5.30). All of the energy input is in the form of heat. Utilization of direct heat for heating cooling or refrigeration replaces the use of large amounts of fossil fuel reducing the CO_2 emission significantly. This type of refrigerator has silent operations, higher heat efficiency, no moving parts and portability.

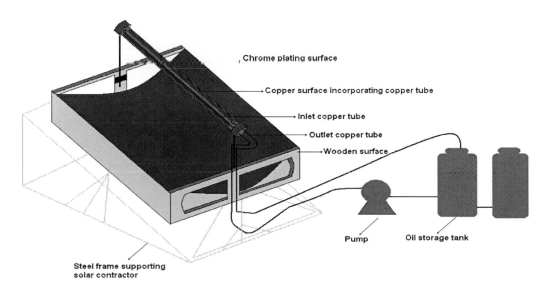

Figure 2.5.30. Details of solar heating unit (After Khan et al., 2005b).

Chhetri et al., (2007a) discussed a model for zero waste stove in order to utilize the waste (Figure 2.5.31). At present saw dust is considered a waste, and management of waste always involves cost. Utilizing the waste saw dust enhances the value addition of the waste material and generates valuable energy as well. The particulates of the wood burning are collected in an oil-water trap which is a valuable nano-material for many industrial applications. This soot material can also be used as an ingredient for non toxic paint. The fuel is waste material from industries as an input. The CO_2 emitted from saw dust burning is necessary for plants for photosynthesis.

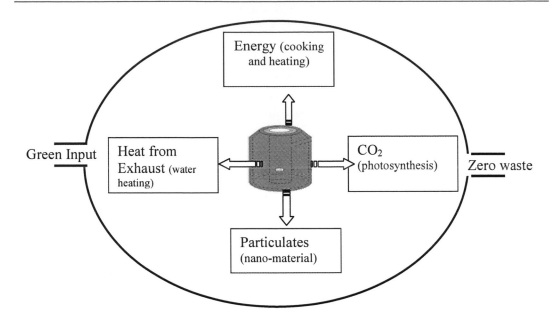

Figure 2.5.31. Pictorial view of zero-waste models for wood stove (after Chhetri et al., 2007a).

A high efficiency jet engine is also an example of zero waste technology (Vafaei 2006). This jet engine can use practically any type of solid fuel such as waste sawdust, and liquid fuel such as waste vegetable oil and crude oil to run the engine. This engine for the first time offers opportunity for the direct combustion of crude oil. Khan et al. (2007e) proposed an approach for zero-waste (mass) utilization for typical urban setting including processing and regeneration of solid, liquid and gas. In this process, kitchen waste and sewage waste are utilized for various purposes including biogas production, desalination, water heating from flue gas and good fertilizer for agricultural production. The carbon dioxide generated from biogas burning is utilized for desalination plant. This process achieves zero-waste in mass utilization. The process is shown in Figure 2.5.32. The technology development in this line has no negative impact on global warming.

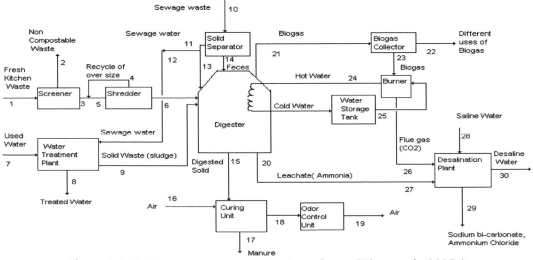

Figure 2.5.32. Zero-waste mass utilization scheme (Khan et al., 2007e).

Role of Technology Development to Reverse Global Warming

Global warming is the consequence of use of natural resources in an un-natural way. The CO_2 produced from industrial activities is the principal cause of global warming. Conventional energy sources, such as fossil fuel contribute to greenhouse gases emissions. Because various toxic chemicals and catalysts are used for refining/processing oil and natural gas, the emitted CO_2 is a toxic product. In addition, fossil fuels have greater properties of carbon isotope ^{13}C making them mere likely to be readily absorbed by plants. This leads to the alteration of characteristic recycle period of carbon dioxide, causing delays that result in an increase in total CO_2 in the atmosphere. Billions of people in the world use traditional stoves fueled by biomass, for their cooking and space heating requirement. It is widely held that wood burning stoves emit more pollution into the atmosphere compared with oil and natural gas burning stoves. However, a small intervention in wood burning stoves will result in the emission of natural CO_2, which is essential for natural processes. Identifying the limitations of conventional stoves, a new technique has been developed to achieve zero-waste in such technologies. This line of development will have great impact on technological development in industrial and other sectors as well.

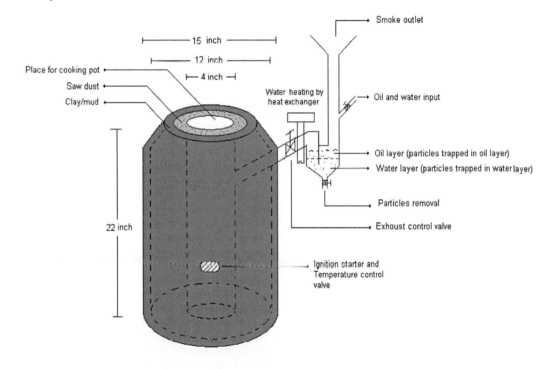

Figure 2.5.33. Sawdust packed stove (after Khan et al, 2007a).

Figure 2.5.33 is a saw dust packed cookstove developed by Khan et al. (2007a). This is a highly efficient clay stove that has no waste. Even though not all by-products are captured and value added, this stove is still considered to be a zero waste stove as it produces only organic gases that are readily absorbed by the environment in order to produce useful final products. This has a special oil-water trapping mechanism that captures the particulates of incomplete combustion in an oil water mixture. A heat exchanger is designed to trap the heat from the flue gas that is utilized for water heating. As all the particulates are trapped, the CO_2

emitted is a clean and natural CO_2 that is an essential feedstock for plant for photosynthesis. The particulates trapped may be used as paint material. This can also be an excellent source of nano material for industrial application. This technology offers solutions for the production of a natural form of CO_2 which is readily synthesized by plants. The other emissions such as methane and oxides of nitrogen are not harmful, unlike those emitted from petroleum based fuels.

The production of green biodiesel and bioethanol discussed earlier are key elements in the production of natural CO_2, which does not contribute to the global warming. Only non toxic chemicals and catalysts are used in the processes to produce biodiesel and bioethanol. Even the benzene, NO_x, methane and other emissions are not harmful as there is no toxic chemicals are involved during the production. These fuels are derived from renewable sources such as plants and vegetables. Plant and vegetables are essential components of natural food cycles for both the plants and animal kingdoms. It has been reported that petroleum fuels are being exhausted within the next few decades, whereas renewable biofuel sources continue for infinite time. These biofuels could replace all petroleum fuels provided the biomass farming is planned in a sustainable way. Replacing the petroleum fuels with clean biofuels in a sustainable way, can eventually lead to the reversal of global warming. This reversal can be accelerated if processing of fossil fuel is rendered non toxic by avoiding the use of toxic additives (Khan and Islam, 2007a; Al Darby et al., 2002). Recent studies indicated that crude oil refining can be avoided altogether with some design modification of the combustion engine (Chhetri and Islam, 2007c)

Energy systems are classified based on their global efficiencies. According to Chhetri (2007), global efficiency is one of the major indicators to be considered while selecting the technology choice for any energy systems. For instance, conventional oil heated steam turbine to electricity production, has a global efficiency of approximately 16%. For combined heat and power turbines, the global efficiency is approximately 18%. Similarly, the global efficiency of a coal fired power system is approximately 15%, for hydropower systems it is 43%, from biomass to electricity conversion is 13%, and nuclear power plant has a global efficiency of approximately 5%. The environmental cost due to these technologies has not been added up yet which further reduces the global efficiency of these technologies. The solar photovoltaic conversion efficiency is reported to be around 15% (Islam et al., 2006). This system also uses toxic batteries and synthetic silicon cells which includes toxic heavy metals inside solar cells. Their efficiency starts decreasing when we store them in the batteries. The efficiency of a battery itself is not very high and batteries contain toxic compounds in it. The inert gas filled tubes radiate very toxic light. The 15% global efficiency of a systems means that for every 100 units of energy produced, 85% energy is lost in the process. This indicates that the prevailing technologies have a very high waste generation. Most of these systems produce toxic CO_2 that cause the global warming problems. Moreover, the CO_2 emissions from embodied energy associated with all the massive equipment production and manufacturing is also very high.

Direct application of solar energy for heating, is of the highest efficiency. Solar energy is a free source and it has no environmental impact at all. Similarly, wood combustion in a simple stove has also a very high global efficiency due to the use of by-products and waste heat. The CO_2 from wood combustion is also an essential ingredient for maintaining the photosynthesis process. The energy systems which have highest efficiency have the lowest environmental impacts.

Considering the long term impacts of various energy systems, the CO_2 emissions during combustion of oil and gas, coal, embodied energy and associated CO_2 emission for hydropower and photovoltaic systems has been ranked based on the quality of CO_2. Similarly, the CO_2 emission from geothermal energy, biomass burning has also been ranked. Based on this ranking, natural CO_2 which does not contribute to global warming is deducted from the Industrial CO_2 which contributed global warming. Series of technological interventions discussed here are truly instrumental in order to reverse the global warming problem.

3. INDUSTRY AND TRANSPORTATION FUELS

The industry and the transportation sector are the most energy consuming sectors in the world. These sectors are the major contributors of greenhouse gas emissions in the atmosphere. Current energy supply mode is based on the use of processed fossil fuels which are contaminated by various types of heavy metals and synthetic chemicals during their processing and refining. For example, the major problems of emission from gasoline fuelled vehicles are the lead, chromium and other heavy metal emission along with toxic greenhouse gases. As natural gas is treated with glycol and amines during their processing, burning of natural gas produces carbon monoxide and a number of low concentration chemicals that are poisonous and are the precursor to numerous health problems including asthma and cancer. Hence, switching from gasoline or diesel to natural gas does not solve any problems encountered by the society today. The only way to reverse the current mode of energy use in industrial and transportation sector is two fold: design vehicles to use crude oil without refining or develop processing technologies environmentally appealing (Khan and Islam, 2007a). The truly–sustainable technologies, which foster the development of natural products in terms of technology development and fuel processing, would help solve the current environmental crisis. In this Chapter, various types of technologies which are inherently sustainable are discussed. The use of direct crude oil in a newly designed jet engine has been discussed in other chapter of this book.

3.1. BIODIESEL

Biodiesel Definition and Controversy

Biodiesel fuels are the mono-alkyl esters of fatty acid derived by the transesterification of plant/vegetable oils and animal fats by using alcohol such as methanol and catalysts such as hydroxide of potassium and sodium heating at certain temperature. When vegetable oil or animal fat is chemically reacted with an alcohol, it produces fatty acid alkyl esters and glycerol. Except oil and fats as feedstocks, all materials used to make conventional biodiesel are from synthetic origin, yet, they are called biodiesel. Biodiesel is considered as an alternative fuel for petrodiesel but still biodiesel production utilizes fossil fuel for its synthesis. If fossil fuels are considered exhaustible, the life of biodiesel will remain until fossil fuels are available. Hence, conventional biodiesel cannot be an alternative to petrodiesel as touted by its proponents. In addition to this, the catalysts and chemicals used to process vegetable oils and fats into biodiesel are highly toxic chemicals of synthetic origin. Moreover, since the biodiesel production has fossil fuels input from agriculture farming to fuel transportation, this is not necessarily a green fuel. To define it as biodiesel and to make it green, the catalysts and chemicals should be non-toxic, derived from biological origin and input energy should be derived from clean energy sources such as direct solar application.

Biodiesel as an Alternate Fuel to Petrodiesel

The world is already witnessing several environmental problems including global warming, ozone layer depletion and climate change among others. This is largely due to the consumption of huge amounts of fossil fuels. The CO_2 produced by burning fossil fuel is not acceptable for plants and builds up in the atmosphere. For these reasons, biodiesel production from renewable plants and vegetable sources has been considered one of the most viable alternative fuels to substitute for petroleum diesel (Giridhar et al., 2004, Meher et al., 2004). The total worldwide production of biodiesel has reached to 2.2 billion gallon (Martinot, 2005). Diesel fuel is used in transportation, agriculture, commercial, domestic and industrial sectors for the generation of power. Department of Environment and Heritage (2005) reported that each kg of diesel fuel consumption produces 2.7 kg of CO_2. Similarly, one kg of biodiesel consumption produces 0.72 kg of CO_2 (Carraretto et al., 2004). Thus, even a small fraction of alternative fuels will have a significant impact on the world economy and environment (Barnwal and Sharma 2005). Nabi et al. (2006) reported that the emissions tests showed a 54% decrease in HC, 46% decrease in CO, 14.7% decrease in NOx, and 0.5% increase in CO_2 when biodiesel was used compared to petrodiesel. However, since the biodiesel production follows similar model with petrodiesel, reducing emission is not a big accomplishment. In order to fully get the benefit from biodiesel, the current production process should be completely reversed into natural and non-toxic model.

Biodiesel can generally be burnt efficiently and simply in existing diesel engines without any modification. This fuel can also be used in home heating, marine, jet application, furnaces and boilers and oil fueled lighting equipment (Tickell, 2003). Biodiesel has become more attractive recently because of its environmental benefits and the fact that it is derived from renewable resources. Burning biodiesel does not increase current net atmospheric levels of CO_2, a greenhouse gas (Du et al., 2004). A biological source such as green biodiesel produces fresh CO_2 which is readily synthesized by plants (Chhetri et al., 2007a; Khan and Islam, 2007a). It is safely biodegradable, offers scope for re-cycling waste oils and produces far less air pollutants than fossil diesel (Xiaoling and Wu, 2006). Biodiesel is simple to manufacture and provides excellent engine performance. This has good lubricating properties with respect to petrodiesel, higher density, greater cetane number, low sulfur emission and low flash point making it the safest fuel to handle (Carraretto et al., 2004; Randall, 1999). Carraretto et al. (2004) reported the typical chemical and physical properties of commercial biodiesel and petrodiesel (Table 3.1).

Table 3.1. Chemical and physical properties of commercial biodiesel and petrodiesel (Carraretto et al., 2004)

Properties	Units	Biodiesel sample	Petrodiesel sample
Density at 15^0C	Kg/m^3	886.1	829.0
Viscosity at 40^0C	Mm^2/s	4.3	2.40
Carbonious residue	%m/m	0.18	0.01
Ester content	%m/m	98.9	-
Glycerol content	%m/m	0.2	-
CFPP	0C	-4	-4
LHV	MJ/kg	37.54	42.99
Phosphorus	Mg/kg	274	0.001
Sulfur	%m/m	0.007	
Iodine number			
Oxidation stability			

Biodiesel Feedstocks

The main feedstocks for biodiesel are vegetable oils, animal fats and waste cooking oil. These are the mono alkyl esters of fatty acids derived from vegetable oil or animal fat. The fuels derived may be alcohols, ethers, esters and other chemicals made from cellulosic biomass and waste products, such as agricultural and forestry residues, aquatic plants (microalgae), fast growing trees and grasses, municipal and industrial wastes. Subramanyam et al. (2005) reported that there are more than 350 oil-bearing crops identified, which can be utilized to make biodiesel. Beef and sheep tallow, rapeseed oil, sunflower oil, canola oil, coconut oil, olive oil, soybean oil, cottonseed oil, mustard oil, hemp oil, linseed oil, microalgae oil, peanut oil and waste cooking oil are considered as potential alternative feedstocks for biodiesel production (Demirba, 2003). However, the main sources of biodiesel are rapeseed and soybean oil, and to certain extent, animal fat with rapeseed accounting for nearly 84 % of the total production (Demirba, 2003). Henning (2004) reported that Jatropha Curcus has also a great potential to yield biodiesel. Chhetri et al. (2007b) reported that Jatropha is a multipurpose tree that the oil can be used for medicinal and other purposes. The UK alone produces about 200,000 tones of waste cooking oil each year (Carter et al., 2005). This provides a good opportunity to utilize waste into energy.

Various types of algae, some of which have oil content of more than 60% by their body weight in the form of tryacylglycerols are the potential sources for biodiesel production (Sheehan et al., 1998). Many species of algae can be successfully grown in wastewater ponds and saline water ponds utilizing CO_2 from power plants as their food. Utilizing CO_2 from power plants to grow algae helps sequester CO_2 for productive use and at the same time reduced the build up of CO_2 in the atmosphere. Waste cooking oil is also considered a viable option for biodiesel feedstock. Utilizing waste cooking oil to convert into biodiesel also solves environmental problems caused by its disposal to water courses. Sometimes it is blamed that biodiesel production competes with food production. Thus utilizing the waste cooking oil and non edible oil will help to solve such problems. The Earth is a big reservoir of various plants oils which can be tapped for biodiesel production in the future.

Advantages of Biodiesel Fuel

There are numerous advantages to biodiesel. Some of the major ones are discussed below.

1. *It provides a market for excess production of vegetable oils and animal fats.*
   Thereis an increase demand of protein from soybean meal around the world. The growers would be more encouraged if they have alternate market for the soybean crop. Biodiesel industry would be an option for the farmers that can increase soybean oil production, rendering it a cheap feedstock for biodiesel fuel. Similarly, the animal fat has limited application in today's market. Provided the biodiesel industries are established, the excess fats will get enough market for its proper use. Moreover, because of heavy use of antibiotics and various diseases (such as mad cow diseases), the use of fats in food products have been restricted. Hence producing biodiesel from these fats would offer cheaper feedstock for biodiesel and at the same time waste material is utilized for useful work.

2. *It decreases the country's dependence on imported petroleum.*
   Petroleum market is extremely sensitive in terms of supply and price. Excess edible and non-edible oils are available in many countries which can be converted into biodiesel for industrial and transportation application. Hence, this will help reduce the dependency of petroleum import from abroad. Since biodiesel can be produced in communities and homes, this will empower the local economy of any place provided proper policies are set.

3. *Biodiesel is renewable and does not contribute to global warming*
   It is considered that biodiesel emission does not contribute to global warming as the plants producing vegetable oil use the CO_2 making a closed carbon cycle. However, the current method of biodiesel production is not green and fossil free. This is true only when biodiesel is produced in natural way using natural catalysts and non-toxic chemicals. The CO_2 produced from biodiesel, despite being from organic origin, is contaminated from the toxic chemicals which are not easily accepted by plants (Chhetri et al., 2007a). Making the biodiesel production truly green would help to combat global warming (Chhetri and Islam, 2007a; Chhetri and Islam, 2006b).

4. *The exhaust emissions from biodiesel are lower than with regular diesel fuel.*
   It is widely considered that biodiesel leads substantial reductions in carbon monoxide, unburned hydrocarbons, and particulate emissions from diesel engines. Biodiesel fuels offer reduction in particulate emissions, especially the black soot portion. However, only reducing emission is not a big accomplishment. The biodiesel production process should be turned completely green so that emission of exhaust gases is not of prime concern. The toxicity of current biodiesel emission is very similar with that of petrodiesel due to the use of highly toxic chemicals and catalysts during production. If the natural catalysts and non-toxic chemicals are used, the emission of clean CO_2 is essential for plants. The emission of nitrous oxides will not be a toxic compound from a green biodiesel process. The benzene, formaldehyde and other hydrocarbons from the biological origin is not the same as that of synthetic origin (Chhetri and Islam, 2006b). The unburned particulates matters can be trapped

by using oil and water trap which can later on be used as industrial nano-material and non-toxic paint (Chhetri et al., 2007a).

5. *Biodiesel has excellent lubricating properties.*
    Biodiesel has better lubricating properties than petrodiesel. This will enhance the performance even if 1-2% of biodiesel is added to conventional diesel (Gerpen et al, 2004).

6. *Positive Energy Balance*
    Biodiesel has a net positive energy balance based on its life cycle/ energy balance analysis (e.g., for soybean production and conversion to biodiesel). The U.S. Department of Energy (DOE) and the U.S. Department of Agriculture (USDA) carried out a detailed study on the life cycle energy balance of soybean, and reported that for every unit of fossil energy used in the entire production cycle, 3.2 units of energy are gained when the fuel is burned that is, or a positive energy balance of 320% (USDA/DOE, 1998). This is lighted in Figure 3.1. It is also reported that this study started with bare soil and took into account all the energy inputs associated with growing and harvesting soybeans, transporting and processing the soybeans into oil and meal, transportation and production of the soybean oil into biodiesel, and transportation of the biodiesel to the end user. It is conceivable that process would be even more appealing if the vegetable oil is produced through truly organic means, such as the use of organic fertilizer in stead of chemical fertilizer.

Current Biodiesel Production Procedures

Conventionally, biodiesel is produced either in a single-stage or double-stage batch process or by a continuous-flow type transesterification process. These processes are generally of the following three types.

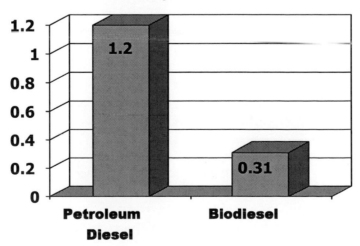

Figure 3.1. Mega Joule (MJ) fossil used per MJ fuel (Adopted from USDA/DOE, 1998).

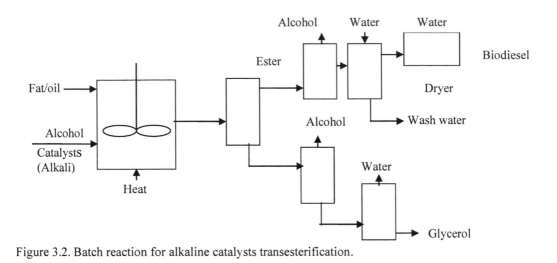

Figure 3.2. Batch reaction for alkaline catalysts transesterification.

1. Alkali/Base Catalyzed Reaction

Alkali catalyzed transesterification reactions are those for which alkalis are used as catalysts. Alkali catalysts help to generate faster reaction than other catalysts, hence all commercial biodiesel producers prefer to use this process (Ma and Hanna, 1999). The alkalis generally used in the process include NaOH, KOH, and sodium methoxide. For an alkali-catalyzed transesterification, the glycerides and alcohol must be anhydrous because water makes the reaction partially changed to saponification, which produces soap. The soap lowers the yield of esters and makes the separation of biodiesel and glycerin complicated. The typical alcohol used is methanol with a 6:1 molar ratio (100% excess). Typical base concentrations are 0.3 to 1.5% based on the weight of oil. When sodium methoxide is used, the concentration can be 0.5% or less (Gerpen et al., 2004). Figure 3.2 is the schematics of batch process for alkali catalyzed transesterification.

The combination of alcohol and catalysts are mixed with oil or fats and heated up to 65^{0}C. However, the temperature varies depending on the type of oil, catalysts and type of alcohol used. To bring the oil, catalyst and alcohol into intimate contact, thorough mixing is necessary at the beginning of the reaction. Reaction completions of 85 to 94 % are reported in alkali catalyzed reactions. It was also reported that 95% of conversion is possible in two step reaction where separate glycerol removal step is used. Higher temperatures and higher alcohol:oil ratios also can enhance the percent conversion. Typical reaction times range from 20 minutes to more than one hour (Gerpen et al., 2004). A continuous or plug flow reaction process reaches up to 98% conversion of oil or fats into esters.

2. Acid Catalyzed Reactions

The acids generally used are sulfonic acid and sulfuric acid. These acids give very high yields in alkyl esters but these reactions are slow, requiring high temperature above 100^{0}C and more than three hours to complete the conversion (Schuchardt, 1998). Acid catalyzed process is used for direct esterification of free fatty acids for high free fatty acids (FFA) feedstock. This process can also be used to produce esters from a soap stock. Figure 3.3 is the schematic for the pre-treating high FFA feedstocks before sending into alkali catalyzed transesterification process. The process also requires removal of water during the reaction.

Very high alcohol to fatty acid ratios, about 40:1, are required and acid amounts equal to 5 to 25% of the FFA level may be needed (Gerpen et al., 2004).

3. Supercritical Methanol Method (without Catalysts)

No catalyst is used in the case of supercritical methanol method, for which the methanol and oil mixture is superheated to more than 350^0C and the reaction complete in 3-5 minutes to form esters and glycerol. Saka and Kudsiana, (2001) carried out series of experiments to study the effects of reaction temperature, pressure and molar ratio of methanol to glycosides in methyl ester formation and their results revealed supercritical treatment of 350^0C, 30 MPa and 240 sec with molar ratio of 42 in methanol is the best condition for transesterification of rapeseed oil for biodiesel production. Schematic diagram of supercritical methanol method is shown in Figure 3.4

Besides these methods, there are other methods such as enzymatic transesterification, co-solvent method and heterogeneous catalysts method. In enzyme catalysed transesterification, bio enzymes are used for the reaction. This method has been very popular recently as this has no negative environmental impacts. In co-solvent method, different types of co-solvents such as tetrahydrofuran (THF) are used to emulsify alcohol and vegetable oil. THF creates one phase mixture of oil and reaction can occur in room temperature. In heterogeneous catalysts method, insoluble solid catalysts such as calcium carbonate have been successfully used in bench scale. However, these methods are not used in commercial scales. The details of chemistry of transesterification reaction is described below.

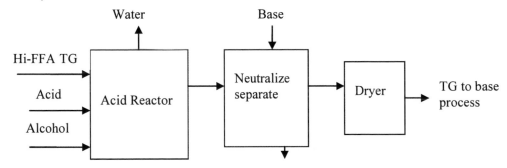

Figure 3.3. Acid catalyzed Transesterification Process.

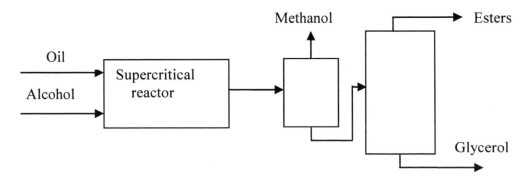

Figure 3.4. Supercritical methanol method.

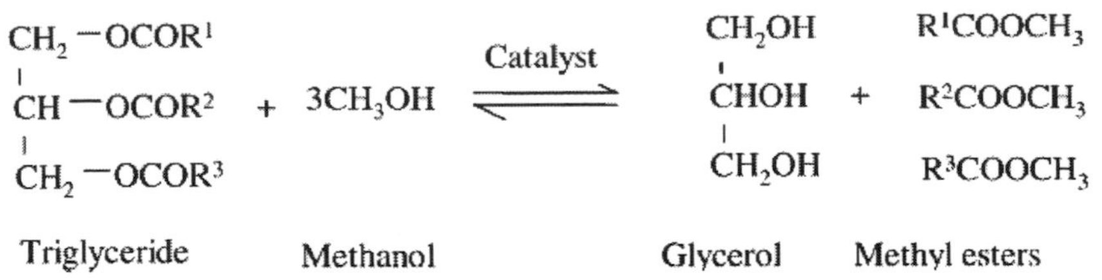

$$
\begin{array}{ll}
CH_2-OCOR^1 & \\
| & \\
CH-OCOR^2 \quad + \quad 3CH_3OH \xrightleftharpoons[]{Catalyst} & CHOH \quad + \\
| & \\
CH_2-OCOR^3 & \\
\end{array}
\quad
\begin{array}{ll}
CH_2OH & R^1COOCH_3 \\
| & \\
CHOH \quad + & R^2COOCH_3 \\
| & \\
CH_2OH & R^3COOCH_3 \\
\end{array}
$$

Triglyceride   Methanol   Glycerol   Methyl esters

Figure 3.5. Typical equation for transesterification where R1, R2, R3 are the different hydrocarbon chains.

The Chemistry of Transesterification

The major objective of transesterification is to breakdown the long chain of fatty acid molecules into simple molecules and reduce the viscosity considerably in order to increase the lubricity of the fuel. The transesterification process is the reaction of a triglyceride (fat/oil) with an alcohol using a catalyst to form esters and glycerol. A triglyceride has a glycerin molecule as its base with three long chain fatty acids attached. During the esterification process, the triglyceride is broken down with alcohol in the presence of a catalyst, usually a strong alkaline like sodium hydroxide. The alcohol reacts with the fatty acids to form the mono-alkyl ester, or biodiesel and crude glycerol. In most production, methanol or ethanol is the alcohol used and is base catalyzed by either potassium or sodium hydroxide. After completion of transesterification reaction, the glycerin and biodiesel are separated (gravity separation). The glycerin is either re-used as feedstock for methane production or refined and used in pharmaceutical products. A typical transesterification process is given in Figure 3.5.

The alkali-catalyzed transesterification mechanism is shown in Figure 3.6. As a first step, the alkoxide ion attack to the carbonyl carbon of the triglyceride molecule, which results in the formation of a tetrahedral intermediate. The reaction of this intermediate with an alcohol produces the alkoxide ion in the next step. In the last step the rearrangement of the tetrahedral intermediate gives rise to an ester and a diglyceride. Similar process continues until glycerol and mono-alkyl ester molecules are formed (Ma and Hanna, 1999).

Figure 3.7 shows the kinetics of acid catalyzed process. The acids generally used in acid catalysed process are brownsted acids, such as sulfonic and sulfuric acids. This process is very slow requiring about 100^0C but yields high alkyl esters and needs more than 3 hours to complete the conversion (Schuchardt et al, 1998).

In addition to the conventional methods, various other methods have been developed to make the biodiesel production technically feasible and economical. Boocock et al. (1996) developed a method for biodiesel production at room temperature without any additional heat. This process uses methanol as alcoholysis medium, tetrahydrofuran (THF) from biological origin to create oil dominant one phase system in which methanolysis speeds up dramatically faster. The separation of THF is also not difficult as its boiling point is similar to that of methanol. Mahajan et al. (2006) reported that using THF as a co-solvent, the mass transfer problems from during the transesterification reaction for developing methanol oil system as oil dominated one phase system. The main objective of mixing THF is to convert low acid number vegetable oils into a standard biodiesel in a single chemical reaction using certain catalysts. Mixing THF reduces the mechanical mixing that is conventionally done during transesterification reaction. It was recently reported that excellent results are obtained for biodiesel making from an alkaline transesterification reaction of soybean oil using ultrasonic mixing (Colucci et al., 2005). Ultrasonic agitation offers complete mixing at lower temperature (25-60^{0}C) and increases the reaction rate for to five times higher than those reported for mechanical agitation. The possible reasons for this was considered due to the increase in interfacial area and activity of microscopic and macroscopic bubbles formed when ultrasonic waves of 20 kHz were applied in two phase reaction system (Mustafiz et al., 2007).

Similar study reported that by using ultrasounds (28-40 kHz) for mixing, catalysts requirements were reduced 2-3 times lower than conventional methods and reaction took place in much shorter (10-40 minutes) time (Stavarache et al., 2006). Biodiesel yields obtained when 28 kHz frequency was 98-99%. Zhu and Tsuchiya (2005) reported that using ultrasound for biodiesel production does not need external heating and stirring apparatus leading to a compact design for producing biodiesel fuels. Even though ultrasound could play big role in processing and economics of biodiesel, the catalysts and fossil methanol being used for the reaction still remains problematic due to their toxicity. Generating ultrasound energy using fossil fuels could eventually lead to the environmental problems. Hence some natural source for creating ultrasound energy using solar energy could be a better option for its long term sustainability. Recently it has been reported sugar, which is a non-toxic and inexpensive, can be used as catalysts for biodiesel production (Toda et al., 2005).

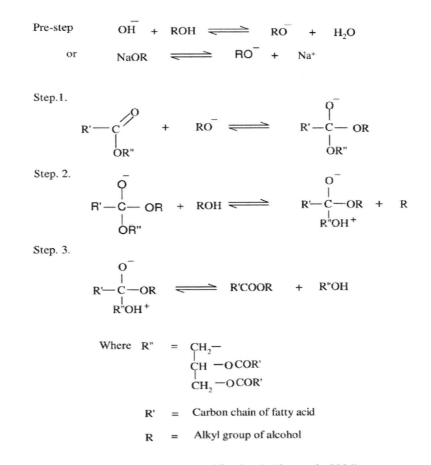

Figure 3.6. Mechanism for base catalyzed transesterification (Meher et al., 2004).

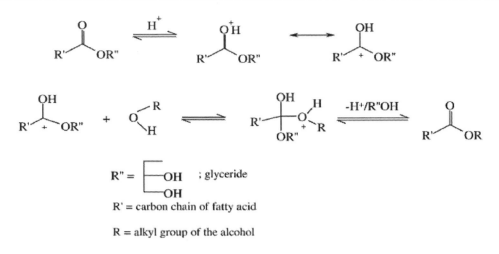

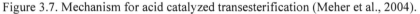

R" = ⌐—OH   ; glyceride
     └—OH
R' = carbon chain of fatty acid

R = alkyl group of the alcohol

Figure 3.7. Mechanism for acid catalyzed transesterification (Meher et al., 2004).

Variables Affecting Transesterification Process

Transestrification reaction is affected by various factors that vary on reaction conditions. The amount of free fatty acid (FFA) and moisture content in the reactants is of great concerns. The higher FFA lowers the conversion efficiency significantly (Meher et al., 2004). The presence of moisture, higher or lower amount of catalysts may cause formation of soap during the reaction. Types of catalysts and their concentration are also very important parameter. Generally used catalysts are acid, alkali, enzyme, and heterogeneous catalysts. Acid catalysts such as sulfuric acid, phosphoric acid, hydrochloric acid or organic sulfonic acid are useful if the feedstock has higher FFA. If the oil has lower FFA, alkali catalysts such as sodium hydroxide, sodium methoxide, potassium hydroxide, potassium methoxide are considered more effective (Ma and Hanna, 1999). It was reported that NaOH was found effective for beef tallow transesterification. Sodium methoxide causes the formation of several by-products mainly sodium salts, which are to be treated as a waste. Enzymatic catalysts such as lipases are able to effectively catalyze the transesterification of triglycerides in either aqueous or non-aqueous systems efficiently. Lipases enhance the production significantly. Molar ratio between the alcohol and oil is also very important factor. The stoichiometric ratio for transesterification reaction requires three molesof alcohols and one mole of triglyceride to yield three moles of fatty acid alkyl esters and one mole of glycerol (Figure 3.5). Since the transesterification reaction is a reversible reaction, excess alcohol is generally beneficial in order to drive the reaction forward to form esters.

High molar ratio of alcohol to vegetable oil helps the separation of glycerin because there is an increase in solubility. The molar ratio necessary for the complete conversion depends on various types of oils or fats. Hence molar ratio, type of alcohol and type of feedstock are important parameters for the higher conversion of mono-alkyl esters. Because the oil and alcohol are not mixed easily, mixing intensity also affects the reaction. Some of the co-solvents such as THF help to make the single phase for oil and alcohol making it easy for the reaction in room temperature. Recently ultrasound mixing has been found to be very effective method for creating emulsion between the oil and alcohol. The other important variables that affect the transesterification process are time and temperature. The reaction rate generally increases with time. For different oil and alcohol used, formation of esters occurs at optimum temperature. For the transesterification of refined oil with methanol (6:1) and 1% NaOH, the ester yields were 94, 87 and 64% for 60, 45 and 32 8C, respectively for reaction time for 0.1 hour. After 1 hour, ester formation was identical for 60 and 45^{0}C runs and only slightly lower for the 32^{0}C run (Ma and Hanna, 1999).

Biodiesel in Industrial Application

The use of biodiesel fuel has been mostly limited in transportation vehicle use. Carraretto et al. (2004) reported a field experience with biodiesel burning and mentioned that adapted burners involve less emission of pollutants and fouling problems. This can be an important fuel for isolated areas where other fuel sources are not available. However, conventional biodiesel is less stable in terms of storage due to oxidation. Moreover, early weathering occurs on the rubberized parts of engine such as gaskets.

Problems with Conventional Biodiesel Production

1. Use of Toxic Catalysts and Chemicals

The catalysts and chemicals used in biodiesel processing are NaOH, KOH, H_2SO_4 among others. These synthetic chemicals are highly toxic. Haynes (1976) reported that a dose of 1.95 grams of sodium hydroxide can cause death. The most serious effects of sodium hydroxide at 50% by weight of active ingredient are corrosion of body tissues. Eye and skin contact can cause very serious burns. It has been reported that concentration of sodium hydroxide of 10 g/l cause nervousness, sore eyes, diarrhea and retarded growth in rats (Haynes, 1976). The synthetic potassium hydroxides also has similar toxicity. Sulfuric and sulfonic acids used in acid catalysed transesterification are highly toxic acids. These are not only hazardous for handling but also create several environmental problems with the waste water streams from the industrial process. Removing many of these chemicals is impossible from the water streams and even if removed, it involves a huge cost. Methanol is derived from a refined fossil fuel and is highly poisonous. It kills the nerves before one feels the pain. Production of methanol from natural gas reforming use toxic catalysts making the environment unsafe.

2. Biodiesel is Dependent of Fossil fuel

The current biodiesel production uses fossil fuel at various stages such as agriculture, crushing, transportation and the process itself (Carraretto, et al., 2004). Figure 3.8 shows the share of energy use at different stages from farming to biodiesel production. Approximately 35% of the primary energy is consumed during the life cycle from agriculture farming to biodiesel production. This energy comes from fossil fuels. To make the biodiesel completely green, this portion of energy has also to be derived from renewable sources. For energy conversion and crushing, direct solar energy can be effectively used while renewable biofuels can be used for transportation and agriculture.

point is also another property at which temperature the fuel can still move. French and Italian biodiesel specifications specify pour point whereas others specify CFPP.

Storage of biodiesel fuel has become a great concern. Vegetable oil derivatives especially tend to deteriorate owing to hydrolytic and oxidative reactions. Their degree of unsaturation makes them susceptible to thermal and/or oxidative polymerization, which may lead to the formation of insoluble products that cause problems within the fuel system, especially in the injection pump (Meher et al., 2004). Even though common mechanism of sediment formation in different fuel oils are diverse, it generally involves in some chemical species. These species include indoles, pyrroles, aromatic thiols, heterocyclic aromatics and carbozoles (Hiley and Pedley, 1998). The absence of these chemicals in biodiesel indicates that the oxidation mechanism is different from petrodiesel. Oxidation of biodiesel results in the formation of hydroperoxides. One of the major concerns of biodiesel users and sellers is chemical attack of fuel system components.

Esters are subjected to oxidation forming hydroperoxide due to their exposure in air which is the addition of oxygen to a carbon atom adjacent to a carbon-carbon double bond. After certain time, peroxide splits and forms short chain acids and aldehydes. When the antioxidants available in the fuel are completely consumed, oxidation of fuel is accelerated. The peroxidation can induce polymerization of the esters and form insoluble gums and sediments which are the major problems forming corrosion in injector pump and injector seal. The hydroxides and alcohols used in the transesterifcation process could be other reasons for their oxidation and corrosion of the parts.

A New Approach to Render the Biodiesel Production Truly Green

Chhetri and Islam, (2006b) developed a new approach to render the biodiesel production process truly green. This new approach is based on the use of alcohol produced from renewable sources. Methanol can be produced by utilizing microbes to convert methane to methanol. Methane produced from anaerobic digestion, is acted upon by methanotrophs that convert methane into methanol (Figure 3.9). Hanson and Hanson (1996) and Murrell (1994) reported that methanotrophs are aerobic bacteria which utilize methane as their sole carbon and energy source. Methanotrophs are physically versatile and can be effectively utilize to produce methanol from wide variety of wastes. Use of ethyl alcohol fermented from grain-based biomass such as corn or sweet sorghum and molasses from sugar for alcoholysis of vegetable oils or fats is also a sustainable option (Figure 3.10). Both of these alternatives eliminate the consumption of huge amount of natural gas to make methanol. No expensive and toxic chemicals are involved in these processes. Khan et al.(2006b) analyzed the sustainability for biodiesel based on economic, environment and social criteria and showed that a truly green biodiesel is a sustainable technology.

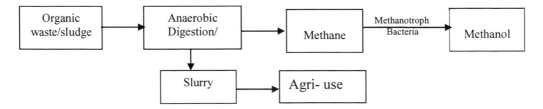

Figure 3.9. Production of methanol from methane by microbial conversion.

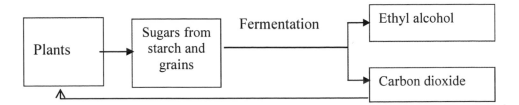

Figure 3.10. Flow process for production of ethyl alcohol.

Figure 3.11 is the schematic diagram of new process for biodiesel production. In this process, potassium hydroxide derived from wood ash or sodium hydroxide derived from sea salt is used as catalyst along with bio-based methanol or ethyl alcohol. Waste cooking oil is preheated up to 50^0 C before mixing the methanol and potassium hydroxide mixture in it. After mixing, the mixture is heated to 60^0 C at which the reaction takes place to form biodiesel and glycerin. The glycerin is separated by gravity separation. The crude biodiesel is heated to 65^0 C to evaporate and recover methanol to reuse in the process. In case ethyl alcohol is used as medium for alcoholysis; it should be heated to 80^0C to evaporate the ethyl alcohol. The biodiesel is then washed with either mist or bubbles and then dried to evaporate all water vapor before sending to storage or use.

The biodiesel produced from this process is a non toxic product because all the chemicals and catalysts are non toxic. The CO_2 produced is 'new' CO_2 with lighter isotopes and it is not contaminated by any chemicals because the biological sources produce new CO_2 (Islam, 2005). Plants will synthesize this 'fresh' CO_2 and complete the carbon cycle. Similarly, the NOx and CO produced during combustion of non toxic biodiesel is not harmful compared to the petrodiesel and conventional biodiesel. Formaldehyde and other emissions from biodiesel combustion are different from those emitted from petrodiesel or conventional biodiesel.

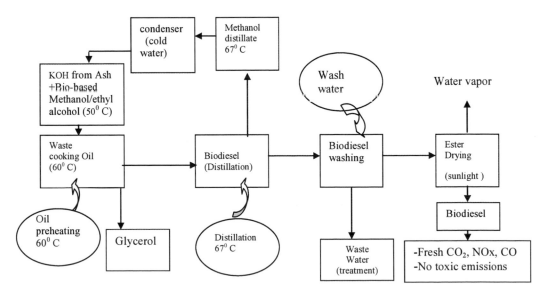

Figure 3.11. Schematic diagram of proposed biodiesel production process (Chhetri and Islam, 2006b).

Economics of the New Approach

The economic feasibility of conventional biodiesel depends on crude petroleum price and transportation of diesel over long distances. It is evident that the cost of diesel will increase in the future owing to the increase in its demand and limited supply. Furthermore, the strict regulations on the aromatic and sulfur contents of diesel fuels makes diesel costlier, as the removal of aromatics from distillate fractions needs costly processing equipment and continuous high operational cost since large amounts of hydrogen are required for such processes. Similarly, reducing the sulfur content of diesel fuel is also a challenge for the industries. Currently, biodiesel is comparatively more expensive than petrodiesel in the market. Major cost of biodiesel is feedstock which is about 80% of total operating cost (Coltrain, 2002). The other components that affect the production cost are chemicals and catalysts. The cost of biodiesel production can be significantly reduced by considering non-edible oils, animal and fish fat, and used frying oils (Barnwal and Sharma, 2005). Non-edible oils from sources such as Neem, Mahua, Pongamia, Jatropha are easily available in many parts of the world and are inexpensive compared to edible oils. The use of waste cooking oil instead of virgin oil to produce biodiesel is an effective way to reduce the feedstock cost because it is estimated to be about half the price of virgin oil (Supple et al.,1999). This will in turn help to reduce the cost of water treatment in the sewerage system and assist in the recycling of resources.

In producing biodiesel from vegetable oils, the return on investment and processing cost are essentially compensated by the by-product credits such as glycerin. Other most important factors that contribute the cost of biodiesel are the cost of methanol, synthetic sodium and potassium hydroxide and conversion energy cost. Methanol, sodium and potassium hydroxide come from a different market which is not related to biodiesel. Thus outside market would significantly affect the cost of biodiesel production. Methanol produced by fermentation is a renewable process and can be produced even from the household waste. This methanol is not bad for environment as it is easily biodegradable.

This new method of biodiesel production from waste vegetable oils and fats and use of inexpensive and natural catalysts, which are free of any toxic chemicals, proves this fuel to be economical in long run as this process has little or no negative impact on environment and public health. Extraction of sodium hydroxide from sea salt is neither expensive not has negative environmental impact. Billions of people are using wood for their cooking and wood ash is abundantly available in many parts of the world. The wood ash is a good and cheap source of potassium and sodium hydroxide. These are non toxic catalyst. The direct application of solar energy for biodiesel convention will make the process economically promising. Khan et al. (2005b) demonstrated that oil heated by direct solar energy can be effectively utilized to with higher efficiency. This will help to reduce the energy cost for biodiesel production.

It was reported that increasing the size of the production output can potentially reduce the cost of biodiesel by as much as 30 % (Environment Canada, 2003). Shumaker et al. (2003) studied a biodiesel plant in Georgia, USA, and reported the direct output of a 15 million gallon plant is $17.4 million annually. Indirect sales in the Georgia economy amounted $16.9 million, and the total economic impact of sales was $34.3 million. The plant's operation created a total of 132 jobs. State and local non-education tax revenues increased by $2 million per year. The total input for the project was $22.947 million and the plant was designed for

25years. This created a positive economic benefit in the locale of the plant. EPA (2002) reported that a 20% blend of biodiesel will reduce 0.9-2.1 % of fuel use in miles per gallon. Similarly a 100% biodiesel replacement will reduce 4.6 -10.6 % fuel consumption miles per gallon of fuel used. Reduction in overall fuel consumption will reduce the cost of biodiesel. In many countries such as USA, there is a tax incentive for various blends of biodiesel used. The production and use of biodiesel will reduce country's foreign dependency for the fossil fuel import and increases the energy security. Considering the overall life cycle cost, green biodiesel has a positive impact in the economy and the environment.

Recently it has been reported sugar, which is a non-toxic and inexpensive, can be used as catalysts for biodiesel production (Toda et al., 2005). However, they used sulfuric acid for the sulphonation to form the aromatic rings to use as catalysts. Biodiesel could be contaminated by the sulfuric acid creating similar problems as that of conventional biodiesel. If sugar can be used from natural origin which has no synthetic chemicals in it and without sulphonation, this could become a good non-toxic catalyst. It has also been reported that charred sugar as solid catalysts could be reused for several time. Using natural sugar as natural catalysts could help in reducing the toxicity in the waste stream. The feedstock for biodiesel has a great role to play in order to reduce the higher cost of biodiesel. Non edible oils such as Jatropha, pongamia and others can revolutionize the biodiesel industry as this will not have competition with the food for humans.

3.2. BIO-ETHANOL

Bio-ethanol is an alternate fuel to gasoline. This can be used in the pure form or any other combination with gasoline. In countries like Brazil, vehicles are running on pure bio-ethanol. Ethanol derived from plant and crops is called bio-ethanol. This is readily obtained from the startch or sugar from a wide variety of crops. Ethanol is obtained by the fermentation of carbon based feedstocks. Glucose is evoled into carbon dioxide and ethanol during fermentation.

$$C_6H_{12}O_6 \text{ (l)} + H_2O \text{ (l)} + heat = 2C_2H_5OH \text{ (l)} + 2CO_2 \text{ (g)} + H_2O \text{ (l)}$$

Ethanol can be produced from a variety of biomass feedstocks such as sugarcane, bagasse, sugar beets, sorghum, switchgrass, barley, hemp, potatoes, cassava, sunflower, molasses, among others. However, most of current ethanol production is primarily from sugar, corn and sugar beets. Bioethanol is a colorless liquid, easily biodegradable, low toxicity has several environmental benefits over gasoline. Ethanol burns to produce energy leaving carbon dioxide and water as by-products. Ethanol can be blended with gasoline to oxygenate the fuel mixture in order to facilitate complete combustion that reduces emission of particulates of incomplete combustion.

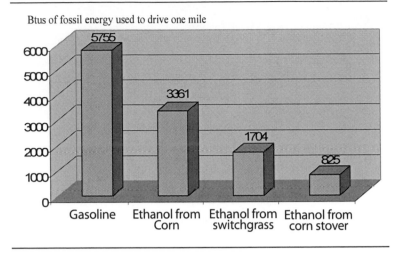

Figure 3.12. The Fossil fuel energy to drive one mile by from different sources (Riley, 2002).

Conventionally, ethanol from corn stover consumes lowest fossil fuel among others to drive one mile in a car (Figure 3.12). Ethanol among biofuels has drawn considerable attention recently due to the disadvantages of fossil fuels (emission of greenhouse gases, unsustainable supply, and increasing price) that produce large amount of CO_2 during a combustion process. Among the liquid biofuels, ethanol has the major contribution in the transportation sector. Lignocellulosic biomass contains 40-60% of cellulose and 20-40% of hemi cellulose two third of which are polysaccharides that can be hydrolyzed to sugars and then fermented to ethanol. Ethanol can be easily burned in today's internal combustion engines to substitute gasoline.

The worldwide gasoline use in transportation industry is about 1200 billion liters/year (Martinot, 2005). The total ethanol production as of 2004 was approximately 32 billion litres/year. Brazil is the leading country to use ethanol as transportation fuel. Globally, there is a huge gap between the gasoline use and supply of ethanol to substitute the gasoline in the current market. Ethanol is being produced from various biomass sources such as corn, sugarcane, sweet sorghum, switch grass and other food grains. Figure 3.13 is the schematic process for hydrolysis fermentation process. During the pretreatment, the biomass is sized, cleaned and pretreated with low concentration acid to hydrolyze the hemicellulose and expose for hydrolysis.

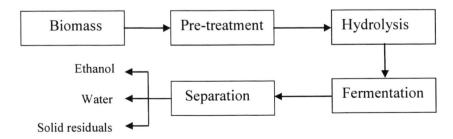

Figure 3.13. Hydrolytic fermentation process (Chhetri, 2007).

Table 3.3. Comparison of various pretreatment options (Martinot, 2005)

Pre-treatment method	Chemicals used for pretreatment	Temperature/ Pressure	Xylose Yield
Dilute acid hydrolysis	acid	>160^{0}C	75-90%
Alkaline hydrolysis	base	-	60-75%
Unanalyzed steam explosion	-	160-260^{0}C	45-65%
Acid catalyzed steam explosion	acid	160-220^{0}C	88%
Liquid hot water	none	190-230^{0}C, p>p$_{sat}$	88-98%
Ammonia fiber explosion	ammonia	90^{0}C	50-98%
CO$_2$ explosion	CO$_2$	56.2 bar	-

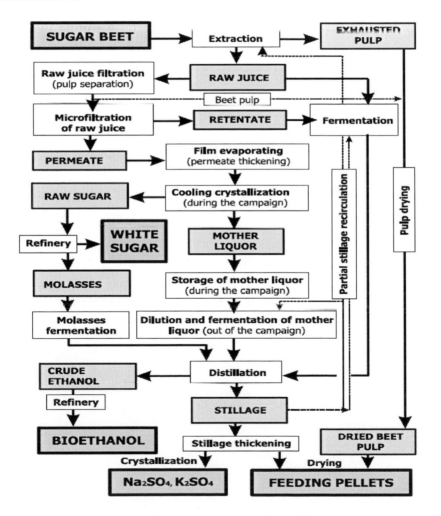

Figure 3.14. Complete technological scheme for sugar and ethanol production (Hinkova and Bubník, 2001).

Table 3.3 shows the chemicals, temperature and pressure used for the pretreatment of the biomass before converting to ethanol. Different kinds of acids, bases, high temperature steam and carbon dioxides are used for pretreatment. In acid hydrolysis, dilute sulfuric acid, hydrochloric acid or nitric acids are used. In alkaline treatment, sodium hydroxide and calcium hydroxide are most common. One of the major objectives of the pretreatments is to remove the lignin part, which cannot be fermented and convert the hemicellulose into fermentable sugars. Physical methods of pretreatment include high steam pressure explosion process, CO_2 explosion, nitrogen explosion and hot water treatment. Biological pretreatment includes treatment of biomass by fungus. After the pretreatment, the cellulose is hydrolyzed into glucose sugar, the reaction is generally catalyzed by dilute or concentrated acid or by enzymes. The common method of hydrolysis is the use of concentrated hydrochloric or sulfuric acid. Enzymatic hydrolysis is technically feasible and environmentally sound but acid hydrolysis is available more commercially. Hinkova and Bubnık (2001) developed a flow process that shows the different steps for the production of ethanol and sugar from sugar beets (Figure 3.14). The by-products are also useful which are also utilized for other purposes.

Problems with Current Ethanol Production

In the United States, 90% of ethanol is produced from corn and corn needs more chemicals fertilizers, insecticides and herbicides than other comparable crops such as soybean (Pica, 2003). Corn farming needs 5.8 times chemical fertilizer and 1.6 times more soil conditioners than soybean. This huge amount of chemicals contaminates soil and ground and surface water near farming areas. Moreover, ethanol conversion process has negative impacts on both water and air. Twelve gallons of waste water is produced per gallon of ethanol produced (Pica, 2003). The waste water consists of various types of toxic chemicals such as concentrated sulfuric acids and others which are used for pretreatment and hydrolysis and emit various types of volatile compounds harmful to human health and the environment.

The ethanol production from hydrolytic process uses highly toxic chemicals in series of processes. Hydrochloric and sulfuric acids, synthetic sodium hydroxide and calcium hydroxide are highly toxic and corrosive chemicals. Even though there are enzymatic hydrolysis methods developed, they use various synthetic surfactants to accelerate the reaction. Agblevor et al. (2006) studied the ethanol production process using the flocculating yeast Saccharomyces cerevisiae strain KF-7 which was genetically modified strain with acid hydrolysate of wood biomass. Despite some experimental results, it is impossible to practically achieve these results as the process uses genetically modified strains in large scale production of bioethanol due to various factors such as growth requirements, growth conditions, ethanol yield, ethanol productivity, and ethanol tolerance (Dien et al., 2003). Bakker et al., (2004) studied the ethanol production from willow and switch with acid hydrolysis. In this process, concentrated sulfuric acid was used for the hydrolysis as acid biomass ratio of 2:1-4:1 (willow) and 2:1-4:1(switchgrass). Significant amount of fermentable sugars including glucose and xylose by simple impregnation of these acids, the ethanol fermentation were 38% lowered compared to standard glucose fermentation. This is due to the formation of fermentation inhibitors such as acetic acid and furfural acid formation. The products of burning such contaminated fuel would emit toxic pollutants and pose severe environmental and health problems. These toxic chemicals contribute to water pollution that makes water treatment process very expensive. The pretreatment, hydrolysis and other processes use elevated heat and pressure, which themselves require fossil fuel combustion. Agblevor et al. (2006) carried out a study on ethanol production from cotton gin waste in USA as this caused significant disposal problems. However, concentrated acid was used for the hydrolysis again. Even then, 21-24% was acid insoluble fraction and making ethanol from cotton gin waste did not solve the problem of waste management despite reduction in waste volume. Thus the conventional method of using the fossil fuel as primary energy input to methanol production makes the whole process unsustainable. Despite ethanol can be one of the best alternatives for the gasoline from the energy and environment point of view, the synthetic mode of ethanol production using toxic chemicals and use of fossil fuels as primary energy source in various stages make ethanol an unsustainable product.

Sustainability of Ethanol as Transportation Fuel

For bioethanol production from hydrolysis of woody biomass from coniferous trees from traditional Saccharomyces yeasts offer great advantages (though they cannot ferment pentose sugars) due to their high ethanol yield, high productivity, and high ethanol tolerance (Agblevor et al. (2006). The remaining residues can be used for the production of methane in anaerobic digesters. Switchgrass has very good potential for ethanol production. This can be grown in barren lands in harsh climate and is not grazed by animals. However, because of its nature and low efficiency of large acid biomass ratio necessary for its hydrolysis makes this feedstock not feasible as other soft biomass, instead ethanol production creates large amount of wastes. Further research is necessary to find the suitable yeast for its natural fermentation that will have no environmental impacts.

Brazil is the country that has sufficiently progressed in producing ethanol as gasoline substitute from sugar cane. It has been reported that Brazilian ethanol has a positive energy balance considering the inputs and outputs. According to (Wyman, 2004), about 197 to 222 mega joules of fossil energy are used for providing seeds, labor, and power for agricultural operations, agricultural equipment, fertilizers, lime, herbicides, insecticides, and cane transportation to grow a metric tonne of sugarcane (169,000 to 191,000 Btu/ton) in Brazil. Most of the energy for sugar extraction and fermentation is provided through bagasse left after processing. Yet, 40 to 70 mega joules/metric tonne of fossil fuel is used for electricity generation, chemicals and lubricants manufacturing, erection of buildings and manufacturing of equipment that makes about 237 to 292 mega joules of fossil energy are consumed per tonne of ethanol production. Ethanol fuel has 1707 to 1941 mega joules of energy in a metric tonne (1.470×10^6 to 1.669×10^6 Btu/ton). It is however, obvious that despite Brazil's independence of foreign fuel import, the use of fossil fuel still continues contributing to the greenhouse gas emission. Moreover, the use of synthetic herbicides, insecticides, chemicals fertilizers and acid treatment of the effluent from ethanol processing create several environmental problems. It has been recently reported that genetically modified food has been linked to the "Colony Collapse Disorder" which is the phenomenon of mass disappearance of honey bee in North America (Zatzman et al., 2007a; Zatzman et al., 2007b; Zatzman et al., 2007c).

Considerable attention has been paid to develop ethanol production from cellulosic biomass recently. Cellulosic biomass is abundant with prominent examples including agricultural residues (e.g., corn stover, sugarcane bagasse), forestry residues (e.g., forest thinnings), industrial wastes (e.g., paper sludge), major portions of municipal solid waste (e.g., waste paper), herbaceous plants (e.g., switchgrass), and woody species (e.g., poplar) (Wyman, 2004). Cellulosic biomass can be grown with low energy inputs. The use of sulfuric and other acids for the conversion of cellulose into fermentable sugars is a common practice. The use of acids for the breaking down to cellulose would produce toxic waste making the whole process unsustainable. However, enzymes such as cellulase for cellulose hydrolyze and hemicellulase for hemicelluloses can be used for their breakdown into fermentable sugars and then into ethanol production. This enzymatic process could be the best environment friendly process provided that acid pre-treatment are not carried out. Enzymes which are derived from the same material could make the process sustainable for the long-term.

The production of ethanol from biomass source as an alternative fuel alone is not a big accomplishment if this is still dependent on synthetic chemicals which are inherent to the current environmental problems. Despite large quantities of ethanol is produced in Brazil, USA and other countries, large quantities of fossil fuels are involved in the production of biomass at different stages. Fossil fuels are involved in building of equipment and infrastructure, transporting the biomass up to processing facility, producing lubricants, and production operations. The use of chemicals such as concentrated acids which are inherent to the pre-treatment and hydrolysis can not be considered sustainable. Moreover, the use of fossil fuels to produce synthetic fertilizers, pesticides and surfactants makes the entire ethanol production process. The CO_2 produced by burning ethanol which is contaminated by synthetic chemicals will not be recycled by plants, hence creates similar, if not worse, environmental problems as the fossil fuels do. Production of ethanol by the use of enzymes and fermentation through the naturally available yeast are key to make the process environmental friendly and sustainable. Use of biological waste products from the waste streams of industries and municipal waste in a natural way without using synthetic chemicals could help make bioethanol production a zero waste process. Thus, the only hope to make the ethanol production process sustainable is to develop the process that fosters the use of truly natural products without creating any environmental problems in the long-term (Sapiro et al., 2007).

3.3. STRAIGHT VEGETABLE OIL AS FUEL

Straight vegetable oil was first used as fuel for diesel engine 100 years ago by Rudolph Diesel, inventor of the diesel engine (Nelson et al., 1996). He tested the peanut oil as an alternative fuels in his compression ignition engine. He said, "The use of vegetable oils for engine fuels may seem insignificant today. But such oils may in course of time be as important as petroleum and the coal tar products of the present time". His remark has been true by now and vegetable oil has been an important source of energy either in straight use or in its transformed form as biodiesel. Despite several efforts to use straight vegetable oil to run diesel engine, there are many problems associated with using it directly in diesel engine particularly for direct injection engines.

Most of the research focusing on the vegetable oil as an alternative fuel showed coking and trumpet formation on the injectors to such an extent that fuel atomization does not occur properly or even ceases completely (Pinto et al., 2005). Other disadvantages include oil ring sticking, thickening or gelling of the lubricating oil as a result of vegetable oils due to high viscosity and lower volatility that causes carbon deposits and incomplete combustion lowering the thermal output of engine (Meher et al., 2004). These problems are associated with large triglyceride molecule and its higher molecular mass. However, some engines modified by Elsbett in Germany and Malaysia and Diesel Morten und Geraetebau GmbH (DMS) in Germany and in USA show a good performance when fuelled with vegetable oils of different composition and grades (Canakci and Gerpen, 1999). Burning vegetable oil at high temperatures can create some problems with polymerization of unsaturated fatty acids resulting in the formation of gum. In fat this is not the problem because the unsaturated fatty acid in fats is in lower concentration. However, fats due to their high melting properties and viscosity cannot be used as fuel for engines directly. Fats and oils are primarily composed of triglycerides, esters of glycerol (mono-and diglyceride). Table 3.4 shows the chemical properties of different vegetable oils.

It has been reported that vegetable oil can be used in a diesel engine if it is heated to reduce its viscosity so that it will perform in a similar fashion to diesel fuel. A number of studies and ever growing empirical experiences have shown that the use of such systems with many engines can give operating characteristics and reliability similar to those associated with diesel fuels. Emissions and power have been reported to be comparable or improved. There are several engines that have been attached with the conversion kits to use straight vegetable oil as fuel. These kits use electric heating and often replaced injectors to insure that right condition for combustion can be obtained. A simple way to run an engine in vegetable oil is to make duel engine arrangement (Figure 3.15). The engine is to be started on biodiesel and the waste heat from the engine can be used to heat the vegetable oil. This will not only reduces the viscosity of oil but also avoid the cold start problem of vegetable oil. Once the temperature indicator shows enough temperature to heat the oil, then it can be switched into vegetable oil tank. Care must be taken that before shutting down the engine, it should again be switched into biodiesel and allowed to run for a while. This will solve most of the problems associated with the vegetable oil. However, due to the unsaturated oil molecules, large glycerides molecules, polymerization and carbon formation still becomes a problem using straight vegetable oil as an engine fuel.

Table 3.4. Typical chemical properties of vegetable oil (Khan, 2002)

Vegetable Oil	Fatty acid composition, % by wt.						Acid value
	palmitic	strearic	oleic	linoleic	linolenic	arachidic	
	16:00	18:00	18:01	18:02	18:03	20:00	
Corn	11.67	1.85	25.16	60.6	0.48	0.24	0.11
Cottonseed	28.33	0.89	13.27	57.51	0	0	0.07
Crambe	2.07	0.7	18.86	9	6.85	2.09	0.36
Peanut	11.38	2.39	48.28	31.95	0.93	1.32	0.2
Rapeseed	3.49	0.85	84.4	23.3	8.23	0	1.14
Soybean	11.75	3.15	23.26	55.53	6.31	0	0.2
Sunflower	6.08	3.26	16.93	73.73	0	0	0.15

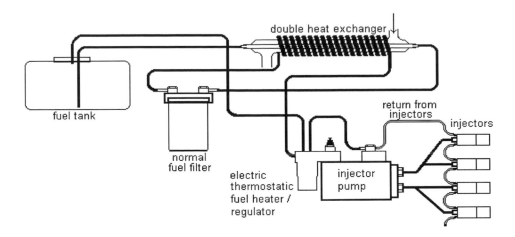

Figure 3.15. Two tank system (Biopower, 2002).

Allen (2002) tested Crude Palm Oil with petrodiesel blend and ran the Kuboto Diesel engine. The modification to the engine was just to bring the exhaust back to the tank to heat the fuel tank once it starts. Principally, it is a dual tank system which starts on diesel engine and when it is heated, it runs with vegetable oil. The test was carried out with 50:50, 80:20 and 100 %. The oil used was refined palm oil. Palm oil was de-gummed with phosphoric acid (H_2PO_4) and fatty acids were removed by saponification with sodium hydroxide (NaOH). The engine lasted less than 300 hours before it packed in with a big cloud of black smoke and an even bigger bang. Dismantling the engine showed erosion around the inlet port and on the piston head itself. The chemicals such as H_2PO_4 and NaOH, make the exhaust gas even more toxic. There must be some natural ways of deguimming and specification. To neutralize the free fatty acids, the seaweed ash, wood ash or natural potash might be alternatives.

Due to the formation of coke and polymerization in the engines, it is not feasible for vegetable oil to use in conventional or modified engines. The only best way to use these vegetable oils directly is to create jet of vegetable oil with bigger surface area so as to allow complete burning. Moreover, creating jet in higher temperature may solve the problems occurred in vegetable oil burning. Moreover, burning vegetable oil in high temperature industrial furnace could also eliminate coke formation and polymerization.

3.4. BIOGAS

Natural gas has been one of the most popular fuels for running transportation and stationary engines. Natural gas is essentially composed of methane, which can be also obtained through anaerobic fermentation of different organic products yielding more than 60% methane (De Carvalho, 1985). Biogas is a mixture of gas produced after decomposition of organic material by anaerobic bacteria. Biogas is mainly composed of 60–70% methane, 30–40% carbon dioxide and some other gases. Biogas can be used for cooking, heating and lighting, refrigeration, stationery and mobile engine operation and electricity generation. The role of methane produced from the organic materials has is increasing as it can be easily produced in locally constructed digesters around most part of the world. Biogas from anaerobic digestion is a promising means of achieving multiple environmental benefits. Substituting fossil fuels with biogas not only reduces greenhouse gas emission but also nitrogen oxides, hydrocarbons, and particulates. The use of slurry as fertilizer on farming can improve the utilization of plant nutrients which offers organic products recirculation. Biogas can directly be used for cooking, heating and all other applications for which natural gas is currently used. The production of biogas not only offers the energy benefits but also makes use of waste which otherwise consumes resources for its treatment.

Khan et al. (2007e) analyzed the energy requirement for 100 apartment buildings in Nova Scotia which can be self reliant in energy use. They developed a comprehensive zero waste energy system for inherently sustainable living. They showed that biogas can be used in fuel cells technology. Fuel cells are highly efficient electro-chemical energy conversion devices that convert chemical energy directly into electricity. Hydrogen gas is the best fuel for these cells but the generation of pure hydrogen gas is very costly. Instead, the use of natural gas has been utilized but the presence of CO in the natural gas limited the use as platinum anode which easily poisoned by CO. So, upon removing the CO (if any) biogas can be a source of fuel for fuel cell. The ammonia (leachate) and CO_2 produced in the anaerobic composting process can be used for desalination plant. The sewage water also contains significant amount of ammonia. Exhaust gas from sewage and leachate liquid are good candidates for desalination of salty water (Khan et al., 2005b). Hossain and Islam (2006) showed that use of biogas in transportation can significantly reduce the greenhouse gas emission, the global warming precursors. Burning biogas is inherently clean and the CO_2 emitted from biogas burning is of biological origin and easily recycled by plants for their photosynthesis.

Feedstocks for Biogas Production

Landfill Gas

Disposal of biodegradable waste into landfills have been of great environmental concern lately. Instead of disposing this waste into landfills, they can be digested to produce methane which can be used for industrial and transportation purposes. Approximately 5 PJ of biogas is produced per annum in Sweden alone contributing significant amount of energy requirements. The biogas produced from the waste has been used mainly for heat production and as a transportation fuel in busses, distribution vehicles, taxis and private cars (Borjesson and Berglund, 2006). Biogas from the landfills is the result of decomposition of cellulose contained in municipal and industrial solid waste. Unlike in manure digesters in controlled conditions, the digestion in landfill in uncontrolled and natural process of biomass decomposition. The efficiency of the process depends on the waste composition, moisture content of the waste, temperature and other materials. Due to mixed composition of landfill waste, the methane formed in the landfill is approximately 50% of the gases. A landfill system consists of series of wells drilled into the landfills with a piping system that connects the wells collecting the gas. Moistures and other impurities are removed before they are sent to use. This can be sent to fuel vehicles, an engine generator or gas turbine to produce electricity. It can also be used to fuel boiler to produce heat or steam. This gas can be used to make hydrogen to use in a fuel cell technology. This can also be sent to the natural gas grid systems. In addition, there are indirect environmental impacts that can be of great importance.

Borjesson and Berglund, (2006) reported the amount of biogas content in various biomass feedstocks in Spain (Table 3.5)

Biogas from Municipal Sewage

Municipal sewage contains several organic biomass solids. Currently many wastewater treatment plants use anaerobic digestion to reduce the volume of these solids. Anaerobic digestion stabilizes sewage sludge and destroys harmful pathogens. Sludge digestion produces biogas containing 60-percent to 70-percent methane, with an energy content of about 600 Btu per cubic foot. Most wastewater treatment plants that use anaerobic digesters burn the gas for heat to maintain digester temperatures and to heat building space. Unused gas is burned off as waste but could be used for fuel in an engine-generator or fuel cell to produce electric power.

Manure Digestion

Biogas production from household and farm manure has been the most popular as this is a very simple and economical technology. The production of biogas for family cooking is sufficient with manure from a cow or buffalo for a family of 4-5 people. This system has been in place in many institutional buildings such as universities, apartments, office building in countries like Nepal. The anaerobic digestion of crop residues and manure reduces the plant nutrient leaching from arable land. Moreover, the use of slurry in farming reduces the need for chemical fertilizers. Figure 3.16 is the plan and sectional view of dome type biogas digester commonly used in Nepal. The feedstock could be either from manure or from any other organic waste including water hyacinth. This consists of a concrete dome plastered around the digester. The digesters can be of various sizes depending upon the size of family. The dimensions of digestor depending on the size of the family are given in Table 3.6. Recently, the concept of community or institutional biogas plants has been envisaged to utilize the waste in community buildings, hospitals, and large apartment buildings to utilize the waste.

Table 3.5. Raw materials and biogas production potential (Borjesson and Berglund, 2006)

Raw material	Dry matter content (%)	Biogas Yield	
		GJ/dry tonne	GJ/tonne raw material
Ley crops	23	10.6	2.4
Straw	82	7.1	5.8
Sugar beet leaves and tops	19	10.6	2.0
Liquid manure (pig)	8.0	7.0	0.56
Food industry waste	8.0	16	1.3
Municipal organic waste sorted	30	12.4	3.7

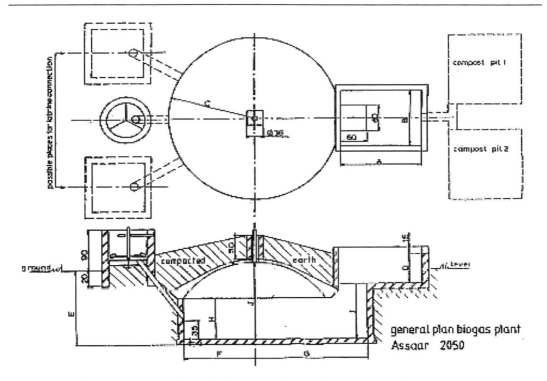

Figure 3.16. Plan and sectional view of a dome type biogas digester (BSP, 2000).

Cleaning of Organic Industrial Waste Streams

Various process industries such as agricultural and food industries discharge large amount of organic wastes in their waste streams. Treating these wastes to meet the effluent requirement involve a large investment. However, using the anaerobic digestion methods for reducing the volume of waste can significantly reduce the amount of waste treated, generating highly valuable biogas energy at the same time. The methane can be utilised to produce electricity and heat in local co-generation plants. This can also be used in home heating, cooking and similar other purposes.

Table 3.6. Size (mm) of the different parts of the biogas plant of different Capacities (BSP, 2000)

Parts	Capacity of the plant (Cubic Meter)					
of the plants	4	6	8	10	15	20
A	140	150	170	180	248	264
B	120	120	130	125	125	176
C	135	151	170	183	205	233
D	50	60	65	68	84	86
E	154	155	172	168	180	203
F	102	122	135	154	175	199
G	185	208	221	240	261	288
H	86	92	105	94	115	115
I	112	116	127	124	132	137
J	151	160	175	171	193	203

Biogas as a Cooking Fuel

Biogas has been used as one of the major cooking fuels in Nepalese rural sectors as an alternative to fuelwood. Approximately 150,000 digesters ranging from 4 m^3 to 10 m^3 have been installed. The local efficiency of biogas stove varies from 30-50% depending on various controlled conditions (CES, 2001). However, the global efficiency of the biogas stove could be more than 75% as it utilizes the material which otherwise used to be a waste. After the introduction of biogas, there has been significant reduction in fuelwood use. BSP (2002) reported that there was a decrease of 3.39 kg fuelwood per household per day in summer and 7.55 kg fuelwood per household per day in winter in southern plain areas of Nepal. The corresponding figures for the northern hills are 5.54 kg and 6.47 kg in summer and in winter respectively.

Cooking from biogas does not produce particulate matters as this is the clean gas. The carbon dioxide emitted from methane burning is a clean carbon dioxide which is recycled by plants. The trace amount of methane leaking from the stoves or from the digester will not contribute to global warming because this is from biological origin. It is generally misunderstood and the methane from biogas digester is calculated as a greenhouse gas. In Canada, organic CH_4 is not considered as greenhouse gas. It greatly depends on the pathway and source from which it is originated. Any gas emitted from biological origin will not contribute to global warming. However, if the waste or the organic products is contaminated with synthetic chemicals such as fertilizers, and pesticides, the methane may not easily break down to carbon dioxide and carbon dioxide may not be recycled by plants because of the toxic contamination. As plants are considered to have lives, they selectively absorb the lighter potion of carbon dioxide from atmosphere for their photosynthesis.

Biogas as a Fuel for Lighting

Biogas has been one of the major alternatives to imported kerosene for lighting. In most of the rural areas of developing countries, kerosene is used as major fuel for lighting. Burning kerosene produces toxic gases and particulate matters which severely affects the respiratory systems of the inhabitants. A study carried out by Biogas Support Program (BSP, 2002) reported that after the introduction of biogas plants the consumption of kerosene has been reduced by 0.30 litres and 0.33 litres per day per household in Terai in summer and winter, respectively. Similarly, the kerosene consumption in the Hills is decreased by 0.36 litres per day per household in summer and 0.37 litres in winter. Prior to the installation of the biogas plants, majority of the households were dependent upon the traditional cooking stoves (96.7%) followed by the kerosene stoves (21.3%). Because of biogas installation, the traditional and the kerosene stoves were substituted to a great extent by biogas stoves. The Ujeli lamps are most popular lamp in Nepal to burn biogas for lighting. The gas consumption of these lamps is between 150 and 200 liters per hour. The light produced by biogas fed Ujeli lamps are comparable with that of a 60-watt light bulb.

Advantages of Biogas Production and Use

Biogas is a clean gas produced by the decomposition of with organic matters by microbes. There are no additional chemicals or catalysts necessary for the biogas production. Biogas fuel has the following advantages over other fuels.

1. Positive Impact on Health, Sanitation and Safety

In order to enhance the biogas production, most of the households build and connect the toilets to the biogas digesters. This gives an opportunity for better management of human excreta and prevents the contamination of water and food products. The water contamination otherwise could cause dysentery and tapeworm infestation (BSP, 2002). The study showed that the incidence of these problems were higher in non-biogas household than the households having biogas digesters. The study further showed that inhabitants who have biogas significantly lowered the incidence of symptomatic eye infection and cough related to kerosene. The danger of burning from kerosene stove accidents was also considerably lowered after the introduction of biogas stoves in the study area. Hence biogas systems have also positive impact on increased household safety.

2. Benefit on Agriculture and Sustainable Land Use

The biogas slurry is an important source of nutrients for agriculture. In the areas where biogas plants were installed, the use of liquid and composted biogas slurry increased considerably. Due to the use of bio-slurry as a fertilizer, the use of chemical fertilizer was reduced by about 9 percent (BSP, 2002). About 10 percent increase in corn yield and 18 percent increase in cabbage yield were reported with the application of digested slurry. Due to the convenience in cooking, collection of firewood declined sharply, more than 50% in many cases.

3. Environmental Benefits

The introduction of biogas digesters help reduce the deforestation, helping to maintain the ecosystem intact. BSP (2002) reported that there was 253 and 278 g equivalent of carbon reduction per day per household during summer and winter respectively in Terai of Nepal. Similarly, 304 and 312 g equivalent of carbon per day per household in summer and in winter in the hills of Nepal, respectively. This emission is an avoided emission from kerosene and fuelwood burning for lighting and cooking in the study area. However, there is a misconception that CO_2 emission from wood burning is a greenhouse gas and greenhouse gas can be reduced by avoiding fuelwood burning. CO_2 emission from wood burning produces natural CO_2 which is essential for plants for its photosynthesis. However, if the wood is treated with various chemicals while making pallets or charcoal or briquettes, the CO_2 produced is not natural and contribute to greenhouse gas. Using biogas fuels, deforestation can be reduced which has positive impact in the environment.

4. Socio-economic Benefits

Biogas can be produced in any small scale in the household to big scale in the landfills and municipal waste treatment systems. Making biogas digesters does not need highly skilled work force. Hence local people in the communities can themselves be the resource persons for biogas digesters construction and make their living working in the communities. The other advantage is that once the people's health is not affected, people can be socially motivated for their own and community works. Because of the production of good fertilizer, more people have practiced farming enhancing their economy. Since their energy is produced from the waste, they can utilize their money for other enterprises. Conventionally, women are considered responsible for collecting firewood for their cooking in developing countries. After the biogas installation, the long hours needed for collecting firewood is saved and this time is usually utilized other productive purposes such as kitchen gardening and adult learning. It was also reported that the time saved was used for taking care of their children, cleaning their household area and maintaining their regular household affairs.

Despite several uses discussed above, biogas is most popular in many countries to use in transportation vehicles. Biogas can be used in heavy duty and light duty vehicles. In light duty vehicles, biogas can be directly used without any modifications. Where as to heavy duty vehicles, may need some adjustments if they run alternatively on natural gas and biogas (Jonsson and Persson, 2003). Sweden is the only country in the world where there is national standard for biogas as vehicle fuel. This standard states that the methane gas to be used in vehicles should be at least 95% along with dew point, sulfur content and other constituents. Biogas is also considered a possible pathway for gradually changing into hydrogen vehicles. Biogas is a potential fuel to considerably reduce the emission from transportation sector. The use of biogas in stationery engines would also pave the way for reducing emission from industries. Because of many reasons stated above, it can be concluded that biogas is an inherently sustainable technology and it has no negative environmental impact and has significant social and economic impact to the society.

3.5. Direct Heat from Solar Energy

Solar energy is the most abundant energy source on Earth. This is free and inexhaustible energy source. Solar energy is clean energy and offers a viable alternative to the fossil fuel burning that currently pollutes our air, water and soil, threaten our public health and contribute to global warming. Currently solar energy is being used to generate electricity through the photovoltaic cells and batteries. The direct use of solar energy is limited to home water heating as well as passive heating of buildings. These photovoltaic cells are constructed of several metals such as silicon (Si), copper indium diselenide (CIS) and cadmium telluride (CdTe). Among these metals, silicon is the most common in use for photovoltaic cells. Silica itself is second most abundant element in the Earth's crust. Silicon does not freely occur in nature but occurs in minerals consisting of pure silicon dioxide in the form of silicon dioxides form such as quartz and silicates such as feldspars. These minerals occur in clay, sand and various types of rocks such as granite and sandstone. Pure silicon is used for photovoltaic cell manufacturing. Silicon is purified by converting to a silicon compound, which is then converted into silicon of high purity. When high purity silicon rods are exposed to one of the silicon compounds such as trichlorosilane, silicon tetrachloride and silane gases at very high temperature (over 1100^0C), additional silicon is deposited onto the silicon rods ($2HSiCl_3= Si+2HCl+SiCl_4$). Physically, silicon is produced from the acid leaching of metallurgical grade silicon. In both cases, either using acid leaching or chemicals synthesis, the silicon is converted into the pure form or concentrated at a level not available in nature. Because of the high heat used and acid contamination, the silicon becomes inherently toxic compounds which are the building blocks of current generation solar cells.

It has been well documented that the inhalation of various forms of crystalline silica may result in acute and chronic silicosis (Ziskind et al., 1976). Silicosis is a pulmonary disease that has affected miners, foundry man and heavy construction workers who chronically inhale silica containing dust. Moreover, any material containing silica is a poison (Seal et al., 2001). On the basis of anecdotal evidence and public concern, the US Food and Drug Administration has banned the use of silicone gel-filled SBI (silicon breast implants) in USA. Since the solar photovoltaic cells are mainly composed of silicon, the extraction, production and synthesis of silicon during manufacturing of solar cells causes emission and leakage of silicon in air and water bodies. Management of these silicon solar cells is of prime concerns today as they are not readily biodegradable. Hence the use of synthetic silicon materials in the solar cells causes several health and environmental problems. Besides the silicon solar cells, it has been reported that a copper indium diselenide (CIS) and cadmium telluride (CdTe) have also several health impacts as they are from synthetically made metals.

Batteries are the major components of photovoltaic electricity conversion. Lead-Acid batteries, Nickel Cadmium and Nickel Iron batteries are the batteries in use as rechargeable batteries in solar cells are. Among these batteries, Lead-Acid batteries are most common in use. Lead-Acid battery which is considered to have higher efficiency among other, essentially consists of Lead, concentrated sulfuric acid. At full discharge, the acid concentration is 30%. Batteries also consist of other heavy metals such as aluminum, Zinc, chromium, palladium, mercury, platinum etc. Once these batteries are used up in the solar cells or any other utilities, they are eventually discharged into the environment. Disposal of these heavy metals and acids into the natural environment form different types of metal oxides and ions in air and water which are harmful to health and pollute the natural environment. These metals and acids are difficult to detect in lower concentrations and continue to damage the water and soil quality in the places where these toxic elements of batteries are discharged. Since these metals are from synthetic origin, there are no methods as such so as to treat these chemicals in water and soil and damages the environment irreversibly. Neither the silicon cells nor the batteries used in solar electric conversion systems are beneficial to the society in the long-term, hence, this technology does not have any future prospect to be used in transportation and industrial applications. The only option for solar energy use could be if the heat is trapped directly without converting it into electricity.

Direct application of solar energy is generally limited to water heating and passive building heating. Water heating is one of the most efficient uses of direct solar energy as there are no conversion systems, instead it only has heat transfer systems between the metal surface of pipe and water and the flow of water occurs due to density difference between the hot and cold liquids. Water heating systems have higher efficiency than the electric conversion of solar energy. However, water heating has a limitation that the maximum temperature can reach is 100^0C. The efficiency of such system can be increased if the heating fluid considered is vegetable oil instead of water. By concentrating the solar energy by solar collectors, the temperature of the vegetable oil can reach over 300^0C (Khan et al., 2007d). Hence the efficiency of the systems can be increased at least by 3 times than in conventional water heating. Solar collectors can be used to concentrate the solar energy just by tracking them by the gravity of evaporating fluid without using any electric devices (Website 8).

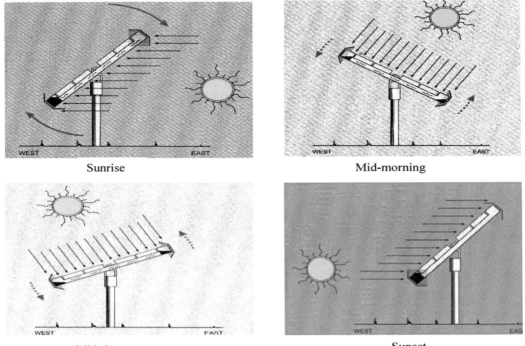

Figure 3.17. Solar tracking without using electro-mechanical equipment (Website 8).

Figure 3.17 shows orientation of tracking the solar collectors depending on the orientation of sun at different times of the day. In the morning, when sun rises from east, it heats the unshaded west-side with both direct and reflected rays forcing liquid into the shaded east-side. As liquid moves to the east-side, the tracker rotates so that it faces east, thus tracking the solar rays coming from the east. The tracker is moved by shifting the weight of liquid flowing from one side of the tracker to the other side through a copper tube connecting the east and west side canisters. The movement of the liquid can be controlled by the aluminum shadow plates. When one side of canister is exposed to the sun more than the other side, its vapor pressure increases, forcing liquid to the cooler, shaded side. The shifting weight of the liquid causes the rack to rotate until the canisters are equally shaded. As the sun moves with time, the tracker follows continually seeking equilibrium as liquid moves from one side of the tracker to the other. The tracker completes its daily cycle facing in the west and remains in that position overnight. From the next morning, the similar daily cycles continues to work. This is a cheap and environment-friendly way to utilize the maximum sun light for direct heating purpose.

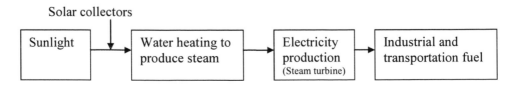

Figure 3.18. Direct solar energy to produce electricity for industrial and transportation use.

A model for direct solar energy to electricity conversion for industrial and transportation purpose is shown in Figure 3.18. Large solar collectors can work as a solar thermal generator because it is run by heat. The huge curve mirror dish focuses sunlight onto a central container where superheated steam is produced. The superheated steam is used to drive the turbine that produces electricity. Various configurations for solar thermal electric generation consist of central receiver or power tower, parabolic dish, solar ponds etc. Electricity generation from solar heating is generally operated in isolated areas that may or may not be connected to grid (Australian Greenhouse Office, 2005).

Direct solar thermal technologies are of two types: high temperature generators for electricity generation and medium temperature for industrial process heat. An Australia consulting company called Sinclair Knight Merz (SKM) estimated that the world solar market for solar thermal electric technologies to be significant by 2020 (Table 3.7). This estimation is based on the current trend of development of the solar thermal electric power in the world.

Generation of electricity from solar power towers consists of large field of sun tracking mirrors called heliostats that focus solar energy on a receiver of a centrally located tower in the middle of all heliostats (Figure 3.19). It has been reported that concentration of energy at the central tower can produce temperature of approximately 550^0C to 1500^0C. The thermal energy gained at the central tower can be used for heating water or molten salt, which saves the energy for later use (Figure 3.19). At this temperature, the steam is superheated and is used to run electric turbine generator. The efficiency of this heat storage system reaches up to 99%. Solar energy could also be a potential power source for splitting water to generate hydrogen energy. Hydrogen energy is considered to be the cleanest form of energy as burning of hydrogen produces huge amount of energy and forms water after combustion.

It is considered that solar thermal energy production is expensive based on the baseload electricity from grid. However, this can be very effective in supplementing day time industrial peak loads, resulting in higher benefits. Moreover, hybrid electric and thermal systems could be more economical systems. Solar thermal electric system has clear environmental benefits among others. The global efficiency of the systems is significantly high as it has no environmental cost. There are no hazardous gaseous or liquid emissions released during operation of the solar power tower plant. If the cost of environmental impact is considered for its counter parts such as oil, coal, gas and nuclear, it is obvious that the solar thermal electric systems are economically attractive and environmentally appealing. Solar energy is the most sustainable source of energy and if the direct application of solar energy used, the process becomes very high-efficient one.

Table 3.7. World potential for solar thermal electric

Year	Capacity (MW)
2000	424
2010	5,977
2020	50,809

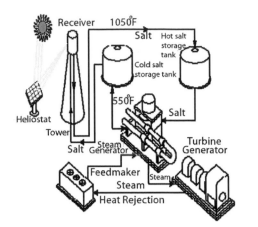 

Figure 3.19. Solar towers (Website 9).

3.6. WATER POWER

Humans have used power of water to supply energy for thousands of years. Rivers and streams are among the most powerful forces in nature. Besides river and streams, there are ocean waves, tides, and currents that move unimaginable amounts of water every moment. The energy of falling water is used mainly to drive electrical generators at hydroelectric dams. Energy from water is a clean source of power that provides electrical as well as mechanical energy. Hydropower is cheap and clean, and the energy source will last for ever, hence it is a renewable source. Currently, about 20% of world's electricity demand is met by hydropower. Canada has about 60% of electricity supplied by hydropower alone (Natural Resource Canada, 2005). Conventional hydropower systems can be brought into operation in few minutes. Due to this reason, hydropower is an ideal source of energy to meet peak energy demands. However, large hydro power projects have several environmental implications. In larger hydropower projects, it requires to construct a large storage dam to store water to maintain head as well to meet the peak load requirement for industrial as well as other utilities (Figure 3.20).

Environmental, Social and Economic Impacts of Hydropower Projects

Despite water power being clean source of energy, development of large hydropower projects has several impacts on the ecology of the river upstream and downstream of the dam. In large storage dam projects, areas of forest or farmland are submerged by stored water. Submergence of farmland will have great negative impact on the local economy. Due to the water retention in the dams, natural migration of fish and other aquatic lives will be affected in the upstream and downstream of the river system. Operation of storage dam and generating unit cause irregular water level rise and fall over time. Several aquatic species are not adapted to such abrupt changes in water levels. In such places, there will be significant reduction of aquatic species affecting the overall biodiversity of the area. Downstream water quality may also be deteriorated. Moreover, bacteria present in the decaying vegetation can also change in the mercury level present in the reservoir rocks into soluble form affecting the aquatic species such as fish that may intoxicate the food. Clearing of the trees in the reservoir area can result in soil erosion and landslides. Spilling of water from the spillways cause in the supersaturation of water with atmospheric gases that can cause fish death. Even though hydropower projects do not emit CO_2 directly, the use of fossil fuels to produce the turbine, generators and transmission lines would contribute CO_2 emission. Hence, the CO_2 avoidance from hydropower projects should take into consideration for the energy consumed for its component parts.

Millions of people may need to be relocated due to the construction of large reservoirs. It is generally experienced that the wellbeing and health of the relocated people are degraded after relocation. The cohesive nature of existing communities is dismantled and people lose their social support network, livelihood and ways of lives they were living due to disperse relocation. Large hydropower dams are managed by governments or corporations, the public resources become more centrally controlled and people eventually lose their control over their natural resources. Dams create good habitat for water borne pathogens and malaria affecting the people's health. The society becomes vulnerable to cultural breakdown all due to relocation. The gestation period for a hydropower project is quite long and the construction of dams is expensive, there is no guarantee that local people will get benefits from the hydropower projects. It may increase inequalities among the people of the areas creating more gaps between the poor and the rich. Despite being clean energy source, the development of hydropower is not always feasible from environmental, social and economic perspective. Especially the larger storage dam projects are not considered beneficial for the long term. In this setting, small, mini and micro hydro power projects which have no large storage reservoirs and are of 'run-of-the-river' type are to be considered for the long-term sustainability even when the effects of electricity is ignored.

Figure 3.20. Large-scale hydropower project in Columbia River in Washington State (Website 10).

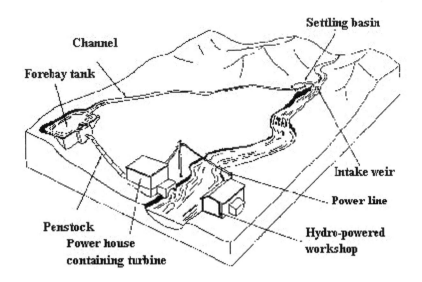

Figure 3.21. Schematic of micro-hydro system (Image courtesy ITDG).

Decentralised Micro-hydro System and their Sustainability

Due to the large storage dams and their impacts to ecology, big hydro projects are considered not beneficial from environmental considerations. However, small, mini and micro hydropower projects have several advantages over the big hydropower projects. These projects are generally 'run-of-the-river' type projects and do not need dams to store water (Figure 3.21). Microhydro turbines constitute the most environment-friendly way to produce electricity. These are very small turbines consisting of spoonshaped cups arranged around the center of wheel. The wheel is mounted on a shaft that turns gently on sealed bearings. The jet of high pressure water from the penstock pipe falls on the bucket causing the wheel to spin at high speed. This spinning can be used to generate electricity through generators, mills to grind grains, operating wood working tools, pumps, fans and other industrial operation.

Micro-hydro plants have a number of environmental and social advantages. It is simple to install and maintain. The pipes, generators, and other parts are usually inexpensive, can be locally manufactured, and are small enough to be handled without heavy equipment. These plants offer flexibility for transportation in difficult terrains where complex structures are difficult to build and become expensive. Micro-hydro system produces no pollution and does not create ecosystem loss as it requires only very slight changes to the flow of a small stream. There is no large dam or reservoir construction involved and hence is an environmentally friendly technology. Electricity is produced very close to the place where the community is located avoiding expensive electrical transmission to carry electricity to the community from far away. Micro-hydro systems are built with simple and indigenous technology making it possible for local people with basic training to maintain their own power systems. With micro-hydro in operation, community's dependency on outside sources of energy is significantly reduced. This also creates jobs for local and enhances the local economy.

Installation of micro-hydro systems in the communities offers people to develop their own micro enterprises such as grinding mills, knitting industries, poultry farming among others.

Sustainability of Decentralized Micro-hydro Projects

The issue of sustainability of any project is not limited with economic and energy systems but the biodiversity considering economic system as a subsystem of the whole ecological world. Energy from our ecological system is used as an input to economic process and emissions of such energy are also given back to ecology. So economic process or development is just 'intermediate means' (Daly, 1977) and prime mover of such process is energy. Daly (1999) further mentioned that the future generations have ownership claims to as much natural capital as the present generation, that is, the rule is to keep natural capital intact. Pokharel et al. (2007) derived that for any projects to be sustainable, total beneficial output from a system should not be less than the input and can be represented by Figure 3.22. Goodland (1992), Costanza et al. (1997) put forward for sustainability in the way that the 'critical natural resources' (Pearce et al., 1990) be conserved, waste produced due to human activities be within the assimilative capacity of the ecosystem, economic development should be qualitative not the quantitative and future generation's ownership on natural resources must be ascertained. Costanza et al. (1997), Hohmeyer (1997), Daly (1991) mentioned that the scale, carrying capacity and equity are the prime concern of any activities that allocate the scarce resources. Decentralized micro-hydro projects (MHPs) system can be considered fulfilling all such criteria.

Islam (2005) defined that any energy systems could only be considered sustainable if it is socially responsible, economically attractive and environmentally appealing. Khan and Islam (2007a and 2007b), Khan et al. (2007b) have further mentioned that those technologies are sustainable that follow the natural path for infinite time horizon. Pokharel et al. (2003) and Khan et al. (2007b) developed criteria to consider a technology to be sustainable. According to them, any energy system should fulfill economical, social and environmental criteria for the infinite time horizon. Based on strong sustainability criteria, sustainable development is the function of Natural Capital (Cn), Economic Capital (Cc), Social Capital (Cs);

D = f (Cn, Cc, Cs) for unlimited time horizon.

Capital stock environment/ecology {*energy resources are part of this*} (Cn) + Capital stock economy (Cc) + Capital stock Society (Cs) ≥ Constant for infinity

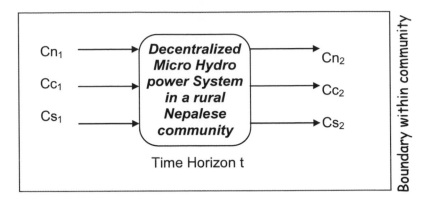

Figure 3.22. Input and output capitals to an energy system within a defined boundary (Pokharel et al., 2007).

Table 3.8. Kerosene and Electricity in rural lighting from environmental perspective

	Before MHP (one kerosene wick lamp)	After MHP (one 25-watt incandescent bulb)	Remarks
Source of lighting	Kerosene	Electricity	Majority of cases
Type of Lamp	Kerosene Wick	Incandescent bulb	Majority of users
Fuel Consumption* per year	86.4 litre (equal to 838 kWh)	54 kWh	1 Litre kerosene = 9.7 kWh
Nominal Consumption	400 watt	25 watt	Energy content of kerosene is 37 MJ/l
Nominal Output of luminous flux	40 Lumen (lm)	500 Lumen (lm)	Kerosene wick lamp 25% efficient
GHG emissionϕ/ year (CO_2 equivalent)	218.64 x 10-3 ton from one wick- lamp	0.5475 x 10-3 ton from one 25-watt incandescent bulb	25-watt bulb emits about 218.0925 x 10-3 ton less CO_2/ year.
Local air pollution	Not estimated	No	Various studies & reports, mentioned that MHP has minor & insignificant impacts
Water pollution	Not known	Very minor	
Local ecological impact	Not estimated	Minor	

Source: calculation based on authors experience and Banskota and Sharma, 1997, Broek and Lemmes, 1997, World Bank, 1996, Plas and De Graaff, 1988).

* Considering 6 hours of lighting in case of kerosene wick lamp and consumption of kerosene per wick lamp is about 0.041 liter/hr (e.g. Broek and Lemmes, 1997). For electricity, 25-watt bulb is considered for 6 hours of lighting. But while calculating CO_2 emission it is considered that the electric lamp lights whole year- as CO_2/kWh emission of MHP is based on life cycle.

ϕ CO_2 emission of MHP-life cycle is 0.0025Kg/kWh, Kerosene is 0.0723 T/GJ.

For strong sustainability in any development process

Natural Capital + Economic capital + Social capital ≥ Constant for all time horizons

Mathematically,

$D_t \geq (Cn + Cc + Cs)_t \geq$ constant at any time t during the development process, provided that $dCn_t/dt \geq 0$, $dCc_t/dt \geq 0$, $dCs_t/dt \geq 0$

A. Condition one: Environmental Condition, $dC_{nt}/dt \geq 0$, (from Figure 3.22 $Cn_2 - Cn_1 \geq 0$)

This condition, in case of decentralised MHP, indicates that the change in environmental capital must be greater than or equal to zero after the system being installed, operated and used. Natural capitals as input to the system are water and surrounding environment. From existing literatures and studies there are no irreversible impacts on these resources as well as no depletion of such natural capital. Output of the MHP are electricity and/or mechanical energy, which, normally in the context of hilly and rural regions of Nepal, replace kerosene, used for domestic lighting, diesel used for agro processing and human labour. Table 3.7 shows how environmental benefits even after considering MHP life-cycle CO_2 emission benefits are outweighing the kerosene use. In other words, environmental capital could be considered increased after installation, operation and use of MHP. So the condition of constant or increased natural capital is well satisfied.

B. Condition Two: Economic Condition, $dCc_t/dt \geq 0$, (from Figure 3.22 $Cc_2 - Cc_1 \geq 0$)

Economic capitals as input to the MHP system are financial capital and physical components. To encourage the development of decentralized MHP, Nepalese government has introduced subsidy for the entrepreneurs or the community. However, several studies including that of ITDG (Khennas and Barnett 2000) has mentioned that financial recovery from the MHP system is possible even without subsidies. The components of the system could be recycled partially after about 30 years and some economical capital will be recovered although most of the analyses of MHP designate zero salvage value. Apart from that the employment benefits, revenues or tax collected by government from manufactures, reduced burden in terms of trade due to reduced import of fossil fuel are some of the economic benefits since all micro hydro parts are manufactured locally in Nepal. Banskota and Sharma (1997) reported that in the tourism industry, especially in the mountain region of Nepal, marginal benefits of lodge owners in trekking route will be increased after electrification and have also small positive employment effect raising local people's income. Several studies, report and publications (Banddyopadhyay and Gyawali, 1994), Pokharel (1999) have mentioned positive benefits of such small-scale inventions. So, economic capital that is economic benefits will be explicitly more than before. So the condition of constant or increased economic capital is also excellently satisfied.

C. Condition Three: Social Condition, $dCs_t/dt \geq 0$, (from Figure 3.22 $Cs_2 - Cs_1 \geq 0$)

Invested social capital to the system will be outweighed by social output that is social benefit. Community or local villagers will invest their labour, time, and other social capitals to the decentralised MHP systems. But in return, they will get following benefits (Figure 3.23) (Pearce, 1987, Hourcade et al., 1990, Aguado-monsonet and Ciscar-Martinez, 1997, Shrestha and Amatya, 1998, Rijal, 1998a; Rijal, 1998b, World Bank, 1996, Banskota and Sharma, 1997).

- Better lighting of houses, which diminishes the likelihood of fire at homes from kerosene.
- Access to audio-visual services (radio and television), which may play a role in developing the informational and educational level of the rural population.
- Lighting of schools and home, which can improve the education of the children and enhance adult education program.
- Better preservation of medicines, and availability of permanent and reliable energy supply in health centers would have positive impact on health system of the community.
- Lighting of roads and trails around the villages could enhance public security.
- Agro processing like grinding, hulling etc, which would reduce the drudgery of people, especially women and children.
- Small number of local employment opportunity would be noticed.
- Enhanced empowerment process due to decentralized systems.

The above-mentioned social capitals are hard to quantify and monetarize but they are strongly implicit benefits to the local communities. So the condition of constant or increased social capital is well fulfilled by MHP system.

Pokharel et al., (2007) evaluated the sustainability of a micro-hydro project and showed that micro-hydro projects are sustainable in terms of environmental, economic and social criteria (Figure 3.24). Hence, micro-hydro systems are inherently sustainable technologies without having any negative environmental impacts. Micro-hydro systems can support local small industries to power. Operation of big industrial districts could also be possible developing series of micro-hydro projects. Compared to fossil fuel burning, even the big hydro projects could stand better if these projects are developed with the least environmental impacts because the water is free natural source which needs no processing. Other hydro operations for power generation such as wave energy, ocean thermal and tidal power are also important sources for energy development, the potential of which are discussed elsewhere in this book.

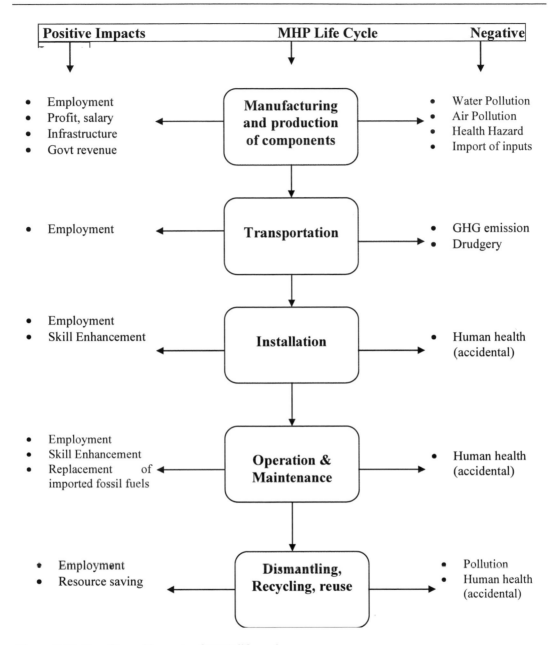

Figure 3.23. Benefits and impacts of MHP life cycle.

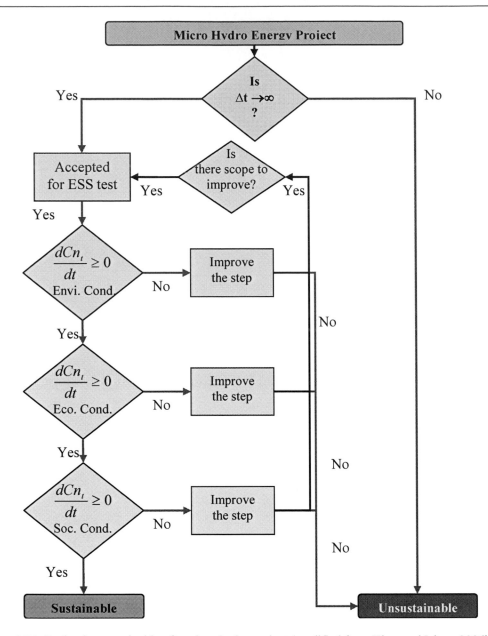

Figure 3.24. Evaluating sustainable of a micro-hydro project (modified from Khan and Islam, 2006b).

4. WATER AND WASTE WATER MANAGEMENT

4.1. INTRODUCTION

Along with air to breath, water is the most essential as well as the most abundant ingredient of life. Just like 70% of earth's surface is covered with water, 70% of human body is constituted of water. Even though the value and sanctity of water is well known for thousands of years in the eastern culture, scientists in the Eurocentric western culture are only beginning to break out of "chemicals are chemicals" mode and discuss that water has memory and the numerous intangibles (most notably the pathway and intention behind human intervention) are important factors in defining the value of water (Islam, 2006). In a commercial level, however, preposterous treatment practices continue. Examples are: the addition of chlorine to 'purify'; the use toxic chemicals (soap) to get rid of dirt (the most potent natural cleaning agent); the use of glycol (very toxic) for freezing or drying (getting rid of water) a product; use of non-organic CO_2 to render water into dehydrating agent (opposite to what is promoted as 'refreshing'), then again demineralization followed by the addition of extra oxygen and ozone to 'vitalize'; the list truly continues for ever. To make the situation worse, many western cities continue to promote fluoride addition to water (original intention was to grow better teeth) even when fluoride-free tooth pastes make brisk sales. Similar to what happened to food products (we call that the HSSA, Honey → Sugar → Saccharine → Aspartame, syndrome) that show spiral down degradation of quality in recent decades, water management shows continuing degradation in both value and efficiency (Chhetri and Islam, 2006c; Islam, 2006b).

Many anthropogenic activities, including urbanization, use of synthetic chemicals in various industrial products, and unsustainable manufacturing processes have contributed to groundwater contamination around the world. Practically all commercial and industrial practices of the post industrial revolution era are mired in over-extraction, improper utilization, and the introduction of toxic chemicals in all phases of technology development. In this modus operandi, water resources have been most negatively affected. Synthetic chemical additives have been introduced in drinking water even though the long term impact is immeasurably harmful to human health. In terms of water management, little regard has been paid to community needs, giving preference to top-down corporate models.

At present, irrigation is the largest water consumer using about 69% of water available, followed by the industry using 23%, while merely 8% of fresh water is consumed by humans.

It is generally believed that more than a billion people in the world especially in developing countries lack access to safe drinking water supply. In this, 'safe' refers to groundwater and/or treated water. In developing countries, some people have access to untreated ground water. In the west, practically no one has access to untreated ground water. Even when people resort to bottled water in order to avoid drinking chlorinated water, the water suffers from at least two shortcomings. They are: 1) the water is not fresh (the water is in the market for a year after bottling); 2) the water is in contact with plastic that is invariably made of toxic materials, such as PET, even when the bottles are touted to be conforming to 'standards'. Therefore, in scientific term, practically 100% of the people of the west have no access to natural drinking water. It is estimated that by the year 2050, 65% of the world population will live in areas of water shortage (Milburn, 1996). This number if optimistic and is not scientific as it does not include the fact that the current water treatment technologies are worse than so-called polluted water that contains organic contaminants. In fact, recent findings of Miralai (Miralai, 2006) shows that organic contaminants cause tangible harm to human health, meaning it can be cured easily, whereas added chemicals that are of non-organic origin by design `cause long-term damages that have no cure and is not recognized by human immune system, rendering the body defenseless. In summary, the 'water shortage' that is currently talked about is more about selling chemicals in order to 'purify' natural water sources than scientific investigation into real water need of the future generation. However, our research indicates that there is indeed a severe water shortage at this moment and this is because of the obsession of the post-industrial revolution society with waste (Islam, 2004). At present, wasting is synonymous with civilization both in eastern and western societies. As examples, two extreme cases can be cited (Islam et al., 2006). Canada is the best country to live in (as ranked no. 1 five years in a row by UN) and it is also the most wasteful nation (with highest per capita energy consumption). Bangladesh, on the other hand is one of the poorest countries in the world and indeed it is the least wasteful nation (with lowest per capita energy consumption in the world). The current technological mindset dictates that the consumption of water will increase along with the generation of waste water. This will involve contamination of water sources caused by the release of chemicals from the chemical industries, leakage from the sources, transportation and storage. Most, if not all, of these contaminants are imposed on the global water system by design.

Definition of Fresh Water and Sustainability

Nature dictates that fresh is better than old. If 'fresh' is defined as a state closer to the natural (without human intervention) state, fresh drinking water chemically would be the water that is extracted from groundwater source. Current models consider artificial chilling as the symbol of freshness. A knowledge based model would consider treated surface water that is transported through toxic pipelines, stored in plastic containers within a confine of toxic fume-generating refrigeration unit to be farthest away from being fresh. For cleaning purpose, the rain offers the freshest source of water. Following this, other surface water such that lake, pond, river would follow. With this criterion, desalinated water that is stripped of all essential minerals would be considered unsuitable for drinking (Khan et al., 2007e).

The effect of refrigeration and microwave irradiation on water has been discussed else where (Chhetri et al., 2006b). Both electrical/microwave heating and refrigeration have the negative effect of turning drinking water into toxic pollution. Even though the effect of microwave is being studied by various researchers, at least for complex molecules, few studies have investigated the effect of electrical heating on the quality of water. Many countries use electrical heating for destroying bacteria, followed by refrigeration to bring back 'freshness' in water. Both these processes create avenues of further contamination of water. Similar statement can be made about natural gas heating. During cooking or heating of water in order to decontaminate, natural gas oxidizes and releases numerous oxides, many of which are harmful in the long term (Chhetri and Islam, 2006a). Ironically, most of these toxins are released from chemical additives that are used to 'process' natural gas. For instance, it is common to use glycol to dry a natural gas and amides to remove sulfides. Even though most of these additives are separated, even traces of them are quite toxic, especially when they are oxidized, as is the case for cooking. Such problem is not encountered if biogas is used to heat water or cook.

4.2. WATER MANAGEMENT

Early human civilization developed primarily along the banks of rivers especially when humans began to develop agriculture. Their aim was to get enough water supplies for drinking and agricultural purposes. However, modern industrial civilization not only drew up extensive amounts of water but also became the major source of water contamination. Even thought water is most abundant substance in the world and more than 70% of the earth's surface is covered by water, the total freshwater available is around 3% (UNWWDR, 2003). The rest is saline water. The total available freshwater in different regions of the world is given in Figure 4.1 Asia is home for more than 60% of world's population whereas total global fresh water availability is approximately 36% of the total freshwater available in the world. More than 65% of this population has not been connected with water systems (Figure 4.2). The water supplied to the remaining 35% of the population is also not contamination free, causing many health problems. This is due to improper water management practices. Water management practices are conventionally a top down corporate approach that does not involve the user community as the major part of the management system.

Between 1900 to 1995, water use in the world has increased by a factor of six that is more than double the rate of population (WHO, 1998). This increase, along with the fact that so-called developed countries (for which the population is declining) continue to use manifold more water per capita than the rest of the world, demonstrates clearly that 'population' explosion is not the reason that there will be a global water crisis in this world. It is, in fact, the addition to wasting habit and shear lack of regard for the environment would be the reasons behind this water crisis.

The global water consumption share in domestic, industrial and agricultural uses is shown in Figure 4.3 Billions of tons of fossil fuels are consumed each year to produce these chemicals which are the major sources of water and air pollution. The majority of these chemicals are synthetic, toxic and radioactive. Some of these chemicals are used to disinfect water and produce very harmful by-products. The chemicals also reach bodies water by leakage, transportation loss and as by-products. The industrial wastes which are contaminated with these chemicals end up in a body of water. Some contaminates may not even be detectable through the current technologies available.

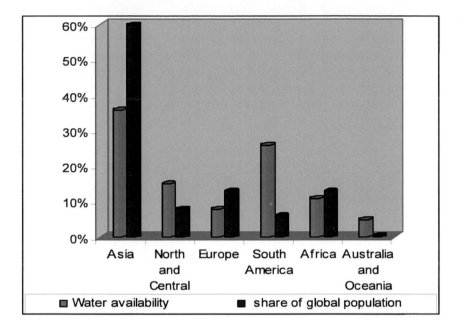

Figure 4.1. Global water availability and population (UNWWDR, 2003).

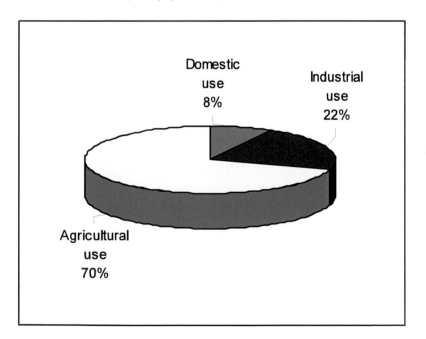

Figure 4.2. Global water end uses (UNWWDR, 2003).

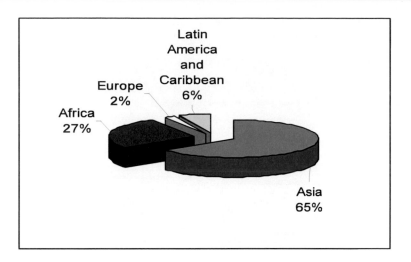

Figure 4.3 Water supply, distribution for unserved populations (UNWWDR, 2003).

It is reported that 90-95% of domestic sewage and 70% of industrial waste are discharged into the surface water resources in third world countries without treatment. However, these countries have the lowest share of waste disposal in terms of global industrial waste. Approximately 2 million tons of waste are from industries chemicals, human waste and agricultural wastes (pesticide, fertilizers and herbicides residue) per day are disposed within receiving water worldwide (UNWWDR, 2003). The water pollution due to the disposal of such waste is even worse in the case of developed countries as most of the chemical industries are located in these countries. The abundance of various diseases among the people in the developed world is one of the key indicators that the pollution from the synthetic chemicals is severe in human and environment

Conventional Guiding Principles in Water Supply and Management

As mandated by United Nations Conference on Environment and Development (UNCED) in Rio de Janeiro in June 1992, the 1992 Dublin Principles emerged as guiding principles for water management (Solanes and Gonzalez-Villarreal, 1999). These principles state that 1) fresh water is a finite and vulnerable, 2) water has an economic value, 3) Water development and management should be based on a participatory approach, involving users, planners and policy-makers at all levels 4) women play central role in water management. Some of these principles are irrelevant. Fresh water is not a finite and vulnerable resource, instead it is a renewable resource. The way we manage and use water makes it finite and vulnerable. Water is a resource which is truly recycled according to the principle of global water cycle. However, current mode of application of synthetic chemicals in water and waste water treatment, agricultural farming and industrial application irreversibly damage the quality of water. Since the water is considered to have memory, contamination of water through synthetic chemicals is contributing water contamination leading to finite and vulnerable source.

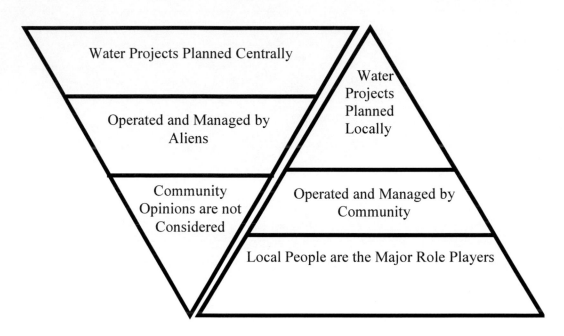

Figure 4.4. Centralized and Decentralized Water Management Approach (After Khan et al., 2007a).

The second principle that considers water as an economic good is also problematic. Water is a free natural source for which each inhabitant of the Earth has equal right for its use. This is a social and natural entity and should be based on the possible distribution for every people on Earth. Considering water as an economic good eventually lead to the partition between those who can and can not afford water to buy. It is undeniable that management of water involves some development, operation and management costs. However, some of these costs can be contributed by users in terms of labor contribution and other local resources making water development and management cost low. Hence, water management and supply services should be imparted considering water as a social good. The Dublin principle of considering water as an economic good should be reconsidered.

The third principle that states water development and management should be based on a participatory approach, involving users, planners and policy-makers at all levels is the most extensive in principle. However, the current water development is primarily driven by corporate approach that largely ignores the role of users or community while planning, designing, project implementation and tariff setting. The corporate models generally do not account the impacts of the projects in the ecosystem locally as well as globally. The local people's right to participate in the decision making, planning and project implementation is jeopardized in corporate models. These corporate whether they are government or private sector would act similar from the people's perspectives. Moreover, one of the largely ignored parts of the water management is integration of water management with renewable energy technologies such as solar application for disinfection, direct solar heat and wind energy use for water heating, pumping and other uses. Integration of sustainable technologies with planning and management could better result in the overall sustainability of water systems. The only solution to the current water management problems could be to design water projects where beneficiaries are the key players in all aspects of project cycle. Most appropriately, decentralized water systems are cost effective and reliable when users are involved in the planning, execution, operation, and maintenance of water systems (Wilderer, 2004; Khan and Islam, 2007a). In suburban communities, decentralized water systems will be more economical than extending the centralized system to those communities (Rebhan and Schroll, 2003).

Khan et al.(2007a) developed a community based energy model where community people are the key role players during planning, designing, operation and management. This model is equally applicable to any other projects including water management. Figure 4.4 represents centrally managed and decentralized projects. The decentralized approach involves raising awareness of the importance of water among policy-makers and the general public. It means that decisions are taken at the lowest appropriate level, with full public consultation and involvement of users in the planning and implementation of water projects. Islam and Kahkonen (2001) studied the determining factors for effectives of community Based Water Projects in Central Java Indonesia. The study revealed that the performance and impact of community based water services are associated with demand responsiveness of their design and existence of mechanisms to monitor household contributions for the construction, operation and maintenance. The results further indicated that the villages with higher level of social capital, particularly with active village group and associations have more household participation in the system design and more effective monitoring mechanisms. The active involvement of users results in a sustainable management and operation of water systems. Kyessi (2005) reported the impact of community based urban water management in fringe neighbourhoods: the case of Dar es Salaam, Tanzania. This area was left by the central authorities without providing any water services to the people. However, a notable phenomenon had emerged in informal and formal settlements where the communities, through self-help and local governance in their own neighbourhood associations, organised to fill the gaps in infrastructure services left by the centralised institutions. The community groups mobilize and organize fund-raising, mutual self-help and external technical assistance to provide water supply and sanitation, roads and drainage channels within the immediate area. This trend was replicated in infrastructure improvement in poor neighbourhoods including fringe settlements. The efforts of the villagers was able to attract involvement of Dar es Salaam City Council (DCC), the civil societies including political party organizations and private individuals as well as youth and women groups, and the donor community. This area not only was able to bring the people and organizations of different interests together but was instrumental in imparting the indigenous knowledge and appropriate technology. Raising the awareness of the water users on the impact of water contamination will help to keep the water source clean. Involving the community from planning to decision making and project implementation to maintenance of the system is a bottom up approach and help to make the water management practices sustainable in the long term. Hence, decentralized and community based water projects are sustainable in the long-term as the users are involved and feel their ownership towards their own projects.

The forth principle of water management stated by Dublin Conference is the central role of women for management and safeguarding water. The conference considered that women have pivotal role as providers and users of water and guardians of the living environment. Implementation of this principle requires positive policies to empower women to facilitate their participation at all levels of water management programs including planning, decision making and project implementation. O'Reilly (2003) analyzed the connections between women and water in a Rajasthani drinking water supply project as a significant part of drinking water's commodification. Women being main users and managers of water as well as main care providers in family, it is important that they be involved in all aspect of water management. However, several studies revealed that building gender neutral practices help to yield high value products. Women have several roles as public representatives, powerful household managers, and public standpost caretakers. Its not enough formulating policies to involve women in water management, these should match in the prevailing socio-cultural context. Singh (2006) argued that the importance of understanding the contextual perspective of gender relations and ideologies in analyzing the transformation of women's role in water management, with such analysis based upon a holistic study of the situation of women (in relation to men) as located in their given socio-cultural context. Existing roles can be effectively modified only when policy interventions are built upon realistic, workable strategies that are meaningful and acceptable to the women and their communities. Hence, empowering women by involving them at different stages of projects cycles respecting their socio-cultural context would lead to a sustainable water management.

Water Reuse

The practice of using domestic waste water for irrigation dates back to thousands of years. Reusing waste water is very important component of water demand management. This provides opportunities to conserve freshwater for higher value use. The resuse of waste water offers two advantages: first, this reduces waste water treatment cost and environmental effects and second, this will help to enhance agriculture production avoiding use of chemical fertilizer because of the nutrients available in the waste water (Miller, 2006). However, reuse of water which is exposed to synthetic chemicals during its treatment would offer no benefits. Water has memory and it is impossible to decontaminate the synthetic chemicals completely to make the water drinkable. Despite reuse of water is important from the water conservation point of view, the risk of hundreds of chemicals at low contamination level could lead to serious health concerns.

Water Privatization

In projects where private sector has been introduced, management has been strengthened, productive efficiency has improved quickly, and sound commercial practices have increased revenues. Water losses have been minimized and attention to customers has improved significantly. Many of these initial successes have resulted from relatively simple management improvements that did not required large investments or sophisticated technologies. Private firms have shown a remarkable capability to optimize the existing infrastructures in a short time. For example, in Buenos Aires, two and a half years after the private sector partner began operation, an additional 570,000 inhabitants have been connected to the water system and 340,000 to the sewage system. During the same period, water production capacity was augmented from 3.4 million to 4.2 million cubic meters a day (Rivera, 1996). On the other hand, when Bolivia invited a subsidiary of San Francisco-based Bechtel Corp. to take over water management in the city of Cochabamba, it failed to protect its poorest citizens from prohibitive water charges. Thousands of people demonstrated against the government's water privatization policy. Bechtel recently abandoned the project but sued the Bolivian government for $25 million, claiming the loss of its expected profits amounted to an 'expropriated investment'.

Despite it has been widely discussed that private sector participation has led to improved service quality and expanded coverage, it largely ignores the low income level people's right to get water at their paying capacity. Private investments are driven solely on profit making. Private companies can operate and maintain water systems, but they can never own the water (Cooper, 2003). Obviously, privatization is not a universal solution. However, accompanying privatization with additional measures, such as a sustained favorable economic environment, legitimate regulatory decision and effective service provision, improved design of projects and targets, and complementary structural and institutional reforms can make privatization beneficial. However, supplying water cannot be perceived as competitive market commodity for profit making, rather it should be viewed as a natural resource that belongs to all inhabitants of the earth. Making profit out of water can not be considered social justice. This is where privatization of water development becomes failure. The only solution to sustainable management of water and waste water is to involve users in all stages of project cycles.

Water Pricing

Water pricing, however, is an extremely sensitive and highly charged political issue. Setting water price through the government and big corporations in terms of their investment strategies makes the situation worse. The recognition of the social and economical value of water and freshwater ecosystems allows the resources to be compared with other social and economic goods and reinforces their status as scarce and essential resources. If water is seen as a truly free good, the incentive for conserving it may be absent. Introduction of water pricing can help develop, efficient water use habits especially in developed countries which generate more waste water. In addition, efficient practices in the collection of water fees may generate surplus revenues, more than is required for regular operation and maintenance of existing systems, and can contribute to financing new systems development. Moreover, flexible strategies that allow in-kind contributions such as labor may be important in financing water development in poorest communities. The users and their local organizations should be involved during the water project development and pricing process (Chhetri et al., 2006c). The best water pricing is to follow a natural law, good intension and social jurisdiction (Shapiro et al., 2006)

4.3. WATER AND WASTEWATER TREATMENT

Chemicals Used in Water and Wastewater Treatment

More than 85,000 synthetic chemicals have been registered for usage in USA and 2000 new synthetic chemicals are introduced in the market each year, most with no or inadequate testing (Global Pesticide Campaigner, 2004). Many of these chemicals are eventually discharged into water body through various means that result in the contamination of water and wastewater sources. A simple fugacity-based model can demonstrate, any contamination of water always accompanies numerous incidents of pollution and starts a chain reaction, on setting a spiral down mode (Khan, 2006). Industrial waste contains large amount of wastewater with various toxic chemicals discharged or leaked from the industries. Moreover, the water sources also get contaminated due to the use of disinfectants or chemicals used during the treatment of water and waste water. Various chemicals, such as aluminum sulfate, ferric chloride, hypochlorite, chlorine dioxide, hydrogen peroxide, bromines, fluorides, activated carbons are used for waste water treatment. These chemicals produce various by-products that are harmful to human health and the environment. The activated carbon uses toxic additives during its production that also adds toxicity in the treated water. Due to these reasons, conventional water and wastewater management are not sustainable (Khan, 2006; Khan, and Islam, 2007b; Chhetri and Islam, 2006c).

Chlorine treatment of water is common in the west and is synonymous with western civilization. Similarly, transportation in copper pipe and distribution through stainless steel (enforced with heavy metal), storage in synthetic plastic containers and metal tanks, and mixing of ground water with surface water (itself collected from 'purified' sewage water) are common practices in 'developed' countries. More recent 'innovations' such as Ozone, UV and even H_2O_2 are proving to be worse than any other technology. Even then, developing countries are engaged in taking pride in introducing these technologies, often paid with borrowed (at very high interest rate) money, much of which is spent on hiring consultants from 'donor' countries. The obsession with synthetic chemicals is so intense that some are calling for the addition of lipitor and aspirin to drinking water so that people can be 'helped' against obesity and other heath problems that arise from the very western lifestyle! Overall, water remains the most abundant resource, yet 'water war' is considered to be the most certain destiny of the 21st century. What Robert Curl (A Novel Laureate in Chemistry) termed as a 'technological disaster', the modern technology development scheme seems to have targeted the most abundant resource. This can only have the most profound devastation to human civilization. It has been discussed that the current mode of water and waste water management is totally unsustainable (Khan and Islam, 2007a).

Many chemical contaminants have been identified in surface drinking water and they are derived from industrial, agricultural and disinfectants (Mittelstaedt, 2006a; Khan and Islam, 2005a). According to World Health Organization (WHO), several chronic effects on the health of the public occur due to the use of agrochemicals, such as pesticides and fertilizers (WHO, 1997). Moreover, the use of lead pipes, fittings and soldering leads to elevated toxic chemical level in drinking water (WHO, 1997). It is generally referred that people in the developing countries are severely affected by the water contamination problems. However, water contamination is also severe in the developed world because of the chemicals derived form the industrial and agricultural activities as well as the use of disinfectants. Water treatment systems usually involve in using synthetic chemicals for its disinfection. Chlorine is one of the most widely used disinfectants for water and waste water treatment. Chlorine industry is one of the largest electrochemical industries in the world. In 1998, more than 35% of the world's total chlorine equivalent to 43.4 million metric tons was produced electrolytically using mercury cells (CMAI, 2005). In US alone, 18% of the chlorine was produced electrolytically usually mercury cells (Figure 4.5).

The residual chlorine in treated water even at low concentrations is highly toxic and corrosive to human and aquatic life (Solomon et al., 1998). The handling, storage and shipping poses safety risks because all forms of chlorine are highly corrosive and toxic. It is likely that chlorine oxidizes organic matters in waste water creating compounds such as trihalomethanes (THMs) that are harmful to humans and the environment. Chlorine residuals are unstable in the presence of high concentrations of chlorine-demanding materials, thus requiring higher doses to effect adequate disinfection. The residual chlorine may precipitates proteins and change the chemical arrangement of enzymes or inactivate them directly.

It has also been reported that certain types of microorganisms have shown resistance to low doses of chlorine. Ibuprofen used as an analgesic, was detected in surface and ground water and waste water treatment plant effluents in many places in Europe, especially in the UK. Similarly, in USA, 200ng/l of ibuprofen was reported in surface water (Koutsouba et al., 2003; Cahill ct al., 2004). Various other pharmaceutical products including estrogens which is used as birth control pill, cyclophosphamidae antineoplastic drug applied in cancer chomotherapy having a mutagenic action to the cells have been reported in significant quantities. Nitrosodimethylamine (NDMA) is a probable human carcinogen (EPA, 2002). This is produced when municipal wastewater effluent is disinfected with chloramines. Chlorite, trihalomethanes, bromate, chloramines and chlorine dioxides that cause diseases like, anemia, nervous system damage, liver and kidney damage and increases the risk of cancer. Conventional models do not take into account these social, environmental and techno-economics aspects of the technology development for the long term. These technologies are also the major causes of the global environmental problems (Chhetri and Islam, 2007a). A summary of some primary water disinfectants, common sources of water contamination and their potential health impacts is presented in Table 4.1.

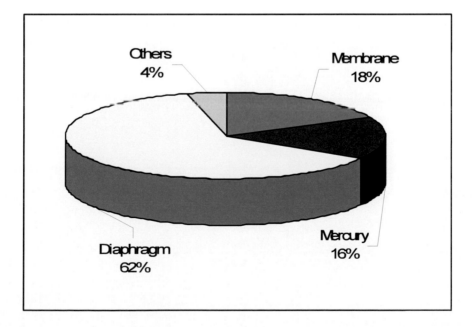

Figure 4.5. US Chlorine cell technology.

Table 4.1. Primary water disinfectants and their impacts (EPA, 2002)

Contaminants	Potential health effects from exposure above the MCL	Common sources of contaminant in drinking water
Arsenic	Skin damage or problems with circulatory systems, and may have increased risk of getting cancer	Erosion of natural deposits; runoff from orchards, runoff from glass & electronics production wastes
Benzene	Anemia; decrease in blood platelets; increased risk of cancer	Discharge from factories; leaching from gas storage tanks and landfills
Benzo(a)pyrene (PAHs)	Reproductive difficulties; increased risk of cancer	Leaching from linings of water storage tanks and distribution lines
Bromate	Increased risk of cancer	Byproduct of drinking water disinfection
Cadmium	Kidney damage	discharge from metal refineries; runoff from waste batteries and paints
Carbon tetrachloride	Liver problems; increased risk of cancer	Discharge from chemical plants and other industrial activities
Chloramines (as Cl_2)	Eye/nose irritation; stomach discomfort, anemia	Water additive used to control microbes
Chlorite	Anemia; infants & young children: nervous system effects	Byproduct of drinking water disinfection
Chlorobenzene	Liver and kidney damage	Discharge from chemical and agricultural chemical factories
Cyanide (as free cyanide)	Nerve damage or thyroid problems	Discharge from steel/metal factories; discharge from plastic and fertilizer factories
1,1-Dichloroethylene, cis-1,2-Dichloroethylene, trans-1,2 Dichloroethylene	Liver problems	Discharge from industrial chemical factories
Dichloromethane, 1,2-Dichloropropane	increased risk of cancer	Discharge from drug and chemical factories
Trihalomethanes	Liver, kidney or central nervous system problems; increased risk of cancer	Byproduct of drinking water disinfectant
1,1,2-Trichloroethane	Liver, kidney, or immune system problems	Discharge from industrial chemical factories
Vinyl chloride	Increased risk of cancer	Leaching from PVC pipes; discharge from plastic factories
Chlorine(Cl_2),Chlorine dioxide (ClO_2)	Eye/nose irritation; stomach discomfort, Anemia; infants & young children:	Water additive used to control microbes

It has been reported that 100% pure have been produced by using reverse osmosis and deionization process to completely remove dissolved salts, nitrates, heavy metals, chemical pollutants, pesticides and disease causing waterborne bacteria and virus (Website 11). Such water is also intended to be used as cleaning agent for sophisticated equipment. Apart from the absurdity of 100% composition of anything, let alone a very reactive and most abundantly natural compound, water, it must be noted that 'pure' water is not suitable for drinking. Drinking water should have various minerals for body. These minerals are available only in the ground water sources. This is the reason why ground water is the best for drinking purposes. The surface water as well as rain water is not suitable for drinking because the mineral content is not balanced. Thus, mixing ground water and surface water together as a drinking water source is not a good management practice. Treatment of water with ultraviolet rays has been promoted for long time (Elyasi, and Taghipour, 2006). However, these ultraviolet rays are from artificial source and there are many toxic effects which may add to the treat the water. An in-depth comparison would reveal that the artificial UV source is exactly opposite to the natural UV source, the sun. Note that artificial vitamin D, Vitamin C, Chromium, and numerous other commercial non-organic chemicals are found to be performing exactly the opposite way as to those that are from natural sources. Considering these, it can be stated that, none of the conventional models of water and waste water treatment is sustainable. Similar principle is applied for wastewater management processes. It has been reported that sunlight can be a good source for disinfection for water and waste water management (Al-Maghrabi et al., 1998).

4.4. Current Water and Wastewater Management Models

In the Modern Age, many forms of what we termed as the aphenomenal model are used in every aspect of daily life (Zatzman, and Islam, 2007a). With this model, social progress is measured in terms of GDP (gross domestic product). Because, this index does no differentiate between waste and investment or short-term and long-term investment, wasting habits, government spending in war and other destructive avenues can show up as an indicator of GDP growth. What is termed as the 'chemicals are chemicals' mantra in technology development manifests itself as 'money is money' in economic terms. Water management is indeed a business that follows this same model. Billions of dollars are spend to add chemicals to water to irreversibly damage the entire pathway of water while profiting the chemical companies who later are trusted to clean up the water for an additional fee. Vast majority of waste water is toxic and comes in contact with water through numerous pathways. Because human engineered pathways make the process even worse, as the cycles of water distribution continues, water becomes continuously more contaminated. Today, some of the most developed nations are reporting some of the worst status of drinking water. The Arsenic problem in United States is well known (Erickson, and Barnes, 2006). United Kingdom recently reported the presence of chemicals used for birth control in drinking water (Fawellm et al., 2001). A study on Romanian rivers detected various pharmaceutical care products such as analgesics, antiepileptic, psychiatric, stimulants, anticoagulants, antineoplastic and disinfectants (Moldovan, 2006). Of course, these are only more recent developments in water crisis. The entire world is still paying for the mess created by DDT that was banned some 35 years ago. A well known environmental engineer, Prof. T.F. Yen said, "We have DDT in every meal we take" (Khan, and Islam, 2007a). It is only conceivable that in 50 years, another environmental engineering professor would be writing, "We have Birth control pill in every meal we take". On the other hand, the developing countries have paid high prices for emulating the technologies initiated by developed countries. For instance, nearly 100 million people are considered to be affected by Arsenic in the Bangal Basin because of the contamination of the ground water that came in contact with atmospheric oxygen due to the sinking of numerous tube wells (Rahman et al., 2004).

Figure 4.6 shows various pathways for water contamination from different chemical sources. Even though, human body is not designed to cope with synthetic chemicals, we are exposed to a cocktail of chemicals designed to kill insects, weeds, pests and other industrial chemicals. These chemicals are exposed to our body through various means at levels which are barely detectable by the most sophisticated monitoring equipment (Global Pesticide Campaigner, 2004). Unfortunately, most of these chemicals cause cancer, disrupt our hormone systems, decrease fertility, causes birth defects, weaken immune system. The magnitude of this devastation is particularly higher when it comes to lower concentration (Miralai, 2006). So much for the mantra: *dilution is the solution to pollution*! This also points out how flawed the entire scheme of allowing chemicals to be consumed as long as the concentration is below certain limit. With the current standard, long-term impacts are not even studied prior to authorizing the use of a chemical even as a food additive. This is in sharp contrast to what Khan and Islam (2007a) termed a screening criterion that would allow the inclusion of any impact for a very long range in time (such as infinity). The common misconception in the current water management practice is: if the concentration is small (preferably below 'detection limit' that in itself depends on the current state-of-the-art of technology) the chemicals will not be harmful. This misconception is easily refuted by the fact that as concentration is decreased the accessibility of a chemical into an organic body increases, thereby increasing the long-term vulnerability of a living organism.

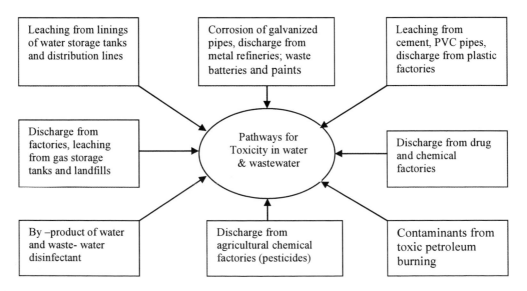

Figure 4.6. Pathways for chemical contamination of water (Redrawn from Chhetri and Islam, 2006c).

We live in a chemical world, ingesting, inhaling and absorbing non-organic (synthetic) chemicals in almost every part of our lives. A recent review by federal government regulators in Canada has determined that over 4000 chemicals once thought to be benign are potentially dangerous for the physical health of Canadians (Mittelstaedt, 2006b). The lists includes some types of perfluorocarbons which are made to make non stick, stain resistant or water repellent products and is commonly found in fast food packaging and cookware. These compounds are widely used to make everyday products ranging from hair driers to water bottles, fast food wrappers, TV, computer casings and inside of tin cans. More recently, it was reported that chemicals used in water bottles are linked to prostate cancer (Fawellm, 2001). This discovery is considered to be the first direct scientific evidence connecting prostate cancer to bisphenol A, a chemical used to make the polycarbonate for hard plastic water bottles, baby bottles and dental sealants used on children's teeth. Bisphenol A is the basic building block of polycarbonate plastic which is used to make water bottles, water cooling jugs, tin can lining inside and coatings on compact disks. This series of chemicals could be in the market because regulations are based on 'detection limit' rather than long-term implications. None of these chemicals would be even manufactured if proper selection criteria were in place (Moldovan, 2006).

Conventional water and wastewater management model is largely dominated by the corporate approach. It is reported that over 74% of the US production accounted for private sector corporations and 1% of the businesses controls 88% of the US private sector production (Global Pesticide Campaigner, 2004). Thus, the economic decisions are at the hands of corporations. These corporations also have deep political and other social influence and have secured constitutional and other rights. However, in corporate decision making, social and environmental costs are largely ignored as their only objective is making profit in the short term (Zatzman, and Islam, 2007). Corporate decisions are explicitly based on considerations of the firm's own short-term costs and benefit, while costs and benefits to society (long-term) are largely ignored. Despite of these facts, the large corporations are not sustainable as they never look back the interests of their customer (Enron Energy Company is an example). Without involving the users in the planning, production and processing and distribution, none of the projects are sustainable in the long-term (Khan, 2006; Khan, and Islam, 2007a).

Water and Waste Water Contamination due to Storage and Transportation Materials

The use of numerous chemicals during water and waste water treatment has numerous problems. The chemical-based water treatment techniques, which were promoted as water purification, have taken a spiral-down turn. Chlorine, which is the most commonly used chemical as water disinfectant has several by-products in the treated water. Chlorite, trihalomethanes, bromate, chloramines and chlorine dioxides are some of the by-products of the chlorine treatment of water and cause diseases, such as, anemia, nervous system damage, liver and kidney damage and increase the risk of cancer.

Storage of water in the cement concrete reservoirs has impacts on the quality of water. Winder and Carmody (2002) reported that cement has constituents that produce both irritant contact dermatitis and corrosive effects (due to the presence of alkaline ingredients such as lime) and sensitization, leading to allergic contact dermatitis (from ingredients such as chromium). They suggested that cement and concrete should be treated as hazardous materials, and that workers handling such products should reduce exposure wherever possible. In order to hydrate the cement, various heavy metals such as cadmium, chromium, lead and zinc (Rossetti and Medici, 1995). Chromate salts are used in machinery and cement contains certain amount of chromate, chromium sensitivity is considered and industrial pollution (WHO, 1998). Storage of water in cement concrete reservoir may increase the chromium and other heavy metal release into water and contamination in drinking water which has several health impacts as it is one of the toxic heavy metals. Hence constructing the water reservoirs, break pressure tanks, and distribution tanks with cement concrete contaminates water with different heavy metals deteriorating the quality of water.

Storage and transportation of water in plastic pipes also has several problems. Oxidation of plastics has been known to produce more than 4000 toxic chemicals, with more than 80 known carcinogens (Islam, 2004). Even in the low temperature, the plastic oxidation continues emitting dioxin and other toxic chemicals. Hence, storage of water in plastic tanks and transportation in PVC or polyethylene pipes will emit various toxins such as thermo plastics and others. In addition to this, transportation of water in stainless steel pipes or copper pipe may stimulate formation of trihalomethanes (THMs) and other by-products which are known carcinogens. Use of chlorine for water disinfection and transporting water in copper pipe at higher temperature could result in the formation of for THMs (McDonald, 2006). Hence, use of these plastic materials will deteriorate the water quality causing serious health implications. Figure 4.7 shows the various components in any water system from reservoir to end use devices due to the materials used for storage, transportation and utilities. Release of metals from cement, pipe materials and plastic molecules into water makes water unsuitable for drinking. Also not sustainable is bottling in synthetic plastic containers. Irrespective of what the standard says, plastic containers release toxins and turn drinking water into toxic pollution. Putting the container in a refrigerator or in a microwave (hot beverages) makes the problem worse making water exposed to various toxins.

Similar model can explain contamination in waste water systems. By-products of different chemicals used for water treatment, addition of synthetic detergents and soaps in bath rooms the waste water. In waste water systems, the concrete sewer pipes are used for conveyance of sewage material. The waste water is further contaminated after the exposure with heavy metals and plastic pipe materials.

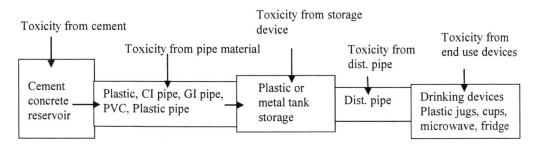

Figure 4.7. Toxicity from different components of water system.

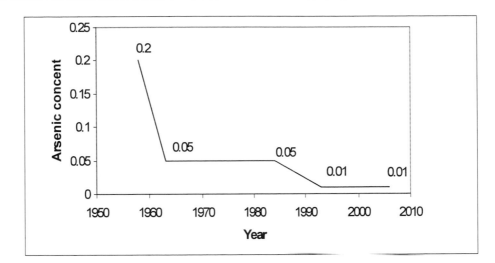

Figure 4.8. WHO standards for As conc. (mg.l).

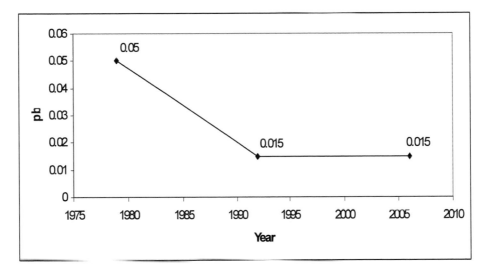

Figure 4.9. EPA standards for Pb conc. (mg/l).

International Standards and Guideline for Water Contamination

There are several national and international standards for the concentration of contaminants in water. International standards which are applicable in general for all countries. National standards are based on the guideline of international standards but are adjusted according to the countries situation and own standards. Figure 4.8 shows the change of international standard for water contamination from Arsenic at different times. The allowable Arsenic concentration in 1958 was 0.2 mg/l, changing over time, the concentration now is 0.01 mg/l. Similar shift is seen in case of Lead concentration over time (Figure 4.9). Miralai (2006) reported that the impact in health could be higher in case of lower concentration of synthetic chemicals in the long term. Lower concentration of such chemicals is not detectable and continuous ingestion could lead to serious health damage. However, if the standards were set for long term, then such changes would not have existed. Considering the long-term health impacts, the standards should be set zero tolerance so that it really becomes standard. Achieving the zero tolerance only will assures the risk free from any chemical contamination

4.5. KNOWLEDGE BASED WATER AND WASTEWATER MANAGEMENT MODEL

It is evident that current practices of water management and distribution are no longer feasible in this rapidly changing world. The distribution of water resources must be carried out based on natural law. Water is a free resource to everybody in the Earth. It is a prerequisite for every living thing to survive. Getting clean and safe water is the right of everyone. However, extensive use of water from industries and big agricultural farms for the benefit of certain private or government corporations have created the world water related problem. Industries not only use excessive water resources but also contaminate water bodies by discharging the waste from industries and agricultural farms (herbicide and pesticides, fertilizers). The common people who are struggling to get their drinking water ended up paying large amounts of water tariff for treatments created by the corporations to succeed in their business operations. The intention counts a lot. The comodification of water is anti-natural. Equitable water resource distribution among every section of the population is a basic natural law and right.

It is obvious that the chemicals used during the water and waste-water treatment, the industrial chemicals leaching from manufacturing, transportation and storage, contamination of oxidation products of various petroleum derivatives associated with water and waste-water are the major causes for deteriorating human health. These management models are unsustainable for the long-term because they are based on short- term benefits only.

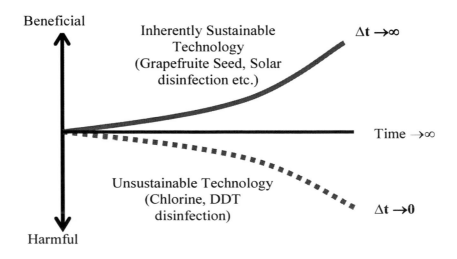

Figure 4.10. Knowledge based technology development model (After Islam, 2004).

In nature, plants produce essential oils to protect themselves from harmful germs, similar to the antibodies produced by white blood cells in human body. These essential oils have been used in medicine as disinfectants for thousands of years. The germs never build up a tolerance or resistance to the antimicrobial action of essential oils, thus the concentration of essential oils to kill bacteria has not changed. However, current practice of destroying bacteria has lead to highly resistant germs, which require stronger, more toxic chemicals and complicated sterilizing procedures are necessary. In addition, the products that are produced after bacteria have been destroyed with toxic chemicals are harmful to the environment. Such is not the case when bacteria are destroyed with natural bactericides. A natural process continues to produce chemicals that are beneficial to the environment. Recently, a study reported that the grapefruit seed extract, mango seed etc. can be used as water disinfectants (Miralai, 2006). These natural disinfectants are environment-friendly and available in nature that can be easily extracted through some natural processes. Only technologies that follow the natural path are sustainable (Khan et al., 2006b). Figure 4.10 shows the direction of nature-based, inherently sustainable technology, as contrasted with an unsustainable technology.

In nature, all functions or techniques are inherently sustainable, efficient and functional for an unlimited time period. Only nature-based water and waste water treatment technologies that have no negative impact on health and environment are to be allowed. Conventional chemical addition has to be dispensed with and technologies and management models are to be developed based on the natural principles. Natural ingredients, such as grapefruit seed extract and essential oils from plant extract can be used as disinfectants. Disinfection of water from solar energy could lead to a long –term solution. There are thousands of such plant oils in nature that can work as disinfectants, herbicides and insecticides. However, we need to understand nature in order to find which is suitable for particular purpose. Knowledge is an ability to understand nature and natural functions. A knowledge based water and waste-water management model requires the integration of social, economic, and environmental concerns in order to achieve the true sustainability in technological development. This would mean the use of local and natural products which will have no emission of toxicity during storage, transportation and end uses, minimization of bottling, storage, and transportation of drinking water. Only natural containers, such as leather, clay, glass (not crystal), wood, straw (tightly packed to prevent leaks, as was practiced by the aboriginal community in North America), and others are suitable and quite inexpensive for the long term. A knowledge based water and waste-water management model that fulfills the sustainability criteria are considered to be sustainable (Chhetri and Islam, 2006c).

Chapter 5

AGRO-PROCESSING

5.1. HUSKING

Rice is one of the world's most used food items that need husking before use. Husking involves the removal of husk from rice by some kind of shear or impact forces. Traditionally rice husking used to be one of the tedious works done in households daily with a level type wooden husk. Traditional wooden husking had never problems of damaging the grain as a wooden lever was used. Modern husking methods involve the use of impeller and rubber roll huskers (Juliano, 1985; Yamashita, 1993). The grain is subjected to various forces during husking, may also result in grain damage depending on the direction of grain feed (Yoshizaki and Miyahara, 1984). The husking and resulting rice depends on the efficiency and energy used during husking. This also depends on the grain size, moisture content of rice and other factors. The value of rice changes depending on whether it has bran in the grain after husking or not or whether it is clean grain or damaged grain. Hence, several factors are to be considered to get the desired rice quality.

Figure 5.1 (a) shows the traditional wooden husking lever operated manually pushed by legs. Figure 5.1 (b) is also a wooden husker with handle operated by hand. This system continued in mountain part of Nepal and some part of India. However, in modern world, these huskers are mechanized using impeller and roller huskers. Shitanda et al. (2000) studied the effect of impeller and roller huskers in the husking characteristics of different varieties of rice. The performance analysis of short grain rice has higher husking energy efficiency in impeller and rubber roll huskers compared to long grain rice. The study further showed that the husking energy efficiency of rubber roll husker for single grain feed was reported to be higher than that for impeller husker irrespective of the rice variety. Rubber roll husker is more suitable for husking short and long grain rice compared to impeller husker when considering husking energy efficiency and grain damage. However, the rubber huskers which are made of plastics have the possibility of contaminating the husked rice from plastic or rubber molecules and may affect the health of the consumers.

Figure 5.1. (a) and (b) Traditional rice huskers (Dhiki) in Nepal (Website 12).

Rice bran is an important source of nutrient. The traditional husking does not destroy rice bran from the rice and is considered healthy way of husking. However, in modern husking, the brand is destroyed due to excessive force and heat generated during husking. The traditional huskers are made of wood and there is no possibility of contaminating the rice grain from wood molecules. Hence, the modernization has moved from good to bad situation. The change that modern husker brought is lessen the human drudgery physically. These machines are operated by fossil fuels using generators that may contaminate the food grains and pollute the environment. They also consume large amount of energy. Hence modern husking techniques are not sustainable for the long-term. Despite traditional technique husking is less efficient, they can be mechanized to more efficient technologies using motive force of water and wind power to run improved machines. There is several water husking mills operated by water power using its potential difference. Machinery blades are connected with the belts which are connected to the rotor run by flowing water. Husking in this matter has no environmental and health impacts and hence are sustainable.

5.2. MILLING, GRINDING AND EXTRACTION

Milling is one of the important agro-processing activities for the farming communities in the world. The traditional milling and grinding devices are manually operated, pain staking and very low efficiency devices like '*Dhiki*' *(Figure 5.1a)* and '*Janto*'*(two stone drinder)*. 'Dhiki' and '*Janto*'are the main agro-processing devices used by majority of the people in rural Nepal and India. Similar devices are still in use in other developing countries for agro-processing. With the change in technological development, people are trying for mechanizing these traditional tolls for easiness and comfort.

In order to mechanize these grinding and milling technologies, several improvements are in place. Hydropower, in the form of traditional (wooden blades) low power output water mill has been in use in Nepal for centuries for grinding purposes. These traditional water mills, located at the bank of streams and rivers, have been the part of villagers' life and are used as an important source of energy in the mid hills of the country. Agro-processing of rural households depends to a large extent on these water mills for their daily life activities. As the rural communities frequently require food-processing services, in the form of cereal grinding, paddy hulling, and oil extraction etc., any disturbance in the river and stream would significantly affect their lives. It is considered that the availability and reliability of these services to a large extent determine the quality of rural lives (CRT, 2005).

Availability of adequate milling services does not only reduce the burden of carrying loads over a long distance but also stimulate and diversify local agricultural production. Figure 5.2 (a) is the wooden penstock to drop the water at high speed and 5.2 (b) is the two stone grinder which is run by the energy of falling water. Millet, corn, wheat, barley and other cereal grains are grinded by this stone grinder. There is no external fuels or processing involved and the operations are truly natural phenomenon.

It is estimated that some 25,000-40,000 traditional water mills are in operation throughout the country in Nepal (Bachman and Nakarmi, 1983). Although these traditional water mills have been part of villages for centuries, due to its low efficiency (generally producing 0.5 kW) it has not been able to meet the increasing processing needs and other energy requirements of the rural communities. Due to this reason, diesel mills are swiftly penetrating in high agro -processing demand areas. In addition to polluting the local environment, these diesel mills have not only disturbed the self-reliant set up of the villages but have also increased the dependency on imported machinery and diesel. Moreover, it has also been responsible for the wastage of a freely available natural resource, whose utility can be highly enhanced through the introduction of a better and more efficient technology such as improved water wheels.

Traditional water mills are operated by diverting the stream through simple construction of stones or brush wood weirs. The earthen channel is extended and led towards the water mill through wooden chute (Figure 5.1a). It has a provision for a safety overflow through a gate. A wooden wedge is inserted at the end of the chute in order to direct the water towards runner. The center piece of the turbine runner is massive boss in which forged steel tip which is driven into the lower cone. The runner wooden blades of turbine are fixed tightly into the center piece. The boss is coupled to its counterparts with wooden wedge and then led to the shaft and key at the top. The whole runner rests on a steel plate with conic depression. The shaft of the runner projects above the bottom of the grinding stone in which the key is inserted. The key exactly fits at the slot in the upper grinding stone and runs the grinder. The power output ranges from 0.2 kW to 0.5 kW and the grinding capacity ranges from 10-20 kg corn per hour (Shrestha and Shrestha, 1998).

An Improved Water Mill (IWM) is an intermediate technology based on the principle of existing mills that improves performance (generating up to 3 kW) as well as reliability of the mills (Shrestha and Shrestha, 1998). The IWM can be used for a longer period in the dry season –and through their increased energy output. This will improve the quality of the milling service offered to the local community. The improved service quality is transformed into a higher agro-processing capacity (milling capacity often doubles) and/or diversified range of services (hulling, oil expelling, saw milling). Moreover, an IWM offers the opportunity to generate electricity for local lighting purposes, depending upon the flow and head availability. The technology has been tested extensively over the last two decades and proves appropriate and compatible with the rural environment, hence is a truly sustainable technology.

Figure 5.2. (a) and (b) Nepali mountain people engineering: a water powered flour grinder with corn feeder (Website 12).

The introduction of IWM induces positive changes in the socio-economic conditions of the local millers and the community at large. For the community, benefits include time saved spent on grinding, the reduction of the workload of women, local agro-processing-employment generation and market development (Shrestha and Amatya, 1998). Improvement of traditional water mills undoubtedly is one of the most efficient options for to assist its local communities in improving the quality of their livelihood (Rijal, 1998b). Similar models can be applied in the other part of the world harnessing the water and wind powers in order to provide services needed by people in agro-processing sector.

Improvement of water mills can also be used in extraction of oil from the grains such as mustard, soybean, and others. As with improved water mills connected to the conveyor belts and the rotating shaft can turn the expelling wheel. Hence power of flowing water can be used for oil expelling. There are not chemicals involved in extraction which other wise could contaminate the end product from the extracting chemicals.

5.3. USE OF MOTIVE POWER

Temptation to use imported fossil fuels has not only ruined the economy of the users but also added threats to the natural environment. Pollution of environment due to human activities, specifically due to use of refined fossil fuels is one of the major cause of several health problems the humanity is facing today. The claim that we are making today to be civilized or advanced can not be proved if we compare the humanitarian values, social factors and environmental well being we had before. Evaluating the environmental problems we are facing today, the diseases emerging up such as diabetes, cancer, AIDS, cardiovascular etc are at the highest level of the entire civilization. Everything we are developing today works only for 'today' not even for tomorrow. The gas we burn today to cook causes several diseases tomorrow, the diesel we drive today is a killer, the coal we burn today to power homes makes the situation worst than not having power. None of the engineering approaches we are taking today is valid for tomorrow. The short term comfort we are taking today is the killer for future generations. Yet, we claim that we have made progress and we are far more advanced than we were earlier. It has been taught that reinventing wheel is not an accomplishment. However, the inventions that we are making today are not bringing us in the right path. It is thus the correct we have to reinventing the wheel again.

The modern energy sources and the technologies to exploit them are not sustainable. Natural has solutions of any problems in many ways. Use of motive power of either wind or water was once the ultimate power source. However, we diverted this mode of energy development so far that we created a mesh to the environment. Now turning back to the motive power of wind, water, tidal, ocean thermal and others have become attractive and non polluting sources of energy. Hence, use of motive power for agro-processing, electricity generation, generating mechanical power and others should be re-visited and the development efforts should be oriented in such a way that only non- chemicals based and natural energy sources are exploited so that there will no additional burden to the natural environment and humanity.

6. FOOD PRODUCTION AND PROCESSING

INTRODUCTION

The growing concern on the quality of food items available in the market is an indication of questionable practice in food engineering, instituted by the food industry. It is being increasingly clear that the welfare and health of general public cannot be assured by most commercial practices of food production, processing and preservation. It is important to add transparency to the process of food marketing starting from food production. It is equally important that people be informed on the way food products are produced, processed and preserved. It has been reported that majority of the food products available in the market of western society including Canadian and USA are genetically modified. While the emergence of 'organic' practices has added some transparency to the process, the practices related to genetic engineering remain inaccessible. A systematic analysis of pathways of food production, processing, packaging and preservation of potato chips adds clarity and transparency. Use of synthetic pesticides and chemicals has several impacts on the food quality. Various additives used during the food engineering process needed to be studied individually tracking them from the source to the final discharge as a waste after consumption. Role of various cooking process (e.g. electric heating, microwave) on the food pathway followed by a food product gives some indication of the impact of cooking technologies on food processing. It is found that most products that emerge after 'denaturing' are carcinogens. Various theories advanced on their possible link with the cancer due to the use of commercial food products are important aspects of the society.

6.1. FOOD PRODUCTION PROCESS

The worldwide commercial food production has increasing exponentially. In developing countries, people are moving towards urban and semi urban areas in search of better services. However, it has turned out that agriculture production in the rural areas has decreased significantly due to this migration. In urban areas, due to limited availability of land, the larger population is dependent on the commercially produced food imported from abroad. In developed countries, food production is highly commercialized. Moreover, due to the changed life style, fast foods are increasingly becoming popular in every part of the world. Potato is one of the food items which is widely used to produce the fast food components, such as french fries, potato chips, etc. Potato is taken as the major source of carbohydrate for the human body. Potato production has been increased both in developing countries and developed countries.

All food production processes follow certain pathways. Plants and vegetables need nutrients to grow. Fertilizers are used as sources of nutrients by plants. Fertilizers are used from the beginning of the production process starting from soil preparation. These fertilizers are usually of synthetic origin except in the cases where organic farming is practiced. Figure 6.1 shows the general production pathway of any food product. During the plant growth, various types of fungicides and herbicides are also used to protect the plant from the weeds and insects. These herbicides and fengicides are from synthetic origin and are very toxic chemicals. Here, 'toxicity' does not refer to regulatory requirement. Instead, 'toxicity' referes to anti-natural qualities of these chemicals.

The world has become a large reserve of the toxic chemicals, fertilizers, pesticides and fungicides. Most of the chemicals are manufactured synthetically. Petroleum products are used as base material to produce these chemicals. Petroleum products themselves become toxic as various types of chemcials and catalysts such as leads, chromium, hydrofluoric acid, hydrochloric acids, glycols, amines are used during their refining (Khan and Islam, 2007a). More than 80,000 synthetic chemicals have been registered for usage in USA and 2000 new synthetic chemicals are introduced in the market each year, most of them with no or inadequate testing (Global Pesticide Campaigner, 2004). A recent review by feredal government regulators in Canada has determined that over 4000 chemicals once throught to be benign are potentially dangerous for the health of Canadians (Mittelstaedt, 2006a). The list includes some types of perfluorocarbons that are made to produce non stick, stain resistant or water repellent products and are commonly found in fast food packaging and cookwares. These are used to make everyday products from water bottles, fast food wrappers and other materials associated with food items. Moreover, these chemicals in one or the other way ended up being discharged into water bodies which are used for irrigation or drinking water sources. The fruit and vegetable matters of any affected plants will be chemically contamination. This will have profound impact on human health.

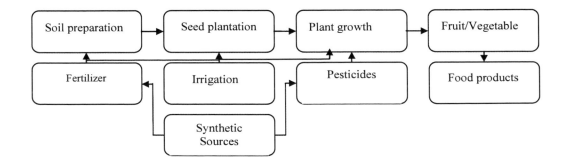

Figure 6.1. Food production pathways (Chhetri et al, 2007d).

6.2. ORGANIC AND NON ORGANIC FOOD

The consumers' inclination towards looking for 'organic' food products gives a good indication on how consumers are looking for alternatives of commercially available food production and processing practices. Consumers want to know that their food is safe and it has been produced in an environmentally responsible manner. Food derived from genetically modified crops is often perceived disparagingly by consumers because the practices related to the genetic modification and their impacts are inaccessible to them. The long term potential effects of genetically modified food on human health and environment have not been well disseminated. Genetic engineering in general is dependent on erratic rather than predictive results despite significant advances in direct or indirect gene transfer techniques. This is because the transgene integration in plants occurs through illegitimate recombination of the genes. The genetic modification results in the natural gene disruptions, changes in the natural sequence of plant metabolism and production of new protein due to the recombination event (Rischer and Oksman-Caldentey, 2006).

Major slogans for the genetic modification of the plants are to develop the new traits, improve the quality and to increase the crop yield. However, for centuries, conventional plant breeding has produced new traits, improve the quality and higher yields. It is obvious that natural genetic variations within the species and between the species have been a major source for crop improvement for centuries (Rischer and Oksman-Caldentey, 2006). Nature has its own way to continuously change and improve the quality of its species without any external intervention. Any anthropogenic intervention against the natural path is anti natural and cannot be sustained in the long term (Khan, 2006).

Organic foods are considered good for health and the natural environment. In case of organic food production, only organic fertilizers that do not pose any serious health risk to humans, use of no pesticides or biopesticides, processed without addition of synthetic chemicals and packaged in an organic container. This is the truly natural way of producing food and such technology is sustainable for infinite time horizon. The synthetic based or non-organic production is not sustainable for the long-term.

6.3. USE OF ORGANIC AND SYNTHETIC FERTILIZERS

Modern farming practices use various types of fertilizers as nutrients for the plants to grow. Nitrogen based fertilizer products such as ammonia, ammonium nitrate, ammonium sulphate, urea; phosphate products such as diammonium phosphate, monoammonium phosphate, concentrated super phosphate, phosphate rock, phosphoric acid and potash based fertilizers such as potassium chloride are common in use (Chemical and Engineering News, 1998). The major source of nitrogen fertilizer is synthesis of ammonia from the hydrogen of natural gas and the nitrogen of the atmosphere. Phosphate fertilizer comes mainly from phosphate rock in widely distributed marine deposits. It becomes superphosphate when treated with sulfuric acid and used as fertilizers. The potassium chloride (KCL) which is called Muriate of Potash is a refined red or greyesh red fertilizer used to supplement potash for the plant growth. The natural potash is refined using hydrochloric acid to form potassium chloride.

Conventional theories are based on the "chemicals are chemicals" approach of the two time Nobel Laureate Linus Pauling's vitamin C and antioxidant experiments. This approach advanced the principle that whether it is from natural or synthetic sources and irrespective of the pathways it travels, vitamin C is the same. However, it is clear that synthetic vitamins do not offer similar benefits as that of natural vitamins for human health. This approach essentially disconnects a chemical product from its historical pathway. In the same way, the synthetic fertilizers are not same as organic fertilizers. These synthetic fertilizers are highly toxic chemicals. When the plants synthesize these fertilizers, the fruits, leaves and other parts are contaminated with these chemicals from various toxins which ultimately affect the users' health. Due to contamination with hydrochloric acid during the production of phosphate and potash, it has toxic effects in soil organisms and plants.

6.4. IMPACTS OF PESTICIDES IN FOOD QUALITY

During the food production, chemical fertilizers, herbicides and pesticides are generally applied. The fertilizers applied during farming play major role in determining the quality of the products. The pesticides, insecticides and herbicides will also have severe impacts on the quality of food. Even though the pesticides are intended to remove pest species only, the application also remove non-pest species, which will have significant impact on the biodiversity of the area. The pesticides can enter into the human body either by air or through the contaminated food. This will have impact on the other parts of ecosystem such as water and soil. The indirect impacts of using the pesticides are the disruption of ecological food chain both in the terrestrial and aquatic environment threatening the survival of many birds, fish, insects, and small aquatic organisms that form the basis of natural the food web.

The use of pesticide is steadily growing in developing as well as in developed countries because more food is to be grown for increased world population. Pesticides are toxic chemicals used in agriculture, urban areas and for public health purposes. Pesticides are substances used to repel, kill, or control any species designated a 'pest' including weeds, insects, rodents, fungi, bacteria, or other organisms. The family of pesticides includes herbicides, insecticides, rodenticides, fungicides, and bactericides. Pesticides are intended to kill living organisms and plants, they are also inherently harmful to human, animals and ecosystems, often killing plants and animals other than the ones they were meant to control. The widespread introduction of pesticides into the environment, often without adequate safeguards create several problems such as human poisoning, livestock and wildlife death, residue in food, water contamination, loss of biodiversity due to environmental hazard and increase resistance among the pests. There are several consequences of pesticide poisoning in human and animals making the world a vulnerable place.

Human health consequences of pesticide poisoning range from acute short-term effects such as respiratory problems, irritation of skin, eyes, throat, and digestive problems to chronic and long-term effects such as cancer, birth defects, and neurological afflictions. Both acute and chronic pesticide poisonings have seriously impact on health and livelihoods. Pesticide poisoning is a commonly under diagnosed illness even in the US. Some of the major chemical pesticides in use today are Organophosphate (affect the nervous system by disrupting the enzyme that regulates acetylcholine, a neurotransmitter), Carbamate Pesticides (affect the nervous system by disupting an enzyme that regulates acetylcholine, a neurotransmitter), organochlorine insecticides (banned in many parts of the world due to severe health and environmental hazard) and Pyrethroid Pesticides (toxic to nervous system) (EPA, 2006). Organophosphate compounds include some of the most toxic chemicals used in agriculture such as parathion, malathion, phorate and others (DNR, 2006). These insecticides are esters, amides, derivatives of phosphoric and thiophosphoric acids. Malathion, paraoxon, parathion, and potasan act as contact poisons, while dimefox, mipafox, and schradan are selective systemic insecticides which are absorbed into the plant sap and remain active for long periods of time.

Carbamate pesticides are derived from carbamic acid and destroy insects in a similar fashion as organophosphate insecticides. They are widely used in homes, gardens and agriculture. Their mode of action is inhibition of cholinesterase enzymes, affecting nerve impulse transmission. Organochlorine insecticides include benzene hexachloride (BHC), DDT, aldrine, chlorodane. Some of these insecticides are banned. It has been reported that DDT is linked with breast cancer in women (Wolff et al., 1993). Children are more vulnerable than adults to dangers of all kinds including the pesticides (PANUPS, 2006).

It is reported that children are 164 times more sensitive than adults to pesticides that frequently contaminate agricultural communities. This is because the children are born with lower levels of our bodies' natural defenses against toxic pesticides. Yet many organizations including EPA too often ignore the clear scientific evidence and fail to protect the most vulnerable people from these dangerous chemicals. Thus, modern food production pathway analysis shows that production of food does not follow a sustainable path. In addition to the inherent toxicity of pesticides and other chemicals, none of the medical procedures or drugs used in treating poisonings and other 'side effects' follows a natural pathway.

6.5. FOOD PROCESSING

Most of the food items are processed in some way before they are consumed. Food processing is the process by which raw ingredients are converted to useable food for consumption. Food processing is an important task of the food cycle. This step is the most vulnerable to the nutrients loss if precautions are not taken. Food processing includes several activties such as removing outer layer, chopping, slicing, liquifaction, cooking, boiling, broiling, frying, steaming, grilling, mixing, etc.

Food processing involves one a combination of various types of technologies including continuous heating, radio-frequency heating, microwave heating, ohmic heating, high pressure heating and infrared heating (Richardson, 2005). Food processing is a thermal treatment of food which is one of the most important processes in the food industry. Thermal processing is based on heating food for a certain length of time at a specific temperature. Maintenance of high quality and safety of thermally processed foods have been some of the major challenges in the food processing industry.

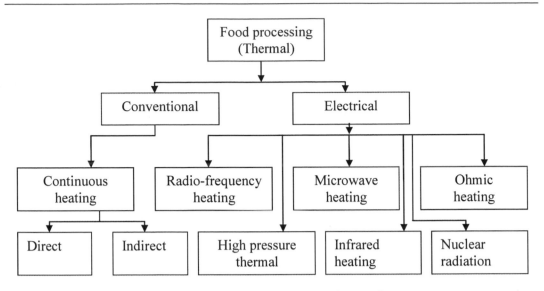

Figure 6.2. Thermal food processing methods (After Chhetri et al., 2007d).

Thermal processing techniques are used to improve quality and safety of the food products. This process involves the production, transformation and preservation of processed items. Stearialization and Pasteraurization are the heating process to inactivate or destroy enzymes and microbiological activities in the foods. Cooking, baking, roasting and frying are heating processes applied for different food items. Dehydration and drying are the thermal process to remove the water content in the food items. Figure 6.2 shows various thermal methods of food processing based on different type of heat sources. In conventional heating method, the processing occurs due to the conduction and convection process. First the cooking pot is heated and then the heat is transferred in the food from the edge to the food particles to be heated. However, in electrial heating, various methods such as radio frequency, microwave, infrared heating, high pressure heating and ohmic resistance are used. In conventional heating methods, processing occurs due to the surfacial heat transfer from one end to another while in electrical and electromagnetic heating the microwaves generated interact at molecular level (Chhetri et al., 2007d). It has been reported that microwave heating produces several carcinogens. Lopez et al.(2004) reported that microwave processing of the avogado produces aldehydes, millards, keytones and polycyclic aeromatic hydrocarbons. Aldehydes such as formaldyhide, millards are blamed to be human carcinogens. Vallejo et al (2003) showed that 55% loss of chlorogenic acid occurred in potato, 65% quercetin content loss was found in tomato and 97% of the flavonoids were lost when fresh broccoli was microwaved.

6.6. ADDITIVES IN FOOD PROCESSING

Food production, processing and preservation involve various kinds of additives. The food preservation also involves some kind of additives or low temperature which may change the properties of the food products. Addition of various additives during processing of the food can alter the intrinsic properties of food. The processed food is also preserved to make it so called fresh in low temperature with some additives. The food products are in most cases packaged in plastic containers either in bags or in containers. These plastic containers or the bags are toxic and can contaminate the food items (Chhetri et al., 2007d). Moreover, these plastic containers contain thermoplastics which easily release its molecules leaving severe impacts on the food quality.

6.7. GENETIC MODIFICATION/FORTIFIED FOODS AND HEALTH IMPACTS

Despite food engineering practices to produce commercial food products in the market are being questioned, the commercialization of the genetically modified (GM) food is accelerating rapidly because the conventional regulatory process is indifferent to the consumer concern as the food production and processing methods are opaque to the public. In Europe, the commercialization of genetically modified food is slow because of the complex regulatory process and higher consumer concerns. North America has the most dominated market share for the genetically modified food among other regions.

In the western world, genetically engineered food is taking over the natural food production. In Canada, more than 30,000 food items available in the commercial market are genetically modified (CBC, 2004). More than 60% of processed food contain genetic modification. It was reported that contaminated genetically engineered papaya were being sold illegally in Thailand (Greenpeace, 2006). Subsequent investigations by an independent constitutional body and by NGOs confirmed GE contamination in the environment in Thailand. During genetic modification of food, the genetic material of an organism is pasted from other organisms.

Some foods are enriched or fortified for vitamins or mineral supplement. It is generally stated that the nutrients lost during the processing can be enriched. However, a natural nutrients inheretted into the food, once lost cannot be enriched with synthetic nutrients. The pathway of synthetic elements and natural elements are entirely different and natural nutrients cannot be replaced by synthetic one to have the same benefit (Chhetri and Islam, 2007d). It is generally stated that fortified milk has more nutrients than original milk. Not only it is not beneficial, actually it is harmful. However, in North America where fortified milk is mostly used, has the highest number of ostoporosis per capita in the world. This is because the nutirents in the milk can never be regained by fortification. Human intervention of natural pathway of any product is not beneficial for the long term. Table 6.1 shows that despite having similar chemical name or compound, the properties of any chemical or compound depends on the pathway it travels and the origin from where it originates from. For example, it has been widely accepted that organic foods are better than foods grown using synthetic fertilizers. Even though the major nutritients nitrogen, phosphorus and potash in both the cases, food grown with synthetic fertilizer are harmful to human and the environment. Similar is the case for Vitamin C which is well known for fighting cancer in the human. However, it has been reported that the synthetic Vitamin C instead could potentially stimulate the cancer (Agus et al., 1999). The synthetic antioxidants are reporeted to give lung cancer unlike natural antioxidants fights agains aging. There are several other chemicals which exhibit different properties despite the similar name or formula.

Table 6.1. Chemicals/compounds that have same chemical name but behave defferently (Chhetri and Islam, 2007d)

Chemicals/ compounds	Natural/organic/bio-based	Denatured/synthetic
Calories	Traditional calories provide energy to body	Chemical calories increases obesity, fattening effect (Baillie-Hamilton, 2003)
Vitamin C	Fights cancer	Stimulates cancer (Agus et al.,1999)
Chromium	Enhances metabolism	Toxic to body (Preuss and Anderson, 1998)
Anti-oxidants	Reduces aging symptoms	Gives lung cancer (Islam, 2004)
Carbon dioxide	Essential for life cycle and biodiversity	Responsible for global warming (Chhetri and Islam, 2006a)
Hydrogen sulfide	Prevents Alzheimer	Fatal/toxic (Takeda et al., 2004)
Alcohol (C_2H_5OH)	Has antioxidants	Highly toxic (MSDS, 2001a)
Pesticides	Kills insects, no negative impacts	Kills insects, numerous negative impacts (Bjornstad and Anderson, 2005)
Fertilizers	Stimulates growth, healthy food products	Stimulates growth, chemically contaminates food, deteriorates health (Bjornstad and Anderson, 2005)
Light	Has several useful vitamins and useful elements	Toxic, stimulates depression, used for torturing prisoners (Islam, 2004)
Plastic	No negative impacts to health and environment	Numerous negative impacts to health and environment (Khan et al., 2006b)
Detergents	Good for health and environment	Several negative impacts to health and environment (Chhetri et al., 2007c)
Milk	Natural milk contains several vitamins and minerals, prevents many diseases	Homogenized milk has fewer and lesser vitamins and minerals, allergic to children (Michalski, and Januel, 2006)
Dye	good for health and environment	toxic to health and environment (Chhetri et al., 2006a)
Heat	Direct solar/wood combustion heating do not have health negative impacts	Microwave heating destroys 97% flavonoids in Broccoli (Vallejo et al., 2004)
Food	Natural/organic- not any unintended effects	Genetically modified –several unintended effects (Cellini et al., 2004)
Antibiotics	natural -treats infections	Synthetic- creates more infections than it treats (Tollefson and Karp, 2004)
Pneumonia	Bacterial- can be treated	Chemical-difficult to treat (Varkey, Kutty, 1998)
Estrogens	Inherently necessary for body functions	Proved to have feminizing effect on fish, amphibians, reptiles, and birds (Coveney et al., 2001)
Any process	Inherently sustainable	Inherently unsustainable, creates several problems (Chhetri et al., 2007a)

Behera et al (2004) compared the changes in aldehyde level, monoterpenes, alcohols and other hydrocarbons with conventional heating and microwave heating (Table 6.2). The experimental results reported that GC analysis confirmed the presence of major constituents; terpene hydrocarbons (a-pinene, b-pinene, sabinene, p-cymene, terpinene), aldehydes (cuminaldehyde, p-mentha-1,3-dien-7-al, p-mentha-1,4-dien-7-al) and alcohols (cumin alcohol, perilla alcohol, trans-verbenol, fenchol). In another study, destruction of vitamin C was reported in the microwave-dried sample followed by higher loss of moisture (Khraisheh et al., 2004). Microwave heating causes insufficient moisture content in food. A similar study reported that about 70% of the Vitamin C is destroyed during microwave cooking of the potato dish and loss of the same further increased due to reduced moisture and longer cooking time (Burg and Fraile, 1995). More than 80 volatile compounds were detected after baking of eight cultivars of potato in a microwave oven. It was reported that the lipid degradation and maillard reaction of sugar degradation were the main sources of more than 80 flavour volatile components identified. Some of the volatile compounds identified after the microwave baking were Hexane, Ethylbenzene, Dimethylbenzenes, Propylbenzene, Benzaldehydes and several others. The sources of these volatiles were the lipids in the potato flesh. The other volatiles found after the maillard reaction or sugar degradation were furfural, phenylacetaldehyde, methylbutanal and several others. Sulfur compounds identified after microwave baking of potato were dimethyl sulfide, disulfide, trisulfide and tetrasulfide along with several other compounds from methoxypyrazines. However, the study does not differentiate the volatiles before and after the microwave baking of different cultivars of potato flesh (Chhetri et al., 2006b). Chhetri et al. (2007a) argued that even the heat produced by different heat sources will have profound impact on the quality of food produced.

Sierra (2000) carried out a study on the effects of continuous-flow microwave heating of milk on the stability of vitamins B1 and B2. The analysis carried out by ion-pair reverse-phase high-performance liquid chromatography at 90 °C holding time was raised to 30 s or 60 s, the content of vitamin B1 was lowered (3% and 5%, respectively). Microwave application for heating milk and milk products caused formation of significant amount of Cholesterol Oxidation Products (COPs) which are very harmful for the human health (Herzallah, 2005). This also makes to think of the other similar food products which may produce similar harmful products due to microwave treatment. Thus microwave heating is considered not beneficial for food processing.

Table 6.2. Comparison of fresh and processed cumin seeds after conventional and microwave by GC analysis of the hydrocarbon and aldehyde presence after Behera et al (2004)

Compounds	Fresh Sample %	Conventional roasting (1250C,10 min)(%)	Microwave heating (*730W,10min)%
Monoterpenes	56.4	58.1	45.0
Sesquiterpenes	0.108	-	0.085
Aldehydes	43.2	41.0	50.0
Alcohols	0.3	0.73	7.68
Ratio of Aldehyde/ hydrocarbons	0.765	0.705	1.11

Heating of food by Radio Frequency (RF) has also been developed. During RF process, heat is generated within the product due to molecular friction resulting from oscillating molecules and ions caused by the applied alternating electric field (Piyasena et al., 2003). RF heating is influenced principally by the dielectric properties of the product when other conditions are kept constant. It is evident that frequency level, temperature and properties of food, such as viscosity, water content and chemical composition affect the dielectric properties and thus the RF heating of foods. Similar to microwave heating, there is likely chances of formation of various unknown products due to oscillating molecules and ionization caused by the applied alternating electric field during RF heating as well as infra-red heating.

Microorganisms are an integral part of the food processing system during the production of fermented food. Many traits important for commercial food applications include sensory quality such as flavor, aroma and visual appearance, bacteriophase virus resistance in case of dairy formentations and ability to produce antimicrobial compounds for the inhibition of undesirable microorganisms. It was reported that various natural toxins (cyanogenic glucosides in cassava), mycotoxins (in cereal fermentations) and anti-nutritional factors (e.g. phytates) are formed during the food processing by fermentation (FAO, 2004). HT2 and T2, mycotoxins caused by *F. sporotrichoides, F. poae,* and *F.langsethiae,* affect the immune system and semen quality. Zearalenone, a mycotoxin also caused by *F. graminearum* and *F. culmorum*, is not very toxic, but has oestrogenic effects and may affect reproductive cycles (Bjornstad and Anderson, 2005). The study further reported that the increase of mycotoxin is a side effect of less-till soil protection. Residues left in the field contaminate the following year's crop. The impact of mycotoxins is compounded by high nitrogen and fungicide levels. This clearly indicates that the use of synthetic chemicals as fungicide accelerated the toxins in the food. The use of chemical fertilizers during the crop production could be another possible reason of mycotoxins in the food products.

6.8. FAST FOOD PRODUCTS

Fast food industry has infiltrated every corner in the developed society. Fast food is now served at restaurants and drive-throughs, at stadiums, airports, zoos, schools and universities, on cruise-ships, trains and airplanes, at Wal-Marts, gas stations and hospital cafeterias etc. It was reported that American spending increased from $ 6 billion in 1970 to $110 billion in 2001 in fast food (Schlosser, 2002). An American average family spends more money on fast foods than on higher education, personal computers, software or new cars.

There is no doubt that these fast foods have changed the people's life style in the developed countries. There are several factors that tempted people to use fast food. The job structures, massive population residing in the cities, industries is far away than residences and the job is on hourly basis. Eating fast food has made life easy, as most westerner dine outside in the fast food restaurants and cafes. However, the way fast food is prepared and preserved has several health impacts. West is not only the places for fast food culture but also the home where most people with obesity are found. The items used in the fast food are commercially produced in masses and several therapeutic and non-therapeutic chemicals such as antibiotics, synthetic pesticides and fertilizers. Various organophosphates chemicals used during food production and processing are the 'fattening' chemicals that are highly toxic to human (Baillie-Hamilton, 2004).

Obesity has been one of the greatest health issues in developed countries especially in USA. Murray (2001) reported that it is the time to stop blaming people or their genes, it's due to an abundance of unhealthy, heavily advertised, low-cost food that underlies the nation's obesity crisis. The problem is caused due to the 'toxic food environment' the strips of fast-food restaurants along America's roadways, the barrage of burger advertising on television and the rows of candies at the checkout counter of any given convenience store. High-fat, high-sugar foods are widely available, taste good and cost less than healthier foods all causing the obesity and several other diseases. The fast food items makes the people dependent on the sugar and fat as they eat such foods regularly and thus foods are considered as addictive as heroin (BBC, 2003). The problem of obesity, high cholesterol and similar diseases are almost non-existent in developing world as their foods do not contain high fats and sugars. Any technology that produces high-fat, high sugars, high cholesterols foods among others are not beneficial to the human. Hence these technologies are not appropriate and the 'ready-to-eat' culture is unsustainable. Development of culture, technology and environment to eat organic and freshly prepared food make the people and their thoughts healthy.

6.9. CHIPS, CHOCOLATES, AND OTHERS READY-TO-EAT FOODS

Chips

Potato and processed potato products are widely consumed foods in the Western Hemisphere. The discovery of the formation of potentially carcinogenic acrylamide in starch foods such as potato poses a significant public-health risk. This paper carried out a comprehensive analysis of the pathways of the various food products especially potato chips. Westney (2002) reported that acrylamide, a compound that causes cancer symptoms in animals is formed during frying and baking of foods. During cooking, many complex chemical reactions take place. Amino acids change their form repeatedly, also producing acrylamide.

Becalski et al. (2003), a group of Health Canada's researchers reported on the major mechanism of formation of acrylamide in food. Figure 6.3 shows the mechanism of acrylamide formation in potato cooking at high temperature. Glucose and a mixture of free amino acids when react with asparagines, acrylamide and other products such as aldehydes were formed when potato was heated at high temperature.

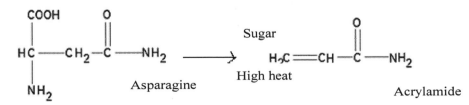

Figure 6.3. Formation pathway of acrylamide in foods (after Becalski et al., 2003).

A study conducted by Health Canada on to find acrylamide levels in parts per billion (ppb) in different food items including potato chips, French fries from various vendors and cereals, bread, coffee, cocoa products (milk chocolate, baking chocolate) are presented in Table 6.3. However, the investigation of trends over time of concentration of acrylamide in varieties of cereals and potato chips suggested that the acrylamide levels fluctuate not only with different food types but also with individual food categories. These variations can be attributed to changes in the concentration of precursors of acrylamide - notably sugars and asparagine - in starting (raw) materials and also to possible changes in process conditions such as heat.

Murkovic (2004) carried out a study on the analysis of acrylamide in foods which is formed from natural ingredients. The highest acrylamide concentrations were found in potato crisps with concentrations of above 1500 ng/g. The contamination of foods with acrylamide originates from a reaction of asparagine with carbohydrates at high temperatures as part of the Maillard reaction (Stadler et al., 2002). Other amino acids, especially methionine can also form acrylamide. Figure 6.4 is the amount of acrylamide in different food products reported by (Murkovic, 2004).

Becalski, et al., (2004) carried out a study to determine the concentration of acrylamide in French fries and of asparagine and sugars in raw wet potato and summarized the values (Table 6.4). The values clearly indicate that the concentration of acrylamide in wet French fries is dependent on the concentration of the value of asparagine and sugars values. It is likely that one of the ways acrylamide formation in French fries can be effectively controlled is by the use of raw products with low sugar (and to a lesser degree, asparagine) content.

Table 6.3. Acrylamide levels in some cereals and potato chip products sampled on various dates in 2002 and 2003 (Health Canada, 2005)

Product	Origin/Type	Acrylamide, ppb					
		Jun-02	Feb-03	Jun-03	Sep-03	Sep-03	Sep-03
Potato Chips	Regular Salted Chips	3700	2500	3400	2160	2620	2640
	Regular Light Potato Chips	1500	790	850	1090	890	1370
	Regular Potato Chips	730	580	500	310	400	320
	Regular Potato Chips	550	1400	1000	1650	1430	1880
	Olive oil with rosemary	530	430	700	1240	1040	1150
	Baked Potato Chips	-	-	300	1830	1780	1650
Cereals	Whole grain oat and whole grain wheat cereal	170	-	88	120	110	110
	Whole grain wheat cereal	120	-	130	90	110	160
	Rice based cereal	100	-	50	70	90	160

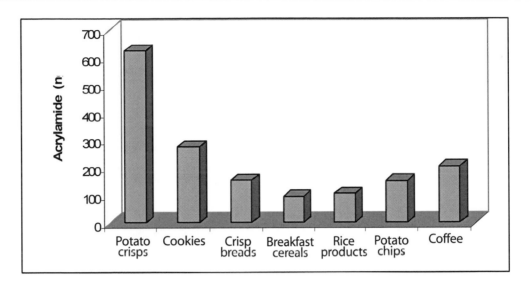

Figure 6.4. Mean value of acrylamide formation in different food groups.

Table 6.4. Concentrations of Acrylamide in French Fries and of Asparagine and Sugars in Raw Potatoes (Wet weight) (Becalski, et al., 2004)

Acrylamide (ng/g)	Asparagine (mg/g)	Glucose (mg/g)	Fructose (mg/g)	sucrose (mg/g)
345	6.67	1.08	0.87	1.6
354	3.74	2.09	1.65	2.76
358	5.07	0.69	0.56	1.05
413	2.68	1.16	0.95	1.65
422	6.41	1.38	1.04	1.82
459	5.65	1.52	1.17	1.93
557	8.35	2.66	2.52	4.25
564	7.38	1.41	1.32	2.65
623	6.27	1.55	1.45	3.34
737	8.3	1.84	1.66	2.44
765	7.94	1.89	1.78	3.02
925	6	3.53	3.24	5.16
934	3.53	4.32	3.88	5.9
999	7.12	1.78	1.69	3.92
1002	3.37	5.39	4.84	7.76
1030	4.37	4.27	4.04	5.37
1062	9.16	3.99	3.78	5.99
1118	5.56	3.51	3.37	5.13
1150	4.92	4.06	3.9	5.52
1242	5.85	5.66	5.21	7.4
1320	3.26	6.28	6.11	10.6
1382	3.12	4.29	4.14	6.66
1485	4.64	5.37	4.39	6.43
1823	8.62	4.82	4.22	6.58

Due to the high nutritive value and wide range of fast food items derived from potato, there is a significant interest in the potato all over the world. The consumption pattern is changing rapidly as the consumers have access to industrially processed potato products. Nutritive value of potato goes on decreasing as the processing steps increases. Some nutrition is removed during the potato peeling. After processing, potatoes available in the market usually contain significantly less glycoalkaloids and nitrates than accepted limits (Peksa et al., 2006). Color of potato chips is considered to be one of the most important factors to be controlled during the chips frying. Santis et al. (2005) reported that the potato strips are soaked in sodium chloride (NaCl) solution prior to frying for certain time which causes osmotic dehydration and desired color can be achieved. However, NaCl is toxic solution and it will form various products during frying due to high temperature oxidation.

Pedreschia, et al. (2004) studies the reduction of acrylamide formation in potato slice during frying. They reported that concentration of acrylamide in the final product was reduced when the potato slice were soaked with de-ionized water, of blanched in hot water or immersed in citric acid solutions for specific time. Glucose content was decreased to 32% in potato slice soaked 1.5 hours in water. Soaked slices showed on average a reduction of acrylamide formation of 27%, 38% and 20% at 150 ^{0}C, 170^{0}C and 190^{0}C, respectively, when they were compared against the control. Blanching reduced on average 76% and 68%. Potato slices blanched at 50^{0}C for 70 min surprisingly had a very low acrylamide content (28 mm/kg) even when they were fried at 190 ^{0}C.

The use of various processing techniques results in the formation of various unwanted products in potato chips and other food items. Besides the processing techniques, there must be improvements from farming practices, production, preservation and packaging. Use of chemical fertilizers during farming, application of chemicals for pest control, refrigeration and freeze drying, packaging in plastic and tin cans make the situation worse. Organic farming, natural pesticides such as pesticides from soap-nut powders, packaging in non-plastic containers and use of natural preservatives for the food preservation are the key to maintain the quality of food including fast foods such as potato chips. However, it is clear that quality of any food items including potato chips varies depending on how the processing and preservation practices are designed.

Chocolates and Others Ready-to-Eat Foods

Chocolates are very popular food and choices of many people either children or adult despite their impacts on health. Including processed cocoa, chocolate has several ingredients such as sugars, milk fats, dairy creams, hydrogenated oil, phenylethylamine, theobromine, anandamide, tyramine, caffeine etc. It is reported that phenylethylamine can cause emotional highs as well as emotional lows (Fenton, 1998). It has also been reported that phenylethylamine migraine and other headaches and causes blood vessel to dilate in the brain causing headache and is responsible for mood swings. Theobromine has been reported to be toxic to dogs and other animals. It is likely that it has some effects to humans too. Cocoa has several times more theobromines than caffeine. Caffeine in the chocolate can cause difficulty in concentrating and cause restlessness. Tyramine is another amino acid group available in chocolate which might cause blood vessels to expand and contract, resulting in dull headaches (Fenton, 1998). Sugar is the integral part of the chocolate production and the bleached and refined sugar has several effects in human body including diabetes and cancers. Sugar content can cause initial increase in insulin level and the rapid decrease in insulin results in the production of excess adrenalin and cortisol, two body chemicals that may cause anxiety. Besides mentioned above, depending on the ingredients, chocolate has several health impacts.

Chocolate as such is not a culprit of any diseases but it truly depends on how it is manufactured and what ingredients the chocolate contains. The cocoa which is made to use chocolate is treated with alkaline to make them dark in color and to reduce the bitterness. The alkaline which is used to treat the sugar to make it white or to bleach creates the health problem as it might contain carcinogens. The cocoa used in the chocolate is usually not natural but is refined before use. A good chocolate can be produced using natural materials such as unrefined cocoa, unrefined sugar or honey, natural pigments for desired color, butters, oils, and other natural ingredients. Any chocolate produced by natural way can boost energy for the users and has no negative health impacts.

It is not enough that chocolate is produced in a natural way, but the packaging is also an important aspect of the preservation system. The plastic packaging could contaminate the chocolate with plastic molecules which is very toxic compounds. Biodegradable plastic or unbleached and naturally manufactured papers are good options to make the chocolate a truly healthy commodity. This model of production and packaging is applicable in any other fast food or canned items. In order to produce good product output, the source of the material from which it is derived such as agriculture farming to the path in which it is manufactured. Other fast food items such as various types of chips, grains, breads and liquid foods also need to be produced, processed and preserved in a natural way without addition of any synthetic chemicals that is non existent in our body.

6.10. QUALITY ASSURANCE OF FOOD PRODUCTS

The use of synthetic chemicals in various industrial, commercial and domestic purposes has several implications in the food quality. Commercial food production is one or the other way involved in the use of synthetic chemicals from the beginning of the plantation to the harvesting, processing and storage. One of the major sources of contamination of food is due to the use of contaminated water. Water is mainly contaminated due to use of pesticides in the crops, discharge of heavy metals from industries, different types of chemicals solvents, industrial and environmental pollutants and discharge and leakage of synthetic chemicals routinely (Baillie-Hamilton, 2004). The chemicals in the food also come from additives, preservatives or the colorants which are deliberately added to food or food crops. Besides this, chemicals enter our food chain from farm animals those are treated with drugs or hormones and antibiotics are added to their feeds. Chemicals leach out into foods from packaging materials as they are mostly made from plastic materials. These synthetic chemicals are the ultimate cause of various diseases and environmental pollution. Non-organic foods are much higher in their chemical calories that fattens out body. Only the organic foods where no chemicals fertilizers and pesticides are used during farming are better for health. Hence, without changing the current practices in all aspects of commercial food and water management, assurance of food quality is impossible.

Modern food production and management practices are unsustainable. The synthetic chemical *modus operandi* is responsbile for all kinds of diseases and environmental problems. Current food production and management models are based on corporate models which have least concerns to human health and environment. These models are based on $\Delta t \to 0$, t='right now' which are not only unsustainable for the long- term but are aphenomenol (Khan et al., 2006; Khan and Islam, 2006a). Only the models which are sustainable for the long-term where $\Delta t \to \infty$. To achieve true quality in food, a paradigm shift in the current practices is necessary. Use of organic fertilizers instead of synthetic fertilizers and biopesticides replaceing the synthetic pesticides are the key to to assure food quality in the long-term (Chhetri et al., 2007d).

There are other practices that makes food unhealthy even if the production process remains good. Food products are preserved and treated with various synthetic chemicals during processing and storage. Moreover, the packaging industry uses synthetic plastic which contaminates the food items continuously throughout the transportation and storage. Hence, use of natural environment and natural products in these processes could significantly contribute to assure the quality of food without any chemical contamination. In nature, eveything has certain characteristics time and violating this time is truly anti-natural (Chhetri, 2007). Perception of treatment of food with high heat and storage in ultra cold temperature is never a means for maintaining a food quality, instead, it deteriorates the food quality significantly. Moreover, our demostic gadgets are such designed that almost everything has synthetic chemical in it. Refrigerators which are aimed to preserve food emits toxic vapours and contaminate the food items. The fuels that are used for cooking food also emit toxic gases. For example, natural gas is widely used in cooking. During the gas processing, glycols and amines are used to dehydrate and eliminate impurities from the natural gas streams. The gas is contaminated with toxic glycols and amines which during burning produces carbon monoxide which is a poisonous gas. Similar is the case while cooking from electricity. Electricity is not a good option for cooking as the electromagetic radiation from electrical field, that may interact at the molecular level of the food items being cooked (Chhetri, 2007).

In nature, everything is function of everyother thing. However, in modern engieering, every solution is obtained after linearizing somewhere in the process. In food quality and management, using a synthetic chemical in any one of the prudtcion or processing chain, could affect the whole food web through land, water and air which is simply ignored. Hence, to completely free the chemical contamination of food, one has to follow the natural path of the products and process. Only pro-nature technologies which are environmentally appealing, economically attractive and socially responsible are the solution to the problems the world is facing today (Islam, 2003; Khan and Islam, 2007a). This model is not only valid for food quality management but also equally valid for each and every technology we develop today.

Chapter 7

FOOD PRESERVATION

INTRODUCTION

Due to the globalization in industries and business including food production and consumption, preservation of food has become a very important issue. In developed countries, the busy lifestyle, driving too far for daily works and obsession towards readymade food has made the preserved food ultimate way to be fed. In the rural and suburban areas of developing countries, food is generally prepared separately for each meal and at least cooked foods are not usually meant for preservation. In the urban areas, the food preservation and fast food culture is emerging. Major aim of preserving food as it is generally understood is to prevent the growth of bacteria, fungi and other microorganisms and retarding the oxidation of fats to avoid rancidity. There are several ways employed for food preservation depending on the type of food and state at which it needs to be preserved. Preservation of food includes heating, drying, freezing, refrigeration, thawing, pasteurization, preservation with chemical additives, canning, packaging, irradiation etc. The preservation methods, their advantages, disadvantages and some natural preservation methods are described in this Chapter.

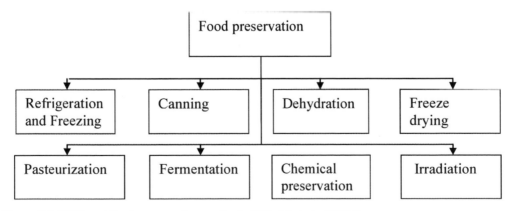

Figure 7.1. Different food preservation methods (Chhetri et al., 2007d).

Many crops are seasonal and many foods can not be grown in certain location due to its specific soil-temperature or weather requirements. Some places are highly fertile and others are not. Due to these reasons, preservation of food is very important step of the food management cycle. Some common methods of food preservation are shown in Figure 7.1.

7.1. FREEZING AND THAWING

Freezing

Freezing is also one of the most commonly used processes domestically and commercially for preserving a very wide variety of food stuffs. Some prepared foods needs freezing (potato waffle) but that would not ave been the case if the same food was uncooked (potato needs just a cool place but not freezing). Even though freezing is an ancient technology for preserving foods, freezing method plays a great role in quality of food to be preserved. Freezing can be done in two ways: fast freezing and slow freezing. In fast freezing, temperature of food is lowered to about -200C at 30 minutes while in slow freezing, desired temperature is achieved within 3-72 hours (Jay et al., 2005). In case of fast freezing, the formation of small intracellular ice crystals occurs. In case of slow freezing, large extra cellular crystals are formed. Sometimes the crystal formation could cause the damage of cell hence limiting the life of the content.

Effect of Freezing on Food Quality

Quality of food after freezing has been a major health concern recently. After harvesting, either we consume immediately (within certain lag time), process or cook and consume (within short time), preserve without processing (like grains), preserve using some processing (for longer shelf-life and business). We are concerned about the 'time' and 'processes' involved from harvesting to consumption. United States Department of Agriculture (USDA) food safety and inspection service reported that the freezing process itself does not destroy nutrients but in meat and poultry products, there is change in nutrient value after the freezer storage (USDA, 2005). Freezing changes in color due to lack of oxygen when wrapped during freezing. This makes clear that the food changes its quality. USDA provided a list of the food and the maximum time that can be stored in freezer, for example meet cooked can be preserved for 2-3 months and meet uncooked and ground can be stored for 3-4 months. Thus it can be inferred that there is degradation in quality of food during freezing. The only thing is that after certain time, there is quantifiable loss in quality.

It has been reported that freezing can slow down or stop some biological reactions for preserving food and sometimes lethal to keeping the quality of food (Tada et al., 2006). There are various internal and external reactions due to food freezing (Montville and Matthews, 2005). Due to food freezing, the extra- and intra-cellular ice formation, osmotic water permeation through cell membrane, deformation of the cell and other behavior occur at microscale and all of these activities bring serious damage connecting to texture and taste of food (Tada et al., 2006). An experiment carried out on tuna fish tissue was reported to produce intracellular and extracellular with significant loss of intracellular components.

Bacillus cereus is a spore-forming pathogen often associated with two kinds of food-borne illnesses, a diarrheal and an emetic syndrome, caused by two distinct toxins. This microorganism is widely distributed in the natural environment and it is easily spread to many types of foods, especially those of plant origin. Consequently, *B. cereus* is frequently isolated from fresh vegetables and ready-to-eat, vegetable-based foods. Psychrotrophic enterotoxigenic strains have also been isolated from Refrigerated Minimally Processed Foods of Extended Durability (RMPFEDs) containing vegetables. Valero et al (2006) showed that at least one of these strains was able to grow at chiller temperatures in carrot and zucchini broths, and cooked carrot puree. So, preserving in the chiller does not mean a total protection from microbial attack. However, antimicrobials from natural essential oils such as benzaldehyde, carvacrol, carvone, 1,8-cineole, cinnamaldehyde, citral, cuminaldehyde, cymene, estragole, eugenol, geranyl acetate, geraniol, isoeugenol, limonene, menthol, perillaldehyde, a-pinene, salicylaldehyde, terpineol, thymol and vanillin have been evaluated for their effects on the growth of food spoilage and foodborne pathogenic microorganisms, including Gram-positive and -negative bacteria and fungi. Valero et al. (2006) found that cinnamaldehyde at 5 µl 100 ml-1 of broth was enough to prevent the development of *B. cereus* in minimally processed carrot broth for more than 60 days, at the moderately abusive storage temperature of 16°C, without adversely affecting the sensory characteristics of the broth. So, smart selection of preservative from natural source may be enough.

Asparagus contains flavonoids (mainly rutin) and other phenolic compounds, which possess strong antioxidant properties. Similar to other vegetables, changes in color, chemical and textural attributes of asparagus occur during thermal treatments such as canning, pasteurization and drying. For example, the degradation of ascorbic acid and change of the green color of asparagus spear surface during thermal treatments are observed. Depending on the type of process, the physical properties of various products, and the time–temperature regimes used, thermal energy can cause varying degrees of loss of vitamin C during drying of green vegetables. Generally, if a process for drying vegetables takes place at a low temperature and within a short time, relatively high retention of the heat-labile vitamin C is expected.

Among the biogenic amines, histamine is potentially hazardous and is believed to be the causative agent in Scombroid poisoning. In the experiments conducted by Ozogul et al (Ozogul et al., 2006), the level of histamine became higher than the hazardous concentration (5 mg/100 g) in eel stored without ice after 6–7 days and, in ice, after 13–14 days of storage. In conclusion, freezing alone might delay the symptoms of hazardous/poisoning process but cannot remove the cause itself. By delaying the symptoms, refrigeration obscures the external features of a degraded food product, making it difficult to assess the quality. Moreover, even at very low temperatures, physical and chemical reactions in the foods can still take place, which will lead to a gradual and irreversible reduction in product quality. Freezing can lead to changes in texture, colour, drip loss, nutritive value and microbial load.

For most chilled foods, storage temperature has a much greater influence on shelf life than all other parameters, and it is of paramount importance for chilled foods that the temperature conditions are correct. Legislation in many countries demands a maximum chill temperature of not more than 4 or 5⁰C. It is usually promoted that temperature abuse in chilled foods can lead to unacceptable growth of spoilage and pathogenic psychrotrophic microorganisms and failure to maintain proper refrigeration is probably the single most cited hazard associated with chilled foods. What is not considered here is the fact that a universal temperature for bacteria inhibition does not exist. Depending on the climate condition, bacterial inhibition temperatures can vary widely. It is likely that food preservation at hotter temperature is more effective for one place and colder temperature for another.

Simultaneous freezing and thawing of food might make some foods more susceptible to microbiological attack due to destruction of antimicrobial barriers and condensation in the product. Consequently, the freezing step should not cause an increase in the microbial load, but may have an influence on subsequent growth in chilled storage of freeze-chilled products. This was not found in the short-term trial but freeze-chilled carrots and green beans had higher total volatile compounds (TVC) values than frozen in the long-term trial (Redmond et al., 2003; Redmond et al., 2004). After harvest and before consumption, vegetables may be stored for varying periods of time and may be processed and prepared under a wide variety of conditions. (Hunter and Fletcher, 2002) studied the effects of storage, processing and cooking on vegetable antioxidant activity.

Among others, time factor is of great importance. Any food always interacts with its surroundings. In return, its physical, chemical and even biological content changes over time. If the change occurs naturally, it is positive as in the case of yogurt formation from milk. At present, preservation is mainly for longer shelve life. That does not stop deteriorating; at best it can slow the process but more likely accelerate the harmful activities, such as, degradation of enzymes, generation of harmful byproducts, etc. Moreover, when we take out the food from the fridge, the damaging rate may explode so much that overall gain may be negative. Due to the several processes being occurred during freezing and the chemicals used for freezing would eventually result in loss of nutrients and quality of food. Freezing the food in more natural way without any chemical addition could help to fulfill the purpose of storing for longer time.

Thawing

Thawing is the process after freezing which creates the environment for the survival or destruction of microbes. Repeated freezing and thawing can destroy bacteria by disrupting cell membranes (Jay et al., 2005). Faster thawing may also increase chances of bacterial survivors. It is because thawing is inherently slower than freezing and the temperature difference for thawing is less than that of freezing. The temperature rises rapidly in thawing and remains for a long course leaving considerable chances for chemicals reaction and microbial growth. It is also considered that microorganisms are usually destroyed during thawing rather than freezing as freezing leads to dehydration, ice nucleation and oxidative damage. Bacteria present on a food before it is frozen can rapidly multiply once the product is thawed. Hence, thawing could be one of the activities which may lead to food poisoning.

Thawing is done in many ways such as in refrigerator, microwave, by cold water, hot water etc. It is considered that thawing in the refrigerator is one of the useful methods of thawing frozen foods. Thawing food in cold water is also considered good options. But the food is to be wrapped before thawed in cold water. Thawing in microwave could be a faster way but as microwave heating is uneven, food should be cooked immediately after thawing. Szymonska and Wodnicka (2005) studied the effect of multiple freezing and thawing of potatoes and concluded that the process changed the enzymatic digestibility of the processed starch changing its functional properties.

Li and Sun (2002) discussed the new developments in food thawing such as high-pressure and microwave thawing, ohmic thawing and acoustic thawing. As the pressure is higher than atmospheric pressure in high pressure thawing, it takes only one third of thawing time. Some research revealed that high-pressure thawing can preserve food quality and reduce the necessary thawing time (Zhao et al., 1998). The study also showed that high-pressure thawing was more effective in texture improvement in frozen tofu than was atmospheric-pressure thawing and recommended that high pressure thawing is good for larger amount of products. However, high pressure thawing is very expensive, there is likely possibility of discoloration due to high pressure and denaturing of proteins.

Microwave thawing requires shorter time and smaller space for processing, and reduces drip loss, microbial problems and chemical deterioration (Virtanen et al., 1997). But due to the preferential absorption of microwaves by liquid water may cause uneven heating of the solid layer and thermal and chemical deterioration of food. In case of microwave thawing, factors such as thermal properties varying with temperature, irregular shapes and heterogeneity of the food make the thawing process more complicated (Taoukis et al., 1987). Thawing of food from microwave heating is also not a natural way of thawing food and could end up generating several anti-natural compounds such as carcinogens during heating. Microwave heating not only has high energy consumption that makes thawing costly but has environmental and health problems.

In ohmic thawing, high electrical resistance is passed through the conduction in the food material being thawed. Ohmic heating is considered more efficient as nearly all of the energy enters the food as heat and ohmic heating has no limitation of penetration depth. Ohmic heating also has advantages over conventional heating such as high heating rate and high energy conversion efficiency (Fellows, 2000). However, due to high electrical resistance, it could possibly damage the protein, cell and vitamins during thawing. Some research showed the potential of acoustic heating for food thawing. More research is necessary to conclude whether it will be beneficial. Hence it is likely that the several constituents of the food items change during freezing and thawing process affecting the inherent quality of food. The only best way is avoid freezing and thawing, if not could be done by using natural air, water and cooling systems.

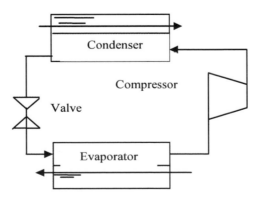

Figure 7.2. Schematic of a typical vapour-compression refrigerator.

7.2. REFRIGERATION

The basic application of refrigeration is food preservation. As we must eat continuously but foods are grown in natural seasonally, compels to go for food storage and transportation for which refrigeration is used since thousands years back. Refrigeration is the process of maintaining the temperature anything below that of its surroundings. It is different than cooling. Cooling is a heat transfer process down the temperature gradient that can be left natural or can be accelerated artificially by blowing. But refrigeration is getting the temperature below the local environment and is always the artificial process that always requires energy consumption. A schematic of a typical vapor compression refrigerator is shown in Figure 7.2. The refrigeration process is used in food preservation, storing chemicals, pharmaceuticals and heating ventilating and air conditioning industries. Refrigeration has an important role in food supply to populations by enabling food preservation at all stages in the cold chain, i.e. during transport, storage, distribution, retail display, and domestic food storage. Refrigeration reduces metabolism of living organism, reduces enzymatic activities but does not kill bacteria. Various food items might need different temperatures to preserve, thus lowest temperature does not mean the food is well preserved.

Refrigeration technology is considered vital in the healthcare sector such as safe vaccine storage and surgery. Refrigeration is also used in transportation equipment, slaughtering yards, fermentation cellars of breweries, ice-cream industry, electronics and precision machinery operations, artificial skating rinks and snow parks. Globally, refrigeration industry is comparable with automobile industry as the largest share of refrigeration sales in 2000 (some 30%) were for mobile applications, with other 25% for fixed air-conditioning, 25% for domestic refrigerators and freezers (some 10^9 units), and 20% for fixed commercial systems (Martinez, 2006). Altogether, refrigeration equipment consumes approximately 15% of world electricity generation. The demand of electricity peaks more frequently during the summer period because of the increasing use of air-conditioning and refrigeration.

Preservation of food is one of the most promising applications of refrigeration. The basic idea is to stop the growth of bacteria and inhibit the activities of spoilage bacteria. Even though food is refrigerated to prolong freshness and inhibit bacterial growth, there is a limit to how long food can be kept in the refrigerator. Pomsa and Tatinib (2001) studied the survival of *Helicobacter pylori* bacteria in various semi-processed and fresh, ready-to-eat foods, and one raw chicken at 4^0C. The study reported that it is unlikely to grow *Helicobacter pylori* in refrigeration condition but they may survive in low acid high moisture environments under refrigeration and pose a possible risk for transmission of infection through foods. Evans et al. (2004) studied the 15 chilled plants used for processing raw meat and salads, Chinese ready meals, dairy products, slicing and packing of cooked meats and catering establishments. Of the 891 sites on evaporators, drip trays and chilled room walls surveyed for total microbes found 336 sites with high counts selecting for Listeria spp., coliforms, enterococci, Staphylococcus aureus and Bacillus cereus. The bacteria count was also found varying depending on the type of products, with raw red meat and poultry or dry ingredients giving highest counts, and raw vegetables and cooked products lowest contamination. Similar study reported that L. *monocytogenes* can easily grow at refrigeration temperature (Grau, 1996). The growth of *C. botulinum* is considered the major potential safety risks for refrigerated pasteurized foods (Mossel and Struijk, 1991). Betts and Gaze (1995) demonstrated its ability to produce toxins in sous-vide foods. Hence, refrigeration does not guarantee the safety against microbial contamination in any case.

It is commonly believed that below 5°C (or below 3°C for cooked foods) the process of spoilage slows down. However, this is a misconception and does not consider scientific facts behind food technology. Refrigeration does not destroy all bacteria and the growth is not arrested. Bacteria that are responsible for food spoilage are indeed inhibited, resulting in degradation by other bacteria. This degradation is not manifested through spoilage, creating illusion that the food has retained its quality. If food quality is defined by its proximity to the preparation time, refrigerated food will invariably become 'old' irrespective of in what temperature it is it has maintained (Chhetri et al., 2007d). For example, Jackson et al (Jackson et al., 2005) found pathogens like, *S. aureus*, *L. monocytogenes*, *E. coli*, and *Y. enterocolitica* from home refrigerators that can survive and grow to clinically significant number. This implies significant risk of eating particularly 'ready-to-eat' foods as they are not cooked (hence, not bacteria treated) before consumption. The presence of *C. botulinum* spores in foods challenges the chilled storage of foods and questions the safety of packaging minimally heat-treated foods (Lindstrom et al., 2006). Moreover, refrigeration consumes significant portion of domestic, commercial and industrial energy that is beyond any justification.

Refrigerant Fluids Used in Refrigeration

Refrigerants are the fluids that are used to produce cold in the systems. These fluids should have large thermal capacity and density, high conductivity, wide temperature margin, low viscosity, compatible with pipe materials and joints, non-flammable and non-toxic with no environmental impacts. There are two types of working fluids in refrigeration: primary and secondary refrigerants. The primary refrigerants are the working fluids of a refrigeration machine such as n-butane, R12, R134a, NH_3 and CO_2 as they give off heat to the sink. Secondary refrigerants are the auxiliary fluids used to transport the low-temperature effect and they may be chilled water down to 0 °C, or antifreeze fluids such as glycols, brines etc. Domestic refrigeration was based on a vapour-compression machine, with R12 R13, R500 (CFCs) as the standard refrigerant fluid from 1930 to 1990 (Martinez, 2006). As R12, R13, R500 were found to cause ozone layer depleting, they were banned afterwards and replaced either by R134a, R600 (n-butane), R600a (iso-butane) or R600b (cyclo-pentane) and others compounds. R22 and R409 are the hydro-chloro-fluoro-carbons (HCFCs) which are also considered to have ozone depleting effects are to be phased out their use completely by 2030.

The use of hydro-fluoro-carbons (HFCs) such as R134a, R410A, R404A, R407C are still allowed to use as refrigerants which are considered having no ozone depleting effects but are the precursors for global warming (Martinez, 2006). Some refrigerants and their ozone layer depletion and global warming potential and mean life in the atmosphere are shown in Table 7.1. Some refrigerants are called natural refrigerants such as air, water, ammonia, carbon dioxide is also considered significant. The industrial carbon dioxide is also a toxic compound to be used as refrigerant. Some hydrocarbon based refrigerants such as propane and butanes are also used but these are highly flammable and toxic. Ammonia can be smell at 5 ppm in air; causing mild eye and respiratory irritation at 50 ppm and severe eye pain at 100 ppm.

7.3. PASTEURIZATION

Pasteurization is the food processing technique by heating to kill the harmful pathogens including bacteria, viruses protozoa, molds and yeasts. Despite pasturization is typically related with milk processing, these days other foods treated with some other heat sources are also called pasteurized. Pasteurization involves the selective removal of a subset of disease causing microbes, which differs from sterilization that involves complete removal of all life forms in the target food. However, endospores of pathogenes such as clostridium botulinum and spoilage organisms such as tyrobutyricum, C. sporogenes or Bacillus cereus can not be destroyed by pasteurization (Montville and Matthews, 2005). Generally, pasteurization uses the temperature below the boiling point of milk. There are two types of pasteurization process in use today: high temperature/short time (HTST) or low temperature long time (LTLT) and ultra high temperature (UHT). In case of LTLT, milk is generally heated to 30 minutes 63^0C where in HTST, milk is heated to 72^0C for 15 seconds. The heating time and temperature is decided on the basis of the thermal death time of most heat resistant non sporeforming milkborne pathogens. In properly pasteurized milk, the naturally occuring enzymes such as alkaline phosphatase is completely destroyed (Vaclavik and Chreistian, 2003).

UHT is another thermal treatment in which 130 ^{0}C temperature is applied for one second at minimum. This treatment kills most of the non sporeforming pathogens and some sporeformers are reduced in number. Despite pasteurized milk does not contain sporeforming pathogens it is not completely sterilized. There are some milk-borne diseases even after the pasteurization. There are several thermoduric gram positive bacteria such as *Enterococcus, Streptococcus, Micobacterium*, and other sporeformers survive even after the pasteurization.

Generally, fresh milk secreted from a healthy cow should be free of any microorganisms. However, there are several microbes found in the milk freshly drawn. Since milk is an excellent nutrient source, raw milk becomes a source of microorganisms too. Pasteurization is done to avoid the possibility of transferring many diseases from animals. Despite the widespread use of pasteurization, milk continues to be a vehicle for some diseases (Montville and Matthews, 2005). Pasteurization was introduced in the 1920s to combat TB, infant diarrhea, undulant fever and other diseases caused by poor animal nutrition and dirty production methods. But with pasteurization, modern equipments such as stainless steel tanks, machines used for milking, refrigerated trucks and inspection methods make pasteurization vulnerable for the public protection. Morover, UHT pasteurization is a violent process that takes milk from a chilled temperature to above the boiling point in a second.

Non of the pasteurization could kill all pathogens, instead due to the high temperature, various nutrients might be damaged. The most important concern these days is the use of therapeutic and non therapeutic antibiotics being used in animals for both purposes. These antibiotics are not completely metabolised by the animals and accumulate in the cells of the animals. Bacteria which are treated with synthetic antibiotics develop resistance and may still be active, which ultimately contaminate the food products such as milk. The use of antibiotics, the synthetic vitamins, reproductive enzymes might have several impacts on the health of the animals. Use of foods grown using synthetic fertilizers are also one of the major causes for many contamination and diseases related to milk.

Nutritional value

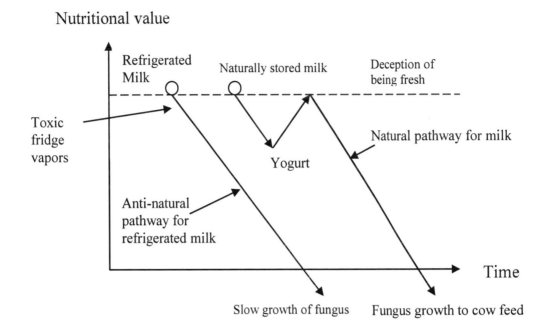

Figure 7.5. Nutritional value vs time for natural and refrigerated milk.

Chherti and Islam (2007d) developed a model for the nutritional value of the raw and refrigerated milk (Figure 7.5). They showed that as the time passes after storing the milk in natural way, the nutrional value as milk goes no decreasing but it forms yogurt. Moreover, the value of nutrition in the yogurt goes on incresing up to certain level. The yogurt also has certain characteristics time but finally rots and probably fugus growth occurs. The fungus could be the feed for cows and finally recycled to the nutritional milk which is a natural pathway for milk. However, when the milk is pasteurized and refrigerated, it violets the characteristics time of milk to convert into yogurt and rots without forming yogurt which is anti-natural pathway. Moreover, the refrigeration have toxic vapours which will the rotton milk also toxic and fungus which can grow in extremely toxic environmentstarts growing.

Half of the world's population living in the villages of the developing countries still depends on hand drawn animal milk and simply heated to boil using wood, biogas or kerosene. This is one of the major nutrients the children in these places depend on. Recently there is some consumer interest in raw milk products in order to get health benefits from the raw milk. As it is perceived that the pasteurized milk destroys the enzymes in the milk, reduced vitamin contents, destroys vitamin C, B12, and B6, denatures fragile milk proteins, kills beneficial bacteria, promotes pathogens and is associated with allergies, increased tooth decay, colic in infants, growth problems in children, osteoporosis, arthritis, heart disease and cancer. Calves fed pasteurized milk do poorly and many die before maturity. Raw milk sours naturally but pasteurized milk turns putrid. As everything has some characteristics time, milk has also certain characteristics time and forms yougort after storing certain time after heating. By pasterurization, freezing and refrigeration, the characteristics time is violeted and it putrified rather than forming yougort.

**Table 7.2. Show the effect of medium on the thermal death of *E-coli*
(Carpenter 1967 in Montville and Matthews, 2005)**

Medium	Thermal Death Point (^{0}C)
Cream	73
Whole Milk	69
Skim Milk	65
Whey	63
Bouillon (broth)	61

Despite several technologies available for milk pasteurization, they have several flaws. It has been reported that North American has the highest percapita ostoporosis affected population disregard of the highet percapita milk consumption (Chhetri and Islam, 2007a). This indicates that the pasteurized milk has no more contrubted to the public health. Since all the enzymes are destroyed, the milk has no enough nutrients in it. Hence, simply heating the milk with conduction method such as wood burning would maintain the nutrients, vitamins and proteins and kill harmful pathogens if any keeping the beneficial pathogens intact. This consumes less energy and is the cheapest and does not harm to the natural environment.

7.4. HEATING AND DRYING

The main principle behind preserving food by heating is using the destructive effects of heat on microorganisms. Preservation by heating means raising the temperature above ambient temperature. Food preservation by heating can be done in two ways: pasteurization and sterilization. In case of pasteurization, harmful pathogens are destroyed by application heat. This will also reduce the number of spoilage bacteria. In case of sterilization, all viable microorganisms are destroyed. Canned foods are sterilized and either the microorganisms are completely destroyed or can not grow due to temperature storage, undesirable pH or oxidation reduction potential (Montville and Matthews, 2005).

Heat treatment for the food preservation is affected by several factors against heat resistant microorganisms. The heat resistance of microbial cells increases with decreasing humidity, moisture or water activity. Due to the presence of fats, there is an increase in the heat resistance of some microorganisms. The effect of salt on the heat resistance of microorganism depends on the type of salts, concentration and other characteristics. Some salts decrease water activity and increase heat resistance by drying. The other factors that affect the treatment of high heat to preserve the food are carbohydrate content of the food, pH, protein and other substances, number of organisms and age of the organisms present on the food. Presence of sugars sometimes causes the heat resistance of microorganisms. Microorganisms are most resistant to heat at their optimum pH growth of average 7.0. It is reported that when pH is lowered though acids such as HCl, the heat resistant of the bacteria increases. When pH is lowered through organic acids such as acetic or lactic acid, a decrease in bacterial heat resistance occurs. The medium at which heat is applied affects the thermal death of microorganisms. Table 7.2 shows the effect of medium on the thermal death of *E-coli*. Foods containing high protein food need greater depth of heating than food containing low protein. The more the number of organisms present, the more heat is necessary to destroy microorganisms. The age of the microorganisms also has great role to play in the heat treatment. Old cells at the stationery phase have higher heat resistance. Time of heat exposure is also an important issue for the heat treatment in food preservation.

Preservation of food by drying based on the principle that water is necessary for microorganisms and enzymes to be active. Drying is carried out to lower the moisture content of the food in such level that the spoilage and food poisoning microbes can not grow. The moisture content is lowered than 20 % by drying by heating, using desiccators, or freeze drying. Drying through the sunlight is the best method to lower the moisture at desired level. For many vegetables, drying up to 60-62 ^{0}C is considered optimum to lower the moisture below 4% (Montville and Matthews, 2005). Drying increase the shrinkage of the food, possibility of nutrient migration, denaturizing proteins and occurs hardening of foods. Bacteria requires relatively high level of moistures for their growth and drying may not always destroy all microorganisms as the process may not be lethal. Careful consideration is necessary for lowering the optimum moisture content. Heating through solar energy is the best method for heating compared electrical heating and the molecular interaction of the food with different heat sources could be different. Fossil fuel heating is not sustainable for drying and create lots of environmental problems. Hence, proper selection of drying heat source plays a great role for the sustainable operation of drying for the food preservation.

7.5. CANNING AND PACKAGING

Canning is used to preserve food for longer duration. In canning, food is boiled in the can to kill all the bacteria and seal the can (either before or while the food is boiling) to prevent any new bacteria from getting in. The food in the can is completely sterile. One problem with canning is that the act of boiling food in the can generally changes its taste and texture as well as its nutritional content. The milk canned is treated with ultra high temperature pasteurization. This process is likely to destroy the nutrients in the milk and since it is boiled, the taste is changed from original.

Mutagens are shown to be present in a variety of commercially heat processed foods (Krone and Iwaoka, 1984). Since these substances are not present in the unheated raw material, it appears that they are produced during processing. Canned salmon and beef broth showed the highest mutagenicity. These findings are considered significant not only because of the large proportion of the food supply which is processed by canning but also because the mutagens in these foods exhibit chemical behaviors and Salmonella strain specificity similar to mutagens in grilled foods which have been shown to be mammalian carcinogens.

Packaging is another important part of the food preservation, the food treated with any other methods needs some kinds of packaging during its storage, transportation and handling. Food packaging is usually done either by papers or by plastics. The papers used for packaging are usually bleached paper and can easily contaminate the food being packaged. Moreover, most food items are packaged in plastics bags. Plastic is a hydrocarbon product of petroleum refinery which is very toxic materials. Islam (2004) reported that oxidation of plastics releases approximately 4000 toxic compounds including dioxins and 80 of these toxins are known carcinogens. These conventional packaging materials are the precursors for several health and environmental problems.

Papers which are naturally produced without using any synthetic chemicals and bleaching materials are the key to the packaging industries. Paper making of the earlier days used to be in this model and still people in many of the developing countries still produce papers naturally from the tree pulps. Similarly, increased production and use of bio-plastics instead of today's synthetic plastics in the packaging industry for food preservation would help to safeguard the public health and the natural environment. Bio-based plastics are totally benign and truly biodegradable. Use of natural papers and bio-plastics would be inherently sustainable for the long-term development of the society.

7.6. IRRADIATION

Food preservation is usually carried out by two types of irradiation: UV irradiation and ionizing irradiation.

UV Radiation

Irradiation of food through ultraviolet rays (UV) is relatively new method of food preservation. UV radiation at wavelengths of 240-280 nm is considered destructive. The radiation of this range damages nucleic acids by cross-linking thymine in DNA (Montville and Matthews, 2005). This radiation easily kills the gram negative bacteria but can not kill the bacterial endospores and molds as they are highly resistant. Viruses are also more resistant than bacteria.

The UV radiation has very low penetration. This also has difficulties in attaining an even exposure level on the food surface that limits its use in food preservation. Generally, UV radiation is used for disinfecting air in filling of liquid food as well as water disinfection.

However, the impact of radiation on the food quality depends on the source of UV radiation. If it is natural radiation from sun, that would not have negative impact but if the UV is generated from the other sources such as electrical sources, this will have much negative impacts on the food quality.

Ionizing Radiation

Unlike UV irradiation, ionizing radiation has high energy and penetrating power. The use of ionizing radiation causes destruction of microbes by generation of free radicals and damaging to DNA, membrane and other cellular structures. It is generally said that ionizing radiation can pasteurize or sterilize foods with out loss in quality and prevents reproduction of microorganism and insects. High electromagnetic radiation with energies up to 5 mega-electron volts (MeV) or electrons from electron accelerator with energies up to 10 MeV are used to irradiate food. Montville and Matthews (2005) also wrote that ionizing radiation affect DNA directly and indirectly and damage the cell. Since this radiation brings chemicals changes in the organism's DNA, it will also affect the structure of the food which is also an organic material like bacterial cell.

The radiolytic products formed from the free radicals are truly anti-natural compounds. The impacts of these compounds are not known yet. However, it is also conceivable that the irradiation with high energy electrons could make the food radioactive producing several impacts. Chhetri and Islam (2006e) reported that electromagnetic irradiation has several problems in plants and in the environment. It is not difficult to imagine that since this irradiation damages living cells of bacteria, it will also harm to the food items. Moreover the high energy irradiation produces radiolytic compounds from free radicals formed from water which are harmful compounds for the long-term. However, the current technology may not detect these impacts right now but one day or the other, these things will come out. It took almost 40 years to know the deadly impacts of DDT, it took almost similar time to understand the effect of CFCs used in the refrigerators, the same way the negative impacts of these technologies would emerge but by the time, people's health and environment will have been already damaged.

7.7. CHEMICAL PRESERVATION

Various chemicals are also used for the food preservation in order to prevent or delay from spoilage. These chemicals are derived from the fact that they are successfully used for treating humans, animals and plants. Although there are large number of chemicals described for potential use as food preservatives, few of have been in use as most of them are toxic and ineffective for preservation. Montville and Matthews (2005) summarized the currently used preservatives which are termed as generally recognized as safe (GRAS) which is presented in Table 7.3.

Various types of chemical dehydrating agents are used to dehydrate different types of food such as milk, potato, fruits and vegetables, meats, soups and sauces, pasta and instant rice. Dried foods are intended to remain for longer time. Drying out foods, such as fruits, can reduce the amount of vitamin C. Dehydrating food also makes the food products more energy dense, which may contribute to obesity. Moreover, drying completely alters the taste and texture of the food.

Sodium benzoic acid is used as antibacterial agent. The activity of benzoic acid is greatest at low pH, meaning high acidity. High acidity alone would be sufficient to prevent the growth of bacteria. Even though it is used as molds and yeast inhibitor, it is considered effective on some bacteria at concentrations of 50-500 ppm range (Montville and Matthews, 2005). However, this is a synthetic chemical and can cause irritation to the respiratory tract, coughing, irritation to gastrointestinal tract, eye, and skin (Chhetri et al., 2006d). Since these chemicals inhibit the growth of bacterial cells, it is obvious that they will also inhibit the human biological functions as contamination of the food items treated to certain concentration can not be avoided. EPA (2006) reported that 3 months exposure of 0.2% benzoic acid in the diet increased the susceptibility of mice to the development of carcinomas following intraperitoneal inoculation with Erlich ascites carcinoma cells. The report further reported that tumors developed in 68.8% of benzoic acid- treated mice.

Table 7.3. Summary of some GRAS chemical food preservatives (Montville and Matthews, 2005)

Preservatives	Maximum tolerance	Organisms affected	Foods
Propionic acid	0.32%	Molds	Bread, cakes, cheese, rope inhibitor in bread dough
Sorbic acid	0.2%	Molds	Hard cheeses, figs, syrups, salad dressings, cakes, jellies
Benzoic acid	0.1%	Yeasts and molds	Margarine, pickle, apple cider, soft drinks, tomato catsup, salad dressings
Parabens	0.1%	Yeasts and molds	Bakery products soft drinks, pickles, salad dressings
SO_2 /sulfites	200-300 ppm	Insect, microbes	Molasses, dried fruits, wine making, lemon juice and other food sources with thiamine sources
Ethylene/propylene oxide	700 ppm	Yeasts, molds, vermin	Fumigant for spice, nuts
Sodium diacetate	0.32%	Molds	Breads
Nisin	1%	Lactics, clostridia	Certain pasteurized cheese
Dehydroacetic acid	65 ppm	Insects	Pesticides of strawberries, squash
Sodium nitrite	120 ppm	Clostridia	Meant-curing preparations
Caprylic acid	-	Molds	Cheese wraps
Sodium lactate	Up to 4.8 %	Bacteria	Pre-cooked meats
Ethyl formate	15-220 ppm	Yeasts and molds	Dried fruits, nuts

Ethylene or propylene oxides and other preservatives are all synthetic based chemicals. Sulfur dioxide and sulfites are used to protect food against molds and yeast. They are also used during wine making. Sulfur dioxide is corrosive when wet and is toxic and fatal at high concentration. The use of sulphites may also have several consequences. Sulphites are generally available in the form of sodium or ammonium sulphite. It is harmful as it is an irritant for respiratory tract. This can also produce asthma-like allergy. MSDS (2003) outlined that toxicological properties not fully investigated. Any chemical compound which is not available naturally is anti-natural and ingestion of these compounds would behave different than their natural alternatives creating several health problems. Because of these toxic chemicals, the chemical preservation of the food can not be considered a safe option of food preservation and may pose health threat in the long run.

7.8. NATURAL FOOD PRESERVATION

The use of synthetic chemicals in various industrial, commercial and domestic purposes has several implications in the food quality. Commercial food production is one or the other way involved in the use of synthetic chemicals from the beginning of the plantation to the harvesting, processing and storage. One of the major sources of contamination of food is due to the use of contaminated water. Water is mainly contaminated due to use of pesticides in the crops, discharge of heavy metals from industries, different types of chemicals solvents, industrial and environmental pollutants and discharge and leakage of synthetic chemicals routinely (Baillie-Hamilton, 2004). The chemicals in the food also come from additives, preservatives or the colorants which are deliberately added to food or food crops. Besides this, chemicals enter our food chain from farm animals those are treated with drugs or hormones and antibiotics are added to their feeds. Chemicals leach out into foods from packaging materials as they are mostly made from plastic materials. These synthetic chemicals are the ultimate cause of various diseases and environmental pollution. Non-organic foods are much higher in their chemical calories that fattens out body. Only the organic foods where no chemicals fertilizers and pesticides are used during farming are better for health. Hence, without changing the current practices in all aspects of commercial food and water management, assurance of food quality is impossible.

There are other practices that makes food unhealthy even if the production process remains good. Food products are preserved and treated with various synthetic chemicals during processing and storage. Moreover, the packaging industry uses synthetic plastic which contaminates the food items continuously throughout the transportation and storage. Hence, use of natural environment and natural products in these processes could significantly contribute to assure the quality of food without any chemical contamination. In nature, eveything has certain characteristics time and violating this time is truly anti-natural (Chhetri, 2007). Perception of treatment of food with high heat and storage in ultra cold temperature is never a means for maintaining a food quality, instead, it deteriorates the food quality significantly. Moreover, our demostic gadgets are such designed that almost everything has synthetic chemical in it. Refrigerators which are aimed to preserve food emits toxic vapours and contaminate the food items. The fuels that are used for cooking food also emit toxic gases. For example, natural gas is widely used in cooking. During the gas processing, glycols and amines are used to dehydrate and eliminate impurities from the natural gas streams. The gas is contaminated with toxic glycols and amines which during burning produces carbon monoxide which is a poisonous gas. Similar is the case while cooking from electricity. Electricity is not a good option for cooking as the electromagetic radiation from electrical field, that may interact at the molecular level of the food items being cooked (Chhetri, 2007).

In nature, everything is function of everyother thing. However, in modern engieering, every solution is obtained after linearizing somewhere in the process. In food quality and management, using a synthetic chemical in any one of the prudtcion or processing chain, could affect the whole food web through land, water and air which is simply ignored. Hence, to completely free the chemical contamination of food, one has to follow the natural path of the products and process. Only pro-nature technologies which are environmentally appealing, economically attractive and socially responsible are the solution to the problems the world is facing today (Islam, 2003; Khan and Islam, 2007a). This model is not only valid for food quality management but also equally valid for each and every technology we develop today.

Natural Cooling System for Preservation

The great misconception exists today is that the costly energy sources such as electricity is the only option used to design the cold storage systems. However, there are truly ways of preserving foods, vegetables and fruits based on the natural principle of thermodynamics that helps to develop natural cooling system. Mohammed Bah Abba developed a "Pot-in-Pot Preservation/Cooling System" device made of earth in Nigeria in 1995 (Website 13). This is a kind of "refrigerator in deserts" that helps subsistence farmers in northern Nigeria by reducing food spoilage and waste and thus increasing their income and limiting the health hazards of decaying foods. This innovative cooling device consists of two earthenware pots of different diameters, one placed inside the other. The space between the two pots is filled with wet sand that is kept constantly moist that helps keeping both pots damp. Fruit, vegetables and other items such as soft drinks are put in the smaller inner pot, which is covered with a damp cloth. The device is then left in a very dry ventilated place. The water contained in the sand between the two pots evaporates towards the outer surface of the larger pot in which the drier outside air is circulating. Based on the principle of thermodynamics, the evaporation process automatically causes a drop in temperature of several degrees. This ultimately helps cooling the inner container, destroys harmful microorganisms and preserves the perishable foods items inside.

The experimental results carried out in this device were overwhelmingly positive. Eggplants stored in this device stayed fresh for 27 days instead of three days without this device, and tomatoes and peppers lasted for three weeks or more. The results of African spinach which usually spoils after a day remained edible after 12 days in the Pot-in-Pot storage device while the outside temperature remains quite high. The cost of each device costs about US 30 cents each, there is no energy input at all as there are no moving parts and no chemicals are used (Lubick, 2000).

7.9. NATURAL PRESERVATIVES

Natural preservatives play a great role in healthy food preservation. However, most products advertised as natural contain potentially harmful chemical and /or synthetic elements (Website 14). There are thousands of essential oils in plants and trees which are powerful natural preservatives. They are derived from flowers, leaves, grasses, and woody plants. Their antiseptic properties of these essential oils were uncovered during the cholera epidemics of the nineteenth century in France when tens of thousands of men, women, and children were affected but only the people working in perfume factories were immune to such diseases. The natural essential oils are such that addition of as little as one drop of sweet orange oil to two ounces of cream will kill all bacteria and fungi in the sample. Essential oils have also been shown to be effective in killing the virus that causes Herpes and assist in healing various diseases. Table 7.4 shows various natural essential oils that can kill bacteria effectively and can be safely used as natural preservatives. Addition of these natural preservatives not only prevents food from bacterial growth but has no negative health impacts unlike in chemical preservatives which are toxic resulting in food poisoning and long term effects.

Table 7.4. Effectiveness of Essential Oils in Killing Bacteria (Website 14)

Essential oil	Minimum Amount in %	Essential oil	Minimum Amount in %
Thyme	0.070	Rosemary	0.430
Origanum	0.100	Cumin	0.450
Sweet Orange	0.120	Neroli	0.475
Lemongrass	0.160	Birch	0.480
Chinese Cinnamon	0.170	Lavender	0.500
Rose	0.180	Melissa Balm	0.520
Clove	0.200	Ylang Ylang	0.560
Eucalyptus	0.225	Juniper	0.600
Peppermint	0.250	Sweet Fennel	0.640
Rose geranium	0.250	Garlic	0.650
Meadowsweet	0.330	Lemon	0.700
Chinese anise	0.370	Cajeput	0.720
Orris	0.380	Sassafras	0.750
Cinnamon	0.400	Heliotrope	0.800
Wild Thyme	0.400	Fir, Pine	0.860
Anise	0.420	Parsley	0.880
Mustard	0.420	Violet	0.900

There are some natural chemical preservatives such as salts (NaCl) and sugars being used since thousands of years. The early use of salt was to preserve meat for longer periods. AT high concentrations, salt exerts drying effects on both food and microorganisms. Due to the equal amount of water and salt on the both side of cell membrane, water moves across the cell membrane equally in both direction (Montville and Matthews, 2005). Due to diffusion process, water passes out of the cell at greater rates than it enters resulting in plasmolysis (shrinkage) inhibiting or death of microorganisms. With higher salt concentration, greater preservative and drying effects are achieved. Similarly, sugars such as sucrose exert their preserving effect in essentially the similar fashion as that of salt. However, it requires more sugars (usually 6 times more) than salt to get the similar preservative and drying effects. Sugar can be used to preserve fruits, candies, condensed milk and similar products (Montville and Matthews, 2005). Sugars help to make water unavailable to microorganisms preventing their growth in the food preserved. Only these natural preservatives are sustainable for the long-term without having any negative health and environmental impacts.

Chapter 8

DRINKING FLUIDS

INTRODUCTION

Various minerals regulate vital body functions and metabolic processes in the human body. Mineral water and spring water available naturally are pure waters and contain various minerals that are essential to the human body. However, addition of artificial or synthetic mineral in water for human consumption does not give benefits of natural minerals. Moreover, it is likely to have negative health impacts as these synthetic minerals can not be metabolized by our body. Hence the distinction between synthetic and natural mineral is very important in relation to the water available naturally or synthesized artificially.

8.1. MINERAL WATER, ULTRA PURE WATER, CHLORINATED WATER

Drinking mineral water has been considered as minimum standard for drinking water in the western society where as in eastern cultures, it has been the symbol of status and healthy water. In order to regulate the various body functions and continue metabolic processes, different minerals are essential for human body. Most of the minerals are available in the natural spring water and ground waters. The most important minerals for our body are sodium, chlorine, potassium, calcium, phosphorus, iodine, manganese, iron, zinc etc. Natural mineral and spring water are non-processed waters obtained from subterranean sources. This source is created by rain water, ground water, and snow melts seeping through the soil. During the percolation, this water absorbs various minerals and other useful substances. Moreover, while the water passing through the clay, sand and other layers of the earth removes pollutants from the water that may take several hundreds of years. The layers of rock and sand work as filters. The minerals are dissolved into water and give some kind of flavor to water. Naturally available mineral water is more refreshing compared to bottled water available in the market.

The mineral water available in the market has been added artificial minerals which are in fact harmful. Human bodies cannot metabolize the synthetic minerals and likely creates several diseases in the long-term. The other important factor is bottled mineral water is stored for a long time and is never a fresh water (Islam, 2006b). Hence in true sense, mineral water should be directly bottled from the underground in the aquifer condition not loose most of its properties. As spring water is already exposed into the atmosphere, this can have much flexibility in transporting and handling. However, storing for a long time would remain no fresh and will loose its natural flavor.

Water is the most essential fluid for living things. It has been reported that 100% pure have been produced by using reverse osmosis and deionization process to completely remove dissolved salts, nitrates, heavy metals, chemical pollutants, pesticides and disease causing waterborne bacteria and virus (website 11). Such water is also intended to be used as cleaning agent for sophisticated equipment. Apart from the absurdity of 100% composition of anything, let alone a very reactive and most abundantly natural compound, water, it must be noted that 'pure' water is not suitable for drinking. However, the type of water we drink plays an important role in our health. Pure water considered to have just the combination of hydrogen and oxygen without any chemicals, mineral and microorganisms. In nature, pure water (H_2O) without some minerals can not be found. It can be produced only in the laboratory synthetically combining molecules of hydrogen and oxygen. However, pure water is also not fully beneficial to health. The water we drink should have several minerals for our body and these minerals are obtained during the seepage of water through the clay, sand and rocks. Hence ultra pure and pure water are not beneficial for human and plants.

Ultra pure water production technology is developed to supply water in some industries such as semiconductor industries. It is reported that semiconductor industries require 15% of its total cost for water (Wakamatsu et al., 1998). Some of the ultra pure water technologies supply over 95% water recovery during purification. However, there is a huge costs involved to purify water. As 75% of the earth is made up of water, development of technology is to be such that natural water could be used in some form. Hence, processing water to produce pure or ultra pure water is anti-natural. Distillation, osmosis and other technologies are used to produce pure water.

Chlorine treatment of water is common in the west and is synonymous with western civilization. Chlorine is a halogen that damages our body enzymes. It is reported that chlorine creates magnesium deficiency the symptoms of which are high blood pressure and chemical sensitivity. Chlorine decreases the absorption increasing the excretion of calcium and phosphorus. As a side effect, an increase loss of calcium into the urine results in osteoporosis. Chlorine contributes to hypertension, pancreas, and bladder and colon cancer, heart and kidney problems.

The residual chlorine in treated water even at low concentrations is highly toxic and corrosive to human and aquatic life (Solomon et al., 1998). Some studies suggested that 10–13% of bladder and colon cancers in Ontario, Canada may be attributable to long-term exposure to by-products of chlorination in household water supplies (Canadian Cancer Society, 2006). It is likely that chlorine oxidizes organic matters in waste water creating compounds such as trihalomethanes (THMs) that are harmful to humans and the environment. Chlorine residuals are unstable in the presence of high concentrations of chlorine-demanding materials, thus requiring higher doses to effect adequate disinfection. The residual chlorine may precipitates proteins and changes the chemical arrangement of enzymes or inactivates them directly. Hence, chlorinated water is never a good drink.

8.2. SPORTS DRINKS

Sports drinks are the beverages to help athletes to rehydrate, replenish energy and nutrients which can be depleted after training or competition. It is generally considered that over consumption of drinking water may reduce electrolytes levels such as potassium, sodium etc. in the body by dilution and may interfare with the nervous system. Gatorade, powerade, all sports, accelerade, little squirts etc are the most popular sports and energy drinks available in the market. Some of the ingredients of sport drinks have been analyzed for their pathways.

Gatorade

Citric Acid

Gatorade consists of water, sucrose syrup, glucose fructose syrup, citric acid, natural and artificial flavors, salt, sodium citrate, monopotassium phosphate, ester gum etc. (Von Peters, 2004). Citric acid is industrially produced as the cultures of *Aspergillus niger* are fed on sucrose to produce citric acid. After the mold is filtered out of the resulting solution, citric acid is isolated by precipitating it with lime (calcium hydroxide) to yield calcium citrate salt, from which citric acid is regenerated by treatment with sulfuric acid (Ali et al., 2002). Figure 8.1 shows the pathways of formation of citir acid. Since it is treated with sulfuric acid, it becomes toxic end product.

MSDS (2004) reported that citric acid causes irritation to the respiratory tract. Symptoms may include coughing, shortness of breath. It also causes irritation to the gastrointestinal tract. Symptoms may include nausea, vomiting and diarrhea. Extremely large oral dosages may produce gastrointestinal disturbances. Calcium deficiency in blood may result in severe cases of ingestion. It is also a skin irritant and causes redness, itching, and pain. The chronic or heavy acute ingestion may cause tooth enamel erosion.

Sodium Benzoate

This causes irritation to the respiratory tract, coughing, shortness of breath if inhaled. Large oral doses may cause irritation to the gastrointestinal tract. This causes irritation with redness and pain eye. Sodium benzoic acid is used as anticorrosive in engines. This is one of the most widely used food preservative. Thus, this would have severe impacts on human health as it interacts with food and inhibits many function of food.

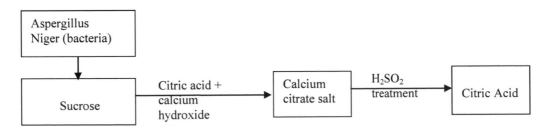

Figure 8.1. Pathway of citric acid formation.

Malic Acid

Malic acid is highly irritant to inhalation, eye and skin for short term exposure. The impacts for long term exposure is not known. Malic acid moderately toxic by ingestion based on LD50 data (LD50 oral mouse: 1600mg/kg).

Artificial Flavor and Modified Corn Starch

The synthetic or artificial flavor is very toxic as it contains some esters from chemicals with volatile compounds which make the sense organs to work. These volatiles compounds are not good for health. The modified corn starch will also not behave same as that of natural corn starch.

Powerade

Major ingredients of powerade are water, high fructose corn syrupmaltodextrin (glucose polymers), citric acid, salt, potassium citrate, modified food starch, potassium phosphate, natural flavors, glycerol ester of wood rosin, guar gum, niacinamide (B3), coconut oil, brominated vegetable oil, pyridoxine hydrochloride (B6), Cyanocobalamin (B12) (Von Peters, 2004). There are polymeric and synthetic compounds in this drink. The extraction process of glycerol ester of wood resin is not transparent. The brominated vegetable oils have several possible chemical contaminations.

Little Squirts

Little Squirts is a children's drink with ingredients such as water, sugar, citric acid, corn syrup solid, modified corn starch, hydrogenated soybean oil, malic acid, ascorbic acid, natural and or artificial flavor, sodium benzoate, color, tricalcium phosphate (for the best results, refrigerate). The pathway of some of these chemicals as explained earlier showed that these drinks are not good both for children and adults, but children will be more susceptible due to the severity of the chemicals in the drinks.

8.3. COCA COLA, PEPSI, SODA, SPRITE OTHER DRINKS

Coca Cola

Coka cola (coke) is a carbonated drink, one of the most popular drinks in the world market. Despite being the number one drink in the world, the real ingredients of coca cola has been kept secret. With general principle of communication, if coca cola contains good things in it, there is no point to keep it secret. The suspicion is that it contains lots of ingredients which are not beneficial to the human health. It is published that coca cola contains or once contained sugar, caramel, caffeine, phosphoric acid, coca leaf and kola nut extract, lime extract, flavoring mixture, vanilla and glycerin (Wikipedia, 2006). The merchandize 7X is considered to be the secret ingredient of coca cola and has remained a secret since its invention in 1886. It has not been clear whether coca cola contains coca leaf in coca cola as the company refusess to comment on this issue. Hence the consumers are kept in dark and might be facing several problems just simply because that they are unknown of its ingredients.

The allergenicity of penicillin in the general population is thought to be at least 10% and this penicilline has been traced in milk, soft drinks and frozen dinners (Murray and Pizzorno, 2005). They suggested that many dietary factors are the causes of osteoporosis including low calcium high phosphate intake, high protein diet, and high acid as diet, high salt intake, and trace mineral deficiencies. The report further suggested that the increased soft drink consumption is a major contributor to osteoporosis. Moreover, soft drinks have been long suspected for leading to lower calcium levels and higher phosphate levels and higher phosphate level in the blood that causes calcium deficiency as calcium is pulled out of bones.

India's highest court has ordered Pepsi and coca-cola to print warnings on their bottles sold in the country that the contents may contain pesticide residues (Mercer, 2006). In February 2003 a parliamentary probe found soft drinks sold in India by the United States beverage giants contained pesticide residues and imposed tougher national health standards. The link between soft between the soft drink and pesticides is considered due to the excessive use of pesticides in the agriculture and attributable to sugar. Sugar is one of the main ingredients in coca cola and it is the cause of several diseases including hyperglycemia (Dufty, 1975). It is also known that sugar is the contributing factor for diabetes, pancreatic cancer in women, becomes a feed for cancer cells among others. Coca cola is considered highly toxic to human being. This is the reason that in India, farmers re using coke as pesticides to kill the bugs.

Nemery et al. (2002) reported that there was a serious outbreak of illness among school children and general public in Belgium in 1999 in relation with the consumption of coca cola and other soft drinks. The major symptoms consisted of abdominal discomfort, headache, nausea, malaise, respiratory problems, trembling, and dizziness. The cause of health problem was due to the use of contaminated CO_2 by carbonyl sulfide that may hydrolyze to hydrogen sulfide. The concentrations were 5–14 mg/l for carbonyl sulfide and 8–17 mg/l for H_2S. Some studies argued that this is a very low concentration to have impacts on human health and cause toxicity. However, it is reported that the lower the concentration of synthetic chemicals, the higher would be the effects Miralai (2006).

It is also considered that coca cola contains phosphoric acid in it. Phosphoric cid contains sulfuric acid along with fluorine, metallic compounds and sulfates. It is highly corrosive and causes severe burns (MSDS, 2005a). It is very destructive to mucous membranes, respiratory tract, eyes and skin. Oxidation products of phosphoric acid are toxic (Hughes et al., 1962). Other possible ingredients of coca cola such as caffeine, flavoring mixtures, glycerin, and carbon dioxide are also chemical based compounds having several health impacts.

Diet Coke

Diet coke has similar ingredients except the aspartame which is used as swweeteing agent instead of sugar. Aspartame has been considered a carcinogen. Consumption of aspartame potentially forms formaldehyde which is also a carcinogen. Despite it has been advertised that diet coke can be consumed by wide range of people with different health problems, this is even worse than reegular coca cola. Aspartame is obtaned by refining saccharine which itself is refined sugar. The production of diet coke is bad to worse mode of coca cola in terms of health impacts.

Pepsi, Soda, Sprite and other Drinks

Pepsi, soda, sprite and other drinks also contain various chemicals including bleached sugar and other artificial sweetner such as saccharine and aspartames. Hence none of these drinks arc good for our health. It was reported that 12 soft drinks including Mountain Dew, Diet Pepsi, Mirinda orange, Mirinda Lemon, Blue Pepsi, 7-Up, Coca Cola, Fanta, Limca, Sprite and Thumbs Up contained cocktail of deadly pesticide residues in them (CSE, 2003). The pesticide residues found in the soft drinks were lindane, DDT, malathion and chlorpyrifos. These pesticides are highly toxic and carcinogenic. The major cause of this contamination is due to the excessive use of pesticides in the agriculture farms especially to grow sugarcane. Some of the pesticides remained in the grains and fruits of the food produced using them and majority of them are eventually discharged into the water bodies. As the water has memory, the contamination will remain despite the water is purified. Moreover, the water treatment also contains some chemicals disinfectants which might ultimately add up the contamination in the final products. Production mode of all soft drinks is similar and has similar health and environmental impacts. The most alarming things with the soft drinks are the plastic bottling which is toxic releasing several toxins including carcinogens. Plastic reacts with its ingredients and produces several anti-natural chemicals. This way, these technologies are inherently unsustainable and anti-natural.

The only best way tomake these soft drinks is to use natural materials. Honey should be used as natural sweetner instead of sugar oraspartame, good carbon dioxide is to be collected from fresh wood burning or biomas burning. Healthy soft drinks including sports drink can only be manufatured supplying all ingredients naturally with out using any synthetic chemicals. The produce should be from organic farming so that it may not contain any synthetic chemicals. Even the bees should be fed the organic flower farming so that the honey could be contamiantrion free. The most important thing is the soft drinks produced naturally should not be stored in plastic bottles. Plastic is very toxic and produces dioxine and other toxins. They should be stored in organic clay or wooden pots tomake them free of chemicals and plastic contamination. If bioplastic is produced naturally, this can be an alternative. Moreover, produce from organic farming and natural materials would sustain for long time.

8.4. BOTTLED AND CANNED JUICES

Bottled or canned juices are aqueous liquid extracted from one or more fruits or vegetables, or any concentrates of such liquid. The juice has a reduced weight and volume through the removal of water from the juice. Various kinds of flavors and sweetening agents are also added in the bottled or canned juice. These sweetening agents range from sugars to aspartame which is a known carcinogen. Water content on any fruit or vegetable is a natural phenomenon and removing water from juice may change the inherent characteristics of what it contains in the fruit or vegetables. Moreover, addition of artificial sweeteners in juice such as sugar or aspartame could lead to several health problems. Preservation of juice for a long time could result in a huge loss in the nutrients levels.

Pesticides are used widely to treat fruits, vegetables, grains, and other foods, and may be present in small amounts as residues on these juice foods (USFDA, 2004). Juice may contain several pesticides residues as many synthetic and non-biodegradable pesticides are used for pest and insect control. Use of lead arsenate in agricultural settings could contaminate the produce with lead contamination. The juice made from such produce could be lead contaminated. Lead contamination in any produce could be possible if the produce were grown at sites where vehicles or equipment are operated using leaded fuel due to its emission. Some incidences have occurred lead contamination of carrot from which juices were prepared (USFDA, 2004). The contamination could also emerge from the use of synthetic fertilizers. Hence the quality of produce is the major factor that determines the quality of any juice from fruits or vegetables.

Joint WHO/FAO Expert Committee on Food Additives, an international food standards organization that establishes safe levels for the protection of consumers, has recently established a maximum level of 50 ppb for lead in ready-to-drink fruit juices, including fruit nectars that are in international trade, to protect the public health. Lead contamination could result due to the use of can soldered by lead. Tin is another metal frequently encountered in canned juices. Tin is used frequently as a coating in unlacquered metal cans used to pack light colored juices, such as pineapple juice. Some tin plating leaches into the juice contaminating the juice. There are various complex factors such as nitrate and sulfate content, amount of residual oxygen in the metal can, the thickness of the tin layer of the container, presence of organic acids and pigments in the juice all affect the leaching of tin into juice. The leaching is also affected by the length of time and the temperature of storage of the juice, the pH and presence of any additives that can affect its pH in the juice. The consumption of juice containing excessive tin levels could cause to acute gastrointestinal illness (USFDA, 2004).

Glass fragments from breakage of glassware and metal fragments resulting from grinding, processing and cutting could also lead various types of other health problems. Plastic bottles and cans used to preserve juice and other foods have severe long term implication in the human health as well as environment. Synthetic plastic is a very toxic material that release dioxins. Plastic emits several carcinogens. Preservation and storage of food in plastic bottles and can could leave to severe plastic poisoning. The chemical preservatives, flavors and synthetic colors added to juice are also not beneficial to health. Hence the current technology of juice production and storage is not sustainable as it has several health problems.

The only way to preserve the juice is to store in bio-plastic or wooden or clay pots. Storage or preservation of juice in clay or wooden pots will not be contaminated with any toxic chemicals. The bio-plastic is a very good alternative as it is biodegradable and will not have health impacts as that of synthetic plastic derived from petroleum residues. There is a misconception that juice can be preserved any duration once it is canned or bottled. It has also been argued that the nutrients we get from the fruits will not be available from juice as processing and contamination would lead to loss of nutrients and may pose health effects. The quality of juice to remain good would be dictated by the characteristics time of any fruits or vegetable to rot or degrade. Hence, direct consumption of vegetables and fruits is the best option. If preservation is needed, natural materials such as wood, clay, bamboo and bio-plastics would be the only sustainable options.

8.5. MILK

Milk has been one of the popular drinking fluids from school children to adults. It is considered that drinking milk will help to quench the thirst, at the same time adds great nutrition. Milk has several nutrients for health including vitamins, calcium, magnesium, phosphorus, zinc, protein and others. However, processing of milks in different ways may loose some of the nutrients. Pasteurization is one of the most common methods of milk processing where heat is used to reduce the bacteria normally present in raw milk. It has been understood that pasteurized milk has less nutrients than un-pasteurized milk, nutrients such as vitamins thiamin, B12 and C will be reduced due to high heat pasteurization. Homogenization of milk inherently loses its characteristics and its nutrients levels. To overcome the loss of nutrients, some synthetic elements such as fortified calcium and vitamins are added. These vitamins and minerals are not same as that of natural ones. This could be one of the reasons why osteoporosis occurrence is high in North America despite being the highest consumer of per capita milk.

Qin et al. (2004) reported some epidemiological studies which suggested that milk consumption is probably as one of the risk factors for prostate cancer. Milk has various levels of estrogen content which is suspected to be the probable cause for cancer. Estrogen comes from the various synthetic hormones and antibiotics used for the cows. Natural estrogens should never be the problems. The synthetic estrogens contaminate the milk and eventually lead to the diseases including cancer. The incidence of prostate cancer is higher in western countries as compared to Asian people. The occurrence of osteoporosis is highest per capita among the US population. Conversely, US is the highest consumer of milk per capita in the world.

To have the real benefit of milk, farm fresh or organic milks is very good for health. It is generally said that unpasteurized milk has risk of exposure to infectious diseases. But this will not be a problem if the cows are grown organically using no chemicals based life and foods. The organic produce of milk will be sustainable for the long term as this has least processing and more nutrients leaving no health problems.

8.6. COFFEE, TEA

Caffeine is the world's most widely ingested stimulant. The average cup of American-style coffee contains about 100 to 150 milligrams of caffeine. The average cup of tea contains about 40 milligrams of caffeine. Caffeine has several health impacts. Caffeine may induce anxiety symptoms and caffeine may mask or mimic anxiety symptoms (Goldberger et al., 2003). Since tea has also higher caffeine content, this will also have similar effect. The impacts of tea or coffee depend on how they are derived. If the coffee and tea are processed naturally without adding any chemicals, limited amount of coffee should not have any health impacts. Coffee has antioxidants essential for the human body. Tea has many ingredients essential for human body. Drinking certain amount of these fluids is not a problem.

Chapter 9

PERSONAL CARE PRODUCTS

INTRODUCTION

Recently it has been revealed that commercial 'health' or personal care products are the source of various diseases. For instance, most cosmetic products have formaldehyde, which is considered to be carcinogen. Similarly, bodymists often contain butane and other hydrocarbon products, the harmfulness of which is well documented. Soap making utilizes a numerous chemical additives which are toxic and have serious health implications. The use of synthetic colouring pigments also makes the products harmful. The list of harmful chemicals used in these products is very long and includes practically all commercially available 'health' or the personal care products as used for skin care, facials, sun screens and others. In this paper, we studied the harmful effects of commercially available health products, focusing on cleansing products, general cosmetics (e.g. lip balm, lipstick, mascara, perfumes) and coloring agents (hair dye, shoe polish, bleaching agents). Development of series of 'healthy' or personal care products such as natural soap, shampoo, tooth paste, hair gels, paints, non toxic shoe polish, sunscreen and other products by non toxic materials and natural way could help to save the health and environment and will be sustainable for the long-term.

Personal care products have been in use for thousands of years. In Persian, Egyptian or Chinese cultures, cosmetic use was common. What sets the modern age apart is the eruption of toxic chemical use in every application. Almost every product including health products, from toys to computers, carpet to clothes, furniture to washing powder are toxic. However, only recently it is becoming known that the list of toxic chemicals is very long and it is considered to be impractical to reverse the life style (Mittelstaedt, 2006b). Most of them are manufactured petroleum derivates and other synthetic chemicals. Today's society is built on the assumption of "chemicals are chemicals"(Khan and Islam, 2007a). Even though this approach is attributed to a Nobel Laureate and Peace activist, Linus Pauling, characterizing chemicals based on the most obvious features is not scientific. It is unscientific to infer that chemicals with similar chemical formula whether they are from natural or synthetic origin, behave similarly. The properties of chemicals will be entirely different from each other depending on the origin and the pathway they travel, during the manufacturing process. Conventional approach does not differentiate between the synthetic chemicals manufactured in an industry and chemicals that are derived from natural elements such as plants. For example, the impact of sodium, derived naturally from sea salt, is different from that of sodium, manufactured in a chemical plant. Synthetic sodium hydroxides are used in many health products including soap production. Similar statements can be made for organic farming and chemical farming; and for every natural process and simulated engineering process (Khan, 2006).

Petroleum products are used as base material or as an additive for almost every product. The petroleum derivates are highly toxic chemicals and have severe impact on human health (Mittelstaedt, 2006b). Perfumes contain very little original musk and mostly synthetic musk and petroleum-based chemicals. More commonly the original musk (fermented flower extract) is entirely replaced by artificial musk and is added to chemical base. An artificial musk is used to replace natural aromas and is added to many products like washing agents, soap and cosmetics (OSPAR, 2004). These compounds are generally polycyclic and evidence indicates that some musks can interfere with hormone communication systems in fish and mammals (Schreurs, 2002). Moreover, cosmetic products also contain formaldehyde and dioxane which are considered to be carcinogen. The body mist contains butane and other petroleum based hydrocarbon ingredients which are highly toxic compounds. Hexachlorophene used in mouthwash and shampoo are also hazardous materials. Mouthwash destroys the essential bacteria and the products that emerge are toxic. In addition, mouthwash base (both alcoholic or non-alcoholic) are extremely abrasive to the delicate tissues inside the mouth and produces toxins from saliva (that otherwise is a natural bactericide). Shampoos are harmful for both hair fibre and the skin. Lipstick or lip balm usually contains aluminum, which is also a known toxin. It was reported that various types of oestrogenic chemicals used in cosmetics are the major sources for women's breast cancer (Darbre, 2006).

Figure 9.1 shows the schematic of pathway of production of conventional health products. Synthetic chemicals are used for almost every health product. The use of these toxic catalysts and chemicals in oil refining result in the toxic contamination of personal care products. These products are eventually exposed to the environment causing water and air pollution. A number of toxic chemicals along with the various coloring pigments are used to make shoe polishes. Certain toxics can be absorbed through the skin and or inhaled (Stimpert, 2006). Some of these toxins are Toluene (C_7H_8), aromatic hydrocarbons, Trichloroethane, Methylene chloride, Nitrobenzene, and other chemicals. Trichloroethane is similar to chloroform. It is commonly used as a solvent and cleaning agent in spot removers during shoe polishing. Trichloroethane can be absorbed by inhalation and ingestion. It is an irritant to the eyes and nose and can result in depression of central nervous system and liver and kidney damage if ingested. Methylene chloride, known also as methylene dichloride and dichloromethane, irritates skin that comes in contact. Memory loss, liver and kidney damage are reported with chronic exposure. This is a known animal carcinogen and a suspected human carcinogen. The use of products containing methylene chloride by people with heart conditions may result in fatal heart attacks (OSHA, 2006). Nitrobenzene, is also a highly toxic substance, found in some shoe polish, furniture polish and floor polish. In addition to this, the coloring pigments used in the health products are mostly industrial and plastic based pigments. These pigments can create allergic reactions, scarring, phototoxic reactions and other adverse effects. These are notoriously toxic and radioactive to human health.

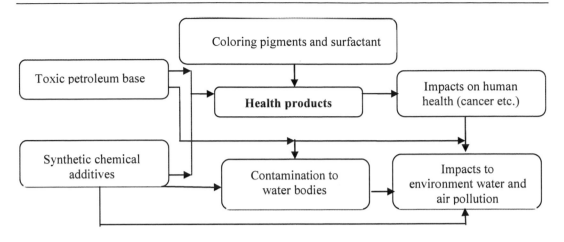

Figure 9.1. Schematic of pathway of production of health products (Chhetri et al., 2007c).

9.1. CHEMICALS AND SURFACTANTS USED IN PERSONAL CARE PRODUCTS

Alkali is one of the heavy chemicals many industries such as petroleum industry, pulp and paper mill, battery industry, cosmetic industry, soap and detergent, leather processing industry, metal processing industry, water treatment plants, biofuel processing industries such as biodiesel and ethanol. Synthetic chlorine and sodium hydroxide are among the top ten chemicals produced in the world and are used in the manufacturing of the wide variety of products including deodorants, detergents, disinfectants, herbicides, pesticides, and plastics. These are also major chemicals used in the various health products. It was reported that the worldwide demand of sodium hydroxide was 44 million tones expressed as NaOH 100% in the year 1999 (CAMI, 2005). The total global demand of alkalis in 2005 was 62 million tones (Figure 9.2). The growth of alkali demand was approximately 3.1% per year.

Alkalis are raw commercial products and needs further processing before application. Huge amount of these chemicals may leak during the transfer from one place to another directly or indirectly polluting the environment. It has also significant effect on human health. Inhalation of dust, mist, or aerosol of sodium hydroxide and other alkalis may cause irritation of the mucous membranes of the nose, throat, and respiratory tract. Exposure to the alkalis solid or solution can cause skin and eye irritation. Direct contact with the solid or with concentrated solutions causes thermal and chemical burns leading to deep-tissue injuries and permanent damage to any tissue (MSDS, 2006).

Personal cleansing products are potential sources of skin drying as this one of the common problem among the dermatologic patients (Ertel et al, 2004). The major reason behind this is due to the use of synthetic detergents. The problem can further be aggravated by the use of synthetic body was and body lotion.

Various surfactants are added to the cleansing products that adhere to skin surface and decrease the amount of friction required to remove unwanted materials. Surfactants are the chemical substances incorporated into cleaning agents considering that the dirt is not effectively removed by water alone even with vigorous washing (Nix, 2000). Anionic surfactants used in the commercial cleaning products specific synthetic surfactants including sodium lauryl sulfate (SLS), triethanolamine lauryl sulfate, ammonium lauryl sulfate, and sodium stearate. Surfactants such as SLS are also found in ointments and creams as well as in cleansers.

Walker et al (2005) studied the acute and short term toxicity of sodium Lauryl sulfate surfactant in the rats. They studied the acute and short-term toxicity in rats have been made on the surfactants sodium lauryl sulphate, sodium lauryl (3EO) ethoxysulphate and their matches C_{12}–C_{15} alcohol sodium sulphate and C_{12}–C_{15} alcohol sodium (3EO) ethoxysulphate. The acute oral LD_{50}s of the four materials were found to range from 1 to 2 g/kg. This clearly indicates the toxicity level of sodium lauryl sulfate. MSDS (2005b) reported that sodium lauryl sulfate is strong oxidizing agent and is very toxic. This causes respiratory, eye and skin irritation. The report also mentioned that it is very harmful if inhaled or swallowed. It also caused sensitization if inhaled.

Therte are several types of chemicasl surfactants used in personal care products (Table 9.1). Sodium Lauryl Sulfate, an anionic surfactant, is prepared by the sulfation of commercially available lauryl alcohol form coconut, with either sulfur trioxide or chlorosulfonic acid (Sodium Lauryl Sulfate, 1983). The product of the reaction is then neutralized with aqueous sodium hydroxide (lye). Carcinogenic nitrates can form in the manufacturing of Sodium Lauryl Sulfate or by its inter reaction with other nitrogen bearing ingredients which shows permanent eye damage in young animals from skin contact in non eye areas. The studies indicated that Sodium Lauryl Sulfate enters and maintains residual levels in the heart, the liver, the lungs and the brain from skin contact. This poses question of it being a serious potential health threat to its use in shampoos, cleansers, and tooth pastes. Some researches further indicated that SLS may be damaging to the immune system, especially within the skin. Skin layers may separate and inflame due to its protein denaturing properties. SLS is used in almost all health products including soaps, shampoos, bubble baths, tooth paste, washing up liquid, Laundry detergent, children soaps and shampoos, stain remover, carpet cleaner, fabric glue, body wash, shaving cream, mascara, mouth wash, skin cleanser, moisturizing lotion and sun screen.

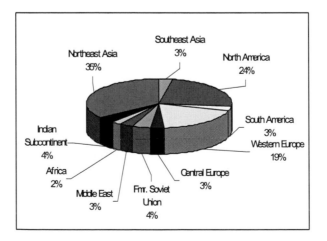

Figure 9.2. Global Chlor-Alkali Production (CMAI, 2005).

Table 9.1. Common surfactant ingredients used in health products (Nix, 2000)

Product	Ingredient	Common uses
Anionic-natural	Natural soap Potassium cocoate	Skin cleansing
Anionic-synthetic	Sodium Lauryl sulfate Tryethanolamine lauryl sulfate Ammonium lauryl sulfate	Ointments, creams Skin cleansing Tooth paste
Cationic	Cetrimide Bemzalkonium chloride	Disinfectants Antimicrobial preservative
Amphoteric	Cocamidopropylbetaine	Baby shampoos Foam boosters
Nonionic	Polysorbate 20 Polysorbate 60	Shampoo/cosmetic Food products Laundry/dishwashing Pharmaceuticals
Antimicrobial	Triclosan Chlorhexidine gluconate Para chloroxylenol	Not available
Humectants/ moisturizers	Glycerin Methyl glucose esters Lactates Lanolin derivatives Mineral oil	Not available
Alcohols	Isopropyl alcohol Benzyl alcohol Cetyl or stearyl alcohol	Antimicrobial, preservatives, Emollients, thickeners in moisturizers and lubricants

9.2. NATURAL SOAPS PRODUCTION

Ancient soap making was a completely natural process. The purpose of the bathing was to stay clean and treat skin diseases. All of the ingredients used came from the natural surroundings. The use of synthetic chemicals began in the late 19th century and expanded and proliferated as a result of military research during the first and second world wars. Since then, the use of synthetic chemicals has become standard in all commodities particularly in personal care products (Chhetri and Islam, 2007c). For example, the synthetic chemicals such as NaOH or KOH as alkaline agents are very toxic and corrosive compounds. Haynes et al. (1976) reported that a dose of 1.95 grams of sodium hydroxide can cause death. The most serious effects of sodium hydroxide at 50% by weight of active ingredient are corrosion of body tissues. Eye and skin contact can cause very serious burns. It has been reported that concentration of sodium hydroxide of 10 g/l cause nervousness, sore eyes, diarrhea and retarded growth in rats (Haynes et al., 1976). Even the vegetable oils that are produced using chemical fertilizers or are refined will have some toxic effects. Similarly, animal fats from animals injected with synthetic hormones also alter the natural course of the animal fat. Figure 9.3 is the schematic for the manufacturing of natural soap.

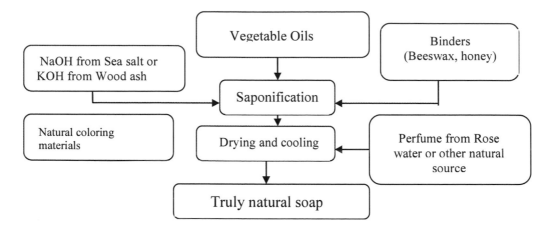

Figure 9.3. Flow process for natural soap making (Chhetri et al., 2007c).

Ingredients of Natural Soap Production

Olive Oil

Olive oil is a triacylglyceride with three fatty acids attached to a glycerol molecule. It is a complex compound of fatty acids, vitamins, volatile compounds, water soluble compounds and some other micro compounds. The primary fatty acids available in olive oil are Oleic acid and linoleic acid with a small amount of linolenic acid. Oleic acid is monounsaturated (55-85%), linoleic acid is polyunsaturated (9%) and linolenic acid is also polyunsaturated with (0-1.5%) (Olive Oil Source, 2006). Olive oil has several other constituents such as tocopherols, chlorophyll and pheophytin, sterols, squalene, aroma and flavour compounds which exhibit a significant impact on human health. It is a highly monounsaturated oil and is therefore resistant to oxidation. The presence of phenols, tocopherols and other natural antioxidants prevent lipid oxidation within the body eliminating the formation of free radicals which may cause cell destruction. Use of olive oil in soap making is characterized by many of its advantages. Thus olive oil soap is very good from health point of view. In this research, olive oil was used as one of the major ingredients of natural soap.

Palm Oil

Palm oil is semi solid at room temperature and is popular for manufacturing solid fat products. Palm oil has been in use for various edible and non edible products. It is also used in chemical, cosmetic and pharmaceutical application. Palm oil olein and stearin are used worldwide in making margarine, confectioneries, and in frying snack foods. The high content of natural antioxidants and its stability at high temperatures make palm oil excellent as a deep frying medium in the food industry. It also gives fried products a longer shelf life, while its bland taste brings out the natural flavors of food. Palm oil is a base material for manufacturing of soap, detergents and surfactants. In addition to this, this is a good raw material to make fatty acids, fatty alcohols, glycerol and other derivatives for the manufacture of cosmetics, pharmaceuticals, household as well as industrial products. Palm oil was also used to make natural soap in this research.

Beeswax and Honey

Beeswax is a product secreted by honey bees. This is a natural product used for several purposes such as medicine, paint, material for shoe polish, candles, sealing materials, natural glue and others. This is a very complex material which contains hundreds of compounds. Honey has inhibitory effects on bacteria, fungi, yeast and viruses (Al-Waili, 2001). Honey application eradicates bacterial infections and accelerates wound healing. Honey is used even for dermatitis and dandruff treatment. Because beeswax and olive oils have similar antibacterial properties, a combination of beeswax, honey and olive oil which contain flavonoids, antioxidants and antibacterial ingredients useful for treatment in skin diseases was used in this study. The study showed that the mixture with honey, olive oil and beeswax (1:1:1) was successful in treating 75%, 71% and 62% of skin disease patients with pityriasis versicolor, (PV), tinea cruris and tinea corporis respectively. Honey mixtures appear to be useful in the management of dermatitis and psoriasis vulgaris. Considering these all benefits to the human health, beeswax and honey were used as ingredients in the soap prepared in this research.

Coloring and Fragrance Materials

The coloring and addition of fragrance of soap have become a tradition over time. However, the colors and fragrance used conventionally are from synthetic pigments or artificial musks. However, in this research, all natural colors and fragrance were used to give the desired colors to the finished products.

Turmeric, Neem Leaf, Cinnamon Powder

Turmeric is a perennial plant with roots or tubers oblong, palmate, and deep orange inside. Turmeric has a peculiar fragrance and bitter, slightly acidic taste exciting warmth in the mouth and colouring the saliva yellow. This is a mild aromatic stimulant and used for coloring. Turmeric tincture is used as a colouring agent. It dyes a rich yellow coating. Turmeric paper is prepared by soaking unglazed white paper in the tincture and drying. This is a completely natural colorant which also has some medicinal value. Coloring the soap with turmeric is beneficial for health. In this research, turmeric powder was used to color the soap and seems aesthetically pleasing. Neem leaf ground in powder form was used to add the natural color in soap. Neem is a tree that can thrive on various climates from 0^0C to 49^0C. It grows in almost all types of soil including clayey, saline and alkaline. The Neem tree thrives on dry, stony, shallow soils, and shallow depth. Neem leaf is used as anti bacterial medicine. To make the gentle green color of soap, Neem leaf was ground into power form to use as colorant. Cinnamon is the inner bark of a tropical evergreen tree. Cinnamon has been is use as spice, medicine and many other products. The lighter color of cinnamon bark has sweet properties gives soap making some flavor. Cinnamon bark was used medicinally and as a flavoring for beverages in ancient Egypt. Cinnamon powder was also used as coloring agent to make the soap.

Natural Fragrance

A natural extract from rose water was used to give the fragrance for the finished soap product. No synthetic chemicals were used in the process.

Production of Natural Soap

Soap was prepared by using all natural ingredients (Figure 9.4 and 9.5). 34.0g with clean water at room temperature, 12.5g of sodium hydroxide (derived by the electrolysis of sea salt), 45.4g olive oil, 10.0g of beeswax, 15.0g of honey, 28.4g coconut oil, 17.0g palm oil, 5g of essential oil (tea oil) were used (Chhetri et al., 2007c). In addition to this, cinnamon powder, turmeric powder, neem leaf powder were used as coloring agent. Natural fragrance could be added at a later stage not to heat. First a salt water solution was heated to 200^{0}F and cooled. Beeswax was melted and mixed with the oil ingredients and stirred. The mixture of olive oil, palm oil, coconut oil and bees wax was stirred. Both mixtures were heated and when both oils and salt water were near similar temperatures around 130^{0}F, then all ingredients were mixed. The honey and essential oils were added and stirred with a glass rod and transfer the mixture into mould. It normally takes 24-48 hours to get the desired hardness of the soap.

The soaps prepared in natural way are truly healthy soaps. In addition to olive oil, other natural oils such as Avogado oil, Caster oil, Coaoa butter, Jajoba oil, Pam oil, Pam kerner oil, Mustard oil, Jatropha oil etc can be used for soap making depending upon which is available. The oils are renewable and non toxic provided that they are extracted naturally and grown organically. The alkali can be extracted from wood ash. As there are no toxic ingredients, using such soaps has no health and environmental impacts. Based on the natural oils and alkali from the wood ash or natural sea salts, this soap making model is inherently sustainable.

Figure 9.4. Natural soap using natural color (Chhetri et al., 2007c).

Figure 9.5. Natural soap without color (Chhetri et al., 2007c).

9.3. Sampoo, Body Mist, Cleansing Products

Most of the shampoos are also made from synthetic chemicals such as sodium laureth, sodium lauryl sulfate, methylisothiazoline, other chemicals and synthetic pigments (Adams, 2005). The experiments on rats have been found that the methylisothiazoline is linked with nervous system damage. The higher level of exposure could cause to Alzheimer diseases. This chemical is considered to be carcinogenic, liver disorders and neurological diseases. Sodium laureth and sodium lauryl sulfate are also synthetic chemicals potential to cause cancer and other diseases including immune system damages. These compounds are also found in various cleansing products. Body mists consists of butane and pentane which are high toxic petroleum products. Hence all personal care products essentially consist of synthetic chemicals which largely ingested through the body skin and create several health problems.

Natural shampoo, body mist and cleansing products can be produced from natural ingredients from plant and flower extracts. Fermented flowers extracts can be used as body mist. Coloring can be extracted from flower or plants extracts. Shampoo can be produced using vegetable or plant based oil ingredients using natural salts. These are natural chemicals and truly biodegradable. They have no negative health and environmental impacts.

9.4. Cosmetics (Lipstick and Nail Polish, Eye Mascara, Hair Coloring Gels, Humectants and Moisturizers etc)

Lipstick and Nail Polish

Personal-care products contain a host of largely unregulated and toxic chemicals as their ingredients. Some of those chemicals used in personal care products such as phthalates, formaldehyde, petroleum, parabens, benzene and lead have been variously linked to breast cancer, endometriosis, reproductive disorders, birth defects and developmental disabilities in children (Mendiratta, 2006). Women and girls are particularly susceptible to such chemicals as they have higher fat than men. Most of these chemicals such as parabens and toluene tend to be more rapidly absorbed and fatty breast tissues could be long term storage site for these persistent toxic chemicals. The alkylphenols found in some of the detergents and bispenol A generally found in hard plastic also contribute for the development of the cancer. These chemicals have environmental problems in addition to the health problems.

The primary ingredients for lipstick are waxes, oil, alcohol and coloring pigments. Various types of waxes are also used, the mostly used being paraffin wax which is cheap and obtained from petroleum by-products. Beeswax, candelilla was and camauba waxes are also used. Candelilla was is a plant wax but the extraction of this wax involves use of sulfuric acid which is a toxic acid. The skimmed waxes are then bleached using alkaline chemicals to give light yellow color before it is processed into desired shape. The oils used are also based on the vegetable and plants oils. Various types of petroleum products such as hexane, ethers and chloroform may also be used during oil extraction which makes the oils toxic to human body as contaminated by anti-natural chemicals. The alcohols used are the refinery grade alcohol from the crude oil refining. Various toxic chemicals and catalysts such as lead and chromium are used during crude oil refining. Using petroleum based alcohol could contaminate the end products with lead or chromium. Lead is a cancer causing metal and can enter into the human body through the skin resulting in cancer in the long term. Johnson (2003) reported that personal care products such as, lipsticks shampoos, deodorants and hair spray contain cancer causing chemicals. Moreover, the coloring pigments used in the lipstick production is also synthetic based pigment.

Johnson (2003) reported that there are two types of compounds being used in cosmetics that pose health risk including cancer. The report further says that there are two types of chemicals related to carcinogens. The first types of chemicals are carcinogenic themselves called 'frank' carcinogens and the other types of chemicals are called 'hidden' carcinogens which are not carcinogenic themselves but under certain conditions may have carcinogenic properties. Over 40 chemicals used in cosmetic and personal care products are 'frank' carcinogens such as Benzyl Acetate, Butylated Hydroxyanisole, Butyl Benzylphthalate, Diaminophenol, Nitrophenylenediamine, Phenyl-p-phenylenediamine, Diethanolamine, Dioctyl Adipate, Formaldehyde, Methylene Chloride, Polyvinyl Pyrrolidone Pyrocatechol, Saccharin, Talc and similar other chemicals. Some 'hidden' carcinogens are the contaminants such as arsenic and lead, chloroaniline, DDT, dieldrin, endrin and other organochlorine pesticides (in lanolin, hydrogenated cottonseed oil, quarternium-26), DEA(1,4-Dioxane: in ethoxylated alcohols), ethylhexylacrylate (in acrylate and methacrylate polymers), Formaldehyde (in polyoxymethylene urea). Some Nitrosamine (NDELA) Precursors such as diethanolamine, bromonitrodioxane, pyroglutamic acid, triethanolamine (TEA), TEA-sodium lauryl sulfate along with some formaldehyde releasers (Johnson, 2003).

Phthalates is mostly used in nail polish making. Bytylated hydroxyanisole is a carcinogenic chemicals used in producing lipstick, glosses and lip pencils. They generally contain in plastic pipe container. Plastic is one of the most toxic material humankind is using. Plastic oxidation produces over 4000 toxic chemicals and 80 of them are known carcinogens (Islam, 2004). The low temperature of oxidation of plastic will also releases various toxins. Thus using such chemicals and plastic containers are one of the several causes of cancer found in the users. Phthalates is a chemicals widely used in making nail polish and other cosmetic products. Duty et al. (2003) the relationship between environmental exposures to phthalates and DNA damage in human sperm. There are other several chemicals used for nail polish.

Coloring pigments are also one of the most important ingredients of nail polish. Various synthetic coloring pigments such as aluminum silicate with sulfur impurities, titanium dioxide, synthetic ultramarine, oxide red, iron oxide, mercury based vermilion etc. are some of the coloring pigments used during manufacturing the personal care products such as limpstick, nail polish and others. Synthetic pigments are toxic and have several health impacts on humans. They are not easily biodegradable and has several environmental impacts.

Production of Natural Lipstick and Nail Polish

Healthy lipstick and nail polish can be made simply using natural ingredients. For lipstick, gloss and lip pencils, good bees wax with no synthetic pesticides treated flowers and plants, plant and vegetable oils with natural extraction or cold press, fermented alcohol and natural coloring pigments are the basis. Plant and vegetable oils are renewable sources and never used up provided they are produced and harvested in a sustainable way. The fermented alcohols have antioxidants and it will help to prevent the lipstick and other products from being rancid. Desired colors can be extracted from plants and flowers. Natural colors are truly non-toxic, biodegradable and they have no side effects at all. The container which these materials are contained should be made from wooden or other non-toxic materials instead of plastic. Thus, natural lipsticks and nail polish can be produced simply by rendering the process to green using the natural ingredients and containers, lipstick, gloss and lip pencils.

Hair Dyeing

There are estimates that close to two out of every five American women and a smaller number of men dye their hair. Various types of synthetic dyes are employed to change the hair coloring as desired. Most of the hair dyes in use today are derived from petroleum sources. Coal-tar (4-methoxy-m-phenylenediamine, and 4-methoxy-m-phenylenediamine sulfate) remained an important hair dyeing agent for a long time. Coal tars and coal tar pitches are known human carcinogens (IARC, 1987). FDA (1993) reported that reducing the use of coal tar dyes will reduce the risk of cancer. The specific components of coal tar used in hair dyes-aromatic amines (DEA, TEA), that have been shown to mutate DNA (IARC, 1993), and to cause cancer in animals (Sontag, 1981). Phenylenediamines (DEA) which is one of the main ingredients of hair drying interacts with nitrites to form carcinogenic nitrosamines.

It was reported that rodents fed either of the chemicals were more likely to develop cancer than animals not fed the substances (Patlak, 1993). Lead-acetate based hair dyeing may cause several other health problems. Women who used permanent hair dyes at least once a month experienced a 2.1-fold risk of bladder cancer relative to non-users (Gago-Dominguez et al., 2001). Some reports indicated that the use of hair color products appeared to increase the risk of non-Hodgkin's lymphona and use of hair coloring products would account for 35% of non-Hodgkin's lymphoma cases in exposed women and 20% in all women. Hence, hair coloring has several impacts on human health and environment.

Bleaching or decolorizing is a chemical process used to make the hair color light. Synthetic hydrogen peroxide (H_2O_2) is also one of the most widely used hair dyeing agents. This has also health implications. Hydrogen peroxide in high concentration (>50%) is highly corrosive, and can cause irritation to the eyes, mucous membrane and skin. Swallowing hydrogen peroxide solutions is particularly dangerous, as decomposition in the stomach releases large quantities of gas (10 times the volume of a 3% solution) and may lead to internal bleeding.

Natural Hair Dyeing

Natural hair dyeing can be produced from the natural oil and bees wax based materials using the natural colors extracted from flowers, natural earth and plants. Production of hair dyes naturally will have no health and environmental problems. Since these are based entirely on natural material and green process, this can continue for ever and will be inherently sustainable.

Eye Mascara, Eye Liner

Saxena et al (2001) reported that eye cosmetics are a common cause of eye lid dermatitis. These products contain coloring pigments, fragrances, resins and preservatives. Eye mascara may cause eye irritant, or allergic contact dermatitis of the eyelids. Black iron oxide used in mascara causes severe reaction to the eyelid. Iron oxide comes in several forms and are used in pigment products. Black iron oxide is known also as magnitite ($Fe_3 O_4$), yellow or brown limonite ($2Fe_2 O_3 3H_2O$) contains 60% Iron, Red hematite (Fe_2O_3) contains 70% iron. Iron oxides are used as pigments in many cosmetics, including mascara, eyeliner, eyeshadows, and lipsticks. However, these pigments are very toxic to the human health (Saxena et al, 2001).

Nikkie (2002) reported that that mascara tubes made by Benson, Lecco (Italy), contains thin film, amorphous polyamide marked Selar PA by DuPont. Polyamide is a thermoplastic polycondensate, a nyclon resin compound and is very much hygroscopic in nature. It spears that this has severe health because the plastic molecules will enter the human body through the skin. Various chemicals used in health products include artificial musks, used to add scent to perfumes and perfumed products, and perfluorinated compounds, used in water-repellent coatings and to prepare non-stick surfaces such as teflon. It was also reorted that flame-retardants suspected of causing learning and behavioural problems in animals, and the antibacterial agent triclosan, were used in antibacterial soap (Peters, 2003).

Permanent eyeliners are also very popular these days. These eyeliners are permanently tatooed onto the eyelids of the consumers making it permanent mark. Using disposable needles, pigments are implanted into the skin at the abse of upper or lower eyelashes. Local anesthetic is oftern given to releave the pain during tatooing. Using the synthetic based colors for eye liner could have several allergic reactions. If the allergic reaction occurs, it may need to take the tatooing whichmay again cause harm to eyes. Hence tatooing or eye lining is is not risk free procedure.

Healthy Eye Mascara and Eye Liner

Eye mascara and eye liners can be made from ingredients such as bees wax, olive oil or other oils obtained from cold pressing, carbon soot collected by burning olive oil and cotton threads. Coloring agents can also be obtained from flower extracts, turmeric, neem leaves, cinnamon power and similar natural products. None of these ingredients have any negative effects on health and environment. These are always available in natural and are thus sustainable for the longer term.

Humectants and Moisturizers

Various types of humectants such as glycerin, methyl glucose esters, lactates, lanolin derivates and mineral oils are added to the skin cleansing products because of their moisturizing properties. These synthetic chemicals are also harmful to the human health and hence the health products.

Most of the chemicals used in the health products (Table 1) are from petroleum derivates. The petroleum products are highly toxic chemicals as their refining process involves using heavy metals and highly toxic chemicals and high temperature (Chhetri et al, 2007a; Khan and Islam, 2007a). For instance, oil refining uses hydrochloric acid and hydrofluoric acid. Similarly, gas processing involves use of glycol, amines and various other chemicals. These are all toxic chemicals and the petroleum derivates are contaminated with these chemicals. The use of these petroleum derivatives which are contaminated with toxic chemicals will have severe health impacts when used in health products manufacturing.

It is clear that most of the health products are dependent of fossil fuels for many of their properties. The petroleum products are the major causes of the global environmental pollution. These health products are inherently unsustainable as the manufacturing process follow the anti-natural path (Khan and Islam, 2007a). Islam (2004) mentioned that only the technologies which follow the natural path are sustainable. Moreover, to consider a technology truly sustainable, this should fulfill the economic, social, environmental and time criteria (Khan et al, 2005a). Any technology which is dependent on the exhaustible fossil fuels is inherently unsustainable. Thus, the ways health products are being manufactured today are neither sustainable nor beneficial to the human and environment.

Production of the glycerin by using natural catalysts from the plant and vegetable oil and replacing the mineral oils with cold press vegetable oils, healthy humectants and moisturizers can be produced. Using such green process, the products will have no negative health implications.

9.5. TOOTHPASTE

Tooth paste is one of the important daily used products from children to adults. Food items remained in and around our teeth could result in the bacterial growth and may potentially destroy the root canal of the teeth. In order to avoid such problems, brushing the teeth with suitable tooth paste is a regular daily activity. However, use of various synthetic chemicals in tooth paste could potentially damage the teeth and will have several other problems linked to the use of such chemicals. These activities depend on what ingredients a tooth paste contains.

There are two types of ingredients used in tooth paste production. Fluorides, triclosan, desensitizing agents, baking soda (Na_2CO_3), glycerin, salts, anti tartar agent and non-sugar sweetener such as xylitol which is considered to enhance remineralization and coloring pigments. Some inactive ingredients in tooth paste are water, detergents to create foam, binding agents, humectants, flavoring agents, preservatives and abrasives for cleaning and polishing.

Use of tooth paste has been a great controversy recently. Fluoride is a powerful poison, more acutely poisonous than lead. This is the reason it is one of the active ingredients in pesticides and rodenticides. Over ingestion of fluorides can cause serious toxic symptoms. Fluoride is one of the important ingredients in tooth paste. Whiteford (1997) reported that there is enough fluoride in a tube of children's fluoride toothpaste to kill an average-weighing child under the age of 9. There are thousands of reports to poison control center in USA related to excessive ingestion of fluoride products from toothpaste, mouth rinses and other supplements. The acute toxic dose of fluoride has been believed to be 2 to 5 mg or 8 mg/kg of body weight (Akiniwa, 1997). Fluoride acute poisoning has several symptoms which are presented in Table 9.2.

Excessive use of fluorides by human can lead to the demineralization of the bone and tooth enamel resulting in a toxic condition which is termed as fluorosis. Bony changes which are described as osteoporosis, exostoses of the spine can be seen only after prolonged high intake of fluorides. This is due to the fact that fluoride is not biodegradable and it accumulates in the body and bones causing toxic or poisoning effects. Excessive ingestion of fluorides in early childhood can damage the tooth forming cells leading to dental fluorosis. A survey found that overall dental fluorosis rate among US school children aged 6 to 9 years oil (Connett, 2005).

The other ingredient used in toothpaste xylitol has also been reported to be toxic in animal test. Xylitol is a sugar alcohol that is being used in sugar free products such as gum and candy. It has been recently reported that xylitol is toxic to dogs. Clinical signs of xylitol are depression, coma, liver dysfunction or failure among others (Animal Medical Center, 2005). This may have similar impacts to humans too.

Triclosan is a chlorophenol which is a class of chemicals suspected for causing cancer in humans. Phenols are toxic compounds that potentially cause severe health impacts including coma or death. This chemical compound is a synthetic, broad-spectrum antimicrobial agent that has exploded onto the consumer market in a wide variety of antibacterial soaps, deodorants, toothpastes, cosmetics, fabrics, plastics, and other products inn recent years (Glaser, 2004). Several studies have linked triclosan to a range of health and environmental effects including skin irritation, bacterial and compounded antibiotic resistant and dioxin contamination to destruction of fragile ecosystem (Glaser, 2004). It has also been reported that triclosan causes an immunotoxic and neurotoxic reaction to humans. Triclosan can bio-accumulate in fatty tissues and can interfere with the thyroid hormones. The chemical structure of triclosan has polychloro phenoxy phenol and due to which it is possible that dioxin can be found in triclosan as synthesis impurities. Hence, use of triclosan in toothpaste is causing health and environmental impacts. The individual analysis of the ingredients in toothpaste shows that the conventional toothpaste is not good for health and environment.

Production of natural toothpastes needs its all ingredients derived from natural substances and green process without using any synthetic chemicals. Natural toothpaste may contain variety of ingredients from ginger oil to seaweed extract. Use of natural oil based tooth paste would have positive health impact. Naturally extracted baking soda (unbleached) does not have any problems. Honey is the best natural sweetener and has several other ingredients including antibacterial properties. Honey is available locally in most part of the world. Use of honey as natural sweetener in toothpaste production will have several advantages.

Table 9.2. Symptoms of acute fluoride poisoning (Akiniwa, 1997)

1. Salivation	2. Nausea
3. Vomiting	4. Abdominal pain
5. Diarrhea	6. Cramps
7. Cardiac arrhythmia	8. Coma

Conventionally, people used to use wood ash as tooth paste. Wood ash contains various metals such as sodium, potassium, calcium, magnesium among others. These are natural component of wood having to negative impact to health and environment. Moreover, Jatropha stem, bamboo twig are very popular as tooth paste even today in many part of the developing countries especially in Asia. Jatropha stem grounded in powder can be directly used as toothpaste powder. Latex from the Jatropha has antibacterial activities and helps to make the mouth fresh. Hence the liquid can also be converted to mouthwash. Natural salts obtained such as sea salts or rock salts can be used instead of synthetic salts. Various extracts from different plants and vegetables including seaweed could be mixed to make natural toothpaste. Glycerin from the breakdown of triglyceride molecule using natural catalysts will be non-toxic glycerin to use in toothpaste. Grounded charcoal can also be used in toothpaste. Mint oil or cinnamon oil can be used to give the good flavor. Hence by using natural materials and rendering the process completely green, natural toothpaste can be produced.

9.6. BABY OILS

Most of the baby oils found in the market are leveled as "For external use only. Keep out of reach of children to avoid ingestion or accidental inhalation, which can cause serious injury". These oils contain mineral oils (paraffin oil) and synthetic fragrance in it. This also contains stearic acid, cetyl alcohol, white petrolatum, polyoxyethylene stearate, propylene glycol, dimethicone copolyol, methyl paraben, butyl paraben and various others ingredients. Mineral oils and alcohols are toxic chemicals unsuitable for any uses in the health products including baby use products. White petrolatum is a skin irritant have a laxative effect if ingested (MSDS, 2000). Synthetic propylene glycol is also a toxic substance and has several health hazards. Glycol oxidation produces carbon monoxide which is a poisonous gas. Other synthetic chemicals which are also used as ingredients of the baby oils are harmful one or the other way.

The best way to produce baby oils is to use the cold pressed olive oil, other plant essential oils and honey. Olive oil and other essential oils from plants have several vitamins and antioxidants and antibacterial properties. Honey also has antibacterial properties and several other natural chemical compounds that helps to soften and treat the skin for the people of any age. The most important thing to be considered here is to use the natural extraction process for oil extraction. There are literatures that reported that chloroform and hexanes are used to extract the oils. Event though the sources of oil are natural, the extraction process using synthetic chemicals make the final product a toxic one. Hence using natural oils, honey, neem extracts and other natural materials can be used to make the healthy baby oil. Baby oil produced in natural way will have no negative health and environmental impact and will be inherently sustainable for long-term.

9.7. SUNSCREEN, FACIAL, TATTOO AND CAMOFLAGE

Sunscreen

The commercially available sunscreen is mostly made from synthetic materials which have several impacts on human health and the environment. The model of natural products manufacturing such as natural soap and non toxic shoe polish can be extended to make natural sunscreen. A mixture of beeswax, honey and olive oil can become an excellent sunscreen material. Beeswax has a high resistance to the passage of heat. This works as a good moisture retainer in the body. Honey, a substance contained in the beeswax is a natural hummectant, which means it draws and holds moisture, and is therefore soothing to dry and damaged skin. As a natural wax, beeswax protects the skin and leaves it feeling healthy and soft. Beeswax reduces inflammation, softens skin, and has antioxidant properties. After processing, beeswax remains a biologically active product retaining anti-bacterial properties. It also contains vitamin A, which is essential for human cell development. Throughout time, people have used it as an antiseptic and for healing wounds. Olive oil has antioxidant properties and absorbs certain ultraviolet rays. The polish material which is made out of beeswax, olive oil and carbon particles can be used as an excellent sunscreen or skin protector.

Facial Care

Various mineral oils and chemicals are used as facial care agents. These mineral oils and synthetic chemicals are toxic and pose several health risks in short and long term. These chemicals are also non-biodegradable and pose environmental risk. Since these products are primarily based on synthetic production mode, they are inherently unsustainable.

Natural facial care agents should be made purely from natural herbal products using plant or vegetable oils such as rose oils, olive oils, honey, ginger, cinnamon powder, neem extracts and several other natural ingredients. These oils should be extracted by using cold pressed method without using synthetic chemicals such as hexane or chloroforms. Lemon wash can also be used as healthy facial care. Lemon wash and natural oils have several vitamins necessary for the skin. These natural herbal products are biodegradable and have no negative health and environmental impacts since there are no synthetic chemicals.

Tattoo and Camouflage

Tattooing has been very popular in the western countries. However, less attention has been paid on the ingredients of the materials used to make the tattoo and their side effects. Different types of multipolymer compounds, alkyd polyester resins, petroleum isoparaffinic hydrocarbons, petrolatum, black iron oxide and synthetic dyes are employed to make the temporary and permanent tattoo. Tattoo ink contains various metals which will also have serious impacts on the long-term health.

Camouflaging is used for army operations, artistic reasons and skin conditionings. Camouflaging for security reasons depends on the local terrain, colors of vegetation and so many other factors, hence color necessary depends on different factors. The camouflaging ink should also be insect repellent. Any synthetic chemical used for making camouflaging could be ingested through the skin which is the largest organ of human body. Hence, use of synthetic chemicals which are toxic in various conditions should be completely avoided. Only natural materials extracted from plants and vegetables or naturally occurring substances should be used to make camouflage. The colors should be extracted from plants and flowers and the alcohols should be made from fermentation.

9.8. PAINTING AND POLISHING

Painting

Conventional Painting

Conventional paints consist of several synthetic chemicals including lead and chromium. Lead, mercury, chromium, mercury, barium, arsenic and other metal based paints are very popular as these metals are used as pigment. It also works drying agent, moisture retainer and increases durability. Lead is extremely toxic to living organisms and especially dangerous to children. Lead causes nervous system damage, hearing loss, kidney damage, dysfunction reproductive organs, stunned growth and relayed development (Gettens et al., 1967). There are several plastic paints in use these days. As plastic is highly toxic materials, the effect of plastic paints could be severe for human and environment. It releases dioxins and carcinogenic materials. Oil based paints are based on toxic mineral oils which also have several heavy metals. These are also not biodegradable and have several other environmental impacts. The asbestos used to give the decorative texture of the paint is a toxic material. All the synthetic materials used in the conventional paints are one or the other way harmful to human and environment.

Non-toxic natural paints can be produced using truly natural materials such as charcoal, the hard wood extracts and other plant extracts. The desired color can be obtained from plant and flower extracts. The mineral based oil paints can be replaced by plant based oils. The conventional milk paints can be extended to natural paint using egg yolk and olive oils. The carbon soots collected by burning wood can also be used as excellent natural paints if mixed with olive oil. There are several way of producing natural paints which are healthy and environmentally friendly.

Non-toxic Shoe Polish

Commercial shoe polish contains various toxic substances. Generally, shoe polish is made from ingredients including naptha, lanolin, wax, bicarbonates of potassium and various types of coloring pigments. It also contains carbonates and bicarbonates of sodium and potassium. The burning of shoe polish will result in the yielding of carbon dioxide and/or carbon monoxide and traces of oxides of nitrogen and various toxic materials depending upon the chemicals, and solvents used to make the shoe polish.

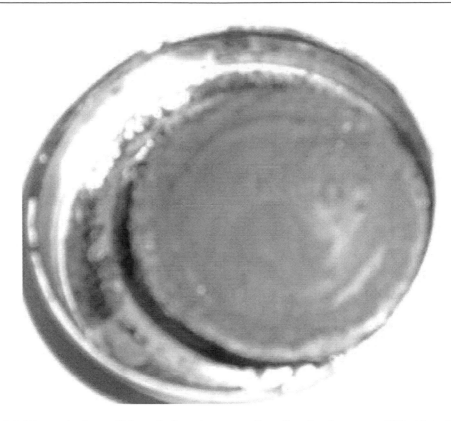

Figure 9.6. Non toxic shoe polish made from beeswax, olive oil and carbon soots (Chhetri et al., 2006a).

To make a good and non-toxic shoe polish, olive oil, beeswax, and carbon soot collected by burning olive oil were used. Beeswax is a tough wax formed from a mixture of several compounds including hydrocarbons (14 %), monoesters (35 %), diesters (14%), trimesters (3%), hydroxy monoesters (4%), hydroxy polyesters (8%), acid esters (1%), acid polyesters (2%), free acids (12%), free alcohols (1%) and some unidentified materials (Honeybee Natural, 2006).

A good black shoe polish was prepared by collecting carbon from burnt olive oil and mixing with olive oil and beeswax (Figure 9.6). The beeswax was melted by heating the pan with hot water. The direct heating of wax results in breaking and color change. The ratio 1:3:3 of beeswax, olive oil and carbon particles will make a good viscous shoe polish. The beeswax, olive oil, carbon mixing ratio depends on the how viscous the polish is to be made. In countries where biomass cookstoves are used, carbon can also be collected from the chimneys of cookstoves by making a water oil trap. Various colors can be extracted from flowers, vegetations and Ocher, the naturally occurring colored earth that yield different colors. Beeswax forms a protective layer over the surface of the shoe and becomes a barrier against water, preventing its absorption by the leather. This beeswax mixed shoe polish is highly effective for use in wet or muddy conditions. This shoe polish has no toxicity and no harmful ingredients. Such shoe polish can be made easily at home. This can also be used for wood polishing and metal polishing.

9.9. DRY CLEANING

Dry cleaning the clothes has been a very popular activity in the urban areas. It has been reported that there are thousands of dry cleaning agents being used in United states and 95% of them use are toxic chemical called perchloroethylene (PERC) as the primary cleaning solvent (Greening planet, 2004). Exposure to the PERC is significant risk to the people involved in cleaning. Moreover, the dried clothes also gives off these toxic chemicals even after the clothes are stored or worn. Perc has several health impacts. Studies indicated that short-term exposure to PERC can cause adverse health effects on the nervous system that include dizziness, fatigue, headaches, sweating, in coordination, and unconsciousness. Long-term exposure has been reported to can cause liver and kidney damage (Greening planet, 2004). The primary hazard from PERC is dermatitis from chronic or acute exposure. Dilute hydrofluoric acid generally found in some products to remove rust stains, may cause severe chemical burns with deep tissue destruction that may not be evident until several hours after prolonged contact (NIOSH, 1998). Exposure to PERC includes depression of the central nervous system, damage to the liver and kidneys, impaired memory, confusion, dizziness, headache, drowsiness, and eye, nose, and throat irritation. NIOSH considers PERC a potential human carcinogen (Earnest, 1997).

PERC is a member of the chlorinated solvents family and is a synthetic chemical. There are no known natural source for this chemical. There is increasing concern about the use of chlorinated compounds such as PERC due to their persistence in the environment and their potential to bioaccumulate. Blackler et al., (1998) reported that the total PERC consumed in dry cleaning sector in 1991 in US reached to 270 million pounds, and approximately two third of this amount (180 million pounds) is released to the atmosphere. The PERC's breakdown compounds such as vinyl chloride and phosgene are toxic to human and trichloroacetic acid is the herbicide that damages forest. The remaining 90 million pounds are captured in the form of a solid waste, reaches to the water bodies washing by percolating water. As these chemicals may not be detected at low level, it is likely that contaminated water is consumed by human and animals finally ingesting into their body. Alternatives developed to PERC are also based on synthetic hydrocarbons, synthetic silicon based and toxic industrial carbon dioxide. Thus, synthetic based dry cleaning agents have health and environmental impacts.

There can be several ways to avoid PRC and related toxic chemicals. Natural CO_2 washing could be a good option instead of industrial CO_2. Natural liquid soaps can be used for dry cleaning purposes. The silicon based compounds will be acceptable if the silicon is extracted from the organic sources such as rice husk. This will be not toxic and completely biodegradable having no environmental and health impacts.

Chapter 10

BIO-PRODUCTS

10.1. INSULATORS

Plastic Insulators

Insulation of the house, industries, office spaces electrical and electronic equipment involve various plastic and organochlorine and their by products. Chlorofluorocarbons or CFCs were used until recently as blowing agents in extruded polystyrene, polyurethane, polyisocyanurate, and phenolic foam. CFCs are considered ozone depleting and greenhouse gases. Extruded polystyrene (XPS) were widely used as building insulating materials but once it was considered toxic, it was replaced by hydrochloro-fluorocarbons (HCFCs) products. Spray polyurethane and some other phenolic foam products were produced for insulating materials foamed with HCFC-141b. However, HCFCs were also regarded as toxic materials as these are also ozone depleting chemicals.

Polyurethane is one of the most common materials used in insulation. Khan et al. (2007c) analyzed and compared the two insulating materials polyurethane and natural wool (Table 10.1). They shoed that polyurethane insulation has several toxic effects and is not readily biodegradable. The use of polyurethane also creates several environmental problems. The pathway analysis of polyurethane and natural wool shows that polyurethane has several environmental implications at different stages of its production. When polyurethane degrades then the most toxic form of PBDEs (penta-BDE) escapes into environment. The PBDEs is traced higher amount in mother's breast milk. It is a highly toxic compound and exposure to it causes adverse health effects including thyroid hormone disruption, permanent learning and memory impairment, behavioral changes, hearing deficits, delayed puberty onset, decreased sperm count, fetal malformations and, possibly, cancer (Lunder and Sharp, 2003). It is reported by Lunder and Sharp (2003) that exposure to PBDEs during infancy leads to more significant harm at a much lower level than exposure during adulthood. Recently, reported breast milk contamination of PBDEs might create a disaster in the near future. Scrap of flexible polyurethane foams from slabstock manufacturing leads to a serious environmental threat (Molero et al., 2006).

Table 10.1. Basic Difference between Polyurethane and Wool Fiber (Khan et al., 2007c)

	Polyurethane	Wool
Type	Artificial fiber; alien products to the nature.	Natural Fiber, which grows in most of the organism.
Composition	Urethane -monomer; it's completely humongous compound and same pattern	Made of alpha-karyotin, which is most valuable protein. However, wool is heterogeneous compound vary from species to species even protein itself is different and complex in a single species.
Diversity	There is no diversity. urethane	Highly diverse. Complex process of synthesis very little is known so far. It's different segments like different monomers
Functionality	Single-functional just as plastic	Multifunctional such as for the protection of organisms, supplies of nutrients,
Adaptability	It is non-adjustable and non-adoptable and can not change itself life the natural products do.	It can adapt with the changes in different conditions, such as temperature, humidity, light intensity. It protects itself and protects the organism where it grows.
Time factor	Non-progressive. It does change with time	It is regressive and changes according to time for example it degrades by time
Perfectness	It creates all kind of problem. From carcinogenic products to unknown product.	It is perfect and does not create problem. Instead solve the problem.

Pathway analysis of polyurethane and natural wool fibres are shown in Figure 10.1 (Khan et al., 2007c). This indicated that there are toxic emission at several stages of polyurethane production which affects human health and environment. Most of these products are also carcinogenic to humans. Oxidation of plastics at various temperatures occur several toxic emission.

There are several other insulating materials in use of buildings and equipment. Polyethylene terephthalate is considered a highly dimensionally stable thermoplastic with good immunity to moisture. Phenolic laminates are widely used for terminal boards, connectors, boxes, and components. These are made from phenolic nylons. Polystyrene are also low loss plastic coil dope used to secure winding and other components. Polyvinylcloride (PVC) is perhaps the most common insulating material is use today. Irradiated PVC has superior strength and resistance to heat. Electrical and electronic housings are commonly molded from PVC. Teflon, thermoplastics, vinyl, nylons, polyesters, polyolefins, silicon rubbers are used as insulating materials.

The list of the insulating materials made out of plastics is never ending. Plastics itself is a toxic material and refined plastic to make foams and insulating materials eventually become more and more toxic due to the addition of processing chemicals. These insulating materials and household products are the major causes of various illnesses. The current technological development mode has made the bad to worse by using wrong process and wrong materials. This mode of development where a perpetual crisis is created to wards plastic use is not sustainable. Only the development of natural insulating materials which are healthy, biodegradable and no negative impacts for environment need to be allowed for use.

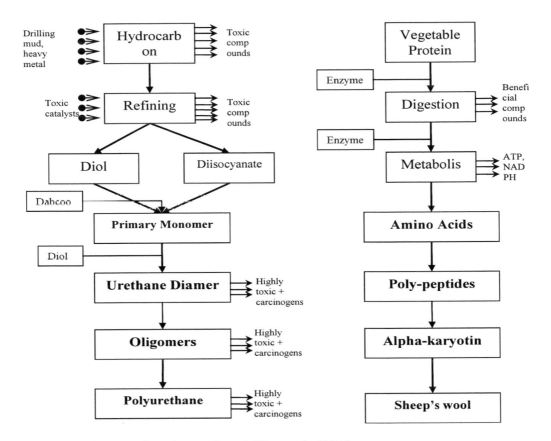

Figure 10.1. Pathways polyurethane and wool (Khan et al., 2007c).

Cotton Insulation

Cotton was the most widely used insulated material before plastics. Cotton can be grown in many places in the world and has several applications including textile making. The waste cotton from textile production can be used as insulating materials for homes, offices, and industries including materials and equipment. As cotton is truly organic product, there is as such no negative health and environmental impact of using cotton unlike its plastic counterpart today which is very toxic and carcinogenic.

In addition to cotton, there are different types of bio-fibers which can be extracted from woody biomass and can be used as insulators. Even the straw, tree leaves have very good insulating properties. There are several types of grassy fibers which are being used as insulating materials in house building and space insulation. Use of cotton insulation will not only provide healthy insulation but also provide carbon sink for CO_2 emission from other activities as cotton seeds could be a large carbon sinks. Other cellulose materials such as papers, paper boards are also non –toxic insulation materials provided that papers are manufactured without using toxic chemicals. Natural fiberglass materials are also excellent natural insulating materials. Use of cottons and other biomaterials are truly natural and sustainable solution to the current environmental problems due to plastic usage.

Natural Hair Insulation

Use of animal wools as insulating materials is not a new science. It has been used since time immemorial. However, these days the use of animal wools has become obsolete and cheap plastic insulators are available in the market. These plastic insulators are highly toxic to the inhabitants and create environmental problems. The animal wools are highly durable but biodegradable materials and work perfectly for the insulation purpose keeping the environment safe. Arabani (2007) studied the insulating property of human hair and animal wool experimentally and showed that human hair and wools have better insulating properties than any synthetic plastic insulators. These natural materials are as durable as plastic materials but at the same time are biodegradable and do not pose any risk to the humans and animals. There are other natural materials that can be used as insulators of such quality. Hence the current development approach should be oriented so as to use foster the development of truly natural products which are inherently sustainable.

10.2. CARPETS

Carpets are one of the most essential items for floor covering from household to office, industries and public and religious places. The most recent development in the carpet is affected by plastics and this dominates most of the carpet market in the world. In earlier days, carpets were made of animal wools and cellulose fibres from the plants such as jute. However, these days, all these carpets are replaced by plastic carpets. Use of plastics in any products including carpets emits toxic gases including volatile organic compounds and several carcinogens.

Synthetic Carpets

The use of plastic based carpets has several volatile organic compounds emission continuously (Dietert and Hedge, 1996). The commercial carpet material consists of various chemicals such as formaldehyde, ethyl benzene, toluene, acrylic oligomers tetrachloroethylene, xylenes, benzene, diphenyl ether, oleylamine, hexamethylene triamine, among others. Nylon is also used in carpet manufacturing. Various kinds of synthetic dyes are also used to make the carpet of desired colors. All of these synthetic chemicals, preservatives and dyes have several health impacts.

Jaakkola et al. (2006) reported that exposure to certain types of surface materials at work appears to increase adults' risk of developing asthma. The study showed that exposure to plastic wall coverings on the job increased asthma risk 2.43-fold, exposure in workplaces with wall-to-wall carpeting were 1.73 times more likely to have developed asthma. Moreover, the risk of developing asthma was quadrupled if molds were presents and there was wall to wall carpeting. Carpet is a major volatile organic compounds (VOCs) source in a resident building which is a major cause for the respiratory illnesses and has significance influence on human health in indoor environment (Denga and Kim, 2007). Several types of VOCs were found to be emitted from the carpets. The concentrated study in the test chamber showed that VOCs reach their peak emission at the beginning, decayed rapidly to a certain level at the beginning and then lasted for longer duration (Shin et al., 2003). This indicates that the carpet emission will continues for ever until there are carpets in the room. Ventilation will help to release volatiles to some extent while it is not the ultimate solution as volatiles will continue polluting the indoor environment.

The analysis shows that all kinds of synthetic carpets are serious threat to the indoor environment and human health. The low temperature oxidation will continue for long duration and the VOCs, plastic and synthetic dyes emission will have several health implications. Hence, the current mode of carpet production is not sustainable and a serious threat to the human health.

Natural Carpets

Unlike synthetic carpets, natural carpets are manufactured from wools, jutes and other natural fibres without using synthetic chemicals. Wool carpets are non-toxic, non-allergic and do not support bacterial growth. It is argued that wool carpet purifies indoor air of common contaminants like formaldehyde, nitrogen dioxide and sulfur dioxide by locking the contaminants deep in the core of the fiber. Wool carpets continually purify indoor air for several years. Wool's naturally crimped shape is the formation of millions of air pockets that act as an insulation to help regulate room temperature. Due to the high moisture content and protein constituents make it naturally flame retardant. Wool carpets also help to control humidity as they have the ability to absorb up to 30% of its own weight in water vapour without feeling wet and therefore. Wool carpets also act as sound insulators in addition to the heat insulators. Wool carpets keep cool in summer and warm in winter because they can absorb or release moisture creating heat. Hence, development of natural carpets and replacement of synthetic carpets by natural carpet has to be taken as an urgent issue.

10.3. TEXTILES

Textile development model is exactly similar as that of carpet. Most of the textiles available in the market have plastics to certain extent if not all such as nylon, polyester and others. They are further added to synthetic dyes to produce in different colors. These are produced from the petroleum derivatives and release toxins all the time and people who wear these clothes are exposed to the toxins released by them. None of these practices are beneficial to human and environment and hence are inherently unsustainable. The synthetic mode of technological development is the culprit to the worsening environmental situation in the globe.

There are natural ways of producing these textiles being practiced from people from thousands of years. Cottons are the sources to produce most healthy textiles. There are several other plant fibers such as jute and others from which healthy and truly biodegradable textiles can be manufactured. There are large number of sources such as flowers and plants from which natural dyes can be extracted. Production of textiles and dyes from the natural materials is an inherently sustainable mode of technological development.

10.4. UTENSILS

Various types of utensils have been developed with time to ease cooking and storing foods. Earlier, people used to cook in stone pots during the start of civilization. Later on, earthen pots became the most ubiquitous in the world followed by cupper and iron pots. After the Industrial Revolution, development of stainless steel tools, equipment and utensils reached at its high level. Most recent development was the development of plastics which replaced almost everything that were in existence. Now the combination of stainless steel and plastics has become the ultimate for any utensils available in the market.

Metal Utensils

Silver, copper, iron, cadmium, aluminum, stainless steel and several alloys are in use to make the cooking and storing utensils and keeping the foods warm for longer duration. There are adverse effects of aluminum ingestion in human body. Adverse effects of aluminum are currently known to be far more chronic (occurring over the long term) than acute (occurring in the short term). Aluminum has been shown to be a neurotoxic compound if it is allowed to enter the bloodstream. Long-term exposure of patients to dialysis water high in aluminum may cause encephalopathy (defect of the brain) and/or bone mineralization disorders (Agriculture and Agrifood Canada, 2003). Water is not only the source for aluminum uptake. Similar health impacts may result if all cooking is done with aluminum pots and utensils.

Cadmium is a heavy metal with a blue-white or gray-black appearance. It is primarily used in silver solder, batteries, plastics and pigments. Cadmium has no known biological function, and is highly toxic to both animals and plants. Contamination could occur due to the soldering of the utensils and ingestion of even lower levels of cadmium over a long period of time can lead to kidney and liver damage, weakening of bone and sense of smell (UNEP, 2001). Cadmium and cadmium compounds are likely carcinogens.

Iron is also a heavy metal which is very reactive chemically. Iron rapidly corrodes in moist air or at elevated temperatures. Ingestion of iron in large amount has been linked to increased risk of cardiovascular disease and colon cancer, can damage the liver and pancreas, leading in some cases to diabetes (UNEP, 2001). Long-term exposure to high levels of chromium (VI) is reported to cause damage to the nose and lungs, and can increase the risk of lung diseases. Ingesting large amounts of chromium can cause ulcers, convulsions, kidney and liver damage, and even death sometimes. Studies also indicated that chromium (VI) is a heavy metal and is considered to be a human carcinogen (UNEP, 2001). Cupper is also one of the most used heavy metal in cooking utensils, water distribution pipes and paints. It has been reported that ingestion of small quantities of copper salts may cause severe abdominal pain, vomiting, diarrhea, blood or protein in the urine, hypertension, convulsions, coma, or even death. Lead is also widely used in solders and in pipes and may contaminate food in many ways affecting the user's health severely. Lead is a serious threat to human health and can adversely affect almost every organ in the human body.

Cooking utensils made of heavy metals, coated with heavy metals, soldered and braced with heavy metals are reactive at elevated temperatures. Despite, it is not visible that these heavy metals contaminate our foods. Exposure to these heavy metals for long duration will cause several diseases. Hence, the current technology development is not in the favor of the human kind and is truly unsustainable.

Plastic Utensils

Plastic utensils or the plastic coated non stick utensils are very popular these days. Most of the plastic utensils are used for storing food for longer duration rather than direct cooking. Exposure to any food item with plastic for a longer time is not good as plastic is continuously oxidized even in low temperature (Islam, 2005b). Moreover, most of the food packaging is made from plastic which is another direct method of plastic exposure to the numerous food items.

With a claim for miraculous solution to waxy, slippery, dirt, fat and water repellent grease encountered in cooking utensils, development of Teflon coating on frying pans and cooking utensils is considered an ultimate in cookware convenience. Teflon coating keeps the food from sticking to the pan, allows diet conscious to use less fat while cooking and makes washing up utensils much easier. However, it is argued that the chemistry of Teflon is not yet fully understood (Thomas, 2005). Teflon consists of several toxic chemicals that can be released from heated pans into the air and into food. The use of Teflon coated pan at high temperature will release the toxins quicker as the coating will break down and emit tiny particles and gases. Teflon, known chemically as polytetrafluoroethylene (PTFE) is a plastic-like substance made up of a complex mixture of perfluorinated chemicals (PFCs) (Thomas, 2005).

Any good non-stick coatings intended to use in cooking are made with PTFE. There are several assumption made for Teflon manufacturing. It was considered that Teflon is not generally volatile, meaning they do not easily airborne, the PCBs are locked into polymers so that they do not leak into the environment, even if they leak, they do not break down and even if they break down, they would remain inert. All these assumptions have been found wrong. Teflon is highly persistent bio accumulative toxins. Teflon is considered to be release in cooking temperature breaking down the coatings due to heat. Since it is plastic like materials, the low temperature oxidation is also likely to occur. Long term Exposure to one of Teflon's breakdown products, perfluorooctanoic acid (PFOA), has led to hypothyroidism (the condition of having an underactive thyroid. A prolonged state of hypothyroidism is a risk for obesity, insulin resistance and thyroid cancer. A recent review by federal government regulators in Canada has determined that over 4000 chemicals once thought to be benign are potentially dangerous for the physical health of Canadians (Mittelstaedt, 2006a). The lists includes some types of perfluorocarbons which are made to make non stick, stain resistant or water repellent products and is commonly found in fast food packaging and cookware. Hence transition from the metals utensils to the use of plastic and plastic ingredients in the cookware makes is bad to worse model of development model and is never a solution.

Earthen and Wooden Utensils

These are still popular in most part of the developing countries. These pots are used for cooking, frying and roasting of foods such as corn, wheat, barley, rice etc. These pots are used to store foods for longer time. These are built from a special type of black cotton soil which is available in most part of the world. Since clay is an organic material, the use of these pots for food preparation and storing has no negative effects on human health. Any contamination in the soil will be stripped off during the high temperature drying of the earthen pots. These are organic materials and they will not have toxic effects even if there is little contamination.

Various types of wooden utensils are also still in use in various part of the world. Wooden utensils are most widely used for yogurt making from milk. Wooden and bamboo utensils were in common use for the storage and fermentation of food whenever necessary. Hence non-treated wood, bamboo and their products are the most appropriate technologies that can not only help to preserve the health and environment but can be produced locally in many areas boosting the local economy leading to sustainable communities.

10.5. THE PLASTIC CULTURE: SYNTHETIC PLASTICS VS BIO-PLASTICS

After the Industrial Revolution, synthetic plastic has been synonymous with civilization. Synthetic plastic personifies the anti-nature model that promised to emulate nature while perpetrating exactly the opposite of the promise. Plastic materials were proposed to ensure flexibility while achieving durability. However, no plastic has ever been manufactured that is as durable as human hair and nails, as strong as bone, as strong or flexible as the muscle that makes up the human tongue, as strong as the spider's web (per unit of cross sectional area), and yet all plastics are toxic even when they are exposed to room temperature (Islam, 2005b). Nature does not produce a single toxic plastic.

It is reported that some 90 million barrels of crude oil is used annually to sustain our live style (Islam, 2004). After all, plastic is made from the solid residue settled during its first phase of the transformation of crude oil into refined products by thermal cracking. Much of this solid residue is used for producing bitumen, tar and related products. Some of this residue is reinforced with metals to produce long-chain molecules in the name of plastic. Figure 10.2 shows the common method of plastic synthesis from residues of petroleum products.

This way, easily biodegradable crude oil is converted into plastic products which are most harmful for the environment over the long term. More than four million metric tons of plastic is produced every day from the 90 million barrels of crude oil consumed. More than 30% of this plastic is used by the packaging industry (Website 15). In United Kingdom alone, three million tons of plastic is disposed every year (Website 16). Most of these plastic materials are either disposed to the environment and are susceptible to oxidation (low-temperature oxidation, LTO, at the very least) a small quantity of it is recycled. Table 10.1 shows the negative impacts of some common synthetic plastic materials.

Crude oil as such is not a culprit for the toxic effect of plastic products. The original ingredient of crude oil is not harmful to living objects and it is not likely that the older form of the same would be harmful, even if it contains trace elements that are individually toxic. It is true that crude oil is easily decomposed by common bacteria, at a rate comparable to the degradation of biological waste (Livingston and Islam, 1999). Even when some toxic chemicals are added to the fractionated crude oil, for instance, motor oil, the degradation rate is found to be rather high (Chaalal *et al.*, 2005). As long as bacteria are present in abundance, it seems, any liquid will be degraded. The problem starts when the crude oil components are either turned into solid residues or burned to generate gaseous products. Unfortunately, the most common use of crude oil is in combustion engines producing energy through thermal conversion, as opposed to the chemical conversion used by practically all living organisms.

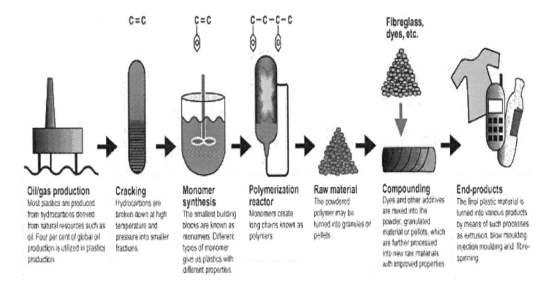

Figure 10.2. Plastic synthesis from petroleum residues (Maske, 2006).

Table 10.1. Negative impacts of some common synthetic plastic materials (Islam, 2005b)

Plastic	Common Uses	Adverse Health Effects
Polyvinyl chloride (#3PVC).	Food packaging, plastic wrap, containers for toiletries, cosmetics, crib bumpers, floor tiles, pacifiers, shower curtains, toys, water pipes, garden hoses, auto upholstery, inflatable swimming pools.	Can cause cancer, birth defects, genetic changes, chronic bronchitis, ulcers, skin diseases, deafness, vision failure, indigestion, and liver dysfunction.
Phthalates (DEHP, DINP, and others)	Softened vinyl products manufactured with phthalates include vinyl clothing, emulsion paint, footwear, printing inks, non-mouthing toys and children's products, product packaging and food wrap, vinyl flooring, blood bags and tubing, IV containers and components, surgical gloves, breathing tubes, general purpose lab ware, inhalation masks, many other medical devices.	Endocrine disruption, linked to asthma, developmental and reproductive effects. Medical waste with PVC and pthalates is regularly incinerated causing public health effects from the release of dioxins and mercury, including cancer, birth defects, hormonal changes, declining sperm counts, infertility, endometriosis, and immune system impairment.

Table 10.1. Continued

Plastic	Common Uses	Adverse Health Effects
Polystyrene	Many food containers for meats, fish, cheeses, yogurt, foam and clear clamshell containers, foam and rigid plates, clear bakery containers, packaging "peanuts", foam packaging, audio cassette housings, CD cases, disposable cutlery, building insulation, flotation devices, ice buckets, wall tile, paints, serving trays, throw-away hot drink cups, toys	Can irritate eyes, nose and throat and can cause dizziness and unconsciousness. Migrates into food and stores in body fat. Elevated rates of lymphatic and hematopoietic cancers for workers.
Polyethelyne (#1 PET).	Water and soda bottles, carpet fiber, chewing gum, coffee stirrers, drinking glasses, food containers and wrappers, heat-sealed plastic packaging, kitchenware, plastic bags, squeeze bottles, toys	Suspected human carcinogen
Polyester.	Bedding, clothing, disposable diapers, food packaging, tampons, upholstery.	Can cause eye and respiratory-tract irritation and acute skin rashes.
Urea-formaldehyde	Particle board, plywood, building insulation, fabric finishes	Formaldehyde is a suspected carcinogen and has been shown to cause birth defects and genetic changes. Inhaling formaldehyde can cause cough, swelling of the throat, watery eyes, breathing problems, headaches, rashes, tiredness
Polyurethane Foam	Cushions, mattresses, pillows	Bronchitis, coughing, skin and eye problems. Can release toluene diisocyanate which can produce severe lung problems
Acrylic	Clothing, blankets, carpets made from acrylic fibers, adhesives, contact lenses, dentures, floor waxes, food preparation equipment, disposable diapers, sanitary napkins, paints	Can cause breathing difficulties, vomiting, diarrhea, nausea, weakness, headache and fatigue
Tetrafluoro-ethelyne	Non-stick coating on cookware, clothes irons, ironing board covers, plumbing and tools	Can irritate eyes, nose and throat and can cause breathing difficulties

Modern life has been completely dependent on plastics products. Households that boast 'wall to wall carpets' are in fact covered with plastic, vast majority of shoe soles are plastic, most clothing is plastic, Television sets, fridges, cars, paints, computer chassis– practically everything that 'modern' civilization has to offer is plastic. The liner that cookware boasting a non-sticky liner is non-sticky because of the plastic coating. The hardwood coating, synthetic wool, the material of medicinal capsule coatings all are plastic. The modern age is synonymous with plastic in exactly the same way as it is synonymous with cancer, AIDS, and other diseases. The biggest problem with plastics, like that of nuclear waste from atomic power plants, is the absence of any environmentally safe method of waste disposal. If disposed of out-of-doors, the respiratory system in any ambient organic life form is threatened. If incinerated, toxic fumes almost as bad as cigarettes are released. Typically, plastic materials will produce some 4000 separately identifiable toxic fumes, including 80 known carcinogens (Islam, 2005b). Hence plastics are the cause of most of the health and environmental problems the world is facing today and use of synthetic plastics is not a sustainable solution.

Natural Plastics

Natural plastics have been used for thousands of years, dating back to the time of the Pharaohs and ancient Chinese civilization. Natural resins, animal shells, horns and other products were more flexible than cotton and more rigid than stone and have been in use for household products, from toys and combs to plastic wraps and drum diaphragms. Until some 50 years ago, natural plastics were being used for making buttons, small cases, knobs, phonograph records, mirror frames, and many coating applications worldwide. There was no evidence that these materials posed any environmental threat. The two-fold problem with natural plastics was that they could not be mass-produced on terms that would yield maximum profit in minimum time according to the demands of a globalized marketing effort, and the modern industrial techniques powering production and marketing on such a scale remained momentarily a monopoly of such a tiny handful of giant corporations in an even smaller handful of powerful Western countries.

There is some awareness of the long-term damage from synthetic plastic products in the West, developing countries are just completing their transition from natural products to plastic materials. This is a disturbing trend and unless the current plastics are turned into 'good' plastic, the mere existence of human race will be jeopardized. 'Good' plastic can be defined as the long-chain polymeric molecules that do not have damaging impact on the environment in either the short-term or the long-term. All biologically available plastic materials are 'good' plastic and it is likely that microbes are used to develop the long-chain molecules of a plastic material will fall under this category. It is also conceivable that even petroleum oil can be the feedstock of 'good' plastic as long as toxic materials are avoided, maximizing the use of additives of biological sources. For instance, if hydrogenation is effected through biological instead of chemically refined products and, as an example, zinc is used instead of lead, the resultant plastic is likely to be environmentally benign or even environmentally friendly.

Bioplastic's best-known building blocks are *polyhydroxyalkanoate* (PHA) and *polyhydroxybutyrate (PHB)*, both entirely biodegradable. In nature, several kinds of bacteria produce these substances. They convert carbohydrates into a polymer and store it in the cell wall. PHB can be heat-formed into a flexible plastic suitable for many applications where biodegradable plastics are desirable, such as packaging. It has been reported from several studies that *Alcaligenes eutrophus*, as well as other bacterial species, produce the organic polymer PHA as a carbon reserve. Moreover, these same microorganisms produce the enzyme necessary to break down the polymer into monomers, metabolized as a carbon source. This natural source of plastic polymer is therefore biodegradable. Moreover, natural plastics can be produced from the starch from cereal grains. Starch can be processed directly into a bioplastic but, because it is soluble in water, articles made from starch will swell and deform when exposed to moisture, limiting its use. This problem can be overcome by modifying the starch into a different polymer. First, starch is harvested from corn, wheat or potatoes, and then microorganisms transform it into lactic acid, a monomer. The lactic acid is chemically treated to cause the molecules of lactic acid to link up into long chains or polymers, which bond together to form a plastic called polylactide (PLA). PLA can be used for products such as plant pots and disposable nappies. Similar principle can be applied to fiberglass and other fabricated materials. Glass in itself is environmentally benign. However, when petroleum-based resins are added to the fiberglass, the final product becomes toxic in the long term. If biological glue, e.g., from fish scale, were used to bond the glass fibers, the product would remain acceptable.

Recycling of Plastic Waste

Today's industrial development has created such a crisis that life without platic is difficult to imagine. Approximately four million metric tons of plastics is produced from crude oil every day (Islam, 2005b). Burning the plastics will produce more than 4000 toxic fumes, 80 of them are know carcinogens. Plastic production itself consumes 8% of the world's total oil production (Website 17). In the UK alone, a total of approximately 4.7 million tonnes of plastic products were used in various economic sectors in 2001 (website 17). Though, there are talks on recycling, only about 7% of the total plastic is recycled today and rest of the plastic are either disposed to the environment or succeptible to oxidation. In fact, good life with plastic is not possible because of its toxic effects into health and environment.

PVC is the major component of the plastic used in the construction sector. High chlorine content (56% of the polymer's weight) in PVC is a major problem in the recycling of PVC. Various hazardous additives are added to the polymer to achieve the desired material quality. These additives include colorants, stabilizers and plasticizers that include toxic components such as lead and cadmium. Studies indicate that plastics contributes 28 percent of all cadmium in municipal solid waste and about 2 % of all lead (EPA, 1989). Recycling of plastic is generally done in two ways.

Mechanical Recycling

This method consists of melting, shredding, or granulation of waste plastic. Though conventionally, plastic is sorted manually, but sophisticated techniques such as X-ray fluorescence, infrared and near infrared spectroscopy, electrostatics and flotation have been introduced recently (Website 17). Sorted plastic material is melted down directly and moulded into a new shape, or melted down after being shredded into flakes to process into granules. Plastic wastes are highly toxic materials, further exposure to X-rays or infrared rays will make the products even more toxic.

Chemical and Thermal Recycling

The chemical process for converting certain plastics back to raw materials is called depolymerization. Chemical recycling process breaks down the polymer into their constituent monomers which are again reused in the refineries, petrochemicals and chemical processes. Pyrolysis, hydrogenation, gasification and thermal cracking are some of the chemical recycling methods. This process is highly energy and cost intensive and requires very large quantities of used plastic for reprocessing to be economically viable. Most of the plastic waste consist not only polyethylene but fiber reinforced materials which cannot be easily recycled simply with conventional processes. These reinforced plastics are thermoset and contain a significant fraction of glass or other fibre and heavy filler materials such as calcium carbonate. In chemical recycling, monomers are broken down into its base components. One such method is the DuPont-patented process called "ammonolysis,". This process depolymerizes plastic by ammonolysis process, where plastic is melt-pumped into a reactor and depolymerized at high temperatures and pressures using a catalyst and ammonia.

Pyrolysis is carried out in absence of oxygen at 500 ^{0}C, which does not allow the plastic to burn and the recycled fibre said to retain its strength. Methanolysis and glycolysis - are used to produce polyethylene terephthalate (PET). With methanolysis, clean post-consumer PET flake is mixed methanol in a chemical process under heat and pressure. PET is converted back into its raw materials (dimethyl terephthalate and ethylene glycol) which can then be purified, mixed with virgin raw materials, and re-reacted to produce PET. With glycolysis, clean post-consumer PET flake is mixed with ethylene glycol in a chemical process under heat and pressure. This process converts the PET back into its monomer to produce PET with 25 per cent recycled content. Environment and Plastics Industry Council (EPIC) developed an important recovery and recycling technique (Figure 10.3) that combines chemical as well as thermal processes for plastic recovery.

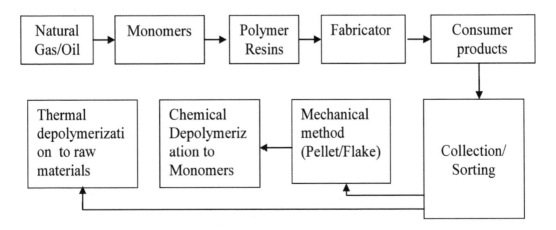

Figure 10.3 Integrated Recycling Systems

Problems in Plastic Recycling

- This recycling technology produces small amounts of solid carbon and toxic gases.
- Hydrolysis of pulverized polycarbonate in supercritical reactors produces Bisphenol A which is a very toxic compound.
- Coloring pigments are highly toxic compounds.
- Dioxins are produced when plastics are incinerated.
- Phthalates are a group of chemicals which are hormone disrupters. Plastic toys made out of PVC are often softened with phthalates and their burning produces toxic fumes.
- Recycling plastic has only single reuse unlike paper or glass materials.
- Huge amount of natural gas is used for depolymerization ammonolysis.

It is thus obvious that recycling of the plastic is not a big accomplishment. This will further worsen the environmental impacts as there are certain additional emission of toxic gases such as bisphenol A and dioxins. Synthetic mode of plastic development is not sustainable in any case. The only sustainable solution is to produce bioplastics from natural materials usning mciroorganisms which offers truly sustainable option for long- term.

Chapter 11

NATURAL COLORS

INTRODUCTION

Colors and dyes remained one of the major components in civilization and phenomenal qualities of the world (Maund, 2006). Colors can be obtained either from natural sources such as flower or plants or can be chemically synthesized. Synthetic colors, though mimic the natural color are not found in nature. Natural colors are extracted from agricultural or biological materials found in nature.

At present many things around us including our food are artificially colored. Over 10,000 dyes and pigments are used worldwide in dyeing and printing industries. The total worldwide colorant production in 2004 was estimated to be 1 million tons in 1994, of which more than 50% were azo dyes (Pandey et al., 2006). Azo dyes are the largest class of synthetic dyes used in commercial applications. These dyes are widely used in a number of industries, such as textile dyeing, food, cosmetics, paper printing, with the textile industry as the largest consumer. All the dyes do not bind to the fabric or other products and its total loss various from 2% in basic dyes to 50% in reactive dyes that leads to severe contamination of surface and ground waters (O'Neill et al., 1999). In average, at least 15% of the used dyes enter the natural environment through various pathways including industrial effluent (Kariminiaae-Hamedaani, 2007).

Most of the synthetic dyes are very stable to light, temperature and microbial attack, making them difficult to biodegrade that blocks the natural ecosystem. Moreover, their discharge into surface water leads to aesthetic problems obstructs light penetration and oxygen transfer into water bodies, hence severely affecting aquatic life. Moreover, many of these dyes are reported to be highly toxic and carcinogenic such as benzidine or other aromatic compounds that might be formed as a result of microbial metabolism (Michaels and Lewis, 1985). Conventional wastewater treatment systems such as municipal sewerage system are also not efficient for decolorization and have several health and environmental impact. Hence removing the synthetic dyes from various industrial waste streams and water is of prime concern today.

Colors are mostly used in food items, drugs and personal care products. Hence colors are directly linked with the human health. Food, drug and cosmetics color pigments are generally made form coal tar and other synthetics. This pigment contains several heavy metal salts that leave toxic by-products on the skin. The animal tests on these colors have indicated that they are cancer causing materials. These colors are mixed with glycerin and polypropylene glycols. Glycol is a toxic substance and glycerin, if not extracted using natural catalysts, consist lots of toxic catalyst components in it making it a toxic product. The only option to make non toxic color is to produce color from natural materials, plants and flower extracts.

11.1. DANDELION AND OAK TREE

Dandelion is one of the most common and problematic weeds of turfgrass and lawns throughout Europe and North America. Dandelion falls under sunflower family. Dandelion also occurs as a weed of container ornamentals, landscapes, nurseries, orchards, and agronomic crops. Chhetri et al. (2007b) studied on the multiple use of Jatropha including color extraction, food and medicinal uses (Figure 11.1). It is a perennial and herbaceous plant with long lance shaped leaves. The roots of dandelion are deeply rooted in the ground. Dandelion yields a yellow composite flower grown in hollow flower stalks. Dandelion can grow in most of the disturbed habitats, lawns, or any open ground. In fact, they grow virtually worldwide. It can grow in adverse condition than their competitors. Dandelion is an excellent food for honey bees. Besides this, dandelion is used as food to make salad. It is one of the most nutrient rich plants among the plant kingdom. It has several mineral contents including potassium, sodium, phosphorus, iron, zinc, magnesium, vitamin A, B, C, D, E. A comprehensive use of dandelion and its different parts for various uses is depicted in Figure 11.1.

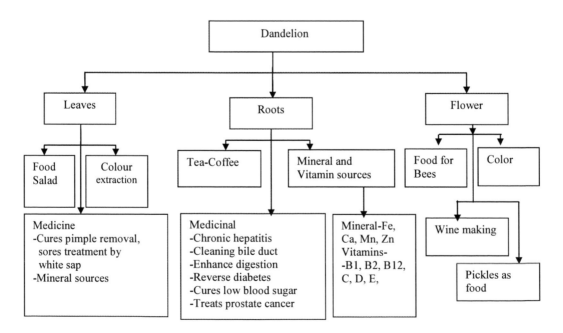

Figure 11.1. Zero-waste multiple use of dandelion.

Pigment Extraction

Pigments can be extracted from the roots, flowers and leaves. The principal pigment found in extract of Taraxacum officinale was a di-esters of taraxanthin with concentration of 350 ppm fresh weight (Booth, 1964). Appreciable amounts of the mono-ester and of free taraxanthin were found in the flowers. Di-ester, mono-ester and free carotenol each had spectral absorption maxima at 420, 442 and 471 mμ in both *n*-hexane and ethanol. Figure 11.2 and 11.3 shows that the color from dandelion flower can be extracted using 95% concentration fermented ethyl alcohol from grains and olive oil and water mixtures. This shows great potential that dandelion which is considered a weed could be useful in producing natural colors. However, the *n*-hexane and petroleum grade extraction results in toxic pigment harmful to human and environment. The organic alcohol and hexane from organic sources such as green peppers would yield non toxic and environmental friendly pigment. Miralai (2006) experimentally showed that the yellow color extracted from grain based natural alcohol remains stable in cotton and other fibers.

Figure 11.2. Color extraction by fermented alcohol (Chhetri et al., 2007b).

Figure 11.3. Color extraction by olive oil and water (Chhetri et al., 2007b).

Oak and other plants have been used for color extraction since a long time in the history of development. The extraction of color from these plants was entirely from natural processes. Traditionally the color is extracted from the leaves and barks by dissolving it into hot water. The extract is further heated to concentrate it. The leaf extract is used for green color where as bark extract is yellowish or brown colors. The color depends on the different parts of the plants used for the color extraction. A knowledge base is necessary to identify the desired color from the different plants including oak tree. Oak tree is one of the oldest plants that were used for color extraction in Asian region.

11.2. PIGMENT FROM EARTH
(ULTRAMARINE, OCHRE, LIME STONE ETC.)

Ultramarine

Earth is the place for getting all kinds of colors. Ultramarine is a naturally occurring blue pigment consisting essentially of a double silicate of aluminum and sodium with some sulfides of sulfates derived from naturally occurring mineral lapis lazuli (Fabian et al., 2006). Natural ultramarine is a blue color which is one of the most complex colors of the mineral pigment. This is a complex sulfur containing sodio-silicate $Na_8 [Al_6Si_6O_{24}]Cl_2$ which is a mineralized limestone containing lazurite, a blue cubic mineral (Hoeniger, 1991). Sodium chloride is also present in these minerals. The blue color is due to the presence of S_3- radical anion containing an unpaired electron. Preparation of ultramarine consisted of ground mineral mixed with melted was, resins and vegetable oils, wrapping the mixture in a cloth and kneading it in a dilute lye solution prepared from wood ash. The blue particles settled at the bottom and impurities and colorless materials remained in the mass. This blue color can then be used to color any thing such as clothes, painting in the temples, houses and heritages (Figure 11.4). The extraction process continued for several times releasing most intense blue particles first and lower grades in subsequent extraction. Even the last extraction can be used as a pigment called ultramarine ash. As this is extracted naturally from natural materials, this is non-toxic and biodegradable having no environmental impacts.

Figure 11.4. Blue colors from ultramarine (website 18).

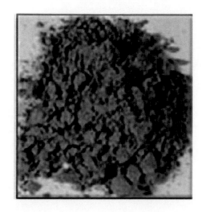

Figure 11.5. Yellow ochre (website 18).

Ultramarine was known for more than 5000 years as coloring pigment. This natural pigment displays a brilliant color and was as valuable as gold in both ancient times and Middle ages (Reinen and Lindner, 1999; Kowalak et al., 2004). There are several kinds of zeolite which can be used as coloring pigments. In addition to this, several other minerals have colors that are extractable to use in daily life purposes.

Ochre

Ochre is a clay earth pigment from naturally occurring minerals. Ochre usually yields golden yellow or light yellow brown color from naturally occurring mineral (Fuller, 1998). It is available in the form of hydrated iron oxide ($Fe_2O_3.H_2O$). This can be made red colored through heating (Fe_2O_3). Brown ochre is a partially hydrated iron oxide which is a kind of rust. Ochre is found throughout the world in many areas. Yellow ochre is a hydrated iron oxide obtained from silica and clay and prepared by grinding and washing the mineral which a rust stained clay (Website 18). Several types of color can be derived from ochre. Hovers et al. (2003) reported that ochre was also used as color in Qafzeh Cave terrace some 92,000 years back at the Middle Paleolithic time. Some geoichemical and petrographic analysis showed that ochre was mined solely to use as color during that time.

Lime

Limestone is also a naturally occurring coloring material being used since a long time. The most important use for this mineral is to use as white paint in the rural homes. This can also be mixed with other color to produce new colors. The color is cement manufacturing is particularly guided by the color of lime. This is environmentally friendly material and has several benefits for local use.

Use of naturally occuring substanbces such as ultramarine, ochre, lime and clay is the most environmentally friendly option to get the natural colors. As synthetic colors have several health and environmental problems, these problems can be overcome by using natural coloring materials such as clay, and other minerals. Extraction of color in this way is a sustainable for infinite time ohorizon as the formation of mineral in the earth surface continues for ever.

11.3. COLOR FROM FUNGI

Fungi, particularly lichens, have a long history as fabric dyes in the world. It was used for red and purple dyes by the people thousands of years ago. The desired orchil purple colors were derived from *Roccella tinctoria*, and other rock lichens of the same genus. Fungus was found to have a natural affinity to woolen and silk textiles. There are several kids of other fungi that are being used as coloring pigment.

Mushrooms also display an infinite variety of size and colors. Mushrooms vary in sizes from pinhead to big basketballs. Practically, the colors of mushrooms include all the colors of the rainbow. Mushrooms are the part of the local ecology of the forest. The growth and survival of mushrooms depends on various factors such as trees animals, insects or birds of any habitat. They are also equally affected by wind rainfall, temperature and other organisms in the subsystem. Mushrooms occur in variety of colors

Including black, brown, pink, white, lilac, and even green. Hence these colors can be extracted and used as natural coloring pigments for the benefits of human beings. As fungus and mushrooms is a part of the ecology, extraction of color from these species is one of the most sustainable options.

11.4. PLANT BASED COLORS

Color extraction from plants was an art from medieval ages. Plant-based colors extracted during that time for human use were from sea buckthorn, berries, turmeric, saffron, charcoal, gum Arabic and others. Even today, plants based colors are the most ubiquitous and there are thousands of plants and flowers that yield varieties of colors. Different types of fruits, fruits peels, extracts such as grape color, beet juice, carrot, beta carotene and others can be used to extract colors. These are used to put the colors in the foods. Various plants have been considered to yield different useful colors. These plants are found in different parts of the world or any plants found in the different parts of the world can be utilized to extract colors (Table 11.1).

Flowers are the most important sources of natural colors. Flowers are available in all kinds of colors of the rainbow. Flowers have blue, purple, red, white, pink, orange, yellow, white, green and brown. There are other flowers with complex or combined colors. Colors from the flowers can be extracted by several ways. Some of these are extracted simply dissolving in hot water, some can be extracted by using fermented alcohols and some by using cold pressed vegetable oil. Some of the colors are extracted by fermentation of the flowers or the plants matters. Hence, to be truly natural and sustainable color, the extraction process should be truly green without using any synthetic chemicals. Since these colors are extracted from the naturally available plants, flowers, minerals, they are inherently sustainable. There are no environmental impacts as well as health impacts from extraction and use.

Table 11.1. Dyes from Common Nova Scotia Plants

Plant	Part used	Place collected	Mordant used				
			Alum	Chrome	Copper	Iron	Tin
Alder (Alnus sp.)	Twigs with leaves	Manganese mines, Colchester Co.	Light yellow		Charcoal gray		
	Twigs with leaves	Maple Lake, Halifax Co.	gold	gold	Dark gold	Dark brown	Orangy yellow
	Twigs with leaves	Sherbrooke, Guys, Co.	Light yellow				
	Twigs with leaves	Halifax, Suburbs	Light brown	medium brown	Dull medium brown		
Balsam Fir (Abies balsamea)	Twigs with needles	Lunenburg Co.	Very warm fawn	brass	Warm fawn	Warm medium brown	Orangy fawn
Bayberry (Myrica pensylvanica)	Whole plant	Halifax, Suburbs	Clear yellow	gold	Olive green khaki		
Beggar-ticks (Bidens sp.)	Whole plant	Halifax City	Orange yellow	Rust golden brown	Golden brown	Dark brown	Orange
Blackberry (Rubus sp.)	Young shoots	Halifax City	Yellow	Dull yellow gold	Light olive green		
Burdock (Arctium minus)	Whole plant	Halifax City	Pale yellow	Yellow grey	Yellow grey	Dull brown	Yellow grey
Maple (Acer sp.)	bark	Halifax City	Beige	Light brown	Medium brown	Grey brown	
Red Oak (Quercus rubra)	Leaves	Halifax City	Beige-green	Golden brown	Dark brown	Deep brown	Golden yellow
Teaberry (gaultheria procumbens)	Whole plant	Halifax Suburbs	Yellow beige	Light gold	Green beige	Medium brown	Yellow beige

Chapter 12

NATURAL PESTICIDES

INTRODUCTION

Pesticides have become ubiquitous facts of life after World War-II. There is not a single place on earth where residues of pesticides are not detectable. As of 2004, more than five billion pounds of pesticides are applied each year, of which 20% are applied in the US alone (USEPA, 2004). Pimentel and Acquay (1992) reported that more than 670 million birds are directly exposed to pesticides each year on U.S. farms alone, 10% of which (67 million birds) die. More than 85,000 synthetic chemicals are registered in USA and 2000 new synthetic chemicals are being added each year for various purposes including antibiotics, pesticides, disinfectants and other purposes, most with no or adequate testing (Global Pesticide Campaigner, 2004). Even though human body is not designed to cope with synthetic chemicals, we are exposed to a cocktail of chemicals designed to kill insects, weeds and other agricultural and household pests. There are several other chemicals which are being used in the industrial processes, water disinfectants and refineries that contaminate our water and food in one or the other way.

U.S. Customs records showed that 3.2 billion pounds of pesticide products were exported in 1997-2000, among which nearly 65 million pounds of the exported pesticides were either forbidden or severely restricted in the United States (Smith, 2001). 2.2 million pounds of pesticides regulated under a treaty on persistent organic pollutants (POPs) were exported between 1997 and 1999. The same study reported that in the period between 1997 -2000, large amount of pesticides designated as 'extremely hazardous' by WHO (89 million pounds), pesticides associated with cancer (170 million pounds) and pesticides associated with endocrine disrupting effects (368 million pounds) were exported, mostly to developing countries (Smith, 2001). Manufacturing and transportation, storage and use of these chemicals have severe impacts to human and the environment. Hence, from public health and environmental perspectives, manufacturing, export and use of these chemicals are unacceptable. Many of these synthetic chemicals including pesticides can cause cancer, disrupt human hormone systems, decrease fertility, cause birth defects or weaken our immune systems. These are just some of the known detrimental effects of particular pesticides at very low levels of exposure. Almost nothing is known about the long-term impacts of these chemicals in the body. Annually, millions of birds and fish species are lost due to the impacts of pesticide use. In addition to the agricultural products in which the pesticides are applied, they contaminate the water and air through many pathways (Figure 12.1).

Despite serious threats posed by pesticides, the production, manufacturing and use of pesticides have never been declined. Some of the toxic chemicals which were once very popular found health threatening and banned later on. Banning of a pesticide often leads to a corresponding increase in use of another synthetic pesticide, as in the case of chlorpyrifos in the name of banning DDT. Chlorpyrifos which is also a toxic chemical is already detected in many rivers of USA and other places. Neurodevelopment tests of chlorpyrifos showed several neurobehavioral and other effects in human and animals (Eskenazi et al., 1999).

Proposing wrong solution for various problems has become progressively worse. Every stage of current development, production and manufacturing pesticide involves the generation of toxic waste. Today, it is becoming increasingly clear that the "chemical addition" that once was synonymous with modern civilization is the principal cause of numerous health problems including cancer and diabetes. Potato farms on Prince Edward Island in eastern Canada are considered a hot bed for cancer (The Epoch Times, 2006). Chlorothalonil, a fungicide, which is widely used in the potato fields, is considered a carcinogen. US EPA has classified chlorothalonil as a known carcinogen that can cause a variety of ill effects including skin and eye irritation, reproductive disorders kidney damage and cancer. Environment Canada (2006) published lists of chemicals which were banned at different times. This indicates that all the toxic chemicals used today are not beneficial and will be banned from use some day. In other words, banning chemical has become a daily affair in the world. However, as in the case of chlorpyrifos which was invented after DDT was banned, each and every new solution has moved from bad to worse. Thus, any synthetic chemical whether it is antibiotics or pesticides are never good for human health and the environment. In contrary to this, nature based products development is the only option in order to reverse the impacts of toxic chemicals to human health and the environment (Chhetri and Islam, 2006c).

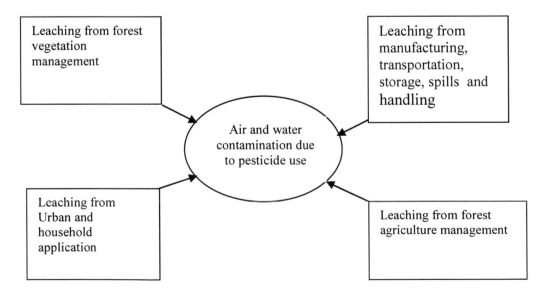

Figure 12.1. Pathways for pesticide contamination in water and air (Chhetri and Islam, 2006c).

12.1 GLOBAL STATUS OF PESTICIDE USE

The world total pesticide consumption is approximately two million tones per year (Gupta, 2004). 24 % of total global pesticide is consumed in USA, 45 % in Europe and 25% in rest of the world. India's share in pesticide use globally is 3.75 %. The intensity of pesticide use in India is about 0.6kg/ha while in Korea and Japan is 6.6 and 12 kg/ha respectively. The worldwide consumption of herbicide is 47.5%, insecticides is, 29.5%, and fungicides, 17.5% and others account for 5.5%. Agrell et al. (2001) estimated that total of 2.6 million tones of DDT was used worldwide between 1950-1995. Approximately 320,000 tons of pesticides were sold in the European Union in 1999 (EC, 2002). Polychlorinated biphenyls (PCBs) are also widely used pesticides which are synthetic chemicals with varying number of substituted chlorine atoms on their aromatic rings. The world production of PCBs (excluding the Soviet Union) totalled 1.5 million tones during their commercial use in 1929–1989 (HELCOM, 2001).

Type of Synthetic Pesticides

There are many classes of synthetic pesticides in the world. However, the major classes consist of organochlorines, organophosphates, carbamates, and pyrethroids (Table 12.1). These are toxic chemicals and exposure to these pesticides can cause acute (short term) or chronic (long term) impacts on animals and humans mainly in the reproductive, endocrine, and central nervous systems. Pesticides are known to cause lymphoma, leukemia, breast cancer, asthma, and other immune system disorders in humans. Moreover, the use of synthetic pesticides has caused to develop resistant for more than 500 species of insects to some pesticides. As a result, the development of new synthetic pesticides will be accelerated. DDT is considered one of the most toxic pesticides which is banned in USA in 1972. But DDT is still in use in several countries in the world where some of the US food supply is grown. Since these synthetic pesticides once enter into the food and water cycle, it is hard to get rid off them. Even if the DDT is banned in USA the population could still be affected from exposure through the food, water and air pathways.

Table 12.1. Types of synthetic pesticides and their potential impacts (UCSD, 2006)

Class	Pesticide	Potential impacts
Organochlorines	DDT, toxaphene, dieldrin, aldrin	Reproductive, nervous, endocrine, and immune system
Organophosphates	Diazinon, glyphosate, malathion	Central nervous system
Carbamates	Carbofuran, aldicarb, carbaryl	Central nervous system
Pyrethroids	Fenpropanthrin, deltamethrin, cypermethrin	Poorly understood

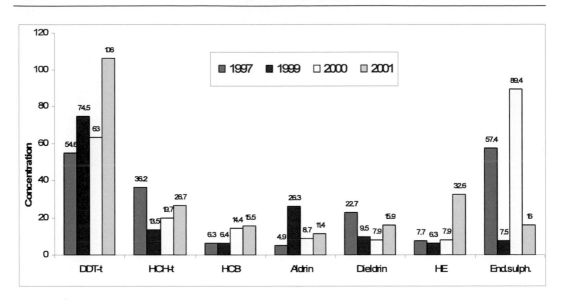

Figure 12.2. Summary of concentration of different organichlorine pesticides in serum (Data from Lino and da Silveira, 2006).

12.2 IMPACTS OF SYNTHETIC BASED PESTICIDES

Papadakis et al. (2006) reported the findings of the study of 16 organochlorine pesticides in the sesame seeds imported to Greece. Heptachlor, heptachlor epoxide, dieldrin, aldrin, endrin, endosulfan I, endosulfan II, endosulfan sulfate, p,p-DDT, p,p-DDD, p,p-DDE were some of them. Organochlorine pesticides are banned in developed countries due to their adverse impact on the environment but are still in use in most of the developing countries for pest control. Hence, the residues of organochlorine pesticides are found in water and various commodities including sesame seeds (Sankararamakrishnan, et al., 2005). Since sesame seeds and oils are mostly used in health food items, they will have severe health consequences. Provided there were any criteria for the items to be selected for the health food items, the products in which pesticide has been applied during production would not have been selected for their negative impacts to health and the environment.

Lino and da Silveira (2006) reported a study carried out to determine the levels of 12 organochlorine pesticides in human serum from Portuguese students of the University of Coimbra between 1997-2001. Various serum samples were analyzed to determine the residues mainly hexachlorocyclohexane (HCH) isomers (a, b, g), aldrin and dieldrin, heptachlor epoxide (HE), hexachlorobenzene (HCB), 1,1,1-trichloro-2,2-bis(p-chorophenyl) ethane (p,p0-DDT), 1,1,1-trichloro-2-(o-chlorophenyl)-2-(p-chlorophenyl) ethane (o,p0-DDT), 1,1-dichloro-2,2-bis(p-chlorophenyl) ethylene (p,p0-DDE), 1,1-dichloro-2,2-bis(p-chlorophenyl) ethane (p,p0-DDD), and endosulfan sulfate. Figure 12.2 is the summary of mean concentrations (measured in μ g/l) of DDT-t, HCH-t, aldrin, dieldrin, HE and endosulfan sulfate in serum. It was observed that DDT concentration in 2001 was found highest in the four years (106 μ g/l) and endosulfan sulfate was found highest in the year 2000(89.4 μ g/l). The concentration of DDT was found almost 5 times highest than HCH in all the years measured. DDT contamination was found higher than other pesticides studied. This result showed that these pesticides contaminate directly into the blood level resulting in the various health problems such as hyperglycemia among others.

Rahimi and Abdollahi (2006) reported that organophosphorus (OP) compounds are the cholinesterase-inhibiting chemicals that are used as pesticides and warfare agents (nerve agents). Exposure to OPs cause a significant number of poisonings and death each year (Abdollahi et al., 1995). This study concluded that hyperglycemia is the outcome of acute or chronic exposure of to OPs due to changes in body glucose metabolism. OPs induce metabolic pathways in different body organs such as brain, skeletal muscles that favor increased glucose production. Moreover, resistance to insulin and disturbance in insulin secretion are the consequences of OPs exposure. Diazinon and Malathion are most common OP compounds that are heavily used in the agriculture as insecticide, to protect home foundation from termites, protect West Nile virus carried by mosquitoes and many people in USA are exposed (Rahimi and Abdollahi, 2006). Table 12.2 is the summary of result of animal studies due to the exposure of OPs.

Table 12.2. Animal studies of Organophosphoruses (OP) exposure in body glucose homeostasis (Abdollahi et al., 1995)

Type of OP	Type of animal	Exposure	Results	References
Malathion	Chick embryos	Subacute	Hypoglycemia	Arsenault et al., 1975
Methyl parathion	A freshwater fish (Brycon cephalus)	Acute	Hepatic glycogen decreases, Gluconeogenesis increases	De Aguiar et al., 2004
Monocrotophos	Broiler chicks	Chronic	Blood glucose level increases	Garg et al., 2004
Malathion	Rats	Subchronic	Hyperglycemia,	Abdollahi et al., 2004
Malathion	Rats	Subchronic	Increases glycogen storage in liver,	Rezg et al., 2006
Malathion	Acute and subchronic	Subchronic	Blood glucose and insulin levels increases	Panahi et al., 2006
Malathion	Rats	Subchronic	Blood glucose and insulin levels increases,	Pournourmohammadi et al., 2005

Leong et al. (2006) carried out a study on organochlorine and organophosphate pesticides in the Selangor River in Malaysia for the year 2002-2003 to determine the concentration of the contaminants. Among the organochlorine pesticides detected were lindane, heptachlor, endosulfan, dieldrin, endosulfan sulfate, o, p'-DDT, p,p' -DDT, o,p' -DDE and p,p'-DDE whereas chlorpyrifos and diazinon were organophosphate pesticides detected. These pesticides have been detected in the rivers though they are banned in Malaysia since a long time. The average concentration was found higher than that of limits set by WHO or US EPA water quality standards. In Malaysia, most of the public water supply source is river water. Due to the higher level of contamination, there is a significant level of risk involved in public health and fish life. Moreover, the wetland ecosystems are also at risk. The major cause of this contamination is the use of pesticides in the agriculture and urban setting for pest control.

A recent study carried out 2002-2003 to determine the concentration of 15 polychlorinated biphenyl congeners and six organochlorine pesticides from the production facility in eastern Slovakia reported that the concentration of these pesticides were significant even after the 20 years after the closure of the facility (Petrik et al., 2006). The sum of 15 PCB congeners was found to be 3105 ng/g of lipid in the Michalovce district versus 871 ng/g of lipid for subjects from the reference districts of Svidnik and Stropkov. The concentration measured in children from the Michalovce district was found to be PCB =766 ng/g of lipid versus 372 ng/g of lipid in children from reference area. Levels of various organochlorine pesticides DDT and its metabolites, hexachlorobenzene were also reported to be elevated Michalovce district due to intensive use of pesticides in agriculture farming in the past. This also indicated that the exposure is still on going from environmental reservoirs and contaminated food. Hence, once these synthetic chemicals are exposed to environment for some reasons, they have several long term impacts in the health and environment.

An acetyl cholinesterase enzyme blood test was conducted for rice farm workers in the Mekong Delta, Vietnam in order to determine the residues of pesticides (Dasgupta et al., 2006). The results showed high presence of pesticide poisoning by organophosphate and carbamate exposure. Over 35% of test subjects experienced acute pesticide poisoning and 21% chronically poisoned. In Vietnam, many banned pesticides such DDT, methamidophos and other synthetic chemicals were found to be used in the survey year 2000 along with illegally imported of counterfeit pesticides. Another survey result revealed that 95% of the farmers disposed the unused pesticides in canals, water courses and ditches. This will not only cause pesticide contamination thought the food in which pesticide is applied but also direct discharge of unused pesticides in water courses raises the ground water contamination level very high. Contamination of water course and soil will have several impacts in human health and the environmental.

Pesticides in Fish and Aquatic Animals

Agrell et al. (2001) studied the effect of DDT and polychlorinated biphenyls (PCBs) in the Baltic marine environment of Finland. Seven PCBs and p,p'-DDT with its metabolites p,p'-DDE and p,p' -DDD, hexachlorocyclohexanes (a-HCH and c-HCH) and hexachlorobenzene (HCB) were determined in muscle of female herring aged two years. The PCBs and DDTs detected in the two year old Baltic herring in 2002 were found in the ranged 2.6–6.3 lg/kg ww (0.08– 0.19 mg/kg lw (lipid weight basis) and 1.4–4.5 lg/kg ww (0.05–0.13

mg/kg lw), respectively. In the same year, concentration ranged for a-HCH, c-HCH and HCB were 0.13–0.24 lg/kg ww (4–7 lg/lg lw), 0.15–0.31 lg/kg ww (4–9 lg/kg lw) and 0.18–0.46 lg/kg ww (5–12 lg/kg lw). This indicated that the pesticides which are applied in agricultural field, urban setting, industrial leakage due to storage and transportation will reach to the water courses and could also affect these marine species.

Yang et al.(2006) carried out the concentration of organochlorine pesticides in fish from remote mountain lakes and Lhasa River in Tibetan Plateau. Total concentrations of DDT, hexachlorocyclohexane (HCH) and hexachlorobenzene (HCB) were 0.78–23 ng/g, 0.13–2.6 ng/g, 0.31–3.2 ng/g based on wet weight respectively. Fish gill were the major areas to accumulate more OCPs due to absorption by its larger surface per tissue. The study also concluded that Tibetan Plateau functions as a regional contaminant convergence zone by long-range atmospheric transport.

An investigation was carried out to determine the concentration of organochlorine pesticides and heavy metal residues in fish and shellfish in Calicut region of India. The studied showed that the highest concentration of OCPs detected in the edible portion of fish were 10.47, 70.57 and 28.35 ng g^{-1} wet weight, in marine, brackish water and freshwater, respectively (Sankar et al., 2006). BHCs was major pesticide residue detected in fresh and brackish water fish whereas BHC and heptachlor epoxide was the major constituent of OCPs in marine water. In all samples, DDT and its metabolites were found in the range of 0.05 to 8 ng g^{-1}. DDT s and other pesticides are persistent in the environment for long time without undergoing degradation and enter into to the food and water cycle through various pathways. Since these pesticides remain in the edible portion of the fish, these residues are ingested through the food into human body and create several health problems.

Wang et al. (2006) investigated and revealed the prevalence of organochlorine pesticide residues in sea mollusks collected from ten coastal cites along the Chinese Bohai Sea from 2002 to 2004. The study showed that OCPs such as p,p' -DDT, p,p' -DDE, b-HCH were widely detected in the mollusks. The study further reported that the content of OCPs in the mollusks did not change in the study period from 2002-2004. This indicates that the sea creators are heavily affected by the pesticides by the application of pesticides in agricultural, commercial and urban areas. The common belief is that when it is diluted in low concentration, it will not be harmful. However, the study showed that even if the pesticides are diluted in the sea, they will still have significant effects. Thus, once the environment is exposed to these synthetic pesticides, it is almost impossible to get rid off these chemicals and will continue affecting food and water cycles creating several health problems.

Pesticides in Food Products

More than 7000 pesticide products and over 500 active ingredients are registered for use in Canada for agriculture application. A study was conducted from 12 May -13 August, 2003 at Bratt's Lake, Hafford, and Waskesiu to determine the contamination of air from different pesticides (Yuan et al., 2006). The study indicated that most of the targeted 11 pesticides were detected with higher frequencies of detections for triallate (97%), bromoxynil (95%), MCPA (94%), 2,4-D (90%), dicamba (90%), and g-HCH (83%). Similar observations were reported in air and water sample studies earlier (Waite et al., 2005). Triallate was the most frequently detected herbicide and was reported at highest level among the 11 target pesticides in the

Prairies in this study (Table 12.3). Trifluralin and ethalfluralin were detected less frequently (68% and 49%) than triallate at the same area.

Table 12.3. Concentrations of pesticides in air and dry deposition samples collected under the Prairie study during the spring and summer of 2003 (Yuan et al., 2006)

Pesticide analyte		Bratt's Lake				Hafford	Waskesiu
		Air sample (1-m)	Air sample (10-m)	Air sample (30-m)	Dry deposition	Air sample (1-m)	Air sample (1-m)
		pgm-3	pgm-3	pgm-3	ngm_2 d_1	pgm-3	pgm-3
g-HCH	Max	479	327	932	0.18	244	220
	Ave	171	182	233	0.07	141	68.5
	Min	68.8	80.9	ND	ND	ND	ND
Triallate	Max	15300	3640	9460	6.63	2190	155
	Ave	2880	1500	1550	1.71	318	52.2
	Min	402	246	54.8	0.15	46.8	ND
MCPA	Max	4960	952	876	7.20	342	160
	Ave	513	223	191	1.00	82	32.8
	Min	9.5	15.5	10.6	0.03	15.4	ND
2,4-D	Max	897	1090	1460	0.84	492	240
	Ave	219	331	331	0.3	117	58.7
	Min	28.6	38	47.8	0.01	ND	ND
Bromoxynil	Max	791	761	722	0.61	804	2546
	Ave	185	199	203	0.14	144	49.1
	Min	8.6	12.1	12.1	ND	ND	ND
Dicamba	Max	615	626	372	0.88	261	35
	Ave	184	187	145	0.22	39.6	10.1
	Min	19	25.8	21.2	0.01	5.2	ND
Trifluralin	Max	811	503	816	0.18	734	24.8
	Ave	170	272	388	0.08	70.6	5.0
	Min	ND	ND	63.7	0.01	ND	ND
Ethalfluralin	Max	453	620	889	0.43	327	ND
	Ave	115	209	308	0.15	27.2	ND
	Min	ND	ND	ND	ND	ND	ND
Atrazine	Max	19.9	41.2	532.1	0.03	ND	ND
	Ave	4.3	9	807	ND	ND	ND
	Min	ND	ND	ND	ND	ND	ND
Alachlor	Max	ND	ND	15.9	0.01	ND	4.9
	Ave	ND	ND	ND	ND	ND	ND
	Min	ND	ND	ND	ND	ND	ND
Metolachlor	Max	ND	10.6	10.9	ND	ND	ND
	Ave	ND	ND	ND	ND	ND	ND
	Min	ND	ND	ND	ND	ND	ND

Note: The method detection limits (MDLs) based on a sample volume of 2500m3 and an extract volume of 1mL for all analytes are 4 pgm, except ethalfluralin (20 pgm^{-3}) ND=Not detected.

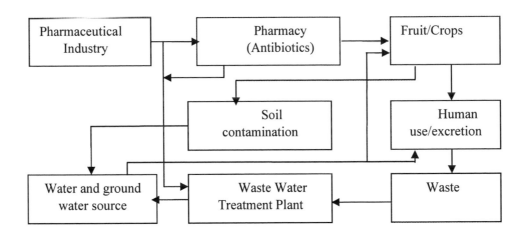

Figure 12.3. Pesticides pathways in human and animals through soil and water resources (Modified from Chhetri and Islam, 2006d).

Lindane which was mainly used as canola seed treatment consisting of at least 99% γ-HCH was continued to be used in Canada until 2004. Even though Lindane was stopped registering in Canada in 2003, it was still found constantly at Bratt's Lake and detected from most samples collected at Hafford and Waskesiu during the sampling period. Except in few cases, atrazine, alachlor and metolachlor were not detected during the study.

Among the several incidents of pesticide contamination in India. In 1958, more than 100 people died in Kerala due to the consumption of wheat flour contaminated with parathion (Gupta, 2004). The same study reported that in India, 51% of food commodities are contaminated with pesticide residues, 20% of which have pesticides residues above the maximum residue level values on a worldwide basis. This means people are continuously exposed with variety of pesticides in their daily life. Suppression of immune system, disruption of hormones, reproductive abnormalities and cancer are some of the results of such contamination. DDT, γ-HCH and malathion are the major pesticides used in India and account for more than 70% of total pesticide used in India. Bhopal disaster which was one of the world's tragic chemical accidents where the accidental release of methyl isocyanate from a pesticide production plant killed over 7000 people immediately and over 15000 people were killed by the effects of toxins later on (AI, 2004). The effects of the toxic gas still suffering people for series of chronic diseases. Hence, any synthetic chemical once exposed in the atmosphere either from accidents or from application as pesticides has long term and health and environmental impacts.

Szyrwinska and Lulek (2006) conducted a study on the exposure of breast fed infants to polychlorinated biphenyls (PCBs) and selected organochlorine pesticides (OCPs) in the Wielkopolska province (Poland) in samples collected in 2000-2001. The result of the analysis showed that median exposure of Wielkopolska first breast-fed infants to OCPs 0.086-3.495 μ g/kg body weight/day). The same study showed the exposure to PCBs of about 0.364 lg/kg body weight/day. These OCPs continue to contaminate the breast milk as mothers are exposed to the environment where these pesticides were applied. According to Rial-Otero et al.(2006), different OCPs, organophosphorus pesticides (OPPs), acaricides fluvalinate, coumaphos and bromopropylate residues were the most common pesticides detected in the samples of honey produced in France, Jordan, Italy, Portugal, Spain and Switzerland. The other two OPPs detected were methidation and methiocarb, in ecological honey from Spain.

Pesticides in Soil and Water Resources

Morvan et al. (2006) carried out a study to determine the contamination of pesticides in the groundwater of a spring draining a sandy aquifer in France from October 1999 to August 2004. In the study area, atrazine (At) was used as pesticides since the sixties until 1999 and At and deethylaltrazine (DEA) were found in quantifiable concentrations, from 0.07 to 0.43 µg l^{-1} for At, and between 0.14 and 1.16 µg l^{-1} for DEA in the outlet of ground water. Isoproturon (0.3 µg l^{-1}) and chlortoluron (0.7 and 2.0 µg l^{-1}) were also detected in some samples. This study showed that the annual mean flux of cumulated At and DEA were found stable which was referred as the indication of long time transfer of these chemicals in unsaturated an saturated zone with continuous leaching of At and DEA accumulated in the soil. Similar study carried out in Hungary to determine the pesticide residues in soil and ground water also indicated the contamination of soil and ground water from the pesticide exposure.

According to Oldal et al. (2006), atrazine was found at a concentration of 0.07 -0.11 µg g^{-1} in 2 of 24 samples evaluated. In ground water samples, concentration of atrazine 166–3067 ng mL^{-1}, acetochlor 307– 2894 ng mL^{-1}, diazinon 15–223 ng mL^{-1}, prometryn 109–160 ng mL^{-1} were detected. In addition to this, 10 other pollutants such as polycyclic aromatic hydrocarbons (PAH), orthorhombic sulphur, 1,3 methano-octahydro-penthalene and others were detected. It can be inferred that this synthetic pesticide has very low degradation and absorption properties as seen in the saturated and unsaturated zone. Even though, ground water is considered good for drinking purposes without treatment, contamination in deep aquifers seen recently in many places of the world by synthetic chemicals is making irreversible damage to the water resources putting in danger the whole ecosystem. The major impacts could be on the human and animal species creating long-term health problems including cancer and diabetes.

Chhetri and Islam (2006d) developed a pathway on how the pesticides and antibiotics from the manufacturing industry and consumption enter into the ground water source and soil after their application (Figure 12.3). The pesticide contamination occurs in the produce which enters into human body their food chain. The pesticide which is blown by wind remains in the atmosphere and inhaled by the people and animals. The soil is also contaminated by pesticides which ultimately leach into the surface ground water source. Water sources also receive contamination from the treated waste water that is discharged into the water bodies.

Pesticides in Fruits

A study carried out to evaluate 10 pesticide residues in oranges and tangerines in Valencia (Spain) reported the occurrence in different concentrations (Blasco et al., 2006). The liquid chromatographic-mass spectrometry (LC–MS) analysis of 10 pesticides namely bitertanol, carbendazim, hexythiazox, imazalil, imidacloprid, methidathion, methiocarb, pyriproxyfen, thiabendazole and trichlorfon were carried out. The results of the analysis are presented in Table 12.4. Carbendazim was detected in more than 50% of the samples and methiocarb was detected only in 2% samples. The result further showed that 63% of the samples contained only one of the carbendazim, hexythiazox, or methidathion, 21% of the samples contained two pesticide residues, 13% samples contained 3 pesticides residues and 2% samples were found to have 4 pesticide residues. The study concluded that the contamination levels of these pesticide residues were not considered a serious public health problem according to European Union (EU) regulations. However, it has been widely reported that pesticides are linked to a spectrum of human health hazards ranging from short-term impacts such as headache and nausea to chronic impacts such as cancer, diabetes, reproductive harms, and hormone disruptions. Chronic health impacts may occur even after minimal exposure to them into the natural environment or ingestion of their residues through food and water (Fong, 1999).

Pesticide and Climate Change

The climate change due to global warming is likely to have several impacts on the fate of pesticide into the environment. Changes in seasonality of rainfall, increases intensity and increased global temperature could be the major climate drivers that may change the pesticide fate and behaviour in the soil and ground water (Bloomfield et al., 2006). However, this relation will not be straight forward as in the case of climate change. Due to increase in rainfall pattern, the flux of pesticide flow could be faster than ever. Due to the temperature rise and subsequent increase in evaporation and evapotranspiration, the transport of pesticides through the water cycle and soil will be different than predicted today. As the temperature and rainfall increases, there will be more weeds, pests and disease in warm and wet climates. More frequent intense rainfall events may increase the erosion of pesticide-rich soil particles from fields to drains and surface waters. Dry soils will have low biodegradation potential than wet soils. This will also have impacts in the pesticide resistance of individual weeds and this can be influenced easily by climate variables. It is likely that the pesticides residues and their metabolites would be more reactive at elevated temperature and may have severe impacts than before. Hence, climate change may have significant impact in the fate of pesticides in the environment.

Table 12.4. Pesticide residue and their concentration in different samples evaluated (Blasco et al., 2006)

Pesticide residue	Occurred in % of samples	Concentration (mg kg^{-1})
Carbendazim	51.9%	0.02–0.04
Hexythiazox	42.3%	0.02–0.05
Imazalil	15.0%	0.02–1.2
Imidacloprid	9.6%	0.02–0.07
Methidathion	32.6%	0.06–1.3
Methiocarb	2%	0.02

Rational for the Development of Natural and Non-toxic Pesticides

The use of synthetic pesticides is growing exponentially in the world. Of the 2.5 million tons of synthetic chemicals, 73% of this amount is produced in ten companies of the five countries: France, the U.S.A., Germany, Britain and Switzerland (Van der Gaag, 2000). These chemicals are designed to often kill many species of living organism in unspecific manner. It is estimated that less than 5% of the pesticides application reach to the target organism and rest are exposed to the non-target organism. More than 95% of these chemicals are composed of many products which are highly toxic. As the organisms develop resistance against these synthetic pesticides, production of new and even more toxic pesticides is increasing continuously. Resistance to DDT occurred after the five years of its application. Today, more drugs are being produced to control multiple drug resistance organisms.

According to WHO, more than 200,000 people worldwide are killed every year as a direct effect of pesticide poisoning which was increased from 30,000 in 1990 (Van der Gaag, 2000). It was further reported that 3000,000 people are poisoned by these pesticides annually and more than 50% of them are children of age 10. Crinnion (2000) reported that pesticides are highly persistent in nature. A national human adipose tissue survey carried out by US EPA since 1976 found DDE which is a primary metabolite of DDT in 93% of the samples in 1982. A survey of adipose tissue levels of toxic compounds in autopsy specimens from elderly Texans found DDE, dieldrin, oxychlordane and heptachlor epoxide in 100% of the samples in 1990. Occurrence of DDT residues in all the samples even after banning of DDT in 1972 clearly indicates that these synthetic pesticides which are highly persistent in the environment are serious threat to the human health and environment in the long term.

Since these pesticides are from synthetic origin, the environmental problems created by these pesticides would further be aggravated due to the resistance developed by organisms and continued production of new pesticides. These synthetic chemicals which are generally the halogenated compounds with very long half-lives, are virtually non-existent in nature and nature can not degrade them easily. As they persist for a long time in the environment, their impact to the living species would continue for hundreds and thousands of years. These synthetic chemicals are hardly biodegradable but will change the course from one medium to another in food chain and natural hydrological cycles. Due to the health and environmental problems created by synthetic pesticides, there is a tremendous pressure to develop more environmentally friendly and non-toxic pesticides. The increasing evidence of pesticides resistance organisms is also fueling the development of new and efficient pesticides. Hence, natural compounds are increasingly becoming the focus in these days.

Due to the toxicity and environmental impacts caused by the synthetic pesticides, search for more environmentally appealing and toxicologically safe natural pesticides has become an urgent need. As the insects develop resistance against synthetic pesticides, there is a need to develop natural pesticides that do not develop resistance. Tens of thousands of secondary products of plants have been identified and there are estimates that hundreds of thousands of these compounds exist in nature (Duke, 1990). These compounds are involved for interacting with other species to defend themselves from other pests. These secondary compounds represent large reservoirs of chemicals with biological function. This is a huge resource to be tapped for use as pesticides. Some pesticides that are derived from plants are already in use. However, in many cases, the natural plant extracts are modified by using synthetic chemicals during extraction and processing. This has always been the case in the development of any products in the past. Since these products will be contaminated by toxic chemicals, this will not offer the similar benefit as those if they were naturally extracted or processed. Lal Chitta from Bangladesh has been tested as natural pesticides Various other plants extracts such as Neem and plant oils such as Jatropha are also discussed in this paper. These plant fruits, extracts and oils are renewable sources leading to a sustainable supply for the long term. Moreover, these plants work as large sink of carbon dioxide.

12.3 BIOPESTICIDES

Application of naturally available microorganisms which has ability to control or suppress pest population has recently received considerable attention. Control or suppression of weeds, fungal or bacterial phytopathogens and invertebrate pests can be achieved by applying high doses of biopesticides to soils, seeds or crops (Hynes and Boyetchko, 2006). Unlike, synthetic pesticides, biopesticides are pest specific and generate little or no toxicity to non-target species. There are several microorganisms which have been successfully applied for the pest control has been presented by Hynes and Boyetchko (2006). Table 12.5 is the summary of some of the registered biopesticides in different countries for specific pest control.

Biopesticides uses increased from 1.4 % in 1995 (Gaugler, 1997) to 2.9% in 2001 (Anonymous, 2002). Despite the numerous environmental threats posed by synthetic pesticides, the development of commercial biopesticides is growing at slow pace as it generates major changes in production techniques and shift in input. Biological pesticides among others include pheromones, plant regulators, and microbial organisms such as *Bacillus thuringiensis* (Bt) as well as pest predators, parasites, and other beneficial organisms (Uri, 1998). It was further indicated that the growth of biopesticide use is always difficult to predict because of regulatory procedures and unknown biopesticide production costs relative to synthetic pesticides. However, as banning of chemicals has almost been a daily affair, and many synthetic chemicals may need to be removed from the market soon, development of biopesticides exist huge potential in the foreseeable future (Chhetri and Islam, 2007a). The European Union has scheduled a 56% reduction of synthetic pesticides of 1991 level by 2008 (Montesinos, 2003). In the US, the Food Quality Protection Act implemented in 1996 requires a reevaluation of all carbamate and organophosphate insecticides by 2006 for compliance to new standards. Similarly, a recent review by federal government regulators in Canada has determined that over 4000 chemicals once thought to be benign are potentially dangerous for the physical health of Canadians (Mittelstaedt, 2006a). The likely outcome of all of these activities necessitates the development of wide range of biopesticides from micro organisms and natural pesticides from plant extracts.

Table 12.5. Registered biopesticides in different countries (Hynes and Boyetchko, 2006)

Beneficial microorganism	Target species	Country of registration
Bacteria		
Agrobacterium radiobacter	Crown gall	Australia, Canada, New Zealand, USA
Bacillus circulans	Damping off (bacterial) diseases	USA
Bacillus subtilis	Damping off (bacterial) diseases	USA, Canada
Bacilum pumilus	Root and leaf fungal diseases	USA
Paenibacillus polymyxa	Damping off, Powdery mildew	Korea, USA
Pseudomonas syringae	Fruit surface molds	USA
Pseudomonas chlororaphis	Cereal leaf diseases	Austria, Finland, Norway, Sweden
Streptomyces griseoviridis	Root and leaf fungal diseases	Canada, Denmark, Finland, Hungary, Iceland, Italy, Netherlands, Norway, Spain, Sweden, Switzerland, USA
Streptomyces lydicus	Several soil borne plant diseases	USA
Fungi		
Ampelomyces quisqualis	Powdery mildew	Korea
Aspergillus flavus	Aspergillus	USA
Fusarium oxysporum	Fusarium oxysporum diseases	Czech Republic
Gliocladium catenulatum	Several fungal diseases	Finland
T. polysporum	Several fungal pathogens	Denmark, Sweden, USA
Bioherbicides—fungi		
Chondrostereum purpureum	Hardwood tree species	Canada, USA
Colletotrichum leave	Black and gold wattle	South Africa
Bacillus thuringiensis	Several insect species	Australia, Canada, France, Greece, Italy, Korea, USA
Beauveria bassiana	Several insect species	Denmark, Italy, Japan, Mexico, Spain, Sweden, USA
Beauveria brongniartii	Sugar cane beetle	France, Switzerland
Lagenidium giganteum	Mosquito	USA
Virus		
Granulosis virus	Codling moth	Austria, Belgium, Germany, Greece, Italy, Spain, Switzerland, USA
Nuclear polyhedrosis virus	Celery looper, Cabbage looper, Diamondback moth and others	Canada, USA

12.4. PLANT BASED OILS AS PESTICIDES

Tens of thousands of secondary products of plants have been identified and there are estimates that hundreds of thousands of these compounds exist naturally (Duke, 1990). These products are involved in the interaction of plants with other species-specially the defense of the plant from plant pests. These compounds represent a large reservoir of chemical structures with numerous biological activities and have yet to be tapped for use as natural pesticides. Plant oils such as olive oil, Jatropha oil, Neem oil and several other oils can be used as natural pesticides (Chhetri et al., 2007e).

All plants produce some compounds that are phytotoxic to other plants. There are several natural products that have been developed as pesticides. However, these natural compounds except in few cases have been modified through some external processing resulting in the alteration of their inherent characteristics. Benzoic acid derived from from the plants is generally made more active by halogen substitution. Some of the benzoic acid derivatives such as dicamba (3,6-dichloro-2-methoxybenzoic acid) are being widely used as herbicides. However, substituting the halogen compounds would eventually make the product more toxic. It is not enough to use the plant derivatives as a source for pesticide but it is also important that these natural extracts are processed in natural way without addition of synthetic chemicals and catalysts. Some of the plant based natural pesticides such as Lal chitta and Soapnut based pesticides have been tested and results have been described. Some of the wider application of Neem based pesticides is also summarized.

Jatropha Oil

Insecticidal and Molluscicidal Properties of Jatropha Oil

Chhetri et al. (2007b) summarized the multiple use of Jatropha. All parts of the Jatropha plant have traditional medicinal uses (both human and veterinary purposes). The oil is a strong purgative, widely used as an antiseptic for cough, skin diseases, and as a pain reliever from rheumatism. Jatropha latex can heal wounds and also has anti-microbial properties. The ground seeds showed molluscicidal activities against the host of liver fluke, a disease found in the Philippines. The oil and oil extracts can be used to treat Schistosomiasis (Bilharziasis) which is a human disease caused by parasitic blood flukes of the genus *Schistosoma*. The use of *J. curcas* oil for the control of cotton insect pests is a promising alternative to hazardous chemicals (Solsoloy, 1993). The study showed that the treatment with *J. curcas* oil extract did not affect the population of beneficial arthropods unlike in chemical treatment. Jatropha *curcas* also showed potential in control of the sorghum pests, the crude oil being more efficient than the methanolic extract (Mengual, 1997).

Saponins are glycosides with foaming characteristics. These can be used as natural pesticides as the saponins have antibacterial characteristics. Use of saponins as natural pesticides would be beneficial to the environment as no synthetic chemicals are introduced. Latex from Jatropha has also antimicrobial properties and can be used to treat wounds and skin infections (Kosasi et al, 1989). Latex from Jatropha carcus is used to treat malaria fever in Nepal (Manandhar, 1989). In Egypt, it is used to treat arthritis, gout and jaundice (Khafagy et al., 1977). Several compounds with anti-tumour activities have also been reported in *Jatropha* species.

Neem Based Pesticides

Neem is a well known herbal plant in the tropical regions of the world. Singh et al. (1996) studied the molluscicidal property of *Azadirachta indica* A. Juss (neem) against the snails *Lymnaea acuminata* and *Indoplanorbis exustus*. They observed that the molluscicidal activity of the leaf, bark, cake, neem oil and the neem-based pesticides, achook and nimbecidine, were both effective pesticides depending on the dose and time of application. The toxic effect of pure azadirachtin (a biopesticide obtained from neem) against both the snails was greater than the synthetic molluscicides. The use of neem products and neem-based pesticides against harmful snails is less expensive and less hazardous to the environment than synthetic molluscicides. Gajalakshmi and Abbasi (2004) study neem as potential fertilizer as well as pesticide. The study showed that the neem leaf composted (vermicompost) worked effectively both as fertilizer as well as pesticide.

Schmutterer (1998) reported that azadirachtin-containing neem seed extracts can cause various effects in insects. They act as antifeedants, growth regulators and sterilants. In addition, azadirachtin is a chitin synthesis inhibitor. Good results in insect control were found with azadirachtin containing seed extracts under field conditions. Inspite of the sensitivity of insects of most orders to azadirachtin, neem products are selective as they do not harm important natural enemies of pests. Neem-seed extracts are considered potential natural pesticides for integrated pest control in developing as well as in developed countries.

Kreutzweiser et al. (2002) evaluated the impact of neem based plant extract azadirachtin in community level disruptions among zooplankton of pond mosocosms in Canada. The result showed that the trends in abundance over time among populations of cladocerans, copepods, and rotifers were found to differ significantly among treatments. At the two highest test concentrations of azadirachtin, adverse effects were observed with significant reductions in several cladoceran species, and near elimination of the three major copepod species present in the sample. Hence it indicates that neem based plant extracts are effective insecticides. The application of this natural extract has no adverse impact in the environment.

Olive Oil

Olive oil has also been reported to have aniti-microbial properties and the ability to inhibit substances that lead to inflammation. Olive oil contains flavonoids that help protect cells and inhibit histamine. It is reported that because of such properties, a natural combination of honey, olive oil, and beeswax can provide significant benefit to people suffering from eczema or psoriasis.

12.5. PLANTS EXTRACTS AS PESCIDES

Lal Chitta as Pesticide

The scientific name of Lal chitta is plumbago Rosea Linn. Locally it is called Lal chitta or Raktachitrak. It is called 'Officinal leadwort or Rosy leadwort. Lal chitta is a tropical tree which is available throughout India, Pakistan and Bangladesh. This tree is generally of 2-3 ft high available perennially with climbing zigzag stems. It has large obovate-ecliptic leaves, tapering to short clasping to stalk. The main stalk is smooth and the flower is 1-2 inch long red calyx covered with granular hairs. Root contains an acrid crystalline principle called 'Plumbagin.' Plumbagin is present in all the varieties of plumbago to a maximum of about 0.91%. It ahs also been reported that root can be used to increase the digestive power and promote appetite. Plumbagin stimulates the central nervous system in small doses, while with larger doses paralysis sets in leading ultimately to death. The tincture of bark of this herb has anti-septic properties that can be used as pesticides.

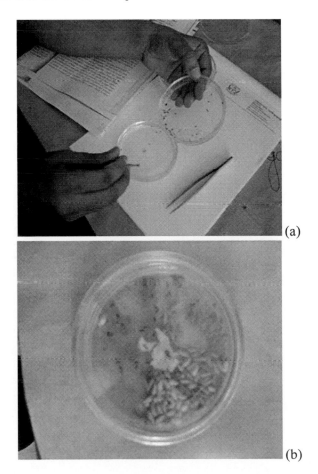

(a)

(b)

Figure 12.4. (a) and (b). Experiment on insecticidal properties of Lal chitta (Mymensing University Bangladesh).

The root of this plant is very acrid, stimulant, diaphoretic, and stomachic, sialogogue, abortifacient and vesicant. It is narcotic and irritant in large doses. This is given in dyspepsia, intermittent fevers, diarrhea, piles, anasarca, skin diseases, skin diseases, rheumatism and paralysis. The paste of the root made with water or some bland oil is applied as an embrocation over rheumatic and paralytic parts. The paste is also used as glandular tumors, buboes, abscesses. If the paste is made with salt and water, it can be used for obstinate skin diseases. The root of this her is used to treat the enlarge spleen. The fresh juice of the root is very acrid and blisters the skin. Hence, in this experiment, the extract from the Lal chitta bark is used as pesticides for treating for rice weevil, pulse beetle and red flour beetle (Figure 12.4 [a, b]). The common hosts for rice weevil are Rice, paddy, rice hulls, wheat, flour, maize, pea, gram, kheshari, mung, for pulse beetle are Pea, gram, kheshari, mung, mashkalai and for red flour beetle are Flour, wheat, rice (broken), suji, gram, mixed feed. These three insects are the major insects that make serious production loss or damage in the mentioned hosts. Figure 12.5 shows the result of the experiment for which the La chitta extract was used as insecticide. In this experiment, 10 insects were taken for the case study in each case. The Lal chitta extract was used in the concentration of 4%, 2%, 1%, 0.5%, and 0.25% weight per ml. Out of 10 rice weevil evaluated for the study, only six remained alive after 6 hours of treatment which is similar for all the three number of experiments. The result of the experiment for 12 hours after treatment and 24 hours after treatment are presented in Figure 12.6 and Figure 12.7. The results for test carried out on pulse beetle are shown in Figure 12.8, 12.9 and 12.10 for six hours, twelve hours and twenty four hours of treatment respectively. Similarly, the results for red flour beetle are shown in Figure 12.11, 12.12 and 12.13 for six, twelve and twenty four hours after treatment respectively. In all cases, all insects were killed when the test was carried out with 0.25% concentration. This can be expanded in the practical application as a complete control of the insects.

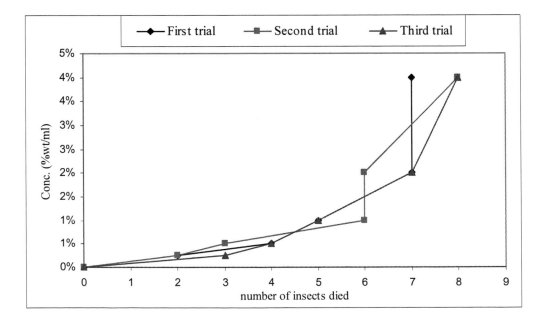

Figure 12.5. Experimental result after six hours of treatment for rice weevil.

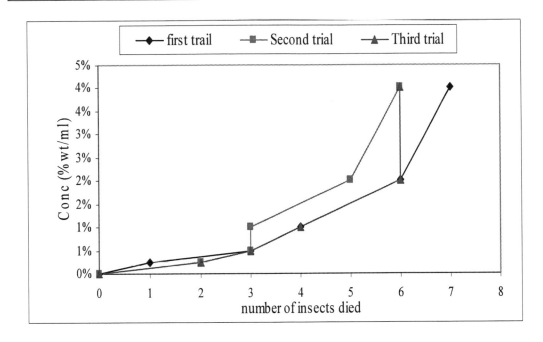

Figure 12.6. Experimental result after twelve hours of treatment for rice weevil.

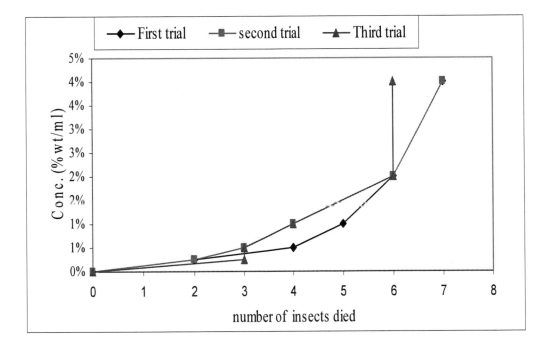

Figure 12.7. Experimental result after twenty four hours of treatment for rice weevil.

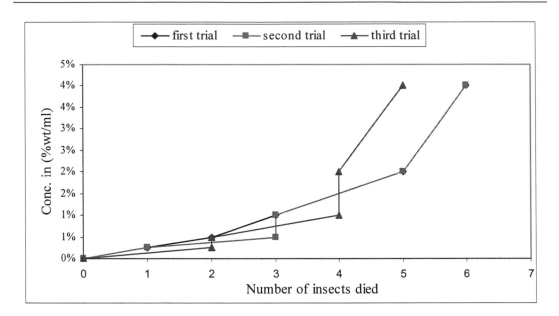

Figure 12.8. Experimental result after six hours of treatment for pulse beetle.

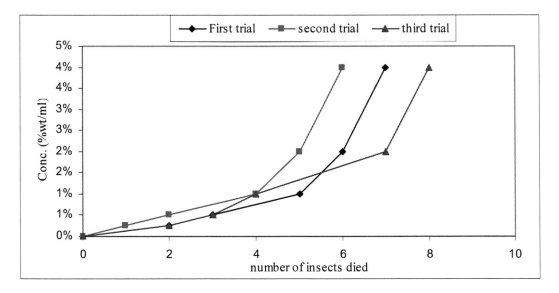

Figure 12.9. Experimental result after twelve hours of treatment for pulse beetle.

Soapnut as Pesticide

Soapnut *(Sapindus Mukorosse)* are fruits of a tropical tree widely available in India, Nepal, Bangladesh and other tropical climates where people have been washing their laundries for hundreds of years. These are basically two types: big (*S. Mukorosse* which are usually cultivated in north India and Nepal) and small (Sapindus Trifoliatus) which is cultivated in south India (Website 19). The soapnut shell contains 'saponins' which works as a naturally available soap when making contact with water. This saponin which has highly cleaning capability repels varmints, fungus and bacteria. The soapnut dry fruit contains 11.5% saponin, 10% carbohydrate and the seeds contain 45.4% oil and 31% protein (Kamra et al., 2006). This is one of the best detergents available naturally. Soapnut is used by the industry to produce soap adding several chemicals in it. The addition of chemicals to soapnut to make soap changes its inherent characteristics making more toxic that it was earlier. However, soapnut can be directly used for various purposes without adding any chemicals. The use of a number of allergic synthetic chemicals is steadily increasing in our society. Most of these synthetic chemicals aggravate the ailment of people with sensitive skin and suffering from neurodermatitis. The chemicals used in the synthetic detergents are mostly allergic creating several skin problems.

Soapnut (Sapindus mukorossi) plant is a rich source of saponins. Soapnuts have unbeatable advantages over synthetic detergents. Soap or detergents from soapnut can be made 100% natural only with soapnut without adding any chemicals (Website 19). Due to this reason, this is perfect to use for those who has sensitive skin, allergies with synthetic detergent and people suffering from neurodermatitis problems. As this does not any chemical addition or any complicated process, soapnut is a cheap option. The laundries washed with soapnut become truly soft. One of the most advantages of soapnut is that it preserves the color of valuable laundry better than any chemical detergents. Soapnut is the best solution for even the finest silk to wash without any damaging effect. Soapnuts are completely biodegradable. The byproducts and unused products do not pollute environment. Production of soapnut is completely renewable as these trees recycle carbon dioxide to produce fresh oxygen.

Figure 12.14. Soapnut fruit

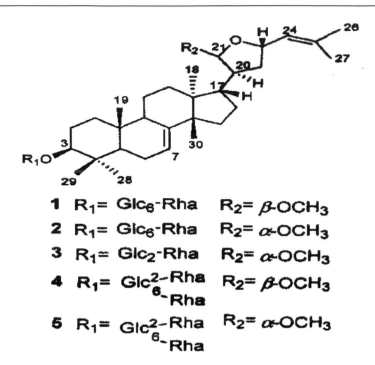

1 R₁= Glc₆-Rha   R₂= β-OCH₃

2 R₁= Glc₆-Rha   R₂= α-OCH₃

3 R₁= Glc₂-Rha   R₂= α-OCH₃

4 R₁= Glc²₆-Rha   R₂= β-OCH₃
           -Rha

5 R₁= Glc²₆-Rha   R₂= α-OCH₃
           -Rha

Figure 12.15. Tirucallane-type saponins assay (Huang et al., 2005).

Planting soapnut is highly sustainable solution to the current synthetic detergents which is environmentally problematic. In general, soapnut tree gives fruits after nine years of plantation, has long life and can be harvested up to ninety years. Soapnut trees are also capable of changing wasteland into fertile soil and help to combat desertification. Besides its use as soap and detergent, it has several applications. This can be use to make shampoo (sud) that fights dandruff (Website 19). As it is natural and does not contain any synthetic chemicals, it will not irritate the scalp. Soapnut can also be used to clean household pets such as dog, cat, and horse. This can also be used for cleaning the utensils, kitchen and bathroom. A highly concentrated soapnut sud can easily be filled into a dispenser to use it as a liquid soap. This can also be used for cleaning the cars. Figure 12. 14 shows the picture of soapnut fruit while Figure 12.5 is the structure of soapnut pericarp shell through NMR.

The saponins derived from soapnuts can also be used as cleanser and detergent. Soapnut has also excellent anti-microbial and anti-inflammatory properties (Focus on surfactant, 2002).

Future Pathway for Natural Pesticides

We live in chemical world, ingesting, inhaling and absorbing synthetic chemicals in almost every activity of our lives. Thousands of chemicals which are involved in daily activities such as pesticides are becoming a great threat to our health and environment. The series of chemicals which are available in the market are based on 'detection limit' rather than long-term implications. The technology today is only capable of detecting certain level of contamination and this eventually become the standard. Miralai (2006) however, showed that the long term effect of a synthetic chemical is higher in lower concentrations unlike in organic chemicals, the long term benefit at lower concentration is actually higher (Figure 12.16). The use of synthetic chemicals is harmful in all cases whether it has low or high concentration. Hence, fulfilling any standard which is based on the detection limit should not be taken as a big accomplishment because as shown in Figure 12.16, the harm at the lower concentration even higher in long-term.

All synthetic pesticides and other chemicals fall under this category and they have to be removed from the market today or tomorrow. However, removing or banning of a chemical has not contributed any good to the society as banning of one chemicals ends up inventing another toxic chemical as in case of DDT which was replaced by chlorpyrifos. Chlorpyrifos also has several toxic effects. Despite several attempts to shift to the natural and biopesticides, the industries are repeating similar mistakes. Taking any chemicals from a natural source is not a solution but the production technology should completely follow a truly natural process without addition of any synthetic chemicals during processing. There are some evidences that in the name of biopesticides, genetically modified microorganisms have been developed to be used as biopesticides. In this case, the results have not been as attractive as it was envisaged earlier. The pests develop resistance against them and the production has not been achieved despite significant investment in the pest control from biological methods.

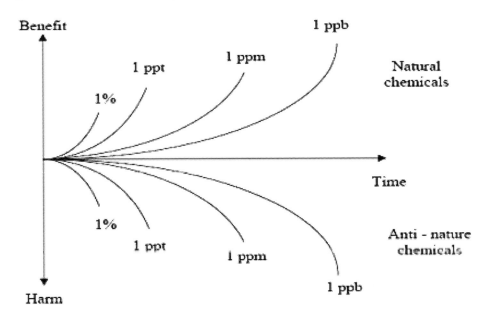

Figure 12.16. Long-term relation between concentration of chemicals and their positive or negative effects (redrawn from Miralai, 2006).

Sharma (2006) reported that farmers in Madhya Pradesh of Indian state are leading the cotton farming in India skipping both the use of pesticides and genetically modified cotton called Bt cotton. He further reported that there are 28 predators of American bollworm which are the main enemies of cotton. These predators will devour the bollworm if synthetic pesticides are not sprayed. Hence, spraying pesticides creates more problems than it was before. Bt was considered as magic bullet in India, however, the suicidal rate among Indian farmers have been highly increased due to the pile of debt they are incurring as they have to pay too much for pesticides as well as for 'technology fee' for the seed companies. The same report indicated that the Chinese farmers who were involved in Bt cotton farming are incurring huge losses due to spurt in secondary pests despite it was earlier projected as silver bullet. The farmers had to spray 20 times more pesticides which considerably increased the production cost. Genetic modification which is anti-natural has never been beneficial in the long term. In case of pesticides, the modified species necessitates the use of more pesticides which finally will develop resistance and the whole system will not be sustainable. Thus, development any technology should completely be based zero tolerance, zero waste and zero emission. Only the natural extracts from plants and biopesticides. Pathways in the whole life cycle ahs a great role to play in order to any product beneficial to the human and environment.

It is well established that the secondary metabolites present in plants provide protection against predators, pathogens and invaders because of their anti-microbial activity. Majority of these compounds found in the plants are lignins, tannins, saponins, volatile essential oils, alkaloids, etc. These compounds have specific anti-microbial activities which can be used to manipulate the rumen fermentation by selective inhibition of a microbial group of the ecosystem (Kamra et al., 2006). Moreover, the ethanol extract of soapnut seed pulp completed inhibited in vitro methane production along with a significant reduction in protozoa count and acetate/propionate ratio.

The experimental results of soapnut and Lal chitta show that they have excellent microbial activities. Soapnut, because of its anti-microbial activities, it can be used as pesticide as well as soap. Lal chitta also has excellent anti-microbial properties and is very much effective in controlling rice weevil, the pulse beetle and the red flour beetle. Neem is similar tree which has anti-microbial properties and are being used as natural pesticide. Hence, natural plant fruit and extract have great potential to be used as natural pesticides. Development of pesticides from plant oil and extracts are inherently sustainable in the long-term as they do not have negative health and environmental impacts.

Chapter 13

OFFICE GADGETS

13.1. TONERS

Toners are used for laser printers and photocopiers. This forms text and images in the paper. Earlier it used to be of carbon but these days, carbon particles are blended with polymer. Polymer particles are melted by the heat causing it to bind to the fibres in the paper. Some examples of such polymers are styrene, acrylate copolymer or a polyester resin. The particle size of the toners are of the range of 8 micrometers which is 600 dots per inch. The modern printer and photocopier catriges are made of plastic materials and creates environmental problems once they are disposed. Toner materials remain suspended in air which is considered toxic and potentially can create irritation, asthma, bronchitis and other diseases. Some of the toners are also considered carcinogenic.

Possible Toxicity Form Toners and Ink

Various petroleum and polymer based carriers, additives and resins are used in ink making. Mineral oils and hydrocarbon resins, UV resins, mineral oils and phenol-formaldehyde rosin esters, polyvinyl alcohol (PVOH) homopolymer, copolymer are also used. Since the polymeric compounds are highly toxic compounds, the ink, printers and toner materials have severe effects on public health. These petroleum based materials are non biodegradable and pose threat in environment. Moreover, the dyes or coloring pigments are also toxic chemicals and have negative environmental effects. Pigments in inks may contain heavy metals, such as lead, which can be harmful to people's health and the environment. This is particularly a concern if the final product will be used by children. Long-term exposure to the volatile organic compounds (VOCs) found in some inks and solvents may cause employee's health problems (Volpe, 1996). It was recently reported that there is a significant health threat for the workers working in laser printer environment and potentially danger of (Bryant, 2007). The study was conducted on Canon, HP Color Laserjet, Ricoh and Toshiba. Even though, this report does not explain the chemical composition of the particulates emitted, it is suspected that the impacts of these particulates range from respiratory irritation to more severe illnesses, such as cancer. As the lasers printer toners are usually made of thermoplastic materials and synthetic dyes, it is likely that the emission contain highly carcinogenic materials.

13.2. INK

In a Christian Science Monitor article published on September 27, 2004 on the development of ink, it was mentioned that the Chinese invented ink 5000 years ago. The ink at that time was a mixture of soot from pine smoke and lamp oil, thickened with gelatin from animal skins and musk. The ancient known writings consist of drawings carved into cave walls. Thousands of years ago, Greek started using bone or metals to scratch marks in wax which made the movement of writings easier than those carved into the walls. Others cultures used to make inks from berries, plants and minerals. Dated back in 2000 BC, it was found that Egyptians, Romans, Greeks, and Hebrews were using paper made from the papyrus plant and parchment made out of animal skins.

Chinese developed a solid ink on about 300 AD, which was in the form of stick or cake. Before using, the cake used to be shaved and melted with water. Iron salts such as ferrous sulfate (treating iron with sulfuric acid) was mixed with tannin from trees with a thickener. In 12th century in Europe, ink was made out of tree barks soaked in water and boiled adding some wine in it. This used to be dried in the sun until it dries. The mixture was mixed with wine and iron salt over a fire to make the final ink.

From 19th century inks are based on new ammonia based aniline dye technology which leads to modern ink. Modern ink uses aniline dye colors with various additives such as ethylene glycol (to maintain flow viscosities) and phenols. Phenols are used to prevent bacterial growth. The offset printing ink consists of many resins and solvents which are toxic. However, the most recent developments in the ink industry are trying to focus on water-based and vegetable oil-based ink which has no health and environmental problems.

Materials Used to Make Ink

An ink consists of base material, colorant, carrier and additives. This is a colorant and a liquid or paste to carry the color to bind it to the base such as paper. Various types of dyes and pigments are used to give color to the ink. Basically all commercial based ink are made out of petroleum based materials, carrier, additives and colorant. In ancient time, to make lasting color of ink, crushed barriers, different types of barks and some plants were used. Certain minerals ground to powder for coloring. Carbon from soot makes a deep black

Inks are composed of three major elements; pigments for color, binders to hold pigments to each other and to the substrate, and solvents that dissolve resins to make the ink fluid. Normally additives such as thinners are added to adjust the viscosity to suit for the particular purpose. The additives for used for UV and plastisol inks are not solvent-based.

- *Oil based Raw materials:* Petroleum oils, Vegetable oils, Soybean oils, solvent vehicles

- *Solvent raw materials:* Alcohols, hydrocarbons, other solvents, water.

- *Colorant Raw materials:* Pigment and dyes

- *Resins:*

  - *Natural resins:* Rosins, nitrocellulose
  - *Synthetic Resins:* Acrylic resins, hydrocarbon resins, Maleic Resins, Phenolic Resins, Polyamide Resins, Sytrene Resins, Thermoplastic Polymers, Vinyl Resins

- *Additives: Wax,* Surfactants, other additives

- *Colorants:* The mutable colorants commonly used are a triaryl methyl dye, monoazo dye, thiazine dye, oxazine dye, naphthalimide dye, azine dye, cyanine dye, indigo dye, coumarin dye, benzimidazole dye, paraquinoidal dye, fluorescein dye, diazonium salt dye, azoic diazo dye, phenylenediamine dye, disazo dye, anthraquinone dye, trisazo dye, xanthene dye, proflavine dye, sulfonephthalein dye, phthalocyanine dye, carotenoid dye, carminic acid dye, azure dye, or acridine dye (Nohr et al, 1997).

- *Organic dye classes include*: dimethylamino, Malachite Green Carbinol hydrochloride, phenylmethylene, 3-benzenediamine monohydrochloride, zinc chloride double salt, dimethylamine, naphthalimide dyes, chlorobenzenediazonium chloride and others (Nohr et al, 1997)

- *Carrier:* Thermoplastics polymer are used as most of the carriers. Thermoplastic polymers as carrier include: polyformaldehyde, trichloroacetaldehyde, acetaldehyde, propionaldehyde, acrylic polymers, polyacrylamide, and tetrafluoroethylene, per fluorinated ethylene-propylene copolymers. Chlorotrifluoroethylene.

Types of Inks

Inks are categorized in four types namely UV (ultraviolet) inks, water-based inks, plastisols, and solvent-based ink. Although the selection of inks is based on the end products, a strong alternative to solvent based inks are being sought as they are hazardous to workers and air pollution concerns. Four categories of inks are described below.

UV inks contain pigments, monomers, oligomers, additives, and modifiers. These inks cure through a photoinitiated radical chain reaction that results in the polymerization of the monomers and oligomers. UV inks are used commonly for printing on plastic, vinyl, metal, and paper. They contain no volatile organic compounds (VOCs) and they will not dry on a press or in the screen reducing the need for cleaning agents. They are limited in flexibility and are not recommended for corrugated surfaces. They are brittle, make finishing operations like die cutting and molding difficult, performance is not as good as traditional solvent based inks in the areas of opacity and color matching. These are not suitable for outdoor use. More care is to be given while handling UV inks since they cause skin sensitivity and contact dermatitis (Volpe, 1996).

Water-based inks contain organic pigments, resins, and additives and can be used on a variety of substrates. These inks are primarily composed of pigments suspended in water, though some still contain up to 15% organic solvents. Water-based inks reduce hazardous material use, VOC emissions, and the amount of solvent needed to clean equipment. However, they can increase drying time and cause paper curl because of the moisture.

Material composition for different color

Color	Materials	Comment
Black	Iron Oxide (Fe_3O_4) Iron Oxide (FeO) Carbon Logwood	Natural black pigment is made from magnetite crystals, powdered jet, wustite, bone black, and amorphous carbon from combustion (soot). Black pigment is commonly made into India ink. Logwood is a heartwood extract from *Haematoxylon campechisnum*, found in Central America and the West Indies.
Brown	Ochre	Ochre is composed of iron (ferric) oxides mixed with clay. Raw ochre is yellowish. When dehydrated through heating, ochre changes to a reddish color.
Red	Cinnabar (HgS) Cadmium Red (CdSe) Iron Oxide (Fe_2O_3) Napthol-AS pigment	Iron oxide is also known as common rust. Cinnabar and cadmium pigments are highly toxic. Napthol reds are synthesized from Naptha. Fewer reactions have been reported with naphthol red than the other pigments, but all reds carry risks of allergic or other reactions.
Orange	disazodiarylide and/or disazopyrazolone cadmium seleno-sulfide	The organics are formed from the condensation of 2 monoazo pigment molecules. They are large molecules with good thermal stability and colorfastness.
Flesh	Ochres (iron oxides mixed with clay)	
Yellow	Cadmium Yellow (CdS, CdZnS) Ochres Curcuma Yellow Chrome Yellow ($PbCrO_4$, often mixed with PbS) disazodiarylide	Curcuma is derived from plants of the ginger family; aka tumeric or curcurmin. Reactions are commonly associated with yellow pigments, in part because more pigment is needed to achieve a bright color.

Color	Materials	Comment
Green	Chromium Oxide (Cr_2O_3), called Casalis Green or Anadomis Green Malachite [$Cu_2(CO_3)(OH)_2$] Ferrocyanides and Ferricyanides Lead chromate Monoazo pigment Cu/Al phthalocyanine Cu phthalocyanine	(Prussian Blue)
Blue	Azure Blue Cobalt Blue Cu-phthalocyanine	Blue pigments from minerals include copper (II) carbonate (azurite), sodium aluminum silicate (lapis lazuli), calcium copper silicate (Egyptian Blue), other cobalt aluminum oxides and chromium oxides. The safest blues and greens are copper salts, such as copper pthalocyanine. Copper pthalocyanine pigments have FDA approval for use in infant furniture and toys and contact lenses. The copper-based pigments are comparatively safer or more stable than cobalt or ultramarine pigments.
Violet	Manganese Violet (manganese ammonium pyrophosphate) Various aluminum salts Quinacridone Dioxazine/carbazole	Some of the purples, especially the bright magentas, are photoreactive and lose their color after prolonged exposure to light. Dioxazine and carbazole result in the most stable purple pigments.

Plastisol inks are used for textiles. These inks are PVC (polyvinyl chloride) resins dispersed in plasticizer that fuse, rather than cure or dry when heated to 320 °F (160 °C) (Kinter, 1992). Plastisol inks release little or no VOC's during fusing. They are popular because they are easy to handle in a variety of climatic conditions. The inks stay wet for long periods of time and can even be left on screens overnight without drying on the screen (Krupinski, 1996).

Conventional *solvent-based inks* consisting of pigments, resins, solvents, and additives are still widely used in screen printing. Solvent-based inks can be used on virtually all substrates. Some substrates, such as styrenes, plastic films, and rubber, can only be printed with solvent-based inks. They are dried by the evaporation of solvent from the ink which results in higher in VOC emissions.

Additives Used in Current Ink

From the evolution of litho printing press, the cleaning became important activity and various types of cleaning agents such as benzenes, aromatic solvents, esters and the blends of these were used. Due to their high vapor pressure and combustibility, the risk was increased.

With 90s environmental regulations, the use of such trichloroethylene or perchloroethylene and other volatile organic compounds were limited. The current low Volatile Organic Compounds cleanings agents are from non aromatic mineral oils or fatty acid esters. Fatty acid esters are preferred because they are renewable, less toxic and biodegradable (Fies,1998). Natural fats and oils are the base materials which comprise fatty acid esters, and there are many different types of these fats and oils available to the chemical industry (Hofer et al., 1997).

The colorants generally used in ink are either dye or pigments. Dye blends with water based solutions which consists of small molecules which stain on paper on molecular level. Whereas Pigmented colorant has larger molecule and is insoluble. However, these days a hybrid of both dye and pigment is generally used in printers like Epson. Besides these, some additives such surfactants, biocides and fungicides are also added.

Environmentally Friendly Inks and Toner Production

Current ink consists of several of toxic polymers, colorants and additives which pose great threat to the environment. These polymeric compounds are non-degradable. Use of bio-based materials for ink and natural colorants is the pre-requisite to produce the environmentally friendly inks and toners. The carbon soot from biomass burning is the non-toxic and most abundant source for toners and inks. Colors from flower extracts and other naturally available materials such as white lime, ochre are some of the colorants naturally available which have no health and environmental impacts. Use of natural colors which are readily biodegradable can reduce the large amount of water treatment cost in the waste streams of toner and ink industries.

13.3. PAPERS

Paper is an important medium indispensable for the communication and information in our lives. However, current paper production has several environmental problems. Over 286 millions tones of paper and board were manufactured in 1994 and 34% of which were derived from recycled materials (World Resource Foundation, 1997). 10 to 17 average sized trees are required to make one tonne of paper. It takes 2.7kg of wood, 130g of calcium carbonate, 8g of sulphur, 40g of chlorine and 300 litres of water to produce 1kg of paper in a large scale paper mill. Pulp and paper industry is the fifth largest industrial consumer of energy leading large amount of CO_2 emission. Paper making industry is one of the highest polluter of toxic liquids with higher biochemical oxygen demand, CO and volatile organic compounds.

Paper is made from the woody and non-woody biomass. Softwood trees such as pine, spruce and hard wood trees such as oak and maple are used for paper making. Plants used for papermaking include cotton, wheat straw, sugar cane waste, flax, bamboo, linen rags, and hemp. Cotton is the most important feedstock to make quality paper. Cellulose fiber component which makes 40-50 % of the biomass is the useful part of the tree to make such papers. Since cellulose is the only part used to make the paper, lignin and other components are to be separated. This process is called pulping.

Paper making is done either by mechanical pulp or chemical pulp. In case of mechanical pulp, pulping is done mechanically or physically. Mechanical pulps are made from wood chips by passing the chips through refiners. Pulps derived mechanically are used to make newsprint and magazine paper, as well as boxes and a variety of other products. Chemical pulping is either done by kraft or sulphate (alkaline) or sulfite (acid or alkaline).

Chemicals Used in Paper Making

Bleaching is one of the major activities in paper making which is used to make the papers white. Bleaching is done by some combination of chlorine, sodium hydroxide, sulfur and hydrogen peroxide as whitening agents. These chemicals are also used as lignin removers. Synthetic chlorine and its compounds are toxic chemicals potentially creating several by products including dioxin. Chlorine is an extremely toxic halogen. It has been reported that potential human exposure to chlorine inhalation occurs in a variety of settings in the workplace due to release from various industrial operation and disinfection uses. A high level exposure to chlorine gas in occupational or environmental settings results in a variety of dose-related lung effects ranging from respiratory mucus membrane irritation to pulmonary edema (Das and Blanc, 1993). The test of pulmonary function after chlorine exposure can reveal either obstructive or restrictive deficits immediately. Due to the use of chlorine during pulping or bleaching process, the waste water stream is contaminated and generally forms trihalomethanes when reacted with other chemicals in water that is carcinogens (Aggazzotti et al., 1998). These trihalomethanes also called organochlorides which do not degrade very well and stored in the fatty tissue of the body such as breast and other fatty areas. These organochlorides cause mutations by altering DNA, suppress immune function and interferes with the natural cell growth.

The other chemicals used in paper manufacturing include sodium hydroxide, sulfur and hydrogen peroxide as whitening agents. These are used to control pH, sizing agents, dry strength adhesives (starch, gums), wet strength resins, fillers (e.g., clay, $CaCO_3$), dyes and pigments, drainage aids, and optical brighteners (McCrady, 2004). Sodium hydroxide may cause eye and skin burn, skin ulcers and corneal damage, permanent damage to the digestive tract, inhalation may lead to chemical pneumonitis, causes chemical burns to the respiratory tract and pulmonary edema (MSDS, 2001). Other chemicals involved in the process have also several toxic effects. The papers have become truly toxic products due to the use of such chemicals. Synthetic dyes and pigments have also several health and environmental problems. Hence current paper production is not environmentally sustainable process.

Environmentally Friendly Paper Production

Paper produced from current production process is toxic and continuously emit the toxic chemicals such as chlorine, sodium hydroxides and some acids. Such papers will more severely affect children's health as they are more vulnerable against toxic chemicals. The synthetic chemicals used in today's paper making are very slow or non biodegradable. The colorants used are also from synthetic sources in addition to the bleaching chemicals. However, earlier paper making before world war were completely natural and non toxic. The papers made from hand or mechanical methods were more durable than the modern papers today. Hence, making environmentally friendly paper is not a new technique but knowledge is necessary to understand the overall impacts of toxic papers into human health and environment.

The major shift necessary to render the current paper production green or environmental friendly needs changes in two things. First, the toxic chemicals should be avoided or replaced with non-toxic or natural chemicals. Second, the coloring agents should be from natural sources such as tree leaves, flowers and other natural dyes. This will not only produce non-toxic paper but will also reduce the treatment cost in the waste streams. The energy to be used for the processing should be derived from the renewable sources such as direct solar, geothermal, and natural biofuels. The CO_2 produces from such sources would be natural CO_2 and essential for the plants to continue photosynthesis. Hence rendering paper production green would reduce health and environmental impacts.

Chapter 14

CONCLUSIONS

14.1. THE SYNTHETIC CHEMICAL ADDICTION

Any substance has certain chemical composition despite the sources and pathways it followed or the phase that it is present in. While this is a common knowledge, it is practically impossible to find a scientist that understands that the composition is constantly changing. It is changing because nature is continuous and any matter must interact with the environment. The interaction is continuous and, hence, time dependent. Therefore, unless it is a matter of arbitrary definition (e.g. sugar and oxidized sugar both being called 'sugar'), there cannot be a matter with constant composition. In addition, any change in composition will invariably affect the reaction rate between a matter and the environment. The property of a matter, therefore, depends on both time and space dimensions. Conventional engineering practices are indifferent to these facts and accept that any natural product/chemicals can be replaced by synthetic product/chemical. Due to this reason, engineering practices, which are supposed to emulate Nature are promoting anti-nature, exactly opposite of what the original promise was. Human engineered pathways make any process worse than it was before intervention. Current technological development mode is, hence, based on the two-time Nobel Laureate Linus Pauling's 'Chemicals are chemicals" approach. This 'Chemicals are chemical" model raises serious questions on whether the current technological development is moving in forward direction or not.

Depending on the origin and pathway, any chemical exhibits different characteristics. For example, it has been believed that vitamin 'C' from natural source can fight cancer, at the same time, synthetic vitamin 'C' has been reported to stimulate cancer because the cancer cells gobbles up the synthetic vitamins. Similarly, estrogens are essential chemicals for human body. However, a recent report showed that synthetic estrogens have a feminizing effect on gonadal differentiation in various species including fish, amphibians, reptiles, and birds. The synthetic fertilizers can never replace organic fertilizers if we consider long-term health and environmental impacts. The simplest example is: If nitrogen from cow dung or tree leafs and Urea synthesized from natural gas is same, why all these people today go for organic food? Hence the biggest misunderstanding today is that current technology development does not differentiate between the natural products and synthetic products if they perform same for short-term.

During the development of synthetic products, the characteristics time of products are violated, hence, the waste products are either not degraded or takes longer time to degrade. Thus, if the life cycles is not considered or simply $\Delta t=0$ is considered, it could be true that both the natural and synthetic products are the same. However, $\Delta t=0$ refers to an aphenomenal state, denoted by time= 'right now'. All synthetic products take longer time to degrade, even after they degrade, they will have negative impacts even in micro level, hence they are inherently unsustainable. The synthetic chemicals addiction has been a great barrier for inherently sustainable technology development as over 85,000 synthetic chemicals are already in the market without considering the long-term impacts into human and the natural environment.

Even though the technology development is intended to help people to increase production and to ease the social life, marketing of technology is carried out based only on some tangible features ignoring its impacts to human and the natural environment. Socially speaking, this means, technologies are currently developed based on tangible gains. Philosophically, this is the 'desire' or 'temptation'driven model that Freud promoted. Scientifically, they are characterized as aphenomenal model, as the promises made are inherently reversed soon after the period of interest or t = 'right now'.

The current technology development mode with miopic approach has offered several ill effects in the modern society. There are some indicators that compel us to conclude that our civilization is not going in the right direction. For example, in last 50 years, the occurrence of cancer went 50 times higher, millions of people are affected by AIDS the cure of which has not yet been found, the osteoporosis, asthma, obesity, Alzheimer, and heart diseases etc have increased in alarming rate. This is due to the synthetic chemical contamination in food items, personal care products, perfumes and ingestion of toxic emissions that contains heavy metals such as lead, chromium, arsenic, aluminum among others. In fact, cancer is nothing but the response of our body against the invasion by synthetic chemicals including synthetic antibiotics. The synthetic based development mode is driving the entire civilization into the wrong path.

Millions of tons of plastics are being produced today as by-products of petroleum refineries. Synthetic plastic which are promoted as the alternative of natural plastic has become one of the most devastating products of this century. Plastic emission is caused either by low temperature oxidation or high temperature oxidation. Cooking pot as a non stick (which is made of Teflon) is made of plastic, which is considered to produce carcinogens that cause cancer. Most of the food items are packaged in plastics which eventually intoxicate the food because of the low temperature plastics oxidation. These plastics are likely to react with the synthetic chemicals which are used to preserve the food items producing several chemical products. Modern engineering structures, insulating materials such as polyurethane and Styrofoam, TV, computer, utensils, clothes, auto parts, tools and equipments are all made of plastic, the list continues for ever. It was recently published in 'science' magazine that the use of plastic carpets is the major causes for developing asthma in adults. The plastic is emission everywhere, the toxic cement in walls, use of highly toxic paints in the structures have left no room where people can escape without inhaling the most toxic elements at every breath they take in. The plastic revolution has created such a perpetual crisis that without plastic life is almost impossible. Most of the synthetic materials invented after the Industrial revolution have one or the other long-term health and environmental impacts. However, nature also produces bio-plastics which are made up of polyhydroxyalkanoate (PHA) and polyhydroxybutyrate (PHB). These plastics are produced naturally by bacteria and hence are entirely biodegradable, non-toxic and can replace the synthetic plastics.

Emission of greenhouse gas particularly CO_2 is of great concern today. Even though CO_2 is considered as one of the major greenhouse gases, production of natural CO_2 is essential for maintaining life on earth. Note that all, CO_2 are not same and plants apparently do not accept all types of CO_2 for photosynthesis. There is a clear difference between the contaminated CO_2 from industrial process and clean CO_2 produced from renewable biofuels such as from wood burning and human respiration. As various toxic chemicals and catalysts are used during fossil fuel refining, the danger of generating CO_2 with higher isotopes cannot be ignored. Hence, it is clear that CO_2 itself is not a culprit for global warming but the industrial CO_2 which is contaminated with catalysts and chemicals, likely becomes heavier with higher isotopes and as a consequence plants cannot accept this CO_2. As the plants have lives as humans have, they always discriminate lighter CO_2 against heavier portion of CO_2 from the atmosphere. While taking in to account the impact of CO_2 for global warming, we must distinguish between natural and industrial CO_2 based on the source from which it is emitted and a pathway of the fuel that emits CO_2 following from source to the combustion.

Current synthetic based technology development is by no means sustainable. The climate change due to global warming has been affecting every species on the globe. Kofi Annan, former Secretary General of UN wrote that based on the available data in UN, greenhouse gas emissions of the major industrialized countries continue to increase bringing the global warming at alarming level. Similarly, Sir Nicholas Stern of Britain, who was the former chief economist of World Bank, referred climate change "the greatest and widest-ranging market failure ever seen," with the potential to shrink the global economy by 20 percent and to cause economic and social disruption at par with the two world wars and the Great Depression. As the current technological development is based on the synthetic development mode, the solution proposed to combat global warming has gone from 'bad' to 'worse' making the world worst place to live in. For example, all the provisions of Kyoto protocol have failed to protect the world's climate change. In the name of emission trading, industrialized countries are 'licensed' to pollute more than ever. Since the warming on earth is a global issue, allowing the production of industrial CO_2 anywhere in the world will eventually have impacts in global scale, thus emission trading can never be a solution to global warming. Of course, until there is no distinction between organic and industrial CO_2, all the solutions to solve the global environmental problems will fail. For example, if we consider the environmental problems created in the last 50 years from human activities and the efforts made to fight against them, there is not a single environmental problem that has been addressed at all, instead, each solution proposed has gone 'bad' to 'worse' mode because they are based on "Chemicals are Chemicals".

14.2. CURING CHEMICAL ADDICTION

The fundamental problem with current technological development is its aphenomenal nature which is based on ignorance or extremely miopic vision. Only knowledge-based technology development can rescue the world from being over flooded from the synthetic chemical addiction. This the approach of obliquity or long-term approach that is based on conscience or good intention (Zatzman and Islam, 2007a). There is not a single synthetic chemical that is not harmful to nature, yet, over 2000 chemicals are being introduced in the market every year. In contrast, banning these synthetic chemicals has also been a daily affair. It is surprising that banning one chemicals results in invention of another chemicals which are not any better. For both cases, the model that is being followed is the same. As the old saying goes, insanity is doing the same thing over and over while expecting different results. This insanity has grasped modern technology development, leading mankind through a spiral down pathway (Zatzman and Islam, 2007b).

Most of modern engineering quests are desperate to look for homogeneity, linearity, single answers to the problems. However, nature operates on diversity, flexibility, heterogeneity, dynamism and multiplicity. Nature works on zero waste and every by-product it produces are the input for another system whereas modern engineering has become synonymous to the hazardous waste generation. Unlike nature which is truly non-static, modern engineering assumes 'static condition' before solving any problems. None of the calculus problem is solvable if we do not assume $\Delta x \to 0$. What would happen if Δx does not tend to zero? Every technology developed today is based on linearization, short-term benefit considering only external or tangible features. Because of synthetic chemicals, which are inherent to the current technology development mode are primarily responsible for every problem on earth, there is no hope for solving these problems without introducing fundamental changes in technology development. A paradigm shift towards knowledge based technology development that truly emulates the science of nature is essential to achieve the long-term sustainability in technology development as well as to avoid chemical addiction. Any technology is considered sustainable only if it is technically feasible, environmentally appealing, economically attractive and socially responsible. The new technology development mode must foster the development of natural products, which are inherently beneficial to the environment. Hence the only way to cure chemical addiction is educate people on the development of nature-based products which are sustainable for the longer term.

14.3. NATURAL SOLUTIONS

Nature has solutions to any problem in the world, because Nature is is perfectly balanced. In other words, nature is inherently sustainable. Sustainability of any technology can be achieved only through emulating Nature. Any time the anti-Nature scheme is implemented, the overall process becomes truly unsustainable. Intention of technology development has a great role to play here as any process starts with intention. If the intention is natural (good) and the process followed is natural (good), the stated objectives could be attained. By emulating nature (from source, i.e., intention to the process, i.e., the pathway, taking into account the global efficiency), all objectives, short-term or long-term, can be achieved. Hence, nature has solutions to any problem and only natural solutions are inherently sustainable.

14.4. BASIS FOR INHERENTLY SUSTAINABLE TECHNOLOGY

Nature thrives on diversity and fl exibility, gaining strength from heterogeneity, whereas the quest for homogeneity seems to motivate much of modern engineering. Nature is non-linear and inherently promotes multiplicity of solutions. Modern Applied Science, however, continues to define problems as linearly as possible, promoting "single"-ness of solution, while particularly avoiding nonlinear problems. Nature is inherently sustainable and promotes zero-waste, both in mass and energy. Engineering solutions today start with a "safety factor" while promoting an obsession with excess (hence, waste). Nature is truly transient, never showing any exact repeatability or steady state. Engineering, however, is obsessed with standards and replication, always seeking "steady-state" solutions.

In nature, all functions are inherently sustainable, efficient and functional for an unlimited time period. In other words, as far as natural processes are concerned, *'time tends to Infinity'*. For example, photosynthesis started to occur as soon as biodiversity started and will continue till then, so as the carbon cycle. This can be expressed as $\Delta t \rightarrow \infty$. By following the same path as the functions inherent in nature, an inherently sustainable technology can be developed. The 'time criterion' is a defining factor in the sustainability and virtually infinite durability of natural functions. The path of sustainable technology is its long-term durability and environmentally wholesome impact, while unsustainable technology is marked by $\Delta t \rightarrow 0$. Presently, the most commonly used theme in technology development is to select technologies that are good for t='right now', or $\Delta t = 0$. In reality, such models are devoid of any real basis and should not be applied in technology development if we seek sustainability for economic, social and environmental purposes.

In order a process to have sustainable, it should fulfill at least three criteria: environmental, economic and social inputs. This means, in any process, the sum of outputs of these three capitals mush have positive outputs for any time horizon after the implementation of the process (Figure 14.2). This can be expressed as:

Natural Capital + Economic capital + Social capital $\geq$ Constant for all time horizons

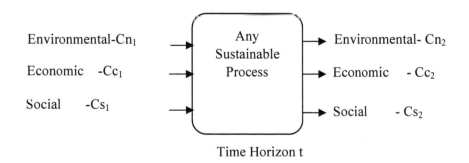

Figure 14.2. A model for sustainable process.

The following criteria have to be fulfilled by any process or technology to be inherently sustainable. The output should be greater at least equal to the respective inputs.

Environmental Condition   : $dCnt/dt \geq 0$, (Figure 14.2. $Cn_2 - Cn_1 \geq 0$)
Economic Condition : $dCc_t/dt \geq 0$, (Figure 14.2. $Cc_2 - Cc_1 \geq 0$)
Social Condition   : $dCs_t/dt \geq 0$, (Figure 14.2. $Cs_2 - Cs_1 \geq 0$)

Environment Criteria is the major criteria to be fulfilled before doing any other assessment in technology development. If the environmental criteria are fulfilled, the technology can continue for infinite time period and hence, will be automatically be economical fulfilling the economic criteria. For social inputs and outputs, the overall change in the society after the implementation of technology should be positive. Only the nature-based technology can fulfill all of these criteria if considered for long-term, hence, becomes the basis for inherently sustainable technology development.

REFERENCES

Alvarez, V., Kershaw, M. E. W., and Medeiros, L. C., 1999. Preserving Beverages: Water, Juice, and Milk. *Ohio State University extension fact sheet. Family and consumer sciences*, 1787 Neil Ave., Columbus, Ohio 43210. HYG-5354-99.

AEHA, 1998. Natural gas may be harmful to your health. Allergy and Environmental Health Association, Nova Scotia. http://www.geocities.com/RainForest/6847/ (Accessed on Dec 29, 2006).

AlDarbi, M.M., Saeed, N.O., Islam, M.R. and Lee, K., 2005. Biodegradation of Natural Oil in Sea Water. *Energy Sources*. 27(1-2):19-34.

Arab, F., 2005. Comprehensive Energy Management. M.SC. Thesis, Faculty of Engineering, Dalhousie University, 78pp.

Agus, D. B. and Vera, J. C. and Golde, D. W. 1999. Stromal Cell Oxidation: A Mechanism by Which Tumors Obtain Vitamin C. *Cancer Research* 59:4555–4558.

Al-Hassani, S.T.S., Woodcock, E., and Saoud, R., 2006. 1001 Inventions: Muslim Heritage in Our World, FSTC, 372 pp.

Associated Press, 2006. Cancer data faked, researcher admits", filed. Toronto Star, http://www.thestar.com/NASApp/cs/ContentServer?pagename=thestar/Layout/Article_T ype1&c=Article&pubid=968163964505&cid=1137279035069&col=968705899037&call _page=TS_News&call_pageid=968332188492&call_pagepath=News/News (acessed on 14 Jan 2006)

Agblevor, F.A., Cundiff, J.S., Mingle, C. and Li, W., 2006. Storage and Characterization of Cotton Gin Waste for Ethanol Production. *Resources, Conservation and Recycling* 46 198–216.

Allen, M., 2002. Straighter-than-straight Vegetable Oils as Diesel Fuels on "Journey for Ever" (http://journeytoforever.org).

Australian Greenhouse Office, 2005. Solar Thermal –Technology Status Overview. *Redding Energy Management* pp 57-64.

Aguado-monsonet, M. A. and Ciscar-martinez, J. C., 1997. The Socio-Economic Impact of Renewable Energy Projects in Southern Mediterranean Countries: Methodology. Task 5 - INTERSUDMED Project. EUR 17668 EN. European Commission.

Al-Maghrabi, I., Chaalal, O., and Islam, M.R., 1998, "A New Technique of Solar Bioremediation", *3rd Int. Conf. Solar Electricity*, Sharjah, UAE, March.

Ali, S., Ul-Haq, I., Qadeer, M.A. and Iqbal, J., 2002. Production of Citric Acid by

Aspergillus Niger Using Cane Molasses in a Stirred Fermentor. Electronic Journal of Biotechnology December 15, 5(3).

Adams, M., 2005. Popular Shampoos Contain Toxic Chemicals Linked to Nerve Damage. News Target.Com (http://www.newstarget.com/z003210.html) (accessed De18, 2006).

Akiniwa, K., 1997. Re-Examination of Acute Toxicity of Fluoride. Research Review. *Fluoride* 30 (2): 89-104.

Al-Waili, N, Al-Alak, J, Haq A, Shabani, M and Akmal, M., 2001. Effects of honey on gram positive and gram negative bacterial growth in vitro. *FASEB J* 15:A586.

Animal Medical Center, 2005. Xylitol toxicity: A Warning to all Dog Owners. Animal *Medical Center Newsletter*, Winter 2004-2005.

Arabani, S.R., 2007. *Use of Natural Materials for Insulation and producing Paints.* M.A.Sc.Thesis, Department of Environmental Engineering, Dalhousie University.

Agriculture and Agrifood Canada (2003). *Aluminum and Health.* www.agr.gc.ca/pfra/water/alhealth_e.htm (Dec 31, 2006).

Abdollahi, M., Jafari, A. and Jalali, N., 1995. Chronic toxicity in organophosphate exposed workers, *M. J. I. R. I.* 9:221–25.

Abdollahi, M., Mostafalou, S., Pournourmohammadi, S. and Shadnia, S. 2004. Oxidative stress and cholinesterase inhibition in saliva and plasma of rats following subchronic exposure to malathion, *Comp. Biochem. Physiol. C. Toxicol. Pharmacol.* 137:29-34.

Arsenault, A.L. Gibson, M.A. and Mader, M.E., 1975. Hypoglycemia in malathion-treated chick embryos, Can. J. Zool. 53:1055-1057.

Agrell, C., Larsson, P., Okla, L., Bremle, G., Johansson, N., Klavins, M., Roots, O., Zelechowska, A., 2001. Atmospheric and river input of PCBs, DDTs and HCHs to the Baltic Sea. In: Wulff, F., Rahm, L., Larsson, P. (Eds.), *A Systems Analysis of the Baltic Sea.* Springer-Verlag, Berlin Heidelberg, pp. 149–175.

Anonymous, 2002. *Pesticides to 2006. Freedonia Industry Study #1523.* The Freedonia Group, Cleveland p. 212.

Armstrong, K., 1994. A History of God, Ballantine Books, Random House, 496 pp.

Amnesty International (AI), 2004. Cloud of injustice-Bhopal disaster 20 years on. http://web.amnesty.org/pages/ec-bhopal-eng (accessed on October, 24, 2006).

Aggazzotti, G., Fantuzzi, G., Righi, E., and Prediery, G., 1998. Blood and Breath Analysis as Biological Indicators of Exposure to Trihalomethanes in Indoor Swimming Pools. *Science of the Total Environment* 217:155-163.

Abou-Kassem, J.H., Zatzman, G.M, and Islam, M.R., 2007. Newtonian Mechanism and the Non-Linear Chaos of Nature: Preliminary Investigations in the Mathematics of Intangibles, J. Nature Sci. and Sust. Tech., in press.

Abou-Kassem, J.H., Farouq Ali, S.M., and Islam, M.R.,2006. Petroleum Reservoir Simulation: A Basic Approach, Gulf Publishing Company, Houston, TX, USA, 480 pp.

Bice, D., 2001. Modeling the Carbon Isotopes. Earthscape. <www.earthscape.org/t1/bid01/bid01f_03.html> <accessed January 31, 2003>

BBC, 2001. Gas Cooking Threat to Lungs. Tuesday, 13 February. http://news.bbc.co.uk/2/hi/health/1167044.stm (accessed on Dec 27, 2006).

Behera, S., Nagarajan, S., and Jagan Mohan Rao, L., 2004. Microwave Heating and Conventional Roasting of Cumin Seeds (*Cuminum cyminum L.*) and Effect on Chemical Composition of Volatiles *Food Chemistry*, 87: 25–29.

Bachman, A., and Nakarmi, A.M., 1983. *New Himalayan Water Wheel,* Sahayogi Press Kathmandu, November, 1983.

Baker, R.J., Hertz-Picciotto, I., Dostal, M., Keller, J.A., Nozicka, J., Kotisovec, F., Dejmek, J., Loomis, D. and Sram, R.J., 2006. Coal Home Heating and Environmental Tobacco Smoke in Relation to Lower Respiratory Illness in Czech Children, from Birth to 3 Years of Age. *Environ Health Perspect* 114(7): 1126–1132, Jul 2006.

Black, R., 2006. Lighting the Key to Energy Saving. BBC News Website, June 29, 2006. (http://news.bbc.co.uk/2/hi/science/nature/5128478.stm).

Business Week Online. 2000. 'As Fuel Prices Heat Up, Social Tensions Could Boil Over.' November 20.

Baskill D., 2006. Lighting is still in the Dark Age. BBC News Website, Thursday, 17 August 2006. http://news.bbc.co.uk/2/hi/science/nature/4794249.stm.

Bodart, M. and De Derde, A., 2002. Global Energy Savings in Offices Buildings by the Use of Daylighting. *Energy and buildings* 34 (5):421-429.

Bosswell, M.J., 2003. Plant Oils: Wealth, Health, Energy and Environment. *International conference of Renewable Energy Technology for rural Development.* 12-14 October, 2003, Kathmandu, Nepal.

Boswell, M.J, Nepal, K. M. and Sulpya, K.M., 2000. *Jatropha Oil Cakes in Rice Cultivation.* Nepal/UK oil seed project, internal report.

BSP, 2002. An Integrated Environment Impact Assessment. June 2002.150p. (unpublished) BSP Lib Temp No.1, (http://www.bspnepal.org.np/pdfs/bsp_30.pdf)

Burg, P., and Fraile, P.,1995. Vitamin C Destruction During the Cooking of a Potato Dish. *Lebensm.-Wiss. u.-Technol.,* 28: 506–514.

Basu, A., Akhtar, J., Rahman, M. H. and. Islam, M. R., 2004. A review of separation of gases using membrane systems. *Petroleum Science and Technology.* 22(9-10):1343–1368.

Beyer, K.H., Jr., Bergfeld, W.F., Berndt, W.O., Boutwell, R.K., Carlton, W.W., Hoffmann, D.K., and Schroeter, A.L. (1983) Final report on the safety assessment of triethanolamine, diethanolamine, and monoethanolamine. *J. Am. Coll. Toxicol.* 2:183-235.

Bakker, R.R., Gosselink, R.J.A., Maas, R.H.W., Vrije, T. de and Jong, E. de. 2004. Biofuel Production

From Acid-Impregnated Willow And Switchgrass, 2nd World Conference on Biomass for Energy, Industry and Climate Protection, 10-14 May 2004, Rome, Italy

Barbier, E., 2002. *Geothermal Energy Technology and Current Status: An Overview.* Renewable and Sustainable Energy Reviews. *Vol.6: 3–65.*

Blask, D. E. Brainard, G.C., Dauchy, R.T., Hanifin, J.P., Davidson, L.K., Krause, J.A., Sauer, L. A., Rivera-Bermudez, M.A., Dubocovich, M.L., Jasser, S.A., Lynch, D.T., Rollag, M.D. and Zalatan, F., 2005. Melatonin-Depleted Blood from Premenopausal Women Exposed to Light at Night Stimulates Growth of Human Breast Cancer Xenografts in Nude Rats. *Cancer Research,* December 1*65:11174-11184.*

Bradley, M., 2006. Spent Nuclear Fuel Edges Closer to Yucca. The Christian Science Monitor. www.truthout.org/docs_2006/072706F.shtml (accessed July 27, 2006).

Butler, N., 2006. The Global Energy Challenge. Council on Foreign Relations, the Corporate Conference. New York, N.Y., March 11, 2005.

Banddyopadhyay, J. and Gyawali, D., 1994. Ecological and Political Aspects of Himalayan Water Resource Management. *Water Nepal.* Vol. 4 Number 1.

Bakker, R.R., Gosselink, R.J.A., Maas, R.H.W., Vrije, T. De, Jong, E. De., Van Groenestijn, J.W., and Hazewinkel, J.H.O., 2004. Biofuel Production from Acid-Impregnated Willow and Switchgrass. *2nd World Conference on Biomass for Energy, Industry and Climate Protection*, 10-14 May 2004, Rome, Italy.

Banskota, K. and Sharma, B., 1997. Impact of Alternative Energy Technology in Reducing Pressure on Forest Resources. Case Studies from Ghandruk. *Discussion Paper.* Series No. MEI 97/5. ICIMOD. Kathmandu. Nepal.

Broek, R. Van-den and Lemmes, L., 1997. Rural Electrification in Tanzania. Constructive use of project appraisal. *Energy Policy* 25 (1) pp 43-54.

Barnwal, B.K and Sharma, M.P., 2005. Prospects of Biodiesel Production from Vegetable Oils in India: *Renewable and Sustainable Energy Reviews,* Vol.9: 363-378

Boocock, D.G.V., Konar, S.K., Maqo, V., and Sidi, H., 1996. Fast One Phase Oil-Rich Processes for the Preparation of Vegetable Oil Methyl Esters. *Biomass and Bioenergy* 11(1):43-50.

Borjesson, P. and Berglund, M., 2006. Environmental Systems Analysis of Biogas Systems-Part I: Fuel-Cycle Emissions. *Biomass and Bioenergy* 30:469–485.

Biopower, 2002. How Can I Know if My Engine Will Run on Straight Vegetable Oil? http://www.bio-power.co.uk/tryit.htm (accessed on Nov 08, 2006). BSP, 2000. *Biogas Annual Report.* Biogas Support Program, Nepal.

Bryant, N., 2007. Office printers 'are health risk'. http://news.bbc.co.uk/2/hi/asia-pacific/6923915.stm (Accessed on July 31, 2007).

Bunny, H. and Besselink, I. 2005. The National Biodigestor Program in Cambodia, in

Relation to the Clean Development Mechanism. http://www.iges.or.jp/en/cdm/pdf/cambodia/activity03/F.pdf (December 10, 2007)

Bernays, E 1928. *Manipulating Public Opinion: the Why and the How* American Journal of Sociology Vol 33 May 1928 http://www.jstor.org/view/00029602/ dm992334/99p 06153/0

Becalski, A., Lau, B. P.Y., Lewis, D. and Seaman, S.W., 2003. Acrylamide in Foods: Occurrence, Sources, and Modeling. *Journal of Agricultural and Food Chemistry* 51(3):802-808.

Bjornstad, A., and Anderson, J., 2005. Mycotoxin Prevention in Cereal Crops by Enhanced Host Plant Resistance. *The Norwegian Research & Technology Forum in the US/Canada, the University of Minnesota,* Minneapolis and St. Paul, September 26-27, 2005.

Becalski, A., Lau, B. P.Y., Lewis, D., Seaman, S.W., Hayward, S., Sahagian, M., Ramesh, M. and Leclerc, Y., 2004. Acrylamide in French Fries: Influence of Free Amino Acids and Sugars. *J. Agric. Food Chem. (52)*:38013806.

Baillie-Hamilton, P., 2004. *The Body Restoration Plan: Eliminate Chemical Calories and Repair Your Body's Natural Slimming System. Avery Pub. Group, ISBN:97811583331873, 320pp.*

BBC, 2003. Fast food 'as Addictive as Heroin. January 30, 2003. http://news.bbc.co.uk/2/hi/health/2707143.stm

Betts, G.D. and Gaze, J.E., 1995. Growth and Heat Resistance of Psychrotropic Clostridium Botulinum in Relation to 'Sous Vide' Products. *Food Control* 6:57–63.

Blackler, C., Denbow, R., Levine, W., Nemsick, K. and Polk, R., 1998. *A Comparative Analysis of Perc Dry Cleaning and an Alternative Wet Cleaning Process: Executive Summary.*

Bernstein, M. 2004. Experts debate benefits, dangers of chlorine in C&EN point-counterpoint.http://www.innovations-report.com/html/reports/life_sciences/report-35026.html (Acessed on December 12, 2007).

Becker, K., Becker, M. and Schwarz, J.H., 2007. String Theory and M-Theory: A Modern Introduction, Cambridge University Press, New York, 756 pp.

Bloomfield, J.P., Williams, R.J., Gooddy, D.C., Cape J.N. and Guha, P., 2006. Impacts of climate change on the fate and behaviour of pesticides in surface and groundwater-a UK perspective. *Science of the Total Environment* 369:163–177.

Burg, P., and Fraile, P.,1995, "Vitamin C destruction during the cooking of a potato dish", Lebensm.-Wiss. u.-Technol., 28: 506–514.

Bear, J., 1972. Dynamics of Fluids in Porous Media, American Elsevier Publishing Co., New York, 761 pp.

Barlow, M. and Clarke, T.. 2002. "Who Owns Water?" in The Nation at: http://www.thenation.com/docPrint.mhtml?i=20020902&s=barlow extracted from: Barlow, Maude & Tony Clarke. 2002.Blue Gold: The Fight to Stop the Corporate Theft of the World's Water (New York: New Press – WW Norton)

Blasco, C., Font, G. and Pico, Y., 2006. Evaluation of 10 pesticide residues in oranges and tangerines from Valencia (Spain) Food Control 17:841–846.

Booth, V.H. 1964. Pigments from roots and leaves.J. Sci. Fd. Agric.15. 342-344.

Chhetri, A.B., Khan, M.I., and Islam, M.R., 2007a. A Novel Sustainably Developed Zero-waste Cooking Stove. J. *Nat.Sci. and Sust.Tech.* In press.

Chhetri, A.B. and Islam, M.R. 2008. Bio-Hydrocarbons as Replacement for Kerosene in Developing Countries. *J. Nat.Sci.and Sust.Tech.* Submitted.

Chhetri A.B., and Islam, M.R., 2006a. Problems Associated with Conventional Natural Gas Processing and Some Innovative Solutions. *Petroleum Science and Technology*. In press.

Chhetri, A.B. and Islam, M.R., 2007a.Reversing Global Warming. J. *Nat.Sci. and Sust.Tech* 1(1):79-114.

Chhetri, A.B. and Islam, M.R., 2007b.A Pathway Analysis of Crude and Refined Oil. *Int. J. Environment and Pollution, Accepted, November, pp 23.*

Chhetri, A.B., Khan, M.I., and Islam, M.R., 2007a. A Novel Sustainably Developed Cooking Stove. *J. Nature Sci. and Sust. Tech.* 1 (4), pp 15.

Chhetri, A.B., Islam, P. and Mann, H., 2007b. Zero-waste Multiple Uses of Jatropha and Dandelion. J. *Nat.Sci. and Sust.Tech.* 1(3):435-460.

Chhetri, A.B., 1997. An Experimental Study of Emission Factors from Domestic Biomass Cookstoves. AIT Master's Degree Thesis no-ET -97-34.

Chhetri, A.B., 2007. Scientific Characterization of Global Energy Sources. *J.of Nat. Sci. and Sust.Tech.* 1(3): 359-395.

Chhetri, A.B. and Islam, M.R., 2006b. Towards Producing Truly Green Biodiesel. Energy Source. In press.

Chhetri, A.B., Adhikari, B.H. and Islam, M.R., 2006a. Wind Power Development in Nepal: Financing Options. *Energy Sources.* In press.

Chhetri, A.B., Adhikari, B.H. and Islam, M.R., 2006c. Increasing Water Demand and Groundwater Contamination. *International Conference on Management of Water, Wastewater and Environment: Challenges for the Developing Countries.* September, 13-15, 2006, Kathmandu, Nepal.

Chhetri, A.B., Rahman, M.S. and Islam, M.R., 2007c. Characterization and Production of Healthy Health Products.*Int. Journal of Material and Products Technology*. Accepted, September, pp 21.

Chhetri, A.B., Rahman, M. S. and Islam, M.R., 2007d. Comprehensive Pathway Analysis and Quality Assurance of 'Healthy' Health and Commercial Food Products. *J Nat.Sci.andSust.Tech*. Accepted. November, pp33.

Chhetri, A.B., Zaman, M.S., and Islam, M.R., 2006b. Effects of Microwave Heating and Refrigeration on Food Quality*2nd International Conference on Appropriate Technology*, July 12-14, 2006, Zimbabwe.

Chhetri, A.B and Islam, M.R., 2006c. Knowledge based water and wastewater management model. A knowledge-based water and wastewater management model. *2nd International Conference on Appropriate Technology*, July 12-14, 2006, Zimbabwe.

Chhetri, A.B. and Islam, M.R.2006d. Impacts of antibiotics in human health and their fate into the natural environment. *Int.J. of Risk Assessment and Management.* Accepted.

Chhetri, A.B. and Islam, M.R., 2006e. A Critical Review of Electromagnetic Heating for Enhanced Oil Recovery. *J. Pet.Sci. and Tech*. Accepted.

Chhetri, A.B., Islam, P. and Islam, M.R., 2007e. Development of Natural Pesticides from Fruits and Plant Extracts. *J. Nat.Sci. and Sust.Tech.* Accepted.

Chhetri, A.B. and Islam, M.R., 2007c. Greening of Petroleum Operations", in *Petroleum Science and Technology Research Advances*, F. Columbus (ed.), Nova Science Publishers, New York, Accepted, November, pp 34.

Chhetri, A.B. and Zatzman, G.M., 2008. Global Warming-A Technical Note. J. of Nat.Sci. and Sust. Tech. In press.

COMEAP, 2004. *Committee on the Medical Effects of Air Pollutants. Guidance on the Effects on Health of Indoor Air Pollutants.* December, 2004.

Carter, B., 2006. There Is a Problem With Global Warming...It Stopped in 1998. The Telegraph,UK.www.telegraph.co.uk/opinion/main.jhtml?xml=/opinion/2006/04/09/do09 07.xml (accessed on June 30, 2006)

Colucci, J.A., Borrero, E.E. and Alape, F., 2005. Biodiesel from Alkaline Transesterification Reaction of Soybean Oil Using Ultrasonic Mixing.

Canakci, M. and Van Gerpen, J.H., 1999.Biodiesel Production via Acid Catalysis. *Transactions of the ASAE*, 42(5):1203-1210.

Cevallos, D., 2006 *Latin America:Big tobacco Fights Back* at www.corpwatch.org (Acessed on January 10, 2006)

Christman, K., 1998. The History of Chlorine, Chlorine Chemistry Council http://c3.org/Chlorine_Knowledge_Center/history.html (Acessed on January 10, 2006)

Connett, M., 2005. Fluorosis on the Rise According to New U.S. Survey. *FAN Science Watch Newsletter*. Issue no 24, August 25, 2005.

Chaalal, O., A. Zekri, and M.R., 2005, Uptake of Heavy Metals by Microorganisms: An Experimental Approach. *Energy Sources*, vol. 27, no. 1-2, 87-100.

Carter, D., Darby, D., Halle, J. and Hunt, P., 2005. *How to Make Biodiesel. Low Impact Living Initiative,* Redfield Community, Winslow, Bucks, UK. ISBN: 0-9549171-0-3

Carraretto, C., Macor, A., Mirandola, A., Stoppato, A., Tonon S., 2004. Biodiesel as alternative fuel: Experimental analysis and energetic evaluations. *Energy* 29: 2195–2211

CES, 2001. A Studies Report on Efficiency Measurement of Biogas, Kerosene and LPG Stoves. Biogas Support Programme 20p BSP Lib Temp No.71.

Cornell, E.A.,2005. What was God Thinking? Science can't Tell, Time, vol.166 (20), November 14

Coltrain, D., 2002, Biodiesel: *Is It Worth Considering? Risk and Profit Conference Kansas State University Holiday Inn,* Manhattan, Kansas August 15-16.

Costanza, R., Cumberland, J., Daly H., Goodland R., Norgaard R. 1997. *An Introduction to Ecological Economics,* International Society for Ecological Economics and St. Lucie Press, Florida.

CRT, 2005. Improved Water Mills. Center for Rural Technologies in Nepal. www.crtnepal.org/new/technologies.php?mode=detail&technologies_id=14 (Dec 30, 2006).

Chemical and Engineering news, 1998. American Chemical Society. http://pubs.acs.org/ hotartcl/cenear/980629/pesttabs.html (accessed on July 02, 2006).

CERHR, 2003. NTP-CERHR, Expert Panel Report on Reproductive and Developmental Toxicity of Propylene Glycol. National Toxicology Program U.S. Department of Health and Human Services. NTP-CERHR-PG-03.

Carey, A., 1995. Taking the Risk out of Democracy:Corporate Propoganda versus Freedom and Liberty (Urbana IL: U. of Illinois)

Clayton, M.A. and Moffat, J.W.,1999. Dynamical Mechanism for Varying Light Velocity as a Solution to Cosmological Problems, Physics Letters B, vol. 460, No.3-4, pp. 263-270

CBC, 2004. Genetically Modified Foods: A primer. CBC Online News, May 11, 2004.

Coriell, S.R., McFadden, G.B., Sekerka, R.F. and Boettinger W.J.,1998. Multiple Similarity Solutions for Solidification and Melting, Journal of Crystal Growth, vol. 191, pp. 573-585

Cellini, F. Chesson, A., Colquhoun, I. Constable, A., Davies, H.V., Engel, K.H. Gatehouse, A.M.R. Karenlampi, S., Kok, E.J., Leguay, J.-J., Lehesranta, S.Noteborn, H.P.J.M., Pedersen and Smith, J. M., 2004. Unintended effects and their detection in genetically modified crops. *Food and Chemical Toxicology* 42:1089–1125.

Chakma, A., 1999. Formulated solvents: new opportunities for energy efficient separation of acid gases. *Energy Sources* 21 (1-2)

Canumir, J. A., Celis, J.E., De Bruijn, J., and Vidal, L.V., 2002.Pasteurization of Apple Juice by Using Microwaves. *Lebensm.-Wiss. u.-Technol.,* 35: 389–392

CHI Associates, 1998. Pellet Stoves and Inserts, Common Sense Internet und Business Consulting, 8 Golden Circle, Southampton, MA 01073- 413-527-5820. <http://hearth. com/what/pelletstoves.html> [Accessed: January 10, 2006]

CMAI, 2005. Chemical Market Associates Incorporated. www.kasteelchemical.com/ slide.cfm< accessed on May 20, 2006>.

Cooper, M.H., 2005, *Water Shortages. Global Issues.* Washington D.C: CQ Press, 319- 323.

Canadian Cancer Society, 2006. www.cancer.ca/ccs/internet/standard/0,3182,3172_372124_ langId-en,00.html (Dec 21, 2006)

CSE, 2003. Pepsi, Coke Contain Pesticides. www.rediff.com/money/2003/aug/05pepsicoke. htm (accessed on Dec 22, 2006).

CBC, 2007. Toxic toys still on store shelves. http://www.cbc.ca/consumer/story/2007 /12/05/lead-testing.html (accessed on December 10, 2007).

Crinnion, W.J.,2000. Environmental medicine, part 1: the human burden of environmental toxins and their common health effects. *Alt Med Review,* January 5:52-63.

Calle, S., Klaba, L., Thomas, D., Perrin, L., and Dufaud, O., 2005, Influence of the size distribution and concentration on wood dust explosion: Experiments and reaction modeling, *Powder Technology*, Vol. 157 (1-3), September, pp. 144-148.

Caroll, S., 2004. Why 3-Dimensions in Space Aren't Just Enough? Invited paper presented at the Annual Meeting of the Philosophy of Science Association, Austin, Texas

Coveney, D., Shaw, G., and Renfree, M.B., 2001. Estrogen-Induced Gonadal Sex Reversal in the Tammar Wallaby. *Biology of Reproduction* 65:613-621.

Cahill, J.D., Furlong, E.T., Burkhardt, M.R., Kolpin, D. and Anderson, L.G., 2004. Determination of pharmaceutical compounds in surfaceand ground-water samples by solid-phase extraction and HPLC electrospray ionisation MS. *J. Chromatogr.* A 1041, 171–180.

Crugg, G.M. and Newman, D.J., 2001. Medicinals for the Millenia: The Historic Record, Annals of the New York Academy of Sciences, vol. 953, pp. 3-25.

De Villiers, L.S., 1994. Natural Micronutrients as Controlling Factors in Western Diseases – A Lesson in Nature-programming. *Medical Hypotheses*, 42: 149-158

Dennekamp, M, Howarth, S., Dick, C.A.J., Cherrie, J.W., Donaldson, K., and Seaton, A., 2001. Ultrafine particles and nitrogen oxides generated by gas and electric cooking. *Occup Environ Med* 58:511-516 (August).

Duncan, N. and Swartman, R.K., 1995. *The Canadian Renewable Energy Guide,* Burnstown: General Store Publishing House, 1995.www.newenergy.org/sesci/ publications/ pamphlets/passive.html (Dec 28, 2006).

Danielo, O., 2005. *An algae -based fuel.* Biofuture, No. 255, May 2005.

Daly, H. E. 1991. Elements of Environmental Macroeconomics in Costanza Robert (Ed): *Ecological Economics: The Science and Management of Sustainability,* Columbia University Press, New York. pp 32-46.

Dorogovtsev, S. N., Mendes, J. F. F., and Samukhin, A. N., 2000. Structure of Growing Networks with Preferential Linking, Phys. Rev. Lett., vol.85, No. 21, pp.4633-4636

Demirba, A., 2003. Biodiesel Fuels From Vegetable Oils Via Catalytic and Non-Catalytic Supercritical Alcohol Transesterifications and Other Methods, a Survey. *Energy Conversion and Management*; Volume 44 (13): 2093-2109.

Dien, B.S., Cotta, M. A, and Jeffries, T.W., 2003. Bacteria Engineered for Fuel Ethanol Production: Current Status. *Appl Microbiol Biotechnol* 63:258–66.

De Carvalho, A.V. Jr., 1985. Natural Gas and Other Alternative Fuels for Transportation Purposes. *Energy* 10(2):187-215.

Department of Environment and Heritage, 2005. Australian Government, Greenhouse Office. Fuel consumption and the environment.<www.greenhouse.gov.au/fuellabel/ environment.html> accessed on February 18, 2006>

Du, W., Xu, Y., Liu, D., Zeng, J. 2004. Comparative study on lipase-catalyzed transformation f soybean oil for biodiesel production with different acyl acceptors. *Journal of Molecular Catalysis B: Enzymatic* 30: 125–129.

Daly, H. E. 1977. *Steady- State Economics.* W.H. Freeman, San Francisco, CA.

Daly, H.E.,1999. *Ecological Economics and the Ecology of Economics: Essays in Criticism,* Cheltenham, UK and Northampton, MA, US: Edward Elgar.

Daly, H. E. 1991. Elements of Environmental Macroeconomics in Costanza Robert (Ed): Ecological Economics: The Science and Management of Sustainability, Columbia University Press, New York. pp 32-46.

DDT, 2006. Dichloro-Diphenyl- Trichloroethane from Wikipedia, the Free Encyclopedia http://en.wikipedia.org/wiki/DDT (October 4, 2006).

Dufty, W., 1975. *Sugar Blues.* New York: Warner Books.

DNR, 2006. Department of Natural Resources. Michigon State. www.michigan.gov/dnr/0,1607,7-153-10370_12150_12220-27249--,00.html.

Darbre, P.D.,2006. Environmental Oestrogens, Cosmetics and Breast Cancer. *Best Practice & Research Clinical Endocrinology & Metabolism* 20 (1):121–143

Duty, S.M., Singh, N.P., Silva, M.J., Barr, D.B., Brock, J.W., Ryan, L., Herrick, R.F., Christiani, D.C. and Hauser, R. 2003. *The relationship between environmental exposures to phthalates and DNA damage in human sperm using the neutral comet assay.* Environmental Health Perspectives *111 (July): 1164-1169.*

Dietert, R.R. and Hedge, A., 1996. Toxicological Considerations in Evaluating Indoor air Quality and Human Health: Impact of New Carpet Emissions. *Critical Reviews in Toxicology*, 26 (6):633-707.

Denga, B and Kim, C.N., 2007. CFD Simulation of VOCs Concentrations in a Resident Building with New Carpet under Different Ventilation Strategies. *Building and Environment* 42:297–303.

Duke, S.O. 1990. Natural pesticides from plants. p. 511-517. In: J. Janick and J.E. Simon (eds.), *Advances in new crops.* Timber Press, Portland, OR.

Dasgupta, S., Meisner, C., Wheeler, D., Xuyen, K., and Lam, N.T., 2006. Pesticide poisoning of farm workers–implications of blood test results from Vietnam. *Int. J. Hyg. Environ.-Health.* In press.

Darnerud et al. 2001. "Polybrominated Diphenyl Ethers: Occurrence, Dietary Exposure, and Toxicology," in Environmental Health Perspectives Vol. 109 Supplement 1 (March 2001): 49-68.

De Aguiar, L.H., Moraes, G., Avilez, I.M., Altran, A.E. and Correa, C.F., 2004. Metabolical effects of Folidol 600 on the neotropical freshwater fish matrinxa, Brycon cephalus, *Environ.* Res. 95:224-230.

Das, R. and Blanc, P.D., 1993. Chlorine Gas Exposure and the Lung: A Review. *Toxicol Ind.Health*. May-Jun, 1993, 9(3):439-55.

EPA, 2006.Office of Pesticide Programs www.epa.gov/pesticides/about/index.htm.

Ertel, K. D., Hartwig, P. and Bacon, R., 2004. Assessing Possible Synergy Between a Moisturizing Body Wash and Lotion. *J Am Cad Dermatol.* p79

EIA, 2004a. Renewable Energy Trends 2004. Renewable Energy Sources: A Consumer's Guide. http://www.eia.doe.gov/neic/brochure/renew05/renewable.html (Dec 29, 2006)

EIA, 2004b. International Energy Outlook. Greenhouse Gases General Information, Energy Information Administration, Environmental Issues and World Energy Use. EI 30, 1000 Independence Avenue, SW, Washinghton, DC, 20585.

EPA, 2002. A Comprehensive analysis of biodiesel impacts on exhaust emissions. Air and radiation. Draft technical report. EPA420-P-02-001.

Environment Canada, 2003. Transportation and environment, Environment Canada <www.ec.gc.ca/transport/publications/biodiesel/biodiesel12.html>[Accessed:November25, 2005]

Environment Canada, 2006. www.ec.gc.ca/international/multilat/rotterdam_e.htm (Acessed on December 05, 2006)

EPA, 2003. *Facts About Burning Stove. Puget Sound Clean Air Agency, Air Resources Department. US.*

Enviroharvest Inc., 2006. Electricity and Health. www.enviroharvest.ca/electricity _and_health.htm (accessed on December 27, 2006).

European Committee for Solar Cooking Research, 1995. Second International Solar Cooker Test. Summary Results. ECSCR, Germany.

EPA global warming site 2001. Climate.http://www.epa.gov/globalwarming/climate/ index.htm.

EIA, 2006. Energy Information Administration, Natural Gas Division, January 2006. www.eia.doe.gov/pub/oil_gas/natural_gas/featurearticles/2006/ngprocess/ngprocess.pdf

EIA, 2006a. Energy Information Administration/International Energy Outlook, 2006. Overview.AEO2006 National Energy Modeling System, run AEO2006. D111905A. (www.eia.doe.gov/oiaf/aeo/pdf/overview.pdf)

EIA, 2006b. Energy Information Administration/International Energy Outlook, 2006. The Energy Challenge. http://www.eia.doe.gov/oiaf/ieo

EIA, 2006c. Energy Information Administration. This Week in Petroleum. http://tonto.eia.doe.gov/oog/info/twip/twip.asp, accessed on August 06, 2006

EIA, 2006d. Energy Information Administration, World Energy Outlook www.eia.doe. gov/oiaf/ieo/world.html <accessed on April 25, 2006>Environment Canada, 2006. www.ec.gc.ca/international/multilat/rotterdam_e.htm

EIA, 2000. U.S. *Crude Oil, Natural Gas and Natural Gas Liquids Reserves 1999 Annual Report.* September 2000, Office of Oil and Gas, US Department of Energy, Washington DC 20858.

EIA, 2002. U.S. *Crude Oil, Natural Gas and Natural Gas Liquids Reserves 2001 Annual Report.* Office of Oil and Gas, US Department of Energy, Washington DC 20858.

EIA, 2005. A*nnual Energy Outlook 2005, Market Trends- Energy Demand, Energy Information Administration, Environmental Issues and World Energy Use.* EI 30, 1000 Independence Avenue, SW, Washington, DC 20585.

Emoto, M., 2004. The Mssages from Water. Conscious Water Crystals: The Power of Prayer Made Visible. www.life-enthusiast.com/twilight/research_emoto.htm <accessed on June 1, 2006>

Erickson, M. L. and Barnes, R. J. 2006.Arsenic concentration variability in public water system wells in Minnesota, USA. *Applied Geochemistry* 21:305–317.

EPA, 2002. US Environmnetal Protection Agency, Integrated Risk Information System (IRIS), Office of Research and Development (ORD), National Center for Environmental Assessment; http://www.epa.gov/ngispgm3/iris/search.htm.

Elyasi, S. and Taghipour, F., 2006. Simulation of UV photoreactor for water disinfection in Eulerian framework. *Chemical Engineering Science* 61(14): 4741-4749.

Evans, J.A, Russell, S.L., James, C. and Corry, J.E.L., 2004. Microbial Contamination of Food Refrigeration Equipment. *Journal of Food Engineering* 62:225–232.

EPA, 2006. Integrated Risk Information System:Benzoic Acid. http://www.epa.gov/ iris/subst/

0355.htm

Ertel, K. D., Hartwig, P. and Bacon, R., 2004. Assessing possible synergy between a moisturizing body wash and lotion. *J Am Cad Dermatol*. p79.

Earnest, G.S., Hayden, C.S., Watkins, D.S., Hagedorn, R.T. and Flesch, J.P., 1997. Control of Exposure to Perchloroethylene in Commercial Drycleaning (Ventilation), www.cdc.gov/niosh/hc19.html (Dec 15, 2006).

Eskenazi, B. Bradman, A., and Castorina, R., 1999. Exposures of Children to Organophosphate Pesticides and Their Potential Adverse Health Effects. Environmental Health Perspectives Supplements 107 (Suppl-3): 409-419, June.

European Commission (EC), 2002. Towards a thematic strategy on the sustainable use of pesticides. Electronic citation available at: http://europa.eu.int/eur lex/en/com/ pdf/2002/com2002_0349en01.pdf.

Editorial, 2007. Borlaug's Revolution, *The Wall Street Journal*, July 17, p. A16

EPA, 1989. Characterization of Products Containing Lead and Cadmium in Municipal Solid Waste In the United States, 1970-2000. Final Report for EPA Municipal Solid Waste Program Prepared by Franklin Associates, Ltd. Prairie Village, Kansas, EPA/5S30-SW-015A.

Enron, 2006. Enron Corporation, an American Energy Company from Wikipedia, the Free Encyclopedia [online] Available: (http://en.wikipedia.org/wiki/Enron) (October 4, 2006).

Fischer, A. and Hahn, C., 2005. Biotic and Abiotic Degradation Behaviour of Ethylene Glycol Monomethyl Ether (EGME). *Water Research*. Vol.39:2002–2007.

Farquhar, G.D., Ehleringer, J.R. and Hubick, K.T. 1989. Carbon Isotope Discrimination and Photosynthesis. *Annu.Rev.Plant Physiol.Plant Mol. Biol.* 40:503-537

Fuchs, H.U. 1999. A Systems View of Natural Processes: Teaching Physics the System Dynamics Way. *The Creative Learning Exchange* 8 (1): 1-9

Fialka, J.J. and Ball, J., 2006. Bush's Latest Energy Solution, Like its Forebears, Faces Hurdles. *The Wall Street Journal,* February 02, 2006.

Farahani, S., Worrell, E. and Bryntse, G. 2004. CO_2-free paper? *Resources, Conservation and Recycling* 42:317–336.

Fernandes, M.B. and Brooks, P., 2003, Characterization of carbonaceous combustion residues: II. Nonpolar organic compounds, *Chemosphere,* Volume 53, Issue 5, November, pages 447-458.

Fraas, L. M., Partain, L. D., McLeod, P. S. and Cape, J. A., 1986. Near-Term Higher Efficiencies with Mechanically Stacked Two-Color Solar Batteries. *Solar Cells* 19 (1):73-83, November.

Fawellm, J. K., Sheahan, Y. D., James, H. A, Hurst, M. and Scott, S. 2001. Oestrogens and oestrogenic activity in raw and treated water in Severn Trent water. *Wat. Res.*35 (5):1240-1244.

FAO, 2004. Biotechnology Applications in Food Processing: Can Developing Countries Benefit? *Electronic Forum on Biotechnology in Food and Agriculture:* Conference 11. 14th June-15th July, 2004.

Freeth, T., Bitsakis, Y., Moussas, X., Seiradakis, J.H., Tselikas, A., Mangou, H., Zafeiropoulou, M., Hadland, R., Bate, D., Ramsey, A., Allen, M., Crawley, A., Hockley, P., Malzbender, T., Gelb, D., Ambrisco, W. and Edmunds, M.G.,2006. Decoding the Ancient Greek Astronomical Calculator Known as the Antikythera Mechanism, Nature, vol. 444, pp. 587-591

Fleischhauer, M.,2007.Indistinguishable from afar, Nature, vol. 445, pp. 605-606

Fenton, C.H., 1998. Chocolate and Anxiety: Your Guide to Anxiety and Panic. http://panicdisorder.about.com/cs/shfitness/a/chocolate.htm (December 12, 2006)

Fellows, P., 2000. Food Processing Technology –Principles and Practice (2nd ed., pp. 369–380). Chichester, UK: Ellis Horwood.

Food and Drug Administration (FDA) (1993). Hair Dye Dilemmas. FDA Consumer. April 1993. Accessed online May 6, 2004 at http://vm.cfsan.fda.gov/~dms/cos-818.html.

Fuller, C.,1998. *Natural Colored Iron Oxide Pigments*, pp. 281-6. In: Pigment Handbook, 2nd Edition. Lewis, P. (ed.). New York: John Wiley & Sons.

Fabian, J., Komiha, N., Linguerri, R. and Rosmus, P., 2006. The absorption wavelengths of sulfur chromophors of ultramarines calculated by time-dependent density functional theory. *Journal of Molecular Structure: THEOCHEM* 801: 63–69.

Fong, W. G., Moye, H. A., Siber, J. N., & Toth, J. P. (Eds.). (1999). *Pesticides residues in food.* New York: John Wiley & Sons, Inc.

Fleischhauer, M., 2007. Indistinguishable from afar, Nature, vol. 445, pp. 605-606

Focus on surfactant, 2002. Soapnut tree extract new from Sabinsa. *Soap and Cosmetics, 78* (1) 24 Jan-Feb.

Ginsberg, N.S., Garner, S.R., Hau, L.V., (2007) Coherent control of optical information with matter wave dynamics, Nature, vol. 445, Feb. 8, pp. 623-626.

Gelderblom, H R.1996. "41. Structure and Classification of Viruses" in Samuel Baron, ed., Medical Microbiology. (Galveston TX: University of Texas Medical Branch. 4th ed. - ISBN 0963117211)

Global Pesticide Campaigner, 2004. Vol.14, No.2, www.panna.org/resources/ gpc/gpc_200408.14.2.pdf

Greenpeace, 2006. *Contamination by Genetically Engineered Papaya in Thailand.* Greenpeace Southeast Asia, May 2006.

Goksu, E. I., Sumnu, G., and Esin, A., 2005. Effect of microwave on fluidized bed drying of macaroni beads. *Journal of Food Engineering*, 66: 463–468.

GTZ, 1997. *Solar Cooker Field Test in South Africa. A Comparative Field Test for the Socio-acceptability of Seven Different Types of Solar Cookers.* GTZ, Pretoria.

Gubitz, G.M., Mittelbach, M. and Trabi, M., 1999. Exploitation of the Tropical Oil Seed Plant *Jatropha curcas L. Bioresource Technology* 67:73-82.

Goldemberg, J., 2003. *Jobs provided in the energy sector.* Adapted from Grassi, G. (1996).

Gilbert, B. and Zhang, H. 2003. Nanoparticles Change Crystal Structure When They Get Wet. Research Shows. *Nature* August 27.

Gale, C.R., martyn, C.N., Winter, P.D. and Cooper, C., 1995. Vitamin C and Risk of Death from Stroke and Coronary Heart Disease in Cohort of Elderly People. *BMJ* 310:1563-1566.

Guo, R. *et al. 2004.* Thermal and Chemical Stabilities of Arsenic in Three Chinese Coals. *Fuel Processing Technology,* 85(8-10): 903-912.

Gerpen, J.V., Pruszko, R., Shanks, B., Clements, D., and Knothe, G., 2004. *Biodiesel Analytical methods.* National Renewable Energy Laboratory. Operated for the U.S. Department of Energy Office of Energy Efficiency and Renewable Energy. NREL/SR-510-36240.

Godoy, J., 2006. Environment: Heat Wave Shows Limits of Nuclear Energy. *Inter Press Service News Agency. July 27, 2006.*

Goldschmidt, V.W.2005. Two Differing Perspectives on Ozone Depletion and Global Warming. *Proceeding of Third International Conference on Energy Research and Development (ICERD-3),* Nov. 21-23, 2005 1:39-46

GWEC, 2006. Global Wind Energy Council, April 2006. www.gwec.net/uploads/media/06-02_PR_Global_Statistics_2005.pdf

Giridhar, M., Kolluru, C., Kumar, R., 2004. Synthesis of Biodiesel in Supercritical Fluids, *Fuel.* 83, 2029-2033.

Gajalakshmi, S. and Abbasi, S.A., 2004. Neem leaves as a source of fertilizer-cum-pesticide vermicompost. *Bioresource Technology* 92:291–296.

Goodland, R. 1992. The Case That the World Has Reached Limits, More precisely that current growth in the global economy cannot be sustained, in R. Goodland, Herman Daly, S.E. Serafy, B. von Droste: *Environmentally Sustainable Economic Development: Building on Brundtland,* UNESCO

Grau, F.H., 1996. Smallgoods and Listeria. *Food Australia,* 48(2):81-83.

Goldberger, B.A., Lessig, M.C., McCusker R.R., Cone, E.J., Gold, M.S., 2003. Evaluation of Current Caffeine Content of Coffee Beverages: Recommendations for Clinicians Regarding Caffeine Exposure. *Society of Biological Psychiatry's Annual Convention and Scientific Program 2003.* San Francisco, California.

Gupta, P.K., 2004. Pesticide exposure-Indian scene. Toxicology 198:83–90.

Gaugler, R., 1997. Alternative paradigms for commercializing biopesticides. Phytoparasitica 25:179–182

Glaser, A., 2004. The Ubiquitous Triclosan: A Common Antibacterial Agent Exposed. Beyond Pesticides/National Coalition Against the Misuse of Pesticides. *Pesticides and You,* 24 (3): 12-17.

Gago-Dominguez, M., Catelao, J.E., Yuan, J., Yu, M.C., Ross, R.K., 2001. Use of permanent hair dyes and bladder-cancer risk. *Int. J. Cancer* 91, 575-579.

Gettens, R.J., Kuhn, H. and Chase, W. T., 1967. Indentification of the Materials of paintings: Lead White. Studies in Conservation *12 (4): 125-139.*

Greening Planet, 2004. PERC-A Stain on the Dry Cleaning Industry. www.grinningplanet.com/2004/02-10/dry-cleaning-alternatives-eco.htm (Accessed on February 10, 04).

Huang, H.C., Liao, S.C., Chang, F.R., Kuo, Y.H. and Wu, Y.C., 2005. Molluscicidal Saponins from Sapindus Mukorossi, Inhibitory Agents of Golden Apple Snails, Pomacea Canaliculata. *J Agric Food Chem.* 51(17):4916-4919.

Ginsberg, N.S., Garner, S.R., Hau, I.V., 2007. Coherent control of optical information with matter wave dynamics, Nature, vol. 445, Feb. 8, pp. 623-626

Gleick, J., 1987. Chaos – Making a New Science, Penguin Books, NY, 352 pp.

Fies, M. 1998. New solvents based on renewable raw materials for cleaning operations in the ink industry.

Hawking, S., 1988. A Brief History of Time, Bantam books, London, UK, 211 pp.

Honeybee Natural, LLC 2006, dba Santa Fe Beeswax Candle Co. http://www.santafecandle.com/learn/beeswax/beeswax.htm (accessed on May 20,2006).

Hinkova, A., & Bubnık, Z., 2001. Sugar beet as a raw material for bioethanol production. Czech Journal of Food Science, 19, 224–234.

Hofer, R., Daute, P., Grutzmacher, R., Westfechtel, A. 1997- A New Raw Material Source for Polyurethane Coatings and Floorings, *Journal of Coatings Technology* No 869, 65.

Herzallah, S.M., 2005. Influence of Microwaving and Conventional Heating of Milk on Cholesterol Contents and Cholesterol Oxides Formation. *Pakistan Journal of Nutrition,* 4 (2): 85-88, (*Asian network for scientific information,* ISSN 1680-5194).

Henning, R., 1997. The Jatropha Project in Mali. Weissensberg, Germany: Rothkreuz 11, D-88138.

Homeopathy, 2006. Homeopathy from Wikipedia, the Free Encyclopedia [online] Available: (http://en.wikipedia.org/wiki/Homeopathy) (October 4, 2006).

Houghton, J.T., Meira Filho, L.G., Callander, B.A., Harris, N., Kattenberg, A. and Maskell, K. *Climate Change 2001: The Scientific Basis. Technical Summary.* Cambridge University Press, Cambridge, UK.

Houghton, J., 2004. *Global Warming: The Complete Briefing.* Third Edition. Cambridge University Press, Cambridge, UK.

Hughes, L. and Scott, S., 1997. Canadian Greenhouse Gas Emissions:1990-2000. *Energy Conversion and Management* 38 (3)

Hall, D.O. and Overend,R.P, 1987. *Biomass: Regenarable Energy.* John Wiley and Sons-A wiley-Interscience publication, pp 504.

Hossain M.E. and Islam, M.R., 2006. Fluid Properties with Memory – A Critical Review and Some Additions. *36th International Conference on Computers and Industrial Engineering (ICCIE) in Taipei, Taiwan,* R.O.C., June 20-23, 2006.

Hall, D.O, Rao K.K., 1999. *Photosynthesis.* 6th edn. 214 pp. Cambridge: Cambridge University Press.

Holden, P.and Thobani, M. 1996. "Tradable Water Rights: A Property Rights Approach to Resolving Water Shortages and Promoting Investment" World Bank Policy Research Working Group No.1627 (Washington DC: The World Bank)

Hadiths of The Prophet, 2007. Collected and Translated by Sahih Bukhari [online] Available:(http://www.usc.edu/dept/MSA/fundamentals/hadithsunnah/bukhari/001.sbt.html) (April 23, 2007)

Hohmeyer, O.1997. Social Costs of Climate Change. Strong Sustainability and Social costs. In: Hohmeyer et al (ed.) *Social Costs and Sustainability. Valuation and Implementation in the energy and transport sector.* Springer Verlag. Germany.

Hourcade, J., Clombier, M., Menanteau, P. 1990. Price Equalization and alternative approaches for rural electrification. *Energy Policy* 18(9). Pp 861-870

Haynes, H.J., Thrasher, L.W., Katz, M.L., Eck, T.R. 1976. Enhanced oil recovery, national petroleum council. *An analysis of the potential for EOR from Known Fields in the United States-*1976-2002.

Hiley, R.W. and Pedley, J.F., 1988. Storage Stability of petroleum-Derived Diesel Fuel 2. The Effect of Sulphonic Acids on the Stability of Diesel Fuels and a Diesel Fuel Extract. *Fuel* 67:469-473.

Hanson, R. S., Hanson, T. E., 1996. Methanotrophic bacteria. *Microbial. Rev.* 60: 439-471.

Hinkova, A., and Bubnık, Z., 2001. Sugar beet as a raw material for bioethanol production. *Czech Journal of Food Science* 19:224–234.

Hossain, M.E. and Islam, M. R., 2006. An Alternative Fuel for Motor Vehicles. *Energy Sources.* Accepted.

Hart, M., 2000. The 100: A Ranking Of The Most Influential Persons In History: A Ranking of the Most Influential Persons in History, Citadel, 540 pp.

Health Canada, 2005. Acrylamide Levels in Selected Canadian foods (www.hc-sc.gc.ca /fn-an/securit/chem-chim/acrylamide/acrylamide_level-acrylamide_niveau_ e.html).

Hunter, K.J., and Fletcher, J.M., 2002. The antioxidant activity and composition of fresh, frozen, jarred and canned vegetables, *Innovative Food Science and Emerging Technologies,* 3:399–406.

Hildbrand, C., Dind, P., Pons, M. and Buchter, F., 2004. A New Solar Powered Adsorption Refrigerator with High Performance. *Solar Energy* 77:311–318.

Hughes JPW, Baron R, Buckland DH, *et al.* 1962. Phosphorus Necrosis of the Jaw: A Present-day Study. *Br. J. Ind. Med.* 19:83-99.

Hoeniger, C., 1991. The Identification of Blue Pigments in Early Sienese Paintings by Color Infrared Photography. *Journal of the American Institute for Conservation* 30(2):115-124.

Hovers, E., Ilani, S., Bar-Yosef, O., Vandermeersch, B., Barham, L., Belfer-Cohen, A., Klein, R.G., Knight, C., Power, C., Watts, I., Mcbrearty, S., Marshack, A., Sagona, A., 2003. An early case of color symbolism: Ochre use by modern humans in Qafzeh cave. *Current anthropology* 44 (4):491-522.

Henning, R. K., 2004. Integrated Rural Development by Utilization of Jatropha Curcas L.

as Raw Material and as Renewable Energy: *Presentation of The Jatropha System "at the international Conference, Renewables 2004" in Bonn, Germany*

HELCOM, 2001. The pesticides selected for immediate priority action, a compilation and evaluation of the information given by the contracting parties with the focus on use and legislation. October 2001. Helsinki Commission, Baltic Marine Environment Protection Commission.

Hooper, K. and McDonald,T., 2000. "The PBDEs: An Emerging Environmental Challenge and Another Reason for Breast-Milk Monitoring Programs," in Environmental Health Perspectives Vol. 108, No. 5 (May 2000): 387-392

Hanson, K., S. Robinson, and G. Schluter. 1993. "Sectoral effects of a world□oil price shock:. Economy-wide Linkages to the Agricultural Sector," US Department of Agriculturre Publication, at: http://www.usda.gov/publications/TB1862/tb1862.pdf

Hynes, R. K. and Boyetchko, S.M., 2006. Research initiatives in the art and science of biopesticide formulations. *Soil Biology & Biochemistry* 38:845–849.

Hau, L.V., Harris, S.E., Dutton, Z., and Behroozi, C.H., (1999) Light Speed Reduction to 17 Metres Per Second in an Ultra Cold Atomic Gas, Nature, vol. 397, pp. 594–598

Islam, M.R., 2005. Knowledge based Technologies for the information age, JICE05 Keynote speech, *Jordan International Chemical Conference* V, 12-14 September 2005, Amman, Jordan.

Islam, M.R., 2004. Unraveling the Mysteries of Chaos and Change: Knowledge-Based Technology Development", EEC Innovation, vol. 2, no. 2 and 3, 45-87.

Islam, M.R., 2003. Unraveling the Mystery of Chaos and Climate Change: The Knowledge-Based Technology Development.Vol 2., No.2 &3, ISSN 1708-307.3006)

Islam, M.R.2006a. Computing for the Information Age. Keynote speech, proceedings of the *36th International Conference on Computer and Industrial Engineering*, Taiwan, June 20-24, 2006.

Islam, 2006b. A Knowledge-Based Water and Waste-Water Management Model. *International Conference on Management of Water, Wastewater and Environment: Challenges for the Developing Countries*, September 13-15, 2006, Kathmandu, Nepal.

Islam, J., and Kahkonen, S, 2001.What Determines the Effectiveness of Community-Based water Projects? Evidence from Central Java, Indonesia on Demand Responsiveness,

Service rules and Social Capital. *Working Paper No 251.* Center for Institutional Reform and the Informal Sector, University of Maryland, College Park, MD.

Islam, M.R., Shapiro, R. and Zatzman, G.M., 2006. *Energy Crunch: What more lies ahead? The Dialogue:Global Dialogue on Natural Resources,* Center for International and Strategic Studies, Washington DC, April 3-4, 2006.

Islam, M.R., 2003. *Unraveling the Mystery of Chaos and Climate Change: The Knowledge-Based Technology Development.*Vol 2., No.2 &3, ISSN 1708-307.

Islam, M.R., 2002. Emerging Technologies in Subsurface Monitoring of Petroleum Reservoirs, *Petroleum Res. J.,* vol. 13, pp. 33-46.

Islam, M.R., 2004. Unraveling the Mysteries of Chaos and Change: Knowledge-Based Technology Development", *EEC Innovation,* vol. 2, no. 2 and 3, 45-87.

Islam, M.R., Zatzman, G.M. & Shapiro. R.2006. *"The Energy Crunch: What More Lies Ahead", in Global Dialogue on Energy* (No. 2 in a series) Washington DC, at the Centre for Strategic and International Studies, 3-4 April 2006.

Islam, M.R., Mousavizadegan, H., Mustafiz, S., and Belhaj, H., 2007. A Handbook of Knowledge-Based Reservoir Simulation, Gulf Publishing Co., Houston, TX, to be published in Jan., 2008.

Islam, M.R., 2005b. Unraveling the Mysteries of Chaos and Change: The Knowledge-Based Technology Development. *Fifth International Conference on Composite Science & Technology and First International Conference on Modeling, Simulation and Applied Optimization,* Sharjah, U.A.E., 1-3 February 2005.

Islam, M.R. and Chilingar, G.V.,1995. Mathematical Modeling of Three-Dimensional Microbial Transport in Porous Media, International Journal of Science & Technology, vol. 2, No. 2, pp. 55-64.

Islam, M.R. and Nandakumar, K., 1990. Transient Convection in Saturated Porous Layers with Internal Heat Sources, Int. J. Heat and Mass Transfer, vol. 33, No.1, pp. 151-161.

IEA, 2006. http://www.iea.org/textbase/press/pressdetail.asp?PRESS_REL_ID=182. (Acessed on December 10, 2006).

IEA, 2007. International Energy Agency:Renewable in global energy supply, an IEA fact sheet, September, 2006. http://www.iea.org/textbase/papers/2006/renewable_ factsheet.pdf

IEA, 2004. International Energy Agency, (Ed). World Energy Outlook 2004. *Organisation for Economic Co-operation and Development,* Paris.

IEA, 2004a. Light's Labor's Lost, Policies for Energy-efficient Lighting. *World Energy Outlook.*

International Agency for the Research on Cancer (IARC) (1989). Occupational Exposures in Petroleum Refining: Crude Oil and Major Petroleum Fuels. IARC Monographs on the Evaluation of Carcinogenic Risks to Humans. Lyon.

Ion, S. E., 1997. *Optimising Our Resources. The Uranium Institute.* Twenty-Second Annual Symposium 3.5 September, London.

IPCC, 2001. Climate Change 2001: The Scientific Basis. Houghton J.T., Ding, Y., Griggs, D.J., Noguer, M., Van der Linden, P.J., Dai, X., Maskell, K. and C.A. Johnson, (eds), Cambridge University Press, Cambridge, UK, 881 pp.

IEO, 2005. Energy Information Administration / International Energy Outlook. Energy-Related Carbon Dioxide Emissions. www.eia.doe.gov/oiaf/ieo/pdf/emissions.pdf <accessed on May 29, 2006>.

IEA, 2005. Energy Information Administration / International Energy Outlook. Worldwide CO_2 Emission from Fossil fuel Consumption and Flaring. www.eia.doe.gov/pub/international/iealf/tableh1co2.xls <accessed on May 30,

International Agency for Research on Cancer (IARC), 1987. Overall evaluations of carcinogenicity. IARC Monographs on the evaluation of carcinogenic risks to humans. Suppl 7. Indiana Department of Environmental Management, 1993.

Juliano, B.O. 1985. *Rice Chemistry and Technology*. St. Paul, Minnesota, USA: merican Association of Cereal Chemists, Inc.

Jonsson, O. and Persson, M., 2003. Biogas as Transportation Fuel. Swedish Gas Center, *Session I,* FVS.

Jarvis, D., Chinn, S., Luczynska, C., Burney, P., 1996. Association of Respiratory Symptoms and Lung Function in Young Adults with Use of Domestic Gas Appliances. *Lancet* 347: 426-31.

Jedrychowski, W., Maugeri, U., Flak, E., Mroz, E., Bianchi, I., 1998. Predisposition to Acute Respiratory Infections among Overweight Preadolescent Children: An Epidemiologic Study in Poland. *Public Health*. 112(3):189–195.

Jash, T., and Basu, S., 1999. Development of a Mini-biogas Digester for Lighting in India.*Energy* 24:409–411.

Josefson, D.2003. Vitamin Supplements Do not Reduce the Incidence of Cancer or Heart Diseases. *BMJ* 327:70

Jackson, V., Blair, I.S., McDowell, D.A., Kennedy, J., Bolton, D.J., 2005. The Incidence of Significant Foodborne Pathogens in Domestic Fefrigerators. Food Control.Available online at www.sciencedirect.com.

Justo, C.E.G. & Veeraragavan, A., 2002.Utilisation of Waste Plastic Bags in Bituminous Mix for Improved Performance of Roads (Bangalore [India]: Centre for Transportation Engineering - university of Bangalore),at:http://www.mindfully.org/Plastic/Recycling/Waste-Plastic-Bituminous-RoadsApr02.htm

Jay, J.M., Loessner, M.J. and Golden, D.A., 2005. Modern Food Microbiology, Seventh Edition. ISBN 0-387-23180-3. Springer Science+Business Media Inc.

Johnson, E. (2003). Cosmetics and the cancer connection. CBC News. January 28, 2003. www.cbc.ca/consumers/market/files/health/cosmetics/ (accessed on Dec17, 06).

Jaakkola, J., J., K, Leromnimon, A and Jaakkola, M.S., 2006. Interior Surface Materials and Asthma in Adults: A Population-based Incident Case-Control Study. *American Journal of Epidemiology*, October 15, 2006.

Johnston, N., 2002. Garlic:A natural antibiotic. Newsbrief,'American ChemicalSociety, http://pubs.acs.org/subscribe/journals/mdd/v05/i04/html/04news4.html(accessed on Aug 02, 2006).

Khraisheh, M.A.M., McMinn, W.A.M. and Magee T.R.A., 2004. Quality and structural changes in starchy foods during microwave and convective drying. *Food Research International*, 37:497–503.

Khan, M.I, 2006.Towards Sustainability in Offshore Oil and Gas Operations. *Ph.D. Dissertation*, Dalhousie University, 442pp.

Khan, M.I., Chhetri, A.B. and Islam, M.R., 2007a. Community-Based Energy Model: A Novel Approach in Developing Sustainable Energy. *Energy Sources,* 2(4):353-370.

Khan, M.M., Prior, D. and Islam, M.R., 2006. A Novel, Sustainable Combined Heating/Cooling/Refrigeration System. *J. Nat. Sci. and Sust. Tech*. 1(1):133-162.

Khan, M.I. and Islam, M.R., 2007a. *Achieving True Sustainability in Technological Development and Natural Resources Management.* Nova Science Publishers, New York, USA: pp384.

Khan, M.I. and Islam, M.R., 2007b. Handbook of Sustainable Oil and Gas Operations Management, Gulf Publishing Company, USA: in press.

Khan, M.I., Chhetri, A.B. and Islam, M.R., 2007b. Analyzing Sustainability of Community-Based Energy Technologies. *Energy Sources,* 2:403-419.

Khan, M.M., Prior, D. and Islam, M.R., 2005b. Direct- usage Solar Refrigeration: from Irreversible Thermodynamics to Sustainable Engineering. *ICEC 2005.* Amman, Jordan, 12 - 14 September 2005.

Khan, M.M., Prior, D. and Islam, M.R., 2007d. A Novel Sustainable Combined Heating/Cooling/Refrigeration System. J. Nat. Sci. and Sust Tech. 1(1):133-162.

Khan, M.I, Zatzman, G. and Islam, M.R., 2005a. New Sustainability Criterion: Development of Single Sustainability Criterion as Applied in Developing Technologies. *Jordan International Chemical Engineering Conference* V, Paper No.: JICEC05-BMC-3-12, Amman, Jordan, 12 - 14 September 2005.

Khan, M.I, and Islam, M.R., 2005a. A Novel Sustainability Criterion as Applied in Developing Technologies and Management Tools. *Sustainable Planning* 2005, 12 - 14 September 2005, Bologna, Italy.

Khan, M.I., and Islam, M.R., 2005b. Assessing the Sustainability of Technological Developments: An Alternative Approach of Selecting Indicators in the Case of Offshore Operations, *ASME International Mechanical Engineering Congress and Exposition (IMECE)*, Orlando, Florida, USA, November.

Khan, M.M., Prior, D. and Islam, M. R., 2007e. Zero-Waste Living with Inherently Sustainable Technologies. *J. Nat.Sci and Sust.Tech* 1(2):271-296.

Khan, M.I. Chhetri A.B.and Lakhal, S. 2007c. A Comparative Pathway Analysis of a Sustainable and an Unsustainable Product. *J. Nature Sci. and Sust. Tech.* 1(2):233-262.

Kaoma, J. and Kasali, G.B., 1994. Efficiency and Emissions of Charcoal use in the Improved Mbuala Cookstoves. Published by the Stockholm Environment Institute in Collaboration with SIDA, ISBN:91 88116: 94 8.

Kvitco, V. 2007. Mathematical Disproof of Lorentz' Mathematics and Einstein's Relativity Theory, *Physics Letters A.* in press.

Khan, A.K., 2002. Research into Biodiesel Kinetic and Catalysts Development. A Thesis Submitted for the Partial Fulfillment of the Requirement for an Individual Inquiry Topic at the University of Queensland, Brisbane, Queensland, Australia.

Kim Oanh, N.T. Nghiem, L.H. and Phyu, Y.L., 2002. Emission of Polycyclic Aromatic Hydrocarbons, Toxicity, and Mutagenicity from Domestic Cooking Using Sawdust Briquettes, Wood, and Kerosene. *Environ. Sci. Technol* 36 (5):833-839.

Khennas, S. and Barnett, A., 2000. Best Practices for Sustainable Development of Micro Hydropower in Developing Countries. Final Synthesis Report. DFID/ITDG, UK. <www.itdg.org> (Accessed: January 25, 2006)

Koutsouba, V., Heberer, T., Fuhrmann, B., Schmidt-Baumler, K., Tsipi, D. and Hiskia, A., 2003. Determination of polar pharmaceuticals in sewage water of Greece by gas chromatography–mass spectrometry. *Chemosphere* 51, 69–75.

Kyessi, A.G., 2005. Community-Based Urban Water Management in Fringe Neighbourhoods: The Case of Dar es Salaam, Tanzania. *Habitat International* 29:1-25.

Khilyuk, L.F. and Chilingar, G.V. 2003. Global Warming: Are We Confusing Cause and Effect? *Energy Sources* 25:357-370

Khilyuk, L.F. and Chilingar, G.V. 2004. Global Warming and Long Term Climatic Changes: A Progress Report. *Environmental Geology* 46(6-7):970-979.

Khilyuk, L.F. and Chilingar, G.V. 2006. On Global Forces of Nature Driving the Earth's Climate. Are Humans Involved? *Environmental Geology*. Published on line.

Khilyuk, L.F., Katz, S.A., Chilingarian, G.V. and Aminzadeh, F. 1994. Global Warming: Are We Confusing Cause and Effect? *Energy Sources* 25:357-370 Kyoto Protocol, 1997. Conference of the Parties Third Session Kyoto, 1-10 December 1997. Kyoto Protocol to the United Nations Framework Convention on Climate Change.

Kuroda, H., 2006. Emerging Asia in the Global Economy: Prospects and Challenges. Remark by President, Asian Development Bank at the Council on Foreign Relations. February 17, 2006, Washington, D.C., USA.

Kondratyev, K.Y.A. and Cracknell, A. P. 1998. *Observing Global Climate Change.* Taylor & Francis. ISBN- 0748401245 pp:544

Kratchanovaa, M., Pavlovaa, E., and Panchevb, I., 2004.The Effect of Microwave Heating of Fresh Orange Peels on the Fruit Tissue and Quality af Extracted Pectin. *Carbohydrate Polymers*, 56:181–185.

Kjallstrand, J. and Olsson, M., 2004. Chimney Emissions From Small-Scale Burning of Pellets and Fuelwood—Examples Referring to Different Combustion Appliances, *Biomass and Bioenergy*, Vol. 27, No. 6: 557-561.

Kline, M., 1972. Mathematical Thought from Ancient to Modern Times, Oxford University Press, New York, USA, 1238 pp.

Katz, S., Chilingar, G.V., and Islam, M.R., 1995. Estimation of Reservoir Porosity and Relative Volume of Pore Filling Components Using Multiple Sources of Geophysical Data, J. Pet. Sci. Eng., vol. 13, No. 2, pp. 103-112

Krone, C. A. and Iwaoka, W. T., 1984. Occurrence of Mutagens in Canned Foods. *Mutation Research Letters* 141 (3-4): 131-134

Kowalak, S., Jankowska, A. and Laczkowska S., 2004. Preparation of various color ultramarine from zeolite A under environment-friendly conditions. *Catalysis Today* 90:167–172.

Kariminiaae-Hamedaani, H.R., Sakurai, A. and Sakakibara, M., 2007. Decolorization of Synthetic Dyes by a New Manganese Peroxidase-Producing White Rot Fungus. *Dyes and Pigments* 72:157-162.

Kreutzweiser, D.P., Back, R.C., Sutton, T.M., Thompson, D.G.and Scarr, T.A., 2002. Community-level disruptions among zooplankton of pond mesocosms treated with a neem (azadirachtin) insecticide. *Aquatic Toxicology* 56:257–273.

Kamra, D.N., Agarwal, N. and Chaudhary, L.C., 2006. Inhibition of ruminal methanogenesis by tropical plants containing secondary compounds. *International Congress Series* 1293:156–163.

Khafagy, S.M., Mohamed, Y.A., Abdel Salam, N.A. and Mahmoud, Z.F., 1977. *Planta Med.* 31, 274.

Kosasi, S., Van der Sluis, W.G., Boelens, R., Hart, L.A. and Labadie, R.P., 1989. Labaditin, a novel cyclic decapeptide from the latex of Jatropha multzfida L. (Euphorbiaceae) isolation and sequence determination by means of two-dimensional NMR. *FEB* (07678) 256 (1, 2): 91-96

Kohn, G. C., 1999. Dictionary of War Fitzroy Dearborn, Chicago, London.

Keenan, J. 2004. New Imperialism for Saharan peoples'Cambridge Review of International Affairs. Publisher:Routledge, part of the Taylor & Francis Group Issue:Volume 17, Number 3 / October, 2004 pp421-436

Kinter, M. 1992. Screen Printing. In *Air Pollution Engineering Manual,* ed. A. Buonicore & W. Davis, 397-401. New York: Van Nostrand Reinhold.

Krupinski, G. 1996. The Formula for Success--The Right Ink. *The Technical Guidebook.* (CD-ROM), 96 (1).

Kamra, D.N., Agarwal, N. and Chaudhary, L.C., 2006. Inhibition of ruminal methanogenesis by tropical plants containing secondary compounds. *International Congress Series* 1293:156–163.

Krupinski, G. 1996. The Formula for Success--The Right Ink. The Technical Guidebook. [CD-ROM], 96 (1).

Kinter, M. 1992. Screen Printing. In Air Pollution Engineering Manual, ed. A. Buonicore & W. Davis, 397-401. New York: Van Nostrand Reinhold.

Khraisheh, M.A.M., McMinn, W.A.M. and Mchanges in starchy foods during microwave and convective drying", Food Research International, 37:497–503.

Kaku, M. and O'Keefe, R.,1994. Hyperspace: a Scientific Odyssey through Parallel Universes, Time Warps, and the Tenth Dimension, Oxford University Press, New York

Ketata, C., Satish, M.G. and Islam, M.R.,2006a. The Meaningful Zero, Proceedings of the 36th International Conference on Computers and Industrial Engineering (ICCIE), Taipei, Taiwan, R.O.C., June 20-23

Ketata, C., Satish, M.G., and Islam, M.R.,2006b. The Meaningful Infinity, Proc. Conference on Computational Intelligence for Modelling, Control and Automation (CIMCA), IEEE Conference, Sydney, Australia, November 28 – December 1

Ketata, C., Satish, M.G., and Islam, M.R.,2006c. Multiple-Solution Nature of Chaos Number-Oriented Equations, Proc. Conference on Computational Intelligence for Modelling, Control and Automation (CIMCA), IEEE Conference, Sydney, Australia, November 28 – December 1

Ketata, C., Satish, M.G., and Islam, M.R., 2006d. Chaos Numbers, Proc. Conference on Computational Intelligence for Modelling, Control and Automation (CIMCA), IEEE Conference, Sydney, Australia, November 28 – December 1.

Ketata, C., Satish, M.G., and Islam, M.R., 2007a. Abacus-Based Calculators, Proc. International Conference of Computational and Experimental Engineering and Sciences (ICCES-2007), Miami, Florida, Jan.

Ketata, C., Satish, M.G., and Islam, M.R.,2007b. Dynamic Numbers for Chaotic Nature, Proc. International Conference of Computational and Experimental Engineering and Sciences (ICCES-2007), Miami, Florida, Jan.

Ketata, C., Satish, M.G. and Islam, M.R.,2007c. Chaos Laws of Motion, Proc. International Conference of Computational and Experimental Engineering and Sciences (ICCES-2007), Miami, Florida, Jan.

Lakhal, S., S. H'mida & R. Islam, 2005. A Green Supply Chain for a Petroleum Company, *Proceedings of 35th International Conference on Computer and Industrial Engineering,* Istanbul, Turkey, June 19-22, 2005, Vol. 2: 1273-1280.

López, M.G., Guzmán, G.R., Dorantes, A.L., 2004. Solid-Phase Microextraction and Gas Chromatography–Mass Spectrometry of Volatile Compounds from Avocado Puree after Microwave Processing. *Journal of Chromatography A*, 1036:87–90

Lewandowicz, G., Fornal, J. and Walkowski, A., 1997. Effect of Microwave Radiation on Physicochemical Properties and Structure of Potato and Tapioca Starches. *Carbohydrate Polymers*, 34(4):213-220.

Louineau, J.P., Dicko, M., Fraenkel, P., Barlow, R. and Bokalders, V., 1994. Rural Lighting, *A guide for Development Workers.* Intermediate Technology Publications in Association with Stockholm Environment Institute, pp.18-32.

Lu, R. 1998. *Enterprises in mountain-specific products in western Sichuan,* China. ICIMOD Discussion Paper Series No. MEI 98/7, Kathmandu, Nepal, ICIMOD.pp 39–41.

Lu, R., 1992. Sea buckthorn: A multipurpose plant species for fragile mountains. International Centre for Integrated Mountain Development. Karmandu, Nepal.

Lu, R.,1990. Research on seabuckthorn (*Hippophae*) resources in China. *Acta Horticulture Sinica* 17(3):177-178.

Latta, 1961. K. Criminal Law - Theft - Colour of Right - Mistaken Belief Alta. L. Rev. 68 (1955-1961).

Lehman-McKeeman. L.D. and Gamsky, E.A. 1999. Diethanolamine Inhibits Chlorine Uptake and Phosphatidylcholine Synthesis in Chinese Hamster Ovary Cells. *Biochem. Biophys. Res. Commun.*262(3):600-604.

Letcher, T. M. and Williamson, A., 2004. Forms and Measurement of Energy. Encyclopedia of Energy, Vol. 2. Elsevier Inc. pp739-748.

Loven, J., 2006. President Touts Hydrogen Powered Cars. The Associated Press, 2006. April, 22. (www.cafcp.org/news_clips/06_04_22_PresBushPress.pdf).

Lindzen, R.S., 2002. Global Warming: The Origin and Nature of the Alleged Scientific Consensus.Regulation:The Cato Review of Business and Government. http://eaps.mit.edu/faculty/lindzen/153_Regulation.pdf

Lindzen, R.S., 2006. Climate Fear. The Opinion Journal, April, 12, 2006. www.opinionjournal.com/ extra/?id=110008220 (Accessed on June, 30, 2006).

Lakhal, S. Y., and H'Mida, S. 2003. A Gap Analysis for Green Supply Chain Benchmarking. In "*32th International Conference on Computers & Industrial Engineering*", Vol. Vol. 1, pp. 1: 44-49, Ireland, August 11- 13th, 2003.

Lean, G and Shawcross, H., 2007. Are mobile phones wiping out our bees? News, The Independent[online]Available:(http://news.independent.co.uk/environment/wildlife/articl e2449968.ece)

Lubick, N., 2000. Desert Fridge: Cooling Foods When There's Not a Socket Around. *Science for Citizen*. November, 2000 issue.

Lindstrom, M., Kiviniemi, K., and Korkeala, H., 2006, "Hazard and control of group II (nonproteolytic) *Clostridium botulinum* in modern food processing", *International J. of Food Microbiology*, 108 (2006): 92 – 104

Li, B. and Sun, D., 2002. Novel Methods for Rapid Freezing and Thawing of Foods-A Review. *Journal of Food Engineering* 54:175–182.

Lemmini, F., and Errougani, A., 2005. Building and Experimentation of a Solar Powered Adsorption Refrigerator. *Renewable Energy* 30:1989–2003.

Lunder, S. and Sharp, R., 2003. Mother's milk, record levels of toxic fire retardants found in American mother's breast milk. Environmental Working Group, Washington, USA.

Livingston, R.J., and Islam, M.R., 1999, "Laboratory Modeling, Field Study and Numerical Simulation of Bioremediation of Petroleum Contaminants", *Energy Sources*, vol. 21 (1/2), 113-130.

Lu, P.J. and Steinhardt, P.J., 2007. Decagonal and Quasicrystalline Tilings in Medieval Islamic Architecture, Science (Washington, DC, United States), vol. 315, pp.1106-1110

Lino, C.M. and da Silveira, M.I.N., 2006. Evaluation of organochlorine pesticides in serum from students in Coimbra, Portugal: 1997–2001. *Environmental Research* 102:339–351.

Leong, K. H., Benjamin Tan, L.L., Mustafa, A. M., 2006. Contamination levels of selected organochlorine and organophosphate pesticides in the Selangor River, Malaysia between 2002 and 2003. *Chemosphere* xxx: xxx–xxx.

Liu, C., Dutton, Z., Behroozi, C.H., and Hau, L.V., 2001. Observation of Coherent Optical Information Storage in an Atomic Medium Using Halted Light Pulses, Nature, vol. 409, pp. 490–493

Matsuoka, K., Iriyama, Y., Abe, T., Matsuoka, M., Ogumi, Z., 2005. Electro-oxidation of Methanol and Ethylene Glycol on Platinum in Alkaline Solution: Poisoning Effects and Product Analysis. *Electrochimica Acta* Vol.51: 1085–1090 MSDS, 2005. Ethylene Glycol Material Data Sheet. www.sciencestuff.com/msds/C1721.html.

Mercola J., 2005. The Hidden Hazards of Microwave Cooking.www.mercola.com/article/microwave/hazards.htm, <accessed on Jan 25, 2006>

Mills, E., 2002. *The $230-billion Global Lighting Energy Bill.* International Association for Energy-Efficient Lighting and Lawrence Berkeley National Laboratory.

Mills, E., 2005. The Specter of Fuel-Based Lighting. *Science* Vol. 308, 27 may 2005.

MNES, 2001. Draft Tenth Five year Plan (2002–2007) and Annual Plan (2002–2003). October 2001. *Ministry of Non-Conventional Energy Sources* (MNES), Government of India, New Delhi.

MoPNG, 2000. Basic Statistics on Indian Petroleum & Natural Gas 1999–2000 Ministry of Petroleum &Natural Gas, Government of India, New Delhi. *Pediatr* 91, 495-8.

Mortimer, N., 1989. Friends of Earth, Vol 9. In: Nuclear Power and Global Warming by Thompson, B., 1997 (http://www.seaus.org.au/powertrip.html).

Mandelbrot, B., 1967. How Long is the Coast of Britain? Statistical Self-Similarity and Fractional Dimension. *Science,* New Series, Vol. 156, No. 3775, May 5, pp. 636-638

Mahajan, S, Konar, S.K. and Boocock, D.G.V., 2006. Standard Biodiesel from Soybean Oil by a Single Chemical Reaction. *J.of American Oil Chemists' Society* 83 (7):641-644.

Mills, A.R., Khan, M.M and Islam, M.R., 2005. High Temperature Reactors for hydrogen Production. Proceeding of the 3rd *International Conference on Energy Research and Development (ICERD-3)* Kuwait 2: 546-555. November 21-23, 2005 Vol.2: Miralai, S., Budge, S. and Islam, M.R. 2006. A novel technique for natural disinfection of contaminated water. *J.of Nat. Sci. and Sust.Tech.* In progress.

Mustafiz, S., 2006. Modeling Certain Complex Phenomenon that occurs within reservoir fluid movements. Ph.D. Dissertation, Faculty of Engineering, Dalhousie University, pp445.

Mustafiz, S., Mousavizadegan, H., and Islam, M.R., 2007. The Knowledge Dimension: Towards Understanding the Mathematics of Intangibles, J. Nat. Sci. Sust. Tech., vol. 1, No. 3

Martinot, E., 2005. Global Renewable Status Report. Paper prepared for the REN21 Network. The Worldwatch Institute.

Meher, L.C., Vidya Sagar, D., Naik, S.N., 2004. Technical aspects of biodiesel production by transesterification-a review. *Renewable and sustainable energy review*: 1-21

Murrell, J. C., 1994. Molecular genetics of methane oxidation. *Biodegradation* 5:145-149

Ma, F. and Hanna, M. A., 1999. Biodiesel production: a review. *Bioresource Technology*, 70:1-15.

Mcdonald, B., 2006. Factors Affecting Copper Corrosion and THM Formation in Low Alkalinity Water. *M.Sc Thesis.* Civil and Resources Engineering, Dalhousie University, Halifax, Canada.

Milburn, A.,1996. A global freshwater convention ± the best means towards sustainable freshwater management. In *Proceedings Stockholm water symposium* (pp. 9-11). 4-9 August.

Miralai, S., 2006. Natural additives for water treatment. *MASc thesis,* Environmental Engineering, Dalhousie University, Halifax, Canada.

Miller, G. W., 2006. Integrated Concepts in Water Reuse: Managing Global Water Needs. *Desalination* 187:65–75.

Moldovan, Z. 2006. Occurrences of pharmaceutical and personal care products as micro pollutants in rivers from Romania. *Chemosphere*. In press.

Mittelstaedt, M., 2006a. Toxic shock: Canada's chemical reaction. *The Globe and Mail*, May, 27.

Mittelstaedt, M., 2006b. Chemical used in water bottles linked to prostate cancer. *The Globe and Mail,* June 09.

Mittelstaedt, M., 2007. 'Inherently Toxic' Chemical Faces Its Future, The Globe and Mail, April 7, pp. A10

Murkovic, M., 2004. Acrylamide in Austrian Foods. *J. Biochem. Biophys. Methods* 61: 161–167.

Michalski, M.C. and Januel, C., 2006. Does Homogenization Affect the Human Health Properties of Cow's Milk? *Trends in Food Science & Technology* 17:423–437

Murray, B., 2001. Fast-food Culture Serves up Super-size Americans. *Monitor on Psychology* 32 (11), American Psychology Association. December 2001.

Montville, T.J. and Matthews, K.R., 2005. Food Microbiology:An Introduction. ASM Press, 1752 N. St.NW, Washington, DC.ISBN:1-55581-308-9.

Martinez, I., 2006. Refrigeration. http://imartinez.etsin.upm.es/bk3/c18/Refrigeration.htm

Mossel, D.A.A. and Struijk, C.B., 1991. Public Health Implication of Refrigerated Pasteurized (sous-vide) Food. *International Journal of Food Microbiology*, 13:187-206.

Murray, M. and Pizzorno, J., 2005. The Health Hazards of Drinking Coca-Cola and other Soft Drinks. Encyclopedia of Natural Medicine, Revised Second Edition http://www.newstarget.com/004416.html

Mendiratta, A., 2006. Is Your Lipstick Safe? Environment. www.msmagazine.com/summer 2006/isyourlipsticksafe.asp (Dec 17, 2006)

MSDS, 2000. *Material Safety Data Sheet: White Petrolatum.* According to ISO 11014-1.

MSDS, 2006. *Material Safety Data Sheet, Canadian Centre for Occupational Health and Safety,* 135 Hunter Street East, Hamilton ON Canada L8N 1M5.

MSDS, 2001. Material Safety Data Sheet Sodium hydroxide, Solid, Pellets or Beads. http://avogadro.chem.iastate.edu/MSDS/NaOH.htm (November 27, 2006).

MSDS, 2001a. Material safety data sheet for ethyl alcohol (C_2H_5OH) (http://www.nafaa. org/ethanol.pdf#search=%22C2H5OH%20MSDS%22).

MSDS, 2003. Safety (MSDS) Data for Ammonium Sulphite.http://physchem. ox.ac. uk/MSDS/AM/ammonium_sulphite.html

MSDS, 2004. Material Safety Data Sheet for Citric Acid. ww.jtbaker.com/msds/ englishhtml/c4730.htm (accessed on Dec 20, 2006).

MSDS, 2005a. *Material Safety Data Sheet for Phosphoric Acid.*

MSDS, 2005b. *Material Safety Data Sheet for Sodium Lauryl Sulfate.* http://www.hillbrothers. com/msds/pdf/phosphoric-acid.pdf (accessed on Dec 10, 2007).

Maske, J., 2006. Life in Plastics, It's Fantastic. Gemini 2005-2006. www.ciwmb. ca.gov/Markets/StatusRpts/plastichtm (accessed on Dec 31, 2006).

Molero, C., Lucas, A. D. and Rodrıguez, J. F., 2006. Recovery of Polyols from Flexible Polyurethane Foam by ''Split-Phase'' Glycolysis: Glycol Influence. *Polymer Degradation and Stability.* Vol. 91: 221-228.

Mercer, C., 2006. More Pesticides found in Coca-Cola, Pepsiko Drinks. Report from Center from Environment Studies, India. http://www.beveragedaily.com/news/ng.asp?id=69609-coca-cola-pesticides-india-soft-drinks (Acessed on December 9, 2007).

Michaels, G.B., Lewis, D.L., 1985 Sorption and Toxicity of Azo and Triphenylmethane Dyes to Aquatic Microbial Populations. *Environ. Toxicol. Chem.* 4:45-50.

Maund, B., 2006. Color. Standardford Encyclopedia of Phylosophy. Sep 18, 2006. http://plato.stanford.edu/entries/color/ (accessed on Dec 23, 2006).

Morvan, X., Mouvet, C., Baran, N. and Gutierrez, A.., 2006. Pesticides in the groundwater of a spring draining a sandy aquifer: Temporal variability of concentrations and fluxes. *Journal of Contaminant Hydrology* 87:176–190.

Montesinos, E., 2003. Development, registration and commercialization of microbial pesticides for plant protection. *International Microbiology* 6:245–252

Mengual, L., 1997. Extraction of bioactive substances from J, curcas L. and bioassays on Zonocerus variegatus, Sesamia calamistis and Busseola fusca for characterization of insecticidal properties. In: B*iofuels and Industrial Products from Jatropha Curcas.* Giibitz, G.M., Mittelbach, M., Trabi, M. (Eds.), pp. 211-215. DBV Graz.

Manandhar, N.P. (1989) *Fitotherapia* 60, 61.

McCrady, E., 2004. Abbey Publications. http://palimpsest.stanford.edu/byorg/abbey/ napp/facts.html (November 26, 2006)

Mandelbrot, B., 1967. How Long is the Coast of Britain? Statistical Self-Similarity and Fractional Dimension. *Science,* New Series, Vol. 156, No. 3775, May 5, pp. 636-638

Miralai, S.2006. Replacing artificial additives with natural alternatives, MASc Thesis,Dalhousie University, Nova Scotia, Canada

Mittelstaedt, M. 2007. Inherently toxic chemical faces its future' *The Globe and Mail*,Sat 7, April 2007, Page A10, www.theglobeandmail.com/servlet/ArticleNews/freeheadlines/ LAC/20070407/CHEMICAL07/national/National.

Mustafiz, S., J. Paddock, and Islam, M.R., 2007.The use of ultrasonic irradiation for oil water separation. *J. Pet. Sci. Tech.* In press.

McLeans, 2005, Dec. issue.

Maclaren, W., 2007. World fast? Australia switches of incandescent bulbshttp, Treehugger[online]Available:(http//www.treehugger.com/files/2007/02/world_first_aus.p hp) (15 April, 2007)

Manders, J. 1978. 4 Arguments for the Elimination of Television William Morrow and Company, NY

National Energy Pricing Overview, 1996. at:http://energytrcnds.pnl.gov/canada/ca004.htm#36 (accessed 15.01/06)

NepalNews.com. 2002. *"Hard Days Ahead."* Vol 20; No. 15. Oct20-26.

Nabi, M.N., Akhter, M. S., Shahadat, M. M. Z., 2006. Improvement of engine emissions with conventional diesel fuel and diesel–biodiesel blends. *Bioresource Technology.* Vol. 97: 372–378

Nelson, L.A., Foglia, T.A. and Marmer, W.N., 1996. Lipase Catalyzed Production of Biodiesel. *JAOCS*, 73(8):1191-1195.

NOAA, 2005. Greenhouse gases, global monitoring division, Earth System Research Laboratory, National Oceanic and Atmospheric Administration, USA

Nott, K. P. and Hall L.D., 1999. Advances in Temperature Validation of Foods. *Trends in Food Science & Technology*, 10: 366-374

NESCAUM, 2005. *Low Sulfur Heating Oil: An Overview of Benefits, Costs and Implementation Issues.*

Natural Resources Canada, 2004. Biomass Heating Project Analysis. Clean Energy Project Analysis Course. RETScreen International. www. retscreen.net.

Nallinson, R.G., 2004. Natural Gas Processing and Products. *Encyclopedia of Energy* Vol. IV, Elsevier Publication. Okhlahama, USA. pp235-247.

NOAA, 2005a. Trends in Atmospheric Carbon Dioxide. NOAA-ESRL Global Monitoring Division. www.cmdl.noaa.gov/ccgg/trends/(accessed on June 04, 2006)

NASA, 1999. Biomass Burning and Global Change. http://asd www.larc.nasa. gov/biomass_burn/biomass_burn.html.

Nix, D.H., 2000. Factors to Consider When Selecting Skin Cleansing Products *JWOCN* Vol.27 (5):260-268.

Nemery, B., Fischler, B., Boogaerts, M., Lison, D. and Willems, J., 2002. The Coca-Cola incident in Belgium, June 1999. *Food and Chemical Toxicology* 40:1657–1667.

Nikkei, N., 2002. http://www.nni.nikkei.co.jp/) <accessed on May 20th, 2006) Nix, D.H., 2000. Factors to Consider When Selecting Skin Cleansing Products *JWOCN* Vol.27 (5):260-268.

NIOSH, 1998. *Control of Spotting Chemical Hazards in Commercial Drycleaning. DHHS (NIOSH) Publication No. 97-158, www.cdc.gov/niosh/hc20.html.* Natural Resources Canada, 1998. Alberta Post-Consumer Plastics Recycling Strategy

Nohr, R. S., MacDonald, J. G., McGinniss, V. D., Whitmore, Jr., Robert S. 1997. Substrate having a mutable colored composition there on, United States Patent 5616443 (http://www.freepatentsonline.com/5616443.html).

Natural Resource Canada, 2005. Improving Energy Performance In Canada – Report To Parliament Under The Energy Efficiency Act - 2003-2004, Chapter 8: Renewable Energy.http://www.oee.nrcan.gc.ca/corporate/statistics/neud/dpa/data_e/parliament03-04/chapter8.cfm?attr=0 (Acessed on December 10, 2007).

OSHA (1999).OSHA Technical Manual. www.osha.gov/dts/osta/otm/otm_iv/otm_iv_2.html (accessed on Dec 24, 2006).

OSHA, 2006. Occupational Safety and Health Administration, US Department of Labor <www.osha.gov/pls/oshaweb/owadisp.show_document (Accessed on June 08, 2006)

Orme, M. and Leksmono, N., 2002. Ventilation Modeling Data Guide, AIVC Guide 5, 2002 80 pp, ISBN 2 9600 355 2 6.

Openshaw, K., 2000. A review of Jatropha curcas: an oil plant of unfulfilled promise. *Biomass and Bioenergy* 19:1-15.

Olsson, M. and Kjällstrand, J., 2004.Emissions from burning of softwood pellets, *Biomass and Bioenergy*, Vol. 27, No. 6: 607-611.

Ozogul, Y., Ozogul, F., Gokbulut, C., 2006, "Quality assessment of wild European eel (*Anguillaanguilla*) stored in ice, *Food Chemistry*, 95: 458–465.

Oruna-Concha, M. J., Bakker, J. and Ames. J. M., 2002. Comparison of the Volatile Components of Eight Cultivars of Potato after Microwave Baking. *Lebensm.-Wiss. u.-Technol.*, 35:80–86.

OSPAR, 2004. Oslo and Paris Convention for the Protection of the Marine Environment of the North-East Atlantic. OSPAR Commission, ISBN 1-904426-36-0.

Olive Oil Source, 2006. Chemical and Nutritional Properties of Olive Oil. 390 Vista Grande, Greenbrae, Ca 94904. www.oliveoilsource.com/olivechemistry.htm (accessed on May 90, 2006).

O'Neill, C., Hawkes, F.R., Hawkes, D.L., Lourenco, N.D., Pinheiro, H.M., Delee, W., 1999. Color in textile effluents sources, measurement, discharge consents and simulation: a review. *Journal of Chemical Technology and Biotechnology* 74, 1009–1018.

Oldal, B., Maloschik, E., Uzinger, N., Anton, A. and Székács, A., 2006. Pesticide residues in Hungarian soils. *Geoderma* 135:163–178.

O'Reilly, K. 2003. Competing Logics of Women's Participation in a Rajasthan Development Project," in Institutions and Social Change, Surjit Singh and Varsha Joshi, eds. Jaipur: Rawat. 272-291.

Pope, C.A. III, Xu, X., 1993. Passive Cigarette Smoke, Coal Heating, and Respiratory Symptoms of Nonsmoking Women in China. *Environ Health Perspect.* 101:314–316.

Piipari R., Tuppurainen, M., Tuomi, T., Mantyla, L., Henriks-Eckerman, M.L.,Keskinen, H., and Nordman, H., 1998. Diethanolamine-induced Occupational Asthma, a Case Report. *Clin. Exp.Allergy* 28(3):358-362.

Pickover, C.A., 2004. The Paradox of God and the Science of Omniscience, Palgrave MacMillan, N.Y., 288 pp.

Pomsa, R. E. and Tatinib, S.R. 2001. Survival of *Helicobacter pylori* in ready-to-eat foods at 4^{0}C. Short communication. *International Journal of Food Microbiology* 63:281–286.

Prescott, M., 2006. Light Bulbs: Not Such a Bright Idea.Viewpoint. BBC News Website, 3 February, 2006. http://news.bbc.co.uk/2/hi/science/nature/4667354.stm.

Pauley, S.M., 2004. Lighting for the Human Circadian Clock: Recent Research Indicates That Lighting Has Become a Public Health Issue.*Medical Hypotheses* 63:588-596.

Pryor, R.W., Hanna, M.A, Schinstock, J.L., Bashford, L.L., 1982. Soybean oil fuel in a small diesel engine. *Trans ASAE* 26:333–8.

Pohkarel, G.R., Chhetri, A.B., Khan, M.I. and Islam, M.R., 2007. Decentralized Micro Hydro Energy Systems in Nepal: En Route to Sustainable Energy Development. *Energy Sources.*In Press.

Pershing, J. and Cedric, P., 2002. Promises and Limits of Financial Assistance and the Clean Development Mechanism. *Beyond Kyoto: Energy Dynamics and Climate Stabilization. Paris: International Energy Agency*, 94-98.

Pica, E., 2003. Power Politics-Linking Congress, Campaign Contributions and Energy Policy. *Friends of Earth*. Vol.4 August 26, 2003.

Pokharel, G.R., Chhetri, A, B., Devkota, S. and Shrestha, P., 2003. En Route to Strong Sustainability: Can Decentralized Community Owned Micro Hydro Energy systems in Nepal Realize the Paradigm? A case study of Thampalkot VDC in Sindhupalchowk District in Nepal. *International Conference on Renewable Energy Technology for Rural Development*. Kathmandu, Nepal.

Pokharel, G. R.1999. Empowerment through AT and Local Resources. A Case Study. AT Forum. Number 12.

PAD, 2006. Protecting Animals in Democracy [online] Available: (http://www.vote4animals.org.uk/farming.htm) (October 4, 2006).

PVC, 2006. Poly Vinyl Chloride, Wikipedia, the Free Encyclopedia [online] Available: (http://en.wikipedia.org/wiki/Polyvinyl_chloride)(October 4, 2006).

Pauling, Linus. 1954. "Nobel Lecture in Chemistry", reproduced at: http://www.nobelprize. org/peace/laureates/1962/pauling-lecture.html

Pearce, D. W., Barbier, E., Markandya, A. 1990. Sustainable Development, Economics and Environment in the third world, Edward Elgar, London, U.K.

Plas, R., Van der and De Graaff, A.,1988. A Comparison of Lamps for domestic lighting in developing countries. The World Bank. Washington, DC.

Pearce, D. W.1987. Rural Electrification in developing countries. A reappraisal. *Energy Policy* 15 (4). Pp 329-338.

PANUPS, 2006. Pesticide Action Network Updates Service (PANUPS). Pesticides - A Greater Threat to Children. www.panna.org/resources/panups/ panup_20060307.dv.html (accessed on July 02, 2003).

Piyasena, P., Dussault, C., Koutchma, T., Ramaswamy, H.S.and Awuah, G.B., 2003. Radio Frequency Heating of Foods: Principles Applications and Related Properties-a review. *Crit Rev Food Sci Nutr.* 43(6):587-606.

Peksa, A., Gołubowska, G., Aniołowski, K., Lisinska, G. and Rytel, E. 2006. Changes of Glycoalkaloids and Nitrate Contents in Potatoes During Chip Processing. *Food Chemistry* 97: 151–156.

Pedreschia, F., Kaackb, K. and Granby, K., 2004. Reduction of Acrylamide Formation in Potato Slices During Frying. *Lebensm.-Wiss. u.-Technol.* 37:679–685.

Preuss H.G, Anderson RA, 1998. Chromium update: Examining Recent Literature 1997-1998. *Curr Opin Clin Nutr Metab Care Nov.*1(6):487-9.

Porcelli, M. et al, 1997. Non-thermal Effects of Microwaves on Proteins: Thermophilic Enzymes as model system", *FEBS Letters*, 402(1997): 102-106.

Peters, J.B., 2003. Hazardous Chemicals in Consumer Products, *TNO Netherlands Organisation for Applied Scientific Research, The Netherlands* pp.1-28.

Patlak, M., 1993. Hair Dye Dilemmas. US Food and Drug Association. http://www. cfsan.fda.gov/~dms/cos-818.html (accessed on Dec 17, 2006).

Pandey, A., Singh, P., and Iyengar, L., 2006. Bacterial Decolorization and Degradation of Azo dyes. *International Biodeterioration & Biodegradation, In press.*

Pimentel, D., & Acquay, H. 1992. The Environmental and Economic Costs of Pesticide Use. *BioScience* 42:750-760.

Papadakis, E.N., Vryzas, Z., and Papadopoulou-Mourkidou, E., 2006. Rapid method for the determination of 16 organochlorine pesticides in sesame seeds by microwave-assisted extraction and analysis of extracts by gas chromatography–mass spectrometry. *Journal of Chromatography A*, 1127: 6–11.

Panahi, P., Vosough-Ghanbari, S., Pournourmohammadi, S., Ostad, S.N, Nikfar, S., Minaie, B. and Abdollahi, M., 2006. Stimulatory effects of malathion on the key enzymes activities of insulin secretion in langerhans islets, glutamate dehydrogenase and glucokinase. *Toxicol. Mech. Methods* 16:161-167.

Pournourmohammadi, S., Farzami, B., Ostad, S.N., Azizi, E. and Abdollahi, M., 2005. Effects of malathion subchronic exposure on rat skeletal muscle glucose metabolism, *Environ. Toxicol. Pharmacol.* 19:191–196.

Petrik, J., Drobna, B., Pavuk, M., Jursa, S., Wimmerova, S. and Chovancova, J., 2006. Serum PCBs and organochlorine pesticides in Slovakia: Age, gender, and residence as determinants of organochlorine concentrations. *Chemosphere* 65:410–418.

Peter, G., 2006. Gender Roles and Relationships: Implications for Water Management. *Physics and Chemistry of the Earth* 31:723–730.

Pinto, A.C., Guarieiro, L.L.N., Rezende, M.J.C., Ribeiro, N.M., Torres, E.A., Lopes, W.A., Pereira, P.A.P., Andrade, J.B., 2005. Biodiesel: an overview. Journal of Brazilian Chemical Society 16, 1313–1330.

Qian Z, Zhang JJ, Korn LR, Wei F, Chapman RS., 2004. Factor Analysis of Household Factors: Are They Associated with Respiratory Conditions in Chinese Children? *Int J Epidemiol* 33(3):582–588.

Qin, L.Q., Wang, P.Y., Kaneko, T., Hoshi, K. and Sato, A., 2004. Estrogen: One of the Risk Factors in Milk for prostate cancer. *Medical Hypotheses* 62:133–142.

Quinn, G.E., Shin, C.H., Maguire, M.G. and Stone, R.A., 1999. Myopia and ambient lighting at night. *Nature* May 13, 1999. 399 (6732):113

Rijal, K.1998a. Sustainable Energy Use for Mountain Areas: Community-level Energy Planning and Management, Issues in Mountain Development, ICIMOD, Kathmandu, Nepal 1998/4.

Rijal, K., 1998b. An Agenda for Formulating and Implementing Policies for RET production in Nepal. Renewable Energy Technologies- A Brighter Future, ICIMOD, Kathmandu, Nepal. May 1998.

Riley, C., 2002. Bioethanol: A Renewable Transportation Fuel from Biomass. *Biotechnology Division for Fuels and Chemicals National Bioenergy Center AIChE Spring Conference* March 12, 2002.

Randall, W., 1999. *Technical handbook for marine biodiesel in recreational boats.* Prepared for report, prepared by system lab services, a division of Williams pipe Lines Company.

Richardson, P. (eds.), 2005. *Thermal Technologies in Food Processing. Campden and Chorleywood Food Research Association,* UK. Woodhead Publishing Limited.

Rischer, H. and Oksman-Caldentey, K.M., 2006. Unintended Effects in Genetically Modified Crops: Revealed by Metabolomics? *TRENDS in Biotechnology* 24(3):102-104.

Reuters, 2004. Night light linked to rise in child leukemia, Disruption of body clock associated with cancer. http://www.msnbc.msn.com/id/5941842/ (accessed on November 25, 2006).

Ritchie, G. D., Still, K. R., Alexander, W. K., Nordholm, A. F., Wilson, C. L., Rossi, J., 3rd and Mattie, D. R., 2001. A Review of the Neurotoxicity Risk of Selected Hydrocarbon Fuels. *J Toxicol Environ Health B Crit Rev* 4:223-312.

Reddy, J.N and Ramesh, A., 2005. Parametric studies for improving the performance of a Jatropha oil-fuelled compression ignition engine. *Renewable Energy*. In Press xx: xx-xx

Refocus, 2005. *World's Highest Altitude Solar Cooking System?* www.re-focus.net.

Rahman, M.S., Hossain, M.E., and Islam, M.R., 2006. An Environment-Friendly Alkaline Solution for Enhanced Oil Recovery (EOR). *J. of Petrolium Sci. and Tech..* Accepted.

Ramesohl, S. and Merten, F., 2006. Energy System Aspects of Hydrogen as an Alternative Fuel in Transport. *Energy Policy* 34:1251–1259.

Rich, B.. 1994. Mortgaging the Earth: The World Bank, Environmental Impoverishment, and the Crisis of Development (Images Publishing James&James/EarthScan).

Rey, L, 2003. Thermoluminescence of Ultra-High Dilutions of Lithium Chloride and Sodium Chloride, Physica A, vol. 323, pp. 67–74.

Ray, D. E., Richardson, J. R., De La Torre Ugarte, D.G. and Tiller, K. H., 1998. Estimating Price Variability in Agriculture: Implications for Decision Makers", at: http://apacweb.ag.utk.edu/ppap/pdf/98/saeaestimate.pdf, Last accessed 15 January 2006

Rao, S and Parulekar, B.B.,1999. Renewable Technology. Non Conventional, Renewable and Conventional. *Khanna Publisher, Delhi, India.* ISBN NO: 81-7409-040-1.

Rivera, D., 1996. *Private sector Participation in the Water Supply and Wastewater Sector: Lessons from the six countries.* Washington, D.C: The World Bank.

Rahman, M. H., Wasiuddin, N.M., Islam, M.R. 2004. Experimental and Numerical Modeling Studies of Arsenic Removal with Wood Ash from Aqueous Streams. *The Canadian Journal of Chemical Engineering 82:968-977* Reilly, K.O., 2006. 'Traditional' women, 'modern' water: Linking gender and Commodification in Rajasthan, India. *Geoforum* 37:958–972.

Rossetti, V. A., and Medici, F., 1995. Inertization of Toxic Metals in Cement Matrices: Effects on Hydration, Setting and Hardening. *Cement and Concrete Research* 2.5(6): 1147-1152.

Rebhan, A. and Schroll, M., 2003. Executive Summary. Decentralized Water Supply, Distribution and Sewage Management Systems in Serbia-Montenegro and Albania. AROW Business and Consulting Works. Mulheimer Str. 43, D47058 Duisberg Germany.

Redmond, G.A., Gormley, T.R., Butler, F., 2003. The effect of short- and long-term freeze-chilling on the quality of mashed potato, *Innovative Food Science and Emerging Technologies,* 4:85-97.

Redmond, G.A., Gormley, T.R., Butler, F., 2004. The effect of short- and long-term freeze-chilling on the quality of cooked green beans and carrots", *Innovative Food Science and Emerging Technologies,* 5: 65–72.

Ravndal, F., 2003. Quintessence from Extra Dimensions, The Gunnar Nordstrom Symposium on Theoretical Physics, Helsinki, Aug. 27-30

Reinen, D. and Lindner, G.-G. Chem. Soc. Rev. 28 (1999) 75: In Fabian, J., Komiha, N., Linguerri, R. and Rosmus, P., 2006. The absorption wavelengths of sulfur chromophors of ultramarines calculated by time-dependent density functional theory. *Journal of Molecular Structure: THEOCHEM* 801: 63–69.

Rahimi, R. and Abdollahi, M., 2006. A review on the mechanisms involved in hyperglycemia induced by organophosphorus pesticides, *Pesticide Biochemistry and Physiology.* In press.

Rey, L, 2003. Thermoluminescence of Ultra-High Dilutions of Lithium Chloride and Sodium Chloride, Physica A, vol. 323, pp. 67–74.

Rezg, R., Mornagui, B., El-Arbi, M., Kamoun, A., El-Fazaa, S. and Gharbi, N., 2006. Effect of subchronic exposure to Malathion on glycogen phosphorylase and hexokinase activities in rat liver using native PAGE, *Toxicology* 223:9-14.

Rial-Otero, R., Gaspar, E.M., Moura, I. and Capelo, J.L., 2006. Chromatographic-based methods for pesticide determination in honey: An overview. *Talanta* xxx: xxx–xxx.

Shapiro, R., Zatzman, G.M. and Mohiuddin, Y., 2007. Towards Understanding Disinformation. *J. Nat.Sci. and Sust.Tech* 1(3):471-504.

Saka, S., and Kudsiana, D., 2001. Methyl esterification of free fatty acids of rapeseed oil as treated in supercritical methanol. *J Chem Eng Jpn,* 34(3): 373-387.

Stavarache, C., Vinatoru, M., Nishimura, R., and Maeda, Y, 2006. Fatty Acids Methyl Esters from vegetable Oil by Means of Ultrasonic Energy. *Ultrasonics Sonochemistry* 12:367-372.

Supple, B., Howard, H.R., Gonzalez, G.E., Leahy, J.J., 1999. The effect of steam treating waste cooking oil on the yield of methyl ester. *J. Am. Oil Soc. Chem.* 79 (2):175–178.

Shrestha, S. and Amatya, V. B.1998. A Case Study of Micro-Hydropower in Nepal. In: Rijal, K.(Ed). *Renewable Energy Technologies- A Brighter Future.* ICIMOD. Kathmandu.

Sheehan, J., Dunahay, T., Benemann, J., Roessler, P., 1998. *A Look Back at the U.S. Department of Energy's Aquatic Species Program—Biodiesel from Algae.* NREL/TP-580-24190.

Shumaker, G.A., McKissick, J., Ferland, C., Doherty, B., 2003. A Study on the Feasibility of Biodiesel Production in Georgia, February 2003, *FR-03-02,* Center of Agribusiness and Economic Development, 26 pp.

Seal, S., Barr, T.L., Krezoski, S., Petering, D., 2001. Surface Modication of Silicon and Silica in Biological Environment: An X-ray Photoelectron Spectroscopy Study. *Applied Surface Science* 173:339-351.

Singh, A.2005. University of Winnipeg, The Bush Doctrine:Creating Discord in International Security Critique:A worldwide journal of politics, http://lilt.ilstu.edu/critique/Fall%202004%20Docs/Singh_Ajit.pdf.

Sierra, I., 2000. Influence of Heating Conditions in Continuous-flow Microwave or Tubular Heat Exchange Systems on the Vitamin B1 and B2 Content of Milk. *Lait,* 80: 601–608.

Stadler RH, Blank I, Varga N, Robert F, Hau J, Guy PA, et al. Acrylamide from Maillard reaction products. *Nature,* 419:449.

Santis, N., Mendoza, F., Moyano, P., Pedreschi, F. and Dejmek, P., 2005. Soaking in a NaCl Solution Produce Paler Potato Chips. *LWT.* In Press.

Schlosser, E., 2002. Fast Food Nation: What the All American Meal is Doing to the World. Penguin Books. ISBN 0 14 100687 0 , pp 400.

Sustainable Building Sourcebook, 2006. Solar Hot Water, Heating and Cooling Systems. *A Sustainable Sourcebook for Green and Sustainable Building,* 1994-2006. www.greenbuilder.com/sourcebook/HeatCool.html (December, 28, 2006)

Singh, R.B. and Mahato, P.K., 2003. Substitution of Imported kerosene Oil by Indigenous and Renewable plant bi-hydrocarbons in Rural Areas of Mid Hills in Nepal. *International conference of Renewable Energy Technology for rural Development.* 12-14 October, 2003, Kathmandu, Nepal.

SLTBR, 2005. Society for Light Treatment and Biological Rhythms. *Abstracts* 17:10-58.

Schroeder, W.R., and Y. Yao. 1995. Sea Buckthorn: A promising multi-purpose crop for Saskatchewan. PFRA Shelterbelt Publication No. 62. Regina, SK: Prairie Farm Rehabilitation Administration. http://www.agr.gc.ca/pfra/shelterbelt/shbpub62.htm (Accessed on November 22, 2006).

Schnepf, M. and Barbeau, W. E., 1989. Survival of Salmonella Typhimurium in Roasting Chickens Cooked in a Microwave, Convention Microwave and Conventional Electric Oven. *J. Food Safety,* 9:245-252.

Service, R.F., 2005. Is it time to shoot for the sun? *Science,* Vol.309:549-551.

Smalley, R.E., 2005. Future Global Energy Prosperity: The Terawatts Challenge. Materials Matters, *MRS Bulletin.* Vol.30 <www.mrs.org/ publications/bulletin>.

Samuel, E. and Steinman, D.,1995. *The Safe Shopper's Bible: A Consumer's Guide to Nontoxic Household Products, Cosmetics and Food.* New York: Macmillan Publishers.

Sugie, H., Sasaki, C., Hashimoto, C., Takeshita, H., Nagai, T., Nakamura, S., Furukawa, M., Nishikawa, T., Kurihara, K., 2004. Three cases of sudden death due to butane or propane gas inhalation: analysis of tissues for gas components. Case report. *Forensic Science International.* Vol. 143. pp: 211–214

Stosur, G., 2000. US Department of Energy, Washington D.C., *Personal Communication with M.R. Islam.*

Schernhammer, E.S., Kroenke, C.H., Laden, F., and Hankinson, S. E., 2006. Night work and risk of breast cancer. *Epidemiology* 17:108-111.

Shastri, C.M., Sangeetha, G. and Ravindranath, N.H. 2002. *Dissemination of Efficient ASTRA stove: case study of a successful entrepreneur in Sirsi, India.* Energy for Sustainable Development.Volume VI., No. 2

Smalley, R.E., 2003. *Our Energy Challenge. Energy and Nano Technology Conference,* Rice University, May 03, 2003.

Salbu, B. Janssens, K., Lind, O.C., Proost, K., Gijsels L., Danesi, P.R.2005. Oxidation States of Uranium in Depleted Uranium Particles from Kuwait. *Journal of Environmental Radioactivity* 78:125–135

Singh, N., 2006. The Changing Role of Women in Water Management: Myths and Realities. *The Changing Role of Women.* Wagadu Vol. 3, Spring 2006.

Shapiro, R., Ahmad, M., Zatzman, G., Satish, M. and. Islam, M.R, 2007. The Role of Intension in Social Progress. *Executive Times.* Bangladesh.

Solanes, M. and Gonzalez-Villarreal, F., 1999. The Dublin Principles for Water as Reflected in a Comparative Assessment of Institutional and Legal Arrangements for Integrated Water Resources Management. Global Water Partnership, Technical Advisory Committee (TAC) *Background Papers No.3* ISSN:1403-5324.

Solomon, C., Casey, P., Mackne, C. and Lake A.,1998. Fact sheet, Chlorine Disinfection. National Small Flows Clearinghouse. *U.S. Environmental Protection Agency under Assistance Agreement* No. CX824652.

Shitanda, D., Nishiyama, Y. and Koide, S. 2000. Husking Characteristics of Different Varieties of Rice. In *Proc. 14th Memorial CIGR World Congress,* 812-816. Tsukuba University, 28-1 December.

Shrestha, G.R. and Shrestha, L.K., 1998. Meeting Energy Needs of Rural Communities Through Improvement of Water Mills (Pani Ghatta) in Rural Areas of Nepal. Proceedings of the International Conference on *Role of Renewable Energy Technology for rural Development,* 12-14 October, 1998, Kathmandu, Nepal.

Szymonska, J. and Wodnicka, K., 2005. Effect of Multiple Freezing and Thawing on the Surface and Functional Properties of Granular Potato Starch. *Food Hydrocolloids* 19:753–760.

Sontag, J.M., 1981. Carcinogenicity of substituted-benzenediamines (phenylenediamines) in rats and mice. *J. Natl. Cancer Inst.* 66, 591-602.

Saxena, M., Warshaw, E. and Ahmed, D. D. F. 2001. Eyelid Allergic Contact Dermatitis to Black Iron Oxide. *American Journal of Contact Dermatitis* Vol. 12(1):38-39

Schreurs, R.H.M.M., Quaedackers, M.E., Seinen, W., van der Burg, B.2002. Transcriptional activation of estrogen receptors ERf and ERg by polycyclic musks is cell type dependent, *Toxicology and Applied Pharmacology* Vol.183 (1):1-9

Stimpert, D., 2006. Caring for Leather Shoes - Shoe Polish & Polishing Leather Shoes. http://shoes.about.com/od/shoe_care/a/c_leather_shoes_4.htm <accessed on May 20, 2006)

Sodium Lauryl Sulfate, 1983. Final Report on the Safety Assessment of Sodium Lauryl Sulfate. *Journal of the American college of toxicology* Vol 2(7).

Sharma, D., 2006. Has the Bt cotton bubble burst ? Opinion/Agriculture. India Together. Sat 28 Oct 2006

Shin, D.M., Kim, C.N., Kim, D.S., 2003. Emission Characteristics of Volatile Organic Compounds (VOCs) from a Carpet. *Journal of SAREK* 15:40-9.

Smith, C., 2001. Pesticide exports from U.S. Ports, 1997-2000, Int. J. Occup. Environ. Health 2001, Oct/Dec 7(4): 266-274.

Soulincode, 2006.http://www.soulincode.com/images/usa_at_night_nasa.jpg) (October 4, 2006).

Schmid, R.E., 2005. Human Pollutants Collect in Bird Droppings, Live Science http://www.livescience.com/environment/ap_050714_bird_droppings.html (October 4, 2006).

Steenhuysen, J., 2007. Mother Nature Still a Rich Source of New Drugs , Environmental News Networks [online] Available: (http://www.enn.com/med.html?id=1442) (April 15, 2007).

Szyrwinska, K. and Lulek, J., 2006. Exposure to specific polychlorinated biphenyls and some chlorinated pesticides via breast milk in Poland. *Chemosphere* xx: xxx–xxx.

Sankar, T.V., Zynudheen, A.A., Anandan, R. and Nair, P.G. V., 2006. Distribution of organochlorine pesticides and heavy metal residues in fish and shellfish from Calicut region, Kerala, India. *Chemosphere* 65:583–590.

Sankararamakrishnan, N., Sharma, A.K and Sanghi, R., 2005. *Environ. Int.* 31(113).

Sharma, D., 2006. Has the Bt cotton bubble burst ? Opinion/Agriculture. India Together. Sat 28 Oct 2006

Singh, K., Singh, A, and Singh, D.K., 1996. Molluscicidal activity of neem *(Azadirachta indica* A.Juss). *Journal of Ethnopharmacology* 52:35-40.

Schmutterer, H., 1998. Potential of azadirachtin-containing pesticides for integrated pest control in developing and industrialized countries. *Journal of Insect Physiology* 713-719.

Solsoloy, A.D., 1993. Insecticidal action of the formulated product and aqueous extract from physic nut, *Jatropha curcas* L. on cotton insect pests. *Cott. Res. J.* (Phil.) 6: 24-35.

Sierra, I., 2000. Influence of heating conditions in continuous-flow microwave or tubular heat exchange systems on the vitamin B1 and B2 content of milk", Lait, 80: 601–608.

Sweis, F.K., 2004, The effect of admixed material on the flaming and smouldering combustion of dust layers, *Journal of Loss Prevention in the Process Industries*, vol. 17 (6), pp. 505-508.

Schewe, P.F. and Stein, B., 1999. Light Has Been Slowed To A Speed of 17 m/s, American Institute of Physics, *Bulletin of Physics News*, no. 415, February 18

Schuchardt, U., Sercheli, R., Vargas, R.M, 1998. Transesterification of vegetable oils: a review. *J Braz Chem Sco,* 9(1): 199-210

Subramanian, A.K., Singal, S.K., Saxena M, Singhal, S., 2005. Utilization of liquid biofuels in automotive diesel engines: An Indian perspective. *Biomass and Bioenergy, 9: 65–72.*

Tarpley, W.G. and Chaitkin, A., 1992. George Bush: The Unauthorized Biography. Washington DC: Executive Intelligence Review, 1992. 659 pages.

Tickell J, 2003. From the fryer to the fuel tank: The complete guide to using vegetable oil as an alternative fuel. Tickell Energy Consultants; 3rd edition, ISBN-13: 978-0970722706, pp162.

Tung, S., Schweikhard, V., and Cornell, E.A., 2006. Observation of Vortex Pinning on Bose-Einstein Condensates, Phys. Rev. Lett., vol. 97, No. 24, pp. 240402

Toda, M., Takagaki, A., Okamura, M., Kondo, J. N., Hayashi, S., Domen, K., and Hara, M, 2005. Biodiesel made with sugar catalyst. Brief Communication. *Nature* 438 (10) November.

Takeda M, Tanaka T, Cacabelos R (eds), 2004. Molecular Neurobiology of Alzheimer Disease and Related Disorders. *Basel, Karger,* 2004, pp 79–83.

Tollefson, L. and Karp, B.E., 2004. Human Health Impact from Antimicrobial Use in Food Animals. Basic Study. *Medecine et maladies infectieuses* 34:514–521.

Tajchakavit, S. and Ramaswamy, H. S. 1995. Continuous-Flow Microwave Heating of Orange Juice:Evidence of Nonthermal Effects. *International Microwave Power Institute*, 30(3): 141-148.

The Lancet,1996. Vol. 347, 17 February 1996, pp. 412, 426-431: In Smith, M. and Htoo, N., 2006. Gas Politics: Shwe Gas Development in Burma. *Watershed* 11(2):9-11, November 2005-June 2006.

Teflon, 2006. Polytetrafluoroethylene from Wikipedia, the Free Encyclopedia [online] Available: (http://en.wikipedia.org/wiki/Teflon) (October 4, 2006).

Triche, E.W., Belanger, K., Bracken, M.B., Beckett, W.S., Holford, T.R., Gent, J.F., McSharry, J.E. and Leaderer, B.P., 2005. Indoor Heating Sources and Respiratory Symptoms in Non Smoking Women. *Epidemiology* 6(3):377-384.

Toninello, A., Pietrangeli P., De Marchi, U. Salvi, M. and Mondov, B., 2006. Amine Oxidases in Apoptosis and Cancer. *Biochimica et Biophysica Acta* 1765:1 – 13.

The New York Times, 2006. Cooking Gas Linked To Children's Minor Breathing Habits. Wednesday, December 27.http://query.nytimes.com/gst/fullpage. html?sec=health&res= 9800E2D91339F93AA25753C1A967948260. (Acessed on December 29, 2006).

The New York Time, 2006a. *Citing Security, Plants Use Safer Chemicals.* April, 25, 2006.

The Globe and Mail, 2006. *Toxic shock: Canada's Chemical reaction.* May 27, Saturday, 2006.

Thomas P. and Nowak, M.A., 2006. Climate Change: All in the Game. *Nature* (441) June 1, 2006.

Tschulakow, A.V., Yan, Y. and Klimek, W., 2005. A New Approach to the Memory of Water. *Homeopathy* 94 (4): 241-247.

The Epoch Times, 2006. *Potato Farms a Hot Bed for Cancer.* March 24-30, 2006. www.theepochtimes.ca.

Toda, M., Takagaki, A., Okamura, M., Kundo, J.N., Hayashi, S., Domen, K. and Hara, Michikazu, 2005. Green Chemistry: Biodiesel made with sugar catalyst. Nature. 438, 178 (November, 2005).

Tanner, D., 1995. Ocean Thermal energy Conversion: Current Overview and Future Outlook. *Renewable Energy* 6(3):367-373.

Thorpe, T.W., 1998. Economic Analysis of Wave Energy Devices", Third European Wave Energy Conference, Patras, Greece.

Taoukis, P., Davis, E. A., Davis, H. T., Gordon, J., and Takmon, Y., 1987. Mathematical Modelling of Microwave Thawing by the Modified Isotherm Migration Method. *Journal of Food Science,* 52(2):455–463.

Tada, Y., Takimoto, A. and Hayashi, Y., 2006. Heat Transfer and Damage During Freezing of Food. *Journal of Biomechanics* 39 (1):384.

Thomas, P., 2005. Teflon out of the frying pan. The Ecologist Online. www.theecologist. org/archive_detail.asp?content_id=475 (Dec 31, 2006).

The Epoch Times, 2006. *Potato Farms a Hot Bed for Cancer.* March 24-30, 2006. www.theepochtimes.ca.

Uranium Enrichment, 2006. Nuclear Issues Briefing Paper 33, March 2006. Uranium Information Centre Ltd, GPO Box 1649N, Melbourne 3001, Australia

Uranium Information Center, 2006. The Economics of Nuclear Power, Briefing Paper no 8, Australia. http://www.uic.com.au/nip08.htm <accessed on June 05, 2006>

USDA/DOE, 1998. Life cycle inventory of biodiesel and petroleum diesel for use in an urban bus: A joint study sponsored by US department of Agriculture and US department of Energy- final report, May, 1998.

USEPA, 1998. Compilation of Air Pollution Emission Factors, Volume I, External Combustion Sources, US Environmental Protection Agency, Publication AP-42, Chapter 1.3, Fuel Oil Combustion, September 1998.

United States Department of Agriculture (USDA) food safety and inspection service, 2005. http://www.fsis.usda.gov/Fact_Sheets/Focus_On_Freezing/index.asp <accessed on Jan 25, 2006>

USFDA, 2004. Juice HACCP Hazards and Controls Guidance, First Edition, Guidance for Industry. www.cfsan.fda.gov/~dms/juicgu10.html (accessed on Dec 22, 2006).

UNWWDR, 2003. United Nations World Water Development Report. Water for People and Water for Life-A Look at the World's Fresh Water Resources. Executive Summary, World Water Assessment Program.

UNEP, 2001. Post-Conflict Environmental Assessment-FYROM. http://enrin.grida.no/ htmls/macedon/reports/postcon/eng/appendix2.htm (Dec 31, 2006).

University of California Sandiego (UCSD), 2006. *Bacillus Thuringensis.* http://www.bt.ucsd. edu/synthetic_pesticide.html (accessed on October 25, 2006).

Uri, N.D., 1998. Government Policy and the Development and Use of Biopesticides. *Futures* 30(5):409–423.

USEPA, 2004. Pesticides Industry Sales and Usage: 2000 and 2001 Market Estimates Washington, DC: T. Kiely, D. Donaldson, & A. Grube.

Van Someren, E.J.W., 2000. Circadian rhythms and sleep in human aging. *Chronobiol. Int.* 17, 233–243.

Van Bommel, W.J.M., 2006. Non-visual Biological Effect of Lighting and the Practical Meaning for Lighting for Work. *Applied Ergonomics* 37:461–466.

Vaziri, H., Zatzman, G.M. and Islam, M.R., 2007. "Preface", Handbook of Sustainable Petroleum Engineering Operations, Gulf Publishing Co., Houston, 452 pp.

Vallejo, F., Tomas-Barberan. F.A. and Garcıa-Viguera, C., 2003. Phenolic Compound Contents in Edible Parts of Broccoli Inflorescences after Domestic Cooking. *J. of the Science of Food and Agriculture,* 83:1511–1516.

Voss, A., 1979. Waves Currents, Tides-Problems and Prospects. *Energy* 4 (5): 823-831.

Varkey, B, Kutty, K., 1998. Pulmonary Aspiration Syndromes. In: *Kochar's Concise Textbook of Medicine.* Baltimore, Md: Lippincott Williams & Wilkins. 902-906

Van Venden, F., 2006. Electricity's Role in Cancer an Eye Opener. Do Electromagnetic Fields Affect Human Health? Electricity and Health. www.enviroharvest.ca/electricity_ and_health.htm (accessed on Dec 27, 2006).

Valero, M. and Giner, M.J., 2006. Effects of antimicrobial components of essential oils on growth of Bacillus cereus INRA L2104 in and the sensory qualities of carrot broth", *International Journal of Food Microbiology,* 106: 90 – 94.

Virtanen, A. J., Goedeken, D. L., and Tong, C. H., 1997. Microwave Assisted Thawing of Model Frozen Foods Using Feed-Back Temperature Control and Surface Cooling. *Journal of Food Science,* 62(1), 150–154.

Von Peters, W., 2004. Sports Drinks-Are They Safe? www.karinya.com/sportsdrinks.htm (accessed on December 20, 2006).

Van der Gaag, N., 2000. Pick Your Poison: the price we pay for using pesticides. *New Internationalist* May, 323:9-11.

Volpe, P. 1996. Ink Toxicity and the Screen Printer. In The Technical Guidebook. (CD-ROM, 96 (1). Fairfax, VA: Screenprinting and Graphic Imaging Association International (SGIA).

Venkataraman, C., Joshi, P., Sethi, V., Kohli, S., and Ravi, M.R., 2004, *Aerosol Science and Technology,* vol. 38, no. 1, 50-61.

VIOXX, 2006. Rofecoxib from Wikipedia, the Free Encyclopedia [online] Available: (http://en.wikipedia.org/wiki/Vioxx) (October 4, 2006)

Van den Bogaard, A, and Stobberingh, E. 2000. Epidemiology of resistance to antibiotics, links between animals and humans, *Int. J. AntimicrobAgents.* 14:327–35.

Vaclavik, V. and Chreistian, E.W., 2003. Essentials of Food Science. Springer; 2nd ed. Edition, pp 500. ISBN-13: 978-0306473630

Wasiuddin, N.M., Tango, M. and Islam, M.R. 2002. A Novel Method for Arsenic Removal at Low Concentrations. *Energy Sources* 24, 1031–1041,

WEC, 2001. Survey of Energy Resources-Geothermal. www.worldenergy.org/wec-geis/publications/reports/ser/hydro/hydro.asp (accessed on July 12, 2006).

WEC, 2005. World Energy Council, Energy Data Center. Global Energy Scenario Between 2050 and Beyond.

WEC, 2006.The World Energy Council: How to Avoid a Billion Tones of CO2 Emission. http://www.worldenergy.org/wec-geis/default.asp <accessed on May 30, 2006>

Wise Uranium Project, 2005. Uranium Radiation Properties. www.wise-uranium.org/ rup.html (accessed on March 19, 2006).

Wyman, C.E., 2004. Ethanol Fuel. *Encyclopedia of Energy* 2: 541-555.

World Bank, 1996. Rural Energy and Development, Improving Energy Supplies for Two Billion People, Washington D.C.

World Health Organisation (WHO), 1998. Chromium Environmental Health Criteria No. 61. WHO, Geneva.

WHO, 1997. Revision of the WHO Guidelines for Drinking Water Quality. Second Edition. Volume 3, Survellance and control of community water supplies. World Health Organization, Geneva, Switzerland.

Winder, C. and Carmody, M., 2002. The dermal toxicity of cement. *Toxicol. ind. health* 18(7):321-331.

Wilderer, P.A., 2004. Applying sustainable water management concepts in rural and urban areas: some thoughts about reasons, means and needs. *Water Sci. Technol.* 49(7):8-16. WMO, 1998. http:/www.wmo.ch.

Wentzel, M and Pouris, A, 2007. The Development Impact of Solar Cookers: A Review of Solar Cooking Impact Research in South Africa. *Energy Policy* 35:1909–1919.

Wilson, A. & Morril, J., 1997. Comparing Values of Various Heating Fuels *Consumer Guide to Home Energy Savings,* American Council for an Energy Efficient Economy, Washington DC.

Wood, P. 2005. Biofuels, out of Africa. Could Jatropha Vegetable Oil be Europe's Biodiesel Feedstock? *Refocus July-August. 6(4):* 40-44.

Wessen, P.S., Liu, H., and Seahra, S.S.,2000. The Big Bang as Higher-Dimensional Shock Wave, Astron. Astrophys., vol. 358, pp.425-427.

Wessen, P.S., 2002. Five Dimensional Realtivity and Two Times, Phys. Lett., B538, pp.159-163

Wakamatsu, H., Kikka, Y. and Tanaka, N., 1998. Introduction of Ultra Pure Water Close System into Semiconductor Plant. Oki Technical Review *Special Issue on Global Environment* 63 (160).

Wikipedia, 2006. Coca-Cola formula. http://en.wikipedia.org/wiki/Coca-Cola_formula (December, 20, 2006).

Whitford, GM., 1987. Fluoride in dental products: safety considerations. *Journal of Dental Research* 66:1056-60.

Walker, A.I.T., Brown,V.K.H., Ferrigan, L.W., Pickering, R.G. and Williams D.A., 2005. Toxicity of sodium lauryl sulphate, sodium lauryl ethoxysulphate and corresponding surfactants derived from synthetic alcohols. *Food and Cosmetics Toxicology* Vol. 5:763-769.

Waite, D.T., Bailey, P., Sproull, J.F., Quiring, D.V., Chau, D.F., Bailey, J., Cessna, A.J., 2005. Atmospheric concentrations and dry and wet deposits of some herbicides currently used on the Canadian Prairies. *Chemosphere* 58, 693–703.

Wang, Y., Yang, R. and Jiang, G., 2006. Investigation of organochlorine pesticides (OCPs) in mollusks collected from coastal sites along the Chinese Bohai Sea from 2002 to 2004. *Environmental Pollution* xx:1-7

World Resource Foundation, 1997. Paper Fact Sheet. In: ITDG Small Scale Paper Making. www.itdg.org/docs/technical_information _service/papermaking.pdf.Wolff, M.S., Tonilo, P.G., Lee et al., 1993. Blood Levels of Organochlorine Residues and Risk of Breast Cancer. *Journal of the National Cancer Institute* 85:648-652.

Westney, C., 2002. Acrylamide Formation in Cooked Foods-*Nature Science Update*, October 01.

WHO, 2003. World Health Organization. Joint FAO/OIE/WHO expert workshop on non-human antimicrobial usage and antimicrobial resistance: scientific assessment, Geneva, 1–5 December'. www.who.int/foodsafety/micro/meetings/nov2003/en/

Wolff, M.S., Toniolo, P, Lee, E.W., Rivera, M., and Dubin, N. 1993. Blood levels. of organochlorine residues and risk of breast cancer. *J Natl Cancer*.Inst 85:8:648–652.

Website 1: Wikipedia site: http://en.wikipedia.org/wiki/Speed_of_light(last accessed August 5, 2007).

Website 2: Wikipedia site: http://en.wikipedia.org/wiki/Satyendranath_Bose, (last accessed August 5, 2007).

Website 3: http://www.emachineshop.com/engine/ (accessed on Dec 29, 2006).

Website 4: http://encarta.msn.com/media_461531189/Oil_Refining_and_Fractional_Distillation.html (accessed on Nov 29, 2006).

Website 4: http://en.wikipedia.org/wiki/Stirling_Engine (accessed on Dec 29, 2006).

Website 5: www.cameco.com/sustainable_development/clean_environment/act.php (accessed on Dec 10, 2006)

Website 6: http://www.wou.edu/las/physci/GS361/Energy_From_Fossil_Fuels.htm (accessed on Nov 29, 2006).

Website 7: http://www.soygold.com/products/Fuels/fuels_intro.htm (accessed on Dec 10, 2007).

Website 8: http://www.emarineinc.com/products/mounts/tracker.html (accessed on November 12, 2006).

Website 9: www-stud.fht esslingen.de/projects/alt_energy/sol_thermal/ powertower.html (accessed on November 12, 2006).

Website 10: www.eere.energy.gov/tribalenergy/guide/images/photo_wannapumdam.jpg (accessed on November 13, 2006)

Website 11: http://www.purewatersystems.com/ (Accessed on December 21, 2006).

Website 12: Nepal-Manaslu- www.shieldsaroundtheworld.com (Accessed on Dec 30, 2006).

Website 13: http://www.varaprasad.htmlplanet.com/custom3.html (accessed on Dec.12, 06).

Website 14: http://www.botanicalworks.com/NaturalPreservatives.htm (accessed on Dec.10, 07)

Website 15: http://www.ciwmb.ca.gov/Markets/StatusRpts/plastichtm (accessed on Dec 29, 2006)

Website 16: www.wasteonline.org.uk/resources/InformationSheets/Plastics.htm (accessed on March 15, 2006)

Website 17: www.oakdenehollins.co.uk/wmr3. New Recycling Technology Provides End- of-Life Solution for Composite Plastics (accessed on March 15, 2006).

Website 18: http://webexhibits.org/pigments/indiv/recipe/yellowochre.html (accessed on March 15, 2006)

Website 19: http://www.lavano.com/en/waschnuss-infos01.htm (accessed on Dec 30, 2006)

Xioling, M., and Wu., Q. 2006. Biodiesel production from heterotrophic microalgal oil: Bioresource Technology, Vol. 97, (6): 841-846.

Yoshizaki, S. and Y. Miyahara. 1984. Husking Properties of Rough Rice Grain (I): Husking Properties by Pseudo-Static Friction Force. *Journal of Japanese Society of Agricultural Machinery*. 46(3): 309-315.

Yamashita, R.1993. *New Technology in Grain Post-harvesting*. Kyoto, Japan: Farm Machinery Industrial Research Cooperation.

Yang, R., Yao, T., Xu, B., Jiang, G. and Xin, X., 2006. Accumulation features of organochlorine pesticides and heavy metals in fish from high mountain lakes and Lhasa River in the Tibetan Plateau.*Environment International* xx (2006) xxx–xxx.

Yuan Yao,Y., Tuduri, L., Harner, T., Blanchard,P., Waite, D., Poissant,L., Murphy, C., Belzer, W., Aulagnier, F., Li, Y.F., and Sverko, E., 2006. Spatial and Temporal Distribution of Pesticide Air Concentrations in Canadian Agricultural Regions. *Atmospheric Environment* 40:4339–4351.

Ziskind, M., Jones, R.N., Weill, H., 1976. *Annu. Rev. Respir. Dis*. 113: 643.

Zhu, N. and Tsuchiya, T., 2005. Study on Synthesizing BDF by Using Ultrasonic Sonochemistry Effect. 3rd International Energy Conversion Engineering Conference 15-18, August 2005. San Francisco, California.

Zou, Y, Zhao, C., Wang, Y., Zhao, W.,Peng, Y. and Shuai, Y., 2006. Characteristics and Origin of Natural Gases in the Kuqa Depression of Tarim Basin, NW China, *Organic Geochemistry*: *in press.*

Zhao, Y. Y., Fores, R. A., & Olson, D. G.,1998. High Hydrostatic Pressure Effects on Rapid Thawing of Frozen Beef. *Journal of Food Science*, 63(2), 272–275.

Zatzman, G.M. and Islam, M.R., 2007a. *Economics of Intangibles,* Nova Science Publishers, New York: in press.

Zatzman, G.M. and Islam, M.R.2007b. Truth, Consequences and Intentions:The Study of Natural and Anti-Natural Starting Points and Their Implications, *J. Nat.Sci.and Sust. Tech.* 1(2):1-38.

Zatzman, G.M., Chhetri, A.B., Khan, M.M., R. Al-Maamari, and M.R. Islam, 2007a. Colony Collapsed Disorder: The Case of Science of Intangibles. Int. J. of Material Products and Technology. Accepted. October, 2007.

Zatzman, G.M., 2007. The Honey→Sugar→Saccharin→Aspartame, HSSA, syndrome:A note, J. Nat. Sci. and Sust.Tech. 1(3):397-402.

Zatzman, G. M, Khan, A.B. Chhetri, A.B. and Islam, M. R, 2007b. Delinearized History of Time, Science, and Truth: Towards Modeling Intangibles. Int. Journal of Material and Product Technology. Accepted, October. Pp50.

Zatzman, G.M., Khan, M.M., Chhetri A.B. and Islam, M.R., 2007c. A Delinearized History of Time and its Roles in Establishing and Unfolding Knowledge of the Truth. J. Nat. Sci. and Sust.Tech. In press.

INDEX

C

D

E

G

I

N

O

P

S

T

X

Y

Z

DATE DUE